The Life of Irène Némirovsky

1903–1942

Olivier Philipponnat
Patrick Lienhardt

Translated from the French by
Euan Cameron

Chatto & Windus
LONDON

Published by Chatto & Windus 2010

2 4 6 8 10 9 7 5 3 1

Originally published as *La Vie d'Irène Némirovsky* in France in 2007
Copyright © Éditions Grasset & Fasquelle, 2007
Copyright © Éditions Denöel, 2007
English translation © Euan Cameron 2010

Olivier Philipponnat and Patrick Lienhardt have asserted their right under the Copyright,
Designs and Patents Act 1988 to be identified as the authors of this work

First published in Great Britain in 2010 by
Chatto & Windus
Random House, 20 Vauxhall Bridge Road,
London SW1V 2SA
www.rbooks.co.uk

Addresses for companies within The Random House Group Limited can be found at:
www.randomhouse.co.uk/offices.htm

The Random House Group Limited Reg. No. 954009

A CIP catalogue record for this book
is available from the British Library

Hardback ISBN 9780701182885
Trade Paperback ISBN 9780701182892

The Random House Group Limited supports The Forest Stewardship
Council (FSC), the leading international forest certification organisation.
All our titles that are printed on Greenpeace approved
FSC certified paper carry the FSC logo. Our paper procurement policy can be
found at www.rbooks.co.uk/environment

Typeset by Palimpsest Book Production Ltd,
Grangemouth, Stirlingshire

Printed and bound in Great Britain by
Clays Ltd St Ives plc

To my dear parents.
To Malika and Kiran.
O.P

To Christine, Théo and Pierre
P.L

Like other such lives, like all lives, this is a tragedy; high hopes, noble efforts; under thickening difficulties and impediments, ever-new nobleness of valiant effort; – and the result, death . . .

Thomas Carlyle, *The Life of John Sterling*, 1851

I should like this to be used as an epitaph when I die, but it's a very vain notion. And, anyway, inscriptions on tombs are expensive.

Irène Némirovsky, 1934

Contents

Note

Irène Némirovsky often alluded to the fact that prior to writing, she began by filling her notebooks with biographical pointers about the least of her characters; it was what she called the 'previous life of the novel'. Then, she reread her notes, criticising and commenting as she went, and at the same time providing some fascinating reflections on her craft as a writer.

In 2004, nothing appeared to survive of these drafts, brimming as they were with personal memories and autobiographical notes, apart from the manuscript of *Suite Française*, one of the least characteristic of her method of working. She had, however, kept most of them. During the course of 2005, we were fortunate to see draft versions surface of *David Golder*, of *Le Pion sur l'échiquier* [The Pawn on the Chessboard], The *Wine of Solitude* [*Le Vin de Solitude*], *Les Echelles du Levant*, or *Le Maitre des âmes* [The Ports of the Levant, or The Master of Souls], *The Dogs and the Wolves* [*Les Chiens et les Loups*], as well as the first sketches for *Captivité*, the third part of *Suite Française*. Among them were an unpublished novel, *Fire in the Blood* [*Chaleur du sang*], at that point in fragments, a number of short stories, some writings from her youth and some separate pages.

Yet, she herself was not the least among the real-life people on whom she based her characters. Thus a number of the pages in the working notebook for *The Wine of Solitude* contain memories of conversations, of asides overheard twenty years previously, reconstructed through an occasionally painful feat of memory, which we reproduce faithfully in the first part of this book. In this way, the 'previous life' of Irène Némirovsky in imperial and revolutionary Russia, that of her parents and grandparents, her exile in Finland and later in Sweden, which until now were only known about because of a few administrative documents and some interviews given to the press in the 1930s, have sprung from oblivion with a wealth of astonishing detail, sometimes corroborated by new archival information and unpublished family testimony.

In this biography, we indicate the source of all quotations taken from the published work of Irène Némirovsky. In certain cases – mostly autobiographical – where the source is not given – they have come from these manuscripts, diaries and working notebooks, all of which are kept at the Institut Mémoire de l'Édition contemporaine (IMEC), at Ardenne Abbey in Normandy.

Translator's Note

When referring to Irène Némirovsky's published work, I have used the English title where the translation is already available or about to be translated; elsewhere, I have used the French title. All the extracts from Irène Némirovsky's novels and short stories included in this biography have been translated by Sandra Smith, the gifted translator of *Suite Française* and other fictional works by Irène Némirovsky published in English. I should like to record my gratitude to Sandra for her advice and collaboration. I should also like to thank Olivier Philipponnat for diligent elucidation and help on certain aspects of his and his co-author Patrick Lienhardt's text, and Dominique Enright for her meticulous and sensitive editing of my manuscript. Others who have kindly come to my aid include Anthea Bell, Robert Chandler, Geraldine D'Amico, Michel Déon, the late Miles Huddleston, Raphaëlle Liebaert, Koukla MacLehose and Nelly Munthe.

E.C.

Prologue

I Think We Are Leaving Today…
(16th/17th July 1942)

That children, women, men, mothers and fathers should be treated like lowly cattle, that members of the same family should be separated from one another and taken off to an unknown destination; it was to be the fate of our age to witness this sad spectacle.

Monseigneur Jules Saliège, Archbishop of Toulouse,
Pastoral letter *Et clamor Jerusalem ascendit*, 23 August 1942

It is a wagon fitted with a sliding door, used for transporting cattle. Straw has been thrown in and a bucket of water placed inside. The small, high air vents have been covered in barbed wire, so that it is impossible to escape once the sliding door has been closed. A prison on wheels, attached to another, which pulls a third, and so on. On 17th July 1942, this convoy is the sixth to leave France. Its nine hundred and twenty-eight passengers have not asked to leave, they have no tickets, they have only a suitcase and a few belongings. They do not know their destination and their loved ones do not know where they are going.

Some of these travellers have been misleadingly 'convened' during the round-up of the Jews in Paris, on 14th May 1941, for 'verification of status'. Since then, they have been stagnating in a very basic camp, from which it would have been so easy to escape had they not been terrified of exposing their families to reprisals. Over the past few weeks, women and children have also been arrested. It was a task made all the simpler since all or nearly all of them declared themselves to the authorities: what did they risk, in France, by conforming to the law? Others, like her, were taken from their homes only a few days previously. They were not surprised at their arrest: ever since October 1940, the police have been authorised to intern Jews in 'special camps', at the discretion of the *préfets*, the local chief commissioners.

For they are all Jews, all foreigners: tantamount to an offence in occupied France. They have walked through Pithiviers in single file, suitcase in hand, past the windows of the local inhabitants. They passed the sugar refinery, stepped over the railway lines, and walked through the wooden gate guarded by a policeman. Once registered, they were led into some large military sheds where bedsteads covered in straw could accommodate about one hundred adults. 'Needless to say, the Loiret region could have done without this gift,' *L'Écho de Pithiviers* regretted on 24th May 1941. 'Nevertheless, carefully supervised, the foreign Jews will not be too dangerous. And it is far preferable, all things considered, to know that they are behind barbed wire fences instead of running our town halls and our important services . . . The purging of France has thus begun in earnest. Let us admit that it was very necessary and that it has not come a moment too soon.'[1]

The French police put in charge of guarding the camp are not bad men. Just disciplinarians. Some of them helped with the visits and the receiving of parcels, and they posed for souvenir photographs with the prisoners. But since the summer of 1941, the rules have been tightened. Refusing to do forced labour in the neighbouring farms, several hundred prisoners eventually absconded. As a retaliatory measure, no further leaves were permitted and visits were cancelled. It became pointless to try to evade the guards, who were stationed in watchtowers and behind the railings. Once they were recaptured, those who had escaped were locked up for a few days in a small prison made of corrugated iron, open to the full sunlight. The German authorities decided to convert this collection of sheds and those at Beaune-la-Rolande, built in 1940 to house potential prisoners of war, into transit camps for the concentration camp of Auschwitz-Birkenau, in Poland. Over there, all these Jews can be herded in their tens of thousands, far from prying eyes, and when the time came – sometimes immediately – murdered in the gas chambers, which have been in operation since earlier in 1942.

On 25th and 28th June 1942, two initial convoys of a thousand people left the camp for an unknown destination. And it is to maintain the full complement that the round-ups and arrests, bureaucratically known as 'regroupment operations', have been increased in the German-occupied zone of France. Between the arrivals and departures, the Pithiviers camp in this early summer looks like a railway station concourse. In the letter she writes to her husband upon her arrival, on Wednesday, 15th July, she does not fail to mention this hustle and bustle:

> My dearest love
>   Don't worry about me. I have arrived safely. For the time being, there is disarray, but the food is very good. I was even astonished . . . A parcel and a letter may be sent once a month.
>   Above all, don't be anxious. Things will settle down, my dearest. I hug you as I do the children with all my heart, with all my love.
>
> Irène

She is not registered until the following morning, 16th July, by Lieutenant Le Vagueresse 'temporary commandant Pithiviers', who cannot be bothered with accuracy and writes in his register: 'Epstein Irène Nimierovski, writer'. This is a list of the one hundred and nineteen women who in a few hours will climb aboard convoy no. 6 for Auschwitz. Furthermore, who is there to appeal to? Nobody knows anything about this destination, but the fact that they will leave at night has not been concealed. Jukiel Obarzanek, a Polish hosier worker, who joined up as a volunteer in 1939, wrote to his family: 'I am writing to tell you that I am leaving this evening. I think we are going away to work . . . There are women among us too, about a hundred of them and they are very brave.'[2] One of the women is 'Irma Irène Epstein, writer', as indicated on her ration card, confiscated after her arrest. She, too, writes a quick note to her family, the last they will receive:

> Thursday morning
> My dearest, my beloved little ones
>   I think we are leaving today. Courage and hope. You are all in my heart, my dears. May God protect us all.

Departure is in fact scheduled for the following morning, 17th July, at 6.15 a.m., under the command of Lieutenant Schneider of the gendarmerie. Everything is more discreet at dawn. Irène Némirovsky has been less than two days at Pithiviers. Room has to be made, and quickly, for the thousands of Jews arrested the previous day and on that same day in Paris, who are temporarily packed into the Vélodrome d'Hiver.

Those deported, 'delivered to the Occupation authorities', are squeezed in eighty to the wagon, sometimes more. The women probably fill only a single wagon. 'We didn't know where we were going, but we knew we were being deported,' Samuel Chymisz, one of the survivors, recounts. 'There was a joke being spread around that we were going to work. Except that they had crammed one hundred and ten of us into each wagon. And very soon the idea occurred to us and went around the wagon: 'If we are going to work in Germany, why have they packed us in, one hundred and ten to the wagon? We'll arrive in shreds!' And they didn't give us any water at all. In July, in enclosed wagons!'[3] This time, they begin to understand. Letters of farewell drop from the window vents. Some of them will reach their destination.

Samuel Chymisz remembers that the first stop was the station of Chalon-sur-Saône, sixty kilometres as the crow flies from Issy-l'Évêque, the small town in the Saône-et-Loire *département* where Irène Némirovsky lived during the first two years of the Occupation, and where she wrote her last novels. At this very moment, Michel Epstein, who is confined at home by the laws of the Vichy regime, is there redoubling his appeals, his telegrams and letters soliciting aid for his wife through all possible channels. All he receives are worrying replies, such as this telegram from an intermediary of the Red Cross, an ironmonger in Pithiviers, on that same 17th July: 'Pointless sending package as haven't seen your wife.'

Convoy no. 6 will take three days and two nights to reach Auschwitz-Birkenau. Samuel Chymisz: 'We stretched out our hands through the vents, there were some French people on the platforms ... "A little water, please, a little water!" Not one French person moved to go and get us a little water. Not one. They were either frightened or they couldn't be bothered, I don't know.'[4] And not once are they given anything to eat, even though the last wagon, curiously, is loaded with food. Across the frontier, in the German stations, civilians laugh when they notice hands and faces through the vents. Some of them spit.

Not everyone is alive when they arrive at the *Judenrampe* (the unloading ramp for Jews) at Auschwitz-Birkenau on 19th July at about 7.00 p.m. Those who suffocated, or have been trampled, or dehydrated, have been unloaded along the way. Others have been killed by SS bullets fired at the wagons to stop the groaning. The survivors, battered from having had to stand, from lack of sleep, the heat, the over-crowding, the inevitable quarrels and the foul stench, can hardly walk. Yet they are obliged to cover the distance to the camp beneath a volley of beatings, lashes from whips, and orders that are barked out. 'We wanted to take our luggage. *Keine Bagage nicht!* We had to leave it on the train. As we got out, we saw what resembled corpses, dressed in striped uniforms, with ridiculous little hats on their heads, who climbed up on to the trains and threw our luggage down to the ground. Then we were immediately put into rows. *Links, rechts*[5] [left, right]!'

The women are separated from the men. Their jewellery and rings are confiscated. They are searched, made to take a shower, shaved and dressed in a coarse, striped material, and tattooed with the numbers 9550 to 9668. The men have the numbers 48880 to 49688. Almost two hundred of them belong to the district of Dijon, but the majority are Parisian artisans: tailors, shoemakers, shopkeepers, tanners, a jeweller, a dry cleaner, a heating engineer, a cabinet maker, a butcher, a riveter, a furrier, a hairdresser, a male nurse, a second-hand dealer, a scrap merchant . . . Really nothing in common with the 'all-powerful' Jews denounced by propaganda as having 'wormed their way into the best jobs'.[6]

Among these men there is a composer, Simon Laks, to whom the SS will entrust the camp's band. And among these women, a novelist, Irène Némirovsky, who has never for a moment imagined she would leave France, 'the most beautiful country in the world',[7] because she was the family's wage-earner and she has dreamed in French for a very long time. She will not survive a month in this new Sakhaline.* No Chekhov here to bear witness to her wretchedness, to 'this seed of madness, cruelty, hatred and death' scattered in fistfuls, and that has reaped 'such terrible harvests'.[8] On 19th August at 3.20 p.m., according to the Auschwitz certificate, Irène Némirovsky falls victim to 'flu'. In concentration-camp language, an epidemic of typhus. She is thirty-nine years old and an asthmatic.

'And so,' she thinks, 'I regret nothing. I have been happy. I have been loved. I am still loved, I know that's true, in spite of the distance between us, in spite of the separation.'[9] She leaves behind a husband and two dearly beloved little girls. As well as an unfinished novel, *Suite Française*, of which the third part was to have been called *Captivité*.

*The island gulag which Chekhov visited and wrote about. [Tr.]

Part I

A Previous Life
(1903–1929)

I

The Most Beautiful Country in the World
(1903–1911)

But those were legendary times, those distant times when the gardens of
the most beautiful city in our Homeland were the preserve of a young,
carefree generation.

    Then, yes, then the conviction took root in the hearts of this genera-
tion that their entire lives would be spent in purity, serenity and calm;
the dawns, the sunsets, the Dnieper, the Kreschatik, the sunny summer
streets and, in winter, snow that did not bring with it cold weather or a
harsh climate, a snow that was thick and gentle . . . And it was the very
opposite that happened.

Mikhail Bulgakov, 'The City of Kiev',
Nakanune [On the Eve] newspaper, 6th July 1923

In Kiev, in about 1910, a florist at the sign of La Flore de Nice was
selling hydrangeas and Christmas roses. Was the business prosperous?
In the Ukrainian capital, 'there were so many lime trees [along the
streets] that in springtime, you walked beneath an archway of blossom
and on a carpet of flowers'.[1] Once winter was over, hyacinths and
dandelions defied the last gusts of snow. In a few days' time, the lime
trees in the old Revny park would take on a fresh pale plumage and
the Marinsky park, poised upon the red clay cliffs that crumble down
into the river, would be filled with copses of mauve. After that came
an explosion of pollens, that covered the Kreschatik, the principal
thoroughfare of the city, in a carpet of pale yellow.

    There is no writer who has not been struck by the mass of vege-
tation that every year floods the Pechersk district, perched high in the
heart of Kiev. When he went back there in 1923, to find it ravaged by
four consecutive years of onslaughts and pillaging, Mikhail Bulgakov,
who was born there thirty years earlier, had not forgotten the joyful
eruption of spring: 'The gardens were white with flowers, the Garden
of the Tsars was covered in green, the sun pierced all the windows,
setting them ablaze.'[2] And Irène Némirovsky: 'How beautiful it is in

springtime, in this land! The streets lined with gardens and the air giving off the scent of lime trees, lilacs, sweet moisture rising from the lawns; these trees, in clusters, release their sugary perfume into the night.'³ So what need was there for a florist from Nice in the city of Kiev, which was so saturated with perfumes that every evening, before the open-air concert in the Kupechesky park, they had first to spray the beds of stocks and tobacco flowers in order to reduce the fragrance and ward off coughing fits?

The smell of the plains

It was in this vast botanical garden, traversed by wide avenues, and adorned with bandstands and balconies with striped awnings, that a little girl, given the name Irma for the synagogue, and Irina, after the Tsar's niece, was born on 11th February 1903. Of the countless bastions of greenery maintained in the heart of the city, this little girl, who became a novelist, listed four: 'Nicholas Square, the Botanical Gardens, and, up on the hills, the Tsar's Garden and the Merchants' Square'.⁴ The second of these, vast and gullied, with its own pond, and criss-crossed with pathways lined with hundred-year-old lime trees, made the strongest impression on her, possibly because it was the closest to Pushkin Street where her parents lived when she was seven years old. 'It was a rather isolated, overgrown spot. Some sleepy animals lived in iron cages: an eagle from the Caucasus crawling with vermin, some wolves, a bear panting with thirst.'⁵ And there was Nicholas I Square, the centenary park of Lycée No. 1, as well as the verdant terraces perched above the Dnieper, the Dvortsovy and the Kupechesky, which afforded a view over the lower town of Podol. Not forgetting the bridges lined with numbered trees, or those areas of open ground preserved in the heart of the city, as if out of nostalgia for the steppe from which a smell of honey blew in on gusts of wind.

But Irotchka, as her family called her, was asthmatic, a hereditary condition. Her attacks were frequent and violent. A bunch of flowers was enough to affect her. At home there would only ever be a single tulip in a vase or some sweet peas on the balcony. In Paris, she was obliged to import inhalers from Switzerland. And her sensory memories of her native city would be those of a child capable of analysing instinctively 'the unique aroma of the air',[6] an acuity that would make her so receptive to Proustian distillation. Thus the narrator of *The Wine of Solitude* [*Le Vin de Solitude*], 'a poorly disguised autobiography' written in 1933, recalls that in Kiev 'the air misty with dust smelled of dung and roses'.[7]

Despite the rococo cupolas of St Andrew and the Marie Palace, which the younger Rastrelli had designed in 1762, the profusion of theatres, the trolleybus lines, which were inaugurated in 1892, it was impossible to forget that Kiev was the capital of an immensely vast field of buckwheat and rye. In the evenings, at harvest time, the dust from the straw in the ploughed fields stuck in one's throat. 'A cloudy red light drifted down from the sky; the wind carried the smell of the Ukrainian plains to the city, a mild but bitter scent of smoke and the coolness of the water and rushes that grew along the riverbanks.'[8] The Dnieper, pausing over this landscape, flowed through it in huge meandering bends. The breaking ice drove back the opposite bank far beyond the horizon. From the hilltop where the statue of Prince Vladimir held aloft his cross, studded with light-bulbs, to guide the boatmen, stretched a sea on which the sun never shone. The journalist Bernard Lecache, who in 1926 had come to record the testimonies of Jews who had survived the 1,300 pogroms of the civil war, could not help contemplating for a moment the splendour of Kiev, 'full of trees, and undulating, like a woman's body, as beautiful as a city can be'.[9]

For the little girl who was short of breath, this botanical paradise would for ever be a stifling greenhouse, an olfactory variation on the well-known Russian excess. 'The hot summer days, the bells of the ice cream seller, the flowers crushed under foot, crumpled in people's hands, too many plants, too many flowers; a perfume that was overly sweet, that troubles and lulls the spirit; too much light, a savage glare, the songs of birds in the sky: this was her land.'[10]

The Ukraine. In Kiev, its capital, the Russia of the Tsars was born. Even Andréi Bely, a Muscovite by birth, but a St Petersburger at heart, for whom other Russian cities were nothing but 'a miserable heap of wood', acknowledged this unreservedly: 'The mother of Russian cities is Kiev.'[11] Prince Oleg, at the conclusion of a victorious siege, established the first *rus* dynasty there in 882. Converted to the Orthodox faith a century later, under the reign of Vladimir, who had all his people baptised through immersion in the Dnieper, Kiev experienced wars and pillaging, but never neglect: a natural waterway from the Baltic to Constantinople, the river had never stopped replenishing the city with men and maintaining commerce there. And thus its status as the cradle of Russia, albeit the ancient and backward Russia, has never been contested.

To see Paris again

Was this really her cradle? In October, the departure of the ships for their winter dry docks heralded the frosts. The Némirovskys then packed their bags for a distant land. Vichy, Plombières, Vittel, Divonne . . . The spa towns, where their little daughter could be treated for her asthma, offered Irina's parents, Anna and Leonid, the supreme benefits of the casino. But they themselves preferred one of those communities in Nice among which Paul Bourget had just set his novel *Le Piège*, and had no qualms about travelling on to the Côte d'Azur, leaving the child in the care of a governess. Irène Némirovsky remembered that when they all returned to Kiev her wheeler-dealer of a father 'played and juggled or became engrossed in an old roulette wheel, brought back from Monte Carlo', a symbol of his gambler's personality. As for her mother, a photograph of her in a satin dress, with a tight-fitting waist, her arms and her hair strewn with black pearls, and an aigrette on her forehead, suggests the desire for approval that she sought in the palaces and gambling rooms: she wished other people to gaze at her apart from her husband, who sparkled with intelligence and determination rather than lust. A satisfied smile betrays her desires. It is this same portrait that her daughter would describe in 1928: 'Little mother, all dressed up for the ball, her shoulders bare, with a naïve, triumphant smile that seemed to say: "Just look at me! Aren't I beautiful? And if you only knew how much pleasure that gives me!"' All in all, an 'exquisite doll'.[12]

Sometimes these French 'winters' lasted four seasons. They began in Paris where Irina, their only child, alighted from the train with her parents and the servants. 'From the age of four, up until the war, I went there regularly every year. The first time, I stayed there for a year. I was in the care of a French teacher, and I always spoke French with my mother.'[13] And one cannot help smiling when Henri de

Régnier, upon closing *The Wine of Solitude* [*Le Vin de Solitude*] in 1935, felt able to say that 'Némirovsky writes Russian in French.'[14] For she was a French writer whom fate had caused to be born in Kiev, and her Russian, less innate than bookish, would remain imperfect. For Irène Némirovsky ('a Russian name, very difficult to pronounce'[15]), Russian would always be that uncivilised 'wild, sweet language'[16] of the East, where she was born. By comparison with the excitement of Paris, the non-stop theatre of the Riviera, and the variety of the French landscape, the Ukraine, whose very name conjures up boundaries, appeared to her as a desert of ploughed fields or snow glimpsed through a car window, 'a very flat land, where one's gaze is not immediately blocked, as in France, by some hill or the rooftops in a village'.[17] You could swear that Chekhov was thinking of the Némirovskys when he wrote: 'for them, Paris is the capital, the home, whereas the rest of Europe is merely a boring, incoherent provincial world you can only look at through the lowered blinds of Grand Hotels'.[18] In France, on the other hand, it was eternal springtime. And so the first known words written by her, scribbled on the back of a badly faded postcard at Vichy railway station, on 12th or 13th August 1912 or 1913, are in French: 'I am sending you the Chomel spring where I go to drink each morning. Maman thanks you for your letter but I think we are going to Biarritz. See you soon. Irène Némirovsky.'[19]

In Kiev, there was the memory of sensations; in Paris, nostalgia of the soul. For 'Kiev was a small provincial town then, peaceful and dismal',[20] whereas Irène 'felt her heart melt with tenderness at the memory of Paris, the Tuileries Gardens, the yellow moon that rose slowly above the column in the Place Vendôme'.[21] In Kiev there lay vague, mysterious, even worrying memories: 'The shouts of the *chouroum-bouroum*, the carpet seller . . . The little red-headed children, the acrobats who came to perform outside the windows in winter . . . And the crazy old man who had sung at the Opera and thought he was still a singer, draping himself with faded fine clothing, a crown of dried leaves on his head, making grand gestures and imagining that he was singing, though not a sound escaped his lips . . .'[22] Of the Paris of her childhood, in 1934 Irène Némirovsky retained a no less misty memory 'of the monkeys in the Jardin des Plantes and their scarlet genitals'; but above all, it was there, at the Tuileries or the Champs-Élysées, that she had played with little French children. 'Maman, it's not possible,' her daughter Denise would object in 1936. 'You could not have experienced that in the old days, because you were a foreigner . . .'[23] And so her life, 'like everyone's life, had its haven of light. Every year, she returned to France, with her mother and Mlle Rose . . . How happy she was to see Paris again! . . . She loved it so much!'[24]

Zézelle

Mademoiselle Rose? In giving her this delicate name, Irène Némirovsky pointed out in 1936 that she had wanted to draw 'as faithful a portrait as possible' of her former governess. 'I say "as faithful as possible", because this character drawn from reality has caused me much more sadness than if I had invented her.'[25] Not that the memory had to be coaxed out, but she was afraid of sullying the memory of her poor French governess, whom she fallen out with ultimately. How she would come to regret her ingratitude! 'Deliberately, and for many long years, I did not utter her name. My clumsy lips refused to speak it. . . . I no longer want to call her Zézelle, it's too sacrosanct. I shall see. Mademoiselle Rose is good, too . . .'

Perhaps Zézelle had a brother. Perhaps she had grown up in the Ursuline convent. Perhaps her skin was soft: if, in *The Wine of Solitude*, invention comes to the aid of memory, it does not betray it. Of southern origin, 'she was tidy, precise, meticulous, a Frenchwoman through and through, a little "aloof", somewhat scornful. Never a fuss. Rarely kissed anyone.'[26] She was so tiny that by the age of twelve Irotchka had almost caught up with her. Anna Némirovsky, as was the fashion at the time, had engaged this fragile upright woman from the French Home in Kiev, an agency that provided the Kiev middle classes with young French nannies.

Marie – to give her her real name – taught the rudiments of her own language to the child who was entrusted to her. 'She sang in a quiet voice, but so clearly and so tunefully. She taught me: "La tour prends garde", "Marlbrough" and "Les bas noirs, les bas noirs . . ." and also "Nous n'irons plus au bois", "Valsez, fillettes, valsez coquettes, marionnettes du gai Paris".' But also French sayings: '*Aide-toi, le ciel t'aidera* [God helps those who help themselves].' A crumpled photograph shows her dressed in black, a Paris newspaper on her knees, although her hands were rarely idle. We cannot see her gold watch and chain on her breast, but her waist, 'whose measurements were those of an earlier age' is of the kind that Irène Némirovsky – whom we can see behind the governess's right shoulder, wearing an apologetic smile, and with two ribbons in her hair – would try to describe twenty years later:

> Nearly always wearing a little blouse with small tucks, fine linen and broderie anglaise, and sometimes a black sateen apron, her delicate feet clad in black boots with buttons. A velvet ribbon around her neck . . . A face that must have once had the graceful, delicate beauty of a grisette, with 'a youthful glow' that passes quickly, but which still retained her extremely pretty, cheerful, kindly, heart-shaped mouth. Small teeth like those of a mouse. The rest of her features were fine and irregular, and, at the age of fifty, revealed small, delicate 'lines', dark, tired eyes, and hair that in spite of her age was a light, deep-chestnut colour, dark with bluish reflections, assembled in smoky ringlets, in the old-fashioned way, over her uncovered head.

The face of France, virtuous and reserved.

Fine soap and oil of violets

Irina knew instinctively that her mother would not sacrifice her thirties to her daughter. Her 'self-made man' of a husband, an unflagging 'gold-digger', promised to become sufficiently wealthy to buy back her youth for her. If in her vanity she had been able to foresee these riches, would she have been foolish enough to burden herself with a little girl 'whom she had to drag about Europe', a living and costly reproach which would never cease to remind her that she was no longer a young woman? Thanks to God or to abortion, Irina would remain this capricious woman's only child.

Before she was ten years old, Irotchka realised that the only affection she could hope for would be from 'Zézelle', whereas her mother restricted herself to scoldings and reprimands, which she delivered twenty times a day:

'You're cold, and you don't say so, you stupid girl! Put on your coat! At once, do you hear, at once! Let me feel your pulse . . . That's all we need, for you to be ill . . . Leave your nose alone, please, when someone is speaking to you . . . Stand up straight!!! How many times do I have say this to you? You'll be the death of me, I swear . . .'[27]

As for caresses, best not to think of them, unless it was to buy forgiveness, for this mean-spirited mother liked to be thought magnanimous. Aware that Zézelle was the only one who looked after her, Irina gave her all her affection, whereas to Anna she pledged an exquisite hatred, which could be aroused by the 'strange smell' of her blouse, 'a mixture of her mother's perfume, that she hated, the scent of tobacco and a richer smell, warmer, one [she] could neither guess nor recognise, but which she breathed in with amazement, with apprehension, with a kind of primitive sense of modesty'.[28] Zézelle, on the other hand, smelled of 'fine soap and oil of violets', the very aroma of the Nice hinterland. She forgave everything. 'During my childhood, she stood for refuge, for light. How often did she console me when I was punished unfairly, dealt with harshly, or scolded. She soothed me, she was full of moderation, of wisdom . . .'

Anna was jealous. Knowing where to strike, she employed the same cowardly threat on each occasion: 'It really is time we found an English woman to teach you how to behave properly!' Irotchka was appalled: 'How can I, after so many years, accurately describe the feeling that welled up in my soul, the storm of resentment, of pain, of wounded pride? It was not so much her words which, if spoken softly, with a smile, might have seemed tolerable, it was her hateful tone that I am unable to convey, the intonation that, in advance, established the mother as the enemy.' And to think that she still had to go on kissing that chalky-white cheek 'which I wanted to dig my nails into' and say: 'Forgive me, Mama, I'm sorry, I won't do it again.' Several novels would be insufficient to staunch this heart full of rancour which obliged her always to put on an act.

From her mother, Irina inherited her shortness, her brown eyes, her weary gaze. But while she had her father's large mouth which she never liked, Anna's mouth was thin, small, tight-lipped, and her lips were 'pallid, never still, never natural except when she was shouting'. She had a pale complexion and that 'predatory jaw' which lent her a 'loathsome beauty'.

On their first visits to Paris, the Némirovskys could not yet afford to stay in the de luxe hotels. Nevertheless, even when Anna was able to spend part of the year in Paris, leaving Leonid to his relentless toil, Irotchka and her governess were housed elsewhere, usually in a second-class hotel. The novelist would have plenty of opportunity to create an unconventional childhood for herself in *L'Ennemie* [The Enemy], an early novel. '[She] knew that it was not always appropriate to cling to her Mama's skirts when she was going for a stroll, through the trees, with some unknown gentleman.'[29] She was that half-orphan girl, however, even though being abandoned gave her a strange pleasure: that of observing one's own life at a distance. In 1938, she would recall once more the Cité du Retiro, in the Faubourg Saint-Honoré, where her mother had dumped her in a poorly heated room, for she had no need of a witness to her pleasures. 'Of all the hotels I knew in my childhood, that one was the worst, precisely because its squalor was cold and appropriate . . . It was . . . let's see . . . in a wonderful district (the Madeleine, that says it all), with gates they closed at night at the end of a courtyard, a kind of blackish building . . . But here the electricity was switched off during the day to save money, and you could smell the foul kitchen, and see shadows passing by, going down the staircase and crossing the little sitting room.' A scene out of Balzac; one that would be used again in *Le Maître des âmes* [The Master of Souls][30] to accommodate the pitiful beginnings of Doctor Asfar.

But amid all this sordidness was Zézelle. 'She had a core of gaiety which persisted, over a long period, beneath the sadness, beneath the pain . . . She was the only person I really loved in the world.' Anna must have loathed this sad angel, while trying to disguise her own bad temper. Zézelle was at risk in this unspoken rivalry, and she would pay dearly for her role as mother substitute . . .

The carnival at Nice

From Paris, via Vichy, the Némirovskys ended the off-season at Cannes or at Biarritz – where, as Chekhov says, 'the whole of Russia complains that there are too many Russians'.[31] At Nice, in February 1906, mother and daughter were able to join in the carnival festivities. The theme, that year, was Harlequin-Sunshine. 'His Majesty', Harlequin, sketched by the highly eccentric Mossa, was represented astride a blue eagle. But it was the parade of masks along the Promenade des Anglais that most affected the youthful imagination of Irotchka, who had just celebrated her third birthday, an age when early memories begin to stick. When, in December 1932, in the margins of her novel *Le Pion sur l'échiquier* [The Pawn on the Chessboard], Irène Némirovsky drew sketches of the 'masks' of her heroes in her Gallia exercise book, it was in memory of those grimacing heads[32] from which only the calves and feet of the revellers protruded. It is not surprising that in 1930 the first readers of *David Golder* were struck by the coarse features of her characters – exaggerated people, out of a Balzac novel – going so far as to refer, as did Theodore Purdy, the well-known columnist from *The Nation*, to 'caricatures, rather than living figures, but drawn with such assurance, such cruelty!'[33] To say nothing of the Jewish characters in her early writings, who would seem to be moulded from pasteboard.

By making Nice their winter quarters, the Némirovskys were merely following the fashion set by Tsarina Alexandra in 1856 – even though a few men of letters, such as Gogol and Lermontov had preceded her. Ever since it was brought under French jurisdiction in 1860, the bay of Villefranche-sur-Mer had become a miniature Crimea, and it was in the Orthodox church in Nice that the body of the Tsarevitch lay. Ironically, the Russian nobility and the imperial court mingled with the nihilists in exile who were striving to get rid of them, much to the displeasure of the English spending the winter season there. After 1905, because of the political thaw, one could witness the comings and goings of aristocrats on holiday and anarchists returning to their homelands, their pockets full of tracts and explosives. Irène Némirovsky would recall this in *The Courilof Affair* [*L'Affaire Courilof*].

It was between 1900 and 1914 that the Russian colony on the Côte d'Azur expanded. The Némirovskys were not among the six hundred or so listed house owners in 1914. They preferred the comfort of the Terminus Hotel or the Ruhl, which had just replaced the former Hôtel des Anglais, and which the *Journal de Saint-Pétersbourg* – a financial newssheet that had been published in French for almost a hundred years, in which selected passages by Vigny and Barrès sometimes appeared – never tired of praising. These palaces put on dances and organised hat competitions or floral exhibitions that Anna would not have missed for the world. At the Nice races, for the first time elegant women wore their tailored jackets, a fashion that began only in 1906. There too, one might catch sight of the Princesses Paléologue or Faucigny-Lucinge, of the Prince de Bourbon, the Duc de Choiseul-Praslin, the Breteuils or the Montebellos, and still believe for an instant that, on the Baie des Anges, privileges had not been abolished. The thrill of such moments, which made her forget the Jewish quarter of Odessa where she had been born, and the Yiddish that rose to her lips whenever she lost her temper, was worth all the Russian Christmases on the Côte d'Azur. Anna Némirovsky, therefore, thought of herself as a Frenchwoman and, by grafting a 'J' or an 'F' on to her first name, she could be known as Jeanne or Fanny.

In *La Vie mondaine*, 'journal of the high-life', published on the Riviera monthly in summer, but weekly in winter, you could check the 'list of foreigners' residing in Nice, Cannes or Menton. It is worth mentioning a few of those who lived the great days of the Côte between 1880 and 1910: Grand-Dukes Vladimir, Alexis, Serge and Paul, the brothers of Alexander III; Count Serge Tolstoy, chamberlain to the Emperor; Madame de Durousov, who kept a very fashionable salon; the Ukrainian artist Marie Bashkirtseff, who shared the Villa Acqua-Viva, on the Promenade des Anglais, with her cats; and also Joseph Kessel, a schoolboy at the Lycée Masséna. And not forgetting Anton Chekhov, who stayed at the Russian boarding house L'Oasis for his health in March 1898; 'the carnival, the French books, even the almanacs which he read with pleasure, everything interested him,'[34] Irène Némirovsky would write, echoing her own marvellous memories of the Riviera: 'Nice. The lawns of the Negresco . . . It is not the luxury that you admire. You imagine a perfect life in which everything is order and beauty . . . well, paradise!'

And that is why, in about 1910, in Kiev, which was more bedecked with flowers than a carnival wagon, a florist opened a shop called 'À la Flore de Nice': France was in vogue in the Ukrainian capital, just as she was in St Petersburg where 'it was the done thing to send one's clothes to be laundered in Paris or in London', while in polite society one 'affected to speak French and to pronounce Russian with a foreign accent'.[35] In Kiev, a woman of taste took tea at La Marquise and bought her supplies from the Chic Parisien, in Teatralnaya Street. In an episode cut from *The Dogs and the Wolves* [*Les Chiens et les Loups*], Irène

Némirovsky also mentions Aline's, a Parisian milliner on the boulevard. So much elegance could not fail to attract Anna Némirovsky, who preferred to be called Anna Ivanovna, like the niece of Peter the Great. The most germanophile of the tsarinas – but 'the most Russian of all the Russian tsarinas' according to Rémizov[36] – who ruled over the Empire with a stone fist from 1730 to 1740, she had been notorious for the thousands of opponents who were arrested and tortured, or deported to Siberia during her reign, but also for her support of the arts – the ballet in particular.

High life

'Refined and authoritarian'[37] was how 'Fanny' would be remembered by the family, and this was how her daughter portrayed her in the novel about her own wretched childhood: 'She was tall, shapely, "of regal bearing".'[38] And yet she was small, five foot three at the most. Her face, even in old age, was always powdered, and she worried that her daughter's kisses might spoil her make-up, but she enjoyed life too, for 'sorrow ages people and ruins the face'.[39] Although her registered date of birth is given as 1 April 1887, Anna Margoulis was born in about 1875.[40] This ruse succeeded in tricking a few lovers, later a few gigolos, and finally a few gold-digging pimps. But she was as lustful and mendacious as she was venal. Even in Kiev, she almost divorced Leonid because she had fallen for a rich Russian. It took this man's lover, a girl of eighteen, the daughter of a Jewish tailor who scraped a living in an upstairs room, to come in person to entreat her to leave the man, before Anna, alarmed, agreed to give up her infatuation.[41]

Anna Némirovsky would not have appreciated a young Jewish girl coming to plead for her cooperation in this way. For, to her considerable chagrin, her own parents were Jewish, just as Leonid was. And Jews, since the time of Catherine II, had been allocated housing zones outside of which they risked being arrested. Furthermore, their civil rights were not always recognised in the Russia of Nicholas II. These humiliating restrictions were known as 'disabilities'. It was solely in Kiev that, unless one was entitled to the privileges accorded to chemists or former soldiers – both highly respected jobs – only those Jewish shopkeepers and financiers of the 'first guild' were entitled to live in the city, and not in the suburbs. This was the case with the banker Leonid Borisovich Némirovsky, just as it was with the jeweller Aron Simonovich, born in Kiev in 1873, who would rise to become Rasputin's financial adviser. Privileges such as these were granted to the most socially advanced Jews by the liberal-minded Alexander II, but his assassination, in 1881, had thrown Russo-Jewish society back into arbitrariness and restrictions.

Well aware of this apartheid, Anna was careful to choose her lovers from among the Gentiles. She also forbade Yiddish from being spoken under her roof, or the preparation of Jewish dishes; these were archaic habits, incompatible with the French furniture brought from the Faubourg Saint-Antoine, the French ballads she sang to her own accompaniment on the piano, the French outfits purchased in the Rue Auber and worn for the first time in Biarritz, and the copies of *Femina* and other fashion magazines published in Paris. In this respect, Anna was not very different from so many of the parvenus from the upper part of town, 'bloated with self-importance', who were only concerned with getting the better of the middle classes, so amusingly described – in Yiddish – by Sholem Aleichem, who lived in Kiev during the Belle Époque: 'People go abroad to take the waters; the ladies walk around clad in gold and velvet; the children ride about on *"vélocipèdes"*; at home, they have governesses, they speak French and play the piano, they eat jam and drink liqueurs; they spend without counting the cost. In a word, it's the high life . . .'[42]

Miss Dragonfly

Anna's parents had given her a perfect education. A gold-medal winner at the Kiev Gymnasium – the top school for girls – she was thus entitled to teach there for a while. She had been taught the piano by teachers from the Conservatoire. Very aware of her own appearance, she adored fur coats, scents and the sweet shops in Pechersk, the famous *tsoukiernas* with their pyramids of Turkish delight and crystallised fruits. This is no doubt where she acquired her 'tendency to be plump, which she fought by using those corsets shaped like a breastplate which women wore at that time and over which their breasts nestled in two satin pockets, like fruit in a basket'.[43] A love of food was inherited from her father, Jonas Margoulis.

Of him, at least, Irina could be proud. Born in 1847, in Odessa, Jonas – whom people preferred to call Iona or Johann – also had nostalgic memories of the carnival at Nice, of the Paris Opéra, which he was mad about, and – not far away, on the Boulevard des Italiens – of the Maison Dorée, the best restaurant in France until it closed in 1902, where he had squandered his inheritance. Irina used to listen dreamily as he recalled this blissful time:

'Every afternoon I would go and take the air on the boulevard. It is lined with trees, and there one encounters the most beautiful women languidly reclining in their open carriages . . .'

So many years later, he still spoke French perfectly, though with a slight accent: 'He would say: "*Ma petite* file" [my little girl] putting a strong stress on the final mispronounced syllable. His was the only conversation that bothered about culture . . .' He had read Racine, Voltaire, Hugo – he pronounced the name 'Hougo' – and, languishing far from France, he could still recite 'Athalie's Dream' or 'La feuille' by Arnault:[44]

> De ta tige détachée,
> Pauvre feuille desséchée,
> Où vas-tu? – Je n'en sais rien . . .*

Iona had not just learnt French and music. He had graduated from the Nicholas I School of Commerce in Odessa. In those days 'he was young and healthy, with his fine teeth, his brisk movements, his blazing eyes, shining with intelligence . . . beneath large, bushy eyebrows'. Already rather dashing and fastidious in his dress, he wore a goatee beard. His wife, Rosa Chedrovich, known as Bella, was a very gentle little woman, shy and devout, and never without her prayer book. Of her, Irène Némirovsky would retain the memory of a small, grey-haired woman, who worried and had nothing to do, whom her daughter and her husband treated badly, who was worn out by sorrows and household duties, was treated like a servant, and who had never been young. 'A poor, slight, scrawny little woman who in my imagination always seemed to be seventy-five years old, limping hurriedly

---

*'Adrift from your stalk,/ Poor withered leaf,/ Where are you going? – I have no idea . . .' [Tr.]

on one leg, with a face that was faded like an old photograph, her features hazy and yellowing, drenched in tears . . .'

Rosa was born in 1854 in the 'new town' of Ekaterinoslav, the cereal capital of the Ukraine, but her family came originally from Alexandrovsk,[45] a hundred kilometres south, on the Dnieper. Her parents, 'important wheat merchants', who were wealthy and had twelve children, one of whom was her twin, had provided her with a tidy little dowry. She willingly acknowledged, however, that the Margoulis family were in another league:

'When I got married, your great-grandfather had a synagogue built in Alexandrovsk . . . My wedding dress had been ordered from Odessa and brought by river, on a boat borrowed for the purpose . . .'

Anna, their elder daughter, was eighteen when, in 1893, Rosa gave birth to a second child, whose name was Victoria. This young aunt was, in a manner of speaking, Irina's elder sister. And this was how they were brought up. When Anna and Leonid decided not to take Irotchka with them to France, she would be entrusted to her grandparents and sent to stay with Victoria.

Victoria, in turn, received the same careful education as her older sister. She learned French. She was enrolled at the Gymnasium in Fundukleyev Street, in the heart of Kiev, at more or less the same period as Anna Akhmatova. 'She was a delightful person and very easy to get on with, very pretty,' her granddaughter Tatiana recalls. 'She was nicknamed "Miss Dragonfly". Because she had been spotted at an officers' ball wearing her school uniform, the establishment was obliged to change the design. And when she returned carrying flowers, it caused a great commotion at home!'[46] Irène Némirovsky confirms this aspect of her character in 'Le Sortilège', a plainly autobiographical short story: 'My aunt was pretty, with soft skin and a slim figure, and as simple as a flower.'[47] Iona, however, had paid out so much money to have Anna sit in front of a piano that, when Victoria wished to imitate her, he replied:

'We have spent too much on your sister. You must ask your husband to pay for them [lessons], when you are married.'

So Victoria, while still very young, made a bad marriage to an older man. Anna did not complain: she did not like having to share the large apartment that Leonid had eventually found for them on Pushkin Street with her sister and her parents. If it had been her decision, she would have dissuaded her husband from taking in Iona and Rosa, whom she would have left on their own in Odessa, where everything reminded her of Jews, from all walks of life, and of the ghetto where the family sprang from. In *The Dogs and the Wolves*, Irène Némirovsky would portray a similar parvenu character 'who was proud to distance [himself] as far away as possible from the people they called (and with such scorn!) the simple Jews, the poor Jews . . .'[48] Victoria, in turn, would forbid her own children from marrying Jews, in order to simplify their lives. And yet, from force of habit, the Némirovskys only mixed with their own kind in Kiev – a hypocritical attitude that Irène would take pleasure in mocking in *Le Bal* by accumulating the names of the Nassans, the Moïssis, the Birnbaums, the Rothwans, the Levinsteins and the Lévy de Brunelleschis on the invitation cards sent out by the Kemps, a couple of Jewish parvenus who are the ghosts of Anna and Leonid . . .

Of mud and black pigs

It was in Odessa, while she was still living with her parents, that Anna made the acquaintance of Leonid Némirovsky towards the end of the century. He had been born on 1st September 1868 at Elisavetgrad, a provincial capital established in the eighteenth century to keep the Turks and the Tartars from the Crimea under control. In the previous year the mother of another French writer, Judaeo-Russian like Irène Némirovsky, had been born there: Nathalie Sarraute. In 1885, the city of green roofs, which had only recently been electrified, was awaiting its first water-tower. Elisavetgrad still consisted of 'mud and black pigs', of lowly shops with windows embossed with ice, a 'free and penniless childhood',[49] which Leonid didn't mind recalling when he was in the right mood or, like Irène Némirovsky's David Golder, when he was racked by nostalgia for stale bread: 'a shop, lit up, on a dark street . . . a candle set behind an icy window, the night, snow falling,, and himself . . .'[50] He actually laughed when he told Irotchka about the day when, in order to put out a fire in a burning house, he had gone out into the street with other children to form a chain: 'We sprayed water on the neighbours' feet, on the women's skirts, and then over each other!'

But in Elisavetgrad, one out of every two children died before reaching adolescence. Jews made up a quarter of the 50,000 registered inhabitants. None of them went to school in 1860; twenty years later, out of a total of 134 pupils, there were 104 Jews, a sign of great social improvement. In the last years of the century, the Jews had come to account for one third of the population of the Ukraine. Their forebears were frequently not 'children of Israel', but distant descendants of the Khazars, a Turkish-speaking tribe that had converted to Judaism in the middle of the eighth century. Because they tolerated mixed marriages, the Khazars had been responsible for an extraordinary expansion of Judaism in southern Russia, and a Judaism that was more spiritual – and material – than ethnic.

Leonid Némirovsky was probably not one of the happier Jewish schoolboys in Elisavetgrad. He lost his father, Boris, whom Irina would never know, when still a child. Leonid would not say a word about this, what is more, merely observing quietly that: 'When I was ten, my father threw me out . . .'[51] He lived alone with his mother, Eudoxia, his brothers, and his sister, Anna Borisovna. Soon afterwards, he had to go to work to help provide for them. He was employed first as an errand boy in a hotel, then as an assistant in a factory in Lodz, in Poland, one of the main textile centres in Eastern Europe, famed for its printed cotton and its miserable ghetto.[52] One night, the factory caught fire. He did not attempt to bring the blaze under control, having guessed that 'the fire had been lit in order to cash in on the insurance premiums'. By the age of twenty, this smart young man had done every type of work, he had roamed around Moscow and travelled across Russia as far as the Pacific Ocean, relying on large swigs of strong alcohol whenever he was unwell. From these feverish years he had developed a hole in one lung which would later lead to his collapse. In Irina's eyes, her father would continue to be the embodiment of the toughness that for her was peculiar to the Jewish spirit, proudly bending destiny to his advantage while others merely submit to chance, pleasure or fate. For certain writers, this domineering quality would be the legacy of the 'Jews of the steppes', the descendants of the distant Khazars, who paid no attention to ritual – a characteristic of a Trotsky or a David Golder; whereas the caricature of the Jew from the ghetto sagging beneath the secular yoke, but grateful to God for his misery, that 'resigned mediocrity'[53] as Irène Némirovsky described it in 1927, was a more ancient type, moulded by twenty centuries of persecution.[54]

An obscure little Jew

What could this Leonid Némirovsky, from such a humble background, really mean to the refined Anna Margoulis, brought up by her parents with a veneration for French culture, still so significant in Odessa? He spoke only Russian and Yiddish. He was, in a word, 'a peasant'[55] who did not deserve his good fortune. He did not come from a 'good family', but from one of those indiscernible lineages 'that rise deviously, instinctively, like certain aquatic plants' until they 'push through the green, thick, muddy surface of a lake'. At least he had risen to the top. He had just taken over the management of a factory that made cotton fabrics whose gaudy designs Irotchka would always remember. She would also retain memories of a factory in Schlüsserburg, to the east of St Petersburg, and of an asphalt factory with 'low, sombre rooms, with trodden earth floors', where the workers were to her child's eyes merely 'voiceless, shapeless shadows'.

Leonid's audacity, his 'powerful, passionate expression' had not failed to intrigue Anna. 'He had suddenly earned enough money and was offering her a sure, stable position. He had seen the young woman, found her beautiful, had taken a gamble after a few drinks, had married her, thus ensuring, without realising it, a lifetime of unhappiness.' If she could not find herself a Russian aristocrat, the Margoulises would still have wished a less dubious suitor for their daughter. But Anna was already acquiring a practical notion of what it was that constituted a 'good family': 'When for three generations, no one had stolen anything, nor been in prison, and they knew how to read or write.' But, more importantly, knew how to earn money. And yet, despite his undeniable material success, Leonid would always be a pariah among the Kiev bourgeoisie. Reflecting on the 'old tarnished kettle' that he liked to use, Anna could not help but compare it to the silver services of their acquaintances. 'Were they richer or not as rich, well respected or less respected? . . . Just one clear feeling, but an extremely vivid one. They were different, they were outsiders, and, strangely, rather marginalised.'

So in about 1902, Leonid placed a large engagement ring on her finger. Victoria, who had kept a watchful eye on the manoeuvrings of the suitor around her elder sister, was their maid of honour. Leonid was climbing another rung on the ladder. Plump and resilient, Anna was very much to his taste. His pride in shaping his life was, however, mingled with the humiliation of being merely tolerated by Anna's parents, and by Anna herself. Because of his tobacco-coloured skin, he had been nicknamed 'the Arab', like Pushkin, who had Abyssinian blood. Irène would inherit his tanned complexion. On her right wrist there was a brownish patch, like a hallmark, which would always remind her that if her destructive trace of snobbery came from her mother, it was to her father, that 'obscure little Jew', that she owed both her tenacity, her great pride, her shrewdness and, above all, her enigmatic capacity for success.

Gradually, by juggling with shares, Leonid grew rich. He owned a match factory in the Baltic States, one of the main centres for the manufacture of non-phosphoric matches after Novgorod.[56] Ever since Serge Witte, the Minister of Finance from 1894 to 1902, had opened up the Empire to foreign capital, it had been a favourable time for entrepreneurs. Within ten years, oil and steel production had seen spectacular expansion. The extension of the rail network and the advent of the trans-Siberian railway made the Far East a new America. The Ukraine had become an industrial Eldorado. Half the cast-iron, iron and coal needed by Russia was mined there. Speculation favoured the emergence of a flourishing middle class, which relied on the creation of the constitutional-democratic party – or 'Cadet' – loyal to the new institutions, but favourable to liberal reforms in the Western mould. As with the revolutionary parties, a number of Jews could be spotted among the Cadets, a consequence of the unwavering anti-Semitism of the tsars. This would not fail to be denounced by the Orthodox reactionaries.

Men are wolves . . .

The liberalism of the Cadets more or less suited Leonid Némirovsky's school of thought, for his sole preoccupation was to prosper, unfettered, and to erect a bulwark of gold between himself and his childhood.

He began to cultivate a discouraging grimace beneath a 'short American moustache' in the Douglas Fairbanks style. If he handled a great deal of business, it was not because of the lure of money, but the early acquired habit of fighting in order to live, of buying the rights that had not been granted to him, and the desire to give his daughter the childhood he had never had.

'I had no time for fun. I had to work. You don't know what that is . . . You have everything. You, *you're a happy child* . . . You eat when you're hungry, you're warm in winter . . . You learn, you'll be an educated woman . . .'

And if he paid little attention to Anna's indiscretions, it was because he wasn't interested. Certainly, 'he didn't hate women, but he treated them with scorn. Only one thing in the world gave him pleasure, gold, he was consumed by a terrible lust for gold.' Bankers' jargon, mixed with fashionable French phrases of the day, was the first language that Irène Némirovsky would have heard. She was brought up amid this confusing prattle: 'Just the figures . . . The price of sugar and wheat . . . "Millions, millions" . . . "Ten million . . .", "One million." "One hundred and twenty-five thousand million" . . . then two words . . . "Debts" and "millions". Sometimes one word dominated, sometimes the other. But, usually, they were used together, like the chorus of a song.'

Because he had been poor and had had to support his own family, Leonid would even provide for the education of his niece and nephew, Ekaterina and Gricha. He would respond to Anna's ever more exorbitant whims, and eventually even take in and provide for her lovers. Having spent his whole life slaving away, what raison d'être remained to him other than wearing himself out even more, to the point of exhaustion, as long as people lived well at his expense? 'The only duty he recognised towards God and men was this: to keep his family alive, raise his children, support the elderly and those who were still of an age to be able to work, to give [them] money – with sarcasm, irony, and often with helpful words . . . but to give, and to keep giving, right down to his last penny.' But he wasn't taken in by scroungers.

'My girl,' he said to Irotchka each day, 'men are wolves. When you are strong, they are frightened of you and flatter you, and as soon as you succumb, they devour you . . .'

And yet he had been a cheerful young man, full of hope and

strength. 'Sometimes, he would sing, plucking at the strings of a guitar, just to entertain, for he had no musical education other than his ear for harmony. Gypsy songs, Ukrainian songs, and, most especially, those marvellous songs from Moldavia.'

The spectre of the ghetto

After Irina's birth, Leonid's position had improved. He owned warehouses in Odessa. For a long time the city had been dominated by Greek ship owners and grain-trading, an occupation that had made Anna's maternal grandparents wealthy. At the turn of the twentieth century, the great port of the Ukraine, founded by Catherine II midway between Athens and St Petersburg, had become a southern Babel of four hundred thousand souls, the population having doubled in twenty years. Not only did all the peoples of southern Russia and the Mediterranean mingle there happily, 'the Levantines who smell of garlic, the tide and spices, people whom the sea had gathered up from every corner of the world and flung there in a torrent of foam',[57] but one could also trade virtually anything and everything there, wheat, wool, exotic produce, herrings, nuts and watermelons, not to mention early Zionist pamphlets.

The Jews of Odessa, almost a third of the city, lived mostly in what was effectively the red-light district of the Moldavanka. They spoke Russian, and the percentage of their children who attended school was five times higher than in Kiev. Since 1870, however, their situation had deteriorated. With the expansion of the railway, the port of Odessa was now in competition for trade with Rostov or Sevastopol. The recession spread through the city, driving the unemployed and the new arrivals into the ghettos, while the newly enriched merchants were terrified that the Jewish curse might catch up with them.

For persecutions had not stopped raining down on these rather too plentiful Jews. In May 1871, an early storm of hatred had ravaged the Jewish quarter, causing the deaths of six people and making thousands homeless. These irrational reprisals aimed to deflect the people's fury towards imagined threats and were known as 'pogroms'. The government regularly unleashed turmoil throughout the ghetto. Any excuse was valid: 'peace, war, a victory, a defeat, the birth of a long-awaited

Imperial heir, an assassination, a trial, revolutionary uprisings or a great need of money . . .'[58] In this apocalyptic carnival, the worst atrocities, worthy of the Conquista, were encouraged – as one witness, Israel Zangwill, said about the pogrom at Milovka: 'an old man scalped with a sharp ladle; a woman whose eye was put out with a white-hot poker; a child's skull trampled by the heel of a real Russian'.[59]

These massacres had doubled following the assassination of Alexander II on 1st March 1881, from bullets fired by a revolutionary. By way of atonement, the 'Jewrys' – as they were called at the time – of Elisavetgrad, Odessa, Kichinev and one hundred and sixty other locations suffered both force and fury. Nothing was spontaneous: the rioters were usually manipulated by government envoys, while the firemen were kept to barracks throughout the duration of the 'disturbances', so that the rioting could be discreetly brought under imperial control. Frequently, it was enough to spread a rumour in order to collect ransoms and then feign leniency. But, at regular intervals, it was necessary to give substance to the threat. The pogroms, in short, were a preposterous means of government, the final manifestation of a retrograde state.

Within thirty years, this scourge had destroyed Odessa, the principal Jewish city in Russia, by sowing insecurity and exile. Irène Némirovsky was barely succumbing to exaggeration when, in 1927, she described the ghetto children she had observed in her childhood: 'They jostled people in the streets; they begged, quarrelled, swore at the passers-by, rolled around half-naked in the mud, fed themselves off vegetable peelings, stole, threw stones at dogs, fought, filled the streets with a hellish din that never let up. . . . As soon as they were a little older . . . they sold watermelons they'd stolen, asked for alms and prospered like those rats that run along the beach, circling the old boats.'[60] The comparison strikes one as repugnant; it is one that Isaac Babel employed, in that same year of 1927, to describe a synagogue invaded by rats.[61] But Gogol, too, had a similar recollection when, in *Taras Bulba*, he described the 'Jewry' of Warsaw in almost identical terms.[62]

In 1910, a cholera epidemic had decimated the Moldavanka. In Odessa the reality discouraged caricature. In *David Golder*, Irène Némirovsky would describe the Jewish quarter of the Marais, in Paris, in the same way, with its dark stalls that 'smelled of fish, dust and rotting straw'.[63] The first person to describe this was Israel Zangwill, the son of a Latvian immigrant, who in 1892 depicted, without contempt or false pride, the ghetto of Whitechapel, in London's East End, with its 'filthy men', its 'unwashed women', its children 'crawling around in gutters or in alleyways . . . in the mud, among the peelings', an entire 'race of semi-barbaric people', and one that was his own. 'Never have the Jews been portrayed so badly as they have by this Jew,' wrote André Spire of Zangwill. 'And yet nothing in his work could be less like that of the professional anti-Semites.'[64] Similarly, from her very earliest writings, Irène Némirovsky would never allow herself to feel pity for people, and yet, at the same time, she never averted her eyes from what Spire calls 'the solemn face of the ghetto'. This was also a concern of 'enlightened' Yiddish writers – Sforim, Peretz, Aleichem: not to depict nostalgia for the *shtetl* and places of Jewish misery, in case they blackened them still further.

In these conditions, one can understand that the Margoulises should have viewed anxiously the prospect of Anna meeting an orphan without a past, a beast of burden who had wasted away his health on suspect jobs, from Lodz to Vladivostok. Even his name, Némirovsky, he 'who knows no peace', symbolised the centuries of snubs endured by the Jews of Russia. Nemirov, an ancient fortified town in Podolia, had long prided itself on the erudition of its rabbis. That was before 10th June 1648, when the hetman Khmelnytsky, the leader of the Zaporague Cossacks, to whom the Polish princes had granted relative autonomy in Ukraine, gave orders to three hundred of his ruffians, brandishing Polish flags as decoys, to slit the throats one by one of the six thousand or so Jews of Nemirov, men, women and children, aided and abetted by the Greeks who lived in the town. A number of the wretched victims were thrown into the Dnieper; only those who wished to convert survived. The synagogue was set alight, the sacred books were trampled or cut into pieces to use as sandals. The Cossacks maintained that by such actions they were freeing themselves from the land rents imposed on them by the Polish overlords, who had cynically given the Jews the duty of raising taxes, including those on marriage and baptism, and had therefore equipped them with the keys of the churches. However, this legend, peddled by Sholem Asch in his romanticised chronicle of the fall of Nemirov, is not based on any historical document. The memory of the Nemirov pogrom, the most terrible one of this period, would still remain so vivid that Polish Jews continued to commemorate it with a day of fasting, the 20th of the month of Sivan.[65]

The scum

Anna had a stomach-turning notion of the ghetto: filth, misery and vice, mired in a dense hubbub of Yiddish. Leonid would never earn enough to make this spectre go away. As a reaction, she cultivated an ideal of purity that she carried to neurotic lengths, one form of which was miserliness – at home, Anna economised on butter and sugar – another, an obsessive concern with her appearance and a fondness for washing herself spotlessly clean. If you don't grow old you won't grow ugly. She always wore make-up, her black hair shone and her eyebrows were finely pencilled. 'I remember my mother's image very clearly,' wrote Irène Némirovsky in 1934. 'How curious it is that, until now, I am unable to write that word without hatred.' Anna, just like Bénia in Babel's *Tales*, must have thought: 'Did the good Lord not make a mistake in settling the Jews in Russia in order that they should be tormented there as if in hell? What harm would there have been in having them live in Switzerland, where they would have been surrounded by well-ordered lakes, mountain air and nothing but French people?'[66] As for her, she would always require more and more jewellery to overcome her obsession with the 'race'. For 'if Papa stopped working,' she explained to Irotchka, 'if he did no more business, they would all become little provincial Jews again, who knows? Similar, perhaps, to the Jews from the Podol.' That was the great fear of the Russified Jews, whether they came from Kiev or St Petersburg.[67]

The Podol, on the banks of the river, was the historical heart of the Ukrainian capital. In more recent times, it had become the quarter reserved for the Jews, those forbidden entry to the upper town of Kiev, which was the preserve of aristocrats, high-ranking civil servants, and Jews who had got where they were through merit, shrewdness or being comfortably off: the home of the Némirovskys. In the Podol, you could hear the sound of cobblers hammering, the wheels of the carts unloading flour, the patter of street pedlars and the cries of slovenly children wearing caps and *paéys*, armed with catapults, running about the broken-down alleyways beneath heaving clotheslines.

'Strange images . . . that nauseating street, and those tanned kids running along in dirty shirts hanging out of their trousers . . .' Whereas Leonid and Anna had long ago forgotten to carry out their ritual obligations – because they had not had time, because she had better things to do – in the Podol there were observant Jews with their Levite fur hats, who held jealously to their customs, 'to such an extent that it would have been just as impossible to extricate themselves from [them] as to live without their beating hearts'.[68] In *The Dogs and the Wolves*, Irène Némirovsky would depict them as they were seen by the 'rich Israelites' from the upper town, in other words, as Anna saw them: they were 'the scum, the unsavoury Jews, self-employed craftsmen, people who rented sordid shops, vagabonds, a mass of children who played in the mud'.[69] Untouchables.

In the description that she gives of the Jewish Kiev of her childhood, Irène Némirovsky has detected the tragic drama that was being waged between the excluded and the elect, who were connected to the former through an unfortunate bond of consanguinity; 'perhaps,' she writes, 'they looked upon the horror and confusion of the Ghetto as if they were at the theatre, with the same superficial shudder of spectators watching a drama, but who almost immediately are appeased by wrapping themselves in a comfortable sense of security: "That would never happen to me. Never." . . . She would not sink that low.'[70]

But there was no need to sink so far as the Podol: the drama sometimes took place in the heart of the city, in a swirl of blood and fire. Irotchka was unable to recall that in October 1905 the pogrom broke its barriers and invaded the streets of Pechersk. Such was the violence that Sholem Aleichem, the 'Jewish Mark Twain', was forced to go into exile. What then had happened to make life unbearable in 'Yehoupets' – the name Aleichem gave Kiev? After the Russian military defeat at the hands of the Japanese in 1905 (in which two Némirovskys from Kiev had paid with their lives), only a screen of Jewish blood could obscure the collapse of tsarism, the ineptitude of the generals and the corruption that was rotting the state. This time, the people's discontent took the form of an insurrection. From Odessa, the general strike spread to all the cities of the Empire. In St Petersburg, people from polite society had to serve themselves in the cafés and maintain the sorting of the mail. In Kiev, the battalion of firemen, who were being shot at by Cossacks, opened fire on the barracks and the governor's palace, before dispersing into the swamps and the forests. On 17th October, such was the pressure that Nicholas II was reluctantly obliged to proclaim a manifesto instituting the Imperial Duma and guaranteeing his subjects equality and civil liberties. But in Odessa, the very next day, hired thugs and dockers, under police protection, laid waste and then methodically set fire to the Moldavanka. It was the seventh pogrom since 1821, but it surpassed all of them in intensity: three hundred and two dead, a sixth of whom came from the ranks of the Samooborona, the Jewish self-defence league in which the pioneers of armed Zionism distinguished themselves. In Kichinev, in Ekaterinoslav and throughout the cities of Ukraine and Russia, eight thousand Jews perished in less than a week.

God was far away . . .

In Kiev, on that same 18th October, General Bezssonov gave just one command: 'You may destroy, you must not loot.' This was intended to show that the anti-Jewish fury was prompted only by the desire to suppress the anarchy propagated by the 'Jewish scum', as the Tsar would explain it to his mother in a letter dated 27th October: 'The people are indignant about the insolence and audacity of the revolutionaries and socialists, and since nine-tenths of them are Jews, all the hatred is directed against them – whence the Jewish pogroms.'[71] In accordance with this political duty, the houses of the Podol were laid waste one by one, street by street, with calculated brutality, and their inhabitants left to fend for themselves. Pechersk was not forgotten. 'The streets of Kiev are full of wailing,' one witness reported; 'the Cossacks and hooligans beat people up, cut our brothers' throats. And there is no one there to defend us.'[72] Since this Apocalyptic wind made no distinction between Jews of the first or second guild, or those who had sold their residential rights, there were a number of citizens of Kiev who protected their neighbours by placing holy icons in their windows. In a chapter removed from *The Dogs and the Wolves*, Irène Némirovsky would imagine that Ada, the heroine who is so like herself, had found refuge with an Orthodox family for a week, in an old dilapidated house where financial worries were unknown. 'They displayed the traditional attitudes of polite Russian society, brought into contact with the Jews through circumstances: "All the yids are bastards but we are poor sinners. Everyone has his faults and Salomon Vronovitch, my doctor, or Arkady Israelitch, my businessman, are not in the least like Jews.'" Irina Némirovsky was not so fortunate herself: it was Macha, the cook, who put an Orthodox cross around her neck and hid her behind a bed, while she prayed that fate would spare her.'[73] Which it did.

The little girl was only two and a half at that time. It was therefore not from memory, but from her belief in the tales told later by her parents or her grandparents, that Irène Némirovsky was able to recreate the barbaric ride in *The Dogs and the Wolves*. 'Hear that, that's a window being broken. Can you hear the glass shattering? That's stones being thrown against the walls, and the iron shutters of the shop. That's everyone laughing. And there's a woman screaming as if her insides were being ripped out. What's going on? . . .'[74]

It is reckoned that forty thousand buildings were destroyed and two hundred thousand Russian Jews chose exile during the twelve months that followed the disturbances in 1905. In Kiev, over four days in October, almost eight thousand passports were issued by the governor. And thus the Némirovskys, for all Anna's efforts to de-Judaise her household, were unable to forget that they were and would remain Jews in the eyes of the fanatical Orthodox priests and the unscrupulous politicians. All the more so, since doctrinal anti-Semitism, bolstered by these early revolutionary warning shots, would subsequently become unbelievably entrenched. Several violent propaganda organisations came into being, the most active being the Union of St Michael the Archangel, run by Deputy Purizhkevich, and the Union of Russian Peoples, established by Pyotr Rachkovsky, the former head of the Kiev secret service, better known as the Black Hundreds, of which the Tsar himself was an honorary member. The slogan of these anti-Jewish Templars, distributed through thousands of pamphlets across the Empire, did not split hairs: 'Lynch the Jews, save Russia'.

Far from reinforcing Anna's and Leonid's Jewish feelings, the threat of anti-Semitism eventually had the effect of discouraging any traditional, and even more so, any religious expression. 'God was far away.' For them, in fact, as for so many Jews on the path to assimilation, emancipation would mean giving up their faith. 'Make it clear that religion does not exist in Hélène's life,' Irène Némirovsky notes in the margins of *The Wine of Solitude*. 'Apart from the evening prayer, the religious side of life is non-existent.' Which was why every evening Leonid would appear in his daughter's bedroom, kneel down with her on the carpet, and recite this materialistic prayer: 'We must pray to God to give good health to your father, your mother, and the daily bread . . .'[75]

Irotchka, her hands joined together, observed her father's dark eyes. 'My unhappy Papa . . . The only one from whom I feel that I, my blood, my restless soul, my strength and my weakness have sprung. His silvery white hair, which was tinged slightly with green, like a moonbeam, his dark complexion, somewhat lined, even when he was young, already creased by strain and reflection, his very deep-set – I wanted to say burning – eyes . . . one cannot describe this glint, this fire of intelligence and passion.' He certainly needed this determination to extricate himself from the death-trap set for Jews by a regime in its death throes.

Sundays with nothing to do

So it was to the very heart of Pechersk that Leonid and Anna had moved, soon to be joined by Victoria, Iona and Rosa. Protected by gold-painted gates, 'the house with its columns, spacious and dignified, in the shade of the ancient lime trees'[76] described in *The Dogs and the Wolves* approximates fairly well to the lavishly furnished one at 11 Pushkin Street,[77] where the Némirovskys came to live in 1910, occupying an apartment that was spacious, but simply furnished, since this aspect did not interest Leonid Némirovsky. From the balcony, which was decked with flowering plants, and was large enough for them to sit out and take supper there, the view stretched over the city and the Dnieper, as far as the hills.

In the gloomy dining room with its worn wooden floor, Irotchka endured without flinching the rebukes of her mother, who lounged about on a battered leather sofa with its stuffing coming out. 'How many meals ended in tears, salty tears that clouded her eyes, ran down her face into her plate, blending with the taste of the meat . . .' In the kitchen, Leonid's guests settled down to play cards by the warmth of the stove. At night, Macha slept there behind an old partition. She was a 'very good woman', who had only one known fault, which nobody had verified: that she slept with her son. Irotchka did not venture into her quarters except on 'Sundays with nothing to do', amid 'the fish scales, the large bunches of black radishes on the tables, and the knife used to pick the pips from the watermelons'.

Pushkin Street was truly 'one of the wealthiest, quietest streets in the city'.[78] The hustle and bustle of Kreschatik Boulevard gently faded away, the further south one travelled. It rose up again further down, in the old Cadet Street, renamed Fundukleyev in 1869, in honour of the governor, and it would become the first street in Russia to bear the name Lenin. It was a thoroughfare frequented by students, who nicknamed the district 'Little Switzerland', because of the bungalows for renting in the area of greenery, to the west, near the Faculty of Anatomy. Along the parallel Boulevard Bibikovsky, bordering the botanical gardens, stood the Alexandrovski *lycées*. On Sundays, the girls 'in straw hats, the tops of their dresses stretched taut beneath their budding breasts, their skirts billowing around their hips' would meet the boys at the bandstand 'in their light shirts, their belts with the Imperial Eagle around their waists and their caps tipped backwards, looking as if they could conquer the world'.[79]

At the crossroads with Pushkin Street stood the Bergonnier Theatre, named after its French architect, where the first screenings of *Illusion* and of short films made by the Lumière brothers had recently been shown, projected on to stretched fabric. Not far away was the terrace of the Café François where Iona, unfurling his French newspaper, took Irotchka to eat ice creams in memory of the Tortoni on the Boulevard des Italiens. While they relished their ices, they listened to the *sharmanshchik*, a parrot on his shoulder, winding the handle of his barrel organ, or to the blind lute (*kobza*) player, led by a barefoot youth, peddling old Ukrainian tales, which were drowned out by the grating of the rattling trams. A bald man selling toothpicks cajoled his customers. But the best-known of the beggars was a toothless Italian woman who played the accordion and who, for a few pennies, would play the Marseillaise.

In his own home, Leonid was happy enough to conform to the French etiquette imposed by his wife. At Easter, if Iona expressed a longing for stuffed pike, he had to persuade Leonid to take him to a Jewish restaurant, since Anna would not put up with the smell. During the day, however, Leonid was more likely to be found sitting at a marble table at Semadani's, the fashionable tea house on the Kreschatik, where the wheeler-dealers met to discuss money more willingly than at the stock exchange.

Such was the daily backdrop to Irène Némirovsky's existence during the first ten years of her life. Unlike her mother and her young aunt, she was not a pupil at the Gymnasium. Anna was too anxious about making a model child of her to allow her to have school friends. From her earliest days, Irotchka experienced 'the boring lessons, the tyranny of the tutor who stays as close to you as a jailer, the kind of discipline you find in prisons, homework every day that you might come to enjoy but which is made hateful because it is forced on you so idiotic-ally'.[80] In her bedroom, alone among her great 'shadow-filled' books, she imagined 'a break in a mountain, between fallen rocks, where the army hid'; there she recited from memory 'phrases from the *Mémorial de Sainte-Hélène*, her favourite book, which she knew almost by heart'.[81] She performed *War and Peace* over to herself in miniature, battling against the boredom of Sundays, and imagining herself leading a French army, Napoleon's Grande Armée, and perhaps dreaming of the Life of the Empress Josephine, which she would start to write one day . . .[82]

Did she really, as it has been claimed, speak Russian, German and French by the age of four, and write in them by the time she was five?[83] One thing is certain: French was her chosen tongue, because it was Zézelle's and, according to her grandfather, the language of the lost paradise itself. 'I spoke French before speaking Russian,' she would observe in 1940 . . . 'I think and I even dream in French. All that is so mixed up with what remains in me of my race and my country, that with the best will in the world, it is impossible for me to tell where one ends and the other begins.'[84]

A bird that came from France

Anna played her part in this tendency, instilling in Irotchka a deep love of French poetry and arranging for her to be given music and elocution lessons, in the fanciful hope of seeing her appear on stage one day. Because Anna was fond both of social gatherings and French culture, she could be seen at the Bergonnier Theatre applauding the latest works of Edmond Rostand. Ever since the Universal Exhibition in Paris, in 1900, Iona had worshipped Sarah Bernhardt, whom he had seen perform the exhausting role of the Aiglon at the Théâtre de la Renaissance. On her first visit to the Ukrainian capital, in 1882, the actress had had to be accompanied back to her hotel by Cossacks on horseback, in order to disperse the crowds that had thronged the route; this delirious welcome did not mean that she was spared gibes, however – for members of the public, unlike American audiences, spoke French so perfectly that they considered themselves entitled to criticise the company.[85] In Odessa, she was greeted with a hail of stones, so that nobody should be unaware of her Jewish origins.[86]

Family legend had it that in 1911 Irotchka was heard by Sarah Bernhardt herself during her later tour of Russia. In actual fact, if the little girl did recite some Rostand, it was at the annual charity fair at the French Home, in the presence of General Sukhomlinov.[87] The military governor of Kiev, Volynia and Podolia, and virtually 'undisputed king of the country' since 1905, was feared by all the Jews of the city, for he had total control over them. Dressed in a replica of the white dress with black collar designed for Sarah Bernhardt by the very young Paul Poiret, Irina recited the Duke of Reichstadt's speech in front of this hero of the war against the Turks. She continued her 'dream of blood, of glory' alone in her bedroom, marshalling her wooden soldiers among her books, which were piled up and made into fortresses:

> Yes. Every day, a book.
> In my bedroom, every evening, I read: I was intoxicated . . .

'At this period,' she would explain, 'I was eight years old and mad about Edmond Rostand . . . After the performance, the governor-general, who was watching, wanted to see me and congratulate me. I was very excited to find myself face to face with this person who, for us, was a symbol of terror, tyranny and cruelty. To my great surprise, I saw a charming man who looked like my grandfather and who had the gentlest eyes imaginable. He asked me how it was that a young Russian girl should speak French so well; I explained that I went to France every year with my parents. Then he said to me, and these were his exact words: "Ah, my child, how I envy you and how I wish I could go back and live my whole life quietly there."'[88]

One should not judge people by their faces: the novelist would remember the lesson. And she would draw her inspiration from this memory when she created the scene of the amateur dramatic show at the Alliance Française in *The Dogs and the Wolves*: 'Their mothers had thick necks, tied their hair in heavy black buns and wore diamond earrings whose brilliance reflected the social success of their husbands. It would have been considered impertinent to wear pearls if he did not hold the position of banker, but diamonds were acceptable for members of the lowest category: merchants of the Second Guild.'[89] On stage, that evening, twenty-five little girls sang the song of Soubise and Boissière in chorus:

> *Sentinelles, ne tirez pas,*
> *C'est un oiseau qui vient de Fra-a-ance!* *

Thus, probably for the first time, beneath the tricolour flags and paper chains, Irotchka felt French by right, a right with which comes a love of a language and a culture. And, once back at home: 'Do sing, Mademoiselle Rose, please. Sing the "Marseillaise". Do you know it? The verse about the little children: "*We shall enter into the pit . . .*" Oh! How I long to be French! – "You're right," agreed Zézelle, nostalgically. "It's the most beautiful country in the world." . . .'[90]

---

*'Sentries, don't shoot,/It's a bird that comes from France. [Tr.]

2

A Vague and Murderous Hope
(1912–1917)

Only the waters of the canal moved; that figure of a woman walking over the bridge, who might have been about to commit suicide, was it not Pushkin's Lisa? No, it was nothing, simply a passer-by; she walked over the canal by the Winter Palace, disappearing past the yellow residence on the banks of the Moïka . . .

Andrei Bely, *Petersburg*

In about 1912, Leonid's energy and his skill among the *'combinazione'* bore fruit. 'Eaten away by a kind of long-standing and muddled ambition', he would soon be able to fill his visiting card with such flattering titles as Chairman of the Commercial Bank of Voronezh, and Director of the Moscow Union Bank, which had branches all over Russia. He began to make money as if he were mining it, by impulse initially, then out of habit, and finally because he liked doing so. Gold – 'does one play in order to earn it?'[1] As for the actual source of his riches and the nature of his business, they remained 'fairly complicated'.[2] 'He had found a job as manager of some gold mines in Siberia, in the Asiatic taiga,'[3] it is suggested in *The Wine of Solitude*. It might, on the other hand, have been in the business of exporting wood from Irkutsk and Ienisseisk to Europe, which was then a flourishing concern. We do not know whether this exile was the result of a bet or, on the contrary, a setback in his career. For Irina, all that changed was the tone of the conversations, as impenetrable as the Yiddish that he sometimes used so that only grown-ups could understand him: 'Copper, silver mines, gold mines . . . phosphates . . . millions, millions, millions',[4] all this uttered calmly and without enthusiasm. 'That weary enthusiasm, that disenchantment, full of passion, that was what was needed. The material side of life, and that alone, was what interested him.' Thus, for her birthday, as well as for Christmas and Easter, which the Némirovskys celebrated, Irina was given jewels, with the following recommendation:

'Look after them and be careful not lose them when you're playing. They were bought last week and they're already worth double.'

A birth certificate

She was almost ten years old. Her thick hair was held back by a bow or pushed underneath a hat. She wore 'a white dress of broderie anglaise, with three layers, a silk belt, and two large, delicate white bows, securely fixed with two pins to the outer skirt of open-weave taffeta',[5] and patent leather shoes. She was taught the piano, without being able to match Anna in Grieg's 'Erotic Song'. And, like her mother, she missed France. 'To be born and grow up there . . . To be at home in Paris . . . To not have to drive for five days to go back to a barbaric country where she didn't really feel at home either . . . because her dresses were based on Paris fashion . . .'[6]

Trimming her nails on the sofa, Anna sighed: 'Some people are fortunate. The Porgès[7] spent three months in Paris, the lucky woman . . .' Leonid moaned: 'You're never satisfied, good God . . . Money, money . . . To bust one's gut for that . . .' The grandmother, diminutive and hobbling, tried clumsily to comfort her daughter: 'I don't know what you're complaining about . . . You're young and beautiful . . . You've got your daughter . . . You've always cheered me up.' Irotchka would never forget the apologetic smile of her little *babushka*, too good to be tolerated under the family roof, nor her eyes that were red from crying, 'always putting her hand up to her flat chest, as if every word made her heart jump'. And what words from Anna: 'The child! Ah yes, the child . . . No, of course I won't forget her. Good God, there's no danger that she'll allow herself to be forgotten . . . So can I never think of myself, of me, no? . . .'

Rosa did not see that Irina, far from arousing tender feelings in her mother, was ageing her, nor did she see that motherhood was hampering Anna's dreams of endless seduction. It seems clear that this child had not been wanted. In *David Golder*, Irène would evoke 'the fear, the terror she [her mother] felt about having a child',[8] but also the lingering suspicion as to whether Leonid was her father. Forever coming between her and her fantasies, Irina was for Anna a reminder of her marriage, a measure of her age, a 'birth certificate'.[9] Worse, a rival: 'I did not ask for much,' observed Irène Némirovsky in 1934. 'But I realise now that I removed quite a number of things, firstly the money, then some of the worries . . .' Which explains Anna's determination to dress her daughter, until she was grown up, in little girl's dresses. Had it not been for Leonid, Irina would have been placed, without any qualms, in a French boarding school, as happened to Nathalie Sarraute.

An overwhelming sadness

In Kiev, during the summer, Irina used to wait until dusk to go to play in the nearby park. When she returned, she would find some 'cold milk in an old, chipped blue bowl on her dressing table': the smell was unforgettable. Or else, with Victoria, she would take the tram to go and call on the Datievs, acquaintances of her parents, given the name Manassé in *The Wine of Solitude*, who lived in a wooden dacha in a green suburb, described in detail in 'Le Sortilège'. The Datievs were Orthodox and from old Russian stock. 'I had never seen such an old house,' wrote Irène Némirovsky . . . 'The chaos, the dilapidation and neglect could be seen everywhere . . . The house smelled of strong tobacco, damp fur and mushrooms, for it was damp.' Able to eat in her bedroom whenever she pleased, to go to bed after midnight, to run barefoot on the floor or in the garden, when she met Nina, the daughter of the house, Irina would sometimes be invited to the Datievs for two or three days where she enjoyed the full freedom of a care-free existence, Russian style, much to Zézelle's indignation: 'But, really, don't they ever work at all?'[10]

For the summer holidays, they chose the beach resorts of the Crimea, much favoured by the St Petersburg middle classes. The journey there seemed longer than travelling to Paris. 'In those days there was no railway to link Simferopol and Yalta, the Russian Nice. It took twelve hours in a horse-drawn carriage and you spent the night at Simferopol.'[11] After a few days, they moved to the less crowded resort of Alushta, on the southern shore of the peninsula. It was situated in a small, rocky bay beneath craggy mountains, lined with low, whitewashed houses, where there was nothing to do except breathe in the fragrant, thuja-scented sea air and make out the flight of the bats. The shingle was littered with watermelon skins, which the rats fought over. These sparse memories of the Black Sea would prove to be useful, in 1940, to sketch in the background for her *Vie de Tchekhov* [*The Life of Chekhov*]: 'It's a mixture of the Riviera and of Asia . . . The fruit is magnificent, the air pure and gentle. In the evenings, the lights from the ships sparkle on the water. The Crimea is unforgettable.'[12] And even there, everything reminded her of France: the Chez Florin patisserie in Yalta, and that suffocating aroma of the Côte d'Azur in the air – a blend of iodine, oleander and the pine trees on the slopes of the hills.

Once autumn came, it was time to return to Kiev, however, and redis-cover 'the silence of this sleepy, provincial city, in the depths of Russia . . . dull, hidden away, overwhelmingly sad'.[13] In three months' time the lamp-lights would be switched on in the streets. The shops seemed 'eerie and mysterious, slightly frightening, with their little lights here and there swaying beneath the shop signs'.[14] Irotchka would go back to the boring routine of supervised leisure activities and private lessons, the sad priv-ilege of a little rich girl. 'When I consider my childhood in Russia, in the twilight of the Tsarist regime, I see a stream of lessons and teachers. Never time to dream or to relax. No frivolous distractions. One hour's skating on Sundays, that was all. I think that the core of pessimism that struck you in my books derives from this rather sad childhood.'[15]

A faint shudder

In the evenings, to take her mind off things, it was always the same games, drawing or cutting out shapes, as she listened to Zézelle humming old French songs, such as 'Malbrough s'en va-t-en guerre' or 'Plaisir d'amour'. On Sundays, books, which she devoured avidly, took her back to France: little volumes of Stendhal, Balzac or Maupassant, which were available from the Idzikovski bookshop on the corner of the Fundukleyev; penny novels, which gave her the illusion that she could see through her mother; 'travel books, a few libertine storytellers of the eighteenth century and a lot of modern novels, the best and the worst',[16] which she read greedily by night-light, in secret, under her pillow, or sitting cross-legged on the floor, one hand in her hair, in the beam of light shining through the half-opened kitchen door, to the sound of mice behind the walls. What demons did boredom unleash in her solitary heart? What responses, true or false, did she find to her problems in books? And, in fact, 'where could her mother be coming from, looking so dishevelled, her eyes shining'?[17]

'It was true that, now and again, reading too much affected [her] as if she were heavily intoxicated.'[18] On one occasion, rummaging around, she brought to light 'a set of erotic books, left there, undoubtedly, after her parents got back from their honeymoon'. Faded, but in one piece. Throughout these pages, women in corsets, semi-naked men, obscene couples dressed in Chinese finery, paraded before her eyes. 'Two women lying on a bed with their arms entwined were kissing one another full on the lips.' Eyes agog, unashamed and in no hurry, Irotchka turned the pages. Her rapt curiosity was followed by amusement: 'How ugly they are, how comical they are . . .' Then repulsion, on seeing 'this girl wearing socks and a schoolgirl's overall, with long, bare legs and stockings rolled down, and, facing her, an enormous pot-bellied man in underpants'. Was this, these 'images of sad and dreary debauchery', the sordidness that her mother called love, this treasure that all women yearned for? 'Love . . . what filth.'

Nevertheless, a 'faint shudder' stirred within her, 'the onset of a sharp, vague pleasure, that suddenly aroused her' for it made her an accomplice. 'She's a woman, she's made for love,' Anna sometimes said. If that was love, Irotchka knew quite enough about it. Instructed too early in the 'shameful mystery' of the flesh, she thought she could dispense with any initiation into love. This would not be the least of her grievances against her mother – since, there could be no question, she had engaged in these farces. From that time on, Irotchka developed a horror of 'beautiful, powdered white arms', of 'lazy, pale hands', of Anna's 'wearing make-up',[19] the screens of her lust. Zézelle, who was so innocent, struck her as being all the more maternal, and her 'oily, wrinkled, soft, creased' skin was softer than Anna's 'snowy white body'. In order to conceal from her mother what she had learnt, Irotchka allowed herself to play the little girl, holding back the adult language she had discovered and using only childish words when with her family. Which is why Anna would say:

'This child is a fool . . .'

When, to her surprise and joy, Leonid went away from home for months on end, Anna believed she had reached the zenith of her femininity. In the same way that her husband lusted after money, this thirster after sensuality did not think herself born 'to be a placid, middle-class woman, satisfied with her husband and child'.[20] Until the spring of 1914, she lived almost continuously in France, between Paris, Biarritz and Nice, believing she was concealing from Irina the secret of her rejuvenation. Her daughter did not keep a count, but each time it was an 'oily Levantine' or a 'dark, greasy Armenian' with 'flat bluish hair, a hooked nose and thick raspberry-coloured lips',[21] who behaved like a peanut vendor. In fact, the sort of people whom Anna pretended she could not abide in Russia, and whom the French referred to as 'métèques'. But how could she refuse the jewels, the gold, the pearls?

At least this way of life spared Irotchka any domestic scenes and reprimands, for Anna did not bother about her any longer. When she encountered her in the mornings on the Allée des Acacias, in the Bois de Boulogne, Irina preferred 'not to see her mother, with her Irish tweed jacket, her polka-dot veil, her skirt sweeping across the dead leaves, walking along, overdressed, as women were at that time, looking like a "horse pulling a hearse", going to meet her latest lover'.[22] But in the evenings, in the prayer taught her by Leonid, she now substituted Zézelle's name, 'with a vague and murderous hope', for that of 'little mother'.[23] Occasionally, she dreamed absent-mindedly of far-off Siberia where her father was hatching goodness knows what. Then, she forgot about him. She closed her eyes, the better to dream of and hear 'deep in her soul, the music made by the wind that she would so love, later on . . . and which cut through her sleep like a great, overwhelming swell, swirled over her, buried her in its waves, then died down, nestling in her heart like the silvery quiver of a flute, and sent her to sleep'.

A sickly odour of filthy water

Dreaming in her bed, in some hotel in France, Irina did not know that she would never again see the gleaming Dnieper, the sorbets from the Café François, and Vladimir's blazing sword. One day in March 1914, after two years away, Leonid turned up in Nice, his fortune made, and announced that before the autumn all three of them would move house to St Petersburg, the capital of the Empire, together with the grandparents and the servants. 'He was stronger, with a swarthy complexion, red lips . . . When he laughed, his face lit up with fiery intelligence and a sort of malicious cheerfulness.'[24] In a photograph from that period, probably taken in a large hotel in Nice, Anna can be seen with bare arms, several necklaces adorning a bosom sheathed in pearl-white, tight-lipped, with a moon-like complexion, a smug expression, and a drink in her hand. Leonid, in a dinner-jacket with shiny lapels, wizened and looking as if he's seen it all before, is holding a cigarette. He appears indifferent to the male escort, with his detachable collar, fine moustache and beaming smile, who is probably playing footsie with his wife. If his patience is being tried, he is concealing it well. And Irotchka? At the hotel, with her governess, 'feeling like a trunk that's been forgotten at the left-luggage office' . . .[25]

This time, Leonid would not forget her. He had just joined the board of directors of the Private Bank of Commerce in St Petersburg. The address must have made Anna turn pale: 1 Nevsky Prospekt. And yet this unique establishment was by no means one of the most important banks in Russia. That summer, overcome by her own vanity, Fanny took possession of the house that Leonid had just acquired on the Angliskaya Prospekt, followed, a few weeks later, by Zézelle and Irina, who had been driven away from France by the end of the holidays – or by the declaration of war. They left the Mediterranean summer for the autumn of a northern Florence, which smelled of must that wafted across from the Finnish marshes. They had not paid attention to Dostoyevsky's warning about St Petersburg: 'There is no other place where the human soul is subjected to such dark and such strange influences.'[26] Irotchka knew immediately what to expect; it was enough to trust her sense of smell: 'It was one of the most grim, damp days of a sad season, when, in these climes, the sun is barely visible . . . How harshly it blew, that day, the biting north wind, and what a sickly odour of filthy water rose from the Neva!'[27]

Ever since the quelling of the first revolution and the dissolution of the Duma in 1906, Russia had well and truly returned to being the 'barbarous country' which it was pointless to pretend one could grow used to, especially if one was a successful Jewish businessman like Leonid. In Kiev, in 1911, the murder of a thirteen-year-old child with a knife had immediately been attributed to a Jewish labourer, accused of having ritually 'calumniated' Christian blood by mixing it with the Passover matzos; due to the relentless propaganda put out by the ultra-conservative, anti-Semitic Black Hundreds, the trial, in 1912, of Mendel Beiliss was broadcast far and wide.*

In the Tsarist capital, the pledges required of Jews were even more draconian than anywhere else. There you could hear the monk Iliodor preaching a crusade against the 'Yids'. In 1911, the proportion of Jewish children in the city's primary schools did not exceed 1 per cent. And if impoverished Jews were not seen in the streets, it was, Gorky would say, 'due to the fact that the police did not allow Jews to beg and even more, I think, because the ever so charitable Orthodox and Catholics would probably prefer to place a stone or a serpent, instead of bread, in the hand of a Jewish beggar'.[28]

If anti-Semite propaganda was more virulent in St Petersburg, there were also fewer victims of it in the city, for it was first and foremost an export item, conjured up in the dens of the Union of Russian People for the 'Jewified' provinces of the Empire. It was in St Petersburg, in 1903, that the murky *Protocols of the Elders of Zion*, presented as the latest proof of a 'Jewish plot', had been doctored and published; but it was in Kiev, Kishinev and Odessa that the contrived coming of a 'Judaeo-Masonic kingdom with an antichrist tsar at its head' was taken seriously. It served no purpose that in 1910 a police investigation ordered by Prime Minister Stolypin revealed that this 'document' was pure fabrication; and it was at the Kiev Opera House, in September of the following year, that Stolypin (no longer Prime Minister), who had made enemies of both Iliodor and Rasputin, was assassinated. The killer was a turned agent of the Okhrana (the secret police) – many blamed the Jews.

Satisfying residential criteria, on the other hand, was a way of ensuring a peaceful and protected existence in St Petersburg. In this still youthful city, with no antiquated ghetto, one did not have to fear waves of drunken Cossacks. Because of this, it was in 'Piter' that the largest proportion of wealthy Jews were to be found: lawyers, contractors, industrialists, rich businessmen and bankers, such as Moses Gunzburg, Boris Kamenka, or Dmitri Rubinstein, president of the board of directors of the Franco-Russian Bank. The latter, who was reported to be the wealthiest man in Russia, was a schemer, well established in government circles, who

---

*Beiliss was acquitted, the evidence against him being too clearly fabricated, even for the seven Black Hundred members in the jury. [Tr.]

would not hesitate, in 1915, to pay off the rent of the muzhik Rasputin, without whose blessing nothing of importance could be done in Russia. In 1915, 'Mitka' Rubinstein also became head of the bank that Leonid had recently joined.[29] Furthermore, he held power of attorney for the Grand-Duke Andrei Vladimirovich, whose affair with the ballerina Mathilde Kschessinskaya, the former favourite of Nicholas II, was notorious. Now, it was from her that Leonid had just bought his house, in the heart of the capital. From these tangled relationships it was clear that the 'obscure little Jew' from Elisavetgrad had climbed the social ladder. In exile in Paris, would it not be his task to entertain the Grand-Dukes Alexander and Boris?

A disparate dwelling

Number 18 Angliskaya Prospekt, in the Kolomna district was a single-storey yellow brick building, ten windows wide, adorned with two capitals at each end, and with a garage – since Leonid now had a car at his disposal – a rare luxury. This was the neighbourhood where the new synagogue was situated, the building of which in itself symbolised the position of Jews in St Petersburg: the first stone had only been allowed to be laid on condition that it was at least five hundred metres away from any church, and that all other places of Jewish worship were pulled down beforehand. It was the smartest district of St Petersburg, where more than 60 per cent of 'citizens with privileged status' lived; in the Angliskaya Prospekt alone there had been the young composer Stravinsky, who had just astounded Paris, and who had lived there until 1910, then, since October 1913, the *starets* Rasputin himself, who held his salon at number 3, when he was not roaming the neighbourhood in search of prostitutes.

In Irène Némirovsky's memory, this characterless home would nevertheless remain 'a large and beautiful house'. The interior resembled a 'thieves' den': a suite of adjoining rooms laid out in such a way that from the entrance hall 'through wide, half-open doors, you could see a line of drawing rooms decorated in gold and white'. Irina's bedroom was peaceful 'with its pink walls, its lacquered furniture, and her little porcelain lamp lit in one corner'. Sturgeon, caviar, servants, service in the French style . . . 'The gold shimmered, the wine flowed', but no one bothered about where the second-hand furniture came from or how it was arranged. The crockery, the knick-knacks and the books were bought in lots at the auction room. Clutter, wreathed in dust, was piled up everywhere, making this home a 'disparate dwelling'.[30] In the midst of this capricious existence, was Irotchka, at the keyboard of a piano as white as her mother's outfits . . .

Sound transactions

In St Petersburg it was possible to obtain fine wines from Champagne, carnations from the Riviera and perfumes from Grasse. What need was there to go back to Paris again, since there was 'L'Ours', 'Le Palmyre', 'La Fontanka' and all the gypsy cabarets from the islands, where it was so good to splash out? Since 18th August, Leonid's bank had been renamed the Private Commercial Bank of Petrograd, in the Russian manner. Behind this show of patriotism, who could pretend to ignore the fact that General Sukhomlinov, the Minister for War, was not striving for victory, or that Mitka Rubinstein was helping the Tsarina to transfer funds to her family in Germany, in order to help her endure the hardships?

For the enlightened bourgeoisie, as for a part of the intelligentsia, this war brought with it a great hope: that of revitalising the sick body of the autocracy by transfusing it with liberal blood. For the Jews – supported by a few of the *intelliguents* such as Gorky – there beckoned the prospect, given their professed patriotism, of soon enjoying normal rights, while at the same time making savings for a revolution which many had originally craved. On 8th August, along with the other 'non-native populations' of the Empire, Russia's Jewish delegates had proclaimed at the Duma their total 'devotion to the state and the Russian people'. And no fewer than seven hundred thousand Jews had enlisted in the army. These calculations were not Leonid's concern; he preferred to count the millions. 'There were pounds sterling, marks, currencies with weird names.' It was Sanskrit to Irotchka's ears, but Anna 'attentive, listened and converted into money, and detailed pictures of dresses and jewellery'.[31]

This fine surge of patriotism did not prevent a number of Jews – whom the troops, on entering Galicia, over-hastily took for Germans due to the simple fact that they spoke Yiddish – from being shot or thrown into the front line against the enemy. The troops did the same a few months later as they beat a retreat, but this time, the Jews had rediscovered their roles as scapegoats. Spies, saboteurs, speculators, anarchists, war profiteers: anything seemed preferable after the military defeat of December 1914 – one million dead! – rather than recognise the occasionally deliberate incompetence of the general staff, the methodical shortages, or the corrupt businessmen who supplied all the warring nations regardless of which side they were on. Was Leonid Némirovsky, a merchant banker, 'invited to join the Committee of wartime industries that tried to speed up the manufacture of armaments and, especially, their transport', as his granddaughter Élisabeth Gille was inclined to think?[32] Or was he one of those speculators in flour, arms and boots, as *The Wine of Solitude* leads us to believe, as does Irène Némirovsky's abiding curiosity in arms manufacturers such as Basil Zaharoff,[33] who profited, without any qualms, from the vast commercial opportunities created by a conflict unprecedented in the history of mankind? 'He had become very rich since the war started, and everyone flattered him . . .'[34]

However, Boris Karol, Leonid's fictional double, was also capable of declaring: 'I don't understand why sound transactions are not carried out more willingly.'[35] One of these transactions presented itself in mid-September 1915, when Prince Alexander Nikolayevich Obolensky, who had been made regional commissioner for the provision of the city, was asked to summon a regional consultative conference on maintaining supplies of food to the capital. It is extremely likely that Leonid was invited since, as his daughter points out: 'When we lived in St Petersburg, my father, because of his job, very often had to deal with the governors and I saw all those people at close hand.'[36] Alexander Obolensky was the civilian governor of the city from 1914. As a major-general in His Majesty's imperial suite, he had direct access to Nicholas II. Born in St Petersburg in 1872, he had been governor-general of Kiev before the war. In 1916, having become chief of police in Petrograd, he was on the best of terms with the French ambassador, who wrote of him in his diary: 'He's an excellent servant of the emperor and I feel great friendship for him.'[37] Coincidentally in 1924, in Paris, his son would marry Irina's closest Russian friend, thereby making her a princess in turn . . .

It was a happy period for financiers. Ever since the appointment of Pavel Bark, one of their own, to the Ministry of Finance in January 1914, the state generously subsidised private banks, thereby encouraging downwards speculation and bizarre stock exchange dealings. The Private Commercial Bank of Petrograd was, in this respect, one of the most dynamic. From 30th November 1912 to 1st November 1915, its assets rose from 137 to 200 million roubles. In August 1917, they would reach 319 million. Five times less, of course, than the principal Russian banks. In the second-hand goods warehouse that now took place at the Némirovskys' home, 'men arrived, morning and evening, pulling out packets from their pockets', as if they were in a gambling den. Those whom Irène Némirovsky remembered were Jewish, but there was also 'the son of one of those fleeting Ministers of War at the period'.[38] On 31st May 1916, Maurice Paléologue reckoned the city was already in the hands of 'a gang of Jewish financiers and corrupt speculators, Rubinstein, Manus, etc.', who were hand in glove with Rasputin and working 'manifestly for Germany'.[39] In Russia, those with anti-Semitic prejudices even contaminated French ambassadors.

A sense of insecurity

A kindly man, Leonid did not intend to enjoy his wealth on his own. Anna agreed that he should provide Iona and Rosa with a pension as a way of ensuring that they did not move in with them. Irina would not see them again until 1922, but the Revolution of 1917 very nearly took them from her. As for Victoria, she was much too careful not to owe anything to her elder sister, despite Leonid's attempts to help her.

Poor grandpapa Iona! 'It's funny, I see him mainly as an old man, tensing his body so as not to appear bent . . . his eyes still lively and his white hair surrounding his large, bald head.' And poor Rosa, so retiring and so scrawny 'with her dry, withered neck, her greying hair, always awry, that streamed abundantly through the steel teeth of her comb'. Her timorous voice, when she asked:

'Macha, quickly, serve the samovar, Macha, take the chops round . . . Come on now, come and kiss your grandmother, my child . . . You're quite right, my girl. Enjoy life while you can. You grow old and there's nothing left. Eat, do you want this? Do you want that? Do you want my seat, my knife, my bread, my portion. Take it. Take it, Léon . . . take it . . . Take my time, my cares, my blood, my flesh . . .'

Pointless sacrifices, so poorly rewarded.

In St Petersburg Irotchka was just as lonely as she had been in Nice before the war, with less sunshine. 'Without her reading, she would have been sick from boredom. Books for her were a substitute for real life.'[40] Her life was monotonous. 'And tomorrow? What would tomorrow bring? Well, let's see, my English lesson, a walk, algebra problems, lunch, a cup of hot chocolate at five o'clock, everything that had always happened, that would continue to happen, just as the earth would continue to spin around.' Sundays dragged on, especially in winter, which lasted for six months. Her neighbours, two grown-up, consumptive sisters, so scrawny and sad that Irina only spoke to them once, lived alone with their father, but he, a small-time lawyer, chose to lock them away so that he could enjoy himself.

And supposing Anna, carrying out her threats of blackmail, were to replace Zézelle with a stricter English *miss*, so as to discipline this arrogant child who had read Stendhal before reading Tolstoy? Irotchka was a big girl now: twelve years old! 'How old one can be at the age of twelve . . .'[41] Would she require a governess for long? This vague apprehension carried with it the stagnant stench of this 'city of manure, of fogs', half crumbling into the bilious waters of the gulf, like a nightmare out of Gérard de Nerval.

It was a period of instability. One ineffective minister followed another, up until Protopopov, who was appointed Minister for the Interior in mid-September 1916. Prince Obolensky himself had just been dismissed, on the slanderous grounds that he had permitted bribery – but more probably because he, in turn, had raised doubts about Rasputin. From the end of 1915 onwards, St Petersburg – now generally known as Petrograd – lived under the permanent threat of a German siege. Wood, food and bread were in short supply, and the winter of 1916 had been particularly harsh. At the front line, desertion was rife. People were terrified that the sporadic strikes observed in the capital might turn to revolt – which was what occurred on 31st October at the Baranovski factories, and afterwards at the Renault factory, to unprecedented cries of 'Down with the French! No more war!' Whereas Irotchka, for her part, was praying: 'Please let the French win the war . . .',[42] since she was half-French.

An abominable hatred

'Now that I think of it,' she wrote in 1934, 'it is not surprising that I should have been left throughout my life with this fear, this feeling of insecurity and threat . . . one never forgets the taste of certain tears . . . However, one has to wait until the wine has grown old.' The early vintages are the bitterest ones.

Sometimes, Irotchka heard her mother return at dawn. 'Of her, I retain one particular image, when she goes out, in the evening, with some officers, and the chambermaid throws over her shoulders an enormous, heavy, dark cloth [cape[43]] . . . and the sound of sleigh bells in the snow.' Described bluntly in *L'Ennemie* [The Enemy], and later in *The Wine of Solitude*, the scene in which Irina catches her mother unaware in unseemly company, has every reason to be considered authentic. This breach of duty, at a time when even the Minister for War was being tried for high treason, had the effect of transforming Anna into an adversary, pursued henceforth by an unspoken grudge. Irina felt herself besmirched. A long time afterwards, the pages of *Le Bal*, *David Golder*, and *Jezebel* [*Jézabel*] would resonate with this 'abominable hatred',[44] released by a wrench in her heart.

How was it possible not to refrain from making further judgements about this woman? How could one obey her? 'What, I'm Napoleon and I have to apologise like a little child!' At the age of eight or ten, Irotchka was inconsolable if she did not obtain her mother's forgiveness, which was so costly to her pride; from now on, it was she who would draw up accounts. The slightest sign of Anna's physical presence filled her with disgust, 'the vague perfume that lingered after she had gone away, or even the shape of her gloves'. This young girl's heart, in which Zézelle had detected a demon, was filled with a hot-tempered spleen, ready to burst, 'vindictive, exasperated, full of hatred, defying the rules'. When she looked at the portrait of her mother as a child, which made her feel twice as envious, she felt murderous. 'She feels only too strongly that she would have pummelled her, she would have been the stronger of the two, she would have dug her nails into the large, soft arms. And, by an amazing whim of fate, she is *her* daughter, and must obey her. Why isn't she dead? . . . Dead, dead . . . What joy . . .'

'What would I have felt if I had seen my mother die?' Irène Némirovsky wondered in 1938. 'As I say: pity, loathing, and horror at my own heartlessness. Desperately knowing that deep down I felt no sorrow, that I was cold and indifferent, that this was not a loss for me, alas, but on the contrary . . .'

Irina responded to betrayal by betrayal. It was not yet a question, aged thirteen, of catching Anna out at her own game by pinching one of her lovers, as happens in *L'Ennemie* and in *The Wine of Solitude*, but simply of showing that she was no longer going to be taken for a ride. In *L'Ennemie*, it is by means of a letter that little Bragance informs her father, Léon, that his wife is being unfaithful to him. In *The Wine*, it is through incriminating words scribbled on the page of a German grammar book that Bella knows her daughter has seen through her. 'In every family there is nothing but greed, lies and mutual mis-understanding. It's the same everywhere. And at our house as well, it's the same. The husband, the wife, the lover.'[45]

This liberating scene, if it did take place, as its obsessive character-istics tend to make one believe, had the most unexpected consequences. Irotchka's jubilation would not last: apart from a predictable explo-sion of fury, Anna's wrath would rain down on poor Zézelle. It was from her, this goody-two-shoes, that Irina got her insolence! Very well, she would never see 'the charming, gentle, weary face of Mademoiselle' again! Supposing she were to separate her from Irina, who was virtually her daughter, she who had never had a child of her own? Zézelle, whose mind had been affected by the unhealthy climate of Petrograd and the very notion of war in France, could not endure it.

I really want to die . . .

In *The Wine of Solitude*,[46] Irène Némirovsky decided to have her gentle governess, terrified by 'the first outbursts of the Revolution', engulfed by mist. In *Snow in Autumn* [*Les Mouches d'automne*], she has her walk quietly into the Seine, in the guise of an old Russian *niania* whose wits have been turned through exile. 'I must carefully describe what I believe I have sensed in her, how all this chaos persists, these people, their cries, right down to this wild country, must have shocked her, terrified her, and, myself, my soul, everything within me . . . that is untamed, passionate. Yes, all that must have saddened her, frightened her.'

Too French for this 'barbaric country', Zézelle threw herself into the icy waters of the Moïka in 1917. Victoria still remembered this fifty years later. In 1931, however, in a publisher's insert in *Snow in Autumn*, Irène Némirovsky lifted the curtain:

> I should like to draw attention to one thing. *Les Mouches d'automne* was published in a limited edition, and the reviewers who have mentioned it have disapproved of the ending, finding it implausible and 'melodramatic'. I think it is interesting to point out that the elderly aunt Tatiana's suicide is the only authentic, absolutely real fact in the story.
>
> My governess died in this way, a simple-hearted and devout woman who brought me up, and whom I loved as a mother. By way of homage to her memory and because I believe one should account for one's errors, I have not wished to alter anything in the present edition.

Gabri throwing herself out of the window in *L'Ennemie* . . . David Golder dying in 'the black, muddy water'[47] . . . Tatiana Ivanovna slipping unnoticed into the foul-smelling Seine[48] . . . Eliane thinking of jumping into the sea in 'Film parlé' . . . The pool in the River Berche in which Henri's lover disappears in 'La Comédie bourgeoise' . . . The 'dark eddies'[49] into which Ginette would throw herself in 'Les Rivages heureux' . . . The 'fear of water' that Colette admits to, and the 'deep river' into which Jean Dorin vanishes in *Fire in the Blood* [*Chaleur du sang*] . . . The 'green, slimy mud'[50] that engulfs Grayer in 'Le Spectateur' [The Spectator] . . . And the lake into which Father Péricand is thrown in *Suite Française*, bombarded by stones . . . People often commit suicide and drown in Irène Némirovsky's work, in waters that are always colder, always darker and more foul: those eternally polluted waters of St Petersburg, with their 'sour smell', were for her 'the very breath of the city'.[51]

Zézelle survives in Irène Némirovsky's work under the delicate name of Mademoiselle Rose. Her suicide succeeded in transforming Anna from someone who was merely corrupt into a criminal, and Leonid into an accomplice, for, confronted with Irotchka's desperate warnings

– 'Oh, Papa, Papa, if you only knew!' – he retreated into denial: 'Enough . . . you don't know what you're saying, my child . . .'[52] She had to bury deep within herself the weighty secret that no one wished to hear. Up until the day in 1934 when, retracing her memories in order to use them in an important apprentice novel, this poorly concealed secret suddenly leapt into her consciousness. Supposing Irène Némirovsky's entire output was based on a suppressed confession?

So abandoned did she feel at this juncture that it would have been surprising if the desire to join Zézelle did not occur to her. 'For a long time, she gazed at the canal waters – I'd happily throw myself in, she thought, I really want to die . . .'[53] But she had uttered or written these words: 'the lover', and had flaunted them like a talisman. She had jeered at the wretched comedy of married life and, by way of a rejoinder, had converted it into tragedy. It made her want to condemn this 'caricature of home life'.[54] Was Leonid resigned to the fact? It therefore fell to Irina to punish the mother's offence. Her heart stirred with her mother's blood, her skin had her father's dark complexion, her soul quivered with a 'hereditary sickness'[55] which made her vain, insolent and jealous; but she was proud enough to know it, to catch adults in the act and to manipulate them from a distance. For '[her] soul was older than [her] body, and it was [her] soul that had been violated'. In her dreams, her parents became her obedient toys. What revenge! What consolation! 'A little girl tells herself stories in the evening, as she is going to sleep. She connects the grown-ups all around her with a thousand unusual adventures in which their familiar faces sometimes take on fantastical features. This little girl thrills every day to her own imagination . . . Mme Irène Némirovsky appears well placed to know this. For this was the way she began to write.'[56]

It was December 1916. Wartime industry had shaken the Russian economy. Famine was threatening the cities. A mad monk was mesmerising the imperial couple. The state passed from hand to hand. Newspapers came out covered with blank columns, to such an extent that it was expected they would disappear from one day to the next. 'Naturally the grown-ups "knew"; they were waiting for something. What?' Very soon, Irina Némirovsky's mental revolt would be 'faced with the most brutal, the most nightmarish realities'. How could anyone believe in the word 'revolution', when no one any longer believed in the word 'love'?

3

The Upheaval of All Life
(1917–1919)

O you my elusive city,
Why did you arise over an abyss?

Alexander Blok, Nemesis, 1914

The year 1917 stormed into Irina's dream life and cast her out into a convulsive present. At the age of almost fourteen, she was still wearing those large blouses, so shapeless and so ugly, bought in Berlin before the war. But her necklace was made of real pearls, which was a comfort to her. 'How has life suddenly stopped being routine? When did politics forsake the newspapers and enter our existence? When has one ever felt so completely that History, "the historic times", was not solely the privilege of previous generations . . . but could intrude on one's life to such an extent that it affected your sleep, changed your future, surrounded you on all sides and enveloped you like dark waves?'

Year One of the Revolution

When? Leonid Némirovsky would probably have known that ever since 10th February a strike had been spreading from the Putilov metal-working factories into the suburbs. The winter was exceptionally harsh, with temperatures of minus 40° Celsius. Some bakeries, most of them empty, had already withstood orderly assaults. Everybody was expecting a laborious repetition of 1905. On the 14th, the 'Workers' Marseillaise', sung by young women, had rung out along the Nevsky Prospekt: 'We shall throw out the old world . . .' The Tsar was openly defied by pamphlets calling for a general strike. 'Stop working and come down to the street – insist on peace and bread, and the abdication of the Tsar – and to hell with the bourgeoisie!'[1] One can imagine what Leonid's and Anna's reactions were to these demands.

On Thursday 23rd February, the demonstrations had grown to an imposing magnitude. During the afternoon, on the pretext that this was 'International Women's Day', thousands of female textile workers and mothers processed in an orderly manner through the streets of the city, yelling out slogans that were shocking in their starkness: 'Our children are dying of hunger! We have nothing to eat!' Onlookers, office workers and even the Cossacks watched them pass by without any hostility, and in solemn curiosity, much as in days gone by they watched tattered files of wandering monks who had walked three thousand kilometres to kiss the holy relics at the lavra in Kiev. A crowd of darkly clad pilgrims, so tightly bunched that they brought traffic to a stop, gathered calmly in front of the Duma and along the Nevsky for a fête without bread or music. Leonid, Anna and Irina were in one of the motor-cars. A female worker leaned through their window. 'She was wearing a rough woollen shawl on her head, and in the fold of her shawl, in the crook of her arm, a small, sleeping child. I looked at the child and thought it was lovely, so I said so aloud, and the woman half smiled, with one of those almost involuntary smiles that barely reached the corners of her lips and lit up her eyes, a smile at once proud and timid that women all over the world reveal, rich or poor, whenever a passer-by in the street ahead of them has looked at their little one.'

'What do they want? What are they saying?'

Irina's curiosity met with no response, apart from the fact that this was not the first gathering of women, but that it surpassed the previous ones in number. 'And, in fact, even when I stood on tip-toes, and looked into the distance, all I could see were women wearing scarves, women in grey skirts, women carrying children on their shoulders, and who walked by at the same slow, rhythmic pace. We did not see the end of the procession. The police had our car pushed into one of the side streets, and we returned home.'

The marches took place again the next day and the day after, with more demands being called for. Half the workers of Petrograd – two hundred thousand men – were on strike and were swarming towards the centre of the city, crossing the frozen Neva and skirting round the police, who were positioned on the bridges. 'Down with war! Down with the autocracy!' The women, as they always do, implored the troops to lower their guns. On the Nevsky, beneath the strong

sunshine, gangs of students and young girls seized the starting keys
of the trams. Residential districts were invaded by the demonstrators.
As the first grenades and shots were being fired, the Cossacks rained
down blows with the *nagaïka* (an instrument used for flogging), as
they did in years gone by. The troops took over from the 'pharaohs',
and killed and arrested people, but in reality the balance was beginning to swing in favour of the rioters, who preserved a ghastly calm.
Only the officer cadets, newly disciplined, failed to see what they
might have gained from disobeying orders.

It was announced that on the night of the 25th the Tsar would
make a hurried return, not to distribute bread – 'one might as well
ask milk from a billy goat,'[2] Trotsky would say – but to be at the
bedside of the sickly Tsarevitch. Irina, to whom nothing had been
explained, was not fully aware of how serious events were. But on
the afternoon of 26th February, one of those endlessly boring Sundays,
while she was at home alone practising the piano, the social unrest
came beating at her window. 'Cries and the sound of whistles being
blown' rang out from the street. She rushed to the window, only too
glad to abandon her scales. 'First I saw women quarrelling, so it seemed
to me, at the door of a bakery, which was closed. Suddenly, these
women began to laugh and clap their hands. There was a barracks
opposite our house. At the top of the wall one, two, three, ten soldiers
appeared, with rifles in their hands, and with cries and jeers they
jumped down into the street, cheered on by the women and
surrounded by children. In this way, I saw the first soldiers joining the
revolutionaries, this entire crowd grew in a flash, ran towards the
adjoining square, and disappeared.'

That evening, the whole of Petrograd was in the streets, which
were covered with placards stating that the disturbances would be
crushed by force. The law courts had been burnt down. Machine guns
were erected on the rooftops. The Arsenal, the Admiralty, the Okhrana,
the Peter and Paul Fortress, the Winter Palace and, above all, the large
barracks had still to be captured. Irina had gone to bed, and did not
feel anxious yet, but she was intrigued, trusting in the apparent serenity
of the grown-ups. It was then that she heard the noise of gunfire for
the first time. It was the Pavlovski regiment responding to the firing
of the machine guns. The army had just turned its guns on the regime's
last repressive trump card.

'Aren't you frightened?' asked Leonid, when he came home.

No, she was not frightened. The French had taken the Bastille, and since then, France had been an earthly paradise. 'These were just the very first moments of the Revolution. One felt sheltered in one's home. At about midnight everything was quiet.' The following morning, all the regiments had mutinied. Political and common-law prisoners were released from gaols. Armoured cars criss-crossed the city. A soviet made up of workers and soldiers challenged the power that the Duma had initially hesitated to seize and proclaimed the victory of the Revolution. Cosily tucked away ever since the 23rd, and still affected by the fine faces of the female workers, Irina reckoned it was a marvellous spectacle. 'The city was decked in red, and this was a sign that told you you were part of the Revolution . . . No blood was spilled; not a single house was destroyed; the sun shone; red paper flowers were sold in the streets and the trams were decorated with scarlet banners. The people were joyful, magnanimous and full of hope.' Furthermore, they started singing La Marseillaise, and Prince Lvov, first minister of the provisional government formed on 2nd March, had his visiting cards printed in French. On 10th March, the death penalty was abolished – though this did not prevent summary executions. And on the 14th, Russia issued a fraternal 'call for peace to fighters the world over'. A generous and universalist 1789 then took place in Russia. No one gave any thought to what Engels predicted: 'When 1789 occurs in such a country, 1793 will soon follow.'

A cry of hatred and madness

The fairy tale was short-lived. Irina suddenly realised '"that something was happening". Something frightening, exciting and strange, which was the Revolution, the upheaval of all life.' It was the day when, from the study, she saw the implacable machine guns pattering from the rooftops, spraying the leisurely crowd that had taken possession of the city, 'making the weekdays seem like Sunday', and treating the Revolution as a fairground. 'For the first time, I heard the cries of terror and pain from those who were wounded, and the long howl that rose from the crowd and demanded blood, the unforgettable cry of hatred and madness.' Then there was the quarry. On the rooftops, soldiers and students wearing red armbands pursued snipers and handed them over to be lynched. At her window-pane, dumbfounded, Irina was watching this outburst of bestiality, when she heard pandemonium from within the building. They were searching for the *dvornik* Ivan, because he had married his daughter to a policeman. This valiant caretaker, 'a stout old man in a white Russian-style shirt', had hidden under his father-in-law's bed. He was pulled out by a squad of jeering but uncompromising soldiers, then dragged into the back-yard. Irina, pale as a sheet, ran to the window in the corridor.

'Don't look!' yelled Anna.

She looked nonetheless, for she had never seen such things. They had thrust Ivan up against a wall and were asking him to bid farewell to his children, who were sobbing toddlers, then they blindfolded him and there was a burst of rifle fire. The *dvornik*, blood running down his face, slumped to the ground. Then he opened his eyes once more and smiled foolishly. 'They had only wanted to give him a fright, to punish him, or, perhaps, the soldiers had aimed badly.' After this cruel chastisement, the resuscitated fellow's wounds were dressed and he was consoled by his assailants, almost as if the stage manager of this macabre farce had forgotten to bring the curtain down. Emerging from the wings, Ivan's wife brought the merry soldiers something to drink. At the window, Irina was not sure whether to applaud this buffoonery or not. How had the crowds, who had been so blissfully happy in February, been transformed into these wild hordes, those innocent people into these maniacs, the righters of wrongs into comic actors? 'Only much later did I realise that I had witnessed the birth of the revolution. I had witnessed the moment when man had not yet cast aside human behaviour, when he was not yet possessed by the demon, who, nevertheless, was already drawing closer, unsettling him and enveloping his soul. What demon? All who have seen war and rioting at close hand or from a distance know him; everyone gives him a different name, but he always has the same face, wild and crazed, and those who have observed him once will never forget him.'[3]

Blurring over this episode in a few lines in *The Wine of Solitude*, Irène Némirovsky would not allow the *dvornik* Ivan to have any luck: 'He'd fallen and was carried away on a stretcher, just as some nameless, dead woman had been carried away, wrapped in her black shawl.'[4] Seeing in their true light the perverse effects of liberty, when they became arbitrary, she was filled with scepticism about the benefits of the Great Evening. Not that she was unaware of the feudal ossification of the autocracy: 'Inane censorship, cruel practices, the revolutionaries and the government matching each other in the cruelty of their attacks and repression, such more or less was the picture of Russian society in the years 80–90.'[5] But this waste of human lives illustrated the fragility of just causes and the appositeness of the old Russian *nitchevo*: '"Eliminate the unjust for the good of the majority". Why should we? And who is just? And how do people treat me?'[6] Yes, what was the point, exactly, of building on blood? What was the point of rectifying evil with evil? And so the 'hereditary evil', which turned little girls into the loathsome replicas of their mothers if they weren't careful, was a universal principle, since poor people could, in their turn, transform themselves into murderers, and soon there would be 'petit-bourgeois Bolshevists'.[7] 'The revolution provided me with holidays . . . but it encouraged me to ponder,'[8] Irène Némirovsky concluded in 1935, with her consummate skill for understatement.

A pied-à-terre in Moscow

Throughout the existence of the Provisional Government, Leonid Némirovsky, reassured by the impressive downward spiral of the new regime, got on with his business, 'timidly to begin with', then with gusto. The Minister for Justice, the socialist Alexander Kerensky, a great tub-thumper whose real name, well-bred people never failed to point out, was Aaron Kirbis,[9] enjoyed a popular acclaim almost equal to that of the deposed Tsar. Whereas not a single imperial eagle and not a single statue of Nicholas II was still standing, the portraits of 'Alexander IV' began to blossom with the spring. In April it had become fashionable to buy 'Kerensky sweets', disgusting confections flavoured with cinnamon and chocolate and shaped in his likeness.[10] On 7th April, *Pravda* had published the 'April Theses' by Lenin, who had returned from exile, which advocated the 'immediate merging of all the country's banks into one national bank placed under the control of soviets of workers' delegates'. But Kerensky appeared safe. Successively, Minister for War, then Prime Minister, he came out of the woods in July, suppressed the demonstrations by sailors and workers, confronted the Bolsheviks and forced

Lenin into exile once more. At the end of August, he thwarted an attempt at a military coup and proclaimed a republic.

Was Russia, in spite of the war, at last becoming a reasonable country? As in France under the Convention, the anti-Jewish tendencies were abolished. A 'foul and bloody stain of infamy',[11] wrote Gorky, had at last been washed away. In the minds of the Bolshevik leaders, who were waiting for the moment to undermine bourgeois institutions, the 'Jewish problem' simply did not exist: it would disappear of its own accord with the emancipation of the whole of society.[12] Even then, Irina relied upon her nose: ever since February, the stench of the canals 'which nobody had dreamed of cleaning since the February revolution',[13] had become intolerable. How can it bode well for a city that neglects itself? 'In Petersburg, people steal and they pillage,' observed the poet Zinaïda Hippius, whose apartment – a kind of anteroom of the Duma – provided a view over the Taurida palace; 'in the army, there's overall breakdown, indiscipline and rebellions.'[14] And as always in such situations, the Jews were accused of all the present evils existing in Russia, just as they had been blamed for past evils. During the last days of September, this extraordinary slogan could be seen on the walls of Petrograd: 'Down with the Jew Kerensky, long live Trotsky!'[15]

Was this a revolution? The Bolsheviks, relying on the restless mass of sailors and anarchists, on common law and on the unemployed hoi polloi, had promised to create a general disturbance aimed at preparing the way for the transfer of total power to the Soviets. This took place. As the ministers who had been arrested at the Winter Palace passed by on their way to the Peter and Paul Fortress, a crowd chanted: 'Into the water!' Newspapers were censored, telephone lines cut, the city was sealed off by the gunfire of the armoured vehicles and warships; there was looting, rape, pillaging, the settling of scores . . . 'In times of war and revolution, nothing is more extravagant than those first moments when you are thrown from one kind of life into another, all the breath knocked out of you, as if you had fallen from a high bridge into a deep river, without understanding what was happening to you, absurd hope still alive in your heart.'[16]

Devastation was spreading through Petrograd, leaving a thirst for blood in its wake. The officers and Junkers loyal to Kerensky, who were subjected to unbelievable tortures, were drowned along with those princes who had not fled or had not joined the Reds. The February festivities were followed by a hellish Mardi Gras: children sporting guns and ransacking wardrobes, caretakers put in charge of their buildings, thieves posing as inquisitors, compulsory purchases for whatever price was decreed, petty crooks lynched in public places under the eyes of children and the powerless city militia, which was made up of students incapable of loading a revolver . . .

The Némirovskys did not have time to discover whether the *dvornik* Ivan, like his fellow caretakers, was appointed supervisor of the building. On 3rd November, the new authorities ordered the closure of all financial firms and, four days later, they began pillaging the State Bank. Lenin had promised to put an end to the 'power of the bankers': it was time for Leonid Némirovsky to flee Petrograd. But in the state of disintegration into which the country had slumped over the past week, there could be no question of reaching Tehran or Constantinople. Dealing with basic necessities first, Leonid set out for Moscow, in the hope of returning to Petrograd once the turmoil was over or when Kerensky, who was nowhere to be found, had restored order *manu militari*. In the old Russian capital Leonid actually had at his disposal a 'pied-à-terre, an apartment that he sub-let, fully furnished, from a guards officer who was seconded to London at the time, to the embassy probably'. This simple fact provides further evidence of his adroitness, just as it does of the antipathy he must have felt for the Bolshevik revolution, because the horse-guards regiment, established under Catherine the Great for the protection of the imperial residence, was an elite ceremonial unit, famous for its civilised way of life. An unmistakable indication of this was the fact that its anthem was taken from a French opera, *La Dame blanche* by Boieldieu.

It should come as no surprise therefore that Irina, who was shut away at home, should have discovered 'Huysmans, Maupassant, Oscar Wilde and Plato' at the lieutenant's flat. Scattered through the little black notebook that she kept with her until 1942 are lists of the books in her library: *The Picture of Dorian Gray, A House of Pomegranates, À rebours, The Jungle Book,* the poetry of Ronsard, du Bellay, Vigny, Verlaine, *Les Fleurs du mal, Claudine en ménage,* Pierre Louÿs's novel *Aphrodite* and his poems *Les Chansons de Bilitis, Les Hors-Nature* by Rachilde . . . *À rebours,* which she did not fully understand, provided her with a vocabulary with which to describe the clutter of her St Petersburg house, 'but this book was a revelation to me, however: it introduced me to the core of the very best contemporary French literature'.[17] *Mont-Oriol* could instruct her on paternal affairs, and *Bel-Ami* on maternal matters; Oscar Wilde, whose aphorisms ('Men marry because they are tired, women because they are curious; both are disappointed'[18]) she copied down in her notebook, on middle-class comedy. Yet it was Kipling who she would say in 1932 had most influenced her childhood.[19]

The aim of my life . . .

The Moscow apartment offered all the guarantees of safety. It was situated in an 'inner house', which one reached by walking through two outer buildings one after the other, in the midst of which was the apartment, set like 'a donjon in an old French castle'. In choosing a stronghold as a refuge, Leonid had not lacked intuition; it was as if he had feared an attack. For in Moscow the 'khouliganism', as they called it, raged more ferociously than in Petrograd. On the night of 26th October, the Kremlin had been fired upon by batteries positioned on a hill. After that, Junkers and Red Guards confronted each other daily in pitched battle. On the 31st, the insurgents fired into the streets with heavy guns. 'The bombardment was so terrible that soldiers who had fought in the war told me that it was more frightening than at the front,'[20] Irène Némirovsky remembered. On 4th November, Bolshevik victory was achieved. 'But life,' wrote Gorky, 'continued much as normal: schoolboys and schoolgirls attended class; people went for walks; they queued in front of shops; curious onlookers gathered in groups of ten or more at street corners, trying to guess where the firing was coming from.'[21]

Between volleys, Princess Irina came down from her 'donjon' to pick up cartridges and bits of shell casing, remnants of the devastation being wreaked outside. Then she went back upstairs to perfect what she had learned, equipping herself with Latin grammars in order to decipher the texts of 'those authors of the decadent period who gave such pleasure to Huysmans' hero'. It was appropriate reading: in the streets, shops that sold wine were besieged as if they were bomb factories, hotels were shelled as if they were military objectives. Anarchy prevailed. 'Curled up on a sofa, I was very proud to be reading *Le Banquet* while the gunfire was raging. My mother was appalled at my indifference and, every time she walked past me, she reprimanded me.'[22] But it was *The Picture of Dorian Gray*, more than any other book, which delighted and moved her, and gave a shape to her suffering. 'It was the passions about whose origin we deceived ourselves that tyrannised most strongly over us,' wrote Wilde. 'Our weakest motives were those of whose nature we were conscious. It often happened that when we thought we were experimenting on others, we were really experimenting on ourselves.'[23] Viewed in this way, the vague resentment she felt for her mother could become a force for self-exploration. In her black notebook, she noted down in English: 'The aim of my life is self-development.'[24] So a way out existed to the mental labyrinth in which Anna had enclosed her. Was there one to the fortress in which Leonid had had the curious idea of hiding his family? For during five days in November 1917, the Némirovskys withstood a real siege, in which they were liable to be summarily raided, denounced or executed by some zealous commissar. 'We lived in Moscow, shut away in our house with a sack of potatoes, boxes of chocolates, and sardines. Fortunately, we had loyal servants who did not betray us.'[25]

On 10th November, the seizure of the banks that had begun in Petrograd reached Moscow; the gold was impounded. Clearly, nowhere was safe any longer. Leonid resolved to arrange their escape and to transfer his assets abroad discreetly. 'As soon as we could,' Irène Némirovsky points out, 'we would return to St Petersburg, but before long a price was put on my father's head; he was obliged to go into hiding; he could no longer live with us.'[26] In mid-December, the banking system was declared a state monopoly. Private banks ceased to exist. If he remained in Russia, Leonid might as well throw his visiting cards in the fire. And, if he lingered any longer, he would have his entire share portfolio, the basis of his wealth, confiscated. But 'a price' put on his head? Had he, like 'Mitka' Rubinstein, been guilty of accruing wealth fraudulently in wartime? Was he so compromised with the Old Regime? We don't know.

Drunken stupors

One month after the uprising, Petrograd was scarcely recognisable. People were beginning to die of hunger there. 'The candles cost a

fortune, oil was scarce, and it was dark from three o'clock in the afternoon until ten in the morning,' John Reed, the left-wing American
journalist, wrote. 'The robberies and burglaries were increasing . . .
To obtain bread, milk, sugar or tobacco, you needed to queue for
hours beneath the freezing rain.'²⁷ And then, there was that orgy, the
pianka: a continuous pogrom, by day and by night, on grocers' shops,
wine merchants, restaurant storerooms, the cellars of the middle
classes, not forgetting that eldorado of alcoholism, the fabled cellars
of the tsars. Officially, it was a matter of 'collectivising' the liquid
opium and of 'looting from the looters' in Lenin's famous phrase: in
practice, it was an endless bacchanalia, which began in the last days
of November and did not stop until January 1918. For two months,
liberty guided the people, and wine governed the army rabble. It was
all very well for *Pravda*, worried by this appalling propaganda, to say
that it was due to 'bourgeois provocations': men's bodies and bottles
in their hundreds were strewn over the Moïka, the crashing of barrels
shattered the night air, and even chemists and perfumery shops were
ransacked for their alcohol. 'All the public thoroughfares were drenched
with wine and I saw with my own eyes a street swilled out with champagne,' one witness recounted.²⁸ In certain cellars where the casks
were enormous, cases of drowning and asphyxia were reported. Even
the steps of the Smolny palace, the seat of government, were iced
over with some excellent clarets. A musty stench of cheap wine and
vomit hovered over the city. But worst of all, cold-blooded murder
came easier when people were driven by alcohol. Every bourgeois
had a cork for a head. It is not known how many peaceful 'counter-
revolutionaries' were murdered, robbed or beaten up because their
attackers were blind drunk.

Seventeen years after these excesses, Irène Némirovsky could still
smell the stench of those autumn days when she described them
in 'Les Fumées du vin'. 'The drunken stupors had stirred up the
entire city,'²⁹ the commanding officer of Petrograd would observe
in his 'Notes on the civil war', recalling that day when the prestigious Preobrajensky and Pavlovski regiments in their turn descended
into drunkenness. The manner in which the 'comrades' in 'Les
Fumées du vin', who are called upon to vandalise the cellars and
to destroy 'this cursed alcohol which had enslaved [*their*] fathers',
soon 'fought one another, threw themselves on the ground, fell

asleep in the snow, drank wine mixed with the frozen water from the stream',[30] conveys Irène Némirovsky's scepticism for the Revolution, which is to history what adolescence is to life: a spasm of pride that makes the burden of heredity bearable. Like the father's features on the face of the rebellious child, the 'Red terror' would not be able to conceal the heavy toll of 'Nicholas-the-Bloody' for long. The deportations of nihilist terrorists by the autocracy were followed by the deportations of the Mensheviks by the Lenin government. When did Irène Némirovsky realise that the Revolution flouted her ideals? For this was the sacrilege that symbolised this orgy: 'men tossing around bottles of an old Burgundy full of the sunshine of France'.[31] In 'Les Fumées du vin', of course, the 'wild and revolting party' ends with a drowning. The young officer, Ivar, betrayed by the jealous Illmanen girls – who resemble Irina's sad St Petersburg neighbours – disappears in the waters of the gulf with the gypsy girls and the young men who were fleeing the drunken horde. 'Comrades, don't drown the Revolution in alcohol,' the posters with their red star had warned.

If the novelist chose to set these scenes of decadence in Finland, it was certainly in Petrograd that she had witnessed them, as is demonstrated in this marginal note in 'Mercredi des cendres': 'The Revolution, and everything that it nurtured in people's hearts, and that *mad* side of the Revolution, which one is almost ashamed to reveal and which existed . . . The evening, the nights, the feeling that everything is about to end, and the night when the swarm of Reds invaded the terror-struck city . . . with a few soldiers . . . the alcohol in the streets . . .' But it was actually Finland, in early January 1918 at the latest, for which the Némirovskys left Petrograd for good, as did over 40,000 Russians up until 1922. On 12th January, in fact, the frontier, which at the time was forty or so kilometres away, was sealed off.[32] Shortly before that date, on the orders of the Russian Bank for foreign trade, Leonid was still trying to buy back at 115 per cent the shares held by Jonas Lied, the manager of the Siberian Company and Norwegian Consul in Siberia, in the Ob and the Yenisei river companies, that is to say 3.1 million Swedish kroner. A futile poker throw by an 'optimistic speculator',[33] who only resolved to leave Russia in the very last resort.

Mustamäki

Annexed in 1808, Finland had enjoyed a degree of autonomy until it was drastically repressed at the beginning of Nicholas II's reign, and the country was recaptured without violence in 1905. But ever since March 1917, the country that Dumas had likened to a sponge, weary of being exploited, had dreamed of seizing its independence. This dream came crashing down on Kerensky, for whom a Red Finland, to the north-west of Petrograd, would have meant strangulation. The Finnish socialists, believing they had been betrayed, moved towards insurrection. From that point on, civil war became inevitable. From November 1917 onwards, however, it was the bourgeoisie that cried out for independence: forty thousand Russian soldiers, now under Bolshevik command, were then stationed in the country. Busy nego-tiating a peace settlement with Germany, Lenin nevertheless granted independence, though he was still not prepared to relinquish his plan to sovietise this backyard of the tsars. Not fooled in the least by this manoeuvre, Lieutenant-General Mannerheim opened hostilities against the Reds on the night of 27th/28th January, in Ostrobothnia. The 'war for the liberation of the national soil' had begun.[34]

Before this latest confrontation, the Némirovskys had quit their apartment in the middle of the night. They took only what was strictly necessary, Anna's jewellery hidden inside the linings of their oldest clothing. Leonid would return to Petrograd very quickly to settle his affairs and take away anything that could be salvaged. Now 'every journey to Petersburg was a feat and an act of madness and heroism'.[35] Their route to the frontier is unclear: 'First,' Irène Némirovsky recalled in 1933, 'I remember the departure from Petersburg, the first day, the night, the jolting movements, the jostling, the snow . . . a smell of abandonment, the cold, me, sitting in the sledge, and the feel of the shawl on my mouth, but it's extremely vague. Then the arrival at Moustamiaki, the station. There, I especially remember the biting sensation of cold, of ice, and the slanting snow . . .'

Mustamäki, which means 'black hill' in Finnish, was an area on the borders of Karelia where, before the Revolution, a number of Petersburg residents owned dachas. Nina Berberova, who stayed there in 1915, has described in her memoirs the frozen lakes, the snowdrifts and the houses that lined the railway track, 'with its sleeping rails, close to the station's little illuminated window'.[36] Lenin had frequently stayed in the nearby hamlet of Neivola, in the Bonch-Bruyeviches' summer house, before the October rising. And it was in Mustamäki that the expressionist novelist Leonid Andreyev had an impressive black and pink dacha built, in which he died on 12th September 1919. This house was then wrecked. It was in one of these 'pleasure dwellings', set alight by the Reds, that the narrator of 'Aïno'[37] – a powerfully auto-biographical story – discovers books by Maeterlinck, Wilde and Henri de Régnier that had been left behind. And it was in this village, more Russian than Finnish, that the Némirovskys set down their luggage one January day in 1918. The choice of Mustamäki – today Yakovlevo, twenty or so kilometres north of Terjoki, the present-day Zelenogorsk,[38] on the Gulf of Finland – is proof moreover that Leonid retained a hope of returning to Petrograd as soon as possible. Another exile who happened to be there at that same time was the young George Sanders, aged twelve, who had also fled from Petrograd with his parents. He would become one of the most famous British actors of the twentieth century.[39]

Like Sanders and his family, the Némirovskys reached Mustamäki by sledge. When she arrived, Irina discovered 'a village consisting of a house and a shop',[40] as well as an old inn where Leonid found rooms. It was 'a long, low, yellowish house, with two wooden beams that had become detached'. The electricity had been cut off since November. Irina was immediately struck by the sweet aroma of sap oozing from the logs. On the ground floor there was a small, poorly lit drawing-room, with windows that were frozen with ice, through which you could just make out the snow falling on the enormous fir trees among which the wind roared. 'Rarely seen anything as wretched, as "sickety", armchairs covered in worn velvet, with lace antimacas-sars, a bamboo rocking-chair, a green plant that was dying, a table with a yellow oil-lamp on top of it, an extremely threadbare carpet. A permanently open upright piano, a little book-case made of black wood or bamboo, with books that were torn. Next door, the dining-room, the dining table, which was clean, an ash or birch wood floor, whitewood furniture, a wooden balcony, where the snow was piled up to the height of a man.'[41] Irina's bedroom, on the floor above, was shaped like a rotunda, equipped with drab furniture, and overlooked a garden containing a red shed. Sledge tracks on the snow, glinting 'like a wall of diamonds or mica', receded into the night. In the distance, below, you could hear the heavy gunfire and see the flames that were ravaging the frontier town of Terjoki.

Finnish landscape

This temporary solution lasted for months, but Mustamäki provided a soothing peacefulness. 'A Finnish landscape,' wrote Irène Némirovsky in 1939, 'is a stretch of sparkling white moorland beneath a crystal-clear sky; it's the magical forests; for the ice transforms every fir tree, every birch tree into a fragile and marvellous building that appears to be made of sugar, pieces of mirror and shards of diamond; it's the smell of newly-cut wood, of smoke that rises from a tiny, solitary house beside a large field of snow.' And how could one forget the sliding of the *potkukelkka*, with its delicate seat fixed to two long wooden sticks, beneath a sky empty of clouds? And the deep sledges that broke your back, in which you lay down under fur blankets as if you were in your own bed, by the light of enormous stars?

'I had no friends,' regrets the narrator of 'Aïno'.[42] Yet the Némirovskys were not the only ones staying at the inn. There they found other exiled people from a variety of backgrounds, with whom they could not fail to sympathise. Some of them appear not to have left a single trace in the work of Irène Némirovsky: the Tobiases, Dr Rabinovitch, those known by the names Simon, Bleaky and Isaac Lievshitz (or Liepshitz), unless it is in the guise of those 'Jews of good family' described in *The Wine of Solitude*, 'who spoke English among themselves and observed the rituals of their religion with a proud humility'.[43] Others, on the other hand, have survived: the sophisti-cated Baron Roehmer and his virago, who are renamed Lennart and who are Russian Jews of Swedish origin; the 'fat Salomon Lévy', much as himself; finally, Rudolf and his wife Bluma who, under the prism of fiction, will become Fred and Xenia Reuss. 'What a pity if one had to change these names,' Irène Némirovsky regretted in 1933 . . .

United through exile and boredom, this small circle of people, who would have paid no attention to one another in St Petersburg, was obliged to fraternise over a game of bridge. When evening came, that is to say after three o'clock, Irina, Bluma's children and the other youngsters played at table-tapping, as in the story 'Magie'.[44] They whiled away the time spying through the windows on the comings and goings of the woodcutters or the soldiers who wandered about. Bluma tinkled away on an old piano that was out of tune. The smell of newly cut wood was reminiscent of 'a country coffin'. Occasionally, the young servant girl informed them about a village dance. Irina allowed herself to be taken there by the handsome and boisterous Rudolf – nicknamed 'Roudia' – to watch the Red Guards empty their cartridge clips into the night air. Roudia was a big lad of thirty, with a mocking expression and fine dark eyes that burned with desire. He once took her to dance in a barn or a cowshed built of fir wood. 'The music? I've forgotten. I remember that the windows were long and high, and that through the panes we could see the night outside. I imagine that it was heated by a stove, and I remember the girls dancing with their red skirts, and the boys bristling with guns like bandits at the cinema.'

Fairy tales

On 1st February 1918, in order to conform to the Gregorian calendar used in the West, the Russian calendar made up for lost time by removing thirteen days. This meant there was no 11th February, which did not prevent Irina reaching her fifteenth birthday. For her parents she was still a little girl, 'slim, dark-haired, with brown arms that were too thin', dressed to go out in boots, with 'a large chamois wool pullover', with two long brown plaits which were 'tucked in over her ears so that the snow should not wet them', and tied up with black ribbons as soon as she returned to the inn. But for the dashing Roudia this child already had the attraction of a woman: 'She had dark skin, a simple face and was so thin that no one noticed her; she was too pale, with the olive colouring of the children of St Petersburg. It was only when you looked closer that you would say: "What a lovely skin! It's wonderful!" And those long, wide green eyes, brighter than her skin, with nicely shaped eyebrows, a little tight mouth that was difficult to open, rows of small, delicate teeth, truly like pearls, slightly transparent at the top.'

To begin with, Irina did not pay much attention to the interest this devilish Roudia took in her. He was a married man, but 'crazy about every woman who came within his reach'. She was too busy reading

Dumas, Gautier and the incomplete set of old volumes of Balzac that lay in the cupboard in the drawing-room, next to the pots of jam, 'mostly empty, alas'.[45] She could even learn and retain snatches of Finnish. But it was because of boredom, purer and more all-encompassing than in Kiev or Petersburg, that she started to tell herself stories, 'all kinds of stories,' she would explain, 'which gave me great pleasure and which I returned to day after day. I began to write them, and ever since, I've always continued.'[46] If she is to be believed, they were only 'unfinished things', which she never took up again 'because they weren't worth the trouble'.[47] 'It wasn't very original: fairy stories, prose poems imitating Wilde . . .'[48] Nevertheless, she did not tear them all up. Collected in her black notebook are some rather tentative poems in Russian, some of which probably date from this period, while others were more likely written in 1920. Of course, they take no account of the spelling reforms of 11th May 1917, which she would never observe. They are chiefly about love letters tucked into copies of the Koran, jewellery boxes lined with silk, caliphs pining with desire, green cats, elves in ankle boots and goblins straight out of Nordic folklore:

> Darkness is behind the window
> Dusk is in the sitting-room
> The gnome with the long beard
> Walks across the floor.

In one of these poems, the damned soul of a marquise, living in exile in the twentieth century, dreams melancholically of masked balls, of minuets and oval portraits:

> That is why now, after so many centuries
> Born among all these different people
> I sometimes think I am a stranger here
> And that I might have had another fate
> That fate to which I devote all my dreams.

In another, entitled 'Contes', Irina, who had fallen into the habit of talking to herself in order to escape from her loneliness, invents 'fifteen, twenty, a hundred' little stories for herself so as to fill her nights with wonders:

> I shall tell you how the black knight
> Fell to pieces on the floor
> They put him in a little cotton coffin
> And the mice buried him at night
> In a drawer in the dresser, a quiet and cosy spot
> Before they removed their traces.[49]

So Irène Némirovsky was only telling a white lie when she confessed in 1931: 'Writing poems seems like a sport to me, one in which I have no skill . . . No, to begin with I wrote fairy tales . . . I made them come and go in my imagination. Afterwards, I wrote these visions down.'[50] Yet these oddly assorted verses, full of boredom and fantasy, contained as much poetry as they did fairy tale. As for the 'long or not so long stories' and the novels to which, we are led to believe, she dedicated herself 'straight away',[51] they are the stories she invented by making use of what went on in the 'little colony' of Mustamäki: Bluma giving birth 'covered in blood', which she would use again in 'Nativité' in 1933; Lievshitz's diamonds; 'the Jews who play cards and make fictitious deals so as not to lose the habit'; but above all, the unexpected contact of a 'cool cheek, flushed by the icy wind', then the 'burning kiss the colour of fire' that the impudent Roudia stole from her in the snow-covered entrance to the inn, lips that aroused in her, suddenly, 'all the poetic and elating sensations of love'.

This attention from an older man revolted her at first, then left her feeling puzzled. 'Making someone lose his mind is the second pleasure in the world, losing one's own is the first,' she would write in French in her notebook. In her working notes for *The Wine of Solitude*, Irène Némirovsky allows a doubt to hover as to the consequences of this chaste kiss: 'His long, gentle woman's hands were so adept at caressing and lulling one.' And in the finished novel: 'She let him kiss her, even leaned towards him, offering her face, her hands, her lips, savouring waves of delight, aching waves of bliss that pierced straight through her body.'[52] The echo of this little fling, fleeting because it was the first, would resonate for a long time in the work to come: 'It's probably because of him that all my heroes have nice mouths and fine hands.' She had just had a glimpse of the sensual pleasures that her mother sought. And she had discovered an underhand weapon with which to avenge herself. A feminine weapon which Anna, now in her forties,

would not always be able to offset with her lotions: a young woman's
wonderful freshness.

In Helsinki

Irina did not have the opportunity to take this any further. In the early
spring of 1918, the front line, which had scarcely shifted since January,
suddenly veered southwards. On 12th April, as the Germans were
entering Helsinki, General Mannerheim, without waiting for reinforce-
ments, surrounded the Russians on the Karelian Isthmus, where the
fighting intensified. 'As soon as dusk fell, the little roads in the forest
became dangerous: fleeing rebels hid behind the trees, in the snow-
filled ravines, and the soldiers of the enemy army chased after them,
tracking them down, routing them out from the undergrowth. They
fired at each other, and if a stray bullet hit a Russian traveller who had
hidden in the area, far from his own revolution . . . well, then! We had
no diplomats to defend us or to tell our family we had died too soon.'[53]
Through the windows of the inn, those marooned in Mustamäki
watched as women searched for bodies in the snow. In May, a further
seventy thousand Red Guards were forced to surrender; eight thousand
were executed; twelve thousand died from hunger or their wounds. On
the 16th, Mannerheim was carried in triumph through the streets of
Helsinki. A monarchical Regency was established.

By this time, the Némirovskys had sensibly reached the Finnish
capital, after an eventful journey through woods and lakes, travelling
in perpetual daylight. In *The Wine of Solitude*, we are led to think that
Irina was sent to board 'with the widow of a minister' by the name
of Martens, who taught her German and read Hawel's *Mother Courage*
to her 'aloud'.[54] In 1939 she remembered above all the 'very Nordic
comfort' of this city that was 'clean, beautiful and cold in appearance', the 'fine shops' and 'those telephones installed everywhere'
which, at the age of fifteen, so impressed her. But what remained
unforgettable was 'a bookshop so large and so sumptuous such as I
don't think I've ever seen anywhere else', offering a wide selection of
French books, 'from classics to the most modern'. Since she was to
remain in Helsinki for almost half a year, she would be well versed
in the very latest developments of the French novel when she arrived

in Paris. These books would not, however, wipe away the memory of Roudia's lips or his arms. On 9th September 1918, she would jot down in Russian in her notebook:

> Hard to read (dream), this intoxicating night
> Full of languor of warmth
> And desire for love
> Troubles the soul.

There was no longer any likelihood of returning to St Petersburg. To begin with, the authority of the board of directors of the banking sector had been dissolved by a decree of 1st April 1918; anyone who held Russian shares was henceforth punishable by death if he refused to place them in the State Bank. Next, the house on the Angliskaya Prospekt had been requisitioned for use as a military base.[55] Finally, even if Russian anti-Semitism had been vanquished, the measures taken by the Bolsheviks were hardly reassuring. For instance, a repressive edict, signed by Lenin on 27th July, stated: 'The Jewish bourgeoisie are not our enemy because they are Jewish, but because they are bourgeois.' On 30th August, an assassination attempt on the leader of the Revolution was the starting signal for the 'Red Terror', announced in the following terms by the *Krasnia Gazeta*: 'A thousand bourgeois heads for one Bolshevik's! We've waited long enough! Death to the bourgeois; that is the slogan of the day!' Russia was entering into a civil war which, due to the famine that resulted, would lead to several million deaths within three years.

It was in Ukraine that the clashes were deadliest. The German forces, advancing quickly, lost no time in setting up a bogus republic, under the leadership of the hetman Skoropadski, as the peace treaty of Brest-Litovsk entitled them to do. But after the armistice on 11th November, the Ukraine, which had been evacuated, became a battle ground where, up until 1922, rival armies confronted one another, constantly supplied with fighting men thanks to the low cost of bread, which was not in such short supply as it was in Moscow. On 26th January, the Reds had recaptured Kiev from General Petlyura, who had proclaimed independence. It is hard to imagine that this glorious city should have been conquered, lost, recaptured and ravaged seventeen times during the civil war by four regiments of horsemen of the

Apocalypse: the Reds of Boudienny, the Whites of Denikin, the nation-alists of 'little father' Petlyura, and the anarchists of Nestor Makhno – not to mention Pilsudsky's Polish troops. And it was back to Kiev, the centre of the unrest, that those who had resisted Bolshevism flooded in their thousands from Moscow and Petrograd. 'You could see bankers, grey-haired at their temples, fleeing with their wives, talented businessmen fleeing, who had given authority to their colleagues in Moscow as well as instructions to maintain contact with this new world that was in the process of being born in the Muscovite kingdom,' wrote Bulgakov in *The White Guard*,[56] while Irène Némirovsky recorded that:

> some detachments were fighting here and there. A woman, an anarchist, fought for two days in the streets of Elisavetgrad with counter-revolutionary inhabitants. Groups of White officers (Drozdovsky's men),[57] who had set off for the Romanian border, crossed Ukraine to reach Kuban. The villages, bristling with machine-guns, defended themselves furiously against everyone . . . In the four years between 1918 and 1922, there was a succession of invasions and uprisings in Kiev.[58]

And as each of these armies surged back and forth, there were unre-strained, systematic pogroms on a scale unknown. At Piatigori, for example, in June 1920, all the Jews in the city were rounded up in the synagogue, which was then sprayed with petrol and set alight. Often carried out on the excuse that they were training exercises, these atroc-ities were responsible for over three hundred thousand Jewish deaths.

A terrible storm

In March 1919, Kiev came under Bolshevik control, and the Némirovskys left Helsinki for Stockholm, their last place of exile before arriving in Paris. We may assume that in the meantime they paid a brief visit to continental Europe, possibly to Lodz, where Leonid had been able to keep some financial interests intact, or even to the Baltic States, where his match factory was situated. This is what seems to be suggested by this 1931 interview, in which Irène Némirovsky mentions the stages of their odyssey: 'Yes, I've already had an eventful life. Russia, Sweden, Central Europe . . . and Paris. With all the mishaps that have happened to me, they could write a screenplay.'[59] From Finland, 'the most mysterious country in the world',[60] she took away the memory of 'good-looking young people' and 'strong and healthy' men, fiercely patriotic, capable of cutting off a thief's wrists, something she had witnessed with her own eyes; and independent, liberated women, ready to 'aspire to all positions, to all diplomas just like boys do', which was no small lesson.

A number of Russian exiles had already found refuge in the Swedish capital, where they scraped a living from depositing their paintings, their porcelain, bronzes or rugs with antique dealers. 'I arrived in Stockholm on a winter morning, with the snow mingling with the icy rain, and a wild wind,' Irène Némirovsky related in 1930. 'I came from Finland and in my memory I still retained the image of a sparkling winter. Stockholm to me seemed dark, cold and sad. I remember my first walk in the Drottninggatan, I think, a vast, wide, well-lit street, where after months of revolution, famine, and an entire year spent deep in a lost village in Finland, I discovered – with such amazement! – Europe, wealth, comfort, civilisation. (I can still see the enormous scarlet lobsters in the shop windows, which we looked at avidly like victims of a shipwreck.) All that was almost too good, and it made us a little frightened. So I approached Stockholm with a kind of hostility and suspicion.'[61]

The Némirovskys set down their baggage at the Grand Hotel, a monumental palace overlooking the port, which had been advertised in the *Journal de Saint-Pétersbourg* since the turn of the century. From this fortress with its hundreds of bedrooms, Irina watched the female students pass by in their white berets and listened to the 'little housemaids' singing in the courtyards, wearing bonnets, which she learned to call *fröken*. At that point, Leonid had already left Scandinavia, from Bergen, to prepare for the arrival of his family in Paris. This at least is what the puzzling dates jotted down by Irina in the back pages of her notebook suggest: Helsinki 5th January, Bergen 8th January, France 9th February 1919. Others are harder to interpret: 'Jerusalem? 9th May' and 'Mar. 1st March 1920 Petrograd'. But it is true that Leonid wrecked his life by moving about, as David Golder – modelled on him – would do, and, in *The Wine of Solitude,* Boris Karol, who 'had crossed Finland, lost five million Swedish Crowns on the exchange rate, got two million back and left again for Paris where his wife, his daughter and Max were meant to meet him'.[62]

At last, at the beginning of the Swedish springtime, which only really breaks through in May, Leonid summoned his wife and daughter to come to Paris. Like all Russian children, Irina was aware that the Nordic spring is 'sudden, blazing, intoxicating' and that 'you have to hurry to savour it, to drink it like wine'. Which she did, before their embarkation, scheduled for about 20th June, by pacing the streets of the city, which overnight were covered with mauve lilac. After that, the visit to Uppsala, its cathedral, and its lilac trees, as well as 'a very old stone monument which is, I think, the tomb of the first kings of Sweden, the fir trees, the calm water . . .'[63] To the rudimentary Finnish she had acquired in Helsinki, she could add a few fragments of Swedish, and the first bars of the national anthem remained with her for ever.

Spring was drawing to a close. Anna and Irina took a first boat to Norrköping, a hundred miles south of Stockholm, where a 'small cargo boat' bound for France awaited them. 'I've liked this country very much,'[64] she would murmur as she watched the coastline recede. The crossing was rough: 'ten days without putting into a port, with a terrible storm which I must have remembered in *David Golder*'.[65] It was enough, in any case, to instil a fear of water to add to her terror of drowning. She herself acknowledged that this perilous journey by sea would remain, along with the scenes of anarchy in Petrograd, the deepest scar on her young soul. 'Fear? Fear? But I'm never afraid . . . I've never been afraid. Except once in Russia during the Revolution . . . And another time on a small cargo boat which took me from Sweden to Rouen . . . We endured a terrible storm, the ship bobbed about, I was frightened of falling in the green water . . .'[66]

Because the cargo boat was unable to dock in Le Havre owing to the bad weather, Anna and Irina travelled to Paris from Rouen through the Normandy countryside, so agreeable when the blossom is out. Irina was back in Arcadia, 'that sweet land, the most beautiful in the world'.[67] And for a long time.

Leonid was waiting for them at the station. He had lost that stockiness that one sees in the pre-war photographs of him, and he appeared lanky, with his sullen moustache, his silvery temples and his detached, drooping, almost sad demeanour. This was the effect of twenty months spent gathering up his assets which had been scattered by turmoil unprecedented in the old world. A good many of his assets had vanished into thin air, those that had not been stolen by the Bolsheviks. In July 1919, however, he was suspected of having speculated on the rouble and on precious metals on behalf of the Reds – which says a great deal about the reputation of Russian bankers in Paris.

Irina was sixteen. The age at which, in Russia, one becomes a woman. As she set foot on the cobbled streets of Paris, Anna became Fanny, Leonid, Léon. And Irma Irina became Irène Némirovsky.

4

Miss Topsy and Mademoiselle Mad
(1919–1924)

If the echo of these frenzied and marvellous nights could pierce the deaf wall of the years.

Joseph Kessel, *Nuit de princes*, preface to the 2nd edition

Crossing the Place Vendôme at night to reach the hotel where Léon had temporarily arranged for them to stay, the Némirovskys' car passed the Hôtel Vendôme where, three months previously, the man who had unintentionally hastened the downfall of Imperial Russia, Prince Yusupov, was living in comfortable exile with his fiancée Irina, the niece of the late Tsar, murdered with his family at Ekaterinburg.

The peace treaty had just been signed at Versailles. Bastille Day 1919 promised to be the best 14th July celebration for a long time, despite the thousands of households that had been destroyed and the wounded war veterans. In the streets of Paris, the jubilation was so intense that the traffic was unable to move. The Marseillaise, which many Russians could not hear without a shiver running down their spines, rang out everywhere. Aristide Briand's government had indeed sided with the Whites and sent an expeditionary force to Odessa of twenty thousand men, but they had been forced to retreat. And beneath the Arc de Triomphe, the former Russian flag did not flutter, even though millions of soldiers had died on the Eastern front fighting the common enemy, before and after February 1917.

Weird foreigners

Fanny complained that Paris had changed. It was she who had grown older. After the storm, Léon counted the damage. He had had the 'good fortune to discover one of his bank's branches, and here he was able to start reconstructing a fortune that had been reduced to nothing'.[1] When he announced that he was going away on business,

Fanny did nothing to stop him: she no longer felt constrained by the bonds of marriage. Before setting off again, Léon, ever understanding, gave her a fine motor-car in which to parade around the Bois de Boulogne, go for drinks in the Pavillon Dauphine, raid the dress shops, dine at the Ritz and change her clothes twice a day. It was the great post-war novelty: there were more luxury cars in the Bois than there were riders on horseback. Irène, with a wary eye on her mother's antics, remembered everything, the monuments, the parks, the light, the dome of the Invalides, the Jardin des Plantes, the smell of the Seine. 'I had already stayed in Paris as a small child. Returning there, I discovered the memories that awaited me.'[2] This lost paradise took her back over the years, almost to the last century, before the curtain fell in 1914. 'Just a few shadows amid all the light: children dressed in mourning clothes, a blind soldier, another in a small carriage, women rushing about, their long black veils billowing behind them. This was all that was left of the war now.'[3]

So that she could be freer in her movements, Fanny arranged for her daughter to be looked after by an English nanny, an elderly woman marooned by the events of 1917. Irène immediately took a strong dislike to Miss Matthews's 'long horse face',[4] her hollow eyes, her mean mouth and her lugubrious air. Not to mention that, from now on, the English lesson lasted from morning till evening, indoors and outside! 'She was a typically English woman, very handsome, very "British", very thin: a bag of bones,' relates Denise Epstein. 'I never knew her with a man. She followed Mother like her shadow.'[5] From being with her, Irène derived a touch of deportment, a reserve in her feelings, 'a certain restraint in her words and gestures that had the effect of making her charming'.[6] Once she grew used to her, Miss Matthews would actually prove to be less sinister and even excellent company, since Irène Némirovsky would retain her in her employment after her own marriage. One of her vices, which she could not keep secret, was an addiction to ether. She was to be caught unawares, bedridden in a clinic, emptying a bottle of Eau de Cologne to stave off withdrawal symptoms.

Another 'lady of the troupe', tall and with a limp, had appeared on the scene. Irène and Fanny did not meet her for some time, because Léon immediately took her with him to New York, where he had business to attend to. Julienne Dumot would be his secretary from now on. This thirty-four-year-old woman from the Landes region had some sound references: in 1902 she had served in the household of the most Petersburgian of young French playwrights, Sacha Guitry, who had then recommended her to the author of *Triplepatte*, Tristan Bernard. Having made these arrangements, Léon was able to leave his family among the assorted comforts of a flat he had spotted in the west of Paris, at 115 rue de la Pompe, opposite the Janson-de-Sailly *lycée*. This furnished apartment was not far from Passy, Étoile and La Muette, a district in which thousands of Russians, whether they were doctors, journalists, officers, writers, students or princes of the blood, made up a fifth of the population of the *quartier*.

'Don't forget the weirdness of the house either. In Paris.' This note from 1934, written in the margins of *The Wine of Solitude*, leads one to think that the picture Irène Némirovsky paints in the book of her parents' first Paris home is not exaggerated. Furnished with armchairs covered in velvet, bearing the coat of arms of an Italian duke married to an American woman, it displayed poor taste and a slovenliness that Léon and Fanny, any more than they had in St Petersburg, never thought of improving. The bulbs in the chandeliers were grimy and half of them were burnt out. 'Roses no one tended died in their vases; a piano whose lid was never raised by anyone had been pushed into a corner, between torn lace curtains full of cigarette burns that had cost a thousand francs a metre. Ashes were scattered over the carpets; the scornful, silent servants set the coffee down on a corner of the desk and disappeared, their bitter smiles passing harsh judgement on these "mad foreigners".'[7] Irène had experienced such makeshift solutions in Russia, but now that they had found 'the most beautiful country in the world', what was the point? Was Léon, like all the Russians in Paris who lived out of their suitcases, waiting for the last twist of the civil war? During 1920, France, alone among western nations, kept alive a last hope by encouraging General Wrangel's White Russian victories, and then recognising his government. This probably explains why, prior to the wholesale rout of the White armies, in November 1920, the Némirovskys did not feel it was necessary to forsake the bizarre lair in the rue de la Pompe for a more luxurious apartment. Irène, for her part, had already made her own priorities clear by pouncing on French books, especially the modern authors: Proust, Larbaud, Chardonne, Maurois...

Ships that pass in the night . . .

In February 1920, back from his travels, Léon took his wife and daughter to spend the winter and spring in Nice. A series of photographs taken on the Promenade des Anglais that are a cross between a fashion parade and a vanity fair date from this period. In front of a casino that is no longer standing today, and that is more reminiscent of Isfahan than of the Baie des Anges, Léon, a vacant look in his eye, is wearing a bowler hat and a fine double-breasted overcoat, gloves and two-tone 'co-respondent' shoes, and gaiters in the pre-war style. Miss Matthews, dressed like a crow, stands guard indulgently beside Irène. The latter, carrying a small handbag in her white gloves, with thick brown ringlets beneath her black hat, and her feet squeezed into uncomfortable slippers, wears a mischievous smile that is not to be trusted. One of her friends would accuse her before long 'of smiling at people while thinking wicked things about them'.[8] This smile must be for her mother, who carries a parasol on her shoulder and is dressed in a bold white kaftan with a geometric design. A third photograph shows father, mother and daughter together: Irène Némirovsky tore it so that she could send just the image of herself to her Aunt Victoria in Moscow; in her white waistless dress beneath a jacket decorated with triskeles, a black sunhat clamped on head, she walks with a confident step. On the back are these simple words: 'To my dear Aunt Vika from her niece who loves her.'

At the Excelsior Hôtel Regina, a gigantic building of four hundred bedrooms constructed in 1896 to welcome Queen Victoria, Irène made the acquaintance of a young Russian girl, two years younger than her, who had fled Petrograd after her father had been murdered at Kronstadt on 30th August 1918. Valerian Boutourline had been only thirty-two, and his wife, in order to remain in France, must have opened a sewing workshop, if we are to believe the short story 'Destinées' into which Irène Némirovsky slipped some authentic details about her friend Olga Valerianovna Boutourline.[9] In another story from 1940, Olga would appear again, as an older woman, 'still beautiful, with dark eyes, sunken cheeks and a sharp, shy look',[10] but having achieved in exile 'what in France they call Slav mysticism'.[11] The two friends promised to see each other again in Paris. Superstitious and dispassionate, like all those who had experienced the Revolution, Olga nevertheless wrote these lines from Longfellow in Irène's notebook on 5th February 1920:

> Ships that pass in the night, and speak each other in passing;
> Only a signal shown and a distant voice in the darkness;
> [So on the ocean of life we pass and speak one another,][12]
> Only a look and a voice; then darkness again and a silence.

Until the defeat in 1940, Olga remained the closest of Irène's Russian friends. Her other friends, for the most part, are only known by their family name or their first name, depending on whether they are mentioned in her notebook or her letters: Sonia, Mousia, Dichran, Vidoff, Mlle Lütolff, Nirode, Tania, handsome Choura Lissianski and Mila Gordon, a stocky girl of Irène's age, who had survived the Revolution living in the cellar of a factory. Her father, Boris Gordon, who had directed *Les Nouvelles de la mer d'Azov* and went about in a Benz, had, under Nicholas II, a virtual monopoly on the sale of tobacco. Mila was the sort of 'little snob' who, at charity balls, would swoon in the arms of old Prince Gagarin, whom Irène, on the contrary, found 'really ugly and old'. Her elder sister Hélène, too, could do nothing without her English governess, 'as in Chekhov plays'.[13] On her return to Paris, Irène kept in touch with both of them, in their large apartment in the Avenue d'Iéna, which was one of the meeting-places of the more important members of the Russian diaspora, those from the business community, who had suffered least from exile and were speculating on the conclusion of the Soviet experience, and coveted the huge markets – particularly where oil was concerned – which would then open up to investors.

In dancing circles

Not all subjects of the 'ghostly Russia' – one hundred and fifty thousand refugees in 1921 – lived on such a footing. In the French capital, as in Stockholm, there was a flourishing black market in jewellery and silverware, usually sold off cheaply by ruined aristocrats, but which also came directly from 'Bolshevia', had been stolen from museums or were the fruits of the general plundering that took place in Year One of the Revolution. Mme Boutourline's studio was not, therefore, an isolated instance. Michael Tolstoy, the son of the author of *War and Peace*, conducted a vocal group here that sang at society tea parties and in music halls; not to mention the countesses in livery, grand dukes who were hotel porters, officers dressed in the blue of the Citroën workshops, women who threaded pearls like Elsa Triolet; or you might hear the popular cry '*Izvoshchik!*' normally used to hail one of the three thousand Russian taxi drivers in the capital. The epitome of this colourful world is conveyed in the stories of Joseph Kessel, who was able to gather together in tiny Montmartre cabarets an entire cast of Jewish violinists, *djiguite* cavalry officers from the Caucasus, guitarists from the 'Piter' islands, gypsy singers, tutors from the nobility, princes driven half-crazy by exile, all of whom had come down in the world, having sold their very souls to 'Pigal', the hub of this 'tribe without a country and without a city'.[14]

Chaperoned by Miss Matthews, taken to luxury hotels in spa towns, dressed in the latest fashions, Irène Némirovsky, at the age of seventeen, seemed far removed from the 'hysterical, perverted and naïve world, intent on pleasure and materialist to a degree'[15] of the Russians in Montmartre. On 8th November 1920, having a diploma equivalent to the *baccalauréat* in France, she enrolled for a Russian literature course at the university, full of studious intentions: 'And it was Paris at last, escape, work freely accepted, the atmosphere of the Sorbonne, the literature degree and the unquenchable thirst for reading appropriate to adolescence.'[16] It was at the Sorbonne, paradoxically, beneath the hazy frescoes of Puvis de Chavanne, that she made the wondrous discovery of great Russian literature – Turgenev, but above all the poets of the Silver Age. In her notebook, the young student mentions the names of some of these 'eternal sputniks': Merezhkovsky, who had arrived from Finland in early 1920; Balmont, also living in exile in Paris; and a third, Klyuev, the decadent muzhik poet. Further on, in these same narrow pages with their black cover, she raises herself quite naturally to their lofty heights: 'The one fault of geniuses such as Oscar Wilde, Nietzsche, Merezhkovsky, the aristocrats of the Mind, was, not so much to write books that are supposedly amoral, but to publish them. They should have kept them for themselves, jealously, as a miser does a priceless treasure, instead of distributing them "*margarita ante porcos*".'

Of course, Irène was at once too young and too French, but she also belonged to a milieu that was too specific – the financial milieu – to have been able to mingle with the frenetic and sometimes half-starved Russian intelligentsia in Paris: people such as Zaitsev, Bunin, Kuprin, Rémizov, Ossorgin, Chestov, Weidlé, the salons of the Vinavers or Mikhail Tseltin, in fact all those whom Lenin, in 1919, had described as 'excrements of the nation'. For the up-and-coming generation – the Tsvetayevas, Khodaseviches and Berberovas – Mr and Mrs Merezhkovsky were outmoded glories, though not for Irène Némirovsky, for whom their poems might not have been written before the war. 'All I've ever written in Russian is academic writing,' she pointed out in 1940.[17] It was nevertheless in a resolutely modernist, syncopated style that she wrote the following verses, melancholy testimony of her trips to the clubs of Montmartre, in Russian:

> There is merely boredom and weariness
> On your very lovely face
> But each time the wild music rings out
> The opal in your ring glitters nervously
>
> Blue circles beneath your eyes
> Tell of a life of shame and privations
> It is truly scarcely credible
> That you are unable to resist the foxtrot
>
> Your amber cigarette-holder
> Trembles between your pale and gentle lips
> The stylish dance and the blare of the jazz band a-a-a-a
> Lures you and entices you
>
> Purely out of habit
> You come here every evening
> To watch the couples dancing
> And to dream that he may come perhaps
>
> Long ago you and he
> Would join the dancing circle
> Forgetting that in the late-night bar
> They were waiting for the startling voice.[18]

This voice was that of the tziganes, at whose harsh tones all the Russians in Paris, heartbroken in their stupor, would feel their blood heat up as though it were a fire on the steppes. As for Irène, who had only ever heard her mother tinkling on the piano in Kiev and her father humming to the guitar, who had never left the bosom of her governesses, the elemental fury of the gypsy singing shook her like a 'nervous tic'; she didn't understand what it meant, but 'this frenzied and dream-like music was like nothing that she had heard until then'.[19] In its urgency, its uncontrollable outpouring, she recognised the innate poetic gift that is the subject of 'L'Enfant génial', one of her first published pieces of writing. Where then did she hear this 'barbaric music that is unlike anything else in the world'?[20] In a concert for impoverished Russians, as she imagines it in L'Ennemie [The Enemy]? At this period, Irène still attended dances at the Cercle Russe, as did all exiles of her age; or she sold tombola tickets for the benefit of destitute refugees for the Russian New Year or the Cirque de Paris charity dances. But she was also eager to go dancing at the fancy dress balls which her friends gave, where she could now be seen 'with her forehead encircled by a crown of medals, a black velvet camisole braided in gold, a lace blouse covered in imitation jewellery and floral underskirts, a tambourine in one hand, with the other raised gracefully to the sky',[21] in the gypsy manner.

Exquisite pleasures but without any danger

Irène developed a passion for dancing. Since the appearance of black jazz bands, the principal weapon of conquest of the American liberators, people had never dared try out so many steps and undulations. 'Don't think,' she pointed out in 1935, 'that my adolescence consisted of nothing but classrooms and exams . . . I did not disdain the pleasures of youth, I travelled a great deal and . . . danced a lot!'[22] Foxtrots, Argentine tangos, the shimmies brought over from the other side of the Atlantic and played by Negro brass bands: the tumult that streamed through Paris in the aftermath of victory put an entire generation into a frenzy and blocked out the echo of the shells. 'The whole world danced to this frantic farandole that had begun just after the war, and which would end between 1930 and 1931 as abruptly as an epic film does in a cinema with continuous showings.' After all, Katherine Mansfield, whose delicate short stories Irène discovered at that time, danced ragtime like no one else . . .

So she began to visit the places where one had fun, the Château Madrid, the Paris-Plage promenade theatres at Le Touquet where you could let your hair down and disguise yourself as a shrimp fisher, the music halls, the recitals given by 'the incomparable Mistinguett with her 60,000 francs' worth of feathered plumes', the cigarettes smoked behind Miss Matthews's back, the latest Charlie Chaplin, each funnier than the last . . . But, above all, dancing: 'To this innocent little girl who had never known love, the dance was almost love itself. The way bodies touched and intertwined, lightly brushing against each other, the slow, rhythmical swaying, the silence of the dancers and the primordial music, all of this evoked exquisite pleasure but without any danger, idealised, veiled, insidious.'[23] Flirting and flinging herself around was also a form of revenge on Fanny's hatefully privileged life: breaking a few people's hearts in this way gave her the illusion of stealing one of her charms. Very soon, this power would be entirely her own.

This inclination took her to some very dubious places, which she experienced without noticing anything apart from the teeth and the arms of the dancers, the gold of the saxophones gleaming on the black faces, and the women's dazzling dresses. She must have grown accustomed to the fusion of brilliantine, champagne, smoke and perspiration, which was the aroma of those 'Roaring Twenties'. In the nightclubs, in the Russian restaurants and the cabarets she began to frequent – the Perroquet, the Caveau, the Café de Paris, the Poisson d'or (Kessel's haunt), and the Pré Catelan, where half-caste gypsies performed – drunken Americans mingled with Russian women selling rag dolls, cocaine addicts, overdressed pimps, 'bizarre couples whose bodies seemed intertwined' and 'plump women wearing make-up pressing short young men who were rather too well dressed tightly against them with the terrifying tenderness of ogresses'.[24] And then 'naturally, the Krauts. The old American women with gold teeth! The gigolos, all the gigolos.' These were impoverished students, whom she came across at private parties, fed on 'foie gras and caviar sandwiches',[25] and they would get annoyed if Irène, who loved their good humour, pretended to pay them. For with her, they danced for pleasure. 'A time of unrefined joy.'

Music halls

For Russians especially, the sounds of early jazz were like the discovery of a continent; they 'experienced a kind of vague horror, a mad rapture. It was another world . . .'[26] In these early 1920s, Irène Némirovsky's mind was too set on dancing to detect the dance of damnation that was taking place all around her, the depravity of the senses, the scoffing at death that followed the four years of mud during which the old world had stagnated.

At Vichy or Plombières, the gilded youth took the waters and the fresh air; once back in Paris, they stocked up on tobacco and sherry-cobblers, wore themselves out practising 'strides' in the fashionable cellar clubs. Tarts the age of Fanny, whose dresses were fit to throw away after five years in the cupboard, defied their years, the laughter and rheumatic pains, jutting out 'their round little bottoms in the tight fitting skirts' – one of those 'white bottoms' that Sem* would sketch in 1927 in his latest album. In February 1934, jotting down a few memories for a substantial story about the age of cabarets, a painting by Grosz** emerges from Irène Némirovsky's pencil, in which vanity is placed under the cruel spotlight of the years of recession:

> . . . The reign of the older women had begun. They had rejected long skirts, hair worn in buns, corsets, all fetters . . . They muse 'Fifty-five . . . sixty years old . . . So what? Who's to know? When the heart is young, of what importance is a birth certificate? How many stars and actresses are sixty, or even older?' They put lipstick on their wrinkled mouths . . . light a cigarette – when they reach out for the lighter, a shadow can be seen beneath their collarbone, and, just for an instant, in the clear light of day that seeps through the Tomb, the Mask of Death seems to settle on their features, then, slowly, disappears . . .

These few lines will serve to create the edifying portrait of Fanny given in 'Ida', a story that tells of the downfall, actual and figurative, of a chorus-line leader who has been caught up by old age and xenophobia

---

*Georges Goursat (1863–1934). French caricaturist, who signed his work 'Sem'. [Tr.]
**George Grosz (1893–1959). German artist and caricaturist, who fled to the USA in 1932 and became an American citizen in 1938. [Tr.]

– 'a face for playing the part of Phèdre',[27] wreathed in creams, but possessed by a demon whose youthful blood still burns beneath the plastered make-up. In the end, the mask of red death always invites itself to the dances given by Irène Némirovsky for the Faustian characters in her books, who are doomed to deny their age or who simply, like Ida, are obliged to do so because of humiliations in their childhood, hunger in their childhood – because of a Jewish childhood.

The past no longer exists

In February 1921, Irène celebrated her eighteenth birthday. It was a time of exhilarating drives in motor-cars or rented landaus, trips to the countryside or rural *'vikendes'* too numerous to describe: the lake with frogs at Ville d'Avray, the rocks at Fontainebleau, the Normandy beaches of Deauville, Trouville or Honfleur ('a charming little place'), Juan-les-Pins, Saint-Jean-de-Luz and, as ever, the luxury hotels: the Rond-Royal in Compiègne; the sumptuous Hôtel du Palais in Biarritz, which was built for the Empress Eugénie, was rebuilt after the fire in 1903, and was greatly valued by Russian aristocrats for its main courtyard designed to imitate Versailles; the one hundred and twenty-five bedrooms of the Eskualduna, built in neo-Basque style and ringed with shopping arcades, at Hendaye-Plage, just opposite the casino, and wedged between the sea and Chingoudy Bay . . . 'These little trips were delightful. In Paris, it was stifling hot; heat rose in the city as if it were a steam bath; a kind of sirocco wind scorched the chestnut trees. But as soon as you got away from Paris, you could see real trees, leafy, full of shadows and birds, and clear, cool rivers.'[28]

Her friends were now called Lili, Marc, Albert, Mlles Renaud and Jouarre, Suchard, Adrienne, all those French names that were so lovely to pronounce, and which she would so like to have as her own: 'To be called Jeanne Fournier, or Loulou Massard, or Henriette Durand, a name easy to understand, easy to remember . . .'[29] One of her friends had this type of name: René Avot. He was a science student, but he frequently came to the Sorbonne, 'perhaps so as to acquire a more cultural side'.[30] Born, like Irène, in 1903, he was the heir to a stern dynasty of papermakers from the Pas-de-Calais. He was a sensible, disciplined young man, not given to loose living. But he was lively, slim, cheerful, faithful, and above all he danced the one-step to perfection, 'which, in those days, was a priceless asset, on a par with high intelligence and great virtue . . .'.[31] Add to this the fact that the Avots' fiefdom was a few kilometres from Paris-Plage, and that René owned a side-car, and we can appreciate his immediate attraction. In 1933, Irène would capture the 'delicate, sharp face', the 'fox-like profile'[32] of her character René Ponsard, in a portrait that was the spitting image of its model.

The apothegms that appear in her notebook dating from this period reflect her exhilaration and a precocious awareness of the transience of those who were dear to her, whom she had recently lost or left behind in Russia: her sweet Zézelle, her young Aunt Victoria, her grandparents. These mischievous aphorisms, parodies of La Rochefoucauld or manuals of polite behaviour, display a *carpe diem* attitude in the style of the period: 'Know how to judge the precise worth of a great philosophical truth and the original cut of a blouse.' Others, which are somewhat more conventional, are packed with good sense: 'Remember each morning as you get up and every evening as you go to bed that the present moment may be the last, that Death awaits you at every turning of your life. The past no longer exists. What's the point of worrying about problems in the future? Enjoy the present moment and know the value of whims.' Others, again, would be of no use to her: 'Remember that yesterday's friends are tomorrow's enemies.' Finally, a product of the moralising turns of phrase that would continue to fill her future novels, a resolution that was to shape the course of her life: 'If happiness does not exist, there is at least a fairly close imitation of it here below – to create; whether it's creating life or art, it matters little, creating is a supra-human joy, creating is the pastime of the gods . . .'

Nonoche and Louloute

It was for fun, and because she had nothing better to do, that during the course of 1921, at night-time, Irène Némirovsky scribbled down her first attempts at prose. These hilarious sketches introduce us to two shrewd flappers, whom we are to imagine in cloche hats, long pearl necklaces round their necks, using coarse language, driving along at full speed in a Hispano and wincing at the name SDRC: 'Société de la Régénération par la Chasteté'.* While Nonoche – from the name of one of Colette's famous cats? – shares more than one characteristic in common with the author, Louloute, on the other hand, may be based on a certain Loulou de Vignoles, mentioned in the letters she wrote as a girl, and probably the model for the cheerful character of Babette in *L'Ennemie* [The Enemy].

In 'Nonoche au vert', Irène Némirovsky is already depicting the shady world of Biarritz's *nouveaux riches*, a portrait that would turn to vitriol in *David Golder*. In 'Nonoche au ciné', a little tart is addressing her devoted escort in the yapping voice of Arletty: 'I'm a post-war girl, I am, where things zip along and we're in a hurry . . . If you want to love, to express it, to prove it, and to break it up, you haven't got time to hang around . . . And as for theatre, it belongs to your time, my poor old chap, totally . . . It goes along slow-slow-slowly . . . It's like the stopping train, isn't it? . . .' Parisian slang became Irène Némirovsky's sixth language.

In 'Nonoche au Louvre', the daft Louloute stops to admire Leonardo da Vinci's *John the Baptist*, thinking that she recognises the most famous Ukrainian Jewess in Paris, the dancer Ida Rubinstein.[33] A stolidly scholarly variation of this same visit to the Louvre is given, under six headings, in Irène's notebook. Here are the final two: '5. Bronzino's *Portrait of a Sculptor* and finally, and above all the *John the Baptist* (6) by Leonardo da Vinci, a pure treasure, vaguely androgynous, that reminds me of Ida Rubinstein.' So by the age of eighteen, Irène Némirovsky knew how to use irony about things that were dear to her, so as to make them worthy of literature. Those dismal critics who, in 1930, would give a cool reception to the Soifers, Fischl and the other grotesque Jews in *David Golder*, ignored this aspect of her character. But it is true that Irène Némirovsky, with youthful unawareness, was practising her self-mockery on all subjects, and was not concerned with sparing herself. 'Life is a farce; he who makes a fuss about it is crazy' was yet another of the maxims she wrote as a girl.

The Nonoche and Louloute dialogues display an astonishing knowledge of the world: 'You see, sweetheart, there's one thing you don't realise, the Spaniards, the Russians, the Americans, they're just bull-

*Society for Regeneration through Chastity. [Tr.]

shit! They don't really exist. Give me a good "nouveau riche", a well-off, a fat, middle-class bloke, whether he's in sugar or in coal. No showing off, no bluffing, but even better; no cheap hotels, but a nice flat in the 16th, no pearls, but lovely diamonds that are the real thing . . .' It is hardly surprising that these lines are signed 'Topsy' at the end: it was Miss Matthews's nickname for her. That Irène Némirovsky should have immediately adopted this pet name shows yet again her sense of self-mockery, but also the affection in which she came to hold this Englishwoman who had been chosen to be her chaperone.

A humorous magazine

The fourth of these dialogues met with a different fate to the first three, which were not published. 'Nonoche chez l'extra-lucide' appeared without any alterations on 1st August 1921 in the bi-weekly *Fantasio*, a 'humorous magazine' for connoisseurs of 'easy girls', rather like plump M. Prud'homme who featured on each of the covers. It was more the kind of bar-room literature for confirmed 'oglers' like Léon, who, due to his wife's infidelities, had something of a wandering eye. For instance, in the same issue, number 348, in which the 'Topsy' dialogue appears on a full page unobtrusively illustrated by Del Marle, one could admire a suggestive drawing captioned as follows: 'Why dresses? A bathing costume is enough.' Other pages were devoted to a risqué article about 'Love in Venice' or else to 'flirtatious photos in stereo'. The scantily clad models and the advertisements for Minos aphrodisiac cream or transplanted goats' glands were clearly directed at gentlemen of mature age; those recommending the 'oriental pill' ('breasts enlarged, reconstituted and toned up in two months'), however, show that this small-circulation magazine also appealed to wives like Fanny, who were anxious to look like virgins still at the age of forty-five. Furthermore, one could read about the latest can-cans in Biarritz, Deauville or Trouville. *Fantasio*, in short, was 'a very Parisian magazine',[34] Irène Némirovsky observed euphemistically in 1931. Not to say bawdy.

One can imagine the amazement of Félix Juven, alias 'Félix Potin', alias 'La Potinière', the managing director, gossip columnist and leader writer of *Fantasio*, and founder of the well-known weekly *Le Rire*, when he saw the young author of some 'comic dialogues' that he had received in the post arriving at the magazine's premises at 1 rue de Choiseul to collect her payment of fifty or sixty francs. 'I was still a kid,' giggled Irène Némirovsky in 1935, 'I had my hair down my back and a respectable Englishwoman accompanied me everywhere. Can you imagine me arriving at *Fantasio* in that sort of rig-out? First of all I had to invent an excuse to get rid of the Englishwoman, which was not so easy, then, on the staircase, I shoved my hair under my hat!'[35]

With inexplicable propriety, Juven, all of whose colleagues were men, chose to publish the least risqué of these dialogues, under the erroneous signature of 'Popsy'. 'It was childish and jolly . . . Imagine . . . I was only seventeeen.'[36] Eighteen, in actual fact: two years younger than Chekhov when his first comic story appeared. Furthermore, beneath its bawdy appearance, *Fantasio* occasionally concealed a worthwhile literary magazine, one that published the short stories of Louis Delluc, Maurice Dekobra, Henry Bataille, Louis Guilloux, and even Pierre Veber and Jean-Jacques Bernard, the brother-in-law and son respectively of Tristan Bernard.

There was another aspect of this publication that could not displease the Némirovskys: its jeering anti-Bolshevism. Lenin was presented in its pages as 'the greatest butcher of men' the world had ever known. As for the column entitled 'Tête de Turc', it was illustrated by Barrère, the creator of the well-known hirsute Bolshevik with a knife between his teeth. In a tone that was always facetious, *Fantasio* was also anti-modernist, anti-Dada, anti-Freud, anti-Proust, anti-fashion, anti-Negro, anti-'Gna Koués',* anti-*métèques*, and, consequently, anti-Semitic in a risqué, but distinct way, which usually derived from its anti-Bolshevism, for, were not the 'Bolshevists' 'all Jews'?[37] Charles Rappoport, the Russian anarchist who became a French communist, naturally acquired 'the horrible *"grasseyement"*** and hoarse intonations of the ghettos of Galicia'.[38] Among the issues published prior to 1st August 1921 that Irène Némirovsky may have seen, and among the many examples of this tendency which the 'humorous magazine' displayed, penned by the war veteran René Benjamin in November 1920, is this instructive

---

*A deeply offensive racist term used in the colonial period. [Tr.]
**The Parisian way of pronouncing 'r's from the back of the throat. [Tr.]

report gleaned from a street in the Marais: 'Long noses, long beards, large legs, long feet; they stretch out so that they're easier to grab. Are they Boches? Are they Russians? Are they from the land of Sion? How did they get here? What vermin do they do business with? Suddenly, one of them pulls a cap from out of his pocket. Ah! Trotsky! So will it be he who succeeds the great man in Moscow?'[39] This was the prose of a Prix Goncourt winner; Jean Bastia and Félix Juven added puns and coarse jokes in similar vein. In this coconut shy, only a few familiar faces remained unscathed, notably that of the victor of Verdun, Marshal Pétain, who was especially revered by Juven.

Irène Némirovsky, who was still dressing in childish frills, must have been particularly heedless to think of publishing frivolous pieces in such a chauvinistic magazine. But what newspaper, other than *L'Humanité*, and what political party, was not slightly anti-Bolshevik, slightly anti-Semitic, in the France of 1921? From *La Croix* to the *Revue des Deux Mondes*, the rumour was rife that even Lenin's real name was Zederblum. In books with print-runs of over one hundred thousand copies, the Tharaud brothers spread the notion that Moscow was the 'new Jerusalem' of rebellious Jews. At the Sorbonne, students on the extreme right and the 'Camelots du Roi'* regularly got into fights with the revolutionary *'métèques'*. The government elected in 1919 was dominated by a 'Bloc national' that embraced the entire political spectrum, from the nationalist right to the republican socialists, and formed a federation based upon patriotism and anti-communism. It was more-over through this coalition that literary figures as notoriously anti-Semitic as Léon Daudet had entered the Palais-Bourbon. At the Sénat, they discussed whether the bacilli of the plague that had broken out in Aubervilliers were not caused by 'the existence of a real ghetto in the middle of Paris', inhabited by Orientals that could not be inte-grated – as distinct from French Jews of the old stock – brought in 'from all the countries where famine and the pogroms made their lives intolerable: Ukraine, Romania, Poland, Hungary, Soviet Russia, anti-Soviet Russia'.[40] In *Action française*, Charles Maurras announced the invasion of the 'new bohemians' streaming in from Central Europe, who carried 'parthogenic microbes'.[41] And, yet again, the Tharaud brothers, in *L'Ombre de la Croix*, which was republished in 1920 with

*A movement of Royalist supporters, founded in 1908 and disbanded in 1936. [Tr.]

huge success, and then in *Un royaume de Dieu*, published in that same year, revealed to French readers the archaic 'Jewish quarters' of Hungary, Galicia and Ukraine, thereby popularising the stereotype of the Jew in a long robe, ragged, but steeped in religious zeal and recalcitrant where civil laws were concerned.

These ghettos in Paris and elsewhere should be considered for what they were: as ghettos, not clubs. But in *La Vieille France*, the publicist Urbain Gohier had just published the wretched *Protocols of the Elders of Zion*, that specious 'Jewish programme for the conquest of the world' which gave a meaning to the absurdity of the war years. Even Albert Londres, in the columns of *Excelsior*, went along with the anti-Bolshevism, that Great Fear of the 1920s, which was a pretext for every kind of fantasy: 'So who rules?' wrote the well-known reporter. 'The Siberian, the Mongol, the Armenian, the Asian rule, and around the corner of every office corridor, behind the partitions, between two pieces of blotting-paper, under the waste-paper basket, the king: the Jew.'[42] Anti-Semitic propaganda was so normal in the France of 1921 that Félix Juven must have choked himself laughing when he read this inoffensive rejoinder from the 'delighted' Nonoche: 'I've got talent, haven't I? And that pig of a Moses who refuses to give me a part in the February show . . .' Thinking she was creating a Sem, the budding caricaturist was unintentionally creating a Caran-d'Ache.* And her talent, which was a very genuine one, was chiefly that of a mimic.

Black melancholia

Nineteen-twenty-one was also the year in which all hope for exiled Russians of returning home expired. In March, the unexpected mutiny at the naval base at Kronstadt, by sailors who were the spearhead of the Revolution, had been ferociously crushed. In September, Léon decided to move into a more respectable town house at 18 Avenue du Président-Wilson, on the Place d'Iéna. Through the windows, one could see the seven gigantic letters of the word 'CITROËN' on the

---

*Caran-d'Ache (after the Russian word for 'pencil') was the pen-name of the famous anti-Dreyfusard Russian-born illustrator and satirical cartoonist Emmanuel Poiré (1859–1909). [Tr.]

Eiffel Tower. In *The Wine of Solitude*, Irène Némirovsky describes furnishings that are just as bizarre as those at rue de la Pompe, though more ostentatious: 'There was stucco everywhere; the carpet, with its blue and white squares, was meant to look like flagstones; artificial flowers stuck out of marble vases and gave off the slight, acrid smell of dust; some alabaster fruit sat in a shell, electrically lit up from the inside. The marble table was freezing to the touch beneath the lace doilies.'[43] At this table, the Némirovskys dined on lobster and champagne. An entire floor, most probably the ground floor, decorated in mock-Directoire style 'pinkish-red and sea green' and liable to be affected by noises from the street outside, was occupied solely by Irène and her governess. She nevertheless wrote to Madeleine Avot, René's younger sister, who had become her confidante, describing their moving-in with a certain excitement: 'Arriving at two o'clock in the morning to the great consternation of the concierge, we found the house empty, the sheets locked up in a chest that we had to break into with coal tongs, my father being unable to find his keys which were actually in his pockets as we observed the next day. Oh, men!' The following year, her parents looked around the neighbourhood for a flat to have as her own, so that they could enjoy their new home to the full.

In the autumn of 1921, 'Irma Némirovsky' enrolled for an arts degree, so that she could convert her knowledge of Russian literature into a diploma. So as to seal their friendship, Madeleine had invited her to spend the All Saints holiday at Lumbres-lez-Douais, at the family home. Despite the fact that she was living in a clutter and that Léon and Fanny were such an ill-matched couple, nothing had prepared 'Topsy' for the pleasure of the comfortably middle-class, provincial, but nonetheless hospitable atmosphere of the Avots' house, in a village of two thousand inhabitants. What a respite these few days of calm must have been in the course of a 'tumultuous, threatening, exciting life',[44] which had lacked only a stable, loving and warm home . . . It was probably a portrait of this house, with its walls 'hung in pink and grey chintz', that Irène wanted to reproduce in her story 'Nativité', which the inclusion of the Irving Berlin song 'Always' enables us to place in 1925, and in which Madeleine seems to emerge through the sturdy features of Yvonne Armand. 'Her hair was dazzling blonde and cut short, but it was so fine and so abundant that it was impossible

not to imagine it tied back into a large bun, as if it were the will of
nature. Her complexion was pale, rosy cheeks beneath fair skin, with
a rather large nose and clear, grey eyes.'[45] This loyal, kindly counte-
nance was that of a France she did not know and which would lull
her with illusions for a long time – the face of a rural, Catholic, industrious France, the one Maurice Barrès depicted of church towers,
ploughshares and factories, the setting for her last novels. This homely
version of a Potemkin-type village would crumble beneath the first
storm of History.

'You cannot believe the emptiness I felt coming back from the
station,' wrote Irène to her new friend on her return to Paris, on
11th November. 'The house seemed sad and gloomy, and I felt
lonely.' The Avots, who sympathised, invited her again for
Christmas. 'Miss', who would be spending the holidays in England,
would drop her at Boulogne, on the Calais road. Ever since All
Saints, Irène had experienced a sophisticated kind of boredom,
without being able to identify it. 'My life is always the same: walk,
tea, Sorbonne . . . On Wednesday I spent the day in bed and ever
since I've been struggling against a black melancholia. The reason?
I haven't a clue! Whether it's heartache or indigestion from lobster,
I am not quite clear.' Madeleine's invitation thrilled her. After this
first Christian midnight mass, her mood had changed. At the Cercle
Russe New Year Ball, she suddenly felt 'disoriented, almost a
stranger' – which did not in the least prevent her from jigging up
and down until half past two in the arms of seven different partners! The youthful blood that stirred in her veins always prevailed.
But it was at Lumbres, she confessed to her friend as soon as she
returned to Paris, where she had just become acquainted with that
undiscovered country: a family circle. 'I shall remember you all
tenderly for a long time, you can be sure of that.' Madeleine, for
her part, was glad to have been able to escape for a few days from
the starchy atmosphere of Lumbres and the beady eye of her grandfather, an uncompromising captain of industry who would rule over
his factories up to the age of eighty-nine. It was at the casino at
Paris-Plage, or the promenade at Le Touquet that Topsy gave
Madeleine the affectionate nickname of 'Mad': two flappers at the
height of the Roaring Twenties.

Boyfriends

Irène went to the theatre, still escorted by Miss Matthews. At the Œuvre, in 1922, she applauded Ibsen's *Hedda Gabler*, whose stubborn heroine somewhat foreshadows the one in *The Wine of Solitude*. There were trips into the hinterland behind Nice, receptions at the Negresco, and dances, dances, dances . . . 'The days go by so quickly in this blessed country that one doesn't have time to do nothing. I rush about like a crazy creature, I'm ashamed to say. I dance morning and evening. Every day there are very smart galas in different hotels, and since my lucky star has rewarded me with a few gigolos, I have a lot of fun.' But whatever she might say about it to 'Mad', the rapture was begin-ning to fade. Other letters, written with the evident aim of astounding 'little Madeleine', contain more of 'Nonoche's' dialogues: 'I've got my dancing partner, Mademoiselle, and he's a good partner, eh! We'll have to make use of him in Paris next year . . . If you knew how good-looking he is! I'd have a crush on him if he was someone from my circle, cross my heart . . . I don't want to "shockinger" you any longer, darling.' The prudish 'Mad' must have giggled when she read these confessions. That was their aim.

Studying stimulated her appetite for writing. Without realising, Topsy was already distancing herself from the 'still very sensible' Mad, whom she informed as follows: 'I could sing "*Ma seule joie, mon seul bonheur, c'est la Sorbonne*" to the tune of "*Mon homme*". I work hard, I don't get too bored – we're a friendly lot, boys and girls, all Russian. Boyfriends emerge from the shadow of dictionaries if I dare put it like that.' In this chaotic existence where one was constantly on the move, Mila and Choura were the ones who worked hardest. But apart from a few 'wild parties' to which she didn't dare invite René 'for fear of shocking and corrupting him', Irène started to work flat out revising for the exams in June 1922. In July, she obtained her certificate of higher education – that is to say her degree in Russian language and literature – with the equivalent of 'higher' and 'lower' second-class honours respectively. In the language exam, her oral marks of 18 and 16 were remarkable. In the written exam and in literature, she only got 13, but she was first in her class. She worked hard and she partied hard: Madeleine wouldn't believe it!

It was at the Hôtel de la Paix, in Plombières, that Irène continued writing her light-hearted banter until mid-August, in between two glasses of fluoridated water, a shower and a massage, while Léon attended to his business affairs and Fanny to her fittings in some suite on the Riviera. The novelist has described the outdated furnishings of this 'grim little resort in the Vosges, crushed in between two mountains whose greenish colour was reminiscent of a cemetery',[46] with its old-fashioned cinema, its gloomy halls and its casino that was 'a soft, pale yellow like a sorbet that seemed to gleam faintly beneath the rain'.[47] But aged nineteen, there was no lack of remedies for her boredom: 'The casino is filthy, the dancing partners are useless. I've decided not to set foot there again. It would spoil my dancing and I prefer to save my strength so that I can give myself a wild time at St Jean de Luz . . . God, who always provides the cure alongside the disease, has sent a family of factory workers from the Vosges to our hotel. Mother, little sister, and two sons, aged twenty-five and eighteen. Both of them are very nice, have a fine motor-car, take me out in it every day and outdo each other flirting. I've got a soft spot for the younger one. You know I rather like kids who are far too young for my age. And besides, he's so good-looking you want to paint him. A little page-boy's face and just as impudent.' In 1992, Yvonne Comesse, the sister of this 'little factory worker', had not forgotten Irène Némirovsky's 'sweet, short-sighted expression', her 'very musical' voice, her 'graceful face crowned with a black mane of neat and tidy hair, kept in place with a lot of combs and hairnets from which an unruly lock was always escaping', nor, above all, her radiant good humour: 'Lively, cheerful, unaffected and particularly healthy looking, she had in a flash fascinated all those staying at the hotel, and had drawn all the young people into a group for whom she organised games and outings intelligently and imaginatively. Not a moment's boredom with "granny", as she playfully liked to be called . . .'[48]

On her return from the Basque coast, where she had gone to meet Fanny, Irène found herself back in autumnal Paris. 'We were a friendly group that divided its time between the Sorbonne, the dance hall and picnics on the grass,' she had written to Madeleine in June 1922, as if she were not going to set foot in the university again. Buckling down, she enrolled once more, however, on 28th October, this time for a comparative literature course, under the aegis of the venerable Fernand Baldensperger, who would remember her in his survey of modern literature.[49] Another of her teachers who was far from boring was Fortunat Strowski, a respected university teacher, member of the Institut, and a man highly regarded by his students, who was also drama critic of *Paris-Midi* and someone who was extremely well-informed about the literary life of his day. An eminent authority on Montaigne, it is perhaps to his teaching that we owe such an echo of the latter's *Essais* in *L'Ennemie* [The Enemy],[50] the result of patient acclimatisation with classical literature. Irène's new friends that year were called Walter ('eternal suitor'), Édouard, Maurice, Jules. Sitting beside her in the lecture-theatre was Jeanne Reuillon, the future translator of Keats and Spender, and the author of essays on Proust and Colette, who would interview her fellow student in 1934 under the radio pseudonym of Marie-Jeanne Viel.

The exile of the *niania*

At that same time, an unforeseen event cast a shadow over 'Topsy's' carefree life: her grandparents, Iona and Rosa, had just arrived in France. Léon, who had never stopped sending them money, had managed to obtain berths for them on a ship. Victoria, however, who lived in Moscow with her second husband, had personally been obliged to extract from the Soviet Minister for Foreign Affairs authorisation for them to leave the Soviet paradise, pleading: 'So do you require the deaths of these two elderly people?'

Iona and Rosa were only seventy-five and sixty-eight years old respectively, but loneliness had affected them badly. Iona, who suffered from inflammation of the lungs, had had to be taken aboard ship on a stretcher.[51] Fanny was not best pleased to see the bed-ridden old man and the old *babushka*, which her parents had become, returning to her. Consequently, while they could easily have lived at the Avenue du Président-Wilson house, Léon was obliged to move them to Nice. Iona would end his days in a Neuilly boarding-house. And Fanny would remain deaf to Victoria's request to accommodate her son Iakov, so that he could continue his studies. Up until August 1939, Irène never stopped corresponding regularly with her young aunt, caught in the Soviet trap. She cursed Fanny all the more because of this.

Iona and Rosa, who had just endured four years of civil war and hardships, had some curious memories to relate. 'But who, among the Russians who sought refuge in Paris, did not have a story capable of being a novel?' Kessel would say.[52] All the evacuees from the Crimea could describe how, in Yalta, during the winter of 1918, the corpses of White officers, thrown into the sea with balls and chains attached to them, had risen to the surface and blocked the port. As she listened to these tales, Irène began to imagine a timeless story which would convey the dereliction of an old Chekhovian *niania* living in exile in Paris, far from the mansion where she had always been in service. The evocation of the Revolution, 'which you never expect, any more than death', would be an excuse for her putting into words for the first time her obsession with drowning: 'One night, they threw corpses that were still warm into the lake, and, among them, those of the two beloved sons; the dark, melancholic water, like a clouded mirror, reflected only the blackened skeleton of the house, a charred plain and an old abandoned little boat which was rotting among the white water-lilies.' The granddaughter of the owners of the manor would be called Natacha, but she would study at the Sorbonne and would live in a flat 'in the fifth arrondissement, near the Ternes'. As for the *niania*, she would have the same features as grandmother Rosa, 'small and thin, bent over her stick', her 'pale eyes . . . worn out by all the visions mirrored in them, by all the tears they had wept'. And, in fact, Rosa had begun to lose her sight at the time Irène met her in Nice, greying and shrivelled, after eight years' separation. At the end of the story, despair and the deceptive odour of the Seine would lure the *niania* beneath the wheels of a taxi.

Was it this cruel and nostalgic story, the first literary account of Zézelle's suicide, that Irène sent to *Le Matin* in 1923, not omitting to add her address at the end: 'Irène Némirovsky. 18, Avenue du Président-Wilson. Paris'? The time was ripe for edifying eye-witness accounts of the former Russian empire, whether written by acrimonious White officers or by Frenchwomen who had taken part and were desperate for a readership. The press teemed with revelations about the massacre at Ekaterinburg, Rasputin's antics, or the dissolute way of life led by the new masters of Russia. This sensational piece of news appeared in *Le Matin* of 21st October 1923: 'The heads of the Tsar, his wife and his children had been cut off, placed in alcohol and carried to Moscow.'

The 'taste for things Russian' extended, however, to colourful accounts of the Siberian taiga, replete with muzhiks, *barines* and isbas. In *Le Matin*, where Colette edited the book column, Liberty, Arthur Toupine and Nina Mdivani were the specialists in this fashionable genre.[53] So Irène Némirovsky's naive adumbration, though clear and restrained, was returned to her at the address indicated, carefully folded in four. A cursory look at the daily column 'Mille et un matins', which at the time published short pieces by women writers such as Colette, Whip or Marguerite Moreno provides the explanation: 'The Niania' was too long. But Irène Némirovsky was proudly attached to her 'Niania', the first ambitious tale she had managed to finish, and one which shows her feelings for the Russian classics. Cut by two-thirds, it was eventually published in *Le Matin* on 9th May 1924, and under her own name too.[54] It meant so much to her that she revised it from top to bottom a few years later and submitted it to the Kra publishing house in the perfected form of *Snow in Autumn* [*Les Mouches d'automne*], one of her simplest and most deeply moving stories.

A sabbath of one hundred thousand devils

When she was twenty, Léon moved his daughter into a furnished apartment in the Rue Boissière, five minutes away on foot. A short distance from the bustling avenues, it was a fairly calm, almost provincial, street where, at number 24, stood a block of rented flats. Irène would occupy an 'elderly bachelor's apartment', on the first floor. Elated by this new-found freedom, she started to lead a riotous existence. On several occasions, she asked 'Mad' to come and live with her, but to no avail. 'Topsy', however, had an irrefutable pretext: 'No exams for me this year. In the end I've done damn all and I don't want to leave myself open to certain failure. So I continue, bravely, doing nothing.' She rose at midday, went to her lectures, came back at four o'clock with René, on foot, to have tea, then every evening, until the small hours, she entertained her Russian friends and had a wild time. When she wasn't travelling to Morocco with her 'little gang' of show-offs, portrayed wearing cravats and immaculate trousers in a photograph from this period, there were twenty-five full-throated voices singing Slav tunes at her home until dawn . . . 'At night, in a

Russian house, nobody thinks of going to sleep,' she would write . . .
'Russian hospitality knows no bounds.'[55]

It so happened that on the mezzanine floor, in a flat entirely painted
in white, which nevertheless had to be lit during the day, there had
lived since 1911 a man of sixty years old, who was courteous and
discreet, but who was full of curiosity about twenty-year-old virgins,
with which he filled his licentious novels according to eighteenth-
century tastes. Irène encountered him occasionally as she raced
downstairs, without recognising him. He was, said the writer Paul
Léautaud, 'a tall, thin, slightly gangling man, . . . high cheekbones, a
thin-lipped mouth topped with a long, drooping moustache, a receding
hairline and a very pronounced chin', with his left eye concealed behind
a monocle that he was forever fixing in place before any discussion.
'To look at, nothing like a man of letters.'[56] Léon Daudet, who did
not care for this Parnassian's poetry, declared that an absent-minded
murderer must have left this 'corpse with a chin like a wooden clog . . .
dressed as a member of the Académie française' behind in the rain.[57]
Who could he be to merit such polite remarks? Irène, who had no
idea, continued to sow her wild oats. How great would be her embarrassment, on opening Le Figaro on 21st June 1934, to come across this
article greeting the publication of Le Pion sur l'échiquier:

> A few years ago, the flat above the one in which I live, having fallen vacant,
> was rented by a 'Russian family'. A change of tenants in a house is always
> something of an event, especially when these tenants are 'upstairs' tenants
> and their wooden floor is in direct contact with your ceiling. Their lives
> inevitably become involved with yours. Without knowing each other, you
> become somewhat answerable to one another, and I soon realised that I
> would have to reckon with these newcomers and that they would not
> exactly be restful. They had scarcely moved in, in fact, than they made
> their presence felt by disturbing comings and goings, the loud slamming
> of doors, noisy conversations, clamorous shuffling, remorseless rushing
> around and stampeding, not just during the day, but late into the night.
> What exercises could this formidable 'Russian family' be conducting?
>
> I had no idea, but I began to detest these people heartily and to curse
> them for all my disturbed sleep. However rowdy they were though, they
> remained more or less invisible. The only member I met was a delightful
> girl who was reserved and shy in appearance. Was it she who was respon-

sible for the almost daily commotion of which I was the victim and which fortunately did not last for very long, for the Russian family left the house after a few months. I forgot my torment and the girl on the stairs and when, later on, I made the acquaintance of Mme Irène Némirovsky, the admired author of *David Golder* confessed that she had been my neighbour and acknowledged her youthful misdeeds. It goes without saying that I have forgiven her for them.

The affable gentleman in Rue Boissière was Henri de Régnier – a major figure in French literature and the son-in-law of José-Maria de Hérédia, as famous for his poetry as he was for his illustrious wife's love affairs[58] – and it was this august academician whose nights had been destroyed for many months by 'Topsy', as she carried on 'a sabbath of one hundred thousand devils' above his head. Overcome with remorse and gratitude, she would deliver a blushing note that very day: 'Dear Maître, . . . I have such admiration for you. Each compliment you pay me fills me with a very deep and very gentle pride . . . and also with embarrassment when I think of the hateful young girl who disturbed your sleep in Rue Boissière, ten or twelve years ago . . .'[59] Henri de Régnier, in return, would applaud each of Irène Némirovsky's new novels.

In 1923, she was unable to take advantage of their being neighbours. She was still behaving like a spoilt child. The best portrait of her at this period is the rough draft she would write ten years later of Hélène Karol, her double in *The Wine of Solitude*:

She appeared to have stopped growing, and at the age of twenty she still had the slight, slender body of a child . . . A mobile and expressive face, but with a rounded, oval, child-like shape, a pretty, delicate nose, an ugly mouth, dazzling teeth, and soft, piercing eyes . . . I should like to give the impression of a silent creature, where everything happens within herself, who only deigns to provide others with occasional bursts of gaiety, who is fairly ironical, who likes to dress simply, in a white dress, her arms always bare, only happy when, having left the hotel early in the morning, after a night of dancing, she goes for a run in the cool, moist morning air, her bare legs in espadrilles, wearing a blue skirt, with a basque beret on her head, biting into an apple. Otherwise, she was like everyone else, she danced, she allowed herself to be caressed on the terrace outside, she

was one of those girls who wear make-up, who hang around the entrances
to the ladies' rooms, still too young to be allowed into the casinos, who
wear jewellery that is too glamorous, who smoke, show off their legs,
their breasts, their backs; she was one of those half-naked girls, tanned
by the sun during the day, exhausted by dancing and caresses at night,
expending their time and their bodies in a sort of mad and pointless
fervour. She would have felt somewhat self-conscious if she had not
imitated them.

A horrible joy

This self-portrait written from a distance, one very similar to that of
Joyce, the brazen daughter of David Golder, is very close to the truth.
Early in 1924, however, this fooling around nearly ended in tragedy.
In July 1923, Irène had spent several days at Deauville, Plombières and
Hendaye, then at the Hôtel du Palais in Biarritz, before winding up
in Vittel for the rest of the summer, leaving her parents in Vichy. Still
just as 'crazy', she slept one night out of two and introduced Madeleine
to her latest crush, someone called Henry La Rochelle: 'If you knew
the mischief we've got up to!' By this she meant the lengthy cavorting
in the hay, in a barn where her little group of friends had tea brought
to them by a startled maid. 'Miss says that I've become a real oaf!'

But at the beginning of 1924, Irène was no longer joking when she
reported to Madeleine that her 'twenty-year-old boyfriend' had come
to see her at Rue Boissière, 'pale and his eyes bulging, looking vicious
and with a revolver in his pocket', adding: 'With this little hothead I
was almost just as likely to be bumped off myself as to see him put
a hole through his head. Well, fortunately, some friends came round
and he left.' What had happened is unclear. Perhaps this young man
in love had taken offence at being used as a summer gigolo by Miss
Topsy, who at this time was only thinking of her Sorbonne and her
Spanish lessons. A similar episode serves as a touchstone in *L'Ennemie*
[The Enemy]: Comte Génia Nikitof, a male escort on the Place Pigalle,
cannot tolerate being rejected by little Gabri, whom he thought he
had won over; he becomes threatening: 'You do not know me . . . I'll
hurt you . . .' This about-turn is followed by 'an unbearably long and
violent struggle': the rape of Gabri by that 'evil monster', Génia. 'It was

horrible, unspeakable, painful, like a nightmare . . . Disgust that was similar to nausea.'[60]

In *L'Ennemie*, Irène Némirovsky, at the age of twenty-five, had, with exceptional bitterness, heaped all the resentment she had accumulated since childhood on a mother who was conceited, vain, pleasure-seeking and spiteful. Since she was unable to express her hatred directly, her anger was turned against herself. How far? The rough drafts of *The Wine of Solitude*, in which the most introspective of Irène Némirovsky's novels is sketched out in the first person, leaves us in little doubt on the matter:

'On the night following the rape, I should take careful note of Hélène's suffering and horror. The extraordinary thing is that I feel more intensely and more truthfully the suffering of David, dear old man, or Courilof than what I've been through. All I remember is a physical discomfort, the pain in the body, the fever, but the interesting thing is not this, what we have to try and show <u>is the categorical imperative</u>. That is to say, she feels she is to blame, that she is wrong to act in this way. There must – oh, how difficult it is – be <u>a struggle full of anger within her</u> between what she feels is right, <u>which is as if it were dictated by an invisible presence</u>, and her <u>questioning</u>: 'But why? Who is bad? Who is good? I've never been taught . . . Since I enjoy humiliating them, . . . why not do so?'

For what else did she do, since her arrival back in Paris, other than accentuate Fanny's physical decline by her frenzied succession of boyfriends, than to take her revenge on this fickle and contemptuous woman by using her own weapons? 'Oh, perhaps show that horrible joy that comes over her, she, who has grown calm and wise, and indifferent to everything, when she observes the astonishing decline of the mother,' Irène Némirovsky suggested to herself in 1933. 'Now that is really autobiography. But as the madman said, this morning: "I've suffered enough from it to make use of it."'

The path of duty

If the degrading experience of rape disgusted her, it was less repugnant to her than was Fanny's indirect responsibility. For the girl felt humiliated to think that she was falling into the same bad habits as her mother. Now, when she gazed in delight at Fanny's 'haggard, withered face', whom she had tried so desperately to make jealous, she could almost hear her crying out: 'Parricide, parricide.'[61] That was what she could not forgive her: to have passed on to her the gene of inconstancy. Which is why, in *L'Ennemie*, we have the name 'Génia', the 'brute' who personifies the hereditary curse. 'I've spent my whole life fighting against my hideous bloodline, but it is within me. It flows through me . . . and if I do not learn how to defeat it, this bitter, cursed blood will win out . . .'[62] By going from one pair of arms to another in this way, to have boasted about it so much by calling upon the innocent Madeleine as a witness, ready to 'shockinger', Irène had the sudden sense of having betrayed her father. At the end of *L'Ennemie*, we can understand why Gabri, in a paroxysm of shame, should throw herself out of the window. And it is virtually certain that the same temptation crossed Irène Némirovsky's mind, at the age of twenty: 'I've often longed to be dead too . . .'[63] All the more so, having learned of the suicide of the former governor of Petrograd, Alexander Nikolayevich Obolensky, who was an acquaintance of Léon's. She could not be unmoved by this shocking death: Alexander Alexandrovich, the governor's son, had just become engaged to her friend Olga . . .

Only an outburst of pride could save her. By a miracle of heredity, this was something she did not lack. Above all, to distance herself from such depravity, she had her writing. It was not a novel to begin with, but a few pithy sayings that were rather more disillusioned than the previous ones: 'It is said that a woman cannot be raped unless she wants to be; I would add that in my view it is never the man who rapes the woman, but the woman who rapes the man.' Fortified by this feminist moralising that put her in control of her destiny, Irène set out, seriously this time, on her way to the Sorbonne. On 2nd January 1924, three weeks before going to visit her grandparents in Nice, she told Madeleine that she was returning 'with difficulty to the path of duty'. On 10th July, she scraped through her certificate of higher education and comparative literature. Questioned in her oral exam on the origins of Russian romanticism and on Pushkin, she only obtained pass marks of 11 and 13 out of 20.

Two events helped her to bid farewell to these four years of partying:

in the first place, Madeleine's engagement, which she greeted in April with a touch of coldness ('I am very glad, my darling, that you are happy; I send you sincere good wishes for your bliss'); then, on 25th August, the wedding of Olga and Alexander Obolensky, a union that meant her friend was now a Russian princess. Irène did not attend Madeleine's wedding; she wrote to her again, probably in 1925, somewhat distantly: 'It's some time since I've had any news from you. How are you? At home, the season of parties is definitely over. I no longer go dancing. I content myself by entertaining in the strictest privacy.' This latter expression meant that after four years of excess, studiousness and fidelity had become her cardinal virtues; but also that she in turn had met a boy who would not merely be her 'twenty-year-old boyfriend' . . .

5

The Demon of Pride
(1925–1929)

What the worm was to the corpse, his sins would be to the painted image on the canvas. They would mar its beauty, and eat away its grace. They would defile it, and make it shameful. And yet the thing would still live on. It would be always alive.

Oscar Wilde, The Picture of Dorian Gray

'I don't know whether you remember Michel Epstein, a small, brown-haired man with very dark skin, who came back with Choura and us in a taxi on that memorable night or rather memorable New Year's Day morning?' wrote Irène Némirovsky to her friend Madeleine, early in 1925. 'He is courting me and, well, I find him attractive. So, since the crush is very intense at the moment, you mustn't ask me to come away, do you understand?'

Michel Epstein was twenty-eight and was indeed not very tall. His was one of the most ancient Judaeo-Russian names. Without him, would Irène have made up her mind to rectify her existence as a curious sort of immigrant? She remained childlike, and was slightly built and small, at most five feet tall. She lived life in a perilously nonchalant way and, trapped in the maternal snare, she struggled against the grip of a 'bitter and cursed bloodline'. She resembled Marion, the crazy virgin whom Paul Morand had just portrayed in his novel *L'Innocente à Paris*, who found it so hard to be free of her mama and papa. Michel allowed her to look ahead to the future and to escape from the distant but tyrannical control of Fanny, who was not best pleased to discover from some joker that her daughter was about to become engaged, something Irène had carefully avoided mentioning to her. A married daughter would mean that she might soon become a grandmother. Léon, during this time, was away on a business trip in Poland. The news must have affected him less: he could not be unaware that Michel Epstein was the son of an important Russian banker, one who was better known than he was.

Exiles

Michel Epstein was born in Moscow on 30th October 1896 and, since the winter of 1920, he had lived in Paris with his parents and his brother and sister in a very large flat on the Avenue Victor-Emmanuel III (the present-day Avenue Franklin-Roosevelt). Aged twenty, he had begun his studies at the physics and mathematics faculty in St Petersburg. After moving to Kiev in 1918, he had attended the School for Higher Education, and had subsequently just entered the Ministry of Finance as an assistant at the moment that the civil war broke out, leaving the capital in ruins. From 17th to 20th October 1919, a pogrom that was more appalling than that of 1905, coming after those conducted by Petlyura, decimated the heart of the capital, the work this time of those remnants of the former Tsarist army recruited by Denikin. Their reckless brutality, and the systematic pounding of Kiev by the rival armies, forced Michel and his family into exile: his elder brother Samuel, born in 1887, reached France with his wife Alexandra Ginzburg and their daughter Natacha after an unbelievable escape; his sister Sofia, known as Mavlik, born in 1895, and her son Victor; and, finally, Paul, his younger brother, born in 1900, a personal friend of the Grand-Duke Dimitri, who would be employed at the Banque Lazard in Paris.

'Micha' had the pointed chin, the mocking laugh and the piercing smile of his father, Efim Moisevitch Epstein, a part-time lecturer at the School of Advanced Business Studies at Moscow and St Petersburg, and non-executive director of the powerful Commercial Bank of Azov-Don, with its sixty-two branches, which had enabled him to survive after the Bolshevik putsch. Efim Epstein was a personal friend of Count Kokovtzov, Minister of Finance from 1904 to 1914. In August 1917, the total assets of the bank amounted to 1,289 billion roubles, making it one of the five largest banks in Russia. In October, its president, Boris A. Kamenka, financial adviser to both the Lvov and Kerensky governments, happened to be in Finland and had been unable to return to St Petersburg, where the headquarters of the bank were situated in a

grandiose Art Nouveau building, built of granite and anthracite, at
3–5 Morskáya Street. Appointed by the French government as a
'specialist in Russian economic problems', Kamenka had moved to
Paris, where he lived in grand style in Avenue du Parc-Monceau, dele-
gating full power in Russia to his colleagues Auguste Kamenka and
Efim Epstein. The latter was made vice-president of the Central
Committee of the Petrograd banks, whose six members were responsible for negotiating with the Bolshevik authorities for the maintenance
of the directors in their former posts, in co-existence with the newly
created People's Bank. A last-ditch meeting in mid-April 1918 ended
in complete failure: from that moment on, directors of private banks
began to stream out of St Petersburg. Efim Epstein continued to keep
the bank running, but at the cost of several arrests. Though he had
been posted to Kiev, Rostov and then Odessa, he was nevertheless
unable to prevent the Bolsheviks from claiming reserves of 12.5 tons
of gold from the Stockhom Enskilda Bank which the Bank of Azov-
Don had deposited there shortly before October 1917 as security for
a loan of 30 million Swedish kroner.

In March 1920, his task having been made impossible with the defeat
of the White forces, Efim Epstein left for France with Michel, Paul
and Sofia. On the 20th of that month, the first meeting of the board
of directors of the Bank of Azov-Don in exile was held in the Square
du Trocadéro in Paris. Until 1925, relying on the Banque des Pays du
Nord to transfer its funds, the Bank of Azov-Don would continually
come to the financial aid of its former members of staff, employees
or customers living in exile, often at a loss to itself, while continuing
to place its trust in the collapse of the USSR. In this hope, within the
Committee of Russian Banks presided over by Count Kokovtzov, Efim
Epstein put the finishing touches to his plan for denationalising the
Russian banks and restoring stocks and shares. But in 1924, the Soviet
Union was recognised by France, which granted Russian exiles the
status of refugees. As for the death of Lenin – announced regularly
ever since 1921[1] – it had not weakened the Bolshevik edifice in the
least; indeed quite the reverse. The Epsteins would never return to
Russia.

In a short work published in August 1925, with a preface written
by the former minister Yves Guyot – ex-managing director of *Le Siècle*
and a Dreyfus supporter from the start – that called for the creation

of an equivalent to the Federal Reserve Board for Russia, Efim Epstein believed that a turn-around was still possible. His little booklet, full of cold anger, is mainly a first-hand account of the 'confiscation' of the Russian banks – he refused to use the word 'nationalisation'. Epstein commented ironically on the incompetence of the Soviets who, upon opening the banks' safe deposits, usually found nothing except devalued portfolios and securities, instead of the piles of gold they hoped for. In passing, he revealed his financial philosophy: that of a free-trader convinced that the failings of capitalism would not have lasted as those of the 'Bolshevist tyranny' would do on 'the infinitely long road that leads to the supreme objective', that is to say social progress, political freedom and universal well-being. 'That is why the elements that strive to prevent the natural evolution of capitalism by force, on the pretext of the so-called need to eradicate this incentive, but who are actually moved precisely by a spirit of spiteful resentment that in their case takes on monstrous forms – these elements lead mankind inevitably towards the most terrifying social and economic disaster the world has ever known. May what has happened to Russia serve as a warning to the civilised world!'[2]

In spite of these prophecies, Efim Epstein was a cheerful little fellow with a handlebar moustache. He had married a chubby woman who was the complete opposite of Fanny Némirovsky: gentle, motherly and friendly. In St Petersburg, where the Epsteins lived on the Moïka embankment, Efim, it appears, had held consistorial duties, but his son Michel had not inherited his religious beliefs. Raïssa Timofeievna, a close relative, had married a Jew who had converted to Protestantism, Alfred Adler, 'the only psychoanalyst whom I have known,' Irène Némirovsky would write in 1938. A feminist, a socialist and an atheist, who was great friends with Trotsky's first wife, 'Aunt Raïssa' must have gone into self-imposed exile in Zurich so that she could study biology and zoology, her Russian university having refused her this indulgence. She had later moved to Vienna with Adler, the eminent disciple of Freud.

As for Samuel Epstein, the eldest of the siblings, he had formed a partnership with Alexander, the elder son of Kamenka, the former director of the Petersburg School of Drama, as soon as he arrived in Paris. Together, they financed the films made by Studios Pathé Albatros de Montreuil, so named because the founder, Ermoliev, had fled Yalta aboard the *Albatros*, with his entire company and all his equipment. In the company's early years, Films de l'Albatros continued to specialise in Slav orientalism, producing some great film-makers in exile. They even obtained genuine success thanks to the expressive gifts of Ivan Mosjoukine, the most famous Russian silent cinema actor. From 1925 onwards, Albatros, which had retained its original motto 'Standing tall despite the storm', was able to produce Feyder and Marcel L'Herbier, while awaiting René Clair and Jean Renoir in the late 1920s. In this way Samuel played his part in one of the most exciting ventures of French cinema before the tidal wave of talking films.[3] And the Epstein family gradually established itself in the economic life of Paris.

A dreamer from the ghetto

In 1923,[4] before she met Michel, Irène had written a new story, in the Russian vein of 'La Niania', resorting this time purely to her imagination. And yet it is difficult not to compare Irma Némirovsky with the young poet of her story, Ismaël Baruch, whose name is the Yiddish equivalent of Boris, her maternal grandfather's name. Born 'one March day' in the Jewish district of 'a large seafaring and trading city in the south of Russia', he wears curled *paéys* on either side of his forehead, whereas Irina kept her long ringlets until she was twenty. Ismaël's father, a scrap merchant from the ghetto, will eventually cut off his curls and wear 'a short, American-style moustache' in order to launch into speculation, as Leonid had done. The 'brilliant child' has begun to write poetry without even thinking. He wastes his talents in 'disreputable' nightclubs and becomes infatuated with 'sly caresses'. Like Irène, he is gripped by the underlying vitality of tzigane singing. Suddenly aware of his gift, he believes he can encourage it by studying the masters, in his case Pushkin and Lermontov, in hers the poets of the Silver Age. He, too, leads 'a life of comfort and ease', which has not protected him against misfortune. For neither is he unaware that he is Jewish, however hard to endure might be the 'kind of vague anxiety' about falling back into the ghetto, however pointless the 'unknown pride' of escaping his lineage.

The most questionable descriptions in 'L'Enfant génial' – those of Jews 'dressed in their grease-stained greatcoats, chatty, obsequious, hopping about like old wading birds that had lost their feathers, and who understood everything, knew everything, sold everything and bought even more' – owe a little to Irotchka's intimidating memories of the 'Jewish quarters' of Podol and the Moldavanka, but much more to Gogol and to the popular stereotypes of Jean and Jérôme Tharaud, whom she would confess to placing among the 'first rank' of French authors.[5] She had probably read, in 1920, the description of Russian Jewry that the two brother-reporters had brought back from the Ukraine; they had written both about the governor Trepov's fits of anti-Jewish rage, and about the Jews of the *shtetl*, 'an entire people who are poor, starving, contorted, crooked, bent double beneath the weight of their destiny, who go around everywhere in their old rags, their filthy black smocks, who stride about from the market to the synagogue and from the synagogue to the market, in pursuit of a meagre profit'.[6] Similarly, she remembered encountering, in *The Picture of Dorian Gray*, that nightmarish Whitechapel shop manager, a 'horrid old Jew' whose hair fell in 'greasy ringlets'.[7] 'Reread "Dorian Gray",' she noted in about 1933 . . . 'Don't forget the dreadful reality of ugliness. In this book that I have so much enjoyed there is just one chapter that affects me deeply – the one about the London docks . . .' Why would this passage affect her so much, unless it was because it recalled the fascinating ugliness of the ghettos glimpsed fleetingly in her childhood? It would not be incorrect to speak of horror or, to quote Freud (1919), of 'uncanny strangeness' (*Unheimlich**), that is to say 'nothing new or alien, but something which is unfamiliar and old-established in the mind and which has become alienated from it only through the process of repression'. A sudden repression, imposed by Fanny, and one that explains the fantasy-like character of such scenes when they reappear in the work of Irène Némirovsky, like so many hidden mirrors reminding the 'assimilated' young woman of her consanguinity with the ghetto.

This kind of imagery, used in 'L'Enfant génial', never expresses an opinion, as it does in the work of the novelist Binet-Valmer. The issue of *Œuvres libres*, in which this 'great unpublished short story' finally appeared in April 1927, also contained the last 'complete unpublished novel' by the author of *Métèques*. Here we meet a character who is a

---

*Freud's *Das Unheimlich* was translated into English by James Strachey as *The Uncanny*. [Tr.]

Jewish banker, Baron Kaufman, whose pretty daughter would express her disapproval of anti-Semitism were this not politically inadvisable. For, as one of Binet's French characters observes, 'we are the opponents of what exists. Jewish power exists, we are its opponents.'[8] This attitude, which was one shared by Action française* and Jeunesses patriotes** finds absolutely no echo in the work of Irène Némirovsky. On the contrary, in 'L'Enfant génial', which is written in the guise of a parable, a genuine knowledge can be seen of Jewish rituals and traditions, as well as of the social reality of the ghetto. The girls there are dishonoured by the goy officers 'without fear or remorse', and as for the father's obsequiousness, she is responding to the Russians' feeling of superiority, those drunkards 'with their long, filthy beards and their gentle eyes in simple faces'.

Whether rich or poor, persecuted or nouveaux riches, Jews in Irène Némirovsky's work will always be 'dreamers of the ghetto'. As André Spire said of Israel Zangwill in 1913, 'his Jews are not from the Parc Monceau clique'.[9] And her caricatures of them, occasionally snipped out of newspapers, are merely 'ghetto comedies', without any hidden meaning.[10] Furthermore, she was not satisfied with the 'little symbolic tale' that was 'L'Enfant génial', perhaps because the symbol, that of her metamorphosis, was too obtrusive. 'Don't mention it to me,' she grumbled in 1930. 'I've just taken a look at it and I closed the book very quickly: I found it so bad!'[11] Benjamin Crémieux, one of the few critics who took the trouble to read this youthful work, excused her because of its precocity: ' "L'Enfant genial" was an adolescent work, bubbling with romanticism.'[12] For what is it really about? Taken from his parents by the widow of a former military governor, snatched away from his own people, removed from the ghetto where he was proud to strut around, Ismaël, without realising it, has become a court poet. All inspiration has deserted him. He can no longer summon up 'the unconscious echo of the sad Jewish songs, welling up from the centuries like an immense sob, burgeoning from age to age, in his child's soul'. If 'L'Enfant génial' is a fable, its moral is crystal clear: it

*Far-right movement founded at the time of the Dreyfus affair and considerably influenced by the political ideas of Charles Maurras (q.v.). [Tr.]
**Right-wing nationalist group whose members were mainly recruited among students. Founded in 1924 by Pierre Taittinger and much influenced by Italian fascism. [Tr.]

is that of perverted grace. It is his genes that make Ismaël 'an ingen-
ious little child'. There is no true art unless it is ingrained in the blood,
however strong and bitter it may be.[13] It was the tzigane lesson. Because
he had realised earlier on that no mineral could equal the gold-bearing
purity of the long Jewish memory, Ismaël would eventually tie the
noose around his neck. And that is also why, at that moment, Irène
Némirovsky turned away from literary exercises to take up a form at
which she would excel: the novel.

A luxurious feeling

We find yet more aphorisms, pastiches and autobiographical echoes
in Le Malentendu [The Misunderstood], Irène Némirovsky's first novel.
This phrase, for example, which serves as her motto: 'Love born of
fear and solitude is sad and strong like death.'[14] Conceived 'in this
month of August of the year of grace 1924'[15] on the beach at Hendaye,
this study of manners confronts us with a society woman and a penniless worker, who have fallen in love over the Basque summer, which
has revealed them to each other as 'agile and naked' like Adam and
Eve. Back in Paris, their affair does not survive post-war circumstances.
Yves Harteloup, the archetype of the office clerk, held back in his
career by the lethargy of comfortable mediocrity, develops a hatred
for Denise Jessaint's opulent lifestyle, for le gai Paris, expensive nightclubs, 'all that idiotic childishness, that forced gaiety, everything,
including Denise'[16] which his empty pockets lead him to regard with
a sullen, moralistic eye. 'An effort . . . failure . . . the end of everything . . . it was very simple.'[17] Denise, for her part, is slow to realise
that the 1920s-type of clerk, worn out by the turmoil of the trenches,
is in fact the 'new poor':[18] Yves is already broke when the sudden pity
shown by his mistress adds to his humiliation. These radically opposed
lovers repel one another precisely because of their powers of attraction. Bogged down in his depression, Yves is soon no more than a
pawn among Denise's Pascalian playthings. Social determinism will
make a tart of her, and he will be a failure, obliged to escape from
his bondage to Finland, like an emigrant.

The moral of the fable is pessimistic: pure love grows lacklustre in
modern life, it is suffocated by social convention, which is very much

the theme of *A Woman of Paris*, made by Charles Chaplin, one of her favourite film directors. 'Ah, love is a luxurious feeling, my darling . . .'[19] Irène Némirovsky was well aware that this 'wretched world-weariness' was an after-effect of the First World War, that spared the ladies of leisure of the Belle Époque only to throw them into the arms of the young war veterans, embittered by the slaughter of Verdun. This is why *Le Malentendu* gives a new lease of life to the middle-brow novel: 'The kind of heroes Bourget describes are finished; they collected women and ties and did nothing. Did nothing! They would die of hunger, Bourget's heroes!!'[20] This young foreigner's gift for sharply depicting French society was what most surprised the book's first well-informed critic, Frédéric Lefèvre: 'I admire the fact that at the age of twenty you should have reflected sufficiently about life to be able to form a lucid and all-encompassing view of these complex problems.'[21] This capacity was one she shared with a Ukrainian-Jewish novice writer, Emmanuel Bobovnikov, known as Bove, whose stories, written at the same time as hers, portray the inappropriateness of modern life to the lofty sentiments that were still de rigueur in the French novel.[22] Like him, Irène Némirovsky would be interested in the corruption of values in a hostile environment, whether it concerned the employees in *Le Pion sur l'échiquier* [The Pawn on the Chessboard] or patriotism in *Suite Française*. The subject of moral decline, which is present in each of her books, takes shape in the metaphor of the tell-tale mirror, that finds its first variation here, in a direct line from *The Picture of Dorian Gray*: 'That morning, his soul was so like the soul of the radiant mornings of his childhood that the reflection of his image in the mirror caused him to feel surprising pain.'[23]

Beneath the impression it gives of being a social novel, *Le Malentendu* conceals much that is borrowed from Irène Némirovsky's life. Yves's uncle, 'a vastly rich industrialist from the Nord' whose factory was bombed in 1915, is inspired by the patriarchal figure of Prudent Avot, the founder of the paper and cardboard manufacturing firm that bears his name. The use of Denise's maiden name, Franchevielle, and her daughter's first name, Francette, are further evidence of this consciousness of being foreign. More authentic are the wondrous landscapes of the Basque coast, with its 'scent of cinnamon and orange blossom borne on the wind from Andalusia'.[24] Henceforth, Irène Némirovsky would spend almost every summer there, until 1939. Crossing the Bidassoa, the Fontarabie procession, the paths that flanked the mountains, the 'wonderful Spanish wine', 'Pierre Loti's little house with its dense garden and its faded green shutters':[25] so many picturesque details depicted from life.

The cosmopolitan funfair

Was Michel Epstein a 'good catch'? There is nothing to indicate that he would become a high-flying banker. During the mid-1930s Irène Némirovsky's income as a writer would be twice that of her husband at the Banque des Pays du Nord. Boris Kamenka, who had sat on the bank's board of directors since April 1914 as Horace Finaly's replacement, had helped 'Micha' join the bank following his formal application, dated 26th March 1925, which ended with these words: 'I have good French and Russian and fairly good English and German.' These linguistic attributes would eventually secure Michel Epstein a respectable position in management, where he was entrusted mainly with 'French and foreign relations and the documentary credit department', and given 'first-grade responsibility'.[26] Once one takes into account that in October 1926, under the management of its president Charles Laurent, the Banque des Pays du Nord decided to house the Franco-German Committee for Information and Documentation, which was founded by the industrialist Émile Mayrisch in order to bring the two peoples together and prevent another war, one can understand why Michel Epstein should have encountered no problems or resistance in serving as an interpreter, during the Occupation, to the German officers billeted in Issy-l'Évêque, the village in Burgundy where his family had found shelter.

In 1912, one year after its foundation by the Swedish banker and politician Knut Wallenberg, with the aim of channelling French capital into the industrial sites of Northern Europe and Scandinavia, the Banque des Pays du Nord – or Norebank-Paris – had set up its headquarters on the corner of Avenue de l'Opéra and Rue Gaillon. In 1920, it was taken over by the Schneider group, as part of the Union européenne industrielle et financière. Shortly after his arrival, Michel Epstein found himself working under the leadership of Gabriel Brizon,

the vice-president of the board of directors, and his four fellow directors, Ferdinand Prior, Henri de Sigalas, Joseph Koehl and Cyrille
Besson.[27] Initially, his duties were not of major importance. Did Irène
Némirovsky draw her inspiration from Michel's necessarily modest
first steps at the bank to reconstruct, in *Le Malentendu*, the industrious
office atmosphere, 'the clatter of the typewriters', and those 'columns
of figures in ever-growing lines'?[28] This seems all the more plausible
since it was only in 1925 that she completed this novel begun during
the previous year.

On 28th October 1924, she enrolled for the last time at the Sorbonne,
but it appears she was more concerned with her 'violent crush' since
all subsequent trace of her is lost in the warren that is the university.
Every evening, after he had finished work, she would meet Michel in
a friendly bar, Chez Martin, on Avenue George-V, where Paul Epstein
and Choura Lissianski would often join them. 'It was an English bar,
tiny, sparkling clean, with a "respectable" and serious atmosphere',[29]
Le Malentendu suggests. If Michel was calmer and more sensible than
Irène, there was nothing of the killjoy about him. He loved Mistinguett,
Joséphine Baker, champagne, brandy and his friends. Among these
was Daria, Boris Kamenka's daughter, who took up literary translation as a career. And 'Micha' had good manners: when he kept Mlle
Ginoux, his secretary, too late in the office, he had her driven home
by taxi, with a bunch of roses.

The summer of 1925 was probably the last that Irène spent with
her parents, in one of those hotels on the Basque coast that she now
looked upon in horror, considering them as artificial as Fanny and
Léon's relationship. A decadent social world mingled there, washed
up from all over the globe, one that was painful for her to contemplate since it reminded her of her past excesses. At Biarritz, 'queen of
resorts and resort of kings', one might glimpse Chaplin or Guitry, of
course, but also gangsters and careerist politicians whose wits had
been softened by the Spanish sunshine. One of the rare birds in this
aviary was a fine-feathered crook, whose parents had fled the pogroms
in 1889. It was common knowledge that he had invested a great deal
of money in the vast hotel-casino of La Roseraie, built between 1926
and 1928 at Ilbarritz, near Bidart. A few years later, the questionable
suicide of this man – Stavisky – threatened to engulf the Republic
itself in disrepute.

The Wine of Solitude lists a few of the specimens from the golden aquarium in which her parents swam: 'oil merchants, international financiers, arms manufacturers, professional dancers, former students of the Page Corps,* expensive women or cheap ones, men who sell opium and little girls . . .'[30] In *Le Malentendu*, to which she put the finishing touches before sending it by ordinary post to *Œuvres libres*, she portrayed Biarritz as one of the 'two most attractive centres of the cosmopolitan funfair',[31] the other being San Sebastian. A comment that was so accurate that when it appeared in February 1926 in the magazine put out by the publisher Fayard – a 'monthly literary selection of hitherto unpublished work' – the novel was placed next to Alfred Savoir's social comedy, *Un homme*, which was set precisely at the Hôtel du Palais, in Biarritz.

It was in this same highly luxurious establishment, where she had also stayed two years previously, that Irène would have Gabri, the young heroine of *L'Ennemie* stay, in a bedroom overlooking 'the magical Ocean, full of shadows, reflections, the smell of salt and crude songs'.[32] Biarritz, in this second novel, is a new Sodom, in the hands of a 'crowd of puppets who dance and make love with beguiling recklessness', to the beat of 'black music, that vibrates eternally beneath a sky that is too blue, transforming the mind into a kind of empty, resonant bell'.[33] The heroine of *The Wine of Solitude* would prefer morning walks on the beach to these artificial pleasures; similarly, Irène, by avoiding the masquerade, discovered, in her long, solitary rambles in the fresh air, the cure for her weariness of this spurious world. 'The best moment was at the crack of dawn, especially when everyone at the hotel was asleep, with her hair floating loosely over her shoulders, dressed in a blue skirt and a Lacoste shirt, wearing espadrilles, with bare legs and bare arms, she climbed up to the hills . . .' There, quite simply, she enjoyed the priceless happiness that her parents' materialism had kept from her.

David Town

One of the most prominent figures in Biarritz in 1926 contrasted strongly with the everyday lives of the nouveaux riches. His sumptuous

*Imperial Russian military establishment for the sons of the aristocracy, 1697–1917. [Tr.]

Villa Bégonia, perched on the edge of the cliffs, with an aircraft hangar alongside it, could not be missed by anyone walking by. This Belgian tycoon, who had no religion but whose father was Jewish, had built his fortune on artificial silk and on electricity networks. Alfred Lœwenstein, who was worn out by the age of fifty, came to the Basque coast because of his heart condition, not to parade among 'the crowd of mediocrities who think they are rich because they have a few hundred thousand francs to spend'.[34] Having persuaded his government to grant him the monopoly of the railways, Lœwenstein was now planning a huge development project at Chiberta, between Biarritz and Bayonne, a sort of Xanadu, with a race-course, casino, dance halls, golf course and tennis courts, and luxury shops. In this Eden, Daniel Halévy tells us, only 'real kings and gold barons were to have been allowed to live'.[35] And to launch this new Monte Carlo, Lœwenstein planned to give twenty extremely luxurious villas to twenty prominent celebrities, by way of advertising the scheme.

This project, which remained unfulfilled, was the talk of the town. It coincided with the first indications of Lœwenstein's eventual ruin, after he had been reckoned to be one of the three richest men in the world. His utopian character, combined with Leonid's experiences, may have inspired Irène Némirovsky with a new idea for a novel. Her main character, David, is a Jewish financier who, having left the family home with twenty thousand roubles of life assurance received on the death of his father, made a fortune in New York and is embarking upon a gigantic building project that consists of creating from top to bottom, on a stretch of dried-out marshland, a city called 'David Town'. This David has done everything: 'slept in the coal holes on the Volga boats', sold sugar, barley, wheat and even rubber from Poland to Siberia. His wife only asks him for one thing: to be taken far away from the Ukraine and to be called Bella rather than Ruth, 'that dreadful Jewish name'. Their daughter, a pretty, scatterbrained creature, who shows no respect or gratitude to her hardworking father, is called Joy, or else Joyce. She hurls at her mother, who doesn't listen to her, remarks such as: 'Mummy, I'm going back with Salvador and Pachito!' But David's business affairs are unsettled, for 'the Jew is rich today and poor tomorrow'. In the end, the tireless 'Davidouchka', aged fifty-four and petrified by the shadow of death, will restore the situation, even becoming the guest of Prince Stephany, the former Russian governor, in Biarritz. The husband and wife, while living in grand style, will sigh as they reminisce about the cruel years of the pogroms, when they were both penniless. 'Do you remember? . . . You were young and poor . . . We had dreams . . . and the boat deck, and the emigrants, do you remember?' The whole forms a parable: an uprooted Jewish family, split apart by wealth and ambition, but drawn together by memories of humiliation. Money and ill health, alas, make poor bedfellows, and 'when the Good Lord gives us nuts, we no longer have teeth to crack them' . . .

These outlines, taken from a manuscript of 160 pages, bound together with a pink ribbon, are the draft for a satirical work that Irène Némirovsky would devote herself to from 1925 to 1929, until she had completed a variant of Ecclesiastes in the field of high finance. In *David Golder* – the title she would eventually give her novel – an uncouth but astute banker, who is loathed, flattered or mocked by those around him, will be reminded at his death of the oath he made during his miserable childhood and of the faith of his forebears, that still survived beneath the burden of wealth. 'I wrote and rewrote it several times,' Irène Némirovsky would observe. 'I can say I spent four years working on it. It was conceived in Biarritz, from the spectacle of all those unhinged and depraved idle rich, from that world of financiers, shady bankers, women seeking pleasure and new sensations, gigolos, courtesans, etc.'[36] It is striking that among the literary figures who greeted this novel in 1930, only Benjamin Crémieux and André Maurois, both of them Jews, were able to grasp the book's moral depth, instead of merely concentrating on the apparent abjectness of her characters, who are all consumed by a cocktail of sins. 'One thinks of certain remarks of Proust about the old age of Swann, who, as death approached, would also hark back to the nihilism of Ecclesiastes,'[37] Maurois would write, whereas Crémieux, who was more explicit, noted that this 'vanity', updated to suit current tastes, those to do with financial speculation and debauchery, was also an allegory of 'the Jewish soul': 'David Golder expresses simultaneously all the voracity and the satiety of the Jew when he abandons himself entirely to the world: he wants everything while knowing that everything is nothing. That is why he can gain control over everything and give up everything, why he can display in turn the ambition of the biblical David and the detachment of Ecclesiastes.'[38] This was very much Irène Némirovsky's intention: to invite a Commendatore to the parasitic feast of Biarritz, with Léon himself in the role of the vengeful statue, upsetting the tables that had been laden thanks to his money and his life's work. David Golder, the 'maker of gold', the rebellious Samson, breaking the chains of gold shackled to his wrists by a grasping wife and a fickle daughter who are enslaved to vice . . .

Irène Némirovsky only gradually realised how she could put Léon's fate to best use by presenting him as a troubled man, who sees his final dignity – fatherhood – ridiculed by hateful revelations. All the reviewers of *David Golder* have emphasised the cynical character of Joyce, who puts on an act of filial devotion for her illegitimate father so that she can extort a motor-car or fifty thousand-franc banknotes from him. It did not occur to anyone that this was a ruthless self-portrait. For Joyce is Nonoche, the brainless little tart who knows how to count. It was rumoured in fact that Joyce was not a fictional creation. The jeering critic from *Chantecler*, for instance, wrote: 'It is said that your own father, also a Jewish banker, served as your model for *David Golder*, and that having recognised himself, he harbours a strong grudge against you; also that Joyce really existed and was just as pretty and "unhinged" as your heroine, and that she committed suicide, aged eighteen, thereby logically bringing to an end, after all, a remarkable life . . .' The author of these lines could not know how accurate he was.[39] 'I regret not having made Joyce more sympathetic,' she would admit in 1930.

The Turgenev method

In 1925–26, *David Golder* had not yet got off the ground. The book had not found the terse voice, the aggressive tone, the harsh language or the moral breadth that would awe its readers. It was still the story of a business adventurer, which only borrowed its most obvious aspects from Irène Némirovsky's life. At the end of the year, 'still without any recommendation',[40] she sent the manuscript of *Le Malentendu* to *Œuvres libres*. This literary review, published by Arthème Fayard, which had serialised the work of Proust and of Carco before publication, as well as books by Morand, Guitry and Bernstein, agreed to print this 'unpublished and complete novel' at the back of the magazine. *Le Malentendu* appeared in February 1926. Critics did not normally pay attention to this type of publication. So it was only with hindsight that Frédéric Lefèvre, in 1930, was able to detect the promise of this book that cast a look of bitter understanding over the stern rules of the 'world'; he also emphasised the incongruous aspects of this melodrama written by a young Russian woman who refused to write yet another lament for a lost paradise: 'In its moderation and its understated common sense, this novel is very French. It repeats a truth that young lovers too often forget: which is that the purest, most intense love affair, the one least shackled by circumstances, risks breaking apart if it does not take these same circumstances into account. And that a love affair, for example, carries within it the seed of death for three quarters of the time if, on a whim, it flowers between people belonging to classes or social backgrounds that are too different.'[41]

Irène and Michel had not taken this risk: they came from exactly the same milieu, that of Jewish financiers who had been forced to flee to Paris by the Bolshevik revolution. Their wedding was celebrated at the town hall of the 16th arrondissement on 31st July 1926, with Irène, who already wore a diamond engagement ring on her left hand, wearing her wedding ring on the finger of her right hand, in the Russian manner. The marriage contract, which was based on separate ownership of property, records that Michel was still 'unemployed', which suggests that, to begin with, his work at the Banque des Pays du Nord was done on a friendly basis. A religious service followed the next day at the temple in the Rue Théry,[42] a non-consistory synagogue. Neither husband nor wife was practising, but Efim Epstein and his wife, who were, were keen to keep up appearances. Michel's niece Natacha, then aged ten, would remember that her uncle was unable to break with his heel the glass wrapped in a napkin – a symbolic act supposed to bring good luck to the young couple.

Once married, husband and wife moved into a quiet flat on the Left Bank, halfway between Montparnasse and Les Invalides, down a cul-de-sac opposite the National Institute for Young Blind People and backing on to the ruins of the former Oiseaux prison, which had been pulled down in 1904. At 8 Avenue Daniel-Lesueur – the nom-de-plume of a writer who died in 1921 – stood a fine modern building, built in 1923. The young couple had two servants who worked for them: a housekeeper and a Basque cook, Joséphine Arozamena, since Michel came home for lunch as often as possible, that is to say almost every day.

In addition to the bathroom and the kitchen, the flat consisted of three bedrooms, a dining-room and a large sitting-room 'of luxurious sophistication, in which the furniture and the expensive items, skilfully spread about, [were] displayed to full effect'. During the daytime, Irène set up her study there, entertaining socially on occasion, 'infinitely charming and welcoming'.[43]

There were few flowers, or just a tall, solitary tulip in a vase; no type-writer yet in the bay window; no table or desk. But there was a large divan on which she stretched out, an exercise book pressed to her knees, in order to conjure up the former life of David Issakitch Golder, the hero of her next novel, who was now at the head of an important company, the 'Franco-American Company for the development and trade in oil, a public limited company with assets of 60,000,000 francs fully paid'. 'I never make a plan,' she would explain. 'I begin by describing for my own purposes the physical appearance and a full biography of all the characters, even the less important ones. In this way, even before getting down to the actual writing itself, I know my characters perfectly, even, it seems to me, down to the way they speak; I know how they will behave, not just in this book but throughout their lives. When this is done, I start to write.'[44] On lined, perforated pages, she copied out in black ink entire paragraphs of specialised research to do with bankruptcy and commercial insolvency, death duties and heart disease. She noted: 'David Golder *may* have asthma (Dr Périneau) only emphasise the pain, the anguish . . . I think one should avoid mentioning asthma by name, but say "difficulty in breathing", "effort", etc.' Then, feeling her way, she sketched the portrait of Marcus, Golder's partner:

What's his name? Of course this first name should not once be mentioned, but I have to know that he has one. Jacob. Jacques. Isaac. Noé. Ezekièl. Israël. Léon. Rodolphe. Or Rudolf. Rodolphe Marcus? Rudolf Marcus. No, that is too Boche. Rodolphe Marcus is better. I want to ignore where he comes from. Golder and he probably knew each other twenty or twenty-five years ago. But before that? Black night. Darkness. The amazing Jewish integration. He is 'a very parvenu figure' in recent years. He has a few good paintings, some wealthy connections, mainly mistresses, women, that's his vice, his oriental appetite for women and the desire to procure them, jewellery, etc.

It is still only a jeu d'esprit. But the features of Golder, the paper figure who will restore Léon's dignity, were becoming strangely familiar to her. Golder's character is eventually summed up in a few words: '[He] must give the impression of a massive stone.' In this way she gave form to her childhood stratagems, turning into a distraction the boredom and anxiety of her early life, but with no intention yet of making writing her career. 'I am not a literary woman,' she would say. 'I don't write for writing's sake. For me writing is such an unusual pleasure that I don't see myself doing it out of duty or because I've decided to do so.'[45] Nonetheless, the Turgenev method – first sketching in her characters in the minutest detail, only inking in the prominent features, then bringing them to life – would be one she would resort to frequently.

Besides, at the age of twenty-three there was still a lot for her to read. An entire wall of the drawing-room was covered in books. Her favourite authors: the Tharauds, Valéry Larbaud and Chardonne's *L'Epithalame* in the 1921 edition, the quiet pace of which reminded her of 'the great Russians'. *Les Demi-Vierges* by Marcel Prévost, with its 1900-style minxes whose traits were inherited by Nonoche, Joyce and Louloute. Marcel Proust, for whom she professed a 'keen admiration': 'I know every detail of his work; I could reel off to you what Odette was wearing and the faintest of nuances in Gilberte's and Marcel's youthful love affair.'[46] *Climats* by André Maurois, in which, in 1928, she would relish the psychological essence that *Le Malentendu* aimed to achieve. But also Colette's *La Fin de Chéri* and, because she adored '"soppy" things',[47] the fragrant novels of Gérard d'Houville, alias Marie de Régnier. Finally, *Contrerimes* by the Basque poet Paul-Jean Toulet, which took her back to Golder:

> *Sur l'océan couleur de fer*
> *Pleurait un chœur immense*
> *Et ces longs cris dont la démence*
> *Semble percer l'enfer.**

*On the iron-tinted ocean / A vast chorus wailed / And those long demented cries / Seem to penetrate hell. [Tr.]

Nobody came to disturb her apart from the enormous cat Kissou, black as a panther, 'long, broad, hirsute and mad'.[48] Then, Michel returning home; even when she was successful, he only allowed her half an hour's writing time in the evening. After nine years living together, this clause in their marriage contract would not be broken: 'My husband is at the bank, he works like any other man, morning and afternoon. What does a woman do during that time? She goes to the shops, tries on clothes, follows the fashions. In my case, instead of all that, I write. What's the difference in time wasted? There isn't any. My husband comes home. I stop my work; from that moment on I am simply the wife . . . Thanks to this combination of my working duties and my wifely duties I achieve a perfect balance.'[49]

Paul and Irène

Among her reading matter, Irène Némirovsky never mentions Paul Morand, the most stylish of the bathers at the Eskualduna. And yet the ballyhoo surrounding the publication by Bernard Grasset of his novel *Lewis et Irène*, launched with a style of advertising that shocked his rival publisher Gallimard, could not have escaped the notice of someone so avid for new books. A slogan as arresting as it was misleading ('Do Irène's hats come from Lewis's?'), display advertisements in all the daily news-papers, sixty thousand copies sold in two months during the winter of 1924: it was a fine effort indeed. In order to create the hero of this short, terse 'business novel', so frequently emulated, Morand had poured 'a little Jewish blood' into the veins of his intrepid businessman. By his own admission, he had also taken his inspiration from living models: the Swedish match king, Ivar Kreuger; the American press tycoon, Randolph Hearst; Henry Deterding, the boss of the Royal Dutch Petroleum Company; but also Alfred Lœwenstein, since Lewis was 'the natural son of a Belgian banker'. Bernard Grasset particularly liked the laconic and nonchalant opening of the novel: '"Fifteen" – said Lewis.' After some hesitation, Irène Némirovsky must have remembered this when she finally jotted down the first line of her own novel: '"No", said Golder.' In this way, she could be sure of catching Grasset's attention.

In April 1925, Paul Morand had published an anti-Bolshevik piece of farce in the magazine *Demain* entitled 'Je brûle Moscou', in which he openly jeered at the vast Jewish revolution that was making Eurasia a new Promised Land, 'the great laboratory of the world'. In it, he portrayed an exceptionally gifted poet, the fifteen-year-old Ioseph Antonovitch Izraïloff, 'the Tom Thumb of Odessa', who had been responsible for spreading cholera around Moscow. In Morand's sketch, the Jews who are spilling over the globe from the 'large reservoirs' of Ukraine are 'passionate, intolerant, Talmudic';[50] in 'L'Enfant génial', which Les Œuvres libres published in April 1927, they are merely wretched and 'bitter', for at the age of twenty, no more than at the age of thirty, Irène Némirovsky had no wish – nor would she ever have – to involve herself in politics.[51]

In Le Malentendu, however, she used the literary device or trope of the 'rich young Jew', an employee of a mean and calculating bank, and his head clerk, with 'a Teutonic accent', 'a flabby and hairy hand' and 'an almost unseemly nose and a filthy grey beard';[52] grotesque caricatures that cannot fail to make one wince in the course of a novel that is realistic to the point of dullness. Was this healthy self-mockery? An anxiety about appearing impartial? Jeering arrogance?[53] The clichés were laboured in any case, and void of any narrative function. But were they anti-Semitic clichés? Irène Némirovsky borrowed these stylistic accessories, almost without thinking, from the Tharaud brothers, as one of the ingredients of French wit that she envied. Even if it meant offending public taste. That a young émigrée writing in French should have taken mimicry so far that she was copying people's prejudices proved only one thing: the triteness of the anti-Semitic cliché. Without it, the French writer's full array of skills would not have been complete. For it is clear that she had not invented these hackneyed stereotypes, which thrived in the pages of the humorous magazine Fantasio. Later, she would regret having borrowed these practices and was determined to show greater subtlety in her descriptions of dubious characters.

Blood is thicker than water

No book was published under her name between April 1927 and December 1929. On 4th July an unexplained incident may have given a fresh impetus to David Golder: having set off from London aboard his private Fokker, Alfred Lœwenstein could not be found when the plane arrived in Belgium. He had fallen, whether accidentally or not, into the English Channel. His disappearance aroused much conjecture. In March 1933, Irène Némirovsky must have still been interested in what had happened, since she had read and kept the special issue of the satirical publication *Crapouillot* devoted to 'Mysterious deaths' that contained an article on the Lœwenstein affair.

Was this drowning the inspiration for the death of David Golder on the high seas, aboard the ship that was supposed to take him to the West? Early readers of the novel would sometimes put forward the name of the Belgian financier,[54] but Irène Némirovsky always discouraged these simplistic parallels. Not that her characters were all pure inventions: 'I have certainly made use of real-life aspects, but sparsely.'[55]

By her own admission, only two characters from *David Golder* would be based on actual people: the old miser Soifer, who unintentionally brings Golder back to the old traditions, and the libidinous Fischl, to whom Joyce was resigned to sell herself. 'I mean that Soifer and Fischl exist in flesh and blood. I know them.'[56] As for Golder, his characteristics owe as much to Lœwenstein as to Léon Némirovsky or Deterding, another of the conquistadors she would have fun dissecting in order to compose her character. Like David Golder, Deterding grew up without a father, had had a difficult childhood and had been round the world. When he took over control of Shell in 1907, he had neutralised his main rival, Marcus Samuel, by making him his partner; Golder would react similarly with Simon Marcus, his alter-ego at Golmar, before destroying him in 1926 when the latter tried to swindle him. In the early 1920s, Golder and Deterding had both speculated on the defeat of the Bolsheviks by acquiring oil shares stolen from their lawful owners; this did not prevent them in the least from negotiating a business or transport contract with the Soviets.

Irène Némirovsky researched these complex subjects fully, as she always would, covering a recent book by Louis Fischer with jottings, 'a fat book, translated from English, I believe, *l'Impérialisme du pétrole*, which I spent many hours with',[57] and consulting back issues of the *Revue pétrolifère*. During the autumn of 1928, this was her main occupation. For all that, are the oil deals described in *David Golder* true to life? Irène Némirovsky maintained that her father, whom she made read the proofs in November 1929, found nothing to object to: 'Come now, blood is thicker than water! I can't see anything very silly.'[58] The average reader is taken in by the whirl of figures and stock exchange jargon. The anonymous columnist in the *Revue pétrolifère*, who discovered the novel in 1930, gave a more professional opinion, one that pays tribute to Irène Némirovsky's skill as an illusionist. If the picture of the oil market seemed to him slightly phantasmagorical, the character of Golder, the speculator who is ignorant of industrial realities, on the other hand, struck him as truer than life: 'Such men have existed. They knew nothing about oil and they operated purely on appearances, on fictions, on the delusions of similar oilfields, these people with wild imaginations were out for the jackpot . . . The last specimens of these rogues have disappeared in any case and the modern economy will certainly do nothing to bring them to life again.'[59]

Similarly, in order to write the chapter in which Golder, dragged along by Soifer to the Rue des Rosiers, resists and then succumbs to the lukewarm nostalgia that the fur hats and the smell of stuffed pike awake in him, Irène Némirovsky visited the Jewish district of the Marais, which she had been told about. But before publishing *David Golder* in *Les Œuvres libres*, which, as usual, she was invited to do, she felt she must rid herself of a dead weight, satisfy a 'hate-filled dream':[60] that of presenting Fanny with the mirror of her sins. This exorcism took the form of a pitiless novel, written in the course of the years 1927–1928, for which she borrowed the title, *L'Ennemie*, from a famous sonnet of Baudelaire's:

> Ma jeunesse ne fut qu'un ténébreux orage
> Traversé çà et là par de brillants soleils;
> Le tonnerre et la pluie ont fait un tel ravage,
> Qu'il reste en mon jardin bien peu de fruits vermeils . . .*

This devastation was her own innocence, destroyed by Fanny, who was more of a rival than a mother. In the psychodrama, in which her daughter lends her the features of Francine Bragance, an unnatural

---

*My youth was but a dark storm / Pierced here and there by sparkling sunbeams; / The thunder and the rain caused such devastation, / That very few rosy fruits remain in my garden . . . [Tr.]

mother who kills her child, Irène Némirovsky handed out some sophisticated humiliation, particularly when she demolishes her proudest asset: 'How many times had she imagined, with bitter and morose delight, the day when Mama would finally be old, and ugly, and it would be her turn to be alone ... She had dreamed about her first wrinkle, her mother's first grey hair, and that thought had always consoled her ...'[61] In *L'Ennemie*, the mother-daughter conflict is reduced to the twists and turns of misfortune in love: so as to take her revenge on Francine, Gabri tries to seduce her lover. 'There, at last, my revenge ... it's no more cunning than that, eh!'[62] But this game of dialectics, instead of liberating her, makes her an inheritor. A deadly trap is set, which will lead to her suicide. For how could she come to terms with corrupted blood? How can she hate a woman of whom she is a replica, without hating herself? 'How could I judge her? Wasn't I like her?'[63]

The demon of revenge

Marriage to Michel, by distancing her from Fanny, had made this determined outcome possible, and it explains the analytical coldness of *L'Ennemie*. 'She felt as if a monstrous sack of venom that had been growing and growing within her soul for years had suddenly just burst ... And it felt so new, so sweet ...'[64] This catharsis culminates in a verbal exchange reminiscent of Henry Bernstein, in which the mother confronts the daughter:

> 'So you have no dignity, or modesty, or principles ...'
>   'Good God, no; I don't think so ... Where would I have learned any of that, I wonder ...'
>   'Gabri, don't you even understand that what you did was bad?'
>   'What is bad? What is good? I can assure you, I have no idea ... No one ever taught me the difference ...'
>   'And to think I had so much faith in you!!'
>   'You were wrong ... You should never have faith in people you don't know.'[65]

Nevertheless, Irène Némirovsky was not so cruel as to publish this slanging match under her maiden name. *L'Ennemie* must remain hidden, behind its crimson curtain, like the picture of Dorian Gray, bloated with depravity. And since it appeared under the undetectable pseudonym of Pierre Nerey – an anagram of Yrène – Fanny would never be able to shatter this informative mirror.

Like no other book by Irène Némirovsky, *L'Ennemie* conveys her phobia of hereditary traits reemerging, of genetic glue, of sexual impulses, of innate characteristics being perverted by motherly manipulation. In her novels, atavism, desire and drunkenness either prevail or are overcome. Why should the 'passionate, soaring, light-hearted grace of extreme youth',[66] that confers love, also incite her to adultery, depravity and sometimes to crime? This ambivalence is at the heart of her work.

L'Ennemie – which is not always free of melodrama – was published in July 1928. 'Pierre Nerey' appeared this time on the same list as writers such as Henry Bernstein and André Foucault, the first person to read 'L'Enfant génial' and *Le Malentendu*. And yet she was never satisfied with this rather Freudian novel, which revealed more of her bitterness than her pride. In this respect, Wilde's epigraph, had she retained it, would have been obvious: 'Children begin by loving their parents; after a time they judge them; rarely, if ever, do they forgive them.' Pride! And yet she had no lack of it, and had once recommended it to her friend Madeleine: 'I too could be sad. A boyfriend of mine has gone away, but I've got too much willpower to whine about it, too much pride as well. I have to "want" not to think about him any more, Mad. I have to be proud.' But it was probably necessary for her to indulge in sadism first. 'Of course,' she would write in 1934, '*L'Ennemie* draws too much attention to the drama of the mother, who is merely a symbol of the loneliness, the rejection, the moral isolation of the child.' *L'Ennemie* was therefore a failure: Irène's own confused emotions had embroiled her in a row with her mother. Would it not have been more dignified to refuse to brawl? This is precisely the point about *David Golder*, which she would never have finished without the daily encouragement of Michel, the first of her readers, who suggested to her that she rise above herself in a novel in which the autobiographical aspect would be one component among many. 'The demon of pride or the demon of revenge, we shall see which will be the stronger! . . .'[67]

Her task accomplished, Irène Némirovsky could at last settle

down to her first proper attempt at writing *David Golder*, during the
second half of 1928. She was now fully aware of Fanny's irreparable
depravity, but also of the spineless blindness of Léon, who preferred
to drown his sorrows at the gaming tables. She saw clearly that her
father, from being a Russian banker, had become a dabbler in shares,
a court jester who refused to acknowledge his physical decline amid
an orgy of rapid losses and gains, just as Fanny deceived herself
with her round of lovers. Between this husband and this wife, what
was left? A daughter and some money. What a subject for a novel,
both modern and romantic, trivial and moral! 'You want to know
why the business world is so much a part of my novels? Well, simply
because I have many personal memories of it. My father was a
banker. The first tragic events I witnessed were to do with arguments about money.'[68]

David Golder opens on a bitter negotiation, a tussle. David, a giant
of the financial world, has not forgotten, however, that he was once
a rag merchant, 'a thin little Jew with red hair, pale, piercing eyes,
worn-out boots and empty pockets...' A miserable youth as a
building worker, from Moscow to New York, had taught him dirty
tricks. His manners are loutish. 'Never a smile, a caress...' In 1926,
the starving emigrant has become a compulsive businessman,
capable of driving his own partner to suicide. Golder has no enemy
who is his equal – not even Gloria, his wife, the daughter of a usurer
from Kichinev, who covets jewellery 'like a barbarian idol', and who
only knows that her first name was previously a Yiddish one, Havké.
In his Biarritz villa, crammed with parasites who live off him, Golder
grumbles as he amasses his successes. 'Make money for others, and
then die, that's why I'm on this wretched earth...' But a deadly
illness lies in wait for Golder: pneumonia, which allows him to
glimpse his death by drowning one anguished night: 'He felt as if
someone were holding his head under water and that it went on
for centuries.' Confronted with death, Golder becomes the horror-
stricken little Jew again. Only a foolish sense of love keeps him alive,
the one he feels for Joyce, his daughter, a perverse and materialistic
creature who cares only for her 'old Dad's' wallet, asking favours
almost incestuously...[69]

The ultimate in books that end badly

Having reached the climax of this tragedy – a hyperbole of her family's past history – Irène Némirovsky suddenly laid it aside. Compressing the setting, she retained only three characters, in what would be a small-scale version of *L'Ennemie* in one act and six scenes, one just as cruel as the original work, but with the addition of a single ingredient that was lacking: cathartic irony. In it, David is reduced to being a small-time investor who has grown rich by chance, and who was merely a doorman at the Banque de Paris to begin with. Alfred Kemp is a 1926 version of Balzac's César Birotteau, totally dumbfounded at having 'arrived', but for the fact that he is 'a dry little Jew with fiery eyes'.[70] His wife Rosine is a former secretary who is constantly disguising her age with make-up. The Kemps profess Christian values, make fun of the snobs and important people, but at the ball they plan to give to 'get ahead in society',[71] these nouveaux riches only manage to invite a woman who likes orgies, a gigolo with a title, 'a hundred or so pimps and old tarts',[72] and a good number of parvenus with newly gallicised names. Here, Irène Némirovsky caricatures a memory of her early years in Paris in the *trompe l'œil* surroundings of the rue de la Pompe: 'Papa plays with paper and pretends it's money . . . We entertain all the Rastas in Paris and call them socialites . . .'[73] The daughter Antoinette, fourteen years old, is not taken in by their ridiculous behaviour. 'Bloody selfish hypocrites, the lot of them . . .' But a dreadful remark by Rosine – 'This kid, this snotty-nosed kid, coming to the ball! Can you just picture it?' – suddenly transforms the mother's expression into the 'cold gaze of a woman, an *enemy* . . .'. Humiliated to the core of her being, tempted by suicide ('I'd rather be dead and buried . . .'), the girl decides on a drastic step: 'Ah! I want them to die.'[74] She would tear this social farce to shreds by tossing the packet of invitations into the Seine from the Alexandre III Bridge – the tsar accursed by the Jews, persecuting the Kemps a quarter of a century after his death!

Mme Kemp's ball would not take place. The clock on the church tower sounds the death knell of her vanity. But Antoinette, having been initiated into evil, has in turn become a woman. She can, if she wishes, dry the hair of 'little mother', whose dreams are wiped away in tears like those of a spoilt child. At the end of this bullfight, she will offer her her pity – 'my poor mama . . .'[75] – and this final thrust is the rediscovered pride of the writer, which exists only to punish or pardon her creations.

The characters in this murderous farce would have had to have been truly recognisable for Irène Némirovsky to think of protecting herself – or sparing them – by using a pseudonym for a second time. This 'unpublished novella', *Le Bal*, appeared in February 1929 in *Les Œuvres libres*, under the by-line of Pierre Nerey. In it, Irène Némirovsky casts off the occasionally pathetic tone of *L'Ennemie* and stifles her sobs in a ferocious burst of laughter. This sarcasm, this talent for trivial but ruthless dialogue, the type of malicious character sketch à la Grosz[76] would be the moral basis for this vicious social satire that characterises her style up until the mid-1930s. For Charles de Noailles, prince of socialites and benefactor of art and literature, *Le Bal*, according to Cocteau, represented 'the ultimate in books that end badly'. After having read it in 1930, he insisted thereafter on knowing the ending of every novel before embarking on it! Cocteau wanted to know the truth; he was forced to admit that with *Le Bal*, Irène Némirovsky had stirred up a nightmare: for 'a botched ball is terrible for a man of the world, even if he has Charles's spiritual elegance'.[77] And Cocteau immediately recommended that his mother read this 'sort of master-piece'.[78]

A child

'I wrote *Le Bal* in between two chapters of *David Golder*,'[79] Irène Némirovsky observed. It is easy to guess the precise point at which she switched course. It is at the very middle of the book, when Golder, who is convalescing, announces his departure: 'The gust of air made the chandelier above the fireplace tinkle rapidly in the silent room.'[80] And here, on the first page of *Le Bal*, Rosine Kemp on entering the study, 'slammed the door behind her with such force that a gust of air made the crystal beads on the chandelier jingle with the pure, light sound of small bells'.[81]

With the digression of *Le Bal* concluded (since it was published under a pseudonym, there was no reaction), Irène Némirovsky was able to pick up the thread of *David Golder* where she had left off.

Looked after by a quack who is paid to conceal the gravity of his illness from him, David is appalled when he realises that Gloria dreads his death less than she does his money drying up. He is a sixty-five-year-old Gatsby discovering how artificial feelings can be. Threatened with ruin, the old 'slave of success', like Bernstein's Samson,[82] plans to use the last of his strength to bring down the edifice of his wealth upon his wife. But how can he allow his darling Joyce, even if she is his daughter by adulterous means, to be forced to marry the vile Fischl, a scoundrel who has been imprisoned in three countries? It is to remove her from the claws of this caviar-sated 'old pig', that Golder, at death's door, will travel to Moscow to extract from the Soviets the oil concession that will protect Joyce from moral abandonment. His final time of going banco.

Golder will not return to Europe: in a small, squalid port on the Black Sea, a ghastly Greek steamer is meant to take him to Constantinople. Death will prevent him from turning his back on his childhood for a second time. The only witness to his passing is a young Jewish emigrant, thirsting for illusions, as he himself was half a century earlier, when he left Russia for ever. Golder expires in the full force of a storm, having uttered the word 'God', in a delirium that brings back images of his native *shtetl* and the muffled voice of his mother, in the falling snow, calling him by his first name. 'It was the last sound he was to hear on this earth.'[83] Golder is already Citizen Kane.

They were the last words of the novel. Irène asked Michel to read it first, then, quite naturally, she sent it to André Foucault, the chief editor of Les Œuvres libres, in the late summer of 1929. This new 200-page work was longer than her previous books: it could not possibly be published in its entirety unless it was cut by fifty pages. Which is what Foucault, who had published several novels and books of reportage with Fayard and Flammarion, tried to make the young author understand:

'What does your husband say about your novel?'

'He says that, from the beginning to the end of the book, the main character keeps repeating the same thing.'

'Well, Madame, your husband is quite right.'[84]

Irène Némirovsky took him at his word. But, aware that she had written a book whose boldness was not suited to the restricted criteria of Les Œuvres libres, she did not wish to shorten it by one iota, nor rewrite it for a fifth time. Furthermore, unexpected bouts of sickness prevented her from dwelling on the matter for long: the child she had been expecting since the end of the winter was keen to make its appearance. Several months before, in preparation for the great event, she had taken out a subscription to La Semaine de Suzette, but had done so in the name of Cécile, her nanny from the Morvan district: were Fanny to discover that Irène was reading the adventures of Bécassine* at the age of twenty-six,[85] all her fantasies about her own young motherhood would have been reinforced.

In the autumn of 1929 she sent off her manuscript to Bernard Grasset, one of the few Paris publishers who she was certain would not be offended by expressions like 'shit', 'snuff it', 'bloody', and risqué innuendos – 'Oh! Alec, your knees are so cold . . .' that were scattered throughout her new book. She scarcely had time to wait for a reply: in October she was obliged to take to her bed to prepare for the baby's delivery, which was expected to be difficult, but how much more delightful than the bitter revenge of her first books! The child that was to be born would be loved and pampered in a way she had never been, for 'it's a crime to bring children into the world and not to give them a shred, an ounce of love!'[86] What upheaval in her life could she expect of the next year, 1930?

---

*One of the earliest of French comic-strip characters, the adventures of Bécassine, a simple Breton housemaid, had charmed readers of La Semaine de Suzette since 1905. [Tr.]

Part II

In the Literary Jungle
(1929–1939)

6

One Ounce of Good Luck
(1929–1931)

Let us be clear. I don't expect to be dazzled from the first page: that is
the exception, the miracle, the charm of chance.

Bernard Grasset, La Chose littéraire, 1929

'When a manuscript arrives at my firm,' Bernard Grasset explained
to readers of *Le Journal* in 1929, 'it is brought to me and put on my
desk. I cut the strings myself, I open the first page, and, generally, I
read this first page straight away. Here I must make a confession to
you. I am an inveterate idealist: I always expect a masterpiece; even
more, from that very first page onwards, I expect a revelation.'

When had lightning not struck at Grasset's publishing house in Rue
des Saints-Pères? In the previous year, *Climats* had easily passed the
one hundred thousand sales mark, but it was neither a revelation –
Maurois was over forty years old – nor the *succès de scandale* that the
Diaghilev of publishing had been waiting for ever since the death of
Raymond Radiguet, six years previously. Heralded as the comet of
the year 1928, Jean Desbordes's shameless confession *J'adore*, did not
obtain the public's approval, in spite of Jean Cocteau's patronage. And
Bernard Grasset waited in vain for his new *Le Diable au corps*. There
was nothing, however, that could discourage him: 'I am waiting for
the masterpiece, but I am always prepared for the worst disappointment . . . And it is therefore with both great hope and great fear that
I approach that mysterious object that is the work of an unknown
author.'

The manuscript found at Rue des Saints-Pères

The first reader of the manuscript that was sent to the publishing
house of Grasset under the name of Epstein, accompanied by a poste

restante address at Paris-Louvre – 'so that in case of rejection, my
family should not know about the steps I had taken'[1] – was not the
publisher himself, but his employee Henry Muller. Having joined
the firm through a recommendation in 1923, he described in a
humorous book of memoirs how he came to discover *David Golder*
late one afternoon.

> A pile of folders had been put on my table with the request that I weed
> through them and in all likelihood turn them down, since the manuscript
> department had too much work; for four hours, my head resting on my
> hand and a cigarette between my lips, I read, yawning all the while, feeling
> bored and moaning about people who believe they have something to
> say, a message to impart! After looking at my watch, I had decided that
> the one I was about to read would be the last. The name of the author:
> Epstein, meant nothing to me and the work bore no title. With a supreme
> effort, I took it out of its folder and began to leaf through it; I had decided
> to devote a brief quarter of an hour to it. And suddenly I came to my
> senses. What I was reading was remarkable for its power and talent; if,
> as I believe, to write a novel is to create a life, the person who had dreamed
> up these pages was a first-rate novelist. I remained absorbed in what I
> was reading until eight o'clock, oblivious to everything else; I reread
> passages, I became more and more convinced and I wrote an enthusiastic
> report.[2]

Without waiting until the next day, Henry Muller – whose father
intended him to go into banking – entrusted this surprising and unusu-
ally harsh portrait of a certain way of life to his 'boss'. It was a 'business
novel' whose impetuousness was reminiscent of Paul Morand, but
tinged with a biblical morality and strewn with unadorned dialogue:
'Yes, but now, in 1926, don't you realise that your Russian oil fields
aren't worth shit to you? Well?'[3] A series of uppercuts, culminating in the
great sadistic scene in which Gloria sees her life of plenty threatened
by the wrath of David, her rebellious slave: 'I've never been unfaithful
to you. You can only be unfaithful to a husband . . . to a man who
actually sleeps with you . . . who satisfies you. As for you! You've been
a sick old man for years . . . a wreck.'[4] This mixture of modernity,
hysteria and triviality was astonishing. There was no respite in this
convulsive two-hundred-page death agony, but above all there was no

stepping back: if *David Golder* was a parable, don't rely on the author to reveal the motive. This was why in the earliest draft of the novel, when Gloria was still called Gladys, which was the version she sent to Grasset, Irène Némirovsky struck out the sentence with which she had at first thought of ending her novel: 'He entered into peace everlasting.' And this is probably why it is impossible to categorise this novel: whether it is an edifying foil or the ultimate in cynicism, it is a book without a vanishing point which polemicists of all opinions will seize on ad nauseam, reactionaries versus modernists, old fuddy-duddies versus feminists, and Jews against anti-Semites.

Grasset read it overnight. In the morning, he wrote an enthusiastic letter to 'M. Epstein', urging him to come quickly to sign a contract with a view to publication. Golder's doggedness very much appealed to this autodidact whose blunt business methods were derided by the playwright Édouard Bourdet in 1927. Whatever his detractors may say, David Golder is in fact neither a miser nor a nabob: if he handles so much money, it is so that he may remain afloat. If he stops waving his arms about, he will go under and all will go down with him. 'The tragedy of his life is that if he can't relax for a moment: if he stopped making money, he would have no more money!'[5] Bernard Grasset, similarly, swore by action alone. In 1928, he had just published a slim volume of *Remarques* on this subject, in which he wrote: 'For someone who is keen on action, money is merely a statement.' Terrified by boredom and routine, one of his frequent sayings was: 'Action is the supreme remedy, the consolation that never fails, the best way of taking your mind off things.'[6] *David Golder* would provide him with the opportunity to test his fox's cunning once more.

Ever since 1923 and the publication of Radiguet's *Le Diable au corps*, Bernard Grasset enshrined the American way of publishing, one that creates its market, dreams up its own clientele to which it recommends its products, just as Dr Knock* prescribed his remedies. A pirate of the publishing world, in much the same way as there are captains of industry, the literary supplement of the *New York Times* had just dubbed him the 'greatest of publishers'. An engineer of the 'news-

---

*Knock ou le Triomphe de la médecine was the title of a play by Jules Romains, first performed in 1923, in which Knock, a village doctor, persuaded all his patients that they were ill. This satire on human credulity and exploitation was made into a memorable film in 1933, with Louis Jouvet in the title role. [Tr.]

worthy event', governed purely by the laws of competition, this theorist of literary speculation saw the possibilities in Proust before the *NRF* [*Nouvelle Revue Française*]; the contents of a book, however, excited him less than its sales, which he viewed in sporting terms. And in this area, ever since *Maria Chapdelaine** (1921), Grasset created records. 'Those who want to be little-known artists, I leave to my confreres,'[7] says a character in Bourdet's play to this 'crocodile' with real teeth and real tears. For this monster also had his flaws: nerves that could be torn to shreds, which led him by turns into anger or depression. Blinkered, demanding and immoderate, he made life impossible for his colleagues. 'When you are near him, you no longer breathe, you no longer exist,' Jacques Chardonne testified. 'He himself suffocates in the space that he fills and quickly goes away to get a little air somewhere else. What he calls action is a way of speaking loudly. He cannot but impose himself.'[8] In a word, a despot, who in politics shared the uncompromising nationalism of Action française, to the extent that he printed Lambelin's *Les Protocoles des sages de Sion* or *Le Péril juif* (1928). But an enlightened despot, who would publish both the very Christian François Mauriac as well as that monument of sin, *David Golder*.

For Grasset was not born yesterday: the 'novel that spelled money' had the wind behind it. Without going back as far as Léon Daudet's *Le Bonheur d'être riche* (1917), he had enjoyed successes such as *Lewis et Irène* by Paul Morand in 1924 and *Inhumains* by Jacques Sahel in 1928. In 1926, in his roman à clef *Bella*, Jean Giraudoux had lent respectability to the 'Jewish businessman' by creating the character of Emmanuel Moïse, with his 'podgy oriental body' and motivated by the 'love of profit',[9] but also loyal and idealistic. All these books were published under the Grasset imprint, but in this year of 1929 it is also worth noting the publication by Kra of Philippe Soupault's *Le Grand Homme*. The subject matter of *David Golder*, in which the financial frenzy of the Roaring Twenties clashes with disinterested love and dignity, was so much 'in the air' that in 1927 Stefan Zweig made it the topic of a gripping short story. In 'Destruction of a Heart', old Salomonsohn, terminally ill and worn out by commerce and travelling since the age of twelve, decides to withdraw from business matters, never mind the fact that in so doing he is depriving an ungrateful wife and a 'brazen

*A very popular, posthumously published novel by Louis Hémon. [Tr.]

daughter' of their wealth. For he feels betrayed by this daughter, who he believes has become a girl of easy virtue. The curses, imbued with fatalism, that he calls down on the world of 'brigands' and the idle rich whom his wife and daughter frequent, anticipate those uttered by *dear old* Golder: 'One day, I will die like a dog, for I know that what is torturing me is not bile . . . it is death that is stirring within me . . . What kind of life have I led, always solely concerned with amassing money, money, money? . . . only ever for other people, and now what use is it to me?'[10] Curiously, the French translation of 'Destruction of a Heart' appeared in Les Œuvres libres in April 1928. Did Irène Némirovsky – who, incidentally, read German perfectly – know of this poignant 'Viennese short story' in which we see an enormously wealthy old lion ridding himself of his money and becoming an introvert? It would not seem unlikely. Yet the worship of materialism as opposed to the spiritual forces is a subject that lies deep in the heart of the 1920s. 'No one can serve two masters, God and Mammon': Mauriac himself had just published an essay on Christian morality on this maxim from the Gospel.[11]

A difficult convalescence

Three weeks passed without the mysterious author of *David Golder* deigning to collect her post. Three weeks during which the financial columns recorded two powerful tremors, the first on the economic front, the second of a political nature. The shock wave of Wall Street's 'Black Thursday', 24th October, would only really be felt in France a few years later, driving thousands of unemployed workers on to the streets; but the fraudulent bankruptcy of the Oustric bank, which specialised in speculative securities, provided the antiparliamentarians with the first weapons with which to castigate the corruption of the Republic. This scandal, exposed by *Le Canard enchaîné* in November 1929, echoed Golder's affairs remarkably. Apart from anything else, it was to provide the book with unfavourable publicity: some would be inclined to see Golder as the kind of banker who has neither belief nor patriotism, prospering dishonestly on the national soil. For ever since the indictment of the banker Marthe Hanau at the end of 1928, and the collapse of the Banque Lévy, which squandered state funds intended to compensate those wounded during the Great War, Jewish bankers had had rather a bad press in France.

October drew to a close, and the mysterious Epstein had still not come forward. 'It had reached such a point,' Muller wrote, 'that faced with this unusual silence, one of us had suggested putting an advertisement in the newspapers: "Seeking author, having sent manuscript to the publisher, Grasset, under the name Epstein."'[12] It seems likely that 'proofs' of the novel had already been circulated when Irène Epstein eventually made herself known at Rue des Saints-Pères after 'a difficult convalescence', because 'the press had been tipped off', she said, and 'everybody was searching for me'.[13] Furthermore, the child was born on 9th November and the young mother must have stayed in her bedroom for 'several weeks' before becoming aware that people were looking for her. For 'already, the publicity had aroused curiosity'.[14] Could they not have waited to meet her before going to press?

In *Les Chiens et les Loups*, Irène Némirovsky recalled this first, painful and premature childbirth: 'But why does it hurt so much? My God, will it never end? The worst moment came at the end of the night, at that moment when the pain seems unbearable, the moment when you fear you will surely die.'[15] It was a little girl. Her parents gave her three decidedly French first names: Denise, France, Catherine. Before setting off for Rue des Saints-Pères, her first outing since giving birth, Irène Némirovsky entrusted her baby to Cécile, the young woman who had just come to work for her and whom they nicknamed 'Néné', appropriately for a wet-nurse. Irène had seen her working at the home of her friend and neighbour, the daughter of the celebrated radiologist Félix Lobligeois. For the first months, however, Denise – 'or Minouche in private' – would be fed by her own mother. 'She doesn't look at all like me,' wrote Irène to her old friend, Madeleine, on 22nd January 1930; 'she is almost blonde with grey eyes but I think they are still changing.'[16]

Cécile Michaud lived in rue Monge, but she was born in a town in the Morvan, Issy-l'Évêque, on 24th November 1904, the same day in the Gregorian calendar, one year apart, as Irène Némirovsky. This coincidence would draw them still closer.

'You know, I'm not rich,' Cécile said to her, describing her social background.

'But you are well off, my dear Néné, well off compared to those who were in Russia!'

These close ties would be stretched quite far: Néné, who was well paid and did not wear a uniform, accompanied her 'boss' to the theatre, to the cinema, on holiday to Mégève or Villars-de-Lans, and even into the secrecy of the study where she wrote. 'I read all her books and I recognised the people . . . She used to say to me: "You must tell me whom this reminds you of" . . . She wrote at any time, without making a fuss. And she always knitted as she read. I knew her friends, Mme Hélène Lazareff, for instance . . .'[17]

If we are to believe the gilded legend of *David Golder*, Irène Némirovsky is supposed to have arrived at the Grasset publishing house three weeks after giving birth, which would have been at the very end of November 1929. The violence of the early pages of the novel, the power of the dialogue, the stock exchange vocabulary, the elimin-ation of any sentimentality led people to imagine that this was another Paul Morand, less sophisticated and gruffer, but a man. It was a woman who was asked into the publisher's office, 'a shy woman, as in the story about the Brontë sisters'.[18] She announced herself with:

'Forgive me for not coming sooner . . . I've just had a baby. I'm the author of *David Golder*: Irène Némirovsky.'[19]

Small, slender and probably exhausted by childbirth: did Bernard Grasset think of her as that 'unattractive, pronounced Jewish type' that certain curiously informed critics reported? 'The dark, heavy-lidded eyes express a sort of mischievous sweetness, but no more than that. Her short plastered-down hair accentuates the narrowness of her head, which protrudes at the back. Her plump lips smile openly. She comports herself with a well-to-do elegance, the result of an irre-proachable early education.'[20] A radiant and blushing young mother, a disillusioned novel about cruel, dark deeds, a Russian émigrée writing in French, a Jewess furthermore, who did no favours to her own people: Grasset was immediately aware of what he might gain from this prodigy. He told the young woman straight away that her novel would be published in the 'Pour mon plaisir' series, a private hunting ground restricted to books that were representative of his own personal tastes and that had recently included *Les Varais* by Jacques Chardonne, Cocteau's *Les Enfants terribles* and Giono's *Un de Beaumugnes*. As he handed her the contracts to be signed, between two puffs of his cigarette, Grasset, ever the flatterer, with his small moustache and drooping lock of hair, spoke to her more or less as follows:

'A publishing house is a large anthill, or, if you prefer, a large and continuous hive of activity, the running of which fully engrosses me. There is actually very little room for dreaming . . . Producing just anything is not my way and I have always aimed at being able to be defined by what I publish . . . I have faith in the talent of women, or certain women, at least.'[21]

In half an hour, she had just bound her fate to the most unpredictable of publishers. Barely one week after this meeting, on 5th December, the first copies of the book had been printed and bound: Grasset obviously did things well, but above all, he did them . . . quickly. Irène dedicated one copy informally to Fanny: 'To my dearest mother, in memory of Riri.'

The Goriot strategy

Bernard Grasset had already finalised his plans. On 7th December, with a publicist's instinct, he put a display advertisement in *Les Nouvelles littéraires* that was intended to stir up rumours. With infallible judgement he tossed the name of Balzac among the arts columns, certain that it would either be followed up or challenged, which amounted to much the same thing:

> Here is a book that, in my judgement, should go far. It is not only a
> fictional creation of great merit, it is a penetrating insight into our times
> and the particular characters who assume the struggle for existence. An
> entire philosophy of love, ambition and money emerges from this novel
> which, in its power and its very subject, recalls *Le Père Goriot* and which
> is nonetheless extremely original.

And, just as he made the author of *Le Diable au corps*, Raymond Radiguet, younger, with the sole purpose of creating gossip, he suggested to the author of *David Golder* that from now on she be born in 1905, a lie she would discharge honourably, confusing the dates only occasionally. During the next few days, serialised extracts appeared in *L'Intransigeant*, *L'Œuvre*, *La Volonté*, *L'Ami du peuple* and numerous other journals, usually accompanied by paragraphs associating the novel with Balzac's 'picturesqueness', but also with the naturalism of Dickens or Zola. It was excessive, but all is fair in love and war: the critics would all be swept into the trap. Mirbeau, Daudet, Bernstein, Shakespeare, Dostoyevsky, Tolstoy, the Tharaud brothers, Giraudoux, Proust, Morand, Kessel, Martin du Gard and even Malraux: rarely had so many writers' names been invoked in order to argue the toss over Grasset's discovery and to assess the talent of a writer who had only her book with which to defend herself. 'Grasset is a publicity ace,' she would admit. 'I'm not going to deny it and I would never dream of complaining about it.'[22] At the time, she had not even read *Le Père Goriot*!

Four days before Christmas, the book was on sale. Price, 15 francs. For two weeks the grapevine did its work, without the public being able to discover anything specific about the mysterious author of *David Golder*, whose name was so difficult to pronounce that some, confusing it with that of Hélène Iswolsky,[23] author of *Vie de Bakounine*, published by Gallimard, as well as a volume of Russian memoirs, confused her first name. The first reviewers went to some trouble to criticise the brouhaha drummed up by Grasset. Almost all of them, however, fell into the trap of playing the game of literary groupings. If the majority of them looked for French parallels, the most perceptive was probably Gaston de Pawlowski, in *Gringoire*, who likened the death of Golder to that of Ivan Ilyich. And in Tolstoy's novella, in fact, Ilyich's wife cannot reconcile herself to seeing her wages disappear with her husband, however much she may secretly long to see him die; while Ilyich discovers, as he deteriorates, that his whole life has been a façade designed to conceal his own fate from him. One might add that Golder's final moments are also reminiscent of those of Vassili Andreevich in *Master and Man* who thinks back to his childhood before giving up the ghost. In 1933, Irène Némirovsky would acknowledge this debt: 'As far as Russia is concerned, I place no one above Tolstoy; he has everything. I believe the French, in general, prefer Dostoyevsky, but I do not share this taste: Dostoyevsky is a purely Russian genre, Tolstoy is human; *The Death of Ivan Ilyich*, for example, can be understood by any man, old and sick and frightened of dying, whereas to put yourself in the mind of Raskolnikov or the Idiot you need a particular mentality and, to tell the truth, to be slightly mad . . .'[24]

Others compared her to Balzac. In *Liberté*, an already established critic, Robert Kemp, one of the first to assess *David Golder*, fell into the trap like a novice: 'An excellent novel reminiscent of Balzac. All the characteristic features are vigorously applied . . . It really is a powerful piece.'[25] The reviewers, even the most perceptive of them, ploughed this furrow, referring, as Maurois did, to an 'illegitimate Père Goriot' or, like Crémieux, to an 'extravagance worthy of Balzac'. If they did break free from the 'Goriot strategy' devised by Grasset, it was in order to compare Golder to Nucingen or Gobsek, which amounted to the same thing. And if they preferred to allude to Daumier, Dickens or Zola in order to prove their point, it was again so as to emphasise Irène Némirovsky's pitiless realism. Even Henri de Régnier in *Le Figaro*, while refusing to be taken in by the 'tricks of extravagant advertising', nevertheless discussed 'the flattering epithet *"balzacien"*' coined by Grasset on the back cover of this novel of 'robust talent' and 'very assured skill'.[26]

Very little, however, was yet known about the author, apart from the fact that she was Jewish, Russian and very young, and that her father was a banker – sufficient distilled information to feed speculations as to the apparent paradoxes of a book devoid of charity. Henry Muller, riding high after his discovery, had praises heaped upon him all over Paris 'for sharing his convictions, expressing his judgement and communicating his enjoyment'.[27] And justifiably so, for at the beginning of 1930, Marcel Thiébaut could write: 'In a few days, *David Golder* has been dignified as the "subject of conversation" in salons . . . Here and there people have spoken of its "torrential power", its "exceptional power", of a book "worthy of Balzac" and of a "masterpiece".'[28]

This word 'masterpiece' was used for the first time in black and white by the well-known writer André Thérive in his weekly column in *Le Temps*, on 10th January 1930: 'There can be no doubt, *David Golder* is a masterpiece.' In this atmosphere of indiscretions and overexcitement, his long article was a model of perception and composure. The only critic to mention the name of Paul Morand, he refuted the parallel with *Père Goriot*. 'David Golder is more human (I am not afraid to say) and has experienced the futility of his existence, the crassness of his illusions. His story is so cruel, so shocking, and so appallingly sad that no epic greatness attaches to him, and yet I wonder whether true greatness lies where there is nothing imposing.'[29] Thérive was one of the few to notice that Golder is as indifferent to money as he is to fresh air, and without once mentioning the word, he refuses to see the book as a portrait of the world of Jewish high finance; it is instead 'the death throes of a true man who hasn't known how to live and doesn't dare die'. 'I think I can safely say,' he concluded, 'that this book barely begins to describe his life and his story.'

This article would serve as a yardstick for all the others. Up until the autumn of 1930, people would not stop discussing this word: a masterpiece. Overcoming his 'distaste for the subjects that are dealt with', the popular Daniel-Rops praised the 'excellent technique'[30] of the tale. The lawyer and writer Pierre Lœwel, in the latest addition to the nationalist press, L'Ordre, used the word 'miracle'.[31] Edmond Jaloux said he was 'astounded'.[32] André Maurois surrendered to this 'tone of truth . . . almost painful'.[33] Paul Reboux, in Paris-Soir, alluded to 'a first-rate etching' and hailed Irène Némirovsky's 'extraordinary importance' and her 'surprising gifts'. Even the ultra-nationalist Action française, in spite of the fact that it was scarcely an appetising subject – these 'princely games that we, Christians, pay for' – had to confess to being won over by the author's daring: 'David Golder does not appeal to the higher parts of our intellect, and the style is not even of the kind to provide us with discerning pleasures, but this novel has the prime virtue of a novel: it is alive.'[34]

A 'fine book that stinks'

On 18th January, weighed down by the laudatory press-cuttings, Grasset was able to put triumphant inserts in the daily press: 'One has to go back a very long way to find similar critical praise coinciding with such enthusiasm from the public . . . The public, who are not taken in by a lot of long words, are discovering that this is the most captivating, most fascinating novel that we have published in ten years.'[35] It was an achievement that was all the more real because Irène Némirovsky, who was careful to write personally to each of the reviewers who had written favourably about her novel, had not yet experienced success. 'In these conditions of penury, one can admit, of course, to not having received any compliments.'[36] In the brief letter she sent to Henri de Régnier, she naturally expressed the 'extraordinary feeling of pride and joy' that his article in *Le Figaro* had given her, but she also revealed her astonishment at the eulogistic welcome from the French press:

> For it certainly never occurred to me that the great writer I admired from so far should not only read a book I had written but speak about it so favourably. I put all this very badly. I don't know whether my career as a writer will be fortunate or not, but you can be sure that I will never forget the effect that your invaluable encouragement has had on me.

Everyone shared her incredulity. Some quite simply refused to believe that the author of this 'dark, hard, granite-like and bleak islet, in the midst of the ocean of life'[37] could be a young woman of twenty-four, as was alleged. '*David Golder* bears the signature of a woman; we must therefore accept that it is by a woman,'[38] admitted André Billy reluctantly. It was therefore not completely by error that *L'Intermédiaire des éditeurs, imprimeurs, libraires, papetiers et interessés de la presse et du livre* announced on 5th January that the author's real name was René Némirovsky! The women's magazines were not in the least disconcerted by this distressing book, which surpassed Colette in audacity. Virility, strength, vigour, cynicism, bitterness, darkness, cruelty, pessimism, power, 'a male grip' and even 'muscle' were the words most frequently used to convey the astonishment of reviewers, who were not used to being treated so brutally by a young foreign woman. The magazine *Fantasio*, where Irène took her first steps as a writer, wondered, with its habitual misogyny, 'how a woman could have written a book in which there is not a single trivial remark, no softness, not an adjective too many', delivering her sentences on the page 'like a steam-hammer on the pavements'.[39] Princesse Bibesco's *Les Quatre Portraits*, which was published at the same time, but also the other new books written by women disappeared from the shelves within six months. Irène Némirovsky knew only too well why this was: 'Young Frenchwomen have not usually had the human experiences that circumstances . . . have allowed me to acquire: the world of Jewish high finance with all the dramas, the bankruptcies and the catastrophes that occur daily, the journeys, revolution . . .'[40]

For more traditionalist or reactionary readers such as André Bellessort, *David Golder* was notable mainly for its monstrous subject – this world of 'rogues' and 'whores' – and for the indecency of the language, unworthy of a young woman. Bellessort claimed that it was misleading to attach manly qualities to flappers of the Irène Némirovsky mould, when the only quality they borrow from men is their coarseness: 'We are returning to a situation similar to that in the middle ages and the sixteenth century, when women used the same crudity in their language, even in their writing, as men.'[41] Many of the second-rate, tight-lipped, often provincial newspapers,[42] exaggerating the theme of filth, forecast the decadence of literature, symptomatic of a corrupt society. 'Are we moving towards a world which will be as ugly in its reality as it is in its writing?'[43] grumbled the daily arts paper *Comœdia*. The elderly Antoine Redier in the ailing *Revue française*, in which Robert Brasillach and his friends first started, disparaged a 'nauseating... dreadful and pernicious book'.[44] Even André Thérive, albeit secretly thrilled, was obliged to point out to his readers that all was not in the 'best taste' in Joyce's very suggestive responses, particularly when she reveals to Golder that Hoyos – her real father – watched her making love with her gigolo ...

We are obliged to recognise that as far as caricature and coarseness were concerned *David Golder* was unparalleled. For some of the Catholic press, the pandemonium, which was not recommended to young, female readers, at least had the merit of providing a contrast: 'You close it and you hate money.'[45] For the more political papers, on the other hand, this repelling portrait of a 'financial bastard'[46] and the rootless Biarritz society had documentary value: 'Irène Némirovsky examines a debased and rotten society like an examining magistrate; her book is the trial of wealth, and of pleasure at all costs.'[47] And through a series of more or less subtle innuendos, the majority of them did not fail to emphasise that the characters in this 'veritable gathering of wild beasts'[48] were an 'old lecherous Jew'[49] and 'a financier's wife from the appalling race of Jezebel'.[50]

The left was no less harsh about the 'repulsive world of business and pleasures' that this 'fine book that stinks'[51] portrays from life. In pure proletarian style, *Le Libertaire* did not fail to detect the state of moral gangrene in the world of high finance, but nevertheless remained tight-lipped as far as the 'filthy language' and the 'display of smut'[52] that the author had accumulated were concerned. Only the right-wing press let drop the words 'Jewish' or 'cosmopolitan' to refer to this portrait of the business world, depending on what position they adopted. André Bellessort, calling a spade a spade, summed up his view in forthright terms: 'It is a brutal portrait of the millionaire underworld, American or Jewish, that spends extravagantly and invests the gold that it pilfers from markets all over the world in jewellery.' Thus, from being the story of a family transfigured by the imagination, *David Golder* was taken, in certain newspapers, as a satire on Jewish finance and the 'dogged know-how of the sons of the ghetto, the conquerors and masters of wealth, in pursuit of their prey'.[53] In an identical misunderstanding, the Marxist press interpreted it as 'a little tirade against the USSR',[54] propagated by the heir of an old-style banker. Communists and anti-Semites both wanted to give the same dog a bad name: so they accused *Golder* of rabies . . .

An authentic tale

On 11th January, however, the 'Némirovsky enigma' was partly lifted. 'A full, sensual mouth, soot-black hair, hard features',[55] her face finally appeared on the front page of *Nouvelles littéraires*, sketched by the cartoonist Jean Texcier whose *Conseils à l'occupé* ('Advice to the Occupied') would be one of the founding texts of the Resistance in August 1940. This portrait illustrated the first interview with the author of *David Golder* by a veteran of literary discussions, Frédéric Lefèvre, who conducted his interviews in the way a general wages battle, sometimes forgetting to turn up – as a result, there were often ellipses in the place of questions he had not asked. At Avenue Daniel-Lesueur, Lefèvre was greeted by a 'good-looking Jewish woman': 'Of medium height, her slender figure swells from a tight-fitting purple velvet dress; her hair, which is as black as jet or a crow – well, the blackest you can imagine – is cut *à la garçonne*; her eyes are black, just as black as her hair; they have that strange softness – at times barely blinking – that creates a slightly short-sighted look.'[56] Throughout 1930, many journalists would want to see this phenomenon with their own eyes, and they would discover, instead of 'the sort of ferocious virago, an intellectual fed on figures, a masculine suffragette'[57] that her novel might lead one to expect, 'an almost fragile appearance, with a very feminine charm, and a soft, bright face',[58] laughing and so natural that you rub your eyes rereading her book.

Lefèvre's article, 'An hour with Irène Némirovsky', would be copiously plagiarised throughout that year. In it the novelist lists her trinity of favourite authors: Proust, Larbaud, Chardonne. Giving a broad outline of her life, she mischievously insists on the date of birth advocated by Grasset, for 'I know you like accuracy'. Lefèvre, who was no fool, echoed the suspicions that inevitably surrounded the premature fairy tale and the meteor that had fallen on Grasset's offices in Rue des Saints-Pères. Two months later, in *Chantecler*, Claude Pierrey voiced the doubts of a large part of the press:

'It is said, Madame . . .'

'What? Tell me . . .'

'Firstly, that you are very rich, and that the publicity, paid for by you, has merely exploited the clever story of the poste restante address, and also the touching one about you having given birth . . .'

'Oh! my God! How amusing . . . Rich? According to . . . I'm not poor, of course. But is this condition a requirement of talent? As to the *story*, it's authentic, whether you like it or not.'[59]

Not everyone would find these responses satisfactory. Sometimes sarcastically, sometimes out of exasperation, a certain number of critics openly criticised the publicity methods used by Grasset, whom the Minister for Trade and Industry had just decorated with the Légion d'honneur. They refused to be bound by his decrees and they rechristened his series 'Notre bon plaisir'.*[60] If they are to be believed, the 'publisher in search of an author'[61] was not content with just putting out 'wanted' posters, he also enlisted the support of columnists and aroused their curiosity by asking them, in a succession of 'memos' sent to the press, to help him find the mysterious 'M. Epstein'. From early September 1929, there were certain gossip columnists who did not beat about the bush and who referred ironically to the international success that was already looming: 'Curiosity is a strange thing! Due to the fact that its author had been lost for a few weeks, the manuscript of the book entitled *David Golder* is already being translated into English, German and Hungarian, before it has even been published in French.'[62] Yet even those who had been most upset by this behaviour, such as Noël Sabord,[63] were obliged to recognise the talent of Irène Némirovsky.

*The phrase suggests the royal injuction: '*Tel est notre bon plaisir*' (Such is our desire). [Tr.]

The great attraction

Some people were already predicting that the Femina prize would be awarded to this 'striking Jewish woman', who within a month had become *the great attraction** at all the parties'. With perfect composure, she responded with a smile: 'Perhaps in the meantime, M. de Rothschild will have set up a prize!'[64] In the end, *David Golder* would not obtain any award. For Paul Reboux this was proof of its importance. In 1928, Grasset pointed out to Mauriac: 'Nowadays, I publish only books that can do very well without the Goncourt!' Seeing the success of his methods, he would soon be able to treat those who complained with scorn.

Though she accepted her triumph with a smile, Irène Némirovsky herself was a little taken aback by it. To Madeleine, who, aware of her sudden celebrity, was offended not to have received an inscribed copy from 'Topsy', she objected with false modesty and feigned indignation: 'How can you suppose that I would forget my old friends like that because of a book which people talk about for a fortnight and which will soon be forgotten just as everything is forgotten in Paris. It's not kind to think that.'[65] In Paris she received compliments from Jacques-Émile Blanche, the artist who painted the portraits of Proust, Gide, Anna de Noailles and the whole of Paris society, who sent her his latest novel and invited her to visit him at the studio of his home in Auteuil. At the same time, the novelist from the Berry province, Gaston Chérau, so distinguished behind his cavalry officer moustache that he could boast about his friendship with both Léon Blum and Léon Daudet, did Irène Némirovsky the honour of recommending her to the Société des Gens de Lettres, which was founded in 1838 to protect authors' interests. The application was supported by Roland Dorgelès, whose recommendation consisted of two lines: 'When you have written *David Golder*, do you need sponsors? I am very happy to support Madame Irène Némirovsky's application.'

All these compliments should have flattered her. In reality, her sudden notoriety was a challenge to her pride. Would she be capable of repeating this masterstroke and prove herself worthy, without publicity, of the critics' respect? 'I wait,' she confessed to the reporter

*In English in text. [Tr.]

from *Paris-Midi*. 'I'm frightened . . .'[66] For almost three years these
qualms would prevent her from writing a second novel. She had
warned Lefèvre moreover: 'I am not a literary woman. I don't want
to write for the sake of writing. Writing for me is such a rare kind of
pleasure that I can't imagine giving myself up to it out of duty or
because I had decided to do so. After *David Golder*, therefore, it will
probably be several years before I start anything else.' In actual fact,
Le Bal – for which Grasset secured an exclusive contract on 4th April
– was already written. *Le Malentendu* [The Misunderstood], published
hurriedly by Fayard in its 'Collection de bibliothèque' series, was not
a new work. *Snow in Autumn* [*Les Mouches d'automne*] was based on
'La Niania'. So we would have to wait for *The Courilof Affair* [*L'Affaire
Courilof*], at the end of 1932, to obtain a clearer idea of Irène
Némirovsky's true talent. In 1930, she found herself furthermore at
the heart of a controversy that further complicated her antinomic
image of a shy young mother and a novelist without scruples. Floated
by the Jewish press, the charge of latent anti-Semitism in *David Golder*
looked as if it were the price she had to pay for her fame. For this
suspicion came not so much from reading the novel as from the opinions it had aroused. These accusations were not really brought until
February, however, when almost everything had already been said
about *David Golder*.

A Jewish novel?

It had clearly not escaped anyone's notice that from old Golder to the
young emigrant boy who helps him as he is dying, all the characters
in the novel – Gloria, his daughter Joyce, Tubingen, Marcus, Soifer
and Fischl – are Jews. For some, this particular feature merely placed
David Golder in the category of 'Jewish novels', often rather laboured
– though instructive – illustrations of various vicissitudes of the 'Jewish
soul' that a certain Jacob Lévy had made popular in the 1920s. But
why, wondered Marcel Thiébaut, for instance, did Irène Némirovsky
feel she had to contribute to the commonplace of greed, personified
by the old miser Soifer, who is mortified at the idea of buying his
wife a hat, when 'the Jews, on the contrary, are thought to have retained
a less self-seeking family spirit'?[67] Even those who worried that the

characters in *David Golder* did harm to Jews did not dispute the truth of such well-worn clichés as 'a liking for money', 'the fear of death' or 'family feeling' among the other characteristics that *Le Courrier littéraire* listed for its readers.[68] Compared sometimes to Ahasuerus, sometimes to Moses or King David, Golder is either a modern version of the colourful Ukrainian Jew or the 'desert pilgrim' out of a story by the Tharaud brothers, with whom she was frequently compared (not without an ulterior motive),[69] or else a patriarch who has renounced worldly goods: 'David Golder is not bothered about himself, or his own happiness. His happiness has been to bring firstly his wife, then later his daughter, over to the Promised Land. To do so, he does not hesitate to work himself to death, to bring things to a conclusion even when he knows there is no hope for him, and one wonders whether this endless *longing* for future joy, expressed so powerfully by the Jewish race, is not, deep down, one that vaguely motivates all men.' In almost every instance, Golder is a Balzac 'type' and the novel is 'the study of a race' (*La Voix*), 'a precise and striking portrait of international Jewry – and particularly those encountered in Biarritz'.[70] For anti-Semites, whether professed or not, this type is the businessman 'pursuing the possession of riches and the joys of this earth all over the world with the same eagerness that they display in the pursuit of heavenly things'.[71] This intention appears all the more blatant in that Irène Némirovsky was not hiding herself away and was, she said, merely scrutinising her own origins:

'If I have been able to reflect the Jewish soul, it is – you may have guessed – because I am Jewish myself. I have known the financial circles all my life, and I thought there was a tempting subject there. And then I think that there are too many young heroes in French novels. Too much romanticism as well . . . Foreign literature, English in particular, pays more attention to the old man . . .'[72]

Many were not surprised by this. André Billy considered *David Golder* much closer to *Les Métèques* by the 'nice Binet-Valmer' than to *Le Père Goriot*: 'I am told moreover that Mme Némirovsky is Jewish. This does not surprise me; only a Jewess could write such a terrible and such a perceptive indictment of the Jewish passion for wealth.'[73] From *Action française* to *Comœdia*, this common-or-garden psychology was widely shared; but it was *Fantasio* again which gloated most crudely about what it took to be a satire on the nouveaux riches seen through the character of Fischl, 'the old, lecherous Jew'. Its columnist – probably Juven – had not taken the trouble to read the novel in detail, merely seeing in it what he wished to see: 'It is likely that Gloria's real name is Agar, Séphora, or something similar: and that of Joyce, Ruth or Bethsabée; but we are not told. Fine Jewish ladies conceal nothing so much of themselves as their Palestinian first name. These ones are dreadful! They are always in need of money.'[74]

Even those writers best disposed to the 'Jewish novel', who likened Irène Némirovsky to Panaït Istrati, Elissa Rhaïs and Lacretelle, saw nothing in *David Golder* other than an exercise in 'particularism', the author's skill consisting entirely in gathering together 'a synthesis of the Jewish spirit'[75] in the principal character. And yet before finally completing her manuscript, she had been careful to tone down this tendency, striking out on the first page of the manuscript the direct reference to Marcus's 'pale and nimble Jewish hands'.[76] But thanks to the Tharauds, Binet and many others, the French public had grown accustomed to recognising instantly the figure of the medieval Jew from imperceptible stereotypes that are as old as literature; similarly, it has been little remarked upon that the cliché of the financier who is 'king of the world' is the same here as the Gundemann whom Zola portrays in *L'Argent* or Maupassant's Andermatt in *Mont-Oriol*. In some ways, even if *David Golder* is not anti-Semitic, it runs the risk of being considered and even appreciated as such. Jean Blaize, in *La Dépêche*, had detected this danger all too clearly: 'If Mme Némirovsky were not Jewish, people would see anti-Semitism in this book. Some will see it in any case.'[77]

Pride and prejudice

'The Jewish public will read *David Golder* with passionate interest,' Lefèvre had prophesied. Except for the fact that the Zionist press was virulent in its reaction. Pierre Paraf, in *L'Illustration juive*, was one of the first to be critical of the businessman, Golder, as being the very embodiment of the 'Jew for anti-Semites'. In *Reveil juif*, a revisionist weekly paper published in Tunisia, the novelist Ida-Rosette See agreed that *David Golder* was 'a masterpiece', but a masterpiece of denial: 'in fact, despite Mme Irène Némirovsky's qualities of style and technique, all the Jews she portrays in *David Golder* are unpleasant ... We know that this image of Jews as "gold or oil tycoons" pleases a large number of anti-Semites, and we don't have sufficient a sense of adulation to add our own poor flattery to that of so many important figures in order to congratulate a Jewish woman (?) for having described loathsome Jews and Jewesses so well! . . .'[78]

What was she blamed for? For having blackened the picture she paints for dramatic ends, on the pretext that literature is not composed of fine feelings. 'Besides, what could be more ridiculous than blowing one's own trumpet?' the journalist Janine Auscher would plead in 1935. 'I realise that what we criticise in a Zangwill or a Némirovsky reveals our frailties to others by making them public; it is quite clear that if these books were just circulated among ourselves, we would not dream of treating them so harshly . . .'[79] But that she should have preferred sarcasm to ingenuousness, and self-mockery to parochialism, that is what struck many as incomprehensible – and it is what justifies, moreover, the literary importance of *David Golder*. This artistic calculation is not the least of the grievances that could be held against her. But Irène Némirovsky was only prepared to consider her own work. 'It is absolutely certain that had there been Hitler, I would have greatly softened *David Golder*, and I would not have written it in the same way,' she was to say after the advent of Nazism. 'And yet I would have been wrong, it would have been a weakness unworthy of a real writer!' This pride – her pride – was in her opinion the best legacy she inherited from her bloodline. So much so that with *David Golder* she believed, on the contrary, that she had exalted the Jewish soul in all its intrepidness and, ultimately, its selflessness: 'How unfair to claim that, even with them, I have only depicted their faults. It seems to me that, on the contrary, and it's something I'm proud of, I've depicted genuinely racial virtues: courage, tenacity, pride – yes, indeed, in its better sense – in a word, "guts".'[80]

This fact was completely overlooked by the 'Jewish public', who criticised her for portraying characters who inspired at best pity, at worst repugnance. Unlike the Zionist newspapers, *L'Univers israélite* was an unofficial mouthpiece of the Central Consistory of Paris and, as such, rather more in favour of Republican assimilation and patriotic Judaism. It, too, had serious reservations and, in late February, sent an embarrassed journalist to Irène Némirovsky's home to cross-question her. There was an indignant response from the novelist:

'I'm accused of anti-Semitism? Come now, that's absurd! For I'm Jewish myself and say so to anyone prepared to listen!'

'But did you know that our enemies are making use of your characters and are drawing some very disagreeable conclusions from them about Jews?' Nina Gourfinkel pressed on . . . 'Aren't you afraid of providing them with a weapon against Jews? . . . Why is there not a single allusion to a more sympathetic Jewish society in your book?'

To each of these criticisms, Irène Némirovsky, much dismayed, countered with the strength of her own evidence: 'Nevertheless, that's the way I saw them . . .'[81]

Those she depicts in this way are not Jews as a whole, but those she observed in 'the corrupt, cosmopolitan circles' of hotels and casinos. Hoyos and Alec, she argued, are scarcely any better, so *David Golder* is more the portrait of a social milieu than it is of a race, in the current terminology. She told herself not to spare anyone and she did not feel bound by any loyalty, or any indulgence just because of the coincidence of her birth. Had *David Golder* been written in 2009 by Bernard Madoff's daughter, who would dream of accusing her of anti-Semitic views? 'What would François Mauriac say if all the people from the Landes suddenly rose up against him and blamed him for portraying them in such a brutal manner? . . . Did the middle-class people of the Marais think of identifying themselves with those from Francis Carco's "milieu"? Then why should French Jews wish to recognise themselves in *David Golder*? The disproportion is the same.'[82] And let no one counter with Silbermann, Lacretelle's good-natured hero, who justifies his Jewish identity not by ancestry, but by his experience of being treated with loathing. 'I like Lacretelle very much. He is a great novelist. But does he know the Jews at close quarters?'[83] From this reply, we can see that Irène Némirovsky was tempted to generalise her own experience, without bothering to embellish it. Would she have had more consideration for the public if she had been able to anticipate her success?

This line of defence – 'that's the way I saw them' – was one Henry Bernstein had favoured when, in 1908, Jews and anti-Semites criticised him with one accord for the caricature of their respective positions in his play *Israël*. 'I am very happy to be a Jew,' the playwright gallantly replied in *Le Matin*. . . . 'I feel strongly that I owe this secret appetite for life that we call temperament, which makes an artist of one, principally to my origins . . . I feel myself totally incapable of putting on stage anything other than a little vague, faltering, bleeding humanity . . . I see it like that . . . It's not my fault! . . .'[84] It is certainly not merely for its mastery of muffled dialogue or its irrepressible energy that a number of critics have compared *David Golder* with *Israël* and *Samson*: no writer since Bernstein had, as Irène Némirovsky had done, refused so forcefully to conform to the so-called communal reactions, nor demolished the myth of Jewish solidarity in such a way by over-exaggerating the behaviour of a decadent fringe which she wholeheartedly condemned, having suffered from its materialism. 'A difficult and precocious experience, an experience that was partial, dreary and narrow',[85] certainly, but which was enough to explain a great deal, as Nina Gourfinkel eventually acknowledged when she took her leave.

Irène Némirovsky was a novelist, not a preacher. That is why she took trouble to remove any moralising from her book. And while Bernstein dealt with such solemn subjects as anti-Semitism (*Israël*) or class prejudice (*Samson*[86]), she added an almost unbearable irony and a good deal of contempt, which shows just how much she was affected by this matter. She was paying now for this freedom of expression. What is more, she was unable to admit for a second that she had put a large amount of herself into *David Golder*, and even more of her mother, so much so that people would do better to accuse her of filial disrespect. Even if, as Paul Reboux maintained in *Paris-Soir*, she had been heard to remark ingenuously: 'I don't know why they are making so much fuss about this little book . . . I simply drew a portrait of papa and mama . . .'

All things considered, the 'Goriot strategy' devised by Bernard Grasset had been the actual cause of the witchcraft proceedings brought against the young novelist. For the vast majority of the critics, who did their utmost to find 'types' in this book that are not there, tried to represent it as a depiction of the 'moneyed Jew' instead of the Tolstoyan fable that the author's own life had inspired. If, indeed, there is a 'type', it is that of the reckless self-made man, dragged by the sleeve out of his own poverty, and here, for the sake of reality, portrayed in the surroundings she knew best, but who is to be found in many different aspects in the rest of her work right up to Daguerne, the very French orphan, in *La Proie* [The Victim], whose ambition alone helps him work his way up to the top through political wheeling and dealing. For David and Gloria are not driven by a craving for gold, but by the threatening memory of their poverty, which he continuously struggles against and she casts aside in terror. How was Irène Némirovsky able to anticipate the totalitarian pogroms prophesied by Albert Londres in a long report, published a month after *David Golder*, which predicted both Auschwitz and Babi Yar? 'In Russia, the Jews expect to be slaughtered. The day that the Soviets give ground, the Red Cross can get its ambulances ready. The Aryan mob will use its fangs.'[87]

In this poisonous climate, one would have had to have been a very perceptive and very phlegmatic reader to see that Irène Némirovsky had simply dealt with a universal subject from her own viewpoint – 'fear of death',[88] 'the Jewish dread of death'[89] possibly, and the panic that it instils in its victims, whether on account of pride (David), lust (Joyce) or greed (Gloria). And this is probably why Henri de Régnier was thanked so warmly for having noticed that her novel was not in any way what it was accused of being:

> With her *David Golder*, Mme Irène Némirovsky introduces us not to the world of Jewish high finance, but to that category of businessmen, speculators and moneymen who operate outside and beneath it and are like its foam and its wash . . . Starting out with nothing, going from pittance to pittance, from rung to rung, he [Golder] has climbed his way to power. He has climbed his way up through his intelligence, his energy, his courage, his obstinacy, without pity for himself or for others. He has lived a hard life and worked ferociously. He has succeeded. A great deal of money has passed through his hands, but David Golder is not a miser, he has not hoarded money. He is a speculator, a business venturer, a gambler who always put back what he has gained for the next game . . . Certainly, the human material that Mme Némirovsky assembles is somewhat repellent, but she has observed it with keen curiosity, and she manages to communicate this curiosity to us, and make us share it. The interest is stronger than the aversion.[90]

Nina Gourfinkel, in order to help guard against the undesirable effects of *David Golder*, reached the same conclusion: Golder, a rootless and amoral creature, had not an atom of Jewishness left in him. He was one of those dregs washed up at Biarritz, 'that ultra-cosmopolitan resort, home of the Internationale of money, that has renounced traditions, breeding, the earth, and everything that does honour to mankind'. The subject of the novel is neither the 'genius' nor the characteristics of Jews, it is the universal theme of human degradation. 'Golder is what he is, not because he is a Jew, but because he has stopped being one.'[91] After her encounter with the novelist, when she was won over by her arguments, Nina Gourfinkel wrote an angry 'non-proven' article in *L'Univers israélite*, pleading immunity for the accused: 'Irène Némirovsky is certainly not anti-Semitic, any more than she is Jewish. For just as one cannot judge the French according to those districts of Paris that are fitted out according to the presumed taste of "foreigners", so one cannot judge a race according to a few individuals who are devoid of all moral sense and whose real homeland is a fashionable beach resort where all the wastrels of every nation mix with one another.'[92] By the end of 1930, the view at last prevailed that any ideological reading of *David Golder* was unjustified. The book is above all a fictional accomplishment, and it was this aspect alone that would interest the American press, whose opinion is summed up by the *New York Herald Tribune*: 'This powerful tale transcends any racial or geographical features, and it unfurls effortlessly and with great power from its frantic opening up to its inevitable conclusion.'[93] A real piece of theatre machinery, which crushes any moral considerations in its way.

A tragedy worthy of Bernstein

An anti-Semitic novel, a Jewish novel, an immoral novel: none of these phrases was accurate, but together they were responsible for turning Irène Némirovsky into another Henry Bernstein, the prince of amorality. Thérive, Crémieux and Lœwel all made this comparison, citing the irritation in the dialogue, the compelling machinations of the plot, the stubbornness of the main characters and the way the supporting cast faded away. All in all, a certain 'dramatic fluency' and 'some theatrical outrageousness',[94] even if Némirovsky is never as relaxed as Bernstein. As a counterpoint to Golder, many critics also alluded to Isidore Lechat, in Octave Mirbeau's play *Les Affaires sont les affaires* (1903), in which another dry-eyed money-dealer, who is disowned by his daughter and, under threat of bankruptcy, is challenged to overcome his adversaries. Whether deliberately or not, these comparisons underline Irène Némirovsky's dramatic vein. Pawlowski even suggested bringing *David Golder* to the stage 'to provide a tragedy worthy of Bernstein'. Did Fernand Nozière read *Gringoire*? Less than a month after this sound advice, on 19th February, the drama rights were sold to this regular supplier to the Paris stage from the Belle Époque onwards.

Nozière, who was fifty-five years old, was bald, chubby-cheeked and short-sighted, and wore a tie with a Windsor knot. Ever since he had shaved off his beard in 1927, his ex-wife no longer recognised him. A close friend of Ida Rubinstein, he was equally well-known for his plays as for his theatre reviews; these appeared in newspapers from *L'Intransigeant* to *Le Matin*, by way of *Gil Blas* and . . . *Fantasio*. In 1923–24, he had written columns on cabaret, under the heading 'Miousics'. His byline then disappeared, possibly because he had expressed his reservations about *Le Juif errant* by Jean Bastia – a pillar of the 'humorous magazine' – a play that was peppered with anti-Semitic puns that had caused a certain embarrassment among Jewish spectators at the Théâtre du Perchoir, those at least who hadn't laughed along with the audience in the stalls. For Fernand Nozière was a Jew and we need look no further for the explanation of his genius than from Paul Léautaud, who could not bring himself to hate him: 'He is like those little tailors who do not know how to make clothes, and who are happy to tidy things up, to patch up and mend. There is no way in which he could do anything individual, of his own. He tidies up other people's things.'[95] In twenty years and more of mending, Nozière had nevertheless earned his stripes as a fixer. In 1907, having portrayed a Jewish family that had converted for the sake of ambition, he came under opposing fire from those who accused him of anti-Semitism and of philo-Semitism, depending on whether it was seen as a satire or a parable. Afterwards, he adapted for the stage Balzac's *Un épisode sous la Terreur* (1908), *La Maison de danses* by Reboux (1909), Maupassant's *Bel-Ami* (1912) and Dostoyevsky's *The Eternal Husband* (1912) and *The Idiot* (1925), and so on as far as *David Golder*. Adaptation was so much his speciality that, before the war, he had himself become a farcical character in *Revue des X* at the Bouffes-Parisiens, where his spitting image appeared on stage singing:

> *Je profane et dénature*
> *Nos plus illustres auteurs,*
> *Rien n'est plus doux, je vous jure*
> *Quand on est adapteur.**

Confronted with *David Golder*, Nozière sensed that there might be trouble in store, but the prospect sent shivers down his anatomist's spine: 'I found myself faced with a splendid "historical novel",' he recalled . . . 'I had to write stage dialogue based on a wonderfully well-structured literary work. What a subject matter for a playwright! Think of it! I took *my* character to the American West, at a time when he was "nothing" and could aspire to becoming "everything". Twenty years later, I brought him to the Place Vendôme when his position is definitely established . . . What a panorama! What a fine business drama.'[96] Without a moment's hesitation, Nozière took out his cutting knife and did his best to ensure that only the most colourful sections survived, those that were shocking in their coarseness. The Jewish aspects of *David Golder* were enhanced still further, as he himself would admit: 'There is the Jew Fischl with his worrying speculations. There is the Jew Soifer, who, under the guise of poverty, conceals his millions . . . There is Golder's partner, Marcus, who is worn out by the lowest forms of pleasure and has not the strength to cope with a change of fortune. These characters are dreadful, but they are comical too. They can and should frequently induce a somewhat cruel gaiety.'[97] *David Golder* would therefore be a disjointed piece of light comedy, intended to prompt cries, laughter and applause. For the sake of local colour, Russian actors would be recruited for the climax of the play, the Moscow business scene.

In order to assist him in his task, Nozière engaged the support of the great actor, Harry Baur, who, not content with shouldering the demanding role of Golder, would take it upon himself to direct the cast in the 'admirable task of trying to create the excitement of a

---

*I profane and distort/Our most illustrious authors/Nothing can be sweeter, I swear/When you are an adapter. [Tr.]

financial venture'.[98] Everything was on course for a fine success, but Nozière had first to finish *Cette vieille canaille*, a rather crude comedy that the Théâtre Michel had commissioned for the month of November. *David Golder* was due to succeed it in December at the Théâtre de la Porte-Saint-Martin. Known as '*la Porte Sublime*' in the trade, the theatre, which had been losing momentum in the mid-1920s, had been taken over by Maurice Lehmann, who brought it success once more by entrusting the role of l'Aiglon (Napoléon II) to a man, an innovation that had become possible following the death of Sarah Bernhardt in 1923. In 1929, Lehmann had just put on a play about the tragic end of the Romanovs, *Le Dernier Tsar*, an honourable success that raised hopes for an enthusiastic public reception for *David Golder*, especially in view of its Russian setting. However, three months after Nozière had first made his cuts, it was announced in *Comœdia* that a second adaptation of *David Golder* was in the pipeline, this time for the cinema, by a thirty-three-year-old director who had already brought Jules Renard's *Poil de carotte* to the screen – starring Harry Baur. The rumours had, in fact, been circulating for several weeks.

Julien Duvivier, who had been in the business for ten years, had just adapted Bataille's *Maman Colibri* and Zola's *Au bonheur des dames*. The poetic realism of his films had earned him a reputation, but it was the talking film that would establish him during the 1930s. Like everyone else, he had read *David Golder*, which had 'bowled him over'. Or better still, bluffed him: 'I picked up the book one evening and I couldn't put it down until I had finished. It's first-rate.'[99] In 1933, however, he admitted that the original idea of adapting the book came from his producer, Marcel Vandal. The fact remains that he refused to see 'the mud' in it that the reporter from *Comœdia* believed smeared the novel. 'It has been exaggerated,' he said in restrained tones. 'The story is certainly gloomy, but there are patches of sunlight and it is not mud all the time. Personally, I am convinced that it would make a fine film, one with substance and ideas.' Quite the reverse of the adaptation by Nozière, a man who favoured light comedy and whose principal concern was to please his audience. Duvivier, on the contrary, explained his vision of the novel and its spiritual dimension without once mentioning the word 'Jewish'. For according to him, *David Golder* was a universal fable: 'In fact, David Golder, with all his millions, is a poor man. Arriving in Paris from an ill-defined Central Europe, he has earned his wealth by hard work and tenacity. Business matters, and his daughter, these are his entire life ... You can see from this what might be done with a subject like that.'

During the spring, accompanied by Vandal, Duvivier therefore paid a visit to Irène Némirovsky to reassure her as to his intentions. He envisaged shooting certain scenes 'fairly far away, very far even', and predicted 'a new film that would be the talk of the town', since *David Golder* would be his first talking film. The novelist, 'hesitant, self-effacing, surprised by her success, who says yes just as she might have said no',[100] but who was on her guard, warned him immediately that she would not allow her book to be altered. The smiling response from Duvivier partially set her mind at rest:

'But no, madame, not all directors necessarily "mess about with" their subjects, and I shall respect this one! This will turn out on screen as it does on paper, you have my word!'[101]

At the end of May, Duvivier let it be known that he had not yet found the actor who would play the part of Golder, that force of nature. It was a white lie that he was happy to give away in an aside by letting drop the name of ... Harry Baur! Nozière and Lehmann, who did not know this, were still working away quite happily, though anxious about the competition from cinema. For the talking film, which appeared on screens during 1929, directly threatened the last unique quality of the theatre. And because this still imperfect process avoided exteriors, shouting and arguments, acrobatics, scenes that were too complicated, and the hurly-burly of life, it was usually reduced to scenes behind closed doors and to muffled exchanges between two or three characters. It was filmed theatre.

Irène Némirovsky, furthermore, willingly acknowledged the influence of cinema. A few critics – Daniel-Rops, Reboux – had actually criticised the book for being written with film adaptation in mind. She was not bothered about this transformation of fictional processes. A habitual frequenter of movie houses, she actually welcomed it confidently, though she thought that the great upheaval would occur 'when children who are now twelve or fifteen years old and who have been fed and filled with cinema since their childhood ... became writers in their turn'.[102]

The pain of the misunderstood

She did not, however, follow the progress of Nozière and Duvivier too closely. With the approach of summer, she needed above all to take a rest from the hullabaloo that had continued unabated since the publication of her novel and to look after her seven-month-old baby to whom, on 26th June, she inscribed one of the 'complimentary copies', that would not be read until later on: 'For my daughter Denise when she grows up.' Of course, the commercial potential of *David Golder* was not exhausted, and Grasset did its best to prolong it by inserting 'Reading tips for your holidays' in the press, where Némirovsky's name appears alongside those of Mauriac, Maurois and Chardonne. On the other side of the Atlantic, the publisher Horace Liveright was preparing the American translation of *David Golder* for the autumn. During this time, she revised the new edition of *Le Bal*, under her real name this time, merely correcting some minor errors[103] and altering Alfred and Rosine Kemp's surname to 'Kampf', possibly out of respect for the critic from *Le Temps*, possibly to indicate that the assimilation of Jews into French society was an endless battle. At the Hôtel Eskualduna in Hendaye, where she continued to stay until 1932, she spent her days on the beach with Michel, Paul, Choura and Cécile in luxurious simplicity. 'They brought the apéritif and the champagne there,' the excellent nanny would recall. 'Paul said to me: "Come now, a little drink, Néné?"' When the weather was bad, the little group set off for Biarritz or Urrugne to watch the rough sea. Irène was still at Hendaye when, in mid-August, Nozière finished copying out his adaptation. A photo of her on holiday, with Denise on her lap, would appear in *L'Intransigeant* on 28th September. In another, less well-known snapshot, beside Irène Némirovsky, we see Comtesse Marie-Laure de Noailles, the patron of the Surrealists, wearing a black bathing costume, with her white Pomeranian dog. Irène, all smiles, is wearing a long, pleated skirt and white sandals.

Le Bal, incorrectly described as the new novel by Irène Némirovsky, came out at the beginning of August. By way of advance, the author earned the sum of 6,000 francs. Pierre Tisné, the company secretary at Grasset's, who, having read *David Golder* read all her earlier work, considered, not without reason, that *Le Bal* was 'the quintessence of *L'Ennemie*', for the author had taken the trouble to substitute bitterness with farce and to replace vengeance with pity, which was far more cruel. Without this devastating humour, the misfortunes of Antoinette, who plays at torturing her mother as she would at dismembering a doll and sewing it together again, would have resembled a sermon by the Comtesse de Ségur. But here, ultimately, it is the childish Rosine who repents of her vanity, whereas her daughter savours her suppressed revenge. In passing, Irène Némirovsky illustrates the notion that bourgeois comedy, that frantic yearning for balls and fine clothing, is a screen for erotic anguish, and that social degradation, for a nouveau-riche couple, is tantamount to the first intimations of death. Which is why so much emphasis is put on Rosine Kampf's physical deterioration, in comparison with the sensual awakening of Antoinette, who is starved of social life. 'It was at this moment, this fleeting moment that their paths crossed "on life's journey". One of them was about to ascend, and the other to plunge downwards into darkness. But neither of them realised it.'[104]

Eagerly awaited, the book was immediately pounced upon by the critics, most of whom were unaware that this was a long short story written two years previously, who declared themselves disappointed by these complacently stretched-out 130 pages, set in large type, as if somehow excused by the 'Series of Short Works' in which the book was published. After the smash hit of *David Golder*, no one expected this ferocious little story, which was reckoned to be pessimistic and depressing, and left one dissatisfied: 'We were promised a main course, and we are given a stick of barley sugar.'[105] Eugène Langevin, in the *Revue française*, considered such slender pickings to be a great waste of talent; furthermore, the book was immoral, for how could one concede any extenuating circumstances to Antoinette, 'a perverted teenager, fiercely contemptuous of everything that was not to do with the pleasures of the flesh'.[106] In the dock was Bernard Grasset, once again, who was suspected of 'forcing the book through production in order to profit from a success', but also Irène Némirovsky, who had not been unwilling to 'search her bottom drawer'.[107] She had nonetheless been careful to anticipate this criticism in a slip-in sheet that read as follows:

I wrote *Le Bal* in between two chapters of *David Golder*, or more precisely having just rewritten for the third time the account of David Golder's first heart attack in the railway carriage. It wasn't working at all, and I couldn't bear my novel any longer. One day, on the Alexandre III bridge, I had noticed a young girl, leaning over the parapet, who was watching the water flowing past, while the person who was with her and who appeared to be an English governess was waiting with obvious anxiety for someone who never came. I was struck by the young girl's hard and unhappy expression. As I watched her, I imagined all sorts of stories. *Le Bal* is one of them.

Only those readers who were as unimpressionable as Reboux, who didn't measure talent by the number of pages, likened this 'jewel', this 'poignant poem inspired by the pain of the misunderstood', to *Paul et Virginie*, *Manon Lescaut*, Flaubert's *Un cœur simple*, Maupassant's *Yvette*, *Aphrodite* by Pierre Louÿs, and even *Adolphe* by Benjamin Constant. And here was Reboux, at the height of his elation, announcing the arrival of a new Colette in the firmament of French literature: 'No other style among those of contemporary writers seems to me to have [. . .] this flavour, this breeding, this class.'[108]

For many others, *Le Bal* was yet another story about Jews, one that was even more cynical and scathing than *David Golder*. Her characters 'repel one by their behaviour, their attitudes, their way of looking at life'.[109] 'Yet another family of Jews who have come from the East, become rich through the stock exchange, and who are hungry for worldly and social importance,' moaned the reviewer for *Fiches du mois*. 'I should like to believe, however, that the author is not solely destined to portray the children of Israel and that she will offer us some other characters: a temperament like this cannot be endlessly satisfied with the same idea . . .'[110] Six months after the 'trial' of *David Golder*, the press was far more inclined to emphasise the similarity of the caustic qualities of *Le Bal* than to misjudge it for a satire on the Jewish lower middle-classes eager for recognition. But if there was any satire, it was borrowed again: one of the acknowledged influences for *Le Bal*, *Les Demi-Vierges* by Marcel Prévost, was full of social anti-Semitism.

Yet *Le Bal* was merely a further transposition of Irène Némirovsky's adolescent struggle. Antoinette is wicked because she is Rosine's daughter. But because the book is shorter, the opinions are more uncompromising. *Mercure de France* saw it almost as an anti-Semitic diatribe, recognising in the character of Antoinette 'the longing for pleasure', but also 'the passion, the pride and the notion of persecution that are peculiar to her race'.[111] Irène Némirovsky thus found herself caught up in the passionate debate unleashed by the *David Golder* 'affair'. She would never be rid of it. This chilly reception was similar to the far more consensual one accorded to *Galeries Lévy & Cie*, the 'sensational talking and singing Jewish film', now forgotten, made by André Hugon, which was first shown on 24th October. From the nationalist *Gringoire* to the Zionist *Menorah*, they all praised this unbelievable rubbish for its kindly and humorous caricature of French Jews, infected as it was with sickly-sweet clichés. We should not ask as much from Irène Némirovsky, who had too many accounts to settle with her past and preferred vinegar to balm. And therefore Nina Gourfinkel was scarcely surprised to discover in *Le Bal* 'not a jot of kindliness, no pity, not an ounce of spontaneous feeling': the author of *David Golder* could not be changed, nor could her 'dispassionately cruel talent': 'Irène Némirovsky is a lancet.'[112]

The Cinema-Theatre affair

Duvivier was starting to make his film at that same moment. In September, shooting was delayed because no suitable actress had been found for Joyce. An announcement about an audition would even appear in the press: among the one hundred '1930 girls' who turned up at the studio, the role of Golder's illegitimate daughter would eventually be played by twenty-four-year-old Jackie Monnier, who was older than the part required. Harry Baur, who was killing two birds with one stone by warming himself up in front of the cameras as his first night on stage approached, played opposite Paule Andral, who was perfect as the badly tamed shrew. She would also play the part in Nozière's play, in December! After shooting a few scenes in Biarritz in late September, the real filming with the cast began at the Épinay studios in October and was completed without any hitches on 9th November.

The backdrops for this 'big talking film', one of the first to be made in France, were the work of Lazare Meerson, assisted on this occasion by a very young Hungarian student by the name of Alexandre Trauner, whose only previous work had been on René Clair's *Sous les toits de Paris*. Walter Goehr, a pupil of Schoenberg's, who had just written the very first opera for radio, *Malpopita*, was commissioned to write the musical score. True to the promise he made the novelist that the film would turn out 'on screen as it does on paper', Duvivier offered the part of the young emigrant to Charles Goldblatt, a twenty-five-year-old actor who was a close friend of the poet Max Jacob and who was not yet known by the name of Charles Dorat. Clearly, there was nothing of the old-fashioned production about *David Golder*.

The editing was completed during a fortnight in November. At the end of the month, Irène Némirovsky, who had not been consulted about the distribution and the direction – even though people were muttering that she had been heavily involved in the shaping of the dialogue – was invited to view a few scenes. The acting of Harry Baur, in particular, struck her as very convincing. The actor had created a Golder who was totally exhausted, but who was equipped with a raw power, similar to the weary titan in the novel. One of the most curious aspects of the film is its expressionism, which sweeps away all references to Balzac's type of realism in a few shots. The staging and the settings are economical, the dialogue is pithy, the lighting effects harsh. The few scenes that were done as silent film were finally discarded. So as to enlighten the audience, the actors in the scene set in Moscow were made to look like Lenin and Trotsky. Only the performance of Jackie Monnier, who was exasperating, left a lot to be desired. But there is an atmosphere of sentimental terror in this *David Golder* that is reminiscent of *L'Âge d'or*, the surrealist film that Buñuel had just made. Finally, and most importantly, the film did not distort the deeper meaning of the novel: the dying Golder's return to his Jewish child-hood. The final scenes are shot in a storm, on the Black Sea, to the strains of a stirring and emotional Hebrew chant. 'So a fine film in prospect.'[113] On 14th November, Irène Némirovsky felt able to express her two-fold gratitude to Bernard Grasset:

I am glad to be able to tell you that our 'David' will be shown at the Théâtre de la Porte St Martin, at Christmas time, with Harry Baur. Let's hope it does well. In any case, believe me, I do not forget that I am indebted largely to you for the fact that it is being put on in the cinema as well as at the theatre . . .

Fully reassured, she was able to leave Paris for a few days at the end of the month to be treated for her asthma in Switzerland, before the grand dress rehearsal of the film. On her return, on 9th December, she was astonished to discover that further proceedings, planned during her absence, were to be instituted against her: this time she was accused of helping Nozière to benefit from Duvivier's screenplay! A letter from Duvivier expressing his reservations about the amount borrowed for the stage adaptation, which had been copied to the Société des auteurs dramatiques, had been divulged to *La Cinématographie française* by Raymond Berner. The novelist, he asserted, had found the film 'far superior to the play', and wished that the latter could have been amended'.[114] The reporter maintained that he had been told this by Harry Baur, who was well placed to compare the two. Duvivier, who was famous for his volatile temperament, took the matter to court, accusing the manager of the Porte-Saint-Martin of having stolen his script!

This skirmish, much to the enjoyment of the specialist journals, was merely a spasm in the supposed death throes of the theatre in its battle against the invasion of the talking film. Did not Pagnol himself pretend to spurn the theatre by turning towards film-making? The press, which was counting the blows, expected a great deal from the row over *David Golder*, which was then being touted for the Goncourt prize. The comparison may help settle this dispute, which was exacerbated by the fact that Nozière, having begun work earlier, had allowed himself to be overtaken by the film studio. In December, *Les Nouvelles littéraires* even announced that a second tussle was looming over *Le Bal*, with Steve Passeur preparing to make a film and Lugné-Poë a play! A rumour that was very revealing of the 'Némirovsky phenomenon'. Torn between the theatre and the cinema, the writer stood up for herself humorously for having favoured whoever it might be, and she put an end to the gossip by addressing an open letter to the editor of *La Cinématographie française*:

> I greatly regret that your contributor was unable to have a discussion with me, as, I believe, had been his intention.
>
> In actual fact, the role he attributes to me in this Cinema-Theatre affair does not tally in any way with the reality . . .
>
> With great indulgence, your contributor wishes to describe an act that

would have consisted in helping the theatre profit from the discoveries of the cinema as 'irresponsible'. I myself would have called that a dishonest act and one that even the state of 'enthusiasm', which he likes to mention, would not have excused.

That is why I stand up for myself vigorously against this accusation; I have never breathed a word of the script to MM. Lehmann and Nozière, any more than it would have occurred to me to talk about the play to MM. Vandal and Duvivier.

I would remind you, what is more, that prior to the theatre and the cinema there was actually my novel, and consequently it would be simpler to go and look in the book and not at the film for the necessary 'ideas'.[115]

The controversy continued unabated. On 17th December, the film was screened at the Théâtre Pigalle for a selected audience. Duvivier had invited a few theatre critics to whom he had handed a note criticising Nozière and Lehmann once more for having 'used a great many of the cast we have chosen'. Those so charged replied the following day in *Comœdia* reminding readers that the play had been written four months before. Good losers, they nonetheless wished the film every success, for they were certain that a commercial failure would be detrimental to them: 'We must all march together, in full agreement, and respect the figure of Mme Irène Némirovsky to whom they owed their film, to whom we owe our play.'[116] Not for a moment did Nozière and Lehmann imagine that their play might close even before the film opened . . .

The most resounding flop of the year

The rehearsals began at the Porte-Saint-Martin on 20th December. On Friday the 26th, the morning of the opening night, Nozière drummed up support in *L'Écho de Paris*, promising a modern and compelling show: 'I like to see strong and colourful characters at the theatre. I dread the colour grey on stage . . . We hope that cinema customers, as well as Mme Némirovsky's readers, enjoy David Golder and his family so much that they will feel they want to see them on the stage.' A few hours later, to her great delight, Irène was present as the curtain was raised – the same evening as the first night of Bernstein's *Jour* at the Théâtre du Gymnase. She asked Cécile Michaud to accompany her and they both enjoyed themselves very much watching this gloomy play in three acts and seven scenes which they knew better than anyone.

If the critics were unanimous in praising the performance of Harry Baur, whose quick-tempered personality was wonderfully suited to the irascible David, most of them, on the other hand, failed to recognise 'the muscular and almost Balzac-like power of the novel'.[117] In spite of the savoir-faire, the play lacked rhythm and dragged along, the harsh grandeur of the novel was stunted, but above all, Nozière's trimming-down emphasised its most grotesque features. Lefèvre considered it simply 'mediocre'.[118] On stage, Franc-Nohain objected, 'all that is left is the ignominy of this Jewish family, united by only one bond, money . . . It is all there, the origins, the bloodline, the craving for pleasure, the struggle to make money, the radiant beauty, the prevailing cynicism and arrogant selfishness.' In L'Écho de Paris, the cartoonist Sennep sketched Golder turning a gold tap grafted on to his side, and Gloria, with her back turned, disdainfully picking up the manna. In the midst of the Oustric* affair, the public was moreover saturated with 'these stories about industrial shares, about oil and land transactions, and deals on the stock exchange'.[119] An opinion that was shared by L'Humanité, which rather enjoyed the scene in which the 'representatives of prole-tariat power' confronted the banker Golder, the symbol of the 'vacuous-ness of capitalist society', responsible for 'the bankruptcies that accumulate, the wars that break out, unemployment and poverty'.[120]

Not helped by the press and word of mouth recommendations, Nozière's play did not last long: twenty performances at the most. 'It was,' Philippe Soupault would say, 'the most resounding flop of the year.'[121] Though not for Nozière, who saw his play put on in Germany and in Central Europe, and could even afford the cost of a minor dispute with Grasset for having negotiated rights with Italy without informing him. It was true that he only had three months to live.

During January the film was shown at previews in various Paris cinemas, notably at the Gaumont Palais-Rochechouart, on the 28th; the stage sets had been stored away a long time before. It was in this

---

*Albert Oustric was a banker who engaged in questionable speculation on the Paris stock exchange. He was accused of bankruptcy fraud in November 1929. [Tr.]

month too, on the 14th, that Irène's grandfather died in the 16th arrondissement. He was buried in the Jewish section of the Père-Lachaise cemetery, in the family plot that Léon had bought for his parents-in-law. Two years previously, Iona had been knocked down by a car. 'Oh, my God,' Irène Némirovsky was to write in 1934, 'how can one forget the two years of agony, and return to the time when he was young and healthy, with his fine teeth, his lively movements, his fiery eyes, gleaming with intelligence . . .' The only thing of his that she kept was a gold watch, and the memory of the French poems he would recite by heart.

An untamed spirit

The official premiere of the 'great French talking film' took place on 6th March 1931 at three o'clock in the afternoon, at the Élysée Gaumont, on the Champs-Élysées. It was a double event, because it was also the first time that this cinema, 'the most elegant' in the capital, opened its doors to the public. At the entrance, ushers handed out to journalists and guests copies fresh off the press of *Le Figaro* or *L'Écho de Paris*, which reproduced the praise of certain people of note whom Duvivier had had the bright idea of inviting to the previews. The managing director of *Annales*, Pierre Brisson, between two puffs of his Lucky Strike, had no qualms about supplying him with a flamboyant quote: 'To my mind, it is the best French talking film to have been made since *Sous les toits de Paris*.' Gaston Chérau, of the Académie Goncourt, considered the ending of the film 'one of the most awe-inspiring subjects ever to have been devised . . . a landmark on the long road undertaken by the art of the screen'. The composers Arthur Honegger and Maurice Ravel noted the 'powerful restraint' and 'the perfection of the technique'. The poet Jules Supervielle was captivated by the Soviet scene. The painter Van Dongen applauded a 'very fine artistic achievement'. Paul Morand, who was sparing in his compliments, seemed almost jealous: '*David Golder*, excellent. It is not a comedy photographed with the minimum of effort, it is a creation, and one of the finest talking films. It is also a great human journey, from the Polish ghetto to the wealth of Biarritz, from poverty to riches, from life to death. A novelist should turn to the cinema and not the theatre if he does not wish to be misinterpreted.' Colette, alone, ventured a reservation: 'A pointless little piece of directorial excess: the room in which Golder washes when he arrives, and the enamel wash-basin with the jug of water. In a villa such as Golder's, all the servants' bedrooms have basins with running water.' But these lines were removed by Duvivier, who only printed her praise in support of the actor. Léon Werth, Charles Vildrac and Maurice Rostand added their voices to the chorus.[122]

This torrent of approbation infuriated *Action française* and its critic Lucien Rebatet: 'Let's just say that these are charitable offerings from literature and music to their bastard children, and that they don't compromise the indulgent donors very much.'[123] It was true that within a few months Irène Némirovsky had become the idol of 'le Tout-Paris'. She nevertheless retained all her sweetest simplicity to congratulate Jacques-Émile Blanche on his latest novel:

> Believe it or not, I had read one or two pages when you gave it to me, but the gloomy tone of the first chapter was too painful for me: my grandfather had just died. I was swamped with images and memories of death . . . I wanted to tell you all this, but there are always so many people at your house, and I am still an untamed spirit as you will have observed.[124]

'Untamed': this was also the opinion of Tisné, at Grasset's, who was irritated by Irène Némirovsky's suspicious interest in the sales of her book. In early January, the 54,000 copy print-run had not yet sold out, but the misleading figure of 114,000 that had just been printed on the covers – a publicity trick which Grasset was not alone in resorting to – rather concerned the author, who did not fail to complain about it. Tisné eventually flew off the handle:

> What you must stop doing now is seek, as you put it, to 'bother' me, by letting it be known that we don't inform you, or that we inform you afterwards, about the numbers printed of your book.
>
> When I spoke to people here the other day about your allusions to this matter, I can assure you there was quite a commotion, and the least I was told was that the literary folk you mix with must have very strange minds if it is from them that you derive this unjustified mistrust.[125]

During the spring of 1931, Tisné announced, *David Golder* went into its 125th reprint. Irène Némirovsky kept a careful eye on the figures. On 1st June, having heard that Ferenczi had put its own edition of the novel on sale eleven months ahead of the contracted date, illustrated with coloured woodcuts, and at a price of 3.50 francs instead of 15, she would be the first to point out the breach of contract to 'whoever it may concern'.

Thinking in images

Meanwhile, Duvivier's film met with varying success. On 18th March, it was shown at the Capitol in Berlin for the benefit of the 'Rapprochement intellectuel franco-allemand'. In France, Harry Baur's realistic and unaffected performance, which was praised by everyone, was often compared to the work of Emil Jannings, the favourite actor of Murnau and Sternberg. Marcel Carné, in *Cinémagazine*, described it as 'a powerful, bitter and harsh film . . . eminently interesting and successful'. The professionally-based *La Revue du cinéma* deplored the pietism of the countryside scenes, shot in the Basque Country. Jackie Monnier was judged too theatrical and was rudely referred back to her drama school. There was unanimity, however, about one scene: that in which Golder negotiates the oilfields with the Soviets. Yet the interpretations differed. For *Poslednija Novosti*, the daily newspaper for White Russians in exile, it was an amusing satire on Bolshevik methods.[126] For *La Revue du cinéma*, it was, on the contrary, 'a real indictment of capitalism', which would be justification enough for France finally giving a certificate to Eisenstein's *The General Line*. This was not a view shared by *L'Humanité*, which saw in it nothing but a picture 'of rare fantasy', full of bourgeois stereotypes about the economic strategy of the USSR; as for Golder, 'this man may die like a dog, but his death throes should not bring a single tear to our eyes. We are not taken in by the theatrical finale of this death enhanced by Jewish chants . . . We reckon David Golder ought to meet his end with a round of bullets to the head – and silence',[127] which is amusing if one considers that *Le Peuple*, the Communist organ of the CGT (the confederation of French trade unions) had just finished serialising the novel . . .

If *David Golder* is a Jewish film, however – which everyone thought it was – it surpassed André Hugon's new film, *Galeries Lévy & Cie*, which hit the screens in January 1931. The poster for that film depicted two caricatures that were dubious to say the least.[128] Whereas the posters for *David Golder* sometimes showed Harry Baur with a scarf around his neck, with Joyce looking at him in a pleading manner, or sometimes portrayed him on his deathbed, watched over by a young emigrant wearing a shapka and ringlets. Duvivier succeeded in avoiding caricature, unlike the majority of his colleagues, all of whom, in the course of 1931, displayed these shortcomings: Edmond Gréville in his short *Histoires juives*, Abel Gance in *La Fin du monde*, which featured a bellicose Jewish financier by the name of Schomberg, and Jean Kemm in *Le Juif polonais* starring Harry Baur, 'a masterpiece of idiocy' according to Antonin Artaud.[129] Lucien Rebatet, too, was not so much upset by the Jewish character of the film, which was banal by and large, as by Duvivier's over-indulgent treatment of the novel: 'We know in any case that a great deal of second-rate literature makes use of Jews these day, just as in former times it made use of parricides and machicolation. Whatever the merits of Mme Némirovsky's novel, the film has merely made a melodrama of it.'[130] Of course, this reservation did not prevent the anti-Semites from seeing everything from their own point of view: for *La Petite Illustration*, Duvivier's film was but a chapter in pictures of the 'Jewish peril' that threatened France, and David Golder one 'among the squalid and foul-smelling herd who shared his religion drawn by the lure of lucre and the conquest of the West'.[131]

For her part, the novelist confessed that she was quite simply 'deeply moved' to have witnessed the character who had stirred in her imagination for four years arise in flesh and bone. As for talking films, she could only see advantages: 'Silent cinema only enabled us to travel among ghosts . . . Thanks very much! Talking films are an amazing improvement . . . Cinema is the art form that most resembles life, that is most closely related to the truth . . .'[132] She liked it so much, and so willingly acknowledged the influence it had on her own art – scene cutting, the ability to frame and position, the sharpness of dialogue, the openness to suggestion, the reluctance to make comments – that she even thought of writing actual scripts and temporarily abandoning the novel, for, as she admitted to the Russian daily *Poslednija Novosti* on 1st May, 'more than anything else I like cinema in which there is talking, dancing and singing . . . At the moment I am not writing a new novel and I am not preparing anything for the theatre. But I am thinking about subjects for new films, for, as ever, I am thinking in images . . .'[133] What is more, Bernard Grasset no longer believed in the novel. 'One has to recognise that the public has grown tired of the novel,' he said. 'Personally, I have decided to discourage quite bluntly those who make the mistake of thinking they have the talents of a novelist. By that I mean, of course, the 9/10ths of those who write novels.'[134]

In July 1931, the first results of this new line of thought appeared in Les Œuvres libres: Irène Némirovsky's long short story entitled 'Film parlé', which claimed to copy the most obvious techniques of the talking film: a telegraphic style that imitated the script, fade-ins and fade-outs, flashbacks and time gaps, jazz and Americanisms that were in vogue: 'Hey, Luke, you taking a snifter?'[135] In the course of one sentence we come across the characters of Louloute and Nonoche, the former 'weeping like a Magdalen'.[136] As for Anne, the spiteful daughter of the old barmaid Éliane, her grievances are extremely reminiscent of those of Gabri in L'Ennemie: 'Leave me alone; why are you torturing me? What have I done wrong? You abandoned me . . . When you have a child, you look after it, you raise it . . .'[137] Dated 'Nice, 1931', could 'Film parlé' have been drafted before 1930?

Twilight

The author of David Golder did not just give interviews to the Russian press: she read it. So on 1st June 1931, ever anxious about her copyrights, she thought she ought to point out to Grasset that an unauthorised adaptation of her novel was being prepared in a theatre in Kichinev, in Moldavia! And although most of Soviet literary production seemed to her to be breeding 'monuments of pretentious nonsense', she nevertheless did her best to keep in touch with the work of young Russian writers, the most outstanding to her mind being the satirist Valentin Kataev, whose Gogol-like novel Rastrachiki (The Frog Eaters) had been published by Gallimard. In 1933, it was another satirist, Zoshchenko, whom she would rate 'above Chekhov', regretting that his short stories, 'marvels of delicate satire',[138] had not yet been translated into French. Though not deluded for a moment by the clumsiness of the Soviet novel, which was committed to 'the narrow path of Marxism', she nonetheless experienced 'the pleasure of knowing about some very strange customs', even if it meant 'abandoning from the start any purely aesthetic satisfaction'.[139] For acclaimed as she was in France, Irène Némirovsky was very much steeped in Russian culture. 'In the future a huge amount of contemporary literature will be seen to have been affected by Russia,' Robert Brasillach had prophesied in *Action française* on 26th February, singling out among the noticeable Slav motifs in recent French literature, 'the fashion for confessions, for old and distorted evangelical memories, occasionally an unconscious sadism, the strong conviction that all effort is pointless and that the individual may not even exist'.[140] This is a good definition of *Snow in Autumn* and *The Courilof Affair*, the two novels that Irène Némirovsky would publish in 1931 and 1933.

Snow in Autumn, a finished version of 'La Niania', was published in May 1931 by Simon Kra, the former manager at the Banque Rothschild, who founded his publishing house in 1919 after sixteen years as a bookseller. The publisher of the surrealists, Kra was a discoverer of talents with a prestigious and determinedly modern catalogue of authors: Max Jacob, Alfred Jarry, Pierre Mac Orlan, Emmanuel Bove . . . He also published a few contemporary Russian authors, such as Gorky, Kuprin and Shklovsky. Inexplicably, it was in English that Léon Pierre-Quint, the publishing firm's chief editor, read the early version of *Snow in Autumn*, in June 1930. He had only one requirement: that this heavily nostalgic text 'should not be less than 61,500 words at the minimum',[141] so that it could feature as the sixth title in the 'Femmes' collection, alongside Paul Morand (*L'Innocente à Paris ou la Jeune Fille de Perth*), Jean Giraudoux (*La Grande Bourgeoise ou Toute femme a la vocation*), Joseph Kessel (*La Femme de maison ou Mariette au désert*), Henri de Régnier (*Lui ou les Femmes et l'amour*) and Colette (*Sido ou les Points cardinaux*). This luxury edition, available to subscribers only, was launched at the end of 1927 with the intention of portraying 'the different types of today's woman' by the 'modern writers most popular with the public'.[142] It was a flattering offer and not to be turned down, especially at six thousand francs, and particularly since Kra would only have exclusive rights in the book until the end of the year.

Irène Némirovsky's story was published under the enigmatic title of *Les Mouches d'automne ou la Femme d'autrefois*. The metaphor alludes to those Russians who live in Neuilly and Passy, steeped in regrets, and who pine away in small furnished flats rather like those large flies that, in autumn, are trapped inside houses and buzz away for ages before dropping dead. 'Were it not for those memories etched deep in their hearts, life would be unbearable . . .'[143] Deceived by the mist, which she takes to be the first snow, Tatiana Ivanovna, the gentle old *niania*, goes out to walk in the street, just as Irène Némirovsky herself did whenever it snowed; but it is during a downpour that she plunges into the Seine, a cold rain, which in Irène Némirovsky's stories always portends a debacle, degradation, a decline in social standing, a humiliation, ostracism, exile, bankruptcy or death. And like Golder and Francine Bragance before her, it is in a mirror yet again that Hélène Vassilievna, the mistress of the house, observes the inner ravages of exile on her face, one of those mirrors which in Irène Némirovsky's work play the role of the old vanitas. The title she wanted to use for this book, before it became part of the 'Femmes' collection, was 'Twilight', while, much later, its English translation was given the title *Snow in Autumn*.

There were very few comments about *Snow in Autumn* when it was published by Kra since the book was only sold to subscribers. Yet Frédéric Lefèvre drew attention to the 'tasty maturing' and the 'supreme rigour'[144] that this splendidly sustained tale displayed. The allegory of the eternal Russia was too emotional, however, for the impervious *NRF* reader, who dismissed it in two lines: 'Sentimental. All that is weakest in Tolstoy updated to 1930; possibly enough to explain, and to justify, the Russian revolution.'[145] And so when *Snow in Autumn* was republished by Grasset in December, Irène Némirovsky would preface it with a few words to excuse the pathos of her book:

> Rereading *Les Mouches d'automne*, just as the book is about to be published, I feel a sort of embarrassment, the sense of propriety one might experience when discussing a private occasion, and one that is excessive and melodramatic into the bargain. This little story is based partly on memories, and partly on purely subjective feelings; memories of revolution, the early years of exile; nostalgia at the first falls of snow, etc.

The critics welcomed this little book therefore for what it appeared to be, a 'Russian story' that 'tells us more about the bewilderment of émigrés and the Russian soul than do many long novels and weighty tomes',[146] but still too anecdotal and too personal to confirm or live up to the expectations raised by *David Golder*. Blinded by so many Tolstoyan patronymics, everyone overlooked the maturity of style, the imaginative power, the skill of the storytelling and its morbid significance, all except André Thérive who, in these pages that are as remarkable for their concision as for their length, sniffed 'the bitter odour . . . of death and solitude'.[147] By the quickest of shortcuts, the Jewish author of *David Golder* and *Le Bal* had become the Russian author of *Snow in Autumn*. How many of them saw that Irène Némirovsky was not a Russian writer expressing herself in French, but a French writer who had embraced a Russian subject? Once again, Robert Brasillach regretted having to give as a model to French women novelists a young woman 'of both Russian and Jewish origin' who could grasp 'the secrets of our race' better than they did. According to the sprightly musketeer of *Action française*, this was not just another miracle of Jewish assimilation: *Snow in Autumn*, like Flaubert's *Un Cœur simple*, was 'a very restrained little book', less coarse than *David Golder*. 'There is an admirable emotion about this story, and at the same time a discretion that is rare today. Mme Némirovski has managed to convey the vast Russian melancholy in a French form, and has almost removed its enervating power. All that remains is this witness to a troubled time, this servant in whom are enshrined the indisputable virtues of fidelity and faith and who dies, a victim of exile . . . People will read and keep this book whose poetic charm is so moving and so truthful.'[148]

A *viennoiserie*

In 1931, Irène Némirovsky spent the summer at the Hôtel Eskualduna, at Hendaye, for the last time. In her mind, the autumn's novelty was not the publication of *Snow in Autumn*, a story that had been in her head for almost ten years, but the screen adaptation of *Le Bal*, which the Austrian film director Wilhelm Thiele had been working on since the beginning of the year. Having been taught a lesson by the Duvivier-Nozière dispute, she was careful to point out in her letter to Grasset of 20th April that she had not written the script, which 'is merely *inspired* by my novella' and she requested, in passing, eight thousand francs for the rights instead of the three thousand that had originally been expected.

Thiele, who had made a speciality of filming the French and German versions simultaneously, using the same set and the same costumes – as he had in 1929 with *Adieu Mascotte* and its twin, *Das Modell vom Montparnasse* – set up his cameras in the Épinay studios in March 1931. The film set was a modern-style drawing-room, with a sofa upon which the two actresses playing the part of Mme Kampf, Germaine Dermoz and Lucie Mannheim, took it in turns to sit. With Antoinette shut away in a Paris apartment which she happened to regard 'as a stage set',[149] *Le Bal* relied more on the direction than did *David Golder*. Reduced to three or four characters, the dialogue for this chamber drama was so well written that scarcely any changes were necessary. The script was nevertheless consigned to Curt Siodmak, and the dialogue to Henri Falk.

The film was screened for the first time at the Gaumont-Palace on 11th September. It was generally agreed that the French version was far superior to the German one, the humorous talents of André Lefaur (Alfred Kampf), with his easy-going air behind his thick moustache, being beyond Reinhold Schünzel. The cruelty and bitterness of the novella, and its vague eroticism, were almost entirely buried beneath the type of comedy of manners that had earned Thiele his reputation. 'In this way, he is very Viennese,' complained the film magazine, *L'Ami du film*. 'He likes striking sweet chords, "pleasantries". He depicts "the optimistic".'[150] Furthermore, unlike the novella, the film has a happy ending: father, mother and daughter, worn down by the psychodrama they have just endured, console one another as they whimper around the buffet that their guests will not touch.

But the film, which was a success with the public, was illuminated by the performance of a young thirteen-year-old actress whose first role this was. Recommended by a pupil of her mother, a singing teacher, Danielle Darrieux was preferred to the other girls who auditioned, all of whom were too old. (One of them, Odette Joyeux, who was almost seventeen at the time, would launch her long and brilliant career that same year.) Wearing a pale-blue suit trimmed with silver-fox, the teenager reported to the production offices without further ado, much to the displeasure of her mother. 'I did my test without really knowing what it was about,' she would write, 'then I went home.'[151] A fortnight later, after a second screen test in which she had to take the cue from an assistant and call her Maman, she learnt that the producers, Delac and Vandal, had listed her in the credits under the pseudonym of Lydie Danielle. All she could do was to cry out: 'I'm going to be in a film, I won't need to go to school!'[152] For three weeks the young girl would fool around without realising that there were microphones present . . . Because she was fresh-faced and had a nice voice, two songs were also written for her, 'Les Beaux Dimanches' and 'Chanson de la poupée', which would turn the film of *Le Bal* into the sort of musical that Irène Némirovsky loved. For, the author confessed, 'I love life, and movement, and dancing, and travelling so much that the more boisterous cinema is, the more I like it. I'm already waiting for images to appear in stereoscope and in the true colours they are in real life . . .'

Never did she appear so young and so cheerful as she did during 1931 when, with the stir created by *David Golder* having finally calmed down, she could enjoy true peace of mind. Her daughter was almost two years old, a blonde and golden little doll whom Cécile walked in her pushchair along the Boulevard des Invalides. 'Denise is beautiful every day,' her mother marvelled. 'In reality and on paper . . .' The reporter from *Pour vous*, who had come to interview her for the promotion of the film, had not expected to find a mischievous and coquettish schoolgirl teasing the photographers so informally:

'Hey there! . . . No . . . I'm telling you, I don't feel a bit photogenic today . . . I'm sorry . . . I'm sorry . . . It's not like my daughter!'[153]

Irène Némirovsky had success. She had talent, and she had the gift of the gab. She had the recognition, the respect, and the affection of her peers, which out of all her blessings was, like Antoinette in *Le Bal*, the one she most craved. The little girl who had jibbed rebelliously behind her bows and her hats had sent them all packing. In Thiele's film, Rosine Kampf had swapped her first name for that of Jeanne, a name that Anna Némirovsky had liked to use to disguise herself. And as in *L'Ennemie*, it is the sudden arrival of a lover that provokes Antoinette's revenge. It was the first time that Irène had dared to stand up to her mother so openly, and on the big screen. Her intention could not be clearer, especially when we add that, in the film, the

Kampfs acquired shares in a company called Victoria, the name of Fanny's younger sister . . . This sadistic concern ought not to surprise us, for if, in her books, Irène is always ready to show her understanding towards the various incarnations of Fanny, in reality she was unsparing. 'How strange it is . . .' she would muse in June 1934. 'In literature I can't help finding attenuating circumstances, even though I portray loathsome people, whereas in life . . .'

But Irène Némirovsky also had good luck, incredible good luck, and she knew it. 'Do you believe in it?' the monthly magazine *Bravo* asked her in February. Her reply was full of false modesty: 'An old Ukrainian saying goes: "One ounce of good luck in a man's life is enough; but, without that ounce, he is nothing." I've had my ounce.'[154] Now she would have to guard it jealously.

7

Enough Memories to Make a Novel
(1932–1935)

And our days which Time with his sandals hurries on
Have flowed away like a deceptively intoxicating wine.

Henri de Régnier, Les Médailles d'argile

A year after the sensational appearance of *David Golder*, Irène Némirovsky remained an enigma. For Robert Brasillach, the author of *Snow in Autumn* – 'quick to integrate' in accordance with her 'breed' – had, whether one liked it or not, succeeded in the miracle of 'conveying the vast Russian melancholy in a form that is French'.[1] For *L'Intransigeant*, on the other hand, there was nothing less Cartesian than this little book steeped in nostalgia: 'With Mme Irène Némirovsky, one has the feeling that Slav stories are no longer intelligible to French minds with their love of structure and logic.'[2]

By and large, readers were disappointed at the slimness and the melancholy of *Le Bal* and *Snow in Autumn*: more had been expected, they had hoped for better things from the author of *David Golder*, for which Grasset had sold rights in countries as far away as Chile. Edmond Jaloux, for one, would have wished for 'a story that was less well-shaped, not so carefully composed, but that had more resonances, more mysterious revelations'.[3] Irène Némirovsky admitted that a successful story should not be entirely made up of 'facts'*, as she liked to put it, but the criticism would not be forgotten; in 1934, just as she was working on the Paris episode in *The Wine of Solitude*, she wrote: 'What is wrong with this fourth part is that there are nothing but facts, and none of what that ass Jaloux, of the Académie française, calls resonances!' Had not Marcel Prévost, another member of the Académie, drawn the attention of readers of *Gringoire* to 'one of the most moving and accomplished works of our time', which 'deserved to survive when many of the books that were made a fuss

*In English in original text.

of had disappeared'?[4] She confessed to being struck above all, on meeting him, by his cadaverous complexion, 'and that's about the only thing that did impress me about him . . . As if he had spent his entire life in a closed room.' More than ever, the 'demon of pride' watched over Irène Némirovsky like some household god. In 1947, Robert Kemp only wished to remember that mixture of vulnerability and assurance: 'She was a petite, pretty woman, with olive skin, whose eyes, which were extremely short-sighted, had a heartrending gentleness. It was impossible to resist that solemn charm, that thoughtful dignity, that fragility, "though full of power".'[5]

How short life is . . .

At Christmas, Irène Némirovsky left Paris, leaving the critics to argue over whether *Snow in Autumn* fulfilled the promise of *David Golder*. In January, she stayed in Mégève with Denise and her nanny. 'She went for walks in the snow in her lovely fur coat and a bonnet on her head,' Cécile remembered. 'She had been trying to find some belongings for me at old mother Némirovsky's.' On her return, Irène found that Michel was 'ill with fairly serious congestion of the lungs'[6] and, at the end of February, she took him to convalesce at Saint-Jean-de-Luz. During these few weeks of rest and relaxation, she came across 'a wonderful book', *Le Nœud de vipères* by François Mauriac, which Grasset had just published. 'It's the finest thing I've read for a long time,' she wrote on 30th March to Tisné, her main contact at the publisher's offices in Rue des Saints-Pères.

The long confession made by Louis, the wealthy lawyer of humble background, wounded for ever by his wife's infidelity, whose fortune has been squandered by his children, and who is overcome with hatred for his family and friends, must have awoken gloomy echoes in Irène's heart. For Léon, her father, knew he was dying. Like Mauriac's hero, he had begun coughing up blood: haemoptysis. Irène would remember the rainy autumn day when, in a hotel room in Nice or Biarritz, her dear papa, his new suit still fitting him well, had stared at death in a wardrobe mirror:

In his hands he held two ebony brushes which he used alternately to brush his hair, his fine, white hair, with its greenish tinge. Suddenly, he stopped and moved closer to the mirror; it still reflected the green light of the park and his pale, yellowish face looked sicklier still, boundlessly ravaged by life's cares. For a long time, he stared at himself, whistling softly . . .:

'Well, my girl, I didn't think it would be over quite so quickly . . . How short life is, I never thought it would stop so soon . . . Yes, my girl . . . that's how it is . . . yes, my love.'

Irène Némirovsky observed: 'Really, there are truly moments when we are tempted to say that heaven pushes us too far, mocks us too cruelly. Deep down, acceptance of life *is a sense of humour*.'* The last time she had seen her father looking healthy was in 1930, in a night-club, 'a narrow hallway where you could smell the tepid aroma of fur coats impregnated with perfume'. Possibly the last pleasant fragrance to have gratified his aching lungs. It was his illness that had inspired the fourth chapter of *David Golder* and that interminable asphyxia that had so touched her readers: 'The thick darkness flowed into his throat with soft, insistent pressure, as if earth was being pushed into his mouth . . .'

For some time, Léon had been frittering away his money on gambling and had neglected his business to such a degree that, in order to preserve his wealth, he had transferred it almost entirely to Fanny's name. She, aged almost sixty, her love affairs ended and her appearance now suffering, had 'changed into a monster'.[7] Money, henceforth, was her cosmetic. She built up provisions in order to hold back the wrinkles. Nothing else could console her.

The effects of age on the desire for love, the frustrations of marriage and the hereditary nature of hypocrisy: these were the subjects of 'La Comédie bourgeoise', which Irène Némirovsky wrote on her return to Paris, and which was published in June in *Les Œuvres libres*. Henri, the protagonist of this short story with Mauriac-like overtones, although 'brought up as a Christian', nonetheless has a mistress and a child when he gets married. But the young engineer is 'a good catch'.[8] In frame after frame, juxtaposed or faded-in/faded-out, Irène Némirovsky's story lays bare the scenario over three generations of the arranged marriage of Henri and Madeleine, who is manipulated

*In English in original text. [Tr.]

by her children, just as she had been by her parents. This new 'talking film', which ends on a fixed frame, begins with a long tracking shot[9] of a road in the Nord. Gliding over the 'flat and melancholy' country-side, the reader is introduced to a small town with 'low, grey' houses, taken across the market square, and past a factory before entering the hallway, dining-room and 'oppressive' drawing-room of a 'middle-class looking' dwelling, before his gaze comes to rest on a young girl at the piano: Madeleine. Her memories of Lumbres and of 'Mad' Avot had crystallised this image of the thrifty and prudent provincial bourgeoisie, the guardian of national values, which the acid rain of *Suite Française* would dissolve. Foremost among these values: material welfare, the delusion that condemns Madeleine to a lifetime of frustration. Money rarely leads to happiness in Irène Némirovsky's work.

In March 1932, Léon Némirovsky's financial situation was in as much jeopardy as his health. Ever since 1928, the Banque française de l'Union, a reincarnation of the Banque de l'Union, of which he was vice-president, had not performed well. 'He had just received a letter informing him about the bankruptcy of a company in which he was the major shareholder,' suggests *The Wine of Solitude*, which mentions first and foremost the 'Brazilian Match Corporation'.[10] In actual fact, Léon owned shares in Imco, the International Match Corporation, founded by the Swedish tycoon Ivar Kreuger, the son of a Russian consul. Built up on a worldwide monopoly of match production, in the 1920s the Kreuger empire went so far as to grant huge loans to bankrupt governments, involving deals that were very often unsecured, in exchange for new monopolies. Yet three years after the stock market crash of 1929, Kreuger's powerful debtors were insolvent. The 'earthly demiurge', as Paul Morand called him,[11] was faltering. In 1932, the 'Napoleon of matches' awaited the spectre of bankruptcy. He knew that it would create countless victims, that it would destabilise the economy of several countries and would bring about the ruin of tens of thousands of Swedes who had put their entire life savings in shares or life insurance policies in one of his businesses (the Ericsson telephone company, notably).

One of the first victims of the Kreuger cyclone was Léon Némirovsky, who had invested in this tottering giant. In a discarded episode of *The Wine of Solitude*, Irène Némirovsky had reconstructed her father's poignant interview with Ivar Kreuger in the Swede's five-bedroom apartment in Paris, on the third floor of 5 Avenue Victor-Emmanuel III – the same street in which the Epstein 'clan' had lived before moving to Rue de Bourgogne. A 'cold and heavy rain' is falling. Kreuger, who is uncompromising, is asking Némirovsky to repay him the fourteen million francs lent to him to fund his factories, or else to sell these back to him. (For Kreuger 'had at his disposal in most countries men of straw who ran his subsidiary companies'.)[12] In the taxi taking him to the place of torture, Léon, who is trembling with fever, says to his daughter with a heavy smile:

'How do I look? Am I very pale? It is important that he doesn't think I am fatally wounded, do you understand? In business, you have to be strong, right up to the very end you have to show you're the strongest . . .'

He could beg Fanny's help, give up the millions that Irène was not expecting from him, but there is no stopping a man when he's down.

'I've never in all my life asked my wife for anything . . . I'm not going to begin doing so at my age . . .'

Kreuger listens to Léon asking him for one year's breathing space. His handkerchief is stained with blood:

'I'm not well. You know me. We've done some big deals together.'

Kreuger unclenches his jaws:

'Yes, yes, I know, but there comes a time when luck deserts us, just at the moment youth does. Think about it. Perhaps that time has come for you? Listen. I can offer you one thousand pounds.'

'I'm not asking for charity,' replies Léon, turning white.

'I'm offering you what I think is appropriate and necessary and enough for you.'

'You're burying me prematurely, it seems to me. We don't know which of us will die first.'

On the afternoon of Friday, 12th March 1932, a few months after this conversation which Irène Némirovsky placed in June, Kreuger took his own life in this same Paris apartment. It was a suicide with incalculable consequences: French losses of 6,645 billion francs on the stock exchange according to Roger Mennevée, a specialist in financial scandals, who would only take a month to publish his conclusions in a book indicting Président Poincaré of having let the wolf into the sheepfold.[13] Throughout that year, the Imco crash and the enormity of Kreuger's fraudulent dealings would cause much ink to flow. When she heard of Kreuger's suspicious death, Irène described how she rushed to her father's bedside:

'Doesn't that solve your problems?'
    'He has died before me, but I am following him . . .'

Six months after Kreuger, as he had predicted, Léon Némirovsky succumbed to his final lung attack at Boulevard de Cimiez, in Nice. His death would serve as the model for that of James Bohun in *Le Pion sur l'échiquier* [The Pawn on the Chessboard]: 'A long, painful sigh rose in his chest . . . Between his panting, dried-out lips, his final breath had slipped away, along with a silent sigh that ended a long, difficult life, full of vain triumphs and obscure disasters.'[14] Poor old Dad.

Inalienable wealth

Léon died on 16th September 1932, four months after Grandmama Rosa, who died on 18th May. Towards the end of her life she had become almost blind and was prone to unbearable headaches. She could spend three days in a row in her room with the curtains drawn, without leaving her flat in Neuilly. In a letter to her Aunt Victoria, Irène would maintain that she had had to sell Iona's gold watch in order to bury her. Had Léon's insolvency reached such proportions? Could not Fanny have done this one thing for her own mother? At the burial, Irène wore a hat lent to her by Cécile. Her grief was un-mitigated, for she loved her grandmother dearly. She would not forget 'the lines of suffering at the corner of her lips, the sunken corners of her mouth, her eyes that were so deep-set and reddened by tears, in such a way that you could no longer see her very old and faded pupils, forever anxious . . .'

Léon was buried in the Belleville cemetery, on a hill to the east of Paris. Irène had just spent the summer with Michel and Paul Epstein at Hendaye. Standing in front of the grave, beneath the rain, she was torn between great sadness and great loathing; neither the one nor the other would filter through the pages of *The Wine of Solitude*, in which the funeral is described, but her working notebook shows that she had decided, that day, to get rid of the last remnants of any feelings of leniency she might have had for Fanny: 'There were very few people. Lots of flowers . . . Bella had been undecided about whether to put on make-up, and her face, beneath the mourning crepe, had that bloated pallor of old prostitutes looking for their last customer . . .'

No sooner had Léon been put in his tomb than his widow moved into a luxurious flat beside the Seine, on the Quai de Passy – the present-day Avenue du Président-Kennedy – where she would spend the next forty years. She went about in a chauffeur-driven Buick and felt indignant that her daughter paid so little attention to her clothing and scarcely ever mixed in society. Irène, in return, would henceforth only consider Fanny as Denise's grandmother. In spite of these scruples, the final concessions to 'cursed blood', the little girl would more readily recall her feathered hats than her effusiveness: 'I called her madame. She never gave me a kiss on the forehead.'[15]

At the end of *David Golder*, Irène Némirovsky gave the *coup de grâce* to her 'poor Dad' beneath the gaze of a young emigrant, and it was like an adventure beginning all over again. From now on, it was she, the foreigner, who found herself, alone of her flesh and blood, exiled among the living and among the French. 'She was like a child of emigrants, forgotten in a port.'[16] Was it not Léon who had brought her from Kiev to St Petersburg, from St Petersburg to Mustamäki, Helsinki and Stockholm and, from there, to Paris? Was it not he who, in the guise of Golder, had made her famous? Who would now put her on the right path? This sense of loneliness would not leave her. But on the threshold of this new life, her solitude would open unknown perspectives for her. The freedom to abandon her mother just as she herself had been abandoned; the freedom to give her adventurous characters the physique of her father, that 'obscure little Jew' who had worked his way to the top of the financial world. The freedom, too, to liberate her work from her own life and to be judged on her gifts alone. The freedom, finally, to be able to describe, in the near future, without using a device or a pseudonym, her long 'years of apprenticeship': '[Those years] had been exceptionally difficult, but strengthened my courage and my pride. They are mine, my enduring blessing. I may be alone, but my solitude is bitter and intoxicating.'[17]

According to Cécile, Léon would only have left his daughter the sum of 600,000 gold francs. As for Fanny, in the absence of a will, she would not give away a crumb of the riches that had been saved. In Irène's case, in January 1933 she would give Michel Epstein a mandate 'for everything' in the presence of a notary. The novelist's financial troubles emanated from this despoiled inheritance, for she had become accustomed to living luxuriously and well beyond her means. This was also the cause for the sudden proliferation of her short stories and feuilletons, from the end of 1933 onwards, in large circulation period-icals such as *Le Figaro*, the *Revue des Deux Mondes*, *Candide* and *Gringoire*, newspapers that were conservative, nationalist, and even xenophobic. But that was the way the French press was and there was nothing she could do about it. The publication of 'Ida' and later *Jezebel* [*Jézabel*] in the left-wing weekly *Marianne*, in 1934 and 1936, showed that the opinion of those who gave her commissions mattered little to her provided they did not cause her any embarrassment. Irène Némirovsky was a writer, not a polemicist. To accuse her of drinking from the same cup as Henri Béraud would be like the wolf sitting in judgement on the lamb . . .

Two men

The speed with which Irène Némirovsky delivered her new novel leads one to think that *The Courilof Affair* was the first of these potboilers. Begun in the summer of 1932, the book was completed by mid-November. Or was it that she was trying to overcome her sorrow and her confusion by working so unflaggingly? This is plausible, particu-larly since the hero and narrator of the novel, a Tolstoyan terrorist in his soul, is called Léon and dies during the first few pages in a house in Nice, in March 1932 . . . His wife, Fanny Zart, is the daughter of a Jewish watchmaker from Odessa. This zealot will end up hanging in her cell. This is not all: the novelist portrays her mother for a second time as the Franco-Russian tart Margot, a coquette and the 'old, old wife' of the minister Courilof: 'she looked like an ageing bird of para-dise: fading, losing its brilliant plumage, but still as dazzling as costume jewellery, the kind they wear in the theatre'.[18] Moreover, for his daughter Irène's twenty-first birthday, the minister had planned to give a ball that would turn out to be social torture, Their Majesties

insisting that they would only make an appearance if the unworthy
Margot were not there.

The Courilof Affair pretends to be the confession of Léon M. who,
passing himself off as a doctor, has been sent to infiltrate the entourage
of the bloodthirsty Minister for Education, Courilof, nicknamed 'le
Cachalot' (the sperm whale), in order to assassinate him. Courilof had
forged his reputation as a tyrant by mercilessly putting down student
demonstrations. It was reminiscent of an actual event: the assassination of Nikolai Bogoliepov, the former Minister for Education, who
was shot by the student Karpovich in February 1901. But the order
for his execution is slow in coming and Léon, who is immersed in
Schopenhauer ('If you could descend into the heart of your most
hated enemy, you would find yourself there') rather than Lenin,
discovers a man who is as certain as he is about the infirmity of
tsarism. In particular, he takes pity on a valetudinarian, whom power
has unnerved, who is terrified by disgrace and by death, who is
receptive to the arts, to philosophy, and whose convictions are as
shaky as his are steadfast. Forced to cohabit, the murderer and his
victim – or the doctor and his patient – eventually grow accustomed
and come to value one another. Knowledge of human nature is the
worst enemy of revolutionary purity: already, in 1907, the terrorist
in Andreyev's Darkness, saw his principles being undermined by the
jibes of a prostitute.

Once again, The Courilof Affair describes a deterioration, that of the
body; an erosion, that of power; a twilight, that of certainties. Courilof
is an oppressor, certainly, but also an able politician, appalled by the
stupidity of the anti-Semitic party, and who is capable of 'rescue[ing]
the mother of a suspicious young Jewish boy' regardless of what people
might say. Is he good, is he bad? In this book, Irène Némirovsky sets
two autocratic and tyrannical Bolshevik princes back to back, both of
them destroyers of human lives. The novel, a vanitas in political terms,
ends on a relativist credo to the strains of Ecclesiastes: 'A revolution
is such a slaughterhouse! Is it really worth it? . . . Nothing's really
worth the trouble; it's true, not even life.'[19]

Irène Némirovsky had originally thought of calling this study of
revolutionary manners 'Épisode', possibly as an allusion to Balzac's
Épisode sous la Terreur. Then she conceived the title 'Deux hommes',
before realising that this was already the title of 'a fine book by

Duhamel'. For the sum of 25,000 francs, Pierre Brisson, the well-known theatre critic, promised to serialise the novel before the end of March in *Annales politiques et littéraires*, which he had run since 1925. However, since the manuscript had been completed in October, he hoped that the author could quickly provide him with a typed copy in order that serialisation could begin in mid-November. She seemed to be in a hurry too: on 23rd October, ten days after Brisson had written promising to publish it, she supplied him with 68 finished pages and requested her cheque, adding casually: 'If certain expressions strike you as unsuitable, I give you full licence to remove them or replace them.'[20] In fact, the first chapter of *The Courilof Affair* would not appear until 30th December, in order to give priority to André Maurois's *L'Instinct du bonheur*, a decision that puts the reputation of Irène Némirovsky at the end of 1932 in context.

The Courilof Affair can strike one as amateurish. And yet, in order to avoid the implausibilities that certain critics had found in *Snow in Autumn*, Irène Némirovsky had never done so much research. 'The period and the background in which *L'Affaire Courilof* takes place ... have the advantage for me of being known from childhood memories and from the great quantity of memoirs and correspondence I have been able to consult,'[21] she pointed out in May 1933, when the book was published by Grasset. Among her childhood memories, she mainly mentioned her brief discussion with the dreaded governor Sukhomlinov. She also admitted having had a teacher who was subservient to the Narodnaya Volya (The People's Will).[22] 'Courilof, of course, is not Sukhomlinov, any more than David Golder was an exact portrait of any particular financier, they are imaginary portraits, though I think that the conflict and the initial idea for the novel must stem from the reflections that this meeting prompted in me.'[23]

As to the nature of her story, Irène Némirovsky put it down to the interest she had acquired in history since 1931. 'I read a huge amount of biographies, memoirs and letters from that period. There is a very large amount of them, as much in Russian as in French. I drew a great many authentic details from them, going so far as to use phrases that were actually spoken or written by people of that time, and which I put into the mouth of my hero.' Among these books, we should mention Trotsky's autobiography, *My Life*, published in 1930, the only one of these works that she names. We can safely assume that she also read *Memoirs of a Terrorist* by the Bolshevik Savinkov, the man who was behind the murder of the Minister for the Interior, Plehve, in 1904, and the more perceptive readers of *The Courilof Affair* would draw attention to this;[24] also the *Memoirs* of Vera Figner, who was responsible for many assassination attempts (among them that on Alexander II in 1881), published by NRF in March 1930, which may have helped shape the character of Fanny Zart; finally and most importantly, *A History of Russian Terrorism* by General Alexander Spiridovich, published by Payot in 1930. In this 650-page instruction manual, the former head of the Kiev Okhrana and the Imperial criminal investigation department takes care not to broadcast the fact that he was suspected of the plot against the minister, Stolypin, who was murdered at the Grand Opera in Kiev on 1st September 1911. The chief of police, the highly anti-Semitic supporter of Rasputin, Lieutenant-General Kourlov, was also named as being one of the conspirators. Vice-President of the Interior since 1909, this Kourlov would himself escape several assassination attempts until he went into exile in 1917.[25] Could his name have caught Irène Némirovsky's attention? Most probably, but it should also be pointed out that a certain Kurilov taught chemistry in the physicomathematics department of the Imperial Academy of Sciences in St Petersburg, at the time that Michel Epstein studied there . . . This may be a key to decoding the very personal inscription that Irène Némirovsky wrote in the copy of the novel that she gave to her husband: 'For my darling Michel, this book which owes its existence to him, to remember his wife.'

The 1933 man

Between December 1932 and February 1933, immediately after *The Courilof Affair*, Irène Némirovsky began work on a new novel about the death, burial and dreadful legacy of James Bohun, the deposed 'king of steel'. Bohun is but a pale image of Léon, whom she did not dare enshroud in a book quite so quickly. 'What is sad and makes me feel ashamed,' she wrote, recalling the final months of her father's life, 'is the coldness with which I describe everything that is so close to me and that I hold so dear. But then again, the wound is still too recent; it's not good to irritate it . . .' Bohun, an impoverished Greek

lad who has risen to become 'master of the world'[26] through speculating on wartime economy, has more in common with Sir Basil
Zaharoff, a portrait of whom appeared in *Le Crapouillot* in March 1932
and served as a trigger for the novel.[27] He symbolises what Irène
Némirovsky, in her rough draft, called 'the Golder era': one of adventurers in finance and industry, of fortunes built on the battlefield, of
waste and depravity.

These years have passed. ' "Grandeur and decadence" appear to be
the family motto.'[28] It is hard not to read into this the bitterness of
the novelist, who was now ground down with worries about money.
After the 'Bohun crash', his son Christophe is merely an employee,
earning two thousand francs, in his father's firm, which has been sold
off cheaply to his former right-hand man, Biruleff, a Romanian Jew
who has anglicised his name to Beryl, 'a foreigner, a man without
family or friends, a *heimatlos*'.[29] A crook to whom she had to forgo
giving the name Tedesco (the patronymic of a number of Italianised
Ashkenazys) because 'this name is dangerous': she was not going to
be accused of anti-Semitism for a second time. Why Beryl? Irène
Némirovsky had encountered him in Katherine Mansfield's stories
'Prelude' and 'At the Bay', which she never stopped rereading . . .

The backround: 'Unemployment . . . crisis . . . budget deficit . . . The
hunger march in London . . . Unemployment . . . crisis . . .'[30] The social
smack in the face of the 1930s in retaliation for the wealthy times in
the 1920s: this is the subject of The Pawn on the Chessboard [*Le Pion
sur l'échiquier*], whose title becomes immediately obvious. The moral
is another biblical moral lesson: 'The fathers have eaten sour grapes,
and the children's teeth are set on edge.'[31] Christophe Bohun, when
he is in a position to blackmail Beryl profitably and cynically take over
from his father, prefers to watch himself die. 'Ah, how I hate life. Shit,
oh shit, shit, shit . . .'[32] Drenched with rain from the first page to the
final storm, *The Pawn on the Chessboard* is the story of a suicide.
Christophe drowns himself in self-induced degradation: 'On some
rainy mornings, when I leave the house, I feel the desire to lie down
in the middle of the road, and wait for the first passing bus to run
over my body.'[33] This world-weariness puts him in the same category
as Emmanuel Bove's eternal death-wishers, the Arnold of *Un suicide*
(March 1933) for instance, who become hermits due to social pressure.
Even Bohun's miserable death is unworthy of his journey to the grave.

A downgraded version of Yves Harteloup (*Le Malentendu*), is he too familiar with death, ever since the trenches, to counter it with money, love, hope and even regret? 'Love, pleasure, they mean so little . . .'[34]

The Pawn on the Chessboard, a parable about the condition of salaries, the proletariat of office life and the 'curse of work',[35] is the first of Irène Némirovsky's novels of which almost complete drafts survive. Hesitant, convoluted and interspersed with long monologues, or admonishments and calls to order ('Careful! I'm losing sight of the original outline!'), with invective and self-criticism ('I could have written "adorable toddler! . . ." Damnation!'), and with comments and quotations in English or in Russian, these congested pages show that the novelist had wanted to create an X-ray picture of the Great Depression and provide an 'image of the 1933 man'. From the beginning, this sociological aspect – which is occasionally heavy-going – is perfectly described: 'It should equally be a novel about the second generation (after D.G.), the father having worked all his life, <u>pointless hard work</u>, and the son, seeing the worthlessness and futility of work, but forced to do it, and hating it . . . It should be *Babbitt de France* . . . It's <u>the man in the street</u> . . . It's the pawn who is moved about the board, and who for 2 or 3 or 4 francs a month gives his time, his health, his soul, and his life.' Vast perspectives, but she did not conceal from herself that, since Léon's death, she herself had become this pawn: 'In short drag myself out of my current anxiety. 1) Worrying about the future. 2) What's the use? 3) Failed long-term considerations. 4) And pleasures destroyed.'

As with *David Golder*, she began by constructing the biography of Christophe Bohun, born in 1893, married in 1916 to a bluestocking to whom he is unfaithful in 1918. Then a carefree life, 'Paris, Nice, Biarritz etc.'; 'A man like any other in appearance who, born into a wealthy family and brought up expensively, retains the manners, clothing, appearance, language.' Her model, concealed behind an initial, was the bachelor, Paul Epstein. For the sake of the plot (although there is very little), Christophe has to neglect his own daughter; but Irène is reluctant to have him do so, 'because of the tender love I have for my own one'. As for the easy-going Philippe, who works at the 'up to date' cinema and who is as boorish as a Paul Morand hero, he is a darker version of Samuel Epstein.

The voice tests then follow. Irène Némirovsky experiments with

Christophe's in a long monologue: 'I hate work . . . No, work is not self-respect, no, work is not freedom! . . . Love bores me rigid, except with some girl or other, in a sleazy hotel, in passing. I hate the whole world . . . I hate the town. I hate people. I hate my timorous conscience that stops me from running away! Most of all I hate these ghosts, these shadowy distractions, that comfort men . . . I should like to be a plant, an animal, a tree!'

Once this 'previous life of the novel'[36] has been completed, comes the first drafting of technical advice, punctuated as if from memory: 'Unequivocal rule, even more unequivocal than for *David*: complete objectivity . . . The only way, is the cinematographic technique.' Then, using a blue and a red pencil, Irène Némirovsky crosses out, underlines and furiously scribbles over her first draft, scattering it with 'no' and 'yes'. 'All the passages that have a circle round them will be ruthlessly deleted. Only the others will remain. A framework? I think that too tight a framework is dangerous, I write the whole book first, the framework then comes of its own accord. That was the way Barrès worked, and I think it's the right way.'[37] Above all, she should not lose sight of the fact that the result of this architecture ought to be comprehensible to the man in the street, for 'I am not writing for Daniel-Rops; I am writing for Mr Everyman, who is more intelligent and less fortunate than Daniel-Rops.' This second draft, finished in the spring of 1933, could now be left for several months, before the ferocious rereading prior to the final version.

The utmost caution

The Courilof Affair – a novel for which Irène Némirovsky would say she had sizeable offers from competing publishers – was published by Grasset at the beginning of May. It was number 1 in the new series 'Pour mon plaisir'. It was also to be her last book for Grasset, for the sales would not be good. In 1936, Michel Epstein would even blame his 'dear Bernard' for not having bothered about the launch of the book. The critics saw it as the author's true second book. But, some notable exceptions apart, the theme of the book was considered to be unattractive, the length of the book was unappealing and the result was 'a failure'.[38] Even Ramon Fernandez, one of the more complimentary reviewers, writing

in *Marianne*, regretted that '[her] gift for telling a story so compe-
tently can sometimes remove from the narrative a sense of necessity,
of involuntary urgency, so to speak, that arouses the attention and
emotions of the reader'.[39] The more forgiving among them agreed to
liken this tale of terrorism to Malraux's *La Condition humaine* or to
Joseph Kessel. Others, such as Marcel Prévost, acquitted themselves
politely: 'It's very good.'[40] There were few eulogies and many
complaints: the book was too long ("There was the wherewithal here
for an excellent hundred-page novella'[41]); it was bewildering ('how far
this neurasthenic and teetering revolutionary really is from the
truth!'[42]); it had been done before ('Ah! How tired we are of these
stories! We have had so many of them!'[43]); and – the height of in-
accuracy – it was poorly documented. Jean-Baptiste Séverac, for
instance, the deputy general secretary of the SFIO (Section française
de l'Internationale ouvrière), who boasted of having met some genuine
Russian revolutionaries in 1905, asserted that he had 'not recognised
in Mme Némirovsky's hero any of the aspects that seemed to me to
have characterised the terrorists of that period'.[44] Once again, the
novelist was the victim of a misunderstanding – as a parable, *The
Courilof Affair* did not claim to be an historical work – but also the
victim of her own fame, for which *Action française* made her pay dearly:
'Mme Némirovsky has drawn out this subject for a short story to two
hundred and seventy-six pages that, from first to last, exude the most
deadly boredom. We can confirm that to continue to the very end
requires courage bordering on heroism . . . It is a curious case, which
shows once again how dangerous critical hyperbole can be. You believe
in your own brilliance, you stop working and you are your own
victim.'[45]

Action française barked, Némirovsky passed on by. Duvivier's film,
shown in August 1932 at the Venice Biennale, came out in the United
States in the autumn – to be met with relative indifference, it is true;
as for Nozière's play, it was put on again in May 1933 by a Russian
company at the Théâtre Moncey. After *Les Annales*, another eminently
Parisian monthly journal, Marcel Thiébaut's *Revue de Paris* – which
published Giraudoux, Morand, Larbaud and Giono – agreed to publish
one of her stories. 'Un déjeuner en septembre' appeared in the 1st
May issue. Thérèse Dallas is forty years old. An unexpected reunion
– a man whom she had once loved – fills her with regret. The ravages

of time are reflected in her lorgnette: 'puffy cheeks, weary eyes, lines' . . . The word 'faded' occurs no less than six times in this meditation on passing time and decay. 'Happiness was like rainy summer holidays at the seaside, when only the last day had been fine, and that was all that was required to be nostalgic for them.'[46] For Robert Brasillach, who would refer to it in 1934, this story was Irène Némirovsky's 'masterpiece', 'as perfect as a Chekhov short story'.[47] Written in triple sequences of words, in a controlled style and with period elegance, in the style of 'La Comédie bourgeoise', this was her second attempt at analysing feelings, possibly influenced by Jacques Chardonne, whose melancholy stories she envied. This can be seen from her letter of thanks sent to the novelist from the Charente on 21st December 1932:

> Dear Sir,
>
> A few days ago I received *L'Amour du prochain* and I couldn't help reading it from end to end 'like a novel': they say one shouldn't read reflections in this way,[48] but, as I say, I couldn't help it . . . yours are admirable and, in addition to their depth and their truth, there is a poetic outcome that I find very moving and which astonishes me and pleases me like a secret I want to procure . . .

Furthermore, she was turning away from the 'modernists' and veering towards classicism. 'It's strange to see how literary admiration changes with age and living conditions,' she confessed in June to Frédéric Lefèvre. 'To begin with, I mostly liked writers of the last half of the nineteenth century, such as Huysmans. Then I had a passionate admiration for Proust; I knew his work in every detail . . . My preferences today are for authors who are generally agreed to be "old-fashioned". For example, in France, George Sand. When one has had quite enough of all the excitement of today's wonderful life, one ought to read *La Petite Fadette*. What a marvellous sense of peace!'[49] This change of course did not prevent her in the least from berating 'that ass Chardonne' in her working notebook.

In the same issue of *Revue de Paris*, there was a disturbing article on 'Anti-Semitism in Germany', predicting the extermination of Israel not 'by pogroms', but 'by asphyxiation'.[50] Since the accession of Hitler to the Chancellery on 30th January 1933, no one was counting prophets of the Apocalypse any more. In October 1932 there was even an essay published announcing the date of the future Nazi offensive.[51] For Irène Némirovsky, there could no longer be any doubt about the outcome, and she talked about it quite openly to Cécile:

'Well! This time there'll be a war. With the arrival of Hitler we'll hear more about it, Néné, and we'll die, you'll see.'

In the spring of 1933, anti-Semitic propaganda was on the rise in France, with the influx of thousands of refugees fleeing the 'thousand-year Reich'. *Action française* accused the Bishop of Lille of opening his arms to the 'Judaeo-Germanic invasion'.[52] This campaign was heeded, because on 2nd August the immigration services were sent a circular warning them to open the border crossings only 'with extreme caution'. In a book due to appear that autumn, the incorrigible Tharaud brothers denied that Hitler had invented German anti-Semitism, and gave credit for this to Kant, Fichte and Hegel. They even allowed the Brownshirts extenuating circumstances, since the boycotts and the 'violence to individuals', which had been exaggerated by those brainwashed by socialism, were not yet comparable 'by a long chalk, to what had been seen not long ago in Russia, to those pogroms, those systematic killings, organised by the police, on Government orders . . .'[53] What more was needed than auto-da-fés? Uncle Adler, who had moved to the United States in the early thirties, where he was later joined by Raïssa, suggested that the Epsteins do the same. Irène and Michel would do nothing: where is one safer than in the bosom of one's family? And Irène Némirovsky's family, more than ever, was France.

The Monster

At about this time, the idea began to germinate for a new story which, like *Snow in Autumn*, she categorised under the heading 'Déclins'. Her title, 'Le Mercredi des Cendres' [Ash Wednesday], shows that – yet again – it was to do with a conceit. She planned to portray 'the old age of the sinner'. With this in mind, she reread *The Picture of Dorian Gray* and she reluctantly immersed herself in the memoirs of Wilde's lover. Then she outlined the features of her character: 'thick-set and heavy' like a Houdon bust, pale and fair as a Titian, he was born in 1855, but her notes show that he derived his 'barbarous cruelty' from the hetman Petlyura, whose troops recklessly massacred Jews and Bolsheviks during the civil war. 'Is he base and powerful, or, on the contrary, a sort of old-fashioned romantic? No one knows him. Not even me. Perhaps he is simply impulsive and temperamental? He doesn't give a damn about people, quite sincerely and quite deeply . . . Why not make him a well-known minister like Bülow or Witte?'

Suddenly this shifting draft version changes course. Irène Némirovsky remembers Kiev and remembers the war. She remembers her father who died a few months before. She gives her character a Tartar name, Koïré, and conjures up a path for him as a Russian businessman who will sink into poverty. His home is not unlike that of Léon Némirovsky: 'The Koïré family, the father, a little Jew, eaten away by a kind of long and muddled ambition, show his dreams about the need for leather, his *"combinazione"*, sums and the wife . . . Show the life of the Koïrés. He, in particular, who quietly grows richer as a result of it, to begin with, and develops a liking.' This is the first intuition of *The Wine of Solitude* [*Le Vin de Solitude*]. She finished it and corrected it during the summer, which she spent at Urrugne with Michel, his brother Paul – still a bachelor – and the latter's house-keeper. 'It's a delightful and ancient village,' she explained, 'and the house I've managed to rent is an old posthouse from the time of Louis XIV, with huge walls, a vast loft, and with endless cupboards, stair-cases and hiding places. From the way I describe this house, you will guess that I am slightly in love with it, and it's quite true.'[54] The house at Urrugne, on the old road to Spain, was in fact a haven of peace, conducive to creative work, which she summarised in a few words in her working notebook: 'Narrow garden, full of stones. Silence, the distant rumbling of thunder and the sound of feet on the gravel. Flowers both common and dazzling.' During the summer of 1933, she sketched out no less than four new books, one of which, *Deux* [Two], would not be published until 1939 . . .

From 1926 to 1940, Irène Némirovsky wrote only one long, single, continuous novel, an uninterrupted manuscript from which, as they matured, short stories and secondary narratives would detach them-selves. But the trunk that bore these fruits remained and it was none other than the genealogical tree of the Némirovskys. This explains the autobiographical substance of her books, diluted to a greater or lesser degree. *Le Bal* (1929) was a shoot out of *David Golder* (1930), from which grew *The Pawn on the Chessboard* (1933), which was itself an echo of *Le Malentendu* [The Misunderstood] (1926). 'Les Fumées du vin' (1934) was a earlier version of *The Wine of Solitude* (1935), itself a development of *L'Ennemie* [The Enemy] (1928), out of which would stem *Jezebel* [Jézabel] (1936) and *Les Échelles du Levant* [The Ports of the Levant] (1939), in the same way that 'Le Sortilège' was a chapter taken from *The Dogs and the Wolves* (1940). This parthenogenesis comes from the fact that her method of work depended upon improvisation. 'I start writing, as a rough draft, both the novel itself and, at the same time, the thoughts it provokes, the actual diary of the novel, to use André Gide's expression. Then I leave it all to settle and I do my best not to think about literature any more. When I go back to it, every-thing seems to plan and write itself of its own accord.'[55]

One of these 'rough drafts' appeared at Urrugne and Hendaye, born of an impatient womb, brimming with outlines, dead ends, changes of direction and false starts. She entitled this Piranesi-like shambles: 'Le Monstre'. Like Katherine Mansfield's journal, which had just been published by Stock, it was sometimes difficult to disentangle fiction and autobiography. Irène Némirovsky berated herself more than usual: 'Take heart, my girl! You're still young, after all. You have to forge your technique, your method and your tools by yourself.' Holiday homework for the summer of 1933: drag up the greatest number of images of Russia and Finland, 'as if I were fishing for memories with a fish-hook', so as to procure material for two or three years of writing. For, she reckoned, 'there are enough memories and enough poetry in my life to make a novel'.

Although it required a considerable feat of memory ('there are . . . my God . . . 15 years of that. I don't remember very well'), she managed to clear away the snow and obtain unimpaired memories of Mustamäki, enough for at least nine comic, tragic or moving stories, 'of the *Mouches d'automne* type, by polishing up each episode'. She remembered Zézelle's 'slow madness', the 'walks along the Dnieper', the 'lonely Sundays' in Kiev, 'the feeling of envy for other children', 'the mother returning at dawn', her entire youth in fact, 'extracted by force from the past'. Naturally, it would be a good idea to inject into this jumble 'a little apparent inconsistency', while at the same time being careful not to 'deliberately write badly' as Maurois had done in his novel *Le Cercle de famille*, which had an almost identical subject:

the rebellion of a well-brought-up girl who is disgusted by the shallow-ness of family life – 'I'm ashamed of my mother. I don't want to be like her'[56] – and destined for failure because it is in her genes.

Then, despite the beach and the sunshine, Némirovsky would have to force herself to work every day: '2 hours in the morning (10.30 to 12.30) except on days writing articles. Or else walk and 2 hours in the afternoon from 5 to 7.' For in addition to her writing work, Irène Némirovsky had agreed to provide reading notes and cinema reviews to *Rempart*, an 'unattached newspaper' that was fiercely anti-Nazi, and 'independent of government and all governments'. This national daily, founded in March by Paul Lévy, a speculator in politics as well as in the press, would not survive the summer; it was immediately succeeded by *Aujourd'hui*, a mass-market paper whose front page was covered in photographs. This newspaper was noted for its anti-Bolshevism and its blustering patriotism, but also for an anti-Nazism that owed a great deal to the Croix-de-Feu,* which Paul Lévy looked upon approvingly. Léon Pierre-Quint and Jean-Pierre Maxence ran the book page, and René Daumal wrote about cinema. Up until March 1934, Irène Némirovsky wrote theatre reviews for the paper. Her reviews of the latest productions of Steve Passeur, Joseph Bédier, Denys Amiel, Édouard Bourdet, Fernand Crommelynck and Ferdinand Brückner reveal a constant preoccupation of the public and plausibility. 'For, at the theatre, in order to be interested in the characters, they have to arouse pity in us.'[57]

A soul with no resting place

With nothing else to offer, Irène Némirovsky was now obliged to bring forth the stories from her fecund 'Monstre'. 'I have three things on my mind at the moment. "Épisodes", "Deux" and "La Famille Kern". Fortunately, I am quite drawn by the three of them.'

The 'Épisodes', to begin with. Nine, then seven, they would soon

---

*The Croix-de-Feu was an association of right-wing war veterans, founded in 1927. Later, under the leadership of Colonel de La Rocque (*see p.223*), it took on a strong political dimension, and in 1936 it became a political party in its own right, known as the Parti social français (PSF). [Tr.]

be no more than two: the first 'L'Accouchement de Bluma', would be published under the title 'Nativité'; the second, 'Le Vin', is a simple 'prelude' to the 'fictionalised memories' she was thinking about. Real 'hackwork', she sighed, but at least she had 'the excuse of business' . . . In this connection, what would she do with this 'wine' when it was uncorked? 'Ah! It could be published in the *Revue de Paris* (or in *Gringoire* and be given afterwards to Paul Morand for Gallimard!!!).' In the end, it would be submitted in June 1934 to *Le Figaro*, under the title 'Les Fumées du vin'.

Of the three offspring of the 'Monstre', the second was premature: *Deux* was 'not ready yet, and the characters, especially, are extremely vague'. All Irène Némirovsky envisaged was that this novel, 'the first optimistic book I shall write', would have as its subject 'the notion that consists of showing behind the horror, the seeming chaos of life, its beauty and its cohesion'. Faced with the trials and tribulations, the betrayals and the sorrows, *Deux* would be a novel about 'the acceptance of life'. To develop this, she would, alas, need 'a minimum of 2 years'. For, prior to starting work on this antidote to revenge and pity, she would first have to distil the poison, the gall that would be the sap and blood of her third project, the most strikingly truthful one: 'La Famille Kern'. A family which, of course, was her own.

'It would be possible to write a genuine film script with all the episodes of my life . . .'[58] Irène Némirovsky informed the Russian newspaper *Poslednija Novosti* in 1931. It was while she was thinking about Walter Ruttmann's silent documentary film *Mélodie du monde* (1929) that the idea of recreating a universe, her own, came to her: 'One day, later on, a Jewish family, in time and space . . . That would make a fine song of the world . . .' A variety of godparents[59] and literary signposts would be invoked as she tried to describe this first story that would become *The Wine of Solitude*: 'Me. My youth', 'Fictionalised memories', 'A poorly disguised autobiography', 'Fictionalised autobiography in the style of Dickens', '"The Apprenticeship Years" in the style of *Wilhelm Meister*', 'The story of a life', 'A deviated life'. This last title indicates her idea well enough: the evolution of a childish soul bewildered by the hatred of her mother, a hatred 'that must go as far as wanting her to die'. This was the subject of *L'Ennemie*, but since then Léon had died and Irène had no reason to spare Fanny by

▲ As a teenager. 'A dark skin, a simple face and so thin that no one noticed her; she was too pale, with the olive colouring of the children of St Petersburg.' (Notebook, summer 1933) *Tatiana Morozova collection*

▲ Leonid Némirovsky. 'My unhappy Papa … The only one from whom I feel that I, my blood, my restless soul, my strength and my weakness have sprung.' (Notebook for *The Wine of Solitude*) © IMEC

▲ 'Little mother, all dressed up for the ball, her shoulders bare, with a naïve, triumphant smile that seemed to say: "Just look at me! Aren't I beautiful? And if you only knew how much pleasure that gives me!"' (*L'Ennemie*, 1928) *Tatiana Morozova collection*

◀ Irène and her young aunt Victoria. In the foreground is Marie, her French governess. 'I no longer want to call her Zézelle, it's too sacrosanct. I shall see. Mademoiselle Rose is good, too…' (Notebook for *The Wine of Solitude*) *Tatiana Morozova collection*

▶ Iona Margoulis, her maternal grandfather, was the only person who 'spoke French perfectly. He would say: "Ma petite *file*" (my little girl), putting a strong stress on the last syllable of the mispronounced word.' (Notebook for *The Wine of Solitude*) © IMEC

▶ Rosa Chedrovich, known as 'Bella', her maternal grandmother. 'A poor, slender, scrawny little woman, in my imagination […] a face that was faded like an old photograph, her features heavy and yellowing, drenched in tears…' (Notebook for *The Wine of Solitude*) © IMEC

◀ Anna Némirovsky (her mother), known as 'Fanny'. 'What is needed is to show it from the inside, show it in short almost like *Phèdre*, in her impossibility of resisting her vice, her desire, that pride in remaining young and desirable.' (Notebook for *The Wine of Solitude*) © IMEC

▶ General Sukhomlinov, governor of Kiev, in the presence of whom, aged eight, she recited the Duke of Reichstadt's speech from Edmond Rostand's play *L'Aiglon*. 'I was very excited to find myself face to face with this person who, for us, was a symbol of terror, tyranny and cruelty. To my great surprise, I saw a charming man who looked like my grandfather and who had the gentlest eyes imaginable.' (1932) © IMEC

► As a teenager, outside the Excelsior Regina Hotel at Cimiez. '… It is not the luxury that you admire. You imagine a perfect life in which everything is order and beauty…well, paradise!' (7 July 1938) © IMEC

▼ With her mother, pre-1914. 'I think we are going to Biarritz…' (Postcard, 1912 or 1913) © IMEC

▲ 'Papa? The only thing he loves in the world is business, he treasures it far more than he does you or me.'
(Notebook of *The Wine of Solitude*) © IMEC

▼ Irène and her mother. 'A young girl of fifteen, slim, dark, with brown arms that are too thin, and legs that look powerful because they are shaped like those of a woman.'
(Notebook, summer 1933) © IMEC

▶ Anna and Léon, her parents. 'He must have been in love with her. [...] Later on, he must have had more flattering conquests, but at that time he was nothing but an obscure little Jew.'
(Notebook of *The Wine of Solitude*) © IMEC

▼ Anna Némirovsky inscribed this photo to Julie with the initial 'J', for Jeanne. 'If only this scum in the luxury hotels would disappear, there would be no one who would regret it [...].'
(*Aujourd'hui*, n° 285, 31 January 1934) © IMEC

► In Nice, in about 1920, with her father and Miss Matthews. 'Look how you have been brought up, you have lovely dresses, a handsome allowance, a motor car, an Englishwoman… And happiness! You have happiness because you are young…'
(Notebook for *The Wine of Solitude*)
© IMEC

► At Le Touquet. 'She appeared to have stopped growing, and at the age of twenty she still had the slight, slender body of a child. […] A mobile and expressive face, but with a rounded, oval, child-like shape, a pretty, delicate nose, an ugly mouth, dazzling teeth, and soft, piercing eyes.' (*L'Ennemie*, 1928) © IMEC

▼ Dressed up as a gypsy, in about 1920. 'This frenzied and dream-like music was like nothing that she had heard until then.' (*L'Ennemie*, 1928) © IMEC

'She had a horse that was in love with her/ And a pale green cat…' ('Contes', poem in Russian, written in about 1918) © IMEC

'Ah, in the old days!… A woman who flaunted legs like yours every morning, well, after a week she would have had a motor car, a little mansion, the lot!' ('Nonoche au vert', 1921) © IMEC

'Your amber cigarette-holder
Trembles between your pale
and gentle lips
The stylish dance and the blare of the jazz band
a-a-a-a
Lures you and entices you'
(poem in Russian, 1921) © IMEC

◀ (*left*): 'I don't know whether you remember Michel Epstein, a small, brown-haired man with very dark skin […]? He is courting me and, well, I find him attractive.' (Letter to Madeleine Cabour, 1925) © IMEC

◀ 'May what has happened to Russia serve as a warning to the civilised world!' Michel's father, the banker Efim Epstein, wrote in 1925. © IMEC

▶ On a walk in Fontainebleau. 'But as soon as you got away from Paris, you could see real trees, leafy, full of shadows and birds…' (*L'Ennemie*, 1928) © IMEC

◀ Denise Epstein was born in November 1929, a few months before the publication of *David Golder*. 'She doesn't look at all like me; she is almost blonde with grey eyes but I think they are still changing.'
(Letter to Madeleine Cabour, 22 January 1930) © IMEC

▼ Paulette Andral and Harry Baur in the stage version of *David Golder*, caricatured by Sennep.
(*L'Écho de Paris*, 1930)

A LA PORTE-SAINT-MARTIN

▼ 'I have always written. I could never not write.' (*Les Nouvelles littéraires*, 2 November 1935) © *Roger-Viollet*

▲ 'This young mother looks like a girl. [...] Her eyes are black, just as black as her hair; they have that strange softness – at times barely blinking – that creates a slightly short-sighted look.'
(Frédéric Lefèvre, 1930) © IMEC

◀ René Doumic and Henri de Régnier.
© *Sirot-Angel*

▼ Hélène and Paul Morand. DR

▼ Bernard Grasset, 'our friendly little megalomaniac'. DR

▲ Albin Michel. DR

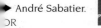

▶ André Sabatier.
DR

▶ 'A happy day is so rare! You will see later on. There will be rainy Thursdays when you won't be able to go out, when you will be nostalgic for this fine summer, when you will think: How good it would be to still be on the beach together! And it will be too late.'
('Comme de grands enfants', 1939) © IMEC

▼ At Hendaye. 'It's a crime to bring children into the world and not to give them a shred, an ounce of love.'
(*The Wine of Solitude*, 1935) © IMEC

▶ At Urrugne, in 1933. 'The house I've managed to rent is an old posthouse from the time of Louis XIV, with huge walls, a vast loft, and with endless cupboards, staircases and hiding-places. From the way I describe the house, you will realise that I am slightly in love with it, and it's quite true.' © IMEC

▲ '7 July 38. [...] We suffocate in the house; we suffocate in the sand. No desire to work, and, at the same time that vague anxiety...' © IMEC

◀ 'How very peculiar we are in the end! Our feeble memory retains only the slightest trace of happiness, so deeply engrained at times that it could almost be called a wound.' ('Les Revenants', 1941) © IMEC

▶ Summer 1939: last holidays at 'Ene Etchea', a rented villa at Hendaye-Plage. © IMEC

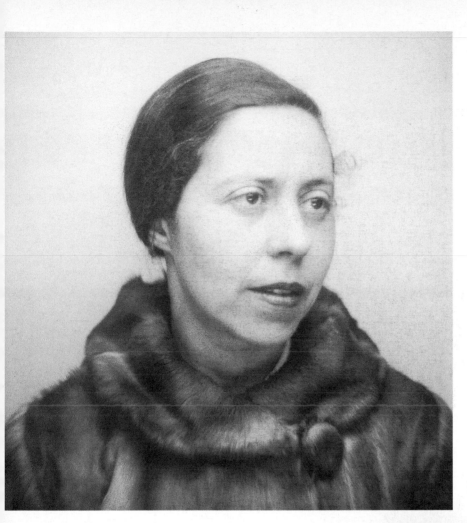

▲ 'When the money is used up, start by selling the fur coats that you will find in our suitcases, which you will certainly recognise…'
(To Julie Dumot, 22 June 1940) © IMEC

▶ With 'Babet', at Issy-l'Evêque. 'This region, in the middle of France, is both wild and rich. Everyone lives in his own house, on his own land, distrusts his neighbours, harvests his wheat, counts his money and doesn't give a thought to the rest of the world.' (*Fire in the Blood*) © IMEC

▲ The manuscript of *Suite française*. 'I've written a great deal lately. I suppose they will be posthumous books but it still makes the time go by.'
(Letter to André Sabatier, 11 July 1942) © IMEC

using a pseudonym. More than a settling of accounts, this new novel would have an oedipal dimension: 'Show that she loved the husband, but could not make up her mind to be faithful to him because of all the bad feelings she has. And how, when the father dies, she breaks off relationships with her mother. After all, life . . . Why not? Nothing holds me back, and nothing, after all, is as good as one's own memories.'

It would merely be a question of changing the names. For herself, Irène Némirovsky was spoilt for choice: Catherine Kern? Or else Marianne, 'which means bitter, bitterness'? Jenny, Annette, Daisy, Élisabeth? 'No, not Élisabeth, a pretty English name, one of those names that were used in smart families.' Ginette, Betsy, Margaret? 'No, it's more a name like Irène that I must look for, Hélène would "sound right".' Mary?' It would be Hélène. Like Ivan Ilyich's daughter. Like the Elena in *The White Guard*. Like the heroine of Turgenev's *Smoke*, Chekhov's *Uncle Vanya*, Joseph Kessel's *Nuits de prince*.[60] A gesture, too, to the number of critics who continued to refer to her as 'Hélène' Némirovsky. 'For my mother, on the other hand, I will describe her and it will be worse than Rosine and all the others.' Fanny, who is rechristened Bella, will, in *The Wine of Solitude*, be 'sometimes a monster, sometimes a pitiful creature you look at with hatred and terror, like the very face of unhappiness, who has weighed down [on me] throughout the past, a face that you don't recognise, that you fear not recognising' . . .

On her return to Paris in September 1933, Irène Némirovsky drafted the outline for her novel: 'I. Russia – Kiev – hatred. II. Petersburg – revenge. III. Paris – pity.' For a moment she even thought of including the episode of the rape, which was so decisive a factor, before changing her mind: 'What is there left in life after this crisis? One is responsible for the fate of one's children. But you cannot demonstrate this by depicting a monster . . .'

Yet *The Wine of Solitude* would be the portrait of a monster. It would also be the tomb of her stolen childhood, from which she was never really cured and which continued to haunt her. 'So this would be the shaping or rather the deviation of a heart. A child who has not been loved, and who, later, never has enough love . . . I believe that the guiding idea should be the following – and everything should be based around it: You do not forgive your childhood. An unhappy childhood is as if your soul had died with no resting place, one that is eternally weeping.'

A long-term engagement

In the autumn of 1933, Irène Némirovsky suddenly parted company with Bernard Grasset so that she could offer *Le Pion sur l'échiquier* to Albin Michel. She was not bothered by the mental state of the publisher, who was prey to megalomaniacal whims and ungovernable rages, torn between the treatments of Doctors Hesnard and Laforgue, and 'reduced to a complete wreck . . . weeping, like a child who refuses to wash or to eat',[61] in the view of Jacques-Émile Blanche, writing in his diary in June 1930. On the contrary, she would be one of the few to testify on his behalf when the time came to defend him in a dispute over trusteeship. And Michel Epstein continued to address him as 'tu' up until the war.

However, *The Courilof Affair* had not been successful: ten thousand copies sold, as against over sixty thousand of *David Golder*, twelve thousand of *Le Bal* and six thousand of *Snow in Autumn* [*Les Mouches d'automne*]. This was a long way from the hundred thousand of Maurois, Mauriac or Morand. Now, following the death of her father, Irène Némirovsky was in need of a regular income, and Albin Michel had proposed an exclusive twenty-year contract, 'both for volume rights and for publication in one or more of its journals'. At the rate of one or two novels a year, she would receive from 1st November onwards, for a renewable period of three years, a monthly amount of 4,000 francs, a guaranteed total sum, in other words, of 144,000 francs. Irène Némirovsky was careful to write to Grasset immediately to inform him of her intentions, and particularly of her reasons:

> You know how unwilling I have always been to undertake long-term commitments. Unfortunately, present circumstances oblige me to do so; I have therefore decided to accept the contract in question, which I must sign before the end of the week. Needless to say, should you be prepared to offer me the same terms, I would give you preference with the greatest of pleasure, and I would be very happy to continue to be connected with your House.[62]

A special clause in her contract, however, allowed her to publish 'a collection of screenplays' with Grasset, as originally agreed, that would consist mainly of 'Film parlé', 'La Comédie bourgeoise' and 'Les Fumées du vin'. The publisher of *David Golder*, who was angry, did nothing about this, which is the reason why the collection *Films parlés* was immediately picked up by NRF, where Paul Morand edited a series of short texts entitled 'Renaissance de la nouvelle'. This alarmed her new publisher, who was distressed to see his latest recruit deserting him already. But Albin Michel knew how to tell someone off humorously: 'Our spiritual marriage is really too recent and it would be unseemly for me to allow you to be unfaithful when our first child has not yet been born!' he wrote to Irène Némirovsky on 13th November. She, somewhat stung, replied with delightful effrontery: 'The wife must submit to her husband. Which is why I am very happy to bow to your decision, and I hope that you will instil in our children after they are born the same feelings that you show towards them in their embryonic stage.' These exchanges were a token of a healthy understanding. And as far as *Films parlés* was concerned, no harm was done: it was agreed with Morand that the collection would contain nothing but 'screenplays' and that it would not be published for another year . . .

Albin Michel had built the reputation of his firm, which was founded in 1901, on an excellent knowledge of bookshops. A man of flair rather than one to pull off coups, he had landed an unexpected Goncourt Prize with *Batouala*, René Maran's '*roman nègre*' in 1921; he had improved his backlist with prestigious classics acquired from his purchase of Ollendorff in 1924; he had taken on 'heavyweight' authors such as Roland Dorgelès, Francis Carco, Henri Béraud and Pierre Benoit; but he had also invested in popular literature, from Félicien Champsaur to Georges Ohnet, as well as the *Claudine* novels of Colette. Irène Némirovsky somewhat epitomised his list: a successful author, of good literary quality, and who was always surprising. She could not have escaped him! No doubt Gaston Chérau and Roland Dorgelès, who were both published by Albin Michel and who were the novelist's sponsors at the Société des Gens de Lettres, would have spoken on her behalf. And so would Henri de Régnier, who formerly edited an in-house series.

On 24th October, Irène Némirovsky took the leap: her signature committed her for life to the firm of Albin Michel. Two days later, *L'Intransigeant*, with a daily circulation of 400,000, began serialising *Le Pion sur l'échiquier*. Gaston Chérau had informed readers about it the previous day in eulogistic terms: 'We may find five hundred authors of novels; one doesn't always find a novelist among that number.' This version of *Le Pion* was not a success, far from it, but the author planned to revise it prior to its publication in book form, scheduled for February 1934. With this in mind, Albin Michel sent her a copy of a report commissioned from one of his readers, which found the novel 'sad' and too 'short on incident' for the wider public. Irène Némirovsky was very close to sharing this diagnosis when she started to reread it, in December. 'I have the sense initially that it lacks sparkle, but that it's quite difficult to remedy it.' The sociological goal of the novel was too obvious, the paint too thick, the pace too slow: 'Much too defined, too explained, too many dots on the "i"s. Pointless.' She had to moderate the style, create more dialogue, 'say in two words what was said in ten, in just one what was said in two, and every word should be sincere, and should say what it means, and eventually say more than it means'. . . . The pawn [*le pion*] was on the chessboard, but the game had begun badly.

To the right or to the left?

Although opposed to the custom whereby writers allowed the publisher to grant first refusal of their works to mass-circulation newspapers, Albin Michel had decided to create his own weekly paper in order to prevent his authors from publishing their work in *Candide* (owned by Fayard), *Les Nouvelles littéraires* (Larousse), *Marianne* (Gallimard) or *Gringoire* (Éditions de France). In December 1933, however, the shape of the new journal, *Noir et Blanc*, was still far from being finalised. Irène Némirovsky wanted to apply to the magazine for the 'vacant position of drama or film critic'. Albin Michel would have preferred some short stories, but meanwhile he could not reasonably prevent her from offering stories to his rivals. Which is what she proceeded to do by taking one of the 'Épisodes' written during the summer and entitled 'Nativité – a title that only came to her two weeks before Christmas – to Horace de Carbuccia, the owner of *Gringoire*.

The short story appeared in the 8th December issue. Irène Némirovsky transposed Bluma's childbirth to a French family that was the spitting image of that of Madeleine Avot. It is an embellishment of the classic tale of the three ages of woman, and it is perfectly summarised in Irène's working notebook for the summer of 1933: 'A little girl kissed for the first time. She is far from being ignorant, but knows things only from an elevated, poeticised point of view, novels, daydreams etc. [. . .] At night, the woman gives birth, "criminal manipulations". Whether she dies or does not die is unimportant. But the profound horror of this child suddenly coming face to face with the realities of life. Then the woman is taken away, the blood is staunched, the child lives and the sense of true beauty which awakes within us.' It is all wreathed 'in a sort of poetic halo', as in Katherine Mansfield's 'At the Bay'.

Gaston de Pawlowski (who had just died), Marcel Augagneur and Marcel Prévost had always given a warm welcome to Irène Némirovsky's novels in *Gringoire*, including *The Courilof Affair*. For a long time she had promised herself that she would discharge this debt. It was not simply a matter of courtesy: in 1934, *Gringoire* had a circulation of about 250,000 copies and Carbuccia was reputed to pay his serial writers royally. Before joining his cousin Marcel Prévost's *Revue de France* in 1927, he had been a playwright. His wife Adry, who came from Polish nobility, was related to the prefect of Paris, Jean Chiappe. In their town house on the Avenue Foch writers used to congregate: Sacha Guitry, Paul Morand, Henri Béraud, Charles Maurras, but also Emmanuel Berl, Francis Carco, Roland Dorgelès, Jean Cocteau and Colette; politicians: Léon Blum, Édouard Herriot, Maurice Sarraut, André Maginot; socialites: Étienne de Beaumont, Boni de Castellane; artists: Yvonne Printemps, André Dunoyer de Segonzac, Max Linder, Charles Chaplin; industrialist and financiers: Horace Finaly, André Citroën. *Gringoire* was the heart of Paris.

Founded in 1928, the 'great Parisian political and literary weekly' devoted only its front page to serious news coverage. The rest was literature, or virtually. Pierre de Régnier, known as 'Tigre', the supposed son of Henri and the author of *Vie de patachon*, published by Grasset in 1930, ran the Paris social page. Jacques de Lacretelle reviewed films, André Salmon covered the arts. All authors who were published by Éditions de France – Kessel, Prévost, Maurice Dekobra

– were *de facto* regular reviewers for the weekly. They wrote for 'Jeff' Kessel, who previously worked at *Revue de France*, and who edited the book pages. In content, these pages had little in common with the front page, which was cantankerous, populist and could not have been more French. It was therefore revanchist and 'anti-Boche': on 16th June, in *Gringoire*, Xavier de Hautecloque was one of the first French journalists to reveal the existence of Hitler's camps.

In 1933, the polemicist, Henri Béraud, who won the Goncourt Prize in 1922, had not yet set the magazine ablaze with his articles castigating Britain, Parliament and the foreign appropriation of French loot. He himself, if we are to believe his memoirs, seems to have regretted the dilettantism of *Gringoire*: 'Fantasies have thick skins! *Gringoire* had no politics or, which amounts to the same thing, it had them in abundance . . .'[63] This was a climb down: under the influence of the dissident Boris Souvarine, a Ukrainian Jew, an anti-Stalinist from the very beginning, and a prophet of the great Soviet holocausts, *Gringoire* was quick to profess its anti-communist stance: not something that would have shocked the author of *Snow in Autumn*! As for Carbuccia, he was a man who had sympathies rather than one who supported political parties. The sympathy he felt for Mussolini could not have been more commonplace, and it was not just because he was right-wing. 'My father,' his son Jean-Luc explains, 'was quite republican, and he was very influenced in his political principles by André Tardieu, the leader of the parliamentary right. So one couldn't talk of the extreme right.'[64] At least, not yet.

It is possible to criticise Irène Némirovsky, who was not politically inclined either, for boarding a dubious ship, on the pretext that the captain gradually changed course, espousing in turn anti-parliamentarianism, the defeatism of Munich, and the anti-Semitism of Vichy. Anton Chekhov had experienced this kind of criticism when he published his work in *Novoe vremia*, which was edited by the reactionary Alexis Suvorin, well known for his anti-Dreyfus views. 'And all these political parties that a beginner had to be subjected to? You had to veer to the left or to the right, be reactionary or liberal. The first step committed your entire future . . . These demands were loathsome, Anton thought, and degrading . . . Ever since childhood, he had wanted to safeguard his inner freedom, his dignity.'[65] These lines taken from *La Vie de Tchekhov*, and written in 1940, were also, and primarily, a defence of her own cause. Was Irène Némirovsky irresponsible? Not everyone was 'Fatty' Béraud, as his friends nicknamed him.

The wine of youth

In spite of her comparative financial difficulties, the early period of the Albin Michel years was a happy time. Irène and Michel Epstein had a nanny, Cécile; a Breton cook, Henriette Quidu, known as 'Kra', as well as a maid. Denise had just celebrated her third birthday, an age at which she could learn from Miss Matthews – Fanny's sole legacy – how to conceal a tiny toffee under her tongue while listening to Mummy reading *Les Petites Filles modèles*, describing the pre-war Champs-Élysées, or reciting 'L'Oreiller' by Marceline Desbordes-Valmore, to help her to fall asleep, without any idea of the portent:

> *Beaucoup, beaucoup d'enfants pauvres et nus, sans mère,*
> *Sans maison, n'ont jamais d'oreiller pour dormir;*
> *Ils ont toujours sommeil. Ô destinée amère!*
> *Maman! Douce maman! Cela me fait gémir.**

In the care of the irreproachable Cécile, Denise led 'the life of a little rich girl',[66] pampered and brought up in a middle-class way, but according to principles that were the opposite of Fanny's: 'I assure you that I shall try to spare my daughter any inappropriate work,' Irène Némirovsky explained in 1934. 'I spend a lot of time with her, and I want her to develop freely, in the fresh air and the sunshine.'[67] Which did not mean she was forbidden strawberry tarts from Rumpelmeyer's or trips to the cinema. Irène Némirovsky liked news-reels, the 'blue beam above our heads, a beam in which the luminous dust dances'. At the theatre, on 16th June 1934, Margaret Kennedy's *Tessa*, adapted by Jean Giraudoux and Louis Jouvet, awoke in her 'old images that I thought had been obliterated' and provided her with the exact tone of voice for *The Wine of Solitude*: 'wild and delightful'.

---

*Many, many poor and naked children, motherless, /And homeless, never have a pillow upon which to sleep; / They are always sleepy. O bitter fate! /Mother! Sweet mother! It makes me want to weep. [Tr.]

Sport? Never. 'She quite freely admitted her weakness for the *dolce far niente*, with a book in her hand . . . But she very much enjoyed long walks across Paris or, in the fresh air, along the Basque coast whose praises she had sung.' Painting? She sat for the Russian portrait painter Krivutz, a pupil of Bakst. Music? 'She declares that she is decidedly unmusical. We discover incidentally, however, that she likes Bach, Mozart, Beethoven and Chopin.'[68] But also Ernest Bloch's *Baal Shem* with 'that vast, deep and disturbing tone, and the poignant sound of the violins that link this Hebrew lament to an entire past of sorrowful bondage'. Not forgetting the *Symphony in D Minor* by César Franck, which, during the first half of 1934, dictated the structure of *The Wine of Solitude*. First movement: Kiev, Petersburg, *Lento – Allegro non troppo*, 'a) sweetness, b) thwarted innocence c) incomprehensible joy'. Second movement: Finland, *Allegretto – Poco più lento*, 'a) meditation, b) anxiety, c) anguish, d) indifference'. Third movement: *Allegro non troppo*, 'a) hatred, b) sadness, c) sorrowful hope, d) trust, e) hope of revenge'. Was she really unmusical?

Naturally, she read a great deal. Denise's children's books. English novels at the Bibliothèque nationale, in Rue Richelieu. The Russians at old Tourguenievka's, in the Rue du Val-de-Grâce, 'one of those streets that are what I like most in the world, – shadows, distant noise, strange faces, the bell on a shop door, a red bar glimpsed from a distance', where the books bequeathed by Turgenev still bore his handwritten annotations. In March 1933, she sent Brisson an anonymous review, for inclusion in *Les Annales*, of the latest novel by her compatriot Dusya Ergaz, to whom critics had sometimes compared *Snow in Autumn*. Her reading notes for the year 1934, probably intended for *La Revue hebdomadaire*, in which some of her reviews appeared, have survived. Evelyn Waugh's humour struck her as too sophisticated in *Vile Bodies*, but *A Handful of Dust* corrected this impression because of its title, 'which describes bitterly and tragically how little we are and the way in which fate plays with us and with our wishes and with our desires'. Alone among American novels, *The Postman Always Rings Twice* by James Cain appealed to her taste for brutal realism and cinematographic punch. In *The Mother* by Pearl Buck, she found a way of answering those who accused her of dwelling on Slavic interests: 'I couldn't care less whether it's true from a Chinese perspective. It probably is but it's absolutely true from a human one.' Finally, Franz Werfel's

The Forty Days of Musa Dagh, the first literary epic to be inspired by the Armenian genocide, would certainly count among the sub-conscious sources of *Les Chiens et les Loups* [*The Dogs and the Wolves*], for 'it is the story in a sense of a man who returns like a stranger among his own people and finds he is bound by ties that are stronger than he had imagined, and who finds himself forced to accept the fate of his race and his country'.

And always, wherever she was – on holiday, in the Square Rodin or at the Tuileries, in the Square Sainte-Clotilde, at the Henri IV pavilion at Saint-Germain, which were her favourite places for walks – Irène Némirovsky would sit down and place on her lap the folder concealed in an imitation old-gold binding, in which the 'diary' of the novel in progress grew thicker. She wrote: 'It is with a certain thrill that I open this exercise book. It is heavy enough, in every sense, and very unwieldy. But so many memories rise from it, more painful than one could believe – that it is very suitable for an evocation of the past . . . Of course, it's affected . . . pathetic. But only the blood from an old wound can give colour to a work of art in the right way. Rise up, rise up in my heart, ancient tears . . .'

From January to July 1934, Irène Némirovsky struggled to start work again on 'the Monster'.[69] She could, in Russian-style, content herself with listing her memories, without bothering to put them in order; 'this would be all right if I didn't have to earn my living. But here, where I am honest with myself, I have to accept the fact that I write in French. I therefore need French readers and, consequently, plots with action.' In order to attract the reader, she would have to recreate a milieu, span the centuries, create life: a saga in the *Buddenbrooks* mould, though not in 600 pages! For the Russian part, it was a ques-tion of technique, and rereading *The Brothers Karamazov*. So as to avoid the 'matter of facts',* she would have to reread André Chevrillon's studies of English literature and the novels of Galsworthy. To create successful portraits, she should reread *Mémoires d'outre-tombe*. And 'for dialogue, reread Proust. No one will ever invent anything better.'

As for her intention, it was quite clear: 'a genuine flesh and blood past, isn't that worth more than anything imagined? . . . My life has been so colourful, so eventful. I need to find a title that can express

*In English in the original. [Tr.]

that.' But 'Le Monstre' was not a title! In *L'Ennemie* [The Enemy], it was to do with that 'mysterious wine', that intoxicating must of childhood, once oblivion has trampled over it. How better to express that harvest of bitterness in which Irène Némirovsky's memory had worn itself out for almost a year? Plagiarise Musset?

> *Poète, prends ton luth; le vin de la jeunesse*
> *Fermente cette nuit dans les veines de Dieu . . .**

Or else 'The Wine of Memory'? 'The Wine of Solitude'? *'Le Vin de Solitude* is a fine title and it has the additional advantage of fixing my mind on the essential. What I think mainly needs to be shown, actually, is this child who grows up in this way, absolutely alone. Place the emphasis on this profound and bitter solitude, on the fantasies that fill her life, on the monstrous appearance this life takes on for her.' This *Wine* could be summed up in an epigraph from Stendhal: 'Our parents and our masters are our natural enemies.' Or to a saying of Némirovsky's: 'Happy childhoods make for a harmonious life. Unhappy childhoods, a productive life.' Of course, her main grudge would be held entirely against Fanny; and in this novel she would make sure she re-established their real difference in age: 'I am eighteen and she is forty-five . . .' But if the substance of her symphony was 'the revenge of a girl on her mother', the leitmotif must continue to be the sense of abandonment, which is all that endures after being punished. Should she invent for herself, as she did in *L'Ennemie*, a younger sister, an abortion, a suicide? The idea was repugnant to her: 'Rightly or wrongly, I have the feeling that there is a line in my life, and almost, already, ready-made chapters and that I must follow this thread. Miraculous! It remains fairly clear, and does not get lost. That's quite rare, I think, in life.' But how difficult it is to remember the sound of voices, and the precise sequence of forgotten conversations! 'As strange as it may seem, I have forgotten the words, and that's just what happens, the fight between reality and the imagination, the words fly over the head of a child.' In *The Wine of Solitude*, however, they are all true, reclaimed inch by inch from oblivion. So true, that Irene Némirovsky did not give up the idea of making a film from it one

*Poet, take your lute; the wine of youth/ Ferments this night in the veins of God . . . [Tr.]

day, and an optimistic film, for 'after the baseness and utter humilia-tion', there followed, 'towards the end, a burst of energy, of confi-dence, of love of life'. *The Wine of Solitude*, like all the earlier novels, is a moral book.

A Golder before Golder

In March 1934, Irène Némirovsky thought for a moment of having a catchy opening scene that was true to life, and full of noise and colour: the Nice carnival of 1906. And for the closing pages? This was far simpler: 'Leave the *conclusion* to God.' Which, in Chapter XI of Part IV, would result in: 'She stood up and, at that moment, the clouds parted; between the pillars of the Arc de Triomphe the blue sky appeared and lit her way.' So God was a Frenchman. Paul Morand said as much, in his own way, in March 1934, in his latest novel: 'France is the Good Lord's concentration camp.'[70] This was also the title under which it would appear in the Nazi weekly *Angriff* in February 1936. But *France la doulce* was not merely a farce, whose 'comic humour'[71] did not escape Irène Némirovsky. In Morand's mind it was very much a condemnation: that of the monopolisation of French studios by that 'swarming riff-raff' that had 'forced its way, among the darkness of Central Europe and the Levant, to the lights of the Champs-Élysées'.[72] Today it is opportune to clear *France la doulce* of any suspicion of xeno-phobia, on the pretext that the book is hilarious. But Morand was not being funny when he told the press: 'Everything that I have written is strictly true. My book is a report: it has the value of a photographic document . . . Those whom I have portrayed do not belong to any one country or, rather, they belong to all of them. They are essentially PARASITES. I consider it is our duty to drive them out.'[73]

So what anthrax-carrying fly had stung the cosmopolitan globe-trotter of *Rien que la Terre*? Perhaps it was the scandal that had gripped France since December, but which did not affect public opinion until 8th January, with the suicide of a certain Stavisky. A forger, a swindler, 'a launderer of cheques', and an unscrupulous businessman, this 'ex-convict who looks like a male escort'[74] posthumously dragged down a swarm of bankers and press barons – among them Paul Lévy, the boss of *Aujourd'hui* – and especially politicians – radicals and socialists, those to the right would say – all of whom had been bribed or sold down the river by this brilliant sorcerer. 'Stavisky shot himself with a bullet fired from three metres away. It helps to have a long arm', ran the headline in *Le Canard enchaîné*. To the great misfortune of France's Jews, Stavisky was a native of Odessa, and this simple fact suddenly unleashed the semi-dormant pamphleteer in Henri Béraud. On 12th January, he took it upon himself to write an editorial in *Gringoire* and cleverly castigated the 'child of the Kiev ghetto'. Swayed by this heavyweight contribution, *Gringoire* gradually veered towards all-out xenophobia. On 6th February, this harmful virus was responsible for ten or more deaths in the Place de la Concorde, in the anti-government riots triggered by the scandal.

So it was with timely relevance that *NRF* came up with the slogan 'The Staviskys of the cinema' to launch *France la doulce*. The affair, what is more, fascinated Irène Némirovsky, who promised herself that she would transform 'the handsome Serge' into a fictional character: 'I shall make use of Stavisky, perhaps, one day . . .' It might be, she further envisaged in her working notebook, 'the career of a businessman. A young D.G.'. This Golder before Golder would see the light of day: he is the Ben Sinner of *The Dogs and the Wolves*, raised to a life of fraud and cynicism through a childhood of misery, humiliation and resourcefulness.

On 17th March 1934, Irène Némirovsky finished reading the proofs of *Le Pion sur l'échiquier*, which she returned to Albin Michel together with a photograph and a brief biographical note. It was a gloomy time of year. 'Nothing is more sad,' she wrote on 24th April, 'nothing gives such a sense of the pointlessness of everything as these cold spring days in Paris, when the cold and heavy rain falls on trees bedecked in their young shoots.' *Le Pion sur l'échiquier*, the most pessimistic of her books, really did appear at the right moment. In spite of its imperfections, she did not underrate it, because Bohun was her blood brother in a way: '*Le Pion sur l'échiquier* is the story of a man whose spiritual life has been stifled by the love of, and need for, material things . . . I must admit I am very fond of my hero, but I think all writers must grow attached to their least attractive characters in this way . . .'[75]

In an introductory note sent to the press, Albin Michel tried, with moderate success, to place the novel within the calamitous atmosphere of that spring: 'The hero's father, a powerful financier, ruined by the crash, had acquired a considerable fortune through fairly shady dealings in which politicians were inculpated. His son, employed in a news agency, who is beset with worries about money, is able to make use of the weapons his father has left him: a folder revealing the complicity of certain characters . . .'[76] Like many French people, Irène Némirovsky was herself a victim of the anti-parliamentary epidemic. On 10th June, during a signing session or a dinner party, she was placed beside the 'fat slob Henri Paté', the former Minister for Education, and vice-president of the Chambre des députés, who, with a great deal of back-slapping, was inscribing copies of his moralising essays on sport and youth. The following day, the novelist jotted down her impressions and provided some indication of the growing discredit of the political class: 'One must admit that this parliamentary world is loathsome, and it seems strange that it can keep going for much longer. I noted the attitude of others, not in the least like the vacuous "Yes, Monsieur le Ministre" of a year ago. I also noted that the politicians I disliked the most (this one was Paul-Boncour) are, by coincidence, precisely those who did not express their admiration to me . . .' Similarly, she was disgusted by rumours about the corruption of a certain newspaper that exchanged its silence or its favours in return for cash. In *Le Pion*, Christophe does not want to read the newspaper any longer, 'because of all these disgraceful scandals, these lawsuits, these contemptible wrecks . . .'[77]

For all these reasons, *Gringoire*'s loud mouth and its calls for moral standards, for national recovery, and its support for Colonel de La Rocque's 'public service', did not intimidate her, particularly since the social reformism of the Croix-de-Feu, the organisation whose prudence had prevented Parliament from falling on 6th February, had no reason to be envious of the parliamentary left and still professed its aversion to anti-Semitism and 'the doctrines of hatred that threaten to divide the French people'.[78] André Maurois and Henry Bernstein were sympathetic to the movement: the latter would even take pride 'in having let the Croix-de-Feu spirit' blow through one of his plays.[79] Irène Némirovsky herself had contributed to the short-lived *Aujourd'hui*, which did not conceal its Croix-de-Feu sympathies. On 8th February, its owner, Paul Lévy, even emerged from his normal reserve to announce the eagerly awaited 'resurrection': 'The national Revolution has begun; nothing can stop it any longer, France wants to become French again, France wants to be governed by men who are worthy of her and to retain her position as a power of the very first rank.' It was a brief crow of national pride, but it gives the tenor of this newspaper for which the pillaging and plundering that took place on the fringes of the large communist demonstrations of 7th February, carried out by 'armed gangs, made up of suspicious-looking foreigners and professional rioters', were the main event of the winter of 1934 . . .

Driven out of Russia by 'the Reds', and a pacifist by temperament, Irène Némirovsky was certainly not a trouble-making socialist. Professionally, she was even driven to mix with little-known men of letters who were not in the habit of raising their fists. Reverting to generalisations in her review of *Les Temps difficiles* by Édouard Bourdet, she wrote a stirring defence of the French bourgeoisie, whose disappearance, she said, would cause more unhappiness in France than the 'scum in the palaces'; for 'the bourgeoisie, whose perilous and tragic position M. Bourdet pinpoints for us in this way, is a strong and admirable part of the country and its misfortunes cannot, and should not, give rise to laughter. They are threatening and dreadful for each one of us.'[80]

A punch

In *Le Pion sur l'échiquier*, which Albin Michel published in May 1934, a financial upheaval opens up a yawning chasm beneath Christophe Bohun's feet. There is no need to go to the ends of the earth to be bored with oneself, as in Paul Morand's novel: a car journey is enough. His suicide is as certain as the war: 'The rolling of the drums, the German soldiers, the peace conference, Italian soldiers, planes, tanks, guns: "Ah, yes, it's true, the war . . . That's all that's missing . . ."'[81] On the radio, Irène Némirovsky emphasised that although her heroes were French, her subject matter had not changed since *David Golder*: 'I continue to depict the kind of society I know best and that is made up of unbalanced people, removed from their background and from the country where they would normally have lived, and who do not adjust to a new life without a shock and some degree of suffering.'[82]

Decadence and materialism, the cruel generation war, the inability to adapt to new circumstances, are also the subject of 'Ida', a long, syncopated story she had written in February at Morand's request, in order to complete her famous collection of 'scenarios'. Irène Némirovsky's idea was taken from Brecht and Weill's *The Seven Deadly Sins* (1933), a theme she had already dealt with vaguely in *Le Malentendu*.[83] In her draft of 'Ida', this aspect appears more clearly still: 'Music halls. Foreigners were rushing around everywhere. They were stacked with money, they wore their gold on their bellies, in their eyes . . . Paris welcomed them greedily like a whore, that's the truth of it, but one mustn't say so.' A caricature? Most certainly, since she herself had scattered her manuscripts with such caricatures and regretted not having 'Sem's wonderful album' to hand to inspire her. On 16th and 23rd May, this 'great unpublished short story' was published in two instalments in the eclectic left-wing weekly *Marianne* (circulation: 120,000), in which *France la doulce* had been serialised. Here we see an 'elderly financier' and an 'ancient chairman of the board' sleeping in turns with an ageing chorus-line leader, who eventually throws herself down her grand staircase: a parable of the decadent 1920s and the 'reign of old women' . . . Ida's moral degradation is the female equivalent to Bohun's collapse, and the fact that she is Jewish does not cushion her fall.

Le Pion sur l'échiquier was published at the same time as 'Ida'. At the last minute, Irène Némirovsky cut the last sentence, which was too explicit: 'A hand had in turn removed from the chessboard the pawn that had become useless, and the game continued without it . . .' The critics were not in the least confused by this novel, which broke with the author's Russian vein. René Lalou considered it to be a 'considerable advance',[84] but then he wrote for *Noir et Blanc*, Albin Michel's stuttering new magazine. Thérive, Lœwel and Franc-Nohain agreed with him. So, too, did Ramon Fernandez, who worked at *Marianne*. Only André Bellessort regretted that the novelist should still be mixing too much with 'this cosmopolitan world of the David Golders, so vulgar and so uninteresting'.[85] In the very nationalistic *Revue hebdomadaire*, the young Élisabeth Zehrfuss, who had admired and understood *France la doulce*, was surprised to have her interest aroused by the most 'frightful' anti-hero imaginable. Finally, Marcel Prévost pointed out a few flaws, but he paid tribute to Irène Némirovsky's 'guts', requesting her to retain her composure and 'not be unsettled by prospective critics who may compare her latest novel unfavourably with her earlier work'.[86]

Wise advice, but it was too late: since 30th May, Irène Némirovsky had been beside herself. Robert Brasillach, the spearhead of the younger reviewers, had demolished *Le Pion* in his 'literary gossip' column in *Action française*:

> The character does not convince us. The sour taste that should surface dilutes into dullness. We had already observed the same danger in *L'Affaire Courilof*: perhaps the author of *David Golder* ought not to write novels. She drags out a simple story, a meagre anecdote, and everything falls apart. Genuine desperation seems to become a literary desperation. All the skill of the writer cannot obscure the vacuity of the subject and the book. And all evocation vanishes.
>
>   . . . Let us ask Mme Némirovsky, whose bitterness is not to our liking, for more *Mouches d'automne*, more lunch parties among newly acquired friends – more short stories. Not everyone succeeds in this difficult art.[87]

Ever since the 6th February disaster, Brasillach had not been himself. His shift towards fascism was well and truly advanced. *France la doulce* had seemed to him to be dealing with a 'serious subject', which was that in a 'supposedly French' film, apart from the shareholders, 'the director is a Ukrainian Jew, the assistants Jews from Frankfurt, the male lead a Spaniard, and the female lead English . . .'[88] But the sophisticated critic of 1934 had not become the lampooner who, during the Occupation, was to recommend that serious thought be given to deporting little Jewish children. And there was nothing ideological about his opinion of *Le Pion*.

Irène Némirovsky was devastated, firstly because she respected the views of this scholarly young man, but also for other reasons, which she jotted down that same day in her working notebook: 'Of course I write too many novels . . . But if people knew what it costs to eat . . . and especially to feed Michel and Denise. It's hard . . . It's true that people couldn't care a f—. I have been a critic myself. I know very well that in such cases, no one is interested, *and that's justice*, and it's because it's a failure. I can feel my heart sinking at times like that, and beating so painfully and with such difficulty, and with a lump in my throat and full of tears.'

Two days later, the wound had not healed and had even become infected:

> I am plunged into the deepest gloom, the very bleakest of moods . . . still the A.F. article. It's not so much being generally slated, but it's the obvious sincerity of young B. which is frightening. Is it really so bad? No, no, I'm only too well aware. I did my best, and it's <u>true</u>. But as usual, it distresses me for the future, the distant as well as the immediate. I feel lost, without heart, without hope, unhappy in the extreme. How I've aged! In the old days, defeat was a whipping: I was angry, I felt stronger. Now it's a punch . . . Defeat knocks me out nowadays . . . I am unable to realise that it will pass, like so many other things . . . And yet, I ought to know that my life is a series of ups and downs, like that of my poor father . . .

One indirect result of this slating was that the book gradually disappeared from window displays a month after publication. 'I am afraid it's a worrying sign,' she wrote to Albin Michel on 27th June. The publisher, who was very reassuring, tactfully referred to the slump that was affecting the market: 'compared to the situation of books in general, sales of *Le Pion sur l'échiquier* are good'. But of the 17,000 copies printed, only 7,000 would be sold in 1942. Would Irène Némirovsky cease to be 'the great attraction' once France sank into a recession?

Supply and demand

Between May and November 1934, Irène Némirovsky published no less than five short stories, some of them quite long. 'At the moment, I have more requests for short stories than I can cope with,' she wrote to her publisher. As Chekhov remarked to those who criticised him for writing too much: 'Mummy and Daddy have to eat' . . .[89]

'Les Fumées du vin', which was finally completed in February, appeared as a foot-of-the-page feature in *Le Figaro* from 12th to 19th June; Brisson, the new editor of the national daily, offered 2,500 francs. For 'Écho', Albin Michel only gave her 400, but he complained about its shortness: it took up only four small columns of *Noir et Blanc*, the weekly magazine that eventually came out in April. It was a condensed version of *The Wine of Solitude*. In it, a writer recalls an episode from his childhood: giving a dying butterfly to his mother, and her indifference to it. 'I believe that this small, insignificant incident was at the heart of my entire love life, and of my books, in which men go about among their fellow men, without being understood by them, each walled up in his own prison.'[90] He himself can't see that he is rebuking his own son. Here, Irène Némirovsky was expressing her own foolish qualms, which she admitted to in April 1934, about not loving Denise sufficiently: 'The truth is, you are not very interested in your children, at least when you are young. You don't love them continuously or every day in the same way, any more than in other loving human relationships. Supply and demand never coincides, any more between parents and children than it does between lovers.'

'Dimanche', which *La Revue de Paris* published on 1st June, draws on the same nostalgia: the naivety of the girl – based on her niece Natacha – who is moved by 'that vigour, that fire in the blood',[91] the disillusionment of the mother whose youth has not lasted long, and the mutual misunderstanding and hypocrisy of the generations. Irène Némirovsky had had the idea for it that Christmas Eve of 1933 when she had made her asthma and her weariness the excuse for staying at home on her own. At the age of thirty, she wrote: 'As a child, I had a premonition of maturity. Now, more than anything else, I have a foreboding about old age. It's comical.' In November 1934, 'Les Rivages heureux' [The Happy Shores] were still those of a carefree youth when she was no longer likely to be waylaid by Ginette, 'the old, faded tart', making up her mind about whether to drown herself in alcohol or in the 'dark eddies' of the Seine.[92]

Irène spent the whole summer at Hendaye, and later at Urrugne, writing *The Wine of Solitude*, only allowing herself a brief trip abroad in early September. At Saint-Jean-de-Luz and the surrounding area, she found confirmation of her fears: there were no more copies of *Le Pion* in the Basque bookshops. Back in Paris in October, Denise and her mother buried their dear fat cat Kissou on the 15th, and learned that same day of the death of Président Poincaré, who was as pot-bellied and moustachioed as the tom-cat had been. At Avenue Daniel-Lesueur, she put the final touches to her manuscript, which Albin Michel planned to publish in January or February. But meanwhile *La Revue de Paris*, which was normally less generous, offered her 20,000 francs.

A 'tidy' little sum, Albin Michel opined knowledgeably, much comforted by the fact that one of his authors had just been awarded the Goncourt prize. A wintry sun finally lit up 1934, Irène Némirovsky's year of gloom.

In the proofs of *The Wine of Solitude*, which she reread during January, the Karol family still have the Tartar name of Koïré that she gave them in 'Le Mercredi des Cendres', at the very start of this auto-biographical venture. 'My plans?' she was asked. '*Le Vin de Solitude*, which will be in the tradition of *Le Bal*.'[93] Serialisation of *The Wine of Solitude*, the most intimate of her novels, began on 1st March; Thiébaut placed it at the front of his magazine, before the unpublished extracts from *La Chartreuse de Parme*.

On its publication, in August 1935, not a single critic would allude to the fact that this work posing as a novel was appearing at the same time as Ivan Bunin's *The Well of Days*, the story of a Russian child-hood disguised as fiction. The difference was that the winner of the Nobel Prize for Literature had relied on his instinctive memory, whereas Némirovsky had had to battle with her memories and train them into the constraints of a symphony. 'This novel,' she explained to her readers, 'is one of those that is written in one's head and in one's heart long before it is written on paper, not one of those that surge forth, ready in the imagination, with a beginning, an end and a definite shape, but one that hesitates and feels its way, and, in short, never end, because every moment spent daydreaming produces possible episodes.'[94] The pains and joys of childbirth: this was the subject of 'Nativité', and now it was the comfort of at last seeing this wine uncorked, stocked in bookshops and poured into the souls of her readers.

'A book about those who have known despair at an age that is supposed to be happy,' read the publicity leaflets inserted into the daily press by Albin Michel, convinced that at last he had another *David Golder*. The foremost critics did not go that far, but Ramon Fernandez admired the delicate touch of the revolutionary back-ground, which was too unreal to distract Hélène from her initiation into love.[95] Jean-Pierre Maxence did not know what to praise most, the balance and robustness of the story, the way the characters stood out, the 'exceptional qualities of colour . . . , the accuracy with which people's behaviour is depicted, the sharpness of the diagnosis, the range of social documentation'.[96] The elderly Henri de Régnier, shocked by Hélène Karol's clear-headedness and staggered by the novelist's wealth of bitterness, regretted only that she 'specialises a little too much in the portrayal of this murky, grasping, fanatical and, in short, rather low form of humanity'.[97]

Curiously, it was only *La Revue de Paris*, in which the book first appeared, that sought to criticise *The Wine of Solitude* for its 'Hebrew pessimism' and its 'Russian recklessness', as well as for the spiteful, self-satisfied and disrespectful characteristics of her heroine: is this the way one should treat a mother who is certainly hard-hearted and vain, but a mother nonetheless? Irène Némirovsky had anticipated this criticism: 'It's wrong from a moral point of view, I know, but it's true, and sincere.' Since her fable *L'Enfant génial*, *The Wine of Solitude* is a profoundly moral book, which has to do with filial feelings and parental responsibility, with contempt and consideration for others, with money, love and hatred. But it is not a book about morality. 'It is not wine, as she says, that solitude has poured over Hélène; it is poison,' quibbled Henri Bidou, who was incapable of understanding that the halo effect that impaired his reading and made Hélène 'ill-defined' for him was merely the misting up of memories: 'It is as if the author was too close to her to see her clearly . . .'[98] So close, in fact, that in 1942 Hélène would prompt Irène to pen this disconcerting dedication, written on the back of the folder containing *Suite Française*: '*Le Vin de Solitude*. By Irène Némirovsky, for Irène Némirovsky.' And also for Fanny, who had never had such a limpid mirror put up to her.

'It's the story,' she would say, 'of a little girl who loathes her mother . . .'

8

How Happy Are the French!
(1935–1938)

To be Jewish and French, how fruitful this union might have been! What hopes I had of it!

Jacques de Lacretelle, *Silbermann*

Without Fanny Némirovsky's avarice and selfishness, would her daughter Irène have written nine new novels, a biography and no less than thirty-eight short stories between 1935 and 1942? Her work, which had been made into films and translated all over the world, was now the principal source of the family income. In 1938, the money she earned was more than three times Michel's annual salary at the Banque des Pays du Nord, which then amounted to 41,850 francs. Michel certainly had other sources of revenue, probably speculative ones, but they had never contemplated reducing their standard of living. Their family doctor was the eminent Louis Vallery-Radot, the grandson of Pasteur and great-grandson of Eugène Sue. Irène Némirovsky therefore had a duty to continue writing, or else she risked jeopardising not only the household budget, but her position in the literary world. Nothing could be further from the truth than her posthumous reputation as a 'banker': the author of *David Golder* lived mainly by her pen. She made a good living, but she did not live alone. And Michel Epstein, who had not yet formed with Albin Michel the friendly relationship he had retained with Grasset, took it upon himself to assist his wife in her business affairs. 'Monsieur Irène Némirovsky,' she joked, 'is not a prince-consort.'[1] In August 1935, he opened a separate account for her at the Banque des Pays du Nord. He brought back paper from the office on which he himself typed out her novels, and in 1937 he made her a present of a Doret pen with which she wrote in 'South Seas Blue' ink. 'I like writing in the morning,' she disclosed, 'but even more so in the evening after five o'clock, when the day is done, in the peace of home and the enchantment of lamplights. I can never work after lunch, but Duhamel, apparently, is like me.

I found that reassuring . . . All I need is my favourite pen.'[2] Michel was
her first reader, draconian but persuasive:

'Why did you write that?'

'But . . .'

'It doesn't work.'[3]

In early June 1935, they moved into another flat, in an identical no-
through road just round the corner, twenty yards from Avenue
Daniel-Lesueur, off the Boulevard des Invalides. The rented flat, on the
sixth and top floor of 10 Avenue Constant-Coquelin, was lighter and
more spacious than the previous one. There was a lift. They could
entertain there and, who knows, accommodate a new baby. An entrance
hall, a corridor, a drawing-room lined with hardback books where
Denise made a hiding-place beneath the curtains. 'I spend my whole
day reading,'[4] the little girl told journalists: the Comtesse de Ségur,
François le Bossu, La Famille Plumet, La Petite Sœur de Trott, rather than
Little Lord Fauntleroy. A photograph of mother and daughter stood in
one corner. There were several bedrooms, a study, a kitchen where the
novelist did not get her hands dirty, but a dining-room where she showed
how greedy she could be. On the sideboard were some magnificent
crystal decanters. Caviar, champagne, evening dresses: 'Our parents lived
in the Russian style. Open house, big parties.'[5] The guests' names were
Fernand Gregh, Paul and Hélène Morand, Tristan Bernard and his son
Jean-Jacques. On Saturday, Paul Epstein and Choura stayed late into the
night. One of the two balconies, which was covered to form a veranda,
echoed with the clinking of glasses: today it is a knitwear and sewing-
machine workshop. The other one, which was a mass of nasturtiums
and sweet-peas, overlooked the kitchen garden of the Saint-Esprit fathers,
an order of missionaries whose founder, Jacob Libermann (1802–1852)
was the son of a rabbi who had converted to Catholicism. In this flat,
where she would live for less than five years, Irène Némirovsky was to
write five novels and would become persuaded that she should forsake
Judaism, though without ridding her books of it.

The dream becomes reality

Promised to Paul Morand one year previously, the anthology *Films
parlés* should have been published as soon as it was printed, in

December 1934; it only appeared three months later, in February 1935. These four visual short stories, designed to look like sequence shots and totally lacking in psychology, stem from an aesthetic appeal that Irène Némirovsky, who had long ago admitted the influence of cinema on her work,[6] no longer subscribed to. None of the scripts she had written for the cinema – one based on 'La Comédie bourgeoise', the others entitled 'La Symphonie de Paris' and 'Carnaval de Nice' – would be filmed. Her disillusion with adapting the art of writing to the artificial light of projectors was obvious, as her working diary makes clear: 'One can no longer delude oneself that cinematographic technique is equipped to bring together a mish-mash of different plots; whatever one says, the real, pure short story sets out to do only one thing: to imitate Mérimée and follow the plumbline.' In this respect, she was ahead of her critics, who were more responsive to her ability as a storyteller than to her avant-gardism. If Fernandez was uncertain whether the 'optic processes'[7] brought anything to the narrative effectiveness, he, like Edmond Jaloux, singled out the 'remarkable study of an ageing woman, worn out by ambition'[8] in the opening story, 'Ida'. Henri de Régnier, for his part, could not understand how such a self-assured talent could have stooped to this 'game without much future'[9] that consisted in aping the camera.

But the younger critics thought well enough of it: unfazed by the screenplay language of *Films parlés*, Jean-Pierre Maxence, who was twenty-nine, detected in this 'excellent collection' the influence of Maupassant in its conception, of Mauriac in the dialogue, and of Chekhov in its bitterness, all without resorting to any subterfuge: 'If she achieves this poetry of gold and ashes, it is as if she were doing so in passing, unintentionally, by chance.'[10] Unlike Brasillach, his former colleague from *Revue française*, and despite his strong nationalist feelings, Maxence would remain loyal to Némirovsky up until the Occupation. In October of the same year, he confessed to being astonished by the evocative power and the rigorous structure of *The Wine of Solitude*, the most accomplished of this 'brilliant novelist's' books: 'When such balance is achieved, one can say of a writer that he is completely fulfilled. . . . The dream becomes reality.'[11]

Albin Michel would sell about ten thousand copies of *The Wine of Solitude*, probably fewer than he had hoped, but the book would be translated into several languages. During 1934, Irène Némirovsky hesitated at first about allowing the book to be published in the *Revue des Deux Mondes*, which had made the proposal, for she considered that the intimate nature of the book and the vindictive character of her heroine were unsuited to such a solemn magazine. And she was not prepared to expurgate her work under any circumstances. 'It is possible to have talent and not write for the *Revue des Deux Mondes*,' remarked Félix Juven ironically in 1921.[12] But the honour of appearing in the venerable *Revue* was not one to be taken lightly. To be co-opted by the sages of this hundred-year-old institution was to receive the French *esprit* from its own custodians: victorious marshals such as Foch or Pétain, heroes of the Republic such as Deschanel and Poincaré, hoary old poets such as Gregh or Régnier, who were likely to have been Irène Némirovsky's sponsors. 'The *Revue* offers us the joyful image of a well-ordered world,' observed the academician André Chaumeix in self-congratulatory mode in 1933. '. . . The editorial office fairly closely resembles a wise Parliament that is mindful of the general interest. The Management represents the monarch, who rules and whose duty it is to watch over the common good of the *Revue*, which has the eminent honour to be the constant reflection of French thinking.'[13] In this antechamber of the Coupole,* which has survived every regime since Charles X without once changing its course or avoiding any sign of ossification, a few young literary figures, such as Jacques de Lacretelle, Francis Carco, Henry de Montherlant and Julien Green were priming themselves for glory. It could be tempting for a foreigner, French in spirit but legally stateless, to shelter behind the pink covers of the unimpeachable and daunting *Revue*, which was well known moreover for its open hostility to Marxist doctrines as well as to German imperialism.

For her first contribution to the *Revue*, Irène Némirovsky chose to submit one of her 'plumbline' stories. In 'Jour d'été', a subtle study of the three stages of life, a little girl of Denise's age, with 'delicate, apricot-coloured skin',[14] enjoys rooting up forget-me-nots. Irène Némirovsky called her Morcenx, after a town at which the train stopped on the Paris–Hendaye line. Her father, who scolds her, is doing his best to tear apart her relationship with him. Lucain, her grandfather, positively enjoys what 'even the tiniest bit of sensual

*A term used to denote the Académie française. [Tr.]

pleasure'[15] can still give him: a walk round the garden, a little drink. All three of them either yearn for life, pursue it or invoke it as it rushes by. As night falls, as in the work of certain Flemish painters, only the rustle of nature answers their prayers. This philosophical vein in Irène Némirovsky's work was not new. It would continue up until the nocturnal hunting in 'Tempête en juin' [Storm in June], the first part of *Suite Française*, with the war raging round them like the eye of a cyclone.

In the issue dated 1st April 1935, Irène Némirovsky found herself in the company of Maurice Genevoix and Alexandre Millerand, the former president of the Republic. During the spring, at the traditional sale on behalf of war veterans, she became friendly with her fellow stallholder Solange Doumic, the daughter of the editor of the *Revue*, René Doumic, whose second marriage to Hérédia's eldest daughter made him Henri de Régnier's brother-in-law. A former fellow student with Bergson and Jaurès at the École normale supérieure, he had neither the intellectual energy of the former, nor the political capability of the latter. With his goatee beard and spectacles, half-hidden beneath the rug he always carried, stooped like a Don Quixote over his novels of chivalry, the seventy-year-old Doumic was, according to Maurras, 'one of those who believed that "life would be tolerable without its pleasures"'.[16] He only used the telephone when he had to and he forecast that the cinema would become extinct. The king-pin of the *Revue* for more than forty years, and its editor since 1915, Doumic, who was a former teacher of rhetoric, displayed a wonderfully steadfast conformism where literature was concerned: opposed until only recently to Baudelaire, Verlaine and Zola, in 1923 he had been known to condemn a work by D'Annunzio because of a passage in which a canoness slept with her cousin. His motto was: 'It is not enough to be young, but it is always a recommendation.'[17] This moralistic attitude followed him in his politics, where Doumic professed the sort of pedantic patriotism that had been traditional at the *Revue* since Ferdinand Brunetière, but its reserved approach had the ability to exasperate *Action française*. And although the *Revue* had paid attention to the blusterings of Mussolini, and later to anti-parliamentarianism, Hitler, on the other hand, aroused its unshakeable patriotism.

Stavisky and Stravinsky

Whether or not Irène Némirovsky shared Doumic's narrow political opinions, she certainly intended to take advantage of the influence of this permanent secretary at the Académie française to further her and her husband's request for naturalisation.

In order to balance the disproportionate pyramid of ages brought about by the war, a law had been introduced on 10th August 1927 that dealt a blow to the sacrosanct 'right of blood' and made it easier to acquire French nationality. On 30th September 1935, four months after Michel had put in his request, Denise became the first member of the family to acquire French nationality by law. This was not a mere whim of fate, but the result of a basic trend caused by the flood of refugees coming from Germany that had taken the immigration authorities by surprise. Since 1931, more than ten thousand foreigners were given French citizenship every year. Russian Jews who had lived on French soil since the end of the war, and whom the USSR did not want, suddenly felt the need to make official the private sense they had that they had become French, for fear of being compared to the undesirable rejects of Nazi anti-Semitism and being looked upon suspiciously by those influenced by opinions cultivated by the nationalist press. In the *Revue des Deux Mondes*, in April 1934, René Pinon demanded that a term be put on the 'outrageous naturalisation which mostly Jews were benefiting from'.[18] On 16th February 1935, Lucien Rebatet, in *Je suis partout*, put the finishing touches to his major anti-assimilationist investigation, entitled: 'Foreigners in France. The invasion'. Blacks, Orientals, Armenians, North Africans are here referred to as 'excrement'. 'Should we tolerate becoming alloyed with this corrupt Oriental blood, diluted by indecipherable mixtures, and by long periods of slaughter, oppression and psychological torment? There is no need to be "racist" to be alarmed.' As for Russian Jews, Rebatet refused to include them among the Slavs. For, he regretted, 'among the 26,000 naturalised Russians, a huge majority of them are Jewish'. A supporter of selective immigration, Rebatet, great music lover that he was, naturally agreed to make an exception with Horowitz – born in Kiev in 1903 – and other 'excellent Jewish virtuosos'.[19] But let us be fair: even in *Marianne*, Emmanuel Berl, who supported a firmer immigration policy, was not opposed to a selective sifting, which he summed up with the phrase: 'There is Stavisky, but there is Stravinsky.'[20] And there was Némirovsky, a literary virtuoso, who was not mentioned by either Berl or Rebatet. But it was in this context that we must consider her decision to apply for French self-respect, and understand the sudden disappearance of all Russian touches from her work.

The novelist had become aware of the advent of Nazism in 1934. Ferdinand Brückner's anti-fascist play, *Die Rassen*, which had greatly upset her, was the inspiration for these visionary lines:

> These 'snapshots of the anti-Jewish war in Germany', as M. Paul Reboux refers to these eight scenes, may appear, as he observes so aptly, strange and even improbable to French readers, and, in fact, the first thing to go through your mind is that these people have all gone mad. But alas, this madness is real and contagious. What is more, it reveals a dreadfully worrying state of mind for the neighbours of a nation where sadism, pride and cruelty are glorified in this way. There never was a more important time to say: 'Let those who have ears listen!' It is true that the Frenchman is too deeply imbued with civilisation to even consider such excesses possible. He did not want to believe at the time in tsarism, nor, later, in the Russian revolution. And yet . . .[21]

She knew therefore what to expect. Looking at *David Golder* again in 1935, she now recognised the brown tinge which, for someone used to anti-Semitic propaganda, this satire of 'fairly cosmopolitan Jews for whom love of money had replaced any other feelings' would take on, in contrast to the 'French Jews settled in their country for generations'. But she was not going to retract anything. To the woman correspondent of *L'Univers israélite*, who had come to give her an anonymous letter from a 'Jewish soul wounded' by reading *Golder*, and to tell her of the suspicions that neither *Le Pion* nor *The Wine of Solitude* had dispersed, Irène Némirovsky, having contained herself and smiled a great deal, replied sharply at last:

'I don't believe I have ever tried to conceal my origins, quite the contrary. Each time I have had an opportunity to do so, I have let it be known that I was a Jew, I have even proclaimed it! I am much too proud of being one ever to have thought of denying it.'[22]

It is a good thing to keep one's flag in one's pocket, so long as no one suspects it of being empty. 'I never boast about my origins except in one situation,' Marc Bloch was to say: 'when confronted by an anti-Semite.' Irène Némirovsky, similarly, was repelled by boastfulness, just as she was by denial. If such confessions, from her mouth, were rare and vehement, it was because it pained her to have to justify herself. She was Jewish and Russian for sure, but she was a French novelist first and foremost. It was by means of such proofs that the France of 1935 – gripped by a frenzy of 'racial' nomenclature that would facilitate the task of the exterminators – each day demanded more of its Jewish nationals. For in order to eliminate, one first has to have subdivided.

Irène Némirovsky confided her intentions to Doumic, whom she had met at dinner in November 1935. He promised to intercede on her behalf with Léon Bérard, a member of the Académie française in the mould of Barrès, who was senator for the Basses-Pyrénées region at the time, who had been Minister of Justice and Education on several previous occasions, and who was an eloquent advocate of the classics. On the 23rd, taking advantage of his kindliness, the novelist sent Doumic her curriculum vitae and Michel's, in order to speed up the naturalisation process. The *Revue des Deux Mondes* was thus ideally disposed towards her. On 1st December, Chaumeix printed a long piece in praise of *The Wine of Solitude*, which only a superstitious mind would think boded ill:

> In our drab age of false dreamers who believe that human goodness stems from nature, she [Irène Némirovsky] unhesitatingly echoes, through her instincts, and through her observational gifts, the most respected philosophers, the most earnest pessimists, the theologians who explain to us the meaning and effects of original sin, and the poets who have best expressed the painful adventure of our earthly life.[23]

Despite the backing of some very well-known names, and applications that continued until 1939, neither Michel Epstein nor, inexplicably, his wife would ever obtain French citizenship.

A trial

When she was a child, Irène Némirovsky recalled in 1934, her grandfather Iona used to make her recite 'Athalie's dream':

My mother Jezebel appeared before me,
Richly attired as on the day of her death;
'Tremble,' she said to me, 'daughter worthy of me;
The cruel God of the Jews will prevail over you too.'

The 'cruel God of the Jews', who went out of his way to refuse her French identity papers, nonetheless never forgot to provide her with subjects for study, however much trouble she took to conceal this source. And so for the first time, in *Jezebel* [*Jézabel*], apart from Sir Mark who 'was Jewish and plebeian by birth',[24] none of the important characters is explicitly Jewish; although Gladys Burnera, Eysenach's wife, the daughter of a wealthy Uruguayan arms dealer, whose dissolute career is traced in this book, belongs to 'that mobile, cosmopolitan society, that has no fixed ties or home anywhere',[25] a definition which, for the French reader, meant more or less the same thing. In this way Irène Némirovsky showed that she could remove the Russian and Jewish aspects while continuing to satirise the corrupt circles of finance, the aristocracy, and now politics. She would also think of adapting *Jezebel* for the stage or screen, as she had in the past with *David Golder*: 'But, in the end, I listened to my friends, who are theatre technicians and who convinced me that the subject did not lend itself to that means of expression ... What's more, what actress would have agreed to play the part of a sixty-year-old woman?'[26]

Cruel Jezebel, the wife of Ahab, king of Israel, was a Phoenician, a lascivious pagan woman who had altars built in Samaria to the idols Baal, Melkart and Astarte. Ultimately, Jehu put an end to her reign of terror by allowing this false Jewish queen, the hated symbol of the depravity of Israel, to be trampled upon by horses' hooves and devoured by dogs. In *Jezebel*, Irène Némirovsky appeared to be deflecting the endless trial she had endured since 1930 towards her mother, and to be laying part of the blame unleashed by these ungracious scenes that portray 'the rich, cosmopolitan class for whom money has gradually destroyed all love of traditions and family',[27] and which are depicted from memory in each of her books, on her. She refers to the 'palace rabble', in the first drafts of this project, while worrying beforehand about depicting 'a milieu, still the same, that of D.G.'. The solution: 'emphasise the "World of *Le*

Bal" side, a caricature of what is real. That's something I know, I've experienced it.'

Is not what has been seen in Irène Némirovsky as denial and recant-ation rather more to do with family drama, with a horror of heredity, with an attempt at emancipation? This is the whole meaning of *Jezebel*, a novel in the form of a legal investigation dossier. There can be no doubt that the infanticide alluded to in the pages of *Marianne* on 2nd October 1935 was another incarnation of Fanny: the mother in *Jezebel* is called Gladys – the first name of David's wife in the earliest draft of *Golder*. Her 'clenched and contorted'[28] lips, her cries of despair in front of the mirror, her hatred of motherhood, her birth certificate that had been altered by ten years, the pity she arouses in her daughter, the proud Marie-Thérèse, belong to 'a monster'.[29] *Jezebel* settled Irène Némirovsky's and Fanny's accounts for once and for all in the minds of her jury of readers. Dominique Desanti relates that she was seven-teen years old when, in 1936, she dared approach the author of *Le Bal* at a dinner for Russian writers. *Jezebel* had just been published. 'So is your mother your tragedy too?' enquired the novelist. 'Mine is that she is never there.' 'Hating an absence and not a presence,' Irène Némirovsky replied to her with a knowing look, 'that's an easier hatred to bear.'[30]

Jezebel is the story of an ogress. Like Mauriac's Génitrix, Gladys Eysenach devours her own child.[31] In order to preserve her 'woman's power'[32] for as long as possible, like a tyrant who refuses to allow her people to grow up, she continues to dress her daughter like a teenager. Even after having postponed her wedding – time for her fiancé to die at the frontline – the only image she wishes to retain of her daughter is that of a little girl 'seven years old, half-naked, with her hair falling over her eyes'.[33] And Fanny, in the same way, denies her age, just as people deny they have cancer. 'I was already born when one day she [my mother] was sent an enormous cuddly bear accompanied by an indecipherable letter,' Denise Epstein recalled. 'This bear was meant for her, my grandmother stubbornly refusing to talk to her except as a very little girl.'[34] In this novel, Irène Némirovsky lays down the truth of this assertion with a wholesome ferocity. It is Bernard Martin, Gladys's illegitimate grandson, who threatens to destroy her position by revealing her age: 'Look, just look,' he says, forcing a mirror in front of her face, 'look at the bags under your eyes that show through your make-up! . . . You're old! . . . You're an old, old woman,' he keeps saying over and over, beside himself, 'How I loathe you!'[35]

Just like 'Ida', *Jezebel* was initially an episode removed from *The Wine of Solitude*, the principal lines of which had been sketched during the first six months of 1934: 'How amusing and topical, and true it would be . . . Show an ordinary, or rather better than ordinary woman, growing older and her despair when her lover drops her. Afterwards, how she becomes a monster and ruins herself, having ruined other human beings.' Topical and true, in fact, for no other period in history had been so beneficial for rejuvenation merchants and other quacks than these fifteen years spent erecting monuments to the dead in every corner of the land. 'Man is shocked by death and considers it the most cruel injustice, because he still retains the inner memory of his immortality,'[36] declared Dr Voronoff in 1920, who claimed to be able to restore man's vitality through the grafting of animal glands. Ten years later, the newspapers were filled with advertisements for elixirs of long life, and ointments 'that make women appear young' and 'protect you from the nightmare of growing old before your time', as Professor Stejskal, the inventor of the renowned Tokalon balm, promised. One might have sworn that Gladys Eysenach had read the advertisement: 'Between the ages of 19 and 50 it will no longer be possible to tell a woman's age.' As we can see, the tyrannical Jezebel is herself a victim of the edicts of creams. 'I am jealous of my youth . . .'[37]

No one is supposed to be unaware of death, but who shows respect for it? This is also the reason why Gladys's trial will be a fair one: as in *Le Bal*, the accused, punished by her own behaviour and humiliated by the public revelation of her lies, eventually arouses sharp pity. 'When I began to write,' Irène Némirovsky admitted in July 1936, I was very severe on my "criminal" . . . And then, the more I wrote, the more attractive I made her, so that in the end I started to find excuses for her . . . If I had to judge her, it would be pity, in my case, that would eventually carry the day . . .'[38] Neither does Marie-Thérèse deny her mother's suffering. In setting up her trial, Irène Némirovsky cannot avoid cross-examining herself. The young Gladys is her self-portrait: 'For eighteen years, she had lived with a cold, strict mother who was nearly insane, an old made-up doll, who was sometimes frivolous and sometimes frightening, who dragged her Persian cats, her daughter, her boredom all over the world.'[39] Out of Fanny, who was embalmed alive, and she herself, already beginning to live on in her books, who would have been the more astonished?

Jezebel is an allegory of arrogance. Human defences are worthless against the onslaught of nothingness; by challenging the natural order of things, you expose yourself to its revenge. By labouring the point, Irène Némirovsky had wanted to raise Fanny's pathetic comedy to the level of a Racine tragedy. Her drafts make this clear: 'What is needed is to show it from the inside, show it in short almost like *Phèdre*, in her impossibility of resisting her vice, her desire, that pride in remaining young and desirable.'

'Facts'

Jezebel was not serialised in *Marianne* until the autumn, but Irène Némirovsky had already sold the exclusive rights to the magazine's editor, Emmanuel Berl, for 35,000 francs in late December 1934. She put the finishing touches to it during the summer of 1935. 'Le Commencement et la Fin', which appeared in *Gringoire* just at the moment that the last extract of *Jezebel* was published, on 20th December, was a variation on the same theme. In this story set in a law court, the prosecutor, Desprez, far from inclining to clemency, becomes twice as harsh and ambitious when he learns that he has a cancerous tumour. Life is a courtroom in which everyone risks his neck. Among the human herd, news of an epidemic does not provoke mutual aid, but a stampede. Each for himself and God for all: it is not hard to see the political moral to be drawn from this, at a time when the French government was closing its frontiers to non-German Jewish refugees.

Not without humour – or pity – Irène Némirovsky gave the prosecutor, Desprez, the features of Bernard Grasset, his 'silvery hair', his 'thin, flat lips and an unusual moustache that was grey like lichen'.[40] It was scarcely a coincidence, since Grasset, too, was eaten away by a cancer, but one of the mind. At the hands of René Laforgue, the pioneer of Freudian teaching in France, the wounded lion, who was prey to terrible attacks of cyclothymia, had fallen into the clutches of various 'butchers of the soul', as he called them. Locked away at the Château de Garches, he spared his staff his irrational rages and allowed himself to lose total control of his publishing house, under pressure from his family and his shareholders.

For the past two years, Irène Némirovsky had kept away from Grasset's office in the Rue des Saints-Pères; but Michel Epstein had formed closer bonds of friendship with the publisher and retained some contact. Towards the end of 1934, Michel had even called one of Grasset's lawyers, so as to ensure that he be kept informed about Grasset's business affairs, since a variety of evidence had led him to believe the contrary. In vain: one year later, the man whom the whole of Paris now took to be a maniac had to undergo incapacity proceedings brought by his sisters. Their case would be dismissed in the spring of 1936. On that occasion, the press would publish a 'Homage to Grasset' on behalf of a hundred or so writers – Gide, Benjamin, Bonnard, Crémieux, Aîné Rosny, Martin du Gard – who wished to 'see him take up as soon as possible his activities in a field in which he had always displayed the most precious virtues of initiative and energy'.[41] Among the signatories of this testimony of 'heartfelt sympathy' and 'gratitude', there were very few writers published by Grasset, but the name of Irène Némirovsky was there among them, in between those of Maurras and Marcel Prévost. This handsome gesture would not prevent Grasset, that spring, from allocating the 5,000 francs from the sale of rights in *The Courilof Affair* [*L'Affaire Courilof*] to the Ferenczi publishing house – 35,000 copies printed! – to fill the deficit in the Némirovsky account. Michel would rebuke him sharply for such unscrupulous behaviour: 'Well,' he wrote to him on 5th May, 'remind your financial directors of everything that the book, film, translation etc. of *David Golder* and *Le Bal* has earned for you.'

So the publisher was not quite so mad. Declared fit to run his firm, he took up the reins once more at the very moment that André Sabatier, who had worked there as an editor since 1929, left. It was not at Grasset that Irène Némirovsky discovered the human and professional qualities of this self-effacing and cultured man, but at Albin Michel, where he had been appointed, on his own terms, to take on a role as 'a sort of chief executive of the literary list'.[42] Sabatier, who was both wise and restrained, and also a devout Protestant, might have suffered further from Grasset's mood-swings had Grasset not added insult to injury by taking a dislike to one of his most promising authors, Jacques Benoist-Méchin, even going so far as to physically throw him out of the office. This young official at the League of Nations, a highly skilled Germanist, was one of Sabatier's proudest recruits. It therefore came as no surprise that in July 1936 Albin Michel should have published his monumental and magisterial *Histoire de l'armée allemande*, much to Bernard Grasset's displeasure . . . Until he was called up for military service and sent to Syria in 1940, Sabatier was Irène Némirovsky's regular editor, and he was far friendlier and more attentive than Tisné had been, a man trained at the rough Grasset school.

The sales of *Films parlés* were acceptable for a book of short stories, and a happy surprise. As for Albin Michel, he declared himself very pleased with *Jezebel*. Irène Némirovsky put the finishing touches to it during the first months of 1936. She paid particular attention to the letters from lawyers pointing out certain procedural errors in the courtroom scene, but not to the numerous letters from strangers who took a firm stand either for or against Gladys! Since the publication date in book form had been postponed until May, she only returned the proofs on 21st April, accompanied by the following suggestion for a publicity band: 'A woman has killed . . . Why?' This concern for effective publicity, this atmosphere of suspense, were the result of her reading, in particular *The Postman Always Rings Twice*, which had been serialised in *Marianne* and for which NRF had asked her to write a preface before the summer. Like *Jezebel*, James Cain's novel is 'the confession of a murderer', but the author of *David Golder* – which had just been translated into Japanese! – was principally attracted by its brutality and its disregard for psychology: 'Here, there are no preparations, no digressions, no breathing space. There are facts. "Facts" . . . Literature that is shaped by the cinema and for the cinema, through the convention of "hot news" and the detective novel, conforms paradoxically to Boileau's precept . . . It is tasty and hard: you experience something healthy, sharp and strong that can be found nowhere else at the present time.'

Strangely enough, her style did not benefit from this in any way. With renewed patience, she indulged in convoluted family intrigues and love affairs; bitterness, regret, and jealousy took the place of violence and 'facts'. 'Un amour en danger' [Love in Danger], which was published in *Le Figaro littéraire* on 22nd February, has very little to do with Cain's 'fisticuff literature'. In it, a man and a woman, in the space of a second, appear to yield to guilty desire. The convulsions of love and the power of a long-held affection are not the same thing; they can follow one another, but rarely combine. 'At the moment of death,' Sylvie imagines, 'will I regret most my love for Hervé, and the painful anxiety of love, or this? . . . a moment of pleasure?' This dilemma makes 'Un amour en danger' a first version of *Deux*, the novel that Irène Némirovsky would start work on in 1937, but which she had been thinking about for two years. The other earlier draft was 'Liens du sang' [Blood Ties], a long story, written during the autumn, which was published in two editions of *Revue des Deux Mondes* on 15th March and 1st April. In it there is the following maxim: 'Love does not give rise to love or, at least, and this is what is so horrible, it only gives rise to an illusion, an *ersatz* love.'[43] What gives rise to this disappointment is age, the calamity that suddenly befalls Anna Demestre's sons, softening or stiffening their egoism according to their characters. Just as there are two kinds of love, there are two kinds of existence: the one, adventurous, which warms the soul and keeps anxiety in check; the other, congealed by comfort, which adheres to the body and the soul. The 'blood ties', for Anna, are the 'appalling silence of old age', which eventually stifles the 'joyful tumult of the soul that you hear resounding noisily when you are young';[44] for Alain, they are the cold family bonds that have buried him alive in his own home.

A 'pitiless compassion'

Turning their backs on death, boredom or poverty, Irène Némirovsky's heroes generally commit irreparable mistakes; they damn themselves, but they have had fun. 'I wanted to describe the moment,' she would say, describing *Jezebel*, 'when that hitherto innocent passion, since it has to do with a very natural wish to please and to be liked, invades the soul, blots out all other feelings, and eventually turns itself into a kind of madness . . . In fact, this tendency of the female heart resembles, in its tyrannical strength, a man's ambition and avarice, and it deserves, I believe, to be studied in the way ambition and avarice have been.'[45] Jean-Luc Daguerne is in this league. What would have become of Bernard Martin if he had survived Gladys's bullet? This was what Irène Némirovsky wanted to find out by giving him a second chance in *La Proie* [The Victim], a novel for which *Gringoire* would offer her

50,000 francs in January for publication in October 1936 – an amount that Albin Michel reckoned to be just about right. Like Martin, Daguerne does not intend to yield an inch to the misfortune of flesh and blood that has made him poor. In the 1930s, Stendhal's Julien Sorel, rechristened Daguerne, is now a child of the economic crisis, a victim of the dazzling successes condemned by the sensationalist press. 'At present, there is a reversal in public opinion concerning financial matters that is very strange to observe',[46] explained Cottu, a politician who feared neither God nor man. 'He is ambitious,' stated Irène Némirovsky. 'He knows that he is courageous and intelligent. Unfortunately, the times in which he lives set little value on these two qualities. They do not even offer this young man a mediocre but secure employment, as they would have done in the past; they offer him absolutely nothing . . . Every day, for nearly a decade, we see this kind of thing happening again and again. This is what my book is about.'[47]

Unfamiliar with the conventions of the crushing social life he has entered into, and despising the weakness that has led him into a marriage entered into out of pride, Daguerne cynically betrays his wife, his son, his friends and himself in order to make his way in the worlds of politics and finance and become the person who does the dirty work for the minister, Langon – another spitting image of Bernard Grasset – and so named in reference to the town in the Gironde where Mauriac set some of his novels. 'But do you think that Mauriac was right to portray people in such an appalling way?'[48] Daguerne's mother-in-law rightly asks, in order to show clearly that *La Proie* is a novel of its time. This book contained an implicit condemnation of corruption that is so blatant that it would upset some critics. As to the moral of the book, it was this: 'Youth is a precious wine that is usually drunk in an ugly glass.'[49] Daguerne wanted crystal, the wine had gone off. And the title, *La Proie*? It was appropriate for a time when everything – feelings, well-being, dignity – was there to be plundered; having been a hunter for a long time, Jean-Luc would himself become 'the victim of the most despicable love',[50] starved by too much hardship. To give in to feelings of love in the middle of an economic crisis is to guarantee it won't last. But youth always gets its reward in the long run. Lying in wait in one of life's corners, it swoops down one day on the parvenu when he no longer expects it, to ruin his job and to insist on love. If it is not too late.

Natural instincts cannot be kept down indefinitely. Unable to control them properly, Gladys Eysenach eventually trains her gun on them. When *Jezebel* appeared in the bookshops in May 1936, Fernandez, Chaumeix and Maxence detected only too well how pathological this case was. René Lalou drew attention to the trouble: fear of the grave.[51] Irène Némirovsky's feat, wrote Henri de Régnier in *Le Figaro*, is to have known how to isolate this 'type' of Faustian woman, afflicted with 'moral deformity', typical 'of an age when the body is king, and we forget the soul'. And that is why Gladys is as much a criminal as a victim, and why Némirovsky has such a gift for 'pitiless compassion',[52] an oxymoron that sums up her feelings for Fanny. Maxence, comparing Gladys to Colette's Léa, emphasised the Racine-like range of *Jezebel*, whose characters, consumed by an inner fire, seem to burn with real life. 'There is no quality that better illustrates a perfect storyteller.'[53]

Albin Michel had forecast that sales would be good: out of a print-run of fifteen thousand copies, twelve thousand would be sold by the end of 1942, and *Jezebel* would be translated into English, German, Norwegian and Serbo-Croat. When Fanny died, in 1972, her granddaughters found a copy in a chest at her home on the Quai de Passy. There are some portraits that are so realistic it is best to hide them.

Foolish hypocrites!

'It is rather amusing to note that there has never been less of a fashion for accepting old age than in our twentieth century,' wrote Henri de Régnier on 23rd May, drawing attention for one last time to the 'powerful talent' and the 'intense gifts of life' of Irène Némirovsky. The very next day, she addressed the following telegram to his home in Rue Boissière: 'Am very sorry to learn of the death of Monsieur Henri de Régnier for whom I felt such friendship and gratitude. Please accept my respectful sympathy and my great sadness.' The academician, who had been so loyal to her, acclaiming every one of her novels in *Le Figaro*, was buried at Saint-Pierre-de-Chaillot amid a host of rosettes, cockades and cocked hats. 'Life is demeaning,' he used to say. 'Is it true?' Irène Némirovsky wondered in 1934. 'In *Le Vin* . . . and later in *Deux* I want to show that it's not always like that. I love life. Deep down, all my worries come from the fact that I'm afraid of not being able to enjoy it fully enough, or for long enough. The days seem too short for me. The sun sets too early. The summers end so quickly. Death comes so quickly.'

Another death was on her mind: that of Pushkin, on 29th January 1837. To celebrate his centenary, Fayard wanted to bring out a biography based on his unpublished letters and certain other documents that had just been published in the Soviet Union by Vikenti Veresaev. On 25th March 1936, instead of writing a review of the book, she provided an account of his marriage and his painful death, two days after his duel with d'Anthès in which he received a bullet in the stomach, for *Marianne*.[54] She appeared to be struck by some noteworthy aspects: his 'unusual precocity', his mixed blood, his pride and his jealousy, his constant 'money worries'. In the book she envisaged, but of which in June not a word had yet been written, she would spare the reader all literary comment, restricting herself 'purely to describing Pushkin, the man, his very romantic life, and the Russian society of his time, and its customs'.[55] It would be an enormous amount of work, a myriad books had already been published on the subject in Russian, not to mention the poet's journal, which was not yet known in France. In May 1936, however, Irène Némirovsky was unwell; furthermore, she had promised to deliver her new novel to *Gringoire* for the autumn. This 'Pushkin' would therefore remain in a draft stage, twenty or so pages intended for 'a passionate Life'. But the technique was not wasted: it would be used later for *La Vie de Tchekhov*.

The Epsteins spent the summer of 1936 at the house in Urrugne, up until 1st October. To amuse readers of *Toute l'édition*, Irène Némirovsky affected nonchalance: 'I am replying to you a little late, for which I apologise, but I have spent my holidays indulging intensely and rationally in the greatest laziness.'[56] In actual fact, she had just put the finishing touches to *La Proie*, a novel of which no drafts survive, despite the fact that Maurice Bourget-Pailleron, the great-grandson of the founder of *Revue des Deux Mondes*, had seen them at Avenue Daniel-Lesueur: there was a large folder 'of more than five hundred pages. The lines were packed closely together, written in a narrow cluster on both sides of each page.'[57] After pruning, all that would be left was a novel of two hundred and fifty pages, the first chapter of which appeared in *Gringoire* on 16th October. A sign of the times, this new book came out at the same time as *Fumier* by Binet-Valmer, a novel whose author claimed that he 'spoke with no fondness for parliamentary circles'.[58]

None of the characters in *La Proie* is Jewish, which is just as well, for they are a shifty lot, constantly at one another's throats. At the end of the book, no one would take offence at Jean-Luc Daguerne's dissolute career, which was far more cynical than that of a Golder. Not that this surprised Irène Némirovsky: 'As I expected, people are a little – not greatly – shocked by the fact that he is French. Foolish hypocrites! But I understand their point of view: what is acceptable from a Dupont or a Durant would not be tolerated coming from some olive-skinned foreigner.' The subject matter stems from *David Golder* and *Le Bal*: what is the secret motivation of those who are socially ambitious? Not the lure of wealth, nor the desire for honours, still less the 'racial' differential, but a Faustian pact that Daguerne signs up to against poverty. Money alone is not enough. 'When success is far away it has a dreamlike quality, but as soon as success enters into the realm of a possibility, it seems sordid and petty.'[59] In order to assert this truth, Irène Némirovsky was now sufficiently sure of herself to be able to place the story in a purely French setting. It was a particularly astute decision for, ever since the victory of the Front Populaire in May, anti-Semitic propaganda had risen a degree. Léon Blum, whom the Camelots du roi* had jostled and bustled in the Boulevard Saint-Germain on 13th February, was now, with the support of the communists, Prime Minister. For the far right, it was not merely a socialist whom France had just entrusted with power, but a Jew; a Jew, that is to say a foreigner, a rebel, the representative of Israel in France. A host of small racist parties fiercely resented the fact that he had granted citizenship for electoral reasons – an imaginary tactic and not in the least Machiavellian, for the polls would not bring him luck. As for La Rocque, blinded by his hostility to Marxism, he held Blum solely and simply responsible for the rampant anti-Semitism that was focused on him and his cabinet. On 6th June, the member for the Ardèche, the war veteran Xavier Vallat, observed in the Chambre: 'For the first time, this old Gallo-Roman land will be governed by a Jew!'[60]

*A royalist fighting squad founded in 1908. Members were frequently disciples of Charles Maurras. The movement was dissolved in 1936. [Tr.]

'It's a change from the Jesuits', retorted André Le Troquer, the socialist member for Paris.

Inassimilability

The times were deteriorating. At the 1935 annual dinner of the *Revue des Deux Mondes*, René Doumic, sensing the storms that lay ahead, suggested a temporary haven: 'The horizon, there is no point in denying it, is heavy with clouds ... The heavier the oppression that weighs over us, the greater the need to escape from it. In order for the brain not to explode or the nerves not to shatter, they need to relax. The *Revue* does not conceal the current difficulties, but it opens up the mind to serene regions, the *templa serena* of high culture.'[61] Hitler, who would reoccupy the Rhineland in March 1936, would not deny this.

Irène Némirovsky did her best to remain calm. 'I am spending my holidays at Urrugne,' she said, 'a delightful little part of the Basque countryside where, at this moment, the chirp of crickets blends pleasantly with ... the noise of machine-guns, a stone's throw from here, in Spain!'[62] The irony did not conceal her anxiety. She unburdened herself on a fictional character, a Jew who is so well assimilated that his first name is Christian, and who is tormented by a secret vulnerability, an apprehension of disaster that he can only put down to outside causes: 'He was one of those people who imagined war every time he heard any dictator give a speech, and not a war that might happen next month or the following year, but tomorrow, immediately.'[63] Christian Rabinovitch, the draft of this story tells us, is a Jew, of the Lœwel-type (2nd or 3rd generation French), or even more worldly, more Haas ... His meeting with a Russian 'yid', who has been driven out by wars and pogroms and who finds himself on a French railway station, sharply awakens his awareness of the 'old heritage' to which he owes his anxiety, this sense of the precariousness at the heart of opulence, like a worm in a fruit. For this 'Pollak's' name is Rabinovitch, just like his. This unpleasant consanguinity of the emigrant and the assimilated is known as Jewishness. 'That is what I suffer from ... That is what I am paying for with my body, with my mind. Centuries of poverty, illness, oppression ... Thousands of poor, weak, tired bones have made me what I am.'[64]

Never had Irène Némirovsky attached such a profound meaning to the image of adulterated blood, 'poisoned' by the 'old leaven of anxieties',[65] nor to that of the tell-tale mirror in which Rabinovitch suddenly recognises his double, motives that sustain her work and find their hidden essence here. The story's title is 'Fraternité'. Was this a way of mocking the 'blood ties', or a way of reminding France of what she stood for? 'In short,' she confides to her working diary, 'I demonstrate inassimilability, Lord, what a word . . . I know that it's true.' But then, of course, her own request for citizenship had got nowhere. This was the argument of the Tharaud brothers: 'Today as yesterday, the Jews will continue to lead their adventurous lives among the other nations. They cannot lose themselves among them: the blood of the race is too strong.'[66] But what the Tharauds challengingly refer to as an 'adventurous life', Irène Némirovsky calls a 'dog's life', a 'flickering façade'.[67] We should distinguish furthermore between 'inassimilability' (the inability to be assimilated) and what an anti-Semitic ideologue like Xavier Vallat calls 'inassimilation' (the inability to assimilate). For her, the inassimilable Jew is not so much the emigrant dressed in a sheepskin coat as Christian Rabinovitch himself who, despite his tweeds, his chauffeur and his good manners, endures his own pogrom in his soul: 'Start again, and once more start all over again, bend your back, and start again, but for the rich man, the man who has had no need of that, his heritage is sickening fear.'

How far away David, arrogant and sure of himself, seems! In early 1938, while attending a production of *Golder* by a Russian company at the Salle Iéna, Irène Némirovsky was struck by the character's obduracy: 'How could I have written something like that?' Money, of course, still had the same smell, but 'the climate has changed a great deal'.[68] In 'Fraternité', she had wanted to create a portrait of a Jew who had become a wealthy Frenchman, but who was always on the alert, to depict 'that race that had not dropped their guard knowing that the roof belonged to them, that their house belonged to them, like a French peasant, but that everything could be taken back'. In short, the self-portrait of a writer whom the critics still hesitated to call 'French' without adding the words 'Russian' or 'Jewish'. Her draft notes on this matter are clear: 'Jewish paternity, pride, the love of his children, the capacity to suffer through them, above all, I think, the need to be loved, for someone who has been hated, the agonising need to be respected, for someone who has been despised and harassed . . . This needs to be purely objective, the impression that I, I should . . . that I, the author, should be a little above my characters.' In spite of this effort, the subjectivity of 'Fraternité' is obvious.

Would people understand it? Irène Némirovsky thought not, but she couldn't help persevering: 'I am certainly going to get myself into trouble again by writing about the Jews again at this time, but oh well! . . .' At this time – that is to say in an atmosphere of paranoia exacerbated by the strikes paralysing the factories, and with the first steps on social issues being taken by the Front Populaire. 'The quietest people began to give strange looks at those with frizzy hair, with hooked noses, who were particularly conspicuous,' Brasillach would write. 'All this is not polemics, it is history.'[69] Ever since June 1936, Action française had been leading a campaign to win over the 'Jewish nationals' and patriots, calling on them to repudiate the stateless and the 'Jewish revolutionaries' who were now in control: Léon Blum, Jean Zay and company. Would Christian Rabinovitch be one of those Jews of the far right, who were openly xenophobic, such as the lawyer Edmond Bloch, a member of the Croix-de-Feu and founder of the Union Patriotique des Français Israélites, who would soon flirt with the Vallats, the Doriots and other French fascists, with predictable results? Not in the least. This middle-class fellow merely yearned to marry his son to an aristocratic woman. It was not hatred, but fear that reminded him of his origins.

The necessities of life

Irène Némirovsky had been right: on 31st October 1936, René Doumic refused to publish 'Fraternité' in *Revue des Deux Mondes*, on the grounds that this short story might be 'anti-Semitic'. Proof of this were Rabinovitch's racial characteristics, his 'excessively long and crooked'[70] nose, his waxy complexion, his febrile temperament, which would be defamatory were it not for the author's affection and gentle irony. If someone who was functionally illiterate were to look at the drawings and caricatures in the special issue of *Crapouillot* devoted to 'the Jews', which appeared on the news stands in September 1936, he might consider it an obscene publication; but quite the contrary, the articles represent an attempt – albeit an occasionally clumsy one – to understand Judaism, its woes and its greatness, its failings as well as the threats that hung over it. 'Fraternité' is another case in point. It is a mirror in which the French Jew sees the first stigmata appearing of the curse of anti-Semitism. Rabinovitch is not a distortion: he is caricatured. He could not rid himself of anti-Semitic misfortune. 'My nose, my mouth, that's nothing,' he declares. 'Only the soul matters!'[71]

Irène Némirovsky chose to laugh off Doumic's response and she had good reasons for doing so. For the *Revue* was not the last magazine to condemn 'the vast revolutionary gathering under the influence of the Soviets', which was what the government of the Front Populaire represented for Doumic.[72] Instead, 'Fraternité' would be published on 5th February 1937 in *Gringoire*, even if it meant distorting the meaning, for the *Gringoire* of the Front Populaire period was not the paper it had once been. In the issue of 25th December, both the final instalment of *La Proie* was printed as well as the rantings of Henri Béraud, who denounced racial nepotism with heavy play on words, and drew up a list of the real or supposed Jews in the 'Blumoche' cabinet, as if their number constituted a cabal. This was the moment that Joseph Kessel, weary of Béraud's specious arithmetic and chilled by his farcical remarks, sent a letter of solidarity 'with all the Jews of France' to the newspaper before slamming the door shut. 'No, Kessel,' Béraud would reply, 'I am not anti-Semitic. I am anti-parasitic.' Thus did the 'anti-Dreyfusards' edge towards 'scientific' racism.

How did Irène Némirovsky come to agree to appear in the same pages alongside such a second-rate mind as Béraud? It should be pointed out that while Béraud was anti-Semitic, *Gringoire* was not – or not yet – and that the polemicist's comments, even if they were tolerated, did not involve the magazine, still less her. Furthermore, could she afford to be difficult? In early October, she received from her publisher the last monthly payment of 4,000 francs of those envisaged in 1933; it was the moment to ask for a reassessment – '. . . for alas,' she wrote to him, 'you can understand the necessities of life for people who, like me, are not wealthy and live purely on what they earn from writing', which was the exact truth. 'If the situation has become very difficult for you, believe me it is even more so for publishers,'[73] replied Albin Michel, who was infuriated by the competition from the weekly magazines and who, since the summer, had been fighting the proposal made by Jean Zay, the Minister for Education, to limit the right of publishers to exploit their own backlists to ten years. 'Very often,' he fulminated, 'we have to wait twenty-five years for a book on which we have spent large sums to become a success with the public and to yield a profit. It's like the cinema. Sometimes I publish books solely because I know that they could be adapted to the screen.'[74] This was precisely the calculation he had made with *Jezebel*, for which he was on the point of selling film rights to Latin America at the begining of 1938. In the meantime, sales of novels had slumped; in 1936, the anxious middle classes preferred to read newspapers, and workers, tracts. Albin Michel had ten thousand copies of *Le Pion sur l'échiquier* in stock, over four thousand copies of *Jezebel*, and Irène Némirovsky's author's account was in debit to the tune of 72,787 francs . . . 'You are now asking me to increase your deficit. I must confess that in these times of severely slack sales I can see no possibility of doing so!'

There was another thing: in mid-October 1936, Irène Némirovsky was four months pregnant. Her apprehension rivalled her joy. 'This child is giving me both fatigue and peace,' she noted on the 8th. 'October freezing, no, radiant. No desire to work, but soon two children to feed . . . Need for a short story and a novel. The novel, nothing yet, not even that, *remote** . . . Nothing . . .' She would publish little in 1937. Apart from 'Fraternité', there was just one short story for *Gringoire*, 'Épilogue', which picks up somewhat listlessly the character of the bar-fly who appears in 'Les Rivages heureux'.

The child was born on 20th March, in the spring of 1937. She was given the names Élisabeth, after her paternal grandmother who had died a few weeks earlier, and Léone, after her grandfather on her mother's side. 'One month ago today my little girl Élisabeth was born,' her mother wrote on 20th April. 'A month of worries, of sorrows, but a great joy. May God protect her. She is very close to my heart.' Every Sunday, Irène Némirovsky could be seen walking her new baby in her pram, in the gardens of the Invalides. She did not know that a passer-by and a neighbour were watching her tenderly. 'See how sweet she is!' he said to his confidante. 'She looks after her children

---

*In English in original text. [Tr.]

so well.'[75] It was Henry de Montherlant, and the young woman who lapped up his words was Élisabeth Zehrfuss, the young critic from *La Revue hebdomadaire*.

The past no longer exists

Irène Némirovsky had just turned thirty-four. She was famous, and yet the grandson of the minister Raphaël Leygues, who used to encounter her at sales organised by the anti-poverty charity, Ligue contre le Taudis, was charmed by her simplicity: '[She] doesn't know Mauriac, or Maurois, or Colette, and yet she is Irène Némirovsky.'[76] The book she started writing, unhurriedly, shortly after Élisabeth was born, was a *Bildungsroman*, the adult phase of *The Wine of Solitude*, which she had described in 1934: '*Deux* is the story of two people, who are crazy, bad and unstable, and whom life, love and marriage improve.' She would follow the intimate fortunes of four sisters of her generation and would observe the resolution of a loving moral code of behaviour disturbed by the chaos of the post-war era. Love doesn't require lovers, their quarrels or their infidelities: it blossoms in spite of them. These experiments in emotional chemistry would make *Deux* a sort of *Elective Affinities* of the inter-war years. With the measured pace of Chardonne, she would also reveal the other side of bourgeois morality, stripping away the mechanics of money and power that were at work behind the good manners. The Carmontels, a family of papermakers, from a long line of Norman country squires, are based on a model that is not denied: 'I wanted a good, solid, middle-class French family, industrialists, who have shared their profits purely between members of the family. The Avots really don't do badly: that very simple life-style conceals ancient wealth and, in particular, a great ability to rise up the ladder.' As for the Segrés, who are more bohemian, they are drawn from a family of impoverished artists, the Namurs, of whom nothing is known apart from these few notes from April 1937: 'They are deeply divided; she, the mother, a life apart, fairly secretive. She must be a beautiful woman, intelligent, for whom certain affairs have been tragic; two lovers killed beneath her if I dare put it like that. He, for many years, [runs] a second household. The two wives are friends (although the lawful wife knows everything) and even the children know one another. In a word, a pleasantly free and easy set-up.'

These outlines cannot keep her anxieties in check. On 5th June, back home from a visit to the Musée Rodin with Denise, she gives way for the first time to a spiritual desire that says a great deal about her state of confusion: 'My Babet continues to have a cold. Anxiety, sadness, a mad desire to be reassured. Yes, that's what I seek, but in vain. Only in Paradise will I find reassurance. I think of Renan's words: "You find peace in God's heart." To be confident and reassured, sheltered in the bosom of God! And yet, I love life. (To think that all this, so sincere, I will probably use to write about.)' For the first time in her adult life, she did not spend the summer on the Basque coast, but near La Ferté-Allais, in the Gâtinais, fifty kilometres from Paris. 'My younger daughter is only six months old and she is too young for long journeys,' she explained. 'So no sea or mountains this year, but fields and woods and a great deal of calm.'[77]

'How did love turn into friendship within married life? When did we stop tearing each other apart and finally want each other to be happy?'[78] Dominique's questions form the subject of *Deux*, which was completed on the eve of 1938. With this occasionally sententious novel – 'love is often merely the memory of love'[79] – which would be serialised in *Gringoire* from April to July, Irène Némirovsky finally exhausted the 'Monster' she had given birth to five years previously, which had supplied her with three novels and several stories. She now had to devise a new narrative matrix for the next five years. This time, autobiography could be of no help to her, or very little. Opening the little black notebook she had neglected since 1921, she could not prevent herself smiling as she read the poems of her adolescence:

> Little goat grazing in the mountains,
> Galya is so happy to be alive.
> The grey wolf will devour the little goat
> But Galya will devour an entire army . . .

'If you ever read this, my daughters, how silly you will think I was!' she wrote. 'Even I think I was silly at that happy age. But it is important to respect the past. So I won't destroy a thing.' Then, carefully numbering each one, she jotted down a list of possible subjects for books and stories she would still like to write, 'if God gives me life'. Nothing would come of some of them: the memory of a dinner with Nozière; 'Mirabeau and his father'; 'Catherine the Great and her son'; 'the marriage of Paul Bourget'; 'grandfather's death in the boarding house'; a piece about Rimbaud in old age; a Lady Macbeth; a portrait of a manly woman 'who only associates with sissies', in the Becky Sharp mould; 'the man who, before he dies, wishes to satisfy his most secret vice'; a gifted child's 'sense of a former life' . . .

Others would lead to a series of nostalgic stories that reveal the dread of giving up the privileges of youth: impatience, foolishness and contempt for experience. Ten years after *Le Bal* Irène Némirovsky tried to share Mme Kampf's point of view, her fleeting dreams, her longing to get her hands on worldly goods, her terror of old age. In 'L'Ogresse',[80] a memory of Plombières in which the name of Danielle Darrieux is slipped in mischievously, a failed actress stubbornly persists in denying fate by involving her daughter in the same dead end. 'Magie' resurrects old memories of Mustamäki and muses about the ironies of life: 'There must have been an error somewhere, a missing stitch, in the threads that weave our destiny.'[81] In 'Le Départ pour la fête', which would not be published until 1940, she set out to describe the fall from the realm of childhood and that sense one has, at the age of forty, 'of being out of one's depth, of sinking into deep water';[82] that moment when the flow of blood decreases and starts to course gently towards death. Finally, in 'L'Incommunicable', which would be published in October 1938 under the title of 'La Confidence', she imagines herself having become an elderly teacher mulling over her memories of St Petersburg and the Crimea. For Colette, her impudent pupil, these were merely dusty fragments of gossip. And yet these two women were alike: one is unaware of her happiness, the other misses it, neither of them enjoys it. 'So this is the end, this is death! Yes, death! What I am feeling is unmistakable. So quickly, my God, so quickly! That was me, that sixteen-year-old child, wearing a grey dress, with my plaits wound in circles around my ears; they were dark blonde, like your hair . . .'[83]

Seventeen years since she had opened her black notebook! It was a gap that left her incredulous. Could she really have been the girl who wrote: 'The past no longer exists. What is the good of worrying about problems in the future? Enjoy the present moment and cherish your fancies.' Her life professed the very opposite: sighs, constancy, anxiety. The subjects that she drafted at the time were for the most part meditations on regret and time slipping away. At random: 'The man who has not lived enough, and who is jealous of his child because he is living', or again: 'The parents who take pleasure in sullying the innocence of children, not in so far as feelings are concerned, of course, but from the point of view of experience of life and, in short, the pleasure of revenge'. And yet more than old age and amnesia, more than these generations of nations at war, more than the bitterness of growing old and the absurdity of life, she always came back to the enigma of Golder: through what alchemical principal did one pull oneself out of the mud and later go on to devour the world? Was it pride? Chance? Was it rather temperament, that pulsation of blood that was rich and thick in those who were prosperous, but thinner and sharper in others, ruined by their own greed? Irène Némirovsky summed up this theory of moods in a single phrase, 'fire in the blood', one virtually synonymous with youth, vigour and destiny. This was the instinct that in its own way shaped the course of life, and led you where your reason told you not to go. The life force unleashed.

'Fire in the blood': these were among the first words she wrote in her newly found notebook, on 6th December 1937. In actual fact, she had been wondering about the enigma of desire and impulsiveness, the blind motive of existence, for a long time. The image threads its way through her work. Just one example, taken from *The Wine of Solitude*: 'I can't change my body, quench that fire that burns in my blood.' What was this secret impulse that ordered her to move on and told her what to write? Was it Fanny's contrasting blood, flowing back to its source? Or Léon's more domineering blood? This imperious fluid was the ink of novels, whose energy the writer has to procure. It was vanity that guided Gladys Eysenach, not sensual pleasure. And it was pride, and not money, that spurred Golder on. Lucre only mattered for 'little people'.

'But what is it actually about those people worthy of the name of men?' wondered Irène Némirovsky on 11th April 1938. 'I believe the great motivation is pride. Tolstoy said so too, probably because he was so forceful at home.' It is with pride that perfect destinies are constructed, those that endeavour to belie one's birth and nature:

witness the irresistible rise of Becky Sharp, the libertine heroine of
Vanity Fair. There was a fictional goldmine there. It might be the career
of a gambler like Ivar Kreuger, about whom she had momentarily
considered writing. Or else the young Bonaparte, 'humiliated, poor, a
simple, embittered adolescent who, in despair, returns home, hammers
his boots on the wooden staircase and yells at the concierge: "Napoléon
Bonaparte"'. Or again, the life of 'a traitor, wheedling his way out of
awkward situations everywhere, a kind of Fouché'.

These archetypal profiles would allow her to illustrate this important
idea, namely that certain lives develop contrary to one's temperament,
as if it were a question of repudiating it. 'This could be very fruitful,
very complex, this contrast – always – that pursues me: between the
public man and the private man.' It might be Dimitri Navachine,
the symbolist poet who had become a representative of the Soviet
State Bank in Paris, and may well have been a secret agent, who
was assassinated at the Porte d'Auteuil in January 1937. No, too
'melodramatic', she decided. Who, on the other hand, would be
better suited to her idea than Léon Blum, who had only just returned
to power after a brief eclipse? This reluctant public speaker was the
very type of man 'whose life is not in harmony with his temperament'.
But Blum 'is a weak-willed, defeated type. Above all, he would be
incomprehensible outside the world of politics, and, really, I don't
know him well enough.'

One way of nevertheless keeping Blum, she reflected, would be to
transpose him into a more universal type of figure, the project on
which her 'heart was most set' at the time: 'Le Juif'. We shall never
know what such a novel would have been like, except through its
likely contents: three portraits of men who took risks, Blum, Stavisky
and Trotsky, each of them motivated by his own creative energy, his
'fire in the blood'. And so what is this burning blood, if it is not that
of 'race', since she did not mind using this word? An unstable, audacious fluid, spurred on by adversity and propelled by otherness. Blum,
the scholarly man, the idealist, who was never destined to change the
fate of a nation. Stavisky, the fox, the *'crooked man'*,* the *'macher'*,**
the eternal urchin from Odessa. 'I should vow to myself to do a Stav,'

*In English in original text. [Tr.]
**A Yiddish term denoting a 'big shot', a person with contacts, a crook. [Tr.]

she noted again on 26th May 1938, 'and not to give a damn about the effect it would have on the condition of the Jews, in general etc. After all, the Jews, for me, I like them as guinea pigs, so!' For she was not going to fall into the trap of commiseration. Trotsky, finally, the most accomplished, the most sincere, the most radical of these pedigree adventurers. *'The aim of my life*.* If I live till I'm very old, if I have enough money to work slowly, to do research etc. "The life of Trotzky" but more as the type of eternally rebellious Jew.' There were several conditions there.

Days of anxiety

'If I have enough money . . .' Irène Némirovsky had less than she ever had, and this was the main reason why she relinquished so many risky projects. 'Obviously,' she concluded reluctantly on 11th April, '"the Jew" would be best, but non-literary considerations are a part of my fear.' Fear of appearing to express an opinion, since talking about the Jews had become a political act. According to Maurras, who was about to be made a member of the Académie française, the time had come for anti-Semitism no longer to be treated instinctively, but rationally, because 'anti-Semitism has no need of racism'.[84] It was not a matter, as it was in Hitler's Germany, of treating the Jews violently, but of banning them from the city, like the outcasts of Athens long ago. Seen from this viewpoint, Irène Némirovsky's character studies could appear to be merely documentary to ill-disposed readers. And a novel is not an exhibit.

As for the 'non-literary considerations' . . . Firstly, there was the declaration of the Anschluss on 11th March 1938, proof that the more the Nazis had, the more they wanted. Paradoxically, the man in the street displayed a growing lack of interest in current affairs. 'Absolute calm everywhere,' observed Irène Némirovsky. 'One can't pretend that one is unaware of all that this may signify, but one can hope nonetheless. What's more, at a certain hurried pace, the "collective brain", if I can put it that way, is unable to react. No government in France, but then we're used to that. Good weather, sunshine, bracing air.' Then, on

*In English in original text. [Tr.]

14th March: 'War, war, will there be war? What a strange time we're living through . . . Logically, war seems very close. Fifty years from now those who read the newspapers of the past few days might think that people were talking to each other excitedly about the news. Not at all. Total indifference, in deeds, in words, a few moans, a few gloomy forecasts . . . and you think about something else.' To trouble a Frenchman, the menace has to be so close that he cannot avoid it. Do we need further proof that temperament is not infallible?

'One can hope nonetheless.' This was precisely the theme of the story that *Gringoire* had asked her for at the end of the month. She would have called it 'Great Expectations', had the title not already been used 'by *my olders and betters*'.* The great expectation in question is none other than achieving French respectability, through money, since the law disapproved of it. In 'Espoirs' – the title under which the story would be published on 19th August – a Russian milliner who was once wealthy scrapes a living in an 'icy little flat' in the Ternes district of Paris; she is based on a dressmaker Irène Némirovsky had known in the Rue de l'Arc-de-Triomphe. She survives by screwing up her face and making her customers feel sorry for her, because a Russian woman, in the eyes of a Frenchwoman, can only blossom in her 'enjoyment of misfortune'. How ideally the Slav soul is made! Her husband Vassili, a *déclassé*, rests his entire hopes on an 'uncle in France' who has risen from nothing, and who will prove to be an aristocrat ruined by fraudulent bankruptcy. And always, the nagging moan of the exile, echoing the application for citizenship for which Irène and Michel Epstein had been waiting for almost three years: 'Ah, how happy are the French! So calm, so fortunate! . . . I think of them with sadness, with envy, yet I admire them. How wonderful, how admirable it is to be happy! . . .'[85]

The novelist had hesitated about calling her heroes Popoff or Arkady, but what did it matter, 'since unfortunately they can't be Lévy or Rabinovitch'? Thus it is in a Jewish context, once again, that we must read this distressing story, modulated on the theme of 'inassimilability'. This time, Irène Némirovsky herself felt the force of the prejudice weighing on her characters. She shared their urgent worries about money, gas, electricity, the telephone bill that had to be paid in three

*In English in original text. [Tr.]

days' time. This embarrassment is the other 'non-literary consider-ation' that prevented her from throwing herself wholeheartedly into a long-term novel. Her diary provides a distressing insight: 'Days of anxiety, the kind of anxiety that money brings, when you don't have any and yet which you know you can earn. A bitter grudge against life. Going about in shoes with holes in them . . . not even having enough money to go and see [a film], a very innocent distraction – and yet one is the author of D.G., a young woman full of talent, etc.'

On 25th June 1938, this really was the material situation in which Irène Némirovsky, the daughter of a banker, found herself. In January, Michel Epstein had spontaneously suggested to Albin Michel that he pay off the overdraft of 65,000 francs still owing on 'their' author's account. 'Although this solution will not bring my wife any money,' he pleaded, 'it will nevertheless allow her to devote herself entirely to her children, only write when she feels she wants to do so, and to receive money for her books each time she writes one.' The publisher was sympathetic, but from now on his payments would not be more than the 3,000 francs per month for the current year, an agreement that was extended until the end of 1940. Only just enough to offset the 'very uncertain' income from the sale of her pre-publication rights.

In actual fact, it seems as if Irène and Michel may have been exerting a form of blackmail, by pretending to hold hostage the manuscript of *La Proie*. The novel, which would sell over ten thousand copies, was put on sale in the spring, at the same time as the first instalments of *Deux*, which continued to be serialised up until 15th July. 'A young man of twenty years of age, with no money and no contacts, but who is intelligent and ambitious, sets out to discover life, in a troubled world: our own . . . A Julien Sorel in a time of crisis',[86] the publicity announced. Edmond Jaloux considered that the socio-political purpose of this novel 'of ideas' was very predictable, but he acknowledged a technique that was 'beyond reproach'[87] and that could only be French; from such an astute literary historian, this was no small praise. Irène Némirovsky, who was relaxing in Hendaye, was grateful even for his reservations: '. . . in the review there is a sentence that will already be useful to me, it is: "It must not be forgotten that surprise is one of the elements of a good story." In other words, the moral of the book should be stated at the end.'

Not everyone shared Jaloux's opinion: for *Les Nouvelles littéraires*, on the contrary, 'the gruesome and vicious aspect of almost all the characters, their fits of violence and their passivity in the face of catastrophes, is very Russian'.[88] The critics confessed to being unsettled by this Balzac-like novel in which neither the word 'Russian', nor the word 'Jew' appeared. A perceptive reader, however, might recognise her reflections on the mystery of blood, for Daguerne is really nothing other than a French-style Stavisky. His hidden motivation, after all, is not so much the lure of profit as it is pride: he will accept ruination to earn the respect of a woman. In this he resembles other heroes of Némirovsky novels: 'Their instinct gets the better of them. In the end it even consumes them without their realising it.'[89] Demonstrating this could be irksome; on the other hand, it was presented by 'a forceful, lucid and truly creative talent', which Maxence reckoned was a hundred times superior to the 'overelaborate, artificial, heavy, even lumbering style'[90] of *La Nausée*, the first philosophical novel by a certain Jean-Paul Sartre.

The positive reception given to *La Proie* did not relieve the Némirovskys' financial difficulties, far from it. By mid-June 1938, they were at rock bottom. She had just discovered that Michel, who, after all, was no more than a 'bank employee', responsible for discounts and stamping cheques, had borrowed 50,000 francs at a punishing rate of interest. What was the point of writing in such circumstances, if the only profit she could derive from it was books? 'In cash, strictly nothing. M. has even taken a month's advance. All hope of salvation lies in selling the novel and even that, if it succeeds, will only be used to pay debts . . . I earn an enormous amount of money, but for eighteen years he has always regularly spent twice what he earned. So, the feeling that there's a deficit to make up firstly, whatever the costs, and then, the feeling, I don't know how to put it, that work itself is perfectly pointless, or more precisely, normal earnings are of no interest because what we have to strive towards are the earnings that come from outside the regular budget. Eg: he earns 300,000 francs a year. Since he knows that he spends 600,000, this 300,000 is nothing, it no longer exists. We need something else; we have to look elsewhere. And that's my life!'

Of course, she could give up non-essentials, spend less. But no: 'I prefer to fight my way out of all these difficulties rather than give up what I consider necessary to live.' The photographer who had come to take a series of portraits at her home was none other than

Albert Harlingue, who had taken pictures of Rodin, Mahler, Debussy, Freud, Claudel, Colette and, by a marvellous coincidence, Katherine Mansfield. No one was going to say that the author of *David Golder* lived beyond her means. Nor that she should give up this superior form of assimilation that her talent had already provided her with. It was a matter of dignity. But from 1938 onwards, the influx of starving immigrants in her work, prepared to do anything to get a job, reveals her state of mind better than anything else. From this period, too, dates the appearance in her notebook of potential 'alimentary stories', mawkish little tales that would mostly be published in the women's weekly *Marie-Claire* in 1939 and 1940, 'purely to earn a few pennies'. Eight years after *David Golder*, it seemed as if Irène Némirovksy had well and truly become her own 'guinea pig'.

9

Children of the Night
(1938–1939)

At many a turning-point in our lives, taking a decision matters more than
taking the better route.

Monseigneur Vladimir Ghika, *Pensées pour la suite des jours*, 1936

Hendaye, late May 1938. 'Blue sky, sunshine, enchantment. Left Paris
in 36°. . . . Read Kipling's memoirs. I believe it's him, bless him, who
has pulled me out of this attack of gloom.' By this date, she had
already begun the book that she would use to repay her household
debts. It was nonetheless possible that her financial embarrassment
was of some use to her, and that urgency provided this novel with
the energy that she appeared to be lacking in *Deux*. 'A great deal of
routine,' she grumbled. 'Be careful. *Facts*. Short, hard sentences, that's
what I need, and it is necessary that the book, though short, should
appear to be filled to bursting with important events . . .' To do so,
she would have to give up following in the footsteps of Mauriac and
Maurois, rediscover the bleakness of *David Golder*, and be prepared to
stumble because: 'I live in a very traditional age and in a land that is
extremely respectful of conventions (in literature).'

How could she rekindle her particular talent? 'I believe the answer
is simple: do my little Honoré [Balzac]. That is to say, devote myself
mainly to depicting characters (and, to a lesser degree) present-day
and post-war situations and deliberately put aside things like *Deux*,
not that I'm unable to do them, but many others can do them as well
and better than me, whereas to show present-day people and depict
them with their slightly exaggerated characteristics (types, no?) well,
there aren't fleets of them.' Hence the opening of 'Le Charlatan', the
provisional title for the novel in progress which does not, fortuitously,
recall that of *Golder*: 'I need money! – I've told you, no.'[1] But this time
the roles are reversed: the child from the ghetto does not become a
banker, he is the poor devil who seeks out the moneylenders and the
pawnbrokers. His name is Asfar and he is indistinguishable from Vassili,

who grumbles in a fit of pique: 'How happy are the French . . .' Even when he has succeeded, and set himself up in a 'dark, expensive, slightly oppressive' house – which is none other than Paul Morand's – Asfar echoes back: 'Yes, you despise me, all of you, you rich French people, you fortunate French; what I wanted was your culture, your morality, your virtues, everything that was greater than me, different from me, different from the muck in which I was born!'[2]

The Master of your Souls

Certainly Asfar is not a Jew; 'non-literary considerations' require it. But he is virtually one, it could be said. He is a *'métèque'*, a stateless person, an 'irascible little foreigner, with feverish eyes', a Levantine from the 'obscure breed', to whom France would do no favours, obliging this generous-hearted and idealistic young doctor to become a charlatan and, from being a 'quarry' to become a 'hunter'. For in this extraordinarily abrupt novel it is not Irène Némirovsky who treats Asfar like a 'dirty foreigner', but her smart neighbours from Avenue Hoche.

The first model for this oriental Knock is Ghedalia, Golder's doctor. It would be enough to resuscitate the cosmopolitan world of Biarritz to make him lifelike; but she was more careful than ever before to avoid the suspicion of anti-Semitism that hovered over her work. Asfar certainly sprang from this 'world of madmen, the one I knew', but, she said, 'I was wrong to think of the world of Golder. Quite the contrary, it is in the most conventional, the most bourgeois of worlds that my charlatan can set himself up, the world of the rich, but the conventionally rich.' This decision would lend more conviction to what she was attempting to demonstrate because Asfar – he suggests as much himself – is not so much a *'métèque'* as 'what you call a *"métèque"'*;[3] this is more or less the same restrictive definition that Sartre would give of a Jew in 1947: 'a man whom others take for a Jew'. In actual fact, it was already Zola's definition: 'The Jews are our charitable work, a charitable work brought about by one thousand, eight hundred years of idiotic persecution.'[4]

When it was begun in April 1938, 'Le Charlatan' resembled a Molière satire. Dario Asfar is the kind of doctor who lives at the expense of his clients. 'He has no ambition, but an almost pathological love of making money. He has a row of foreign decorations. He is not brutal in the way real scientists are (who can be inhuman brutes). He has imagination. He does not merely see phlebitis, general paralysis, etc., but he sees the whole man. Man interests him. It is man whom he wants to win over, conquer or cheat, and not the illness.' Whence his nickname of 'master of souls'. For a time, Irène Némirovsky would actually consider a title, 'The Master of your Souls', before abandoning it as too 'eye-catching'.

Asfar is a manipulator who takes advantage of mental suffering by passing himself off as a modern-day sorcerer, just as Habib, Paul Morand's 'ghastly Levantine', did not long before, curing 'melancholia by faradism' and magnetic tricks.[5] Their clientele were the same: 'wealthy psychotics', overwhelmed with nervous illnesses, phobias or inconsolable grief. The difficulty of existing is an inexhaustible jackpot! 'The charlatan is the man who has understood that the only certain wealth, the only certain means of existence, is to make personal use of other people's emotions.' His entire art consists in only half removing the scars.

This charlatan is a universal character. But neither Jules Romains nor Paul Morand had yet examined the 'actual type' of psychiatrist who locks away his patients in order to keep them under his control. Was Philippe Wardes, like André Citroën, a compulsive gambler? 'On the pretext of giving treatment, [Asfar] maintains this drug habit, sometimes satisfying it, sometimes denying it. He treats imaginary illnesses.' Bernard Grasset did not play baccarat, but his professional cruelty had destroyed him mentally, and because he no longer knew what over-indulgences he could use to 'shake up his nerves', he was one of the acknowledged models for Wardes, the 'Broken Man'. In her diary, she affectionately called her first publisher 'our friendly little megalo-maniac', but she also remembered that Grasset was 'a nasty, ungrateful, thoughtless man'. Was Dario Asfar modelled on Dr Angelo Hesnard, one of the psychiatrists who kept Grasset in virtual seclusion? Irène Némirovsky also recalled the trial of Dr Bougrat, a kind of Stavisky among those who administered intravenous injections, who was sent to prison for misappropriation of funds in 1927, and who had at times been reduced to begging because of his mysterious financial debts. He was the other model for her charlatan.

For all that, this book was not a judgement on Freudianism. Irène Némirovsky had only ever known one analyst, Alfred Adler, who died in 1937, and Asfar's pseudo-theory of the subconscious is mostly based on her own concept of past family history: 'The souls of our ancestors dwell in all of us. It's a question of discovering what belongs to each one of us, through a <u>process</u> which aims to remove that which in our conscience covers the bedrock that is truly our own.'

Originally conceived as a potboiler, which she managed to sell as a project to Carbuccia, 'Le Charlatan' gave rise to feverish planning from April to July 1938. All paths were explored, without self-regulation. 'And now I've got yet another idea. Far too many, Mona, my girl! That will be your downfall.' When her intuition ran ahead of her, she left in her wake a little Russian, a great deal of English, occasionally some German, and a few swear words. No meandering thought escaped the thick draft version, which she then ringed with 'HEAR' or with 'TB' in red pencil. Later, everything became 'far less amusing. I have to correct, prune, go back over the sentences reflecting whether, this time, what I am writing is accessible to the reader . . .'[6]

But first of all, she had to define the main character. Asfar was not a 'suspicious Levantine' at the first attempt. He originally had the name Gabriel Papadopoulos, born in Smyrna of a Greek father and a part Italian, part Russian-Jewish mother. Brought up in Odessa, he did his medical studies in Moscow. In his 'great love of the countryside and of books' he resembles Ismaël, the brilliant little boy, but also in his urchin's education. 'Those he frequented were avaricious, cunning and thought only of money, or else the best of them were consumed by a longing for other countries, other destinies.' Furthermore, what was important was not whether he was Jewish or Greek, but an emigrant born over burning coals. 'I don't know why, but I think of Apollinaire's childhood.'

In this novel about immigration and racism, Irène Némirovsky did not allow herself to make any references to Judaism. Asfar, it goes without saying, is 'scum', a 'badly dressed and unshaven *métèque*', a 'little foreign quack' with 'brown skin', the 'long fingers of an Oriental', with 'features that are not from these parts',[7] but, she made a note to herself, 'I cannot say he belonged to a race of *heimatlos*, because that is another word for Jews'. Asfar is representative of a still more superior type: he is the foreigner who cannot be assimilated, the eternal

rootless man, the 'starving race'.[8] If he has become a charlatan instead
of an honest practitioner, it is probably due to the fact that, since 1935,
there had been laws restricting the practice of medicine purely to
French graduates. Irène Némirovsky, who had done a great deal of
research into the history and laws of medicine, knew this only too
well.[9] 'What I want to create here is the unhappy, proud lad, "for
whom the word soul has a meaning", but who has, to a desperate
degree, the desires and instincts of the contented human being. What
I ought to be doing, in short, is produce the Jew, the Jew who would
like to be humble, good etc. . . . The idea is there, that's for sure.' And
that is why Asfar, far from merely being the universal métèque, is once
again a self-portrait of Irène Némirovsky, torn between her pride as
a writer, her household debts and her status as an undesirable. It is
the pursuit of happiness that corrupts Asfar and that condemns him
to forced labour. 'You can only describe yourself, alas, always your
own more or less disguised mug and your wretched soul.'

When she left with Michel and the girls for Hendaye at the end of
June, with a decent cheque from Gringoire in her pocket and the first
sections of dialogue for 'Le Charlatan' in draft form, she was
temporarily rescued from financial worry and she repeated over in
her mind words from the gospel of Mark: 'Fear not, only believe . . .'
A studious holiday: one chapter a day, which Michel would type out.
'That however means work, real work.' The title of one of these chapters, in the outline drafted in mid-June, gives an idea of the picaresque
novel she had in mind: 'Bardamu'.* For the charlatan was merely a
pretext: Asfar is one of the Némirovsky-like avatars of the modern
rogue, of the cynical parvenu, the product of a hypocritical French
society. 'I don't analyse the type of charlatan, I shove everything that
interests me, everything that affects me behind a label. Unhappy childhood, hatred, love – then hatred of the bourgeois.' In such a way that
the key to the novel is no longer 'how much', as in David Golder, but
rather: 'Do you love me?'

'Le Charlatan' tells of the making of a crook. It is a cruel story
which would accord mitigating circumstances to Stavisky: 'Take a
starving, hunted animal, with a female and young to feed, and throw

*Bardamu is the name of the anti-hero in Louis-Ferdinand Céline's novel Journey to
the End of the Night. [Tr.]

it on to a lush pasture, or sheepfold, with young lambs . . .'[10] Has the
humiliated Asfar, the insulted Asfar, got 'ambitions'? The fire that
burns in his 'restless blood' is pride that is suppressed, stifled and trampled upon, food for his revenge on the bejewelled idiots whom Irène
Némirovsky has rarely treated with such contempt. A parasite out of
obligation, Asfar's curse is also her own: did she not sell her soul to
Gringoire, which persisted in describing her as the phenomenon of
French literature? All of a sudden, the novel took on a Faustian note.
'What does it profit a man if he gains all the treasures of the earth,
but loses his own soul?' This moral was her consolation. A pessimistic
moral, for Asfar becomes precisely what he did not want to be, a
father for whom even filial love is convertible into currency. 'What
will the woolly-minded bastards say?' she worried. '"Mme Némirovsky
remains loyal to the extremely boring type of novel . . ." or some other
nonsense. I ought to be impervious to it, but there you are . . . It's
strange that in 1938 there should still be that desire to see life through
rose-tinted glasses.'

A mental auto-da-fé

'Hendaye 6th July. The most lovely weather . . . feel no more like
working than hanging myself.' In spite of the fact that it is based on
personal experience, 'Le Charlatan' remained a last resort, a saga-like
version of 'Le Juif' deferred to better times. And so it is all the more
astonishing that this novel that was written in fits and starts should
be the result of a four-month clearing-out that was often more
rewarding than the brutal plot she finally battled her way towards.
Irène Némirovsky began to write it almost reluctantly. Did she have
any choice? *Le Figaro* had not followed up her proposal for a short
story: this may have been 'Nous avons été heureux', a poignant tale
of divorce that would appear on 5th August in *Marie-Claire*, the
women's weekly magazine that her friend Hélène Gordon-Lazareff
had launched the previous year. Fee: 2,000 francs. '7th July 38. Boiling
hot; blazing sky, there was a storm a moment ago; long flashes of
silvery rain. We suffocate in the house; we suffocate on the sand. No
desire to work, and, at the same time that vague anxiety . . .'

Irène and Michel Epstein had rented for the summer a villa built in the Basque style whose name, 'Ene Etchea', meant 'my house'. They may have done so to save money, or else, Denise Epstein suggests, because the villa at Urrugne was too far from the sea. Just one street now separated them from the beach, 'a ditch filled with sand that smothers the sound of our footsteps'.[11] Not that Irène was mad about bathing, but her baby was sixteen months old and, she informed her readers, 'building sandcastles for this little girl is my main preoccupation at the moment'.[12] In a tent, dressed in a skirt and striped polo shirt, she read Katherine Mansfield, suddenly aware of the 'tragic joke' that writer's life was, and she reread À l'ombre des jeunes filles en fleurs. Denise, who was so protected that she never learned to swim – nor, in winter, to ski – bathed under the supervision of a nanny. Michel, seated on a folding stool, smoked a cigarette. 'When evening comes, they like to go to Saint-Jean to watch the boats return to port, or else cross the frontier to have dinner in Fontarabia.'[13] The only sight imposed on them was watching Spanish refugees passing over the Bidassoa bridge in lorries, or crossing the river after dusk, guided by French torches. That summer, the Epsteins gave shelter to a young woman who had fled the fighting. 'I don't really know whether her husband had been arrested or shot . . . Her little boy must have been four or five years old. I can still remember the shape of her face. She was a very beautiful, magnificent-looking Spanish woman.'[14] These were unforgettable memories for Denise, who would soon be eight, and who had no idea of the practical difficulties that her parents were making it their duty to ignore.

On 30th July, Irène found the answer to the ending of 'Le Charlatan', by giving it the form of an endless beginning: 'He will be back. For his inheritance.' One month later, the final version was completed. During that same summer, Irène Némirovsky began a new novel which was no more nor less than the Jewish version of 'Le Charlatan'. Its title, 'Enfants de la nuit', was inserted beneath a quotation from the Gospel: 'You are to be children of the light.' It would be, she noted on 21st July, 'the story of a family of Russian Jews – yes, yet again! – in which there would be one son who becomes Stav[isky], the other P.S. and a daughter'. She would show how a Russian Jew, Harry Sinner, who is on the point of marrying a young middle-class Parisienne, shares in the disgrace of his cousin Ben, the spitting image of Stavisky, who drags him down in his moral decline. Is it the émigré's curse or the power of Jewish tropism? At the end of the day, Harry and Ben Sinner, the dog and the wolf, would never be anything in the eyes of the French other than 'two dirty foreigners, two dirty *métèques*',[15] the one who had fallen from the heights, the other who had climbed up from the depths. 'Children of the night: that is to say those who lack grace, who have gone away to be better than others, and who become worse still because the spirit of love was lacking in them.' Irène Némirovsky did not deny that there were Jewish crooks; she simply wanted to dismantle the mechanism that had made neither saints nor fanatics of them, in the way Trotsky did. Ben's cry from the heart, the result of his own fraudulent dealings, strikes the same note as Asfar's lament: 'Ah! All your pretentious Europeans, how I hate them! What you call success, victory, love, hatred, is what I call money! It's just a different word for the same things!'[16]

In fact, Irène Némirovsky had confused these two characters for a long time. On 8th July, for example, Dario Asfar still has a Jewish mother, and 'too bad if there are complaints! She is, and can only be a Jewess, and from Odessa what's more!' Three days later, at the cost of what she described as a 'mental auto-da-fé', 'Enfants de la nuit' became a novel in its own right. Asfar would be the ill-defined *métèque*, and Ben the 'Jewish scum', who had brought bad luck to the gentle French Jews, who had forgotten their tears and their martyrdom. Ada, who was to have been Asfar's fiancée and his companion in exile, becomes Ben's sister. With her extraordinary memory for words and faces, her gloomy, nostalgic nature, her 'sharp irony',[17] it is she, the Jewess from Kiev, who reminds Harry Sinner of the dark and captivating lure of his bloodline. Just as, in 'Le Charlatan', Elinor is the one who, through her charm, and by way of a phonetic anagram,* represents the lure of the Orient. What is more, it is not by chance that Ada is an artist who draws 'cartoons for illustrated newspapers', creating 'a ripple of curiosity around her name'; had not Irène Némirovsky been criticised for making herself known in this way? Ada personifies Irène Némirovsky's latent Judaism, very gentle and very malevolent at one and the same time, at a moment when France believed she could blunt Hitler's fangs by offering territory. French in spirit, if not by decree, a Russian Jewess by birth but not in her culture,

---

*In French, Elinor/L'orient. [Tr.]

Irène Némirovsky actually lived a double exile. In this she was similar to Harry Sinner, 'a foreigner to the French and a foreigner to the Zyromski or Silbermann who caused her so many problems', as she foresaw in January 1938. A child of the night, suspended between two twilights . . .

Wolves are my thing

On 30th July 1938, Irène Némirovsky gave up the idea of ever writing 'Le Juif', many of whose elements were then transferred to 'Enfants de la nuit', in which a subjective picture of European Judaism was emerging. '*Le Juif* needs *a lifetime*,'* she justified herself. 'Terribly provocative too, nevertheless, consider making use of it in case of C. being rejected for ex. But there are other drawbacks: the Jew, unless one ~~makes a caricature of him, or~~ repeats D.G. is not a clear-cut type. I would like to soften the features. I would ruin everything.'

The circumstances were hardly helpful. Since the beginning of the year, numerous voices – among them Brasillach's – had clamoured to put an end to the naturalisation of foreign Jews. On 2nd May, a government edict was open to misinterpretation because it linked 'concerns of national security' to 'the constantly growing number of foreigners residing in France'. Lucien Rebatet, who had spent the summer in Austria, came back dazzled by the Hitlerite pogroms he had witnessed there. In Vienna, the windows of Jewish shopkeepers were not only pasted with prohibitions or invitations for 'urgent cleaning', they were smeared with grease, tar or excrement. The example to follow, if one can believe it, was: 'German anti-Semitism is disrupting the ghetto and quite rightly so. People have felt far too sorry for the little Jewish people . . . I wonder what it might be that prevents us from saying that German and especially Viennese anti-Semitism, provides an example of distributive justice that the Jew-penetrated nations should benefit from rather than veiling their faces and screeching about brutality.'[18]

Feeling sorry for the little Jewish people is exactly what Irène Némirovsky does in 'Enfants de la nuit', by resurrecting the Kiev

*In English in original text. [Tr.]

ghetto, 'self-employed craftsmen, people who rented sordid shops, vagabonds, a mass of children who played in the mud and spoke only Yiddish',[19] the same people whom the photographer Roman Vishniac had tried to immortalise in 1935, with the aim of 'building a monument to Jewish suffering'. In the story, Ada's grandfather, an intellectual who has become a jeweller in order to feed his mother, works secretly on an essay entitled 'The character and rehabilitation of Shylock', with the purpose of rectifying those who are prejudiced; his life's work will be thrown into the fire by the Cossacks. As for the pogrom, it is a 'deluge', a nightmarish 'sabbath', a 'cyclone'[20] more violent than the one Rebatet called for, 'hurling themselves like rams against the walls, hitting them, backing off, furiously battering them to try to knock them down, striking them again and again, in vain'.[21]

It was not an illusion: anti-Semitism was a tide that came from the east. Twenty years after leaving it behind in Russia, here it was licking at the boundaries of France. On 7th September, the Milan publisher, Gemio, sent the following letter to Albin Michel:

> We should be extremely grateful if you could tell us whether Mme Irène Némirovsky is of the Jewish race.
>
> According to Italian law a person should not be considered of Jewish race if one of the parents, the father or the mother, is of the Aryan race.

An undesirable in Russia, Irène Némirovsky did not have the odour of sanctity in Italy either. And in France? As if by coincidence, on 10th November, the day after Kristallnacht – the state pogrom that left several hundred Jewish victims across Germany – the weekly *Gringoire* trumpeted: 'Out with the *métèques*!' Furthermore, on the 12th, Paris announced legislation that limited access to French citizenship, undermined the rights of those who had acquired it, and made the position of 'undesirable foreigners' harder by leaving them liable to internment by the authorities at any moment whether or not they were guilty of an offence. The people thus affected were largely Spanish, Czech, German or Austrian refugees, but Irène and Michel Epstein might well find themselves at the mercy of a pen-pusher. The 'special centres' planned for this purpose would, in her new novel, be given the name they deserved, one that came from Germany: 'concentration camps'.[22]

Irène Némirovsky then abandoned her original title of 'Enfants de la nuit', which was a little too reminiscent of Céline.* For a time, she thought, significantly, of calling it 'L'Étranger' [The Foreigner], as there was little doubt that Ben Sinner would fall within the scope of the new edicts. But the starving Ben is not the only child of this human night; however well assimilated he was, a bout of nostalgia was all it took for Harry to return to his wild ways. Hence the eventual title of the novel *The Dogs and the Wolves* [*Les Chiens et les Loups*], the origin of which we discover in this note of 26th May 1938: 'It's my thing, depicting wolves! I don't just create animals in a pack, or domestic animals.[23] Wolves are my thing, I have a talent for them.'

Was it out of anxiety to be seen as normal that Irène and Michel sent Denise, who up till then had been brought up in a very protected way, to the Collège Victor-Duruy that September? A fall in the playground, followed by water on the knee, would very soon return her to Miss Matthews's supervision, to prepare for the *lycée* entrance exams at home.

A fresh application for citizenship was filed on 23rd November 1938 at the offices of the police headquarters. Michel had the advantage of being recommended by his immediate superiors, Comte Charles-Albert de Boissieu, on behalf of the board of directors, and Consul Philippe de Maizière, who had been a member of the board of directors of the Banque des Pays du Nord since 1930. 'Monsieur Epstein,' they wrote, 'has worked for the firm since March 1925. He is a loyal colleague, whose moral and professional qualities we have valued, and we are convinced of his affection for France, as well as his total honesty.'

As for Irène, she was sponsored by two eminent figures from the world of literature. Jean Vignaud, who came from the region of Saintonge, had been decorated in the war, and was the founder, with Fernand Gregh, of the *Revue d'art dramatique*, as well as a habitué of Parisian editorial offices; he began at *Le Petit Parisien* in 1901 and took over as editor thirty years later. President of the Association de la critique littéraire since 1930, he had had plenty of time to observe how the Némirovsky meteor had burst across the French literary sky, and to do so with particular curiosity since, in 1922, he had been one of the first French novelists to describe the saga of the Russian emigrants.

*The allusion is to Céline's novel *Voyage au bout de la nuit*. [Tr.]

Irène Némirovsky had much to hope for from Vignaud, who in April 1936 was elected to the chairmanship of the Société des Gens de Lettres, and who, through his mandate, intended to 'symbolise among the French-speaking community, in the eyes of the world, the philosophy of the people and the nobility of the national language' . . .[24]

Irène Némirovsky's other supporter was a figure of even greater calibre. André Chaumeix had become the new editor of *Revue des Deux Mondes*, following Doumic's death from a severe attack of bronchitis on 2nd December 1937. The former editor of *Revue de Paris* and editor-in-chief of *Le Figaro*, Chaumeix was 'a very industrious man who doesn't work', according to Maurice Martin du Gard.[25] This explains why at the age of sixty-four, and despite the fact that he was a member of the Académie française, this least secretive of Marie de Régnier's lovers should have written only a handful of brief, scholarly pamphlets on Plato and Roman sculpture, but no literary work in the true sense of the term. He was the epitome of the Third Republic gentleman: a graduate of the École normale, immaculately dressed, British in his bearing, with a twinkle in his roving eye, brilliantined hair, and a perfectly trimmed moustache; the full array of the worldly jack-of-all-trades, who might have been an ambassador, a minister or a member of parliament. Politically, his nationalism, his anti-Marxism and his upright patriotism were rarely faulted. In October 1935, he had been a signatory to the Manifesto for the Defence of the West, in support of Mussolini, alongside a number of ultra-nationalists whom he accompanied to the Vélodrome d'Hiver on 8th July 1937 to acclaim Charles Maurras on his release from prison. Under his editorship, the *Revue des Deux Mondes* would become more political, going so far as to espouse the National Revolution in 1940.

All things considered, Chaumeix was no doubt the man for the job. It was he who would personally deliver Irène and Michel Epstein's petition to the very newly appointed Minister of Justice, Paul Marchandeau, particularly since the latter was the man who drew up the famous law that would shortly make racial defamation in the press illegal, thereby increasing the anti-Semitic paranoia of someone like Brasillach. It was a welcome but insidious law, in the sense that it was the first to introduce in black and white the specious notion of 'race' into the French legislation, which had until then refrained from pronouncements on human biology.

Irène Némirovsky, Chaumeix stated in the letter he wrote to Marchandeau on 30th November, was 'one of the contemporary authors with the most original and forceful talent', while Michel Epstein, the following day, produced all the necessary documents with the exception of their own birth certificates which had vanished in the Soviet night. Was this the reason why their application, which was followed up on several occasions, would remain pending up until the declaration of war? Why, in spite of the support of such prestigious sponsors, and despite her reputation, would Irène Némirovsky never obtain citizenship? Perhaps, Dario Asfar replies, because 'one never escapes one's destiny' . . .[26]

An attempt to feel pity

In late-December 1938, there was nothing to suggest that the application was not being processed. Consulting the stars, *Marie-Claire* even predicted a reassuring 1939 for the women of France, for 'it is thanks to the protecting stars that are placed in the Führer's horoscope that we shall avoid war'.[27] So it was out of excessive prudence, and a form of superstition, that at the same time Irène Némirovsky took an unusual step. For, as she confided to her dear Cécile, who was flabbergasted, 'you never know what the future has in store . . .'

As she did virtually every winter, the novelist had left for the mountains with her daughters. At Besse-en-Chandesse, a medieval town and mountain resort at the foot of the Puy de Sancy in the Auvergne, she made the acquaintance, either that year or the previous one, of a young thirty-eight-year-old priest who had just been entrusted with the deanship of Besse and of Notre-Dame-de-Vassivière, a well-known place of pilgrimage. Abbé Roger Bréchard was ordained priest in 1924 and had originally thought of becoming a missionary in Africa. He discovered his true vocation while in the Boy Scout movement, which he helped establish in the Auvergne from 1926, leading a troop of boys through hell or high water, but mainly through opposition to local customs. For Abbé Bréchard was a curious spirit, cultured, full of charm, and open to change. 'Nothing humdrum about this young priest,' Monseigneur Piguet, the Bishop of Clermont-Ferrand acknowledged, 'neither his conversation, nor his greeting, nor even the simplicity of his modest presbytery, where well-chosen, evocative engravings of religious art, that are void of snobbery and pretension, allow one to discover artistic aspects and considerations that complement the moral virtues of this country priest.'[28]

Called up after the Munich agreements – a guarantee of impotence accorded to Hitler by the democracies – Abbé Bréchard had already returned to his parish by the time that Irène Némirovsky told him of her unexpected wish to be baptised a Catholic. It is tempting to believe that she was only pretending to be a Christian in order to escape the curse that pursued the Jews, since she could now be legally deported. Could it be, however, that her desire for baptism, far from being prompted solely by the fear of what might happen and her longing to be assimilated, reflected a genuine spiritual search? Would her baptism be a recantation, the sort of renouncement of reason that someone like Bergson refused to contemplate in 1937, in case he should be treated as an apostate by the future victims of 'the formidable wave of anti-Semitism that will be unleashed on the world'?[29] Or did it betray a growing abhorrence of Judaism that had reached breaking-point? In that case she would be similar to René Schwob, the most zealous of French converts, who was both averse to Jewish culture, which exasperated him, and the sworn enemy of racial anti-Semitism, which set Jews apart by denying them the right of freedom. But by converting, was she really freeing herself?

Jews converting to Christianity had never really bothered the Judaic authorities during the inter-war period. The phenomenon only affected a tiny number of people, and latter-day Marranos* were not as serious a threat as was the rise in agnosticism and atheism, a trend that revealed both a powerful desire among Jews to sink into the secular swamp and an equally clear refusal to abandon the faith of their ancestors. For a number of immigrants, assimilation was achieved not by apostasy, but purely and simply by forgetting their traditional observance, and the rabbinate was more concerned by this than by the marginal phenomenon of conversions. 'French Judaism today resembles a bloodless, lifeless corpse . . . It is a methodical exodus, an endless flight, an escape from an historical community that has

---

*Spanish or Portuguese Jews who converted to Christianity during the late Middle Ages in order to avoid persecution, but who secretly adhered to Judaism. [Tr.]

not yet achieved its destiny,'[30] wrote Rabbi Vladimir Rabinovich in 1933, predicting a 'tragic awakening' for French Jews who still imagined that a baptism in the trenches had protected them for ever against the bacillus of anti-Semitism.

So what was the point of converting, unless it was for overly superstitious reasons? Since Judaism is not merely a religious statement, conversion would not achieve anything additional. And so it was not so much because he was retracting that Alfred Adler, Irène Némirovsky's 'uncle', became a convert himself, but to escape from ethnic seclusion and to embrace a universal faith; even though he became a Catholic, Adler still remained an unbeliever! Similarly, for a French Jew, conversion was often an imaginative path towards citizenship, hardly ever an inner betrayal. For many converts, what is more, Christ was the one who had come to fulfil the prophecies. Bergson, too, who was tempted to make the leap, saw in Catholicism 'the complete fulfilment of Judaism'.[31] Nor did the majority of converts have the feeling that they had spat upon the Book, since the Church was the daughter of Israel. On the contrary, because they were usually non-believers, they found that the Church, even though they did not always admit it, provided a secret access to the Old Testament and to their own roots. 'They had simply cast off from their shoulders the worn cloak of their fathers,' Jean-Jacques Bernard, a close friend of Irène Némirovsky, would say. 'For them, Judaism had become a word void of any meaning. But when a spiritual impulse opened the doors of the Church or those of the Temple, what did they discover at the very heart of Christianity? Their Judaism!'[32] This is why, in receiving unction, Irène Némirovsky was displaying a Jewish awareness. For nothing was preventing her, after all, from remaining irreligious.

Was it such a paradox that she was setting out on the road to Emmaus at the very moment that *The Dogs and the Wolves* was asserting the ineluctable resurgence of the Jewish character in both the man who had become integrated and the man who had become a Christian, that 'vague and slightly frightening feeling of carrying within oneself a past that was heavier than the past of most men',[33] that sixth sense that is known as *zakhor*? Was it by chance that in this novel she gave the name 'Sinner' to a character who aspired to become French and who is suddenly drawn by his roots to the old

Jewish core? 'Tremendous events such as wars and revolutions have the initial effect, both terrible and admirable, of obliterating what is individual and distinctive in us and bringing to the surface of the soul our hereditary core, which sweeps through the human being in its entirety,'[34] she wrote in 1934. Now, following Hitler's latest show of strength, had not France just recalled its reservists and brought out the gas masks? 'Everyone was waiting for the war to start the way people wait for death: knowing it is inevitable, asking only for a little more time.'[35]

Irène Némirovsky knew moreover that her baptism would not deceive the over-zealous who, unlike old Charles Maurras, did not believe that just because a Jew had become a Christian he had become any less wily. The 'biological' anti-Semites took care solemnly to warn those taking communion: 'The converted Jew remains Jewish, in the same way that the Negro who is baptised retains the colour of his skin and his racial characteristics. The Jewish question is not a religious matter, but a question of race.'[36] Yet had she not taken note, in 1936, of her 'inassimilability'? She knew perfectly well that nothing, not even baptismal water, could wash away her blood. So why, Cécile asked her. 'Why did you change your religion when you are better than a lot of Catholics?'

Even if her work demonstrated that she knew the Gospel well, and even though she abided by the principles of Christian morality – a contempt for the vanities of life, the practice of charitable works – Irène Némirovsky never showed any religious concerns, and the many 'my God!s' that punctuate her working notebooks should not be taken literally. Wedded to the synagogue out of pure convention, she was still not going to abandon the constraints of Judaic ritual for the rosary, incense and genuflections. In *The Wine of Solitude*, she even describes her childish terror at the announcement of the annual procession of pilgrims who had come to worship the relics at the lavra in Kiev, 'preceded by a horrible stench of filth and wounds', bringing with them 'all the diseases'[37] of pagan Russia. Therefore, when Denise asked her when it would be her turn to wear a white vestment and to hold a white candle while scattering rose petals, like the pretty girls making their first communion at the nearby church of Saint-François-Xavier, her mother replied simply: 'You, my darling, never.'[38] Was she being defensive, or was she, rather, expressing a regret? And yet why, on the other hand, did she resolve, in late 1938, that Denise should receive communion one day?

Irène Némirovsky's conversion, coming at the same time as the 'rising tide of perils' and the application for citizenship, reveals an evident need for spiritual consolation that Judaism, which her upbringing had made irrelevant to her, could not provide her with. As to the fact that she also led her daughters and her husband with her to the altar, it does at least indicate that she cared about protecting her family as well as religious considerations. After all, the author of *Jezebel*, an only daughter, was virtually an orphan ever since she had commited fictional matricide. It was even, she admitted implicitly in June 1938, her shame at having loathed this woman so much that now drove her towards a very Christian form of contrition: 'What would I have felt if I had seen my mother die? As I say: pity, terror, and horror at my hardness of heart. Knowing desperately that deep down in my soul I had no grief, that I was cold and indifferent, that it had not been a loss for me, alas, but, on the contrary . . . and the terror-struck spirit pauses at the sacrilege, and fears God. The lips murmur: "I forgive her, I have forgiven her." But in her heart, nothing, not a flicker of grief. A sort of human pity, and that's all, an attempt to feel pity.'

A very mediocre recruit

'I search for souls to give them to Jesus,'[39] said Abbé Bréchard. Being too far from Paris to convert the novelist himself, to her great regret, he chose to send her to Monseigneur Chevrot, who had been priest at Saint-François-Xavier since 1930. But why did he also entrust her to Monseigneur Vladimir Ghika, who officiated not far away, at the diocesan church for foreigners in the Rue de Sèvres? Abbé Bréchard had known this Romanian bishop when he was the apostolic proto-notary. Both of them attended the 'Thursdays' that took place in Meudon, organised by the philosopher Jacques Maritain, a Protestant thinker who had converted to Catholicism in 1906, together with his wife Raïssa, the daughter of a Jewish tailor from eastern Ukraine and an outstanding intellectual drawn ineluctably to the vitality of Catholic renewal. Ever since 1926, Maritain had continued to distance himself from Maurras, going so far as to appear suspect to the theoretician of *'nationalisme intégral'* by proclaiming loud and clear in February 1938 his total opposition to anti-Semitism, which was a forerunner of the 'extermination of the Jews – for that is what it is really about, is it not, when all is said and done'.[40] At Meudon, Abbé Bréchard had formed a particular friendship with the essayist Charles Du Bos, one of the many writers converted or brought back to Christianity through the kindly influence of the Maritains. Did not even the dissolute Jean Cocteau, inflamed by divine grace, join his hands together in prayer, for as long as it took to transform this miracle into literature, and later into sacrilege? From then on, whenever one of his writer friends was upset by a bad review, Abbé Bréchard immediately sent him a consoling letter.

The first letter Irène Némirovsky wrote to Monseigneur Ghika is dated 21st December 1938. Having been recommended by her 'Godfather', she set out simply and straightforwardly her 'strong desire . . . for ourselves and our two children to receive Holy Baptism'. Not only did Monseigneur Ghika agree to her request, but he wished to anoint the catechumen himself. The date was fixed for 2nd February: a decision that meant a great deal of hurry because, in the intervening three weeks, mumps prevented her from going out to prepare for the ceremony.

It was at about Christmas 1938 – celebrated in the Russian style, around a large and magnificently decorated fir tree – that Irène Némirovsky made the acquaintance of this sixty-five-year-old prelate, who would make the most enduring impression on Denise: 'Ah! How good-looking he was . . . Very blue eyes. He was very tall and very slim. He had very white hair that, like Orthodox priests, fell to his shoulders. His robe was violet, and I had to kiss the enormous ring he wore on his finger. He made me feel terribly shy.'[41] For these very reasons, Maritain compared him, in 1936, to 'a latter-day St Nicholas who could endure all sorts of bad weather, who was curious about everything and well informed'.[42] Let us not brush aside the assumption that an orphan might have seen his features as paternal.

According to Pierre Hayet, who has presided over the enquiry into Monseigneur Ghika's beatification since 1992, Irène Némirovsky may have met him earlier, at Queen Nathalie of Serbia's mansion, on the hills above Bidart. The grandson of the last monarch of Moldavia, Ghika, like all the reigning princes, belonged to the Orthodox faith. It was in 1902, after a long period of intellectual development and exacting theological studies at the Vatican, that he 'crossed over' to Catholicism. In 1923, aged fifty, he was finally received into the priesthood, and in the following year he founded a guesthouse for outcasts in the Haute-Marne. At the same time, he settled in Villejuif, in a rudimentary shed in the slums, in order to follow the principles set out in his book, *La Visite des pauvres* – which had earned him the nickname, bestowed by Cardinal Verdier, of 'Prince Vincent de Paul'. Appointed a 'permanent member of the Eucharistic Congress' since 1930, he launched himself into an intense period of pastoral activity that took him from Sydney to the Congo and from Tokyo to Buenos Aires. This meant that he was obliged to hand over his responsibility for the diocesan church for foreigners to a Russian Jew whom Maritain – yet again – had won over to the Catholic faith: the painter, poet, art critic and now a priest, Jean-Pierre Altermann.

Whenever he was in Paris, Monseigneur Ghika continued to mix in literary circles – Claudel, Mauriac, Bergson, Francis Jammes – and he sat for the painter MacAvoy. Thanks to his talents as a writer and his legendary gentleness, he earned himself a reputation as a spiritual director for writers. His *Pensées pour la suite des jours*, published in 1923 and expanded in 1936, blend spiritual improvement with choice phrases. To quote just a few, which must have echoed in the soul of the would-be communicant: 'He who doubts in theory, chooses in practice'; 'Grief is at home amongst us, but like a naturalised foreigner'. Or again: 'The better a road really is, the less do passers-by leave a trace of their footsteps upon it'. These 'fine and noble thoughts' particularly appealed to Irène Némirovsky, especially as dogma did not come easily to her. 'It is not enough to read them,' she would write to him; 'I am well aware that they must be put into practice. How difficult it is!'[43]

All four – Irène, Michel, Denise and Élisabeth Epstein – were received into 'Holy Baptism' on 2nd February 1939, at the chapel of the Abbaye Sainte-Marie, in the 16th arrondissement. Abbé Bréchard, their sponsor, had come specially from Besse, to be a witness. The ceremony very nearly did not take place. 'I've got a bad cold,' Irène Némirovsky wrote to Monseigneur Ghika a week beforehand, 'and I am a little anxious about it being cold in church, for the date of the baptism is approaching and it must not be delayed because of an indisposition.'[44] Two days after the ceremony, the virus had lost none of its virulence, and it prevented her from calling on Monseigneur Ghika as she had promised to do. She posted off a letter of thanks:

Paris, 4th February 1939

Monseigneur

You shall not me see either today or tomorrow to my great regret, since the doctor has forbidden me to go out. I do, in fact, have mumps. We realised this, because, most inconveniently, my husband also has it very badly, which is very tiresome.

What a joy that you were able to baptise us on Thursday!

Monseigneur, be so good as to send us all, in thought, your blessing and believe me very respectfully yours,

Irène Némirovsky-Epstein

Until the summer of 1939, through their correspondence, Irène Némirovsky and Monseigneur Ghika became involved in a curious game of excuses and pleasantries, which had the principal effect of diverting her from her duties. It was a strange sort of parishioner who, when she sent books to the 'monseigneur's' poor, immediately admitted that she would be incapable of expressing her sympathy 'directly'. Very soon, a bout of flu meant cancelling another meeting and, sensing the absurdity of the situation, Irène Némirovsky quickly discovered her irony, which revealed darker concerns than those to do with the holy mass: '. . . The Catholic Church has really found a very mediocre recruit in me! Do not forget me, Monseigneur, for I feel very angry, with others and with myself and very downhearted, and only your blessing can drag me out of it. So give it to me in thought, I beg you. As soon as I am better, I will go to see you.'[45] The visit was constantly postponed. 27th April: 'I will pay you a quick visit as soon as I can.' 4th June: 'Two or three weeks running I went on Fridays to the church for foreigners, but I didn't see you.' As soon as she had to intervene with Paul Morand, with Chaumeix, or Albin Michel about something to do with publishing or to recommend a friend of Monseigneur Ghika's, Irène Némirovsky became more voluble again; but when it was a question of sacred matters, she immediately

became awkward, brusque, even false. Her somewhat clumsy solici-
tude is revealed in this unexpected letter of condolence, written on
10th February:

> Monseigneur
>
> I can't help thinking this evening of the sadness you must be feeling
> after having learnt of the death of His Holiness the Pope.
>
> May I be allowed to express to you here my profound and respectful
> sympathy?
>
> The man who has just died was truly a Saint and a Father for everyone,
> and I think that there can be no 'man of good will' who will not be
> affected this evening.
>
> This is why I am writing to you, Monseigneur.

What this correspondence demonstrates is Irène Némirovsky's ultimate resistance, out of personal pride, to burying herself heart and
soul in religious matters. Even her most sincere evangelical impulses
cannot blot out a slight and understandable remorse – not at having
disowned the Jewish faith, which she knew nothing about, but at
failing her sense of irony by embracing, along with a body of doctrine,
its artifices and ridiculous aspects. In *The Dogs and the Wolves* this
remorse would take the form of a superstition, a simple stain at the
bottom of a dress: 'Nastasia crossed herself when she finished her
prayers, but that was surely sacrilegious, wasn't it? Nevertheless . . .
She couldn't resist; her trembling hand made the sign from her forehead to her chest. She stood up. As she left the junk room, she noticed
with dismay that her dress was dirty and her smock torn at the knees.
But there was nothing to be done.'[46] Nothing, because the mass had
been said.

Anxiety

The writing of *The Dogs and the Wolves* took place at exactly the
same time as Irène Némirovsky's conversion. It even appears, to
judge by a note in the margin of the manuscript, that she settled
on this title ten days before the ceremony, on 24th January: 'The
dogs and the wolves caught between the darkness and the flames

of hell.' Seen in this way, it is hardly surprising that Christianity should be considered not as a fanciful, distant horizon, but as a shelter against anti-Jewish persecution. Thus, in a scene removed from the novel, we see Lilla, Ben and Ada taking refuge for a week with a conventional family, where 'nobody worried about the future'. Security and lack of concern, these appear to be the main assets of Christianity: 'Trust in God for illness and death, and time flies by at a delightfully slow pace.' Whereas, with the Jews, 'everything was done in fits and starts. Happiness and misfortune, wealth and poverty swept over them like thunder from the sky over cattle. It was this that generated both a constant anxiety and an unutterable hope in them.'[47]

These considerations were not to be judged lightly for, at that very moment, anti-Semitic propaganda in the French press had reached a level not seen since the days of Édouard Drumont.* How could Irène Némirovsky, who read *Les Nouvelles littéraires,* have understood, two days after she was baptised, this advertisement for a book just published by Grasset: 'Is anti-Semitism opposed to Christian charity? Is defending oneself against the Jews, on the contrary, the duty of every Christian?'[48] In that same month of February 1939, *Le Crapouillot* objected to 'the extraordinary patronage we give to promoting Jewish artists to the detriment of their purely French colleagues'.[49] And, in *Je suis partout,* this call by Brasillach to deprive 'every Jew, half-Jew, quarter-Jew' of the honour of being French because 'anti-Semitism is a French tradition'.[50] Paris was well worth a mass; was citizenhood worth a baptism?

On top of this pile of worries there was another more secret one that did not weigh lightly upon Irène Némirovsky's surprising fits of religious fervour. After a respite in March, Michel's health deteriorated sharply. Answering questions on the radio about her latest novel (*Deux*), Irène Némirovsky joked mischievously with her interviewer and then, suddenly grave and mysterious, she said: 'There is no end to marriage, except death. There is no other.' In her extreme anxiety

---

*Politician and journalist who, in his fiercely fanatical anti-Semitic manifesto *La France juive, essai d'histoire contemporaine* (1886), attacked Jewish financiers and Jews in general. The book sold in vast numbers and had a great influence on his generation, particularly on Georges Bernanos. [Tr.]

and, as it were, not knowing which saint to address, she turned to Monseigneur Ghika:

> My husband has suddenly fallen ill. They fear pneumonia. He is in a clinic. My doctor reassures me, but I feel very sad and very worried.
>
> Monseigneur, you whom Jesus listens to more than us poor sinners, pray that my husband gets better very quickly, I beg you.[51]

On 27th April, the diagnosis was optimistic. But Irène Némirovsky had truly feared the worst. 'I was so frightened of losing him. I don't know what would have become of me had I not had the great joy of talking to God with trust and hope.'[52] That same day, in fact, the immigration department had just asked them again to supply papers provided six months previously. So everything had to begin again . . .

Yet one had to live. While continuing to develop *The Dogs and the Wolves*, Irène Némirovsky took on many more pot-boiling jobs. From 4th January to 15th March, like other famous writers, she gave a series of six ten-minute 'literary talks' on Radio Paris, on the subject of 'Great foreign women novelists',[53] for 2,000 francs. In March, *Deux* was finally published, with a first printing of fifteen thousand copies and an advance of 40,000 francs. 'Irène Némirovsky's first love story',[54] of which over twenty thousand copies would be sold, was her biggest success since *David Golder*. Furthermore, had it not been for the outbreak of war, Albin Michel would not have abandoned plans to sell the film rights; the publisher knew he must expect the worst, however, for at the same time he published Jacques Benoist-Méchin's *Éclaircissements sur 'Mein Kampf'*, to which Nazi propaganda would soon give an indecent amount of publicity.

Deux was well received by Maxence and by Lalou. Only Lœwel realised what the novel owed to *Les Demi-Vierges* by Marcel Prévost (to whom Irène Némirovsky quickly inscribed a copy) and, in particular, the new prospect it opened up in her work, that of an important novel of social analysis. For far more than a eulogy to conjugal love, *Deux* is the novel of a generation, that of Joyce Golder, who was twenty when the armistice was declared and who was now twice that age. 'Who, better than Mme Némirovsky, and with a more tapered stylet held in a steadier hand, has examined the emotional soul of the youth of 1920, that sort of frenzied passion to live, that fervent and sensual desire to consume oneself in pleasure?' This was before the crisis had transformed the 'despairing search for receding happiness, that damned selfishness of those who claim to be happy'[55] into a fight to the death.

The uncertain times and Michel's going into hospital evidently made her decide to publish 'Le Charlatan' in a slight hurry, without taking the time to remove the repetitions and the weaknesses. This explains the rushed, even obsessive character of this novel in which the words 'Levantine', 'foreigner' and '*métèque*', churned out as if they were an evil charm, eventually induce a sense of nausea. This is precisely what Irène Némirovsky had intended: plunge an idealistic emigrant into the hostile world of Western racism, so that he reemerges a cynical and corrupt creature, and a reluctant crook, determined to acquire honour through trickery and theft. It would be pointless: 'I have a degree in Medicine from France, I am used to living in France, I have obtained French citizenship, but I am treated like a foreigner, and I feel like a foreigner.'[56] These words had a bitter resonance from the pen of 'the great Slav novelist' as *Gringoire* persisted in describing her to its readers, on 18th May 1939! The novel, which would be serialised there until 24th August, had in passing gained a more far-reaching title, *Les Échelles du Levant* [The Ports of the Levant], an allusion to the trading posts in the Middle East that from time immemorial have served as a bridge between Europe and the East. For beyond the quack doctor, it was the question of immigration that enthralled Irène Némirovsky, and the fate of 'those families who come from Syria, from Egypt or from Greece, who spread everywhere and are cast about in such different ways, that within the same generation you find cousins who sell carpets and honey-coated nuts on the beaches of Europe, and well-known lawyers or doctors in New York. (But they don't know one another.) The same race, the same stock, the same anxieties, the ambitions.'[57]

For all that Sennep might represent Hitler as a screaming dwarf on the front page of *Gringoire*, in June 1939 the French wondered whether the summer would bring peace or war; but they suspected that, whichever way, the future would be German. 'There is no further territorial problem in Europe for Germany,' declared Hitler after the Munich agreements. But when, one after the other, he absorbed the Saar, reoccupied the Rhineland, annexed Austria, seized the Sudetenland, and finally invaded what was left of Czechoslovakia in March 1939, the French anxiously wondered what fresh demands would be made by the Führer, who, over the past two years, had devoted two-thirds of his budget to rearmament. A Prussian Poland? Or even Alsace? The USSR, which had been kept out of the European games in Munich, hoped not to have to ask itself these questions . . .

The summer departure for Hendaye-Plage, planned for mid-June, was delayed by a fortnight, time for Denise to pass her entrance exams to the lycée and to receive her First Communion from Monseigneur Ghika on 1st or 2nd July, a ceremony that left her mother with a 'feeling of peace and sweetness'.[58] Before going away, she had taken the trouble to ask Albin Michel for four monthly payments in advance, and she was also busy writing a letter of recommendation for Cécile Michaud, who had just left her employment. So many sudden precautionary measures.

'Yes, the 1939 holidays weren't wonderful.'[59] From that summer in which Irène Némirovsky did not write a novel, there still remained the happy memory of family photographs in the garden of 'Ene Etchea'. Michel, wearing white trousers and a vest, had taken a week's leave; could anyone have guessed, seeing him smiling like this, that his mumps had developed into septicaemia? Irène, in a floral-patterned dress, is clasping an enormous black cat. Denise, in her swimming costume, holds hands with her little sister, who is beginning to stand on her own two feet. A great deal of sunshine and a great many shadows, a precarious photograph 'full of simple joy'.[60]

Then, quite suddenly, on 22nd August, 'like hearing a knock on the door during the night telling you that it was time to get up',[61] came this communiqué from the Deutsches Nachrichten-Büro, the official German news agency, which Irène Némirovsky would take the trouble to reproduce fully in one of her stories: 'The government of the Reich and the Soviet government have decided to draw up a non-aggression pact between them.' These few words meant 'possibly . . . doubtless . . . probably . . . war'.[62] Furthermore, they meant that almost all hopes Irène and Michel Epstein had of being granted French citizenship had vanished. Michel, especially, was worried. On his return to Paris, he appears to have been so prepared for an attack that he asked Albin Michel for a letter of recommendation for his wife which she could use with 'the authorities and the press' in the south-west, in the event of her being prevented from joining him in Paris. Albin Michel's reply was even more alarming and shows that, quite as much as a military offensive, Michel feared a period of nationalist withdrawal and a resurgence of xenophobia. On the 28th, in fact, Irène Némirovsky's publisher wrote to her in Hendaye as follows:

> We are currently living in terrifying times which could become tragic from one day to the next. Furthermore, you are Russian and Jewish, and it could be that people who do not know you – though they must be few and far between given your fame as a writer – might cause problems for you, and so, as we must try to anticipate everything, I thought that my testimony as an editor might be useful to you.
>
> I am therefore prepared to testify that you are a writer of great talent, as is evident, moreover, from the success of your works both in France and abroad where some of your books have been translated.

Less than a week later, Michel's forebodings were realised: since Poland had refused to yield to Hitler's fresh claims and had ordered a general mobilisation, German troops began to attack. On the same day as the invasion, Jean Vignaud wrote once more to the minister, Paul Marchandeau, to remind him of his support – and that of André Chaumeix – for the naturalisation of the Epsteins, which had once been 'welcomed favourably' but was postponed 'due to the circumstances'. Two days later, France and Great Britain, under duress, became caught up in the spiral.

The 3rd of September 1939 was a beautiful day. 'All the French were leaving. They hastily packed their damp swimming costumes and sand-covered sandals into their suitcases, and the women shed tears into the folds of organdie dresses they had carefully set aside to wear on September evenings.'[63]

Part III

Stronger than the Aversion
(1939–1942)

10

French Monsoon
(1939–1941)

And then he knew what he could not believe was true. The houses with everyone in them, men and women, children, babies, grandparents, a whole tiny village, had been swept away completely into the mad current of the roaring river by that first wall.

Louis Bromfield, The Rains Came, 1937

In Irène Némirovsky's notebooks, the first mention of this large market town of over a thousand inhabitants, on the borders of the Nièvre and Saône-et-Loire *départements*, is as early as 25th April 1938: 'Back from Issy-l'Évêque. 4 totally happy days. What more can one ask for? Thank God for that and for hope.' In this Burgundy village with its slate roofs, nestling between forests and valleys, huddled like a cat around its church and its fairground, she recovered from the birth of 'Babet' for the first time. It was in order to leave her with Marie-Louise Mitaine, the mother of 'Néné', a young married woman, that the novelist caught the train to Luzy, from where a car took her to M. Loctin's hotel. We can follow her on foot as far as the prosperous inn on the Grande-Rue: 'I cross the Place du Monument aux Morts, where the image of a soldier stands guard, painted in the brightest pink and blue. Further along there is an avenue lined with lime trees, then ancient darkish ramparts where an arched doorway gives on to open space and lets through a chill north wind, and finally the small square in front of the church. At dusk, you can just make out the round loaves of golden bread in the bakery window, lit up by a lamp with a paper shade. In the grey drizzle and fog, the signs hanging in front of the notary and shoemaker seem to float in the air: the shoemaker has a large clog carved out of light wood the size and shape of a cradle. Over the road is the Hôtel des Voyageurs.'[1]

In this hotel, in late February 1939, Michel came to convalesce for a week. In the kitchen, Mme Loctin prepared copious amounts of food, for the countryside was bountifully provided with poultry, wholemeal bread and cream, which could be enjoyed in the smoke-filled coffee room, heated by a burning-hot stove. The rest of the room was furnished with a few marble-topped tables, a billiards table and a shabby sofa. Hanging on the wall was 'the calendar from 1919 with its picture of an Alsatian woman in white stockings standing between two soldiers'.[2] The peasants came here to play card games or to knock back their drinks. The comfort, however, was relative: in Issy, just before war broke out, water was drawn from the well, and you kept yourself warm by a log fire, wood being as plentiful as butter. At Mme Mitaine's you answered the call of nature in a wooden cabin at the end of the garden. Irène Némirovsky would even refer to 'the most complete lack of comfort'.[3] But this village was a little city-state that was self-sufficient: there was a butcher, a patisserie shop, an ironmonger, a joiner, a post office, a grocer, a notary's practice, a tax office, a tobacconist, a chemist, a school, a police station and even a castle on the Montrifaut hill that overlooked the town. In short, 'an extremely rich region, with large estates, well-fed animals, beautiful children. What are the people like? How can I put it? They're like all the other country folk in the world! Hard on themselves and hard on others.'[4]

Between peace and war

From 1938 onwards, Irène Némirovsky never stopped returning to Issy to forget her weariness and her troubles. At the outskirts of the village she was met by a bitter smell of burnt wood that was intoxicating to her Parisian nostrils. In the clogmaker's workshop, the pervasive aroma of new wood reminded her of the cabins at Mustamäki. The parish priest, Canon Gaufre, was delighted to be able to converse with 'such an intelligent' woman,[5] while walking up Mt Tharot, from which they looked down over the neighbouring hamlets. She loved walking. As far as the orchard belonging to the Montjeu farm, twenty minutes away on the Étang-Neuf path, to eat enormous plums, 'yellow like amber, and that sweet juice dripping over our fingers'.[6] Or else, wrapped in her cloak, she walked up to the property that belonged to the champagne makers, Pol-Roger, then forked north-west towards the Broaille pond, now dried-up; on her way, leaving the castle to her

left, she would stop in the fir-tree woods known as la Maie. The Virgin
of Maublanc would watch over her in the forest as she wrote, lying
in the grass or squatting cross-legged on a blanket of leaves. 'I love
our silent woods. You never meet a soul here ordinarily.'[7] Another of
her favourite walks took her to the place known as the lost Pond,
edged with gorse and glittering with dragonflies, deep in the forest.
How could one imagine the sound of boots beneath this foliage? Had
not the statue to the Virgin of Maublanc been erected to mark the
point where the Prussian troops stopped in 1870?

As soon as war was declared, Irène Némirovsky took the decision
to send her daughters to board at Mme Mitaine's home, far from all
danger. At her request, Cécile went to Hendaye to collect Denise and
'Babet' and take them by train to Luzy, after a night spent at Avenue
Coquelin. Knowing they were safe, their mother immediately set off
for Paris to be with Michel who, without having had time to cure
his septicaemia, had been obliged to cut short his holidays in order
to fill the place of his colleagues Maizière and Pradère-Niquet, who
had been called up. This was meant to be a temporary situation; it
would last until the May 1940 offensive, eight months later.
Throughout this endless false dawn, this 'sort of no man's land
between peace and war',[8] while the nerves grew frayed and the entire
nation began to lose heart, Irène Némirovsky made several visits to
Issy, by train or in her brother-in-law Paul's car, to spend a few days
with her 'evacuated children', as her travel pass stated. Denise, who
went to the local school and attended catechism classes, soon learned
not to stand on ceremony: 'I discovered a new world. I no longer
wore pretty dresses, I could get dirty, I lived among children of my
own age, which had never happened to me before, since I was brought
up by a governess.'[9] For Miss Matthews had been obliged to return
quickly to England. At Issy, there was no more curtsying to distinguished visitors, no more posing for photographers, no more patent
leather shoes or pulled-up socks. And there was this luxury: school
friends! In the class photograph, though, she is the only one wearing
shoes, whereas the other girls are wearing clogs. A Parisienne through
and through!

Out of the events of September 1939 – the declaration of war, her
return to Paris, the anticipation of the disaster – Irène Némirovsky
drew the material for four stories, written during the autumn. In them

we glimpse her mounting anxiety, rising to an apocalyptic vision of 'the bombed towers of Notre-Dame',[10] followed by a flight to the sea that culminates, once again, in a drowning.

The first of these texts,[11] the most light-hearted, carries the hope that the sudden shadow cast by the German-Soviet pact may reconcile the vexed lovers and put an end to their childish quarrelling. The same 'wonderful brotherliness' survives in 'La Nuit en wagon'. The story takes place during a journey from Hendaye to Paris on the night of 3–4 September, and shows a cross-section of France in 1939 gathered together sharing hard-boiled eggs and black coffee, in a train packed with soldiers, children, holiday-makers, peasants and middle-class people temporarily united by their feelings of apprehension. 'You wouldn't think there was a war.'[12] After this scarcely credible initial terror, there followed a night of 'green crystal', criss-crossed with silvery zeppelins 'like huge blind fish', that lends the third of these stories, written in late November, a supernatural tinge. In it, she describes the 'black abyss', the 'yawning night' that covers the capital, darkened, as passive resistance obliged, every night. 'A sleeping Paris, prepared for everything, her guns close by, breathed softly in the darkness.'[13] In 'Le Spectateur', no longer able to restrain herself, Irène Némirovsky finally sacrifices an expiatory victim to the threatening storm. A hedonist, Hugo Grayer, deeply upset by the poetry of ruins, takes a sensual pleasure in the death throes of Europe: 'You could see a country singing as it quivered and died, just as you might feel the heart of a wounded nightingale beating in your hands.' A choice spectacle, and one which the novelist enables him to relish at closer quarters by putting him aboard a liner full of refugees that is torpedoed in the Atlantic, with chaotic scenes of women in mink coats and 'little German-Jewish children'. The unanimity of 'La Nuit en wagon' had been transformed into a nauseating human concoction 'just as you mix alcoholic drinks in a shaker'.[14] Right up to his watery death, this refined individual remains 'curious to know what feelings are aroused by extreme peril'. To punish him for his morbid fascination, Irène Némirovsky submits the very urbane Grayer to the final humiliation, 'the animal, primitive, panic-stricken terror' of drowning. For the war will not merely be a world war: it will be a total war and will brook neither spectator nor 'benevolent neutrality'. 'Le Spectateur' is therefore a fable, one of seven years of not caring a damn in the face of

Nazi arrogance: 'Those crowds were like chickens who let their mothers and sisters get their throats cut while they continued to cluck and peck at their grain, without understanding that it was exactly this passivity, their innate complicity that would hand them over, one day, them as well, to a harsh, strong hand.'[15]

What proof did Irène Némirovsky give, in late 1939, that she would not sit with her arms crossed and wait for the disaster? 'I've thought about what I could best do, and what contribution I might be allowed to make,' she explained. 'It seems to me that the best thing is to restrict oneself to one's specialised field. Now, what I know how to do is write . . . I have therefore written for the foreign press – among others for a Dutch newspaper in Rotterdam – some articles that reveal the magnificent morale of the French, that describe the calm decision made by the soldiers, the calm courage of the women. By gathering together features I have observed every day, I have tried to show the simplicity and bravery of the French. I must also give talks on the radio – broadcasts about women's life. They will consist of biographies of Polish or English heroines who devoted themselves to their country's cause. I hope to be able to do better.'[16]

The script of one of these 'chats' appears to have been preserved. In it, Irène Némirovsky celebrates the spirit and character of Finnish women, the 'delicate and precious balance between manly and feminine qualities'. For, on 30th November, the Red Army had crossed the Finnish frontier. Within twenty-four hours, the Karelian isthmus had fallen to the Soviets. Mustamäki, her temporary exile in 1917, would never again be Finnish. But, she recalled confidently, 'the inhabitants of this country are, generally speaking, strong and healthy. In their character, they are like the granite that the soil of their land is made from: solid and hard . . . I know what I am talking about: I saw them during the civil war of 1920: I can assure you they are formidable enemies.' These well-disposed comments did not prevent Finland from losing one tenth of its territory. Throughout the winter, Irène Némirovsky would anxiously follow the events of this first armed conflict, the stages of which punctuated her working notebook, right down to this foreboding in April 1940: 'Norway and Denmark invaded. Bad feeling.'

A special curse

In Irène Némirovsky's work, the Winter war and the Soviet offensive coincided with a revival of her taste for things Russian, which recent events had made her feel nostalgic about. In 'Aïno', she recalls the civil war in 1918, 'the stench of burning cities'[17] and the heavy gunfire over Terjoki, at the precise moment that the Soviets had just set up a specious 'democratic Republic' subservient to Moscow in this area. In '. . . et je l'aime encore' Olga Obolensky is twenty years younger, 'smiling, wearing a large, 1915-style hat and a pink muslin scarf over her bare neck',[18] and still loyal to the memory of a lover lost, long ago, on a beach in the Crimea. Lastly, 'Le Sortilège', the only one of her stories in which the narrator is called Irène, revives memories of the magic of staying with a Russian girlfriend in an old dacha in the suburbs of Kiev. The master of the house, she remembers, was a retired soldier who 'had known Chekhov very well' and kept on his desk 'a box containing some letters from the writer'.[19] This reminiscence was probably connected to the melancholy and novelistic biography of Chekhov, in the manner of André Maurois and Eugène Semenoff,[20] that she first contemplated in the summer of 1939, and which she began to write in early November, helped by her own memories of Tauris and the Côte d'Azur. For, she wrote, 'it is a great benefit to a writer whose childhood has been unhappy to allow this source of poetry in one's past to spring forth'.[21]

With Denise and Élisabeth far away, the long, solitary days spent at Avenue Coquelin played a large part in this surrender to nostalgia. 'It's not my fault,' explains Ada in The Dogs and the Wolves, which was serialised in the autumn. '. . . It's a unique curse that forces me to remember every trait that ever struck me, every word spoken, every moment of joy and sorrow.'[22] The novel did not appear in Gringoire, but in the pages of Candide, the newspaper to which she had offered an epistolary short story a year ago, 'La Femme de Don Juan', that she had nonchalantly dashed off during the summer of 1938. Why this disloyalty to Gringoire? Because of the 34,000 francs she had been paid at the end of 1938, at a time when Gringoire was already committed to publishing Les Échelles du Levant. The favourite newspaper of the nationalist right, Candide was in fact the other heavyweight of the French press, launched in 1924 by the publisher Fayard, and with a circulation of over 400,000 copies. Thus, while *Gringoire* heaped simultaneous opprobrium on the USSR and its Nazi ally ('Up and at the Nazi-Stalinists!'[23]), *Candide*, formerly pro-Munich and still influenced by the ideas of Maurras, had no doubts about who the enemy was and maintained a fiercely anti-communist line throughout the phoney war. On 11th October, the same day that the serialisation *The Dogs and the Wolves* began, René Benjamin castigated 'the communist Monster' on the front page. Featured on the inside pages, as the weeks went by, were some of the most reactionary names in the French press, Pierre Gaxotte, Alain Laubreaux, Georges Blond and Lucien Rebatet – the latter, it is true, restricted to music criticism. One even comes across André Chaumeix and André Foucault, the 'discoverer' of *David Golder*, who was in charge of news from the French front, that is to say minor news items!

How tiny we are . . .

Irène Némirovsky paid at least two visits to Issy-l'Évêque before May 1940, on about 1st March, then again at the very beginning of April, 'at the bedside of one of her one daughters who was ill'[24] Élisabeth, who had scarlet fever. In the first of the two stories she wrote during this time, one for which the grocer's shop at Issy clearly serves as background, Gilberte is a teenager to whom Denise, having spent part of the winter far away from her mother, seems to have dictated her rebukes: 'There's nothing in this hellish hole! The cursed blindness of parents who force her to remain in the countryside, far from the apartment in Paris . . . !'[25] Similarly, in 'Le Départ pour la fête', little Rosine longs to go and laugh and dance in the neigh-bouring village; but her father, a man who is weary of life, is more preoccupied with other concerns than taking her there: he has just learnt of the suicide of a former mistress. 'The moment you under-stand, for the very first time, that no one actually finds you at all interesting is the moment you cease to be a child.'[26] But the real subject of the story is something else: it is this invisible character that children laugh at and which chills adults' blood; the gradual twilight that begins to envelop life once the age of forty is reached;

that continental drift that places an ocean of misunderstanding between people of the same flesh and blood.

'Jeunes et vieux' [The Young and the Old]: this was precisely the title she planned to give her new novel. No doubt it was motherhood that had brought out this sense of otherness, that had soothed the once eager hot-bloodedness which had switched directions and now coursed through her daughters' veins. Quite simply, Irène Némirovsky was thirty-seven years old. On 10th November, Efim Epstein died. Irène and Michel had definitely stopped being children, for nothing interested Fanny less than her own daughter. On 26th March, in the margin of her story 'Départ pour la fête', she observed: 'I think that from now on I shall only write one thing: what we are becoming. *Cf.* living debases . . . And then that inner detachment. These stories about war, about peace, about life, about love, about death, seen in this light. I've already done this in *Deux*. But it's something I can do, that I <u>should</u> do again continuously.'

Without giving up the notion of a vast meditation on the different ages of life, she wanted to make it a 'French tragedy', to immerse it in the history of the inter-war years and show the continual self-denial that had made the children of the Belle Époque the dupes of 1940, having sacrificed their thwarted desire for earthly pleasures, which were constantly at variance with their sacred duties, to their work, their family and their country. 'It is a destiny that is neither finer nor loftier than any other, the destiny of an ant, but all in all it is man's destiny on this earth, in accordance with the laws of nature. That is why the Frenchman is happy with his lot.' Quoting Chekhov imperfectly, she summed up her initiative in a phrase: 'How these people suffer! How they sacrifice themselves for us.'[27] Was it a question of deriding the conservatism that oppressed youthful impulses? Not at all: this voluntary submission was, on the contrary, the beauty of France, 'their cheerful bravery, their generous modesty, their desire to always give something more than what has been asked of them, not only to help, but an encouraging word, not only a courageous act but an action accomplished with good grace, all in all, everything that makes the French unique in the world'.[28] Was this reckless recognition, at a time when the whole country talked of nothing but the 'fifth column', of that army of obscure traitors who, from ministers to army chiefs, were already speculating on their own defeat? On 26th March, despite being exhausted from illness, Michel solemnly declared himself 'fully at the service of the country'. As for Irène Némirovsky, dreaming of the 'Union sacrée',* she was absorbed in first-hand accounts of the First World War[29] and in *Le Sacrifice* by Henri Massis, whose title alone summed up her state of mind. Could she have any doubts, one month away from the invasion, that the war would be over by the summer, in conditions that were scarcely worthy of the heroic carnage of 1914?

The first inklings of a plot were sketched out on 1st March, at the Hôtel des Voyageurs. A simple, happy life, an appetite for living and for loving disrupted by war, traditions, family matters, 'the mistakes, the regrets, the marriage, the children, the separations, etc.'. The intractable desire to enjoy oneself, curbed by the crushing weight of social heritage and, beyond that, of collective destiny. 'There is one theme in this novel, just one. It is the theme par excellence, and the theme of our times especially: the struggle between man and his destiny. Between the individual and society, if you wish, but not in the sense of Sorel, in a natural way, but between the desire of the individual to live for himself and the destiny that shapes him, that crushes him for its own ends.' Yet one sacrifice is allowed, for 'the Frenchman always sacrifices himself for his children'. Then, this entire futile structure is totally eroded by a new war: twenty years of exhausting effort. The belated anger of the fathers contemplating the ruins, and that of the sons confronted with this legacy. The myth of Sisyphus illustrated by contemporary History. 'In other words, how [19]14 affected [19]40. Why was one the result of the other? Or else, quite simply, the outside world had changed. 14 had nothing to do with it, even though 40 yells at it and holds it responsible. 14 says: Leave me alone. I did what I could. And 40: Since everything's going so badly, you've got something to do with it. The new wine in old skins, that's the basis of the novel.'

Irène Némirovsky sold this ambitious framework to Jean Fayard, who accepted it in April in return for 60,000 francs payable in two amounts. There was just one stipulation: 'Jeunes et Vieux' struck him as no better than the other titles that had been considered, 'La Jeunesse et l'Âge mûr', 'Jeunesse et Maturité', 'Jeunesse et Âge mûr'. 'And I come back to my first idea: a sort of French *Cavalcade*. The only thing

*Président Poincaré's call for unity on the part of all Frenchmen in the face of enemy hostility during the First World War. [Tr.]

that worries me, is the triviality of it, everyone will have had the same idea. Funny too to think that the moment the book's ready, people will say: To hell with the war! And they'll only want racy stories.' *Cavalcade* was the title of a play by Noël Coward, made into a film in 1933: a family saga based on world events over a period of twenty years, from the second Boer War to the Treaty of Versailles, that intertwined a multitude of discordant lives, among them a harmonious blend of the unwavering British aristocracy. Resuming her sketch, she apportioned roles: 'The grandfather, a kind of Avot grandfather, but anticlerical, etc. The father and the mother, much the same as the Avot parents.' A provincial dynasty of papermakers, the incarnation of 'all those nice middle-class people I knew': tough, indestructible, incapable of fulfilling themselves outside the powerful family orbit. One thinks of *Les Thibault* by Roger Martin du Gard, of Georges Duhamel's *Chronique des Pasquiers*; she based herself more on Tolstoy: 'In short, my girl, you want to write your little *War and Peace*.' But also on this sermon, which she had heard at Saint-François-Xavier on one of the first Sundays of September 1939: 'How small we are, my brothers, and how great we are.' This skilful blending of individual destinies and of higher goals would be the hallmark of her last novels.

A story about Jews

Irène Némirovsky sketched out the early scenes of 'Jeunes et Vieux' – which would become *Les Biens de ce monde* [*All Our Worldly Goods*] – in April 1940, at the same time as Albin Michel was announcing the publication of *The Dogs and the Wolves* in deliberately vague terms: 'A tragedy of dark splendour . . . An extraordinary female character.'[30] This was so as to conceal from the reader the precise nature of this tender and cruel book which is another *Cavalcade*, but set in the world of Jewish immigrants, from the ghetto to international finance and vice versa. Tough, idealistic, dissatisfied, daring: such are the Russian Jews in this great novel about non-assimilation to the comfortable French mould, indicated here by the 'slowly simmering soup'.[31] For all that, Irène Némirovsky did not want to be seen to be taken in by middle-class hypocrisy, personified by a banker who is gradually obliged to admit openly the reasons he opposes the marriage of his daughter to the heir of the Sinner bank: 'He wasn't actually xenophobic, no, but . . . every-thing that came from the East aroused an insurmountable mistrust within him. Slavonic, Levantine, Jewish, he didn't know which of these terms disgusted him the most. There was nothing clear about it, nothing certain . . .'[32] Delarcher's long interior monologue, a real array of anti-Semitic views, shows quite clearly that in Irène Némirovsky's novels such opinions always arise from reported speech, 'a technique that has been very useful to me', she noted in the margin of *Dolce* in the spring of 1942. Nevertheless, in order that people should not misunderstand her intentions once again, nor mistake her compassion for loftiness, she thought it wise to write this rather arrogant insert:

> This novel is a story about Jews. I must be clear: not French Jews, but Jews who have come from the East, from the Ukraine or Poland.
>
> Of course, not all Jews are like my hero: the variety in a human race is infinite. I have told a story which, for all sorts of reasons, could only happen to Jews.
>
> I have not written it without some anxiety. Some, I know, will say: 'What do the Jews matter to us?' It is a point of view I understand and, to those people, there is nothing that I can say.
>
> I am more fearful, however, of the objections of Jews themselves: 'Why,' they will say, 'talk about us? Are you unaware of the persecution we suffer, the hatred with which people hound us? If people talk about us, at least, let it be purely to glorify our virtues and to grieve over our misfortunes!'
>
> To that I would reply that no subject is 'taboo' in literature. Why would a people refuse to be seen as they are, with their good qualities and their faults?
>
> I think certain Jews may recognise themselves in my characters. Perhaps they will be angry with me? Yet I know that I am telling the truth.

Since *David Golder*, her argument had not changed: 'This was how I saw them.' What is curious is that at the moment that she gallantly denied having depicted a physiology of the Jew ('the variety in a human race is infinite'), she endeavoured at the same time, in case she were accused of 'impertinence on the part of a foreigner', to depict that of the Frenchman in 'Jeunes et Vieux': 'A Jew,' she said, 'loves money because it is the symbol of what he might do (a sign of power). He loves money sadistically. The Frenchman, be he from the people or the bourgeoisie, does so because he values the respect of his peers.' Even though all hope of acquiring citizenship had disappeared, Irène Némirovsky could not protect herself from 'that genuine and slightly mocking affection that [she] felt for the French' . . . With the invasion a few weeks away, did she actually believe that so many good people would shield her from barbarism? Not really: 'How do I see him exactly, my Frenchman? A little dry except when he is affected to the very depth of his soul. But someone who gives of himself wholeheartedly and immediately? No.'

In spite of reviews that were slapdash and sparse, due to the circumstances, seventeen thousand copies of *The Dogs and the Wolves* would nonetheless be sold. And yet despite the precautions the author took, the book, though appreciated, tended to be misunderstood. *Les Annales*, which ran extracts from this 'novel of Jewish manners', did not take offence at having the hackneyed stereotypes confirmed: on the one side 'the opulent Jews, appeased by wealth and having lost the aggressive features of their race', and on the other 'the starving Jews, who are not well off, and who are determined by every means possible to earn their place in the sun'.[33] On 25th April, Pierre Lœwel detected what was at first sight a roughly accomplished portrait of the characteristics of the 'Jewish soul': 'the perpetual dissatisfaction that stifles it', not to mention 'that morbid appetite for money'.[34] One month later, France had been defeated, and this same Lœwel predicted for Ada, who was liable to be sent to the 'concentration camp', a terrible fate: 'You will learn,' wrote *L'Ordre*'s reviewer, who had suddenly become a prophet, 'how the threat of a resounding collapse will condemn her to the holocaust' . . .[35]

A flock beneath the storm

'The Maginot Line is the most effective barrier against the attacker, it will fulfil its function for as long as may be necessary up until the day that the progress of the war shall dictate for us the form of words imposing final defeat on the adversary,'[36] trumpeted *L'Intransigeant* bombastically in mid-April. Six weeks later, the German breakthrough at Sedan was a memory, and the infallibility of France's defences brought no more a smile to the face than did the slogan for a well-known brand of lingerie: *'Il y a ligne et ligne. Et de toutes les lignes la plus appreciée est celle que donne la gaine Scandale.'*[*][37] Honour had been saved: Paris would always be Paris. At least, until military headquarters declared it to be an open city and handed the Champs-Élysées over to the boots of the Wehrmacht, on 14th June 1940.

Irène Némirovsky had arrived at Issy-l'Évêque two weeks previously, before the wave of civilians fleeing the German steamroller – ten million people, in the words of Marshal Pétain, the new and last Président du Conseil, who added, without labouring the point: 'in indescribable conditions of confusion and hardship'.[38] She had spent the whole of May in Paris in the disappointed expectation of a French counter-attack. 'Let us be patient!' the newspapers nevertheless proclaimed. 'The Germans are not without fears of their own.'[39] One of her stories, 'Destinées', reconstructs the first nights of air-raid warnings in the capital with people peering from their balconies to spot enemy aircraft, instead of hiding in their cellars. Ten days before the initial offensive, a long extract from her *La Vie de Tchekhov*, reduced to two-thirds, had been published in *Les Œuvres libres*. In it, she compares the European of 1940 with a subject of Alexander III, without one being able to tell whether she is thinking of the swastika or the hammer and sickle: 'Evil reigned, then as now; it had not taken apocalyptic forms as it does today, but the spirit of violence, cowardice and corruption was everywhere. Just as it is at the moment, the world was divided into blind torturers and resigned victims, but everything was mean, petty and steeped in mediocrity. People awaited the writer who would discuss this mediocrity without anger, without distaste, but with the pity it deserved.'[40] They still awaited her. But who knows whether she would find the courage . . .

Irène Némirovsky did not have to endure the bombardment, nor the flight from the cities. Around Pentecost, she had moved into the Hôtel des Voyageurs with her daughters, as the 'battle for France' was being waged. She did not yet have the energy to write: 'I rather feel,' she admitted on 6th June, 'that I should write one or two stories, as many as I still can – possibly – and place them, but . . . uncertainty,

*A clever pun on the double meaning of *'ligne'*, which can denote 'line' as well as 'figure'. A loose translation would therefore be: 'There is the line and the figure. And of all the figures/lines the one that is most appreciated is the one provided by the Scandale girdle.' [Tr.]

worry, fear everywhere: the war, Michel, the baby, the little girls, money, the future. The novel, the momentum of the novel totally interrupted. (I want to be honest: the reviewers of *Les Chiens et les Loups* have a point.) So?' So, while the flood of retreating French men and women packed the roads, dragging their elderly and their mattresses on whatever makeshift cart they could lay hands on, exploited by unscrupulous suppliers, starving, exhausted, exasperated, at times reduced to looting and destruction, discouraging the last efforts of an army that was in shambles and that was being pounded from the air, the novelist taught Denise to knit scarves for prisoners of war, inscribed a copy of *Deux* for the patisserie owner's wife, discussed the disadvantages of the 'global method' with the school-teacher and wondered, as did everyone in the village, how to provide education for the dozens of children from the Marne area whose families had been evacuated there by the Pol-Roger champagne company. And what should be done, also, for the hundreds of refugees who had arrived from Paris, from Lyon, from Le Creusot, from Nancy, from Brazey-en-Plaine, and wherever else?

She was worried above all about Michel who, 'at the end of his tether' according to his doctor, had been unable to procure special leave. On 10th June, refusing to stay in Paris any longer, as he had been ordered to do, whereas the rest of the staff of the bank had already moved to Clermont-Ferrand, Michel succeeded in reaching Orléans, from where he sent a telegram on the 11th announcing his arrival at Issy, safe and sound, within three days, accompanied by Paul. By taking this step, he was not unaware that he was putting 43,000 francs of his salary at risk as well as the prospect of imminent promotion. But the circumstances were exceptional. Sufficiently so, his managers would reckon, to do without his services henceforth. For the time being, far from brooding on his disgrace, he made up little rhyming arithmetic problems for Denise as a way of killing time. Denise was delighted to have her parents to herself at last. 'In spite of everything,' she would say, 'those were the happiest years of my life. We lived together, as a family . . .'[41]

Irène Némirovsky first learned of the Exodus, as it was known, through the newspapers, and then from Michel's stories and those of the many refugees – one, in particular, about a woman, who, between 12th and 17th June, had travelled the 120 kilometres separating Juvisy

from Montereau – before seeing them stream through the Issy region
in turn, from 14th to 18th June. Denise recalled the Exodus, too, in
an instructive passage she wrote at school on the 26th: 'From Friday
to Tuesday, we saw thousands of cars pass through our normally fairly
quiet part of the country, driven by people who were fleeing from
the enemy. Most of these vehicles were loaded down with mattresses,
children's toy cars, lingerie and bicycles, which gave this frantic procession of motor-cars an odd appearance that made our hearts sink . . .
No doubt this humiliation will be more useful to the soul of France
and to all the French people than the victory that would have made
us too proud. We will benefit more from defeat.'

This act of contrition, obviously dictated by an adult, coincided
with the arrival of the Germans at Issy-l'Évêque, and later with the
armistice, which was signed on 22nd June. Marshal Pétain, in order
to train the French people to be obedient, openly exhorted them to
repent, and he referred to those really responsible for this Berezina:*
'Our defeat stems from our laxity. The spirit of pleasure has destroyed
what the spirit of sacrifice has constructed.' This indictment was
plagiarised by René Benjamin in his account of the defeat, *Le Printemps
tragique*, which would be one of the documentary sources for *Tempête
en juin* [*Storm in June*]. In Irène Némirovsky's words, the selfish Hugo
Grayer, who is totally indifferent, appears to be deeply distressed by
this revelation; in the first of her stories published after the disaster,
this timid petit-bourgeois, renamed M. Rose but who is still a lover
of porcelain, is nevertheless capable of pity. Alas, he has had to endure
a forced march in the shadow of the Stukas, the treachery of his valet,
hunger, thirst and the loss of all his possessions; and, finally, to give
up his place in a car so as not to desert his companion in misfortune.
In short, to risk his life in order to save it. Sacrifice: it was precisely
this French virtue on which Irène Némirovsky actually based her new
novel. Should she, for want of anything better, have become a
supporter of Marshal Pétain just as she became a Christian? The times
were hard, the consolations few, and Pétain's Passion – 'I make to
France the gift of my person, to attenuate her suffering' – coated the
wounds of the French who were packing the roads or were marooned

*A reference to the retreat of Napoleon's Grande Armée across the River Berezina
(26–29th November 1812). [Tr.]

on the banks of the Loire with a supernatural balm. What greater comfort than 'the instinct that draws the animals of a flock closer beneath the storm'?[42] Who knew whether this catastrophe that she was sharing would not finally unite her with the great family of France?

A great anxiety

But Pétain had announced that 'a new order is beginning'. The immediate effects: the sacrifice of the Republic, ministers imprisoned, the anointment of the leader, an agrarian mystique, 'intellectual and moral recovery', pledges of goodwill to the German authorities. One would have had to be deaf, like Maurras, to detect a 'divine surprise' in this great backward leap, which the antiparliamentarians had wanted for twenty years. This worrying tendency was that much less noticeable in Issy-l'Évêque, still recovering from the reverberations of the chaos in June, particularly since the German soldiers, with their shaved heads and pale complexions, who lived in the Hôtel des Voyageurs were not murderers, but big lads who had not fought in the First World War, and most of whom had not yet encountered any resistance during the Second. They mainly spent their time chopping wood, drinking beer, playing billiards and bouncing 'Élissabeth' on their knees, their teeth sparkling as on the propaganda posters. 'I will enter French homes as a liberator,' Hitler had prophesied. 'We shall present ourselves to the ordinary people as the champions of a social order that is fair and a peace that is eternal . . .' The trap was set. People would almost forget the war: 'The sound of boots, boots, boots . . . white butterflies and flowers like amaranths in the garden, in the sunshine, and a jasmine hedge. Should we talk about the war? Should we? . . .' Irène Némirovsky wondered in early July.

Because he needed to deal with his troubles patiently, Michel, who was the only person in the village to speak fluent German, served as interpreter and even began to get along with two non-commissioned officers, Feldwebel Ewald Hammberger and Lieutenant Franz Hohmann. Not forgetting Paul Spiegel, whom Babet in her ingenuousness called '*mon petit chéri*'. The requirements of the armistice, of course, obliged them to impose a curfew. Futhermore, they gave them the right to requisition vehicles, animals and fodder, foodstuffs and accommodation. But the countryside was fertile and there was no sound of guns. The peace, of course, was German: before the end of June, Feldkommandantur, Kreiskommandantur, Ortskommandantur, Feldgendarmerie and other Feld Geheime Polizei took over from the existing authorities. At least, this was the case in the Occupied Zone of the *département* of Saône-et-Loire, north of a line about twenty kilometres to the south of Issy-l'Évêque. Beyond that, as far as the Mediterranean, stretched the so-called 'Free Zone', which was under French government administration, the German authorities having waived 'all the rights of the occupying power' there, which the armistice agreement entitled them to in the north. Knowing the Aryan concept of the aforesaid rights, a stateless Jewish woman would have every reason to be anxious. On 21st July, furthermore, an initial emergency law had been put in place challenging all naturalisations registered since 1927, thereby depriving six thousand Jews of French nationality. A fortnight later, Irène Némirovsky read in *Le Progrès de l'Allier* that foreign contributors were already undesirable in certain newspapers. 'Do you think that that will affect a foreigner like me who has lived in France since 1920?' she wrote naively to Albin Michel's secretary. 'Does it apply to political writers or to fiction writers as well?' In the absence of her boss, who had taken refuge in the Lot and was too unwell to take charge of his publishing house again, and with no news from André Sabatier since he had been called up, Mlle Le Fur, who was powerless, replied that she had no idea.

To run away, one needs to be aware of a danger; yet what did she have to fear at Issy-l'Évêque, surrounded by these good people who knew her, needed her and sometimes read her? People such as M. Barre, the postmaster-cum-tobacconist, who had been decorated with the Croix de Guerre and was the father of nine children, who asked her to intervene with André Bellessort, the permanent secretary at the Académie française, to help him obtain an Ernest-Cognacq award for large families. And what did these considerations matter compared to the pressing need to feed oneself, to keep warm and to continue to pay the rent on the flat in Paris that had been entrusted to Paul Epstein? Once the offices of Albin Michel had reopened on 1st July, her first concern was to have a 9,000 francs advance on her monthly payments sent to her by postal order, so that she could stave off any new problems. 'Currently, my most serious worry is how to obtain some money,' she wrote on the 12th to Robert Esménard, the publisher's son-in-law and adviser, who had returned to civilian life after the disastrous Belgian campaign. Requested by Michel Epstein on 11th June, when Albin Michel had not yet contemplated closing down his office, the money only reached Issy on 4th August, so disorganised were the postal services. And, with 'Monsieur Rose' completed, Irène encountered every difficulty imaginable in delivering the manuscript to *Candide*, which had moved to Clermont, on the other side of the demarcation line. Yet it was a matter of 3,000 francs, the equivalent of a month's pay! But the frontier, flanked with anti-aircraft batteries, was very secure. It made the exchange of correspondence or sums of money virtually impossible – to say nothing of people moving freely. And there was no way of knowing when *Gringoire*, *Candide* and the large-circulation Paris dailies, which were her main clients, would return to the capital.

Irène Némirovsky was in fact 'completely isolated from people' at Issy-l'Évêque and 'totally unaware of measures that may have been taken recently in the press'. On the other hand, there was a persistent rumour that the demarcation line could be redrawn. The village would then find itself in the southern zone! Many of the farmers whose lives were complicated by this barrier were delighted at the prospect. In actual fact, being a matter for negotiation, the line would fluctuate until the autumn. In late October, Irène Némirovsky was anxiously wondering once more how she would collect her monthly payments if Issy were to be placed under Vichy jurisdiction[43] . . . She therefore chose, deliberately, to remain in the lion's jaws. It was not as absurd a decision as would appear, taking into account the fact that Michel, since his disloyalty to the Banque des Pays du Nord, was also about to see his income decline to nothing. Joseph Koehl, the managing director, would hear of no excuses, neither a medical certificate, nor the military defeat: by refusing to remain at the Paris headquarters of the bank, when everyone else was packing his bag for the Puy-de-Dôme, Michel had signed his own dismissal, after fifteen years of impeccable service. By way of 'termination payment', he would only receive, all in all, 8,027 francs in mid-August, plus a 'bonus' of 5,000 francs at the end of October.

To move to the southern zone, in such conditions, was unthinkable. And the notion of running away like a thief appalled her. To her Aunt

Victoria, in Moscow, she merely explained in a letter that Élisabeth had scarlet fever and was unable to travel. And when Cécile Michaud, who was a local girl, suggested that the Epsteins should cross the line while it was still permitted, she heard herself reply in a half-nonplussed, half-blustering voice: 'But I've done nothing, why would anyone arrest me?' Should the need arise, which was highly unlikely, Irène Némirovsky knew she could count on her connections in Paris; she probably imagined, moreover, as did so many others, that the land that gave the world the rights of man would only legislate reluctantly against the Jews, and that it was advisable to be patient.

It was in this state of mind, trusting too much to proverbial French goodwill and certain of her special status as a writer, that Irène Némirovsky, fully convinced that she had been of service to France, turned spontaneously to Marshal Pétain, the protector of the nation, even when she should have spurned him. Yet the elderly leader had solemnly warned the French people: 'Do not hope for too much from the State. It can only give what it receives.' And what did it receive, if not Nazi inspiration? On 27th August, for example, the Marchandeau law, which punished abuse of a racial nature, was repealed. Thenceforth it became permissible to incite hatred against the Jews in the press, and *Gringoire* immediately made use of this rediscovered law by filling its pages with idiotic cartoons, twisted accusations and unverifiable information, apprising its readers, for example, that on 5th September the 'Jew Lekah, known as Lecache, of Ukrainian parentage, an all-powerful *métèque* from the Place Beauvau in the time of M. Sarraut,* has cynically admitted that France was fighting on behalf of international Jewry'. Yet this same *Gringoire* did not fail to declare its support in due course for Marshal Pétain . . .

But the French, astounded by the insult of the June invasion, wished to believe that the sovereignty of their country was unaffected and that the new regime had not abolished the Republic without reason. When Irène Némirovsky heard that the French government

---

*The Place Beauvau in Paris denotes the Ministry of the Interior. Albert Sarraut was Minister of the Interior from 1926 to 1928, and again, from February to November 1934, and from 1937 to 1940. (He also served two brief stints as Prime Minister, in 1933 and in 1936.) [Tr.]

was to prepare 'measures against stateless people', she believed there must have been a misunderstanding and immediately wrote a puzzled letter to 'monsieur le Maréchal', care of the sub-prefecture at Autun. Why Pétain? In the first place, because she had no way of getting in touch with André Chaumeix, sheltering cosily at the Hôtel Majestic in Royat, on the other side of the demarcation line. And secondly, she felt authorised to do so as a fellow contributor to the *Revue des Deux Mondes*: had not the Marshal just written a 'call to the French people on the subject of state education' for the magazine? It contained the following frank warning to writers: 'We shall strive to destroy the disastrous reputation of a pseudo-culture acquired purely from books, one that promotes indolence and generates useless information.'[44]

Dated 13th September, Irène Némirovsky's letter is a mixture of distress, feigned humility and wounded pride. 'I feel a great anxiety,' she wrote to him, 'at the thought of the fate that awaits us: my family (my husband who has just been gravely ill, my daughters, aged 10 and 3), and myself.' Then, professing her friendship with Chaumeix, Mme Doumic and Marie de Régnier, and reminding him that she had never left French territory since the Russian revolution, she revealed both her panic and her cunning by clumsily resorting to the posturing rhetoric fashionable at the time:

> There is scarcely any need to say that I have never been involved in politics, having written only books of pure literature. In short, whether in foreign newspapers or on the radio, I have done my best to make France known and loved.
>
> I cannot believe, Monsieur le Maréchal, that no distinction is made between those who are unwanted and those respectable foreigners who, if they have been shown princely hospitality by France, are aware of having made every effort to deserve it.
>
> I therefore beg to request that my family and I should be included in this second category of people, that we may be allowed to live freely in France and that I may be allowed to carry out my work as a writer.

It goes without saying that the request, which was sent prior to the announcement of the first decrees making Jews second-rank citizens, could not receive an answer, any more than could the one sent at the same time to the Société des Gens de Lettres, soliciting support. At least this petition was proof that her forebodings were accurate.

Paris lost

Throughout the whole of August, Irène Némirovsky continued to develop 'Jeunes et Vieux'. As in Drieu la Rochelle's *Rêveuse bourgeoisie*, she wanted to depict a seascape for her opening scene with parasols, kites and fireworks, a real Boudin canvas, based on her memories of Paris-Plage that were such a comfort in these troubled times: 'Peace, happy people who look alike, and afterwards, what is going on underneath. I think this opening scene has to be seen from a bird's-eye view. The night was soft, beside the sea, on the grey sand of the dunes . . .' How she missed it, that obstinate, honest, kindly France of the Avots! In this novel, she wanted to 'describe them simply and sympathetically'. She would follow a young couple, married before the First World War, up until 1940; a couple whom fate has established at their property at Lumbres, despite the war and because of it. Jean Fayard's son-in-law, however, did not encourage her on this path, 'since the shortage of paper and the resulting reduction of the number of pages do not allow us to publish serialisations'.[45] But what was the point of stories if they were put in the drawer? While she waited for a better idea, without any conviction she jotted down in her working notebook a few 'subjects for possible stories', to publish 'in any newspaper in Paris or elsewhere, under a pseudonym if necessary'. Paul Bourget's wedding, Mirabeau and his father, a son's biography of his famous father . . . So many projects that would never get off the ground, for how and where could they be published?

In September came days of toil and feasting: in Issy they harvested the wheat. 'Since the morning of the previous day, enormous golden tarts had been baking in the oven, and the children had been picking fruit all week long to decorate them.'[46] As for Irène Némirovsky, she had just put the finishing touches to her *Vie de Tchekhov* [*Life of Chekhov*]. She had enjoyed the writer's friendship with the Jewish painter Levitan, admired his defence of Dreyfus, she had followed him to the penal colony at Sakhalin, had seen through his eyes 'these damp hovels, with their walls teeming with vermin, where chained prisoners lay on a

board . . . Russians, Tartars, Jews, Poles, all races, all religions could
be found there.'[47] Would Albin Michel want to publish this exercise
in admiration, one of the most honest and sensitive books about
Chekhov that one can read? This time, the obstacle came via Robert
Esménard who, citing the generally poor sales and the cancellation of
plans for a film adaptation that his father-in-law had been anticipating,
did not wish to continue making the monthly payments when there
was nothing in writing that obliged him to do so. 'You describe the
current situation to me,' Irène Némirovsky replied, at her wits end.
'Am I to blame for it? If *Les Chiens et les Loups* was put on sale at the
end of May, am I responsible? . . . If you tell me about the poor position the publishing house is in, what shall I say to you about mine?'[48]
Considering the situation to be more serious than his own death,
Michel Epstein was arranging to recoup 46,000 francs from his life
assurance policy.

It would need all Irène Némirovsky's tenacity and persuasion to
force Esménard to be generous and to win his friendship. But the
depressed state of mind of the French people, diagnosed by the good
Doctor Pétain, had never struck her as so glaring. Outraged by the
French laws, and determined never to abandon this country which
was also the land of her childhood, she recognised herself somewhat
in this writer, Chekhov, who 'had the greatest sympathy for France
and seemed to understand and be aware of her virtues more than the
majority of Europeans did'.[49] 'I can see only one thing: reciprocal
undertakings have been made. They must be upheld,' she wrote to
Esménard on 25th September, and this unshakeable faith in the word
as bond was her greatest error of judgement. Evidence of this was
the obligation for all Jews in the Occupied Zone to register with the
state authorities, within the same week, before 20th October. The
qualification for being French no longer depended on values or culture,
under the new regulations they were based on irrelevant genealogical
criteria. Those who would be regarded as Jewish were 'those who
belong or belonged to the Jewish faith or who have more than two
Jewish grandparents'. From now on, Léon Werth noted in his journal,
'the mass no longer removes Jewishness'.[50]

Did Irène Némirovsky realise, at this point, that her baptism no
longer protected her? That her daughters, though naturalised, would
sooner or later have to wear a proof of identity that bore four red

letters spelling the word *'juif'*? Probably not, since on 7th October
Irène and Michel registered at the sub-prefecture of Autun, in common
with 90 per cent of France's Jews, eager to believe that this census
was an act being carried out by a nation jealous of its privileges, and
which would therefore not defer to the Nazis. Michel simply took the
advice of Charles-Albert de Boissieu, a bigwig at the Schneider group
and a director of the Banque des Pays du Nord, who in July had been
appointed Secretary-General to the governmental commission in the
occupied territories – the French Embassy in Paris, as the wits joked.
And Boissieu suggested that he comply. One cannot help observing,
however, that Michel's reemployment, which was on the agenda for
late August, had become undesirable one month later. However much
Michel, who was 'fully restored', might debate matters and collect
testimonies of esteem and friendship from colleagues, M. Koehl's decision was final. It came at the moment that the Banque des Pays du
Nord, one of the leading credit institutions in Paris, was preparing to
hand over its 'Jewish assets' to the economics section of the German
military command.

Had Michel Epstein's employer wanted to dismiss him in the conventional way before being compelled to do so by the racial laws? The
discriminatory *Statut des Juifs* of 3rd October 1940, promulgated on
the 18th, excluded Jews from a large number of jobs in public office,
in teaching, in journalism and in the cinema, but it did not bar them
from the professions. At the same time, it did not abolish the *numerus
clausus* and even authorised, in ambiguous terms, 'the elimination of
supernumary Jews'. As for foreign Jews, they were now liable to internment in 'special camps', at the goodwill of the prefects of the different
départements, who were not appointed without the authorisation of
the occupying authorities. One cannot really pretend that Vichy
encouraged philanthropy.

And here is a legalistic paradox: even though he subjected his family
to this status which he knew to be unjust, Michel did his best to avoid
it himself by requesting special favours, particularly that he be treated
'on equal footing with French Jews'[51] in the face of the conscious threat
of the concentration camp. Writing to Boissieu, a representative of
the government – and offering by way of excuse the state of his health,
his baptism, his financial difficulties, his French children, his nephew
Victor, who was a prisoner of war – all he asked for was a letter of

introduction to the French authorities. A lawyer himself, Boissieu referred to his 'happy memories' and the boundless admiration he had for the work of Irène Némirovsky ... to advise him nonetheless to discharge the 'routine enquiries required by the German authorities'.[52] The stipulations of the first Statut des Juifs, however, were a purely French initiative, albeit copied clumsily from the Nazi Statute of 1935. Two months later, Boissieu would leave public office to take over the management of the Schneider group and of the Union européenne industrielle et financière. As for Michel Epstein, not having received any real help from his colleague Maizière, he was reduced to draining his last savings account at the Caisse des dépôts and, because he had nothing better to do, beginning a translation into French of the Russian biography of Pushkin that Irène had mentioned in Marianne in 1936, for which she intended to write an introduction.

Either through omission or anonymous kindness, the long list of writers proscribed by the occupying power, published on 4th October in Bibliographie de la France under the covert name of the 'Otto list', did not mention Irène Némirovsky's name anywhere. Bernard Grasset, who was a keen supporter of total submission to Nazi censorship, pulped all books by his Jewish authors. The excellent biography of the publisher Albin Michel suggests that he also did this with Irène Némirovsky's novels:[53] this is incorrect, for The Dogs and the Wolves was reprinted in October, and Deux would be reprinted several times up until January 1942.

As far as Jean Fayard, who took over the firm after his father's death in November 1936, was concerned, he did not wait for the Statut des Juifs – which incidentally imposed no obligation on him – to come into effect before taking legal steps. On 8th October, riding roughshod over the contract, he informed Irène Némirovsky that he was no longer prepared to publish her next novel and he graciously relinquished the 30,000 francs already agreed before war broke out: the price of betrayal. She took exception and suggested postponing publication until times were better, and using her former pseudonym of Nerey, as long as the publisher kept his word. Fayard retorted that it was a 'case of force majeure'.[54] 'So is there a law that prevents books by a Jewish writer from being published in the Free Zone?'[55] she protested, chilled at the thought of coping with winter without any income. Until early December she would have to battle to provide evidence for what she was entitled to and, faced with Fayard's grudging attitude, she was obliged to take the matter to the Société des Gens de Lettres. The dispute concerned the wording 'writers for newspapers', specified in the *Statut des Juifs*, a law that was as repugnant as it was slapdash. Did someone who contributed serialised extracts fit into this category? It was a semantic spat upon which the life of an entire family depended, issued on the pronouncement of some pen-pusher.

On 29th October, her back to the wall, the novelist opened her diary and wrote: 'Unbearable anxiety at times. The sensation of a nightmare. Don't believe in reality. Slender and absurd hope. If I could find a way just to get myself and my family out of the woods. Impossible for me to believe that Paris is lost. Impossible. The only solution seems to be "the man of straw", but I have no illusions about the difficulties that this crazy plan entails. Yet, we must.' She did not know that on that same day the legal adviser to the Société des Gens de Lettres had delivered his ruling, quite unequivocally: 'We cannot compare a great writer such as Irène Némirovsky, who is an independent and free person as far as the newspaper is concerned, with a journalist who is a non-manual employee, and the contract by which she assigns publication of a novel to a newspaper cannot be compared to a contract of employment.' It was straightforward advice, which Fayard insolently rejected, suggesting that the government should arbitrate! Severely admonished, the president of the Société, Jean Vignaud, who had backed the novelist in September 1939, was obliged to repudiate his legal adviser in humiliating terms: 'From experience,' he wrote to the novelist on 2nd December, 'I can affirm that for those contributors to our newspaper who are not professional journalists, that is to say novelists or storytellers, we have had to supply proof that these contributors – some of whom are well known – were neither foreigners, nor Jews.' Let us remind ourselves here of Jean Vignaud's solemn undertaking when he took up his duties in 1936: 'As to the material help we have agreed to bring to literature, so harshly affected by the crisis, I want to do what I can immediately.'[56] Four years had passed since then: an eternity. 'You tell me that I forget the situation in which we find ourselves,' the novelist wrote back to him. 'It is precisely because this situation is, for me alas, as for many others, tragic that I am fighting to protect my livelihood and that of my children. But I am beginning to think that this is impossible.'[57]

Irène Némirovsky's novel would not be published in *Candide*. And on 16th November, Jean Fayard would calmly express his thoughts on the new state doctrine he had anticipated so intuitively: 'Collaboration between peoples is the very sign of peace, just as work shared among men is the sign of life. How can we not prefer peace to war, life to death?'[58]

A lacemaker among the barbarians

Irène Némirovsky had persisted in trying to make Jean Fayard see reason: the stoneware casserole had clashed with the cast-iron pot. The *Revue des Deux Mondes* and *Marie-Claire* had not wished to return to Paris. But what about *Gringoire*, where she had not published anything since the defeat? Why had she not thought sooner of Horace de Carbuccia, an ideological weathercock, but a brilliant newspaper salesman? Was it guilt at having taken her last novel to *Candide*, in 1939? Or else because, since the defeat, *Gringoire* had rid itself of its recent qualms? In May, urging readers to become more involved, Henri Béraud again forecast that a German victory would lead to 'mass deportations' and the loss of 'human liberty'. Since the advent of Marshal Pétain, the tone had changed. Georges Mandel, whom the news desk had counted upon on 23rd May to 'destroy the fifth column', was accused on 1st August of 'scheming against the security of the State'. The anti-Semitic cartoonists Carb and Pafer stooped to anything to outdo one another. The collaborationists Laval, Déat and Doriot were portrayed as the betrayed heralds of peace; Jules Moch, Louise Weiss and Georges Boris, as warmongers. All three were Jews. On 26th September, the following catchphrase even appeared in a front-page cartoon that showed Marianne directing a band of hooked noses towards an ocean liner: 'Come on now, get out! France is no longer a land for stateless people.' And it maintained its allegiance to the man without whom this insanity would be illegal: 'Long live Pétain!'[59]

So it really was as a last resort that Irène Némirovsky, immersed in her problems with Fayard and torn by necessity, called upon Carbuccia's friendship. 'I firmly believe,' she told him, 'that if there is anything you can do for me you will do it . . . You alone, dear

Monsieur de Carbuccia, through your influence and the position you hold, can, should we wish it, intervene on my behalf with the government. I honestly do not know what the future holds: all paths appear blocked to me. It is so cruel and unfair that I can't help believing that I will be understood and that people will want to help me.' Horace de Carbuccia was not so influential that he could shield Irène Némirovsky from the decrees of Vichy, but he began by giving her a letter intervening on her behalf with the prefectural authorities of the Saône-et-Loire *département*, with the aim of making matters easier for her. Then, because he had never concealed his friendship for her, he agreed to publish her under a pseudonym: no fewer than eight stories from December 1940 to February 1942, as well as a novel, *All Our Worldly Goods* [*Les Biens de ce monde*], which would be published in April 1941. For the time being, Paul Epstein, who was living at Avenue Coquelin, would receive the payments.

'I always heard my father talk about her in terms of great affection,' Jean-Luc de Carbuccia recalls. 'When the Occupation struck France, he remained loyal to all his contributors. There were some, like Géo London, who had gone into hiding. He helped Henry Torrès's son get out of France. When the problem arose of Jews writing for the press, even in the Free Zone, Irène Némirovsky, who needed to earn her living, suggested to him that she use an assumed name, an "Aryan name". But my father, who had fought in the 1914 war, and who was a *maréchaliste* like the great majority of French people, considered that it would be shameful to give her a pseudonym just because of the pressure of the Occupation. They agreed that the byline for serialised extracts from her novel should read "by a young woman", because that was much more dignified.'[60] It was a barely concealed way of indicating who wrote it. And was it a means of laying in some ammunition should the situation be reversed? Carbuccia, in fact, would candidly admit to having allowed *Gringoire* 'to tease' the Jews in the southern zone 'who changed their names or had themselves baptised', and he would deny ever having mentioned the name of any unidentified Jew or Jewish convert unless it had first been mentioned by the *Officiel* 'or by some *Semaine religieuse*'.[61] A narrow-minded attitude that makes his support of Irène Némirovsky all the more surprising, but a 'great affection' has little to do with logic.

The first story to appear in the new *Gringoire*, on 5th December 1940, under the byline of Pierre Nerey, was 'Destinées', which had probably been written since the summer. A second story would appear in March, 'La Confidente', which was begun in mid-November, without much enthusiasm. A well-guarded secret, a rekindled jealousy, a Machiavellian love affair, that was set in Issy, because it is against 'the little wall in front of the Simons' house'[62] that she chose to crash the car taking the opera singer Flora and her lover to their secret trysts. A subject that was safe, but 'very subtle, too much so, no doubt', since it was so delicate amid the noisy chauvinism of *Gringoire*. 'It would be,' she noted on 19th November, 'like a lace-maker among barbarians.'

The staff of *Aujourd'hui* was not made up of barbarians, but this easy-going daily with a circulation of a hundred thousand copies was blindly *pétainiste*. Its offices were in Place de l'Opéra, however, and that was all that mattered to Irène Némirovsky when, in November 1940, she believed that Paris was lost to her. Up until mid-November, *Aujourd'hui* was a dreary and jingoistic daily paper crammed with inept slogans ('France, her head is at Paris, her feet are at Vichy, but her heart is everywhere'),[63] in which anti-Semitism was reduced to its relevant importance and was even condemned.[64] Louis-Ferdinand Céline would actually accuse it of running 'a yid-loving campaign'![65] The editor, Henri Jeanson, did his best to preserve an apparent freedom of tone, without precluding regular sycophantic outbursts: 'To collaborate is to understand one another. To understand is to be intelligent,' *Aujourd'hui* proclaimed on 8th November. But the name of the graphic artist, who signed himself Bécan, was Kahn, and many of the writers were Jewish. Robert Desnos, who was deeply disappointed by the National Revolution, did not hesitate to criticise strongly the Vichyist 'response' and the 'Order that is euphemistically called moral'.[66] And in a daily column called 'Time for reading . . .', there were regular short stories by writers whose names meant nothing to anyone. It was to this newspaper, for which her admirer Maxence worked, that Irène Némirovsky saw fit to submit a story, entitled 'La Peur', that December. She was certainly unaware that Henri Jeanson, who was no longer in favour, had been obliged to hand over to Georges Suarez, a fanatical pro-German and a determined anti-democrat, and this was no doubt the reason why

'La Peur' would not be printed in *Aujourd'hui*, since the manuscript was returned to the author, with the word 'uncensored' stamped on it.

'La Peur' was based on a real event: two neighbours 'who think that each other is a spy', one of whom kills the other under cover of fog. Irène Némirovsky's first idea was 'a gloomy Zola-like farming community': a peasant who kills his son, who had been discharged from the army, having mistaken him for a burglar. A story 'that hit just the right note', then. To allay any censorship it was signed 'C. Michaud', as was 'Les Cartes'. This was a veiled allusion to Pushkin: a wealthy dancer, having drawn the queen of spades at tarot, is shot coming out of the casino by her maid, who is dismissed for being suspected of the murder. The moral: one never escapes one's fate. This simple little story, which took Irène Némirovsky back to her early work, nevertheless caused her a good deal of strain: 'Great God! What a fuss for such an insignificant and almost desperate effort! What are people talking about in Paris? If only one knew.' In Issy-l'Évêque, she had the feeling that she was losing touch with the latest fashions, that she was no longer able to set her stories in the present day. Exactly as if there had been no war.

Dies Irae

A novel about the war? She thought about it, of course, but only 'if freedom of expression is still possible', for 'nothing is safe, at the moment'. She had certainly not given up the idea of writing her big book about the Jews, but it went without saying that she could not devote herself to it unless a total censorship drove her to do so, and unless she was dying of hunger: conflicting conditions. And so, bolstered by Carbuccia's support, and without precluding the possibility of submitting it to him, she preferred her first idea: a large tableau of the chaotic collapse, which she had just recently sketched out in 'Le Spectateur' and 'Monsieur Rose', in which she would depict 'the struggle between the individual and the community'.

In November 1940 she found herself able to plan the three sections of this 'novel for better times', without ruling out the possibility of

publishing it under a pseudonym. The title would be taken from the
Apocalypse: *'Dies Irae'*. Alas, this was the title of an old novel by 'that
bitch' Camille Santerre! The first part would therefore be called *Panique*,
or *Tempête*, since Zola had used *La Débâcle*. The subject would be identical furthermore: a fictionalised report on the collapse of France,
defeated by the power and proficiency of the enemy, but also by the
extent of her own corruption, her selfishness, and by individual acts
of cowardice. And if examining such matters made one a supporter of
Marshal Pétain, then Zola would have been one too, for his portrait
of France on her knees was scarcely less gloomy! She would also have
to ascertain whether any other uncensored writer had not had the same
idea, though she doubted it: 'The chaotic collapse would be a big book
like *La Mousson* [*The Rains Came*], these few days in June, experienced
by many people. But I have the feeling that, either it will be impossible,
or else, *people will feed upon it.'** In any case, who could tell whether the
war might not be over in six months' time? Then, she imagined, 'it will
be like the other war, we shall want to forget that we've been unhappy,
especially unhappiness like this, this shame. And we shall prefer to split
hairs . . . But these considerations are secondary, particularly at a time
when, as now, I fear I may not be published any more.'

The Rains Came. Did Irène Némirovsky discover this long novel when
it was first published in America in 1937, or did she wait for the film by
Clarence Brown (1939) and the French translation in March 1939? Louis
Bromfield's fine novel, which was a huge success in bookshops, took
as its pretext the earthquake and cataclysmic floods that devastated
Ranchipur in 1936 – causing as many deaths as the defeat in May 1940
– in order to uncover the lives of a hundred characters who are deli-
cately superimposed and are then hurled to the ground like a house of
cards. A jumble of Hindus, Muslims, settlers, English financiers, missionaries and untouchables, adventurers and femmes fatales, masters and
slaves stripped in a flash of all the characteristics of their caste by a
gigantic wave of mud that drops from the skies. It was an ambitious
700-page novel, which she proposed to match: 'Bromf. also wanted to
create a panorama of the eternal India at the beginning and the end,
just as I want to create a panorama of France.' Whence the title, *Tempête*
[*Storm*]: the lightning defeat of 1940 was merely a climactic aberration,

*In English in original text. [Tr.]

a verdigris* squall that blew down in a flash a social structure that was shakier than it had appeared. Like Renoir's 1939 film, *La Règle du jeu*, in some ways, but which took place beneath the driving rain: the proud humbled, hypocrisy exposed, talents suddenly freed, but also an unexpected number of individual acts of bravery, displays of honour and love freely given. What material! What human clay! Until then, Irène Némirovsky had endeavoured to pour scorn on wealthy bankers, smug parvenus or shady politicians, without knocking them off their pedestals; this time she wanted to cast them into a cauldron of fear and absurdity, to besmirch them along the roads of the exodus, to make them rub shoulders unwillingly with the race of untouchables, servants, prostitutes and simple people, until they say: 'How grotesque we must look!'[67]

Irène Némirovsky did not leave herself out of her gallery of flayed victims:

> Peasants, people from the upper middle class, officers, Jewish intellectual refugees, politicians, old people who are forgotten, those whom one professed to respect, and whom one abandons like dogs, mothers who display boundless endurance and self-centredness in order to protect their kids. Those who strut around and chicken out alternately, young people who are battered but not downcast. What fun it would be: that and *the Jews*, what fun it would be! The way things are going, they would be posthumous books, but still. And then, it's easy: normal life, the beginning of May, the crisis, the end, and of course, because otherwise it would be bleak, the perenniality (I think that's what it's called?) of certain values. A lot of room must be made for children for whom this will certainly be enriching, just as the Russian revolution once was for me.

In fact, she had long dreamed of writing her own *War and Peace*, a multi-layered composite of historical events and small upsets linked by what she referred to in 1938 as '*a maze*':** 'some event or other that happens to be at the centre, but, before getting there, the reactions of all those who, however you look at it, take part in the tragedy'. In April 1940, she planned a 'documentary' about the rising perils, which she

Les vert-de-gris was a term used to denote German soldiers during the Second World War. It referred to the colours of their uniforms. [Tr.]
**In English in original text. [Tr.]

would have called 'Notre temps': 'Rambling pages, the ship full of Jews, a children's first communion in a village, Munich, the battlefields of China, of Spain, of France . . . The first day of the 39 war, the Lambeth Walk, the entry of German troops into Vienna and Prague.' It was shelved, due to the hard times. As for the Russian revolution, her memory for precise detail was failing her. Whereas the astonishing spectacle of the Exodus was still on everyone's mind. What bitter comfort it would be to attire these millions of French men and women in the threads of the *heimatlos*, or rootless people, who had been migrating through her books since 1930! What a selfish pleasure, in the general stampede, to condemn the bastards and to comfort the minions! What better medicine, in fact, for forgetting the humiliations endured over the past five months, than to turn them into literature? 'Of course, even though I've lived in the middle of it, God has protected me, and I've seen nothing of that. Then, it's less spectacular than *La Mousson*, but it's fairly easy to imagine the bombing etc. I must show the masses especially. They must be the true hero, the masses of people who suffer without understanding, and their basic feelings of hunger, of anger, of fear. Those who die without knowing why. The horrible waste of men, the squandering of all these forces.' And no love story: 'it's too Hollywood'.

Light and shade

And thus began *Tempête*, the account of the Exodus which Irène Némirovsky anticipated would extend from 8th to 20th of June 1940, without omitting the bombing of Paris on Monday the 3rd in the opening pages. This colossal project ('Oh, but to write these two novels properly, I'll need freedom and ten years of assured life!') was to keep her busy up until the end of the winter, working day and night, since a flask of valerian on her bedside table was evidence of her insomnia. As soon as the pages, drawn from Irène's imagination and covered in minuscule handwriting were ready, Michel typed them out; although he scrutinised them ruthlessly, it was purely from an artistic standpoint. Over a few days in November, the principal characters evolved, some of them were contemptible, and these she relegated to the 'shadows', the others were admirable, and she consigned them to 'the daylight'. For 'when, in a story or a novel, you highlight a hero or an event, you impoverish history; the complexity, the beauty, the depth of the reality depend on those countless bonds that link one man to another, one life to another life, a joy to a sorrow'.[68] This was the simultaneous method, attempted by Zola in his *La Débâcle*.

The first to appear was a politician, 'a stout and important character, in the Herriot mould', accompanied by a 'silly little goose of a mistress'. A man who is 'accustomed to crowds, to public meetings, who made his plans for Europe on paper and was incapable of coping to begin with', but who would always fall on his feet. In order not to add to the timely and relentless attacks on the deposed hierarchy of the Republic, these 'stereotypes of awfulness', Irène Némirovsky replaced him along the way with a well-to-do intellectual, even though it seemed unlikely to her that a man of this kind, like her Corte, should find himself on the road that June: an affected and condescending writer, bloated with vanity, who from his Aventine Hill observes the foul wave of plebeians who are streaming through France. 'Oh, the ugliness, the vulgarity, the horrible crudeness of these people!'[69] The wretched fellow would have to descend to their level, but he maintains his privileged position and instinctively adopts the new manner of speaking, the guarantee of his survival: 'The day of these hedonists, these political wheeler-dealers is over . . .'[70] This acrobat of opportunism, a regular contributor to 'an important Parisian magazine',[71] clearly bears all the distinctive features of André Chaumeix, whose *Revue des Deux Mondes* was now the faithful echo of Pétainist propaganda. In this connection, Marshal Pétain's head of cabinet would recall that Chaumeix paid frequent friendly visits to the Hôtel du Parc, the Marshal's headquarters in Vichy.[72] But Corte, hoist by his own petard, would nevertheless bear out his own maxim: 'In a novel, there is nothing more valuable than teaching the lesson of humility to the heroes.'[73]

The second character from the shadows to withstand Irène Némirovsky's 'monsoon' is none other than the refined collector whom she had successively drowned then revived in two stories from 1939 and 1940. She christened him Langelet, for this chubby *rentier* conceals a demon and a false apostle. Mischievously, she gives him the passionate interests of one of her most attentive readers: the lawyer Pierre Lœwel,[74] the former anti-Munich columnist for *L'Ordre* and great lover of porcelain! Like Louis Bromfield's Miss Hodge, all that Langelet can think about after the ordeal is to check his vases and soup bowls:

'Were there any breakages? Was the tea-set broken?'[75] And, like Corte, he is nauseated at having to be sullied by 'the dregs from Belleville';[76] he had imagined himself more as Pliny the Elder, fleeing the clouds of ash from Vesuvius and taking with him, concealed in his tunic, some rare statuette or 'a bowl modelled on a beautiful breast'.[77] The supreme irony is that it was at Gien* that Irène Némirovsky shattered this statuette and revealed his well-concealed hypocrisy. 'He couldn't be Jewish,' she explains, 'but the absolute intellectual, books, "spiritual values", etc., he leaves a liberal and returns a convinced Hitlerite.' It has been said that the word 'Jewish' does not appear in *Suite Française*. Yet it occurs twice, and it is Langelet who mentions it first, 'with a scornful smile' on the subject of those who had run away to Portugal or South America.[78] Irène Némirovsky would cast this fine fellow beneath the wheels of a car. His death symbolises, she wrote in the margin of the manuscript, 'the end of the liberal bourgeoisie'.

Still among the shadows, there are a couple of upper middle-class Parisians, the Péricands, along with their many offspring and domestic staff. They are loosely modelled on the Deschamps, who were friends of the Epsteins in Paris. The very opposite of the Hardelots in *All Our Worldly Goods*, they are the epitome of 'the Catholic, conservative family', dragging behind them a doddering, but wealthy old man, to whom Irène Némirovsky had originally given the features of her grandpapa Iona, 'or preferably not', she reconsidered, 'a very rich old man, who is fawned upon, feared, etc., and who is now considered to be a burden'. At their first stop on the Exodus, Mme Péricand, who clutches her money and her jewellery to her breast, would soon forget her catechism and reveal the 'bare, arid soul' of a predatory mother: 'She and her children were alone in a hostile world. She needed to feed and protect them. Nothing else mattered any more.'[79] Irène Némirovsky was only mocking hypocrisy here, not true charity; she was simply observing that a great danger is enough to wipe away centuries of civilisation and piety, and that brutish impulses smoulder beneath polite behaviour. This is in fact the lesson of *Tempête en juin* [*Storm in June*]: savagery only threatens human societies when they attain their highest degree of sophistication, that is to say when they are at their least attentive. 'Panic obliterated everything that wasn't animal instinct, involuntary

*A town on the Loire, well known for its porcelain. [Tr.]

physical reaction.'[80] Witness the Péricands' cat, a creature that lives in a flat, which is suddenly let out into the wild night and is exhilarated by the hitherto unknown smell of blood. What Irène Némirovsky, in her drafts, refers to as 'the pure joy' is nothing but innocent cruelty.

The final character from among the shadows is a real 'bastard': Joseph Koehl himself. This man, a financier, is supposed to shoulder the full weight of betrayal. And, so as to remove any ambiguity, his bank will be located on the Avenue de l'Opéra, just like the Pays du Nord. But Irène Némirovsky did not 'see' Koehl. What's more, she was 'sick of businessmen' . . . Only two unscrupulous and lacklustre bankers remain in the novel, the Comte de Furières and Corbin. It is from the latter that the accountant Michaud receives a repellent letter, dated 25th July, informing him of his dismissal in terms fairly similar to those used by Koehl himself to get rid of Michel Epstein in the near future. And for the same reason: leaving his post.

Maurice Michaud is too well acquainted with human nature to be shocked or to arm himself against a sea of troubles for 'it's just been our bad luck to have been born in a century full of storms',[81] and the storm was deaf and blind. His wife does not philosophise in this way: she is a mother and her son is reported missing. Together, they form the 'middle-aged couple' whom Irène Némirovsky has placed in the daylight, because instead of taking away with them a manuscript, museum pieces, jewellery and household linen, they think only of their Jean-Marie. Whereas Mme Péricand, in her flight from the bombing, was able to forget her grand-father. They, the Michauds, do not revert to animal behaviour: they form part of the small number of people, inveterate survivors, who are the stuff of this novel. They are simply unaware that their child is alive, some-where on a farm in Burgundy, in the hamlet of Labarie,[82] lovingly watched over by two farm-girls who speak in dialect, and who were inspired by Louise V. from Issy, but who are secretive and 'securely double-locked'[83] like a peasant's cupboard. One of them is called Cécile, because 'my big Néné must be immortalised'; the other, Madeleine, because Irène Némirovsky had been thinking again about her friend of twenty years ago whom she thought she had unfairly neglected. 'But in these sad times we are living through, we remember our old friends and should like to know that they are all in good health . . .', as she wrote to her on 4th December, so as to renew their friendship.

One final character from the daylight had not initially been foreseen, and yet he is the central figure in this novel, rather as Ransome, the 'slightly weary juvenile lead', was in *The Rains Came*. Irène Némirovsky might not have given him such prominence were it not for this laconic inter-zonal card, posted on 22nd October from Busséol in the Puy-de-Dôme, informing her of the tragic death of Father Bréchard. Irène loved 'the handsome face' of the man she referred to affectionately as 'Godfather'. 'He lived in a manner that was above that of other men,' she wrote to his parents, 'and he died in the same way. I loved and respected him greatly, for he was a true saint.'[84] The priest, who was a lieutenant in the 613th Régiment de Pionniers, was killed on the morning of 20th June, defending the village of Ménil-Tillot in the Vosges, at the head of two sections of his company, confronted by four German armoured cars and thirty or so tanks. 'Some people have said that he took the place at the machine-gun of a soldier who was a father of three,' reported Henri Pourrat, the great novelist of the Auvergne countryside; 'others that having seen one of his men, a family man, wounded, he immediately went to his aid. What is certain is that everyone was of the same opinion, that he had sacrificed himself.'[85]

'Godfather' had been shot full in the face while he was dressing a soldier's wounds. He was found with a crucifix on his lips. He was buried at Ménil, but Irène Némirovsky was to have several masses said in his memory at Issy-l'Évêque, and another in *Tempête*, where he appears undisguised beneath the features of the athletic Father Péricand, a priest from the Puy-de-Dôme, a frustrated missionary, a skier and a hill-walker, just like his model. Why worry, 'since it would only appear, if it appears at all, in peaceful times, or under a pseudonym'? But in November 1940, Irène Némirovsky did not yet know about these terrible details, which she would only be told about nine months later. And this is the reason why, in the early draft of *Tempête*, Philippe Péricand does not die in battle, as he does in a later version, but beneath a hail of stones thrown by his young orphans, who have reverted to a wild state, like dogs that become wolves again. This is also why, in this posthumous homage, he is not merely a dynamic priest, but also a fervent proselytiser, incapable of confronting evil, and literally possessed by 'the desire to gather liberated souls around him, a ripple of urgency which, once he had opened someone's heart to God, propelled him towards other conquests, leaving him forever frustrated, dissatisfied, disappointed with himself'.[86] Did this mean that Irène Némirovsky, two years after her baptism, had the feeling of having been trapped like a fish in the nets of this 'furious fisherman', and transferred to the credit column of the account book of the Catholic Church? Yes, though this did not for a moment undermine her need to believe.

Too pure for the shadows, too ambiguous to cope with full daylight, Father Péricand is the crucified figure of *Suite Française*. He has even experienced temptation, that of abandoning these recalcitrant 'children of Satan'.[87] And it is standing up, his arms held out in a cross, blinded in one eye, with stones and insults raining down on him, that he sinks into the muddy water, like a mocked Christ.

Like a bird waits for a snake

On 21st November 1940, Irène Némirovsky was able to write the first – provisional – sentence of her *Tempête*: 'The clothes and the gas masks had been put away in the small, gloomy room that smelled of mothballs and was used as a walk-in cupboard by the youngest children in the family. The winter, the first since war was declared, was over . . .' Should she cross the demarcation line? She thought less and less about it. In any case, a German decree had made it illegal from now on for Jews who had crossed over into the southern zone to come back to the north, where it was reckoned they would constitute a threat to the occupying forces. Should she go into self-imposed exile? She did not want to be uprooted a second time. 'I have put neither my person, nor my hope outside the soil of France,' Pétain had said. Very well, neither would she! It would not be said that Irène Némirovsky had left France. In Paris, Samuel Epstein was of the same view: 'I have run away enough in my life.' And how would she be able to consult her Paris eye specialist? Move home, why not, but within the northern zone, and in a house that provided a minimum of comfort, as she explained with a touch of self-mockery three days before Christmas to Madeleine, who had taken shelter in a village in the Loir-et-Cher:

> We live in the middle of nowhere like you, with the same inconveniences (deadly boredom, seclusion), and the same priceless advantages, heating and excellent food. But you have one additional advantage because you live in comfort while we live in a small village inn, which is very clean,

but that's all. My daughter Élisabeth, who is three and a half years old, does not know what running water, a lift, etc. are, what's more she's none the worse for it. The elder one goes to the village school. She is only eleven, and it's all right, but the situation must not go on for ever, otherwise she'll only be fit to look after the cows, and since I do not have any cows unfortunately . . .

Bravado? Recklessness? Irène Némirovsky was accustomed to danger, for she had experienced the Kiev pogrom, the Russian Revolution and the Finnish civil war. She had not been frightened. 'I never knew peaceful times,' she explained on the radio in 1934, 'I've always lived in anxiety and often in danger. Well, in spite of everything, I lived the life of a normal young girl, I worked, I read as I do now . . .'[88] Nothing had changed. Shut away in her bedroom at Issy-l'Évêque, she reread Tolstoy, Pushkin and Byron. As she finished the writing of *All Our Worldly Goods*, she tried to analyse the collapse of Parisians threatened by the bombing: 'They waited, without real fear, but with curious fascination, like a bird waits for a snake. You can't run away, but the danger seems too unbelievable. You can't understand it; you can't imagine it.'[89] And furthermore, she had decided to set *Dolce*, the second volume of her *War and Peace*, in Issy-l'Évêque: her village on German time.* Like Chekhov, she would 'sit in the face of the truth, watching it steadily, for a long time, without making any move to chase it away, looking at it so closely that it [would] eventually lose all shape, melt into a sort of mist, dissolve and disappear'.[90] As a novelist Irène Némirovsky possessed the caustic gift of observation to the highest degree. No semblance of virtuousness, courage or harmonious family life could withstand her patient gaze. Her work is a graveyard of lost illusions and undisguised vanity, revealed in Rosine Kampf's mirror: 'I look such a fright . . .'[91] Henri de Régnier, in 1930, had recognised this basic motivation of her genius: 'the interest is stronger than the aversion'.

As the harsh Burgundy winter drew in, she was warmed by an unexpected source of heat: a letter from André Sabatier, who had

---

*A reference to Jean-Louis Bory's novel *Mon village à l'heure allemande*, which won the Prix Goncourt in 1945. The title is a reminder that clocks were set at German time. [Tr.]

returned safe and sound from the Armée du Levant, where, he informed her on 11th December, he had had to 'serve a considerable amount of extra time'. On his return to his office in Rue Huyghens, he naturally took up his role as Irène Némirovsky's editor and friend once more. How could he refuse such support? After the German decree of 12th November, concerning 'the Jewish influence in the economy', the publishing house lived in fear of being placed under the control of an 'administrative manager'. Albin Michel was suspected of being unable to provide certificates of his Aryan roots . . . But the danger passed. The first thing Sabatier did was to persuade Esménard to continue paying Irène Némirovsky's monthly amounts as best he could throughout 1941, if necessary having them cashed by Paul Epstein. The novelist immediately mentioned *La Vie de Tchekhov*, Veresaev's *Pouchkine*, translated by Michel, *All Our Worldly Goods* and also *Tempête*, in a round-about manner, for she was counting on making a visit to Paris shortly – her first since the Occupation – to talk to him more freely about her financial difficulties and her plans. What would his reaction be, for example, to a 'suitably pitched history of *romantik* love', which would be entitled *Le Souffle du Seigneur*?

Sabatier reacted eagerly to the idea of *Pouchkine*; he was probably unaware that a translation already existed, and that Michel had thus worked in vain.[92] There could be no question of publishing *Tempête* yet, but he nevertheless sent her books and newspapers – a collection of *Paris Match* from December 1938 to June 1940 – by way of documentation. As for the *Tchekhov*, it was already scheduled for 1942, illustrated with rare documents that Sabatier had suggested obtaining through the intermediary of the famous dancer Serge Lifar, who was born in Kiev in 1905, was grand master of the Opéra de Paris, and who was on good terms with the Occupation powers; at the time, however, the USSR was still allied to the Third Reich. Meanwhile, Irène Némirovsky suggested, could Sabatier not find a way of announcing the publication of *Tchekhov*? 'That would please me greatly, I must admit, because the people I'm dealing with would then see that I am not "taboo",' she wrote to him on 9th January.

She found the Vichy propaganda tedious, especially the same old chauvinistic broadcasts on the national wavelengths: 'I suppose that French radio is designed to please children.' As for the patriotic loggorhoea of the National Revolution, its constant invocation of the values of order and obedience, its use of the mystique of the képi, and the religious cult of the leader, they prompted increasing distrust. 'Issy-l'Évêque. 12 January 41. They speak of the national community: it will be the age of exacerbated individualism . . . when one man, or two or three at the most, lead the world. The whole question is – of knowing how far the world will allow itself to be led as usual – and, above all: whether we shall be there to see the end of the business.' And yet, 'experience shows that the terrible upheaval that we experienced in June does not allow the individual to survive. Nothing but great flurries from the back of time. But, no doubt fragments of the individual remain.' So from January to April 1941, Irène Némirovsky fine-tuned the individual characters of her novel, hinting here and there at a secret rivalry between Cécile and Madeleine, and at an embrace between 'the little tart' Arlette and Hubert, the Péricands' rebellious son, who is thrown into the midst of the battle for Moulins just as Fabrice del Dongo is at Waterloo in Stendhal's *La Chartreuse de Parme*. But there was little love in the bundles borne by the June refugees.

On 23rd February, the novel was given its final title: *Tempête en juin*. On the same day she drew a large map of the Massif Central on a page of the manuscript, so that she could follow the wanderings of her heroes more closely. Issy-l'Évêque features in the upper corner. This aide-mémoire did not prevent her from making a few mistakes along the way; Corte's arrival at Tours, for example, and his waking up the following morning at Paray-le-Monial*. . .

On 2nd April, a first draft of *Tempête* was completed that was unsatisfactory to her mind: 'How wretched everything seems on rereading it. It's very funny: there are things like "Destinées" that I write effortlessly, or rather, without wanting to do them very well, simply for the money, and which I like when I reread them. And others into which I put my heart and soul . . .' One thing reassured her, however: the Exodus did not appear to have inspired many writers, apart from Colette, whose *Journal à rebours* had just been published by Fayard. Here we find, under the heading 'Late June 1940', a succession of

*Paray-le-Monial is 300km from Tours! [Tr.]

snapshots, not nearly enough with which to construct a novel, and so intermingled that they became cubist:

> The cattle trucks, the hay carts, the large motor-cars wreathed in dust, the wheelbarrows and the open wagons stretched on, beyond the distant line of mountains, the regions darkened by the blue foliage, the fields of ripe grass in which every blade was covered by a cluster of people asleep, a car decked with mattresses, a sleeping child rolled up in a towelling dressing gown, a pair of doves in a cage, a fox terrier tied to a tree, a young girl clasping a man's jacket around her; across the five hundred kilometres of roads that covered a dishevelled France that was collapsing into herself, a credulous, forgetful weariness rid me of any illusion . . .[93]

'If that's all she could get out of June,' Irène Némirovsky was glad to note, 'I'm not worried. But perhaps, in my case, there's too much horror . . .' As for *Dolce*, for which she was beginning to draw up a framework, she merely had to open her eyes to imagine the scenes. On the morning of 24th April, for example, the arrest of two 'soldiers' taken prisoner by the Germans. 'They were given a quarter of an hour to get ready.' It was a bleak omen. And yet the dozen or so Germans staying at the Hôtel des Voyageurs were still as charming and courteous. There were just more of them.

The earth does not lie

The kindness of Carbuccia and Sabatier, a sudden plethora of projects, and the fact that she was gradually becoming used to the inconveniences, had given Irène Némirovsky new heart. For sure, money was short. The tax authorities were harassing the Epstein household. The rent on the Avenue Coquelin flat had not been paid for months, and the landlord was refusing to lower it. The monthly payments from Albin Michel only reached Issy haphazardly. But for her birthday on 24th February, her daughters reminded her of their most precious asset, which was one they had in abundance:

> *Malheureusement, en ce moment,*
> *Le cœur est riche et les sous rares.*

Pour remplacer ces beaux présents
Reçois donc, notre chère maman,
Un don encore beaucoup plus rare:
*Les bons baisers de tes enfants!**

Kisses do not cast the clouds aside. In early April, Denise's sudden attack of peritonitis became a nightmare: since Dr Benoît-Gonin said he was unable to do anything, they were obliged to take her, in a gazogene-fuelled vehicle, to Luzy, where a surgeon agreed to operate in the middle of the night, on a kitchen table! 'You can imagine the turmoil,' wrote her greatly relieved mother to Madeleine Cabour, entreating her more than ever to find her vacant lodgings close to Beaugency, ideally 'a house with three or four bedrooms, furnished, with a garden and the possibility of it being heated in winter'.[94] Irène set further conditions: proximity to a doctor and a chemist, and supplies of meat and butter to feed the children. And above all, no occupying troops! Alas, the rented accommodation spotted by Madeleine at Jailly, in the Nivernais, two hours by road to the north, was not vacant until September. As for the only house available in Issy, it contained no fewer than fourteen rooms and the owner demanded a nine-year lease.

Would she have to put up much longer with the stench of tobacco from 'these gentlemen' that rose up in clouds from the ground floor of the inn?

For want of anything better, Irène Némirovsky was forced to observe these humdrum surroundings, in order to recreate them with 'perfect objectivity' in a series of realistic stories produced in the early spring of 1941, in a style that was closer to Maupassant than to Chekhov. Here, to begin with, is the Loctins' café, drawn from life one Sunday towards the end of March:

Lit with that particular light of cold spring days, a bright greyness that chills the soul, a downcast, shivering greyness. On the horizon, above the sloping grey roofs, that faint orange glimmer. Each time the door is opened it lets in a blast of very cold, very pure air, and a smell of damp lilac and milk,

---

*At the moment, unfortunately, the heart is rich and pennies are few. So instead of these fine presents, accept, dearest Mama, a gift that is richer by far: the loving kisses of your children! [Tr.]

because this is the time they milk the cows (?). The bell summons people
to prayers. At two tables they are playing tarot. Large, ruddy figures, well
fed. Strong, dirty hands that can't be washed so much has the earth worn
into the fissures. On the ground, the floor is made up of tiles (each one
containing the image of a flower that looks like a lily). Beams on the ceiling.
From the kitchen nearby comes the chatter of women who shout very
loudly to cover the noise of the butter that is cooking . . . The air smells of
damp lilac and milk and a very light aroma of fresh bread, because it's
Sunday and the restrictions have not yet affected the countryside. But
perhaps I ought not to mention that. The stove that has not been lit since
the beginning of the month . . . Its smell of cold soot. The marble tables,
the glasses of red wine, the grey and brown tile shaped like a cold, slippery
mosaic. Let's see what comes of that!

Out of that came 'L'Honnête Homme', which *Gringoire* published on
30th May, under the pseudonym of Nerey. It is a gloomy story, in which
we see an old skinflint, M. Mitaine, disinherit his son because he suspects
him of having stolen from him, just as he himself had robbed his own
father when he was young. The moral of the story comes from Joseph
de Maistre: 'I do not know what is felt in the heart of a rogue, but I
understand the heart of an honest man, and it is terrifying.'[95] Irène
Némirovsky explores two of her favourite themes here: inherited vice
and 'the fear that begets the phantom'. Most of all, having come to know
the peasant people of Issy, who were thrifty and hardworking, but also
'discreet, wary, [and had] everything securely double-locked',[96] she could
view the Issy countryside without blinkers. She came to regard the French
peasant as Chekhov did Tolstoy's pure muzhiks: 'There were some gentle,
resigned characters among them, the eternal victims . . . But, in the main,
what stubbornness, what bestiality, what a harsh and wretched life!'[97]
We come across these themes again in 'La Voleuse', a story set at
the Montjeu farm, a former manor house that has fallen to rack and
ruin in the hands of its new owners, wily and money-grabbing peasants, who have turned it into a hovel. Young Marcelle, the family's
adopted granddaughter, has stolen some money. No one is surprised:
her mother was a farm-girl who had been dismissed for stealing a
brooch. In actual fact, the child has hidden her spoils, so as to make
her suspicious grandmother feel ashamed once her innocence is revealed.
The revenge is worthy of *Le Bal*! Marcelle does not know, however, that

her mother was not a thief, but the victim of a jealous plot. No matter, she has inherited the curse. The story – which was unpublished – abounds with real names and, one senses, from a series of familiar observations – 'murmur of melting snow flowing between two stones; billing and cooing of pigeons on the roof; joyful capering of hens in the neighbouring field and the slow cot-cot-cot of the happy fowls pecking at their grains, while a tousled snow-white feather gently rises and falls again' – that Irène Némirovsky jotted down these sketches at the Montjeu farm.

Two other stories from this period are simply potboilers. 'L'Ogresse', written under the inscrutable pseudonym of Charles Blancat, revives memories of the casino at Plombières, and most probably of Léon Ponzio, the baritone from Nice, who is here cast as an elderly failed actress forcing her daughter to rebuild her ruined dreams, like Saturn devouring his offspring, for 'there is nothing more dangerous than a woman's unsatisfied desire'.[98] It would appear in *Gringoire* a few months after *All Our Worldly Goods*, 'an unpublished novel by a young woman' the serialisation of which would keep the reader on tenterhooks from 10th April until 20th June. It is, by far, the longest novel she had written, for 'monsieur de Carbuccia' was not as lavish as he was before the war. Thirty chapters, three decades of French history, dozens of characters, long, patient, fulsome sentences that reflect the Hardelot family, who are always tested, but are never defeated. This, the name of a beach near Le Touquet, is the one Irène Némirovsky gives to the Avot family, on whom, from a distance of twenty years, she bestows an affectionate and mocking glance, one that is less concerned with the family's absurd-ities, but which is infinitely nostalgic and understanding. The Avot factories had, in fact, been completely destroyed by bombing in 1940.

All Our Worldly Goods has neither the diligence of *La Proie*, nor the emotive power of *The Wine of Solitude*, or the passion of *The Dogs and the Wolves*. But its very restraint is poignant. It is Irène Némirovsky's great classic novel. In it, she propounds the secret of France: the unfailing durability of the provincial bourgeoisie, which never allows itself to be broken up and resolutely confronts fate by way of births, marriages and legacies. Could it be that it was the peasant folk of Issy who, by contrast, made the qualities of the Avots, so distant in her memory, that much sharper in focus? From the outset, the theme is sententiously formulated: 'A good middle-class family should be large and hardy enough to stand up to death.'[99] And goodness, how determined death is! Begun before the fighting of 1940, the story ends in a clash of arms that is so deafening that it eventually drowns out every voice, as if she had recast *Deux* on a battlefield. Wonderfully controlled, the process which consists in expanding the perspective at the last moment reduces her characters to the size of microbes, in such a way that, having almost lost sight of them, she cannot prevent her novel celebrating the triumph of darkness. It is a short-lived triumph: 'We'll rebuild. We'll get through. We'll survive.'[100] It is by returning to the land to cultivate our own 'worldly goods' that we reap by the sweat of our brow. A Vichyist refrain? But the earth did not wait for Vichy to hate the lie.*

A new environment

In 'L'Ami et la Femme', a woman who is unfaithful to the memory of her husband, a pilot who died in a desert in Asia, throws herself down two flights of stairs in a suburban restaurant, just as Ida, the chorus-line leader from *Films parlés*, once did. This unpublished short story appears to have been written at the same time as *All Our Worldly Goods* was being planned: we actually find the same idiotic song written by Georges Milton which, with good reason, must have been buzzing around Irène Némirovsky's head:

> *T'en fais pas Bouboule!*
> *Pleure pas comme une moule*
> *Ne t'mets pas les nerfs en boule.*
> *Les tracas ça rend maboule . . .***

And what worries there were. In Europe, Germany was expanding on every front. Marshal Pétain spoke of collaboration with the enemy, but he had sacked his dauphin Pierre Laval, who had set this in

---

*An allusion to Marshal Pétain's speech of 25th June 1940: 'I hate the lies that have done you so much harm.' [Tr.]

**A loose translation might be: 'Don't be upset Bouboule!/Don't cry and be a drip/Don't let yourself become a bundle of nerves./Worry can drive people crazy . . .' [Tr.]

motion. Demanding action, the occupying power succeeded in having Pierre-Étienne Flandin, Laval's successor, replaced by a more zealous *fonctionnaire*, Admiral Darlan. In March 1941, a Commissariat for Jewish Affairs was entrusted to Xavier Vallat, an assiduous and methodical anti-Semite, who was given the responsibility of preparing a new *Statut des Juifs* that would be more restrictive and predatory than the first. Flourishing the spectre of 'collusion between the Jews, the English and the masons', Henri Béraud exhibited astonishing bad faith and coarseness in his efforts to legitimise hatred of the Jews, particularly since the words he used were all the more drastic for having been thought out: 'In a word, is it good, is it right, is it reasonable to call oneself anti-Semitic? Having asked myself the question, I reply: in all conscience, yes, one should be anti-Semitic.'[101]

Béraud even held forth in the pages of *Gringoire*, where *All Our Worldly Goods* was being serialised, exposing the journalists and politicians who were hiding under false names. Certain Parisian papers, such as *Le Pilori* or *Je suis partout*, specialised in the anti-Jewish diatribe, the *ad hominem* insult, denunciation, the call for murder and even genocide.[102] In the capital, flats owned by Jews who were 'absent from Paris' were requisitioned by strangers. Papers would arrive ratifying these assaults. And in a blustering pamphlet published that April, Lucien Rebatet, while castigating 'the theatre and cinema gangs', called for a pure and simple purging of the world of show business. And if he had to provide names: Delac, the co-producer of *David Golder*; Nozière, who adapted it; Duvivier, its director, who was married to a Jewess; and even 'a certain Némirowsky',[103] the owner of two Paris cinemas on the eve of the war . . . As for good old Harry Baur, because he had been unable to provide overwhelming proof of his '*aryanité*', he would be detained for several weeks by the Gestapo. It was as though there was a curse surrounding *David Golder*.

On 26th April, a German decree required French publishers to pay any sums due to Jewish authors into blocked accounts. Late payments from Albin Michel amounted to 24,000 francs at the time, and Irène Némirovsky hastened to have this paid to Paul Epstein. He received the payment on the very same day as the first big round-up of Jews in Paris, 14th May: three thousand seven hundred people were immediately taken to the internment-without-trial camps at Pithiviers and Beaune-la-Rolande, in the Loiret. A technocratic motive had been coined for the occasion: 'An excess number in the national economy'. On 2nd June, the new law governing the status of Jews was announced; it was more draconian than the previous one, and it gave a long list of proscribed jobs, from banker to forestry agent. A new census, a prelude to extermination, was required within a month; the Epsteins, biting their nails, complied stoically. Over the months, a whole catalogue of harassments would be added to this infamous proclamation, decreeing the times at which Jews were allowed to go out, imposing a curfew on them, excluding them from public places or stigmatising their shops – the main effect being that these shops would also be attacked by Parisians, who are always eager for a good tip-off!

But this apart, all was very well:* on 29th May, an 'aryanised' Banque des Pays du Nord was able to hold its first extraordinary general meeting since the defeat. The new chairman of the board, Charles-Albert de Boissieu, and the directors Koehl and Maizière attended. Their final report displayed deeply moving concern:

> The events that have taken place during the current financial year have brought a violent disruption in business trends . . . You will certainly wish to join us in warmly thanking our staff for the courage, dedication and selflessness they have manifested at every level. Thanks to them we have been able – at critical moments – to see through successfully an occasionally difficult clearance of our assets. We regret that a certain number of our colleagues have been captured. We believe you will approve of the benevolent steps we have taken on their behalf, which will allow their families to make use of the benefits that had been allotted to them during the mobilisation.

Not a word about the staff who had been dismissed, but let us take comfort: 'Since the end of the summer of 1940, a certain return to equilibrium is gradually manifesting itself in the affairs of our customers, who are slowly returning to employment in a new environment.' The net profit for the year: 11,451 million francs. As David Golder would say: 'Money was no object, in those days . . .'[104]

---

*Ray Ventura's celebrated song 'Mais à part ça, madame la marquise, tout va très bien' (1935) has become a symbol of French insouciance during the 1930s. [Tr.]

II

Hatred + Contempt
(1941–1942)

A man's eyes are only wide open when he is unhappy.
Anton Chekhov, *Notebooks*

'At the moment of failure, it is human instinct to erect invincible barriers of hope. A feeling of unhappiness must remove these barriers one by one, and only then failure finds its way into man, straight into his very heart. Then, little by little, man recognises his enemy, calls him by his rightful name and is horrified,'[1] wrote Irène Némirovsky in the first of her completed novels that she would not live to see in printed form.

The first of these barriers gave way at dawn on Sunday 22nd June 1941, crushed by the German tanks that had just crossed the Soviet frontier. Irène Némirovsky certainly had no liking for Moscow, but this turnaround threatened the equilibrium that made the German presence bearable in the village of Issy-l'Évêque, where Michel was able to take advantage of his friendship with Spiegel, Hammberger or Hohmann, soldiers who were not anti-Semitic. They were all expecting that, having been kept busy over the past year sounding the curfew, distributing delicacies and being pleasant to the civilian populations, the German soldiers would shortly be posted to the vast Eastern front. Who would replace them?

A bombshell

On the evening of the 21st, the officers, with the more or less voluntary help of the villagers, organised a big party beside the Étang-Neuf, in the grounds of the Château de Montrifaut, to mark the first anniversary of their arrival. It was only that night that these soldiers, who were just beginning to learn French and to adapt to their surroundings, would hear about the 'bombshell' of Operation Barbarossa, which Hitler

believed would lead to victory before the autumn. The party evolved
into drunken revelry. The explosion of champagne corks hailed the final
act of the war and the likely increase in fighting that everyone dreaded.

To think that the summer was expected to be fine. 'Unbelievable
heat,' Irène Némirovsky noted on 25th June. 'The garden is adorned
in June colours – sky-blue, pale green and pink. I've lost my pen. There
are still other anxieties such as the threat of the concentration camp,
the *Statut des Juifs* etc.' Not that she really feared being arrested:
after all, they didn't kill Jews in French camps! But who would look after
Denise? And whom would she inform about the special diet required
to treat Babet's attacks of enteritis? It was to meet such an eventuality that on the 22nd she wrote to Julie Dumot, at Marmande, asking
her to meet them as soon as possible. She left a large sum of money
with the village notary, as well as a letter in the form of a will, giving
her power of attorney:

> . . . When the money is used up, start by selling the fur coats that you
> will find in our suitcases, which you will certainly recognise . . . There is
> also quite a lot of fabric, all pinched from the Quai de Passy. If you are
> able to, keep the sable. There is also some silverware. Sell it after the furs
> and before the jewellery.   •
>
> Finally, in the very last extreme, there will be the manuscript of a novel
> at the Loctins' house which I may not have time to finish and which is
> called *Tempête en juin*.

As for the flat on Avenue Coquelin, she simply authorised her to 'flog'
it if the situation demanded. But why did she rely to such an extent
on Julie, whom she did not like very much and whom she had scarcely
seen in any case since Léon's death in 1932? Because Cécile was pregnant. And because Julie Dumot, who was fifty-six, single, and who
had returned to France in April 1940 after having lived abroad for a
long time, had nothing to do at the time. Furthermore, it was so that
they could move her in permanently to be with them that Irène and
Michel finally decided to rent the large house with four bedrooms,
on the Place du Monument aux Morts, which Monsieur Marius Simon
agreed to lease to them for 4,500 francs annually,[2] as from 11th
November. All that was lacking was firewood, a cooker and a few
pieces of furniture ordered from the joiner Billaut.

It was not too late, however, to cross over secretly into the southern zone where, apparently, 'they couldn't care less about the war' (28th June). 'They could have fled to Switzerland,' Cécile would say later; 'they didn't even try.'³ But Irène Némirovsky continued to depend on the Morands, on Benoist-Méchin and even Grasset who, in case of misfortune, would put in a word with the very courteous ambassador Otto Abetz. In a letter written beforehand, authorising Julie, should the need arise, to retrieve all her Paris furniture, the novelist puts this very point to her landlord's agent: 'I hope that this state of affairs will not last and that our influential friends will succeed in setting us free.' However, she dreaded the consequences of the 'bombshell' of 22nd June: intensification of the politics of collaboration – as illustrated that July by the creation of the Légion des volontaires français contre le bolchevisme – and nazification of the Occupied Zone with the utmost speed. She sensed moreover that by leaving her to grapple with the French authorities, these young, twenty-year-old soldiers, future casualties of war, would cause her to run a greater risk than she would have done under German jurisdiction. That is why, when Issy-l'Évêque learned that 'its' Germans were to be mobilised, Michel's first action was to arrange for Feldwebel Hammberger, their neighbour at the Hôtel des Voyageurs, to deliver to him a letter of recommendation that read as follows: 'We have lived with the Epstein family for a long time and we have known them to be a likeable and honest family. We request that you treat them accordingly. *Heil Hitler!*' One never knew.

The occupying troops left the village on 28th June. 'They had been downhearted for 24 hours, now they are gay, especially when they are together. The little darling said sadly that "the happy times are over". They are sending their parcels home. They are overexcited, that's obvious. Admirable discipline and, I think, deep down no rebelliousness. I make an oath here and now never to heap my grudges, however justified they may be, on to a body of men, whatever their race, religion, conviction, prejudices, wrongs. I feel sorry for these poor children. But I cannot forgive individuals, those who reject me, those who coldly drop us, those who are ready to play dirty tricks on you. Those people . . . if I could get my hands on them one day . . .'

Irène Némirovsky was thinking of Koehl, Boissieu, Vignaud and Fayard, of course, but also of 'l'État français', which she had been reminded of from a 'close reading' of *Le Journal officiel*. It was on

14th June, in fact, that the new 'law governing the status of the Jews', in which Article 5 prevented them from working as a 'writer, even as a local correspondent, in newspapers or periodicals' was published there. The information was ambiguous, and it meant that she would have to resort to silence or trickery. So in July she used the pseudonym 'Pierre Imphy', from the name of a small town in the Nivernais, as her byline for the first story she had written since 22nd June. In this pacifist fable, a French soldier discovers that the enemy he has killed was his half-brother, conceived during the occupation of the Rhineland, twenty years previously. The German's name was Franz Hohmann, a deliberate homage to the lieutenant who had become Irène and Michel Epstein's friend and who had set off either to court death or to cause it somewhere between Kiev and Moscow. '"L'Inconnu", a story written by a young woman' would be published in Gringoire on 8th August. As for Michel, once his 'protectors' had departed, he seized the first opportunity to write to the Kreiskommandantur at Autun on 30th July, enquiring how he should send Hohmann the watch he had left to be repaired 'in the vicinity of Issy-l'Évêque' . . .

Whilst, ever since May, several thousand Jews had been the victims of round-ups in the Occupied Zone, the Epsteins depended more than ever on the loyalty of the occupying forces. They were not necessarily wrong to do so: in July 1941, the mayor of Issy-l'Évêque, M. Cogny, was brutally relieved of his functions for an 'attitude contrary to the line of current conduct' and replaced by M. de Villette, the lord of the manor at Montrifaut, who was more conciliatory. In Dolce, Irène Némirovsky would disguise him as the pusillanimous Vicomte de Montmort, a reluctant collaborator, who imagines that he can shirk his duties, particularly since his wife is a fanatical supporter of the Marshal, is romantically anti-Semitic and a feudalist at heart, and because it is she who owns much of the cultivated land in the area. And this is why Montmort, in the last resort, 'licks the Germans' boots'.[4] At the same time, the local council of Issy, which had an SFIO (French Socialist Party) majority, had its authority terminated by the sub-prefect of Autun, and the gamekeeper was dismissed for 'having made insulting remarks about the person of the head of state'.[5] So Irène Némirovsky had been right: the politics of collaboration was beginning to make itself felt, and although there was an active core of Resistance workers in Issy under the Occupation – at the heart of which were Morlay, the patisserie shop owner, and Lacombre, the baker – the village also had its bunch of informers, at least one of whom was 'dedicated to the rule of the Maréchal', convinced that there were 'anti-nationalist activities', and would be tried and sent to prison for two years at the Liberation.[6]

It was in this gloomy atmosphere that Julie Dumot arrived in Issy-l'Évêque on 11th July 1941. For the girls, she would now take the role that had up till now been played by Cécile Michaud, whose name incidentally Irène Némirovsky crossed out as the author of her un-published stories 'Les cartes' and 'L'Inconnu'. The latter story, which is not as commonplace as it appears, features a novelist who is no longer fashionable, the victim of a persistent admirer who eventually pushes him into marriage. This man Driant, who 'fled Europe because he was repelled by the present-day world', is uncannily reminiscent of Paul Morand, but his name was also the actual patronymic of Captain Danrit (1885–1916), General Boulanger's son-in-law and the author of some ultra-nationalist novels that were successful in the early years of the century.

Irène Némirovsky hoped that because she could conceal her iden-tity under that of Julie, who was free to go to Paris or to publish under her own name, it would now be easier to place the results of the endless days she had spent writing. She had actually just begun to work on *Tempête* again. All that she needed in order to polish her novel and correct its errors, was a little documentation: '1) A very detailed map of France or a Michelin guide. 2) A complete set of French and foreign newspapers from between 1st June and 1st July. 3) A treatise on porce-lain. 4) The birds in June, their names and their songs.' On rereading it, she was struck to see that this teeming panorama of the defeat, whose complexity she reproached herself for, actually represented a cross-section of French society, and that it was not necessarily those she imagined who would emerge the stronger. 30th June: 'Persevere with the characters of the Michauds. Those who always pay the price and the only ones who are truly noble. Strange that the majority of them, the loathsome majority, should be made up in greater part of these good folk. They are none the better, nor are the others worse.'

There are two morals in *Tempête*: the first, which is worthy of La Fontaine, is that the hurricane can bring down a seventy-year-old regime, whereas the social hierarchy merely bends with the times and recovers more firmly; the second, that heroism is futile, but no more so than disgrace. On 24th July, Irène Némirovsky had just learned of the precise circumstances of 'Godfather's' death in June 1940, and all of a sudden the stoning of Father Péricand struck her as cruel, at once 'too melodramatic' and unworthy of his sacrifice. In the new chapter she then wrote, the priest would die just as pointlessly, but this time while giving first aid to a comrade wounded on the Vosges front. It was still a crucifixion, but his faith appeared to have been shaken by the horror unleashed, and death from a stray bullet was a rather pathetic sacrifice. So little blood and so much sin: for whom then did Father Péricand die?

The spirit of the hive

During the summer of 1941, Irène Némirovsky was able to contemplate the second section of her *roman-fleuve*. After the storm, which was *tempestuoso*, in *Dolce* she wanted to see how a French village adapted to the defeat, to what degree it pretended to acquiesce or to fraternise, and this village, Bussy-la-Croix, is none other, of course, than Issy-l'Évêque. The temporary setting was also ready made: the novel, which opens in the early spring of 1941, ends with the departure of the Germans for the Russian front and the reawakening of anti-German feelings that had been dormant or repressed since the beginning of the Occupation.

The real difficulty would lie in linking *Dolce* with *Tempête*. Mme Angellier, who embodies the invincible provincial bourgeoisie, could be 'Mme Péricand's sister'. The Vicomtesse de Montmort, who is steeped in Pétainism, could be involved with the Comte de Furières, the joint manager of the Banque Corbin. Arlette would once again be the 'instrument of fate'. And Corte? And Langelet? 'No! to be got rid of without loss . . .' In the final reckoning, not one character from *Tempête* would remain in *Dolce*. Bussy is merely the village where the Labarie sisters have taken in the soldier Jean-Marie, and where, as we shall discover through an unlikely coincidence, Mme Angellier has put up her parents during the Exodus. Links were retained, which should have made *Dolce* the springtime intermezzo of Irène Némirovsky's *Suite Française*.

Collusion, resistance or rebellion are a matter of circumstances and temperament; as the danger receded and spring drew to an end, the French would find themselves agreeing to hate the Germans. But it is possible to regret the fact that this atavistic instinct, which is more powerful than the temptations of love or universal harmony, should remain for ever insurmountable. *Dolce* generalises the theme of the incompatibility of races, 'these dark impulses of the blood' that neither the heart nor reason manage to control. 'Foreigner! Foreigner! Enemy, in spite of everything. For ever he would be the enemy.'⁷ This is the tragedy of Lucile Angellier, who is prevented by countless conventions and prejudices that are not of her making but are those of the society in which she lives, from yielding to the overtures of Lieutenant Bruno von Falk, who is not for a moment a Nazi. It was probably their idyll that Irène Némirovsky had planned to concentrate on under the title *Nuit et Songes*: 'And yet they could have loved one another, they could have been happy. It would need a lot of poetry, nature, music etc. I'm kidding myself. I know it's unpublishable. So why not leave it, in all honesty, "for afterwards"? That would be the only way.' But in *Dolce*, which was destined to be published after all, Lucile can only turn Bruno down; she cannot forget that he is a soldier: 'I'm told to go somewhere and I go. Told to fight, I fight. Told to get myself killed, I die.'⁸

This is the deeper meaning of the novel: the age of nationalism and the quick march, 'the spirit of the hive' as von Falk calls it, which aims to gather men together by force and not out of any natural fervour. Not only does it forbid bloodlines intermingling, but it creates feelings of repulsion in a young Frenchwoman such as this, who is in love with a German non-commissioned officer. Irène Némirovsky put a great deal of herself into the character of Lucile, who is so unaccustomed to strong political views that she consorts with both the German invader and the French murderer simultaneously. She, who is Jewish, stateless and outside the law, does not fit into any of the cells foreseen by the deeply entrenched ideology that was victorious from Madrid to Moscow. It is very much Irène Némirovsky's own pride that shines forth at the end of *Dolce*, a determined refusal to 'follow the herd', to merge her own destiny with that of France, which is easy to explain if one thinks of so many disappointed attempts to become part of the national community only to end up having the door closed on her by a decree such as the *Statut des Juifs*. 'I hate this community spirit they go on and on about,' says Lucile. 'The Germans, the French, the Gaullists, they all agree on one thing: you have to love, think, live with other people, as part of a state, a country, a political party. Oh, my God! I don't want to do that!'⁹ Was not this fierce individuality the reason for her own indifference to her Jewish roots? In 1938, Virginia Woolf described this as 'freedom from unreal loyalties'.*

Fire in the Blood

This theme of the 'struggle between individual destiny and the destiny of the community' would only manifest itself clearly in 1942, but from the early chapters of *Dolce*, begun in the summer of 1941, it is there, reduced to its simplest expression: the conflict between the sense of duty and the surging impulses of love. It's the serving girl at the Hôtel des Voyageurs, torn between her French dignity and the instinct that courses through her veins as she blushes at the flirtatiousness of the young Germans. It's the town's dressmaker who, refusing to measure her own enjoyment by the general unhappiness, takes up with an 'enemy' soldier, for 'if we did what other people thought we should do, we'd be worse than animals'.¹⁰ What was the use of the old notions of sacred soil or hereditary aversion compared to the all-powerful empire of the senses? Was it not 'the warm, rich blood of youth'¹¹ that had alienated Lucile from her husband Gaston, and not the war which held him prisoner in Germany? Love will conquer or die.

'Fire in the blood'! It had been such a long time since Irène Némirovsky had used the principle of impulsiveness and youth as the mainspring for her novels, diverting from their course destinies that were mapped out. The expression first appears in her work in 1934: 'It is wonderful to be twenty years old. Do all the girls know how to see it as I do, experience that bliss, that fervour, that power, that fire in the blood?'¹² Ever since 1938, she had wanted to show in a story that 'experience', as old people call it, generally results from chance, and that 'wisdom' is a type of wreckage, the breath you have left to beg for

---

*'Freedom from unreal loyalties . . . You must rid yourself of pride of nationality in the first place; also of religious pride, college pride, family pride, sex pride and those unreal loyalties that spring from them.' Virginia Woolf, *Three Guineas* (1938). [Tr.]

mercy when you have followed fantasies all your life. Young lovers make their way through the potholes of love, believing they are choosing their paths, deaf to the warnings of their elders. Even if their parents have been successful, like François and Hélène Érard, the 'fire in the blood' is passed on from generation to generation, like a hereditary illness. For these ravages provide no lesson. And so Silvio, whom a former passion has reduced to nothing, is prepared to endure it all again.

Fire in the Blood [Chaleur du sang], which was begun during the boiling summer of 1941, would amount to an illustration of a famous saying of Proust's: 'We do not receive wisdom, we must discover it for ourselves, after a journey through the wilderness which no one else can make for us, which no one can spare us, for our wisdom is the point of view from which we come at last to regard the world.'[13] Irène Némirovsky set this parable on the ages of man and the unpredictability of fate, which reads like a detective mystery, in Issy-l'Évêque, without bothering to alter the names of the characters and places, almost all of which were real. Furthermore, it is impossible to separate the development of Fire in the Blood from Dolce, where the subject that both have in common is the primacy of instinct, but also the 'marvellously effective malice' of peasant life, a phrase that shows she was not taken in by the rural mythology of Vichy. The earth does not lie, that's a fact . . . but those who live off it! 'This region, in the middle of France, is both wild and rich. Everyone lives in his own house, on his own land, distrusts his neighbours, harvests his wheat, counts his money and doesn't give a thought to the rest of the world.'[14] There is an almost identical phrase at the beginning of Dolce: 'Life in the provinces of central France is affluent and primitive; everyone keeps to himself, rules over his own domain, reaps his own wheat and counts his own money.'[15] An indifference that is noticeable in peacetime. But with the Germans there?

Wounds

Autumn 1941. Denise, who had spent the summer staying with a friend from Bordeaux, returned to Issy-l'Évêque with her primary school diploma in her pocket. She had a kitten called Sara and an attentive friend whose name was André. Because there was no hairdresser, Irène

Némirovsky concealed her long hair beneath a thick velvet hair-net. She missed Paris dreadfully. Her sight was getting worse, her teeth were causing her pain, and she could not have them treated. Rustic joy? 'Not only does this type of life not have anything luxurious about it, but for me it constitutes a deprivation both from a moral as well as a material viewpoint (total lack of comfort, cramped lodgings etc.),'[16] she wrote to the owner of her Paris flat, in order to persuade him to lower the rent. She could already see the day when difficulties would force her to leave it. And there was the taxman who persisted in denying the defeat!

On 5th September, a short, nostalgic story was published in *Gringoire*, under the pseudonym of Nerey, in which the characters and the places – the old Montjeu farm, which had fallen into ruins – are also those in *Fire in the Blood*. 'How very peculiar we are in the end! Our feeble memory retains only the slightest trace of happiness, so deeply engrained at times that it could almost be called a wound.'[17] One of these wounds was a letter, received on 6th August, from a lover of Fanny's (Irène's mother had taken refuge on the Côte d'Azur with forged Latvian papers), demanding the return of the furs that had been 'swiped' from Quai de Passy at the beginning of the year! Nothing would be forthcoming.

> Since you will have the occasion to see my mother [she replied], I should be grateful if you would confirm to her that it is in fact I who have taken the furs she mentioned to you (among other things, a pelisse that belonged to my father) and various other objects. You may also tell her that I sold all this immediately, thereby enabling her granddaughters and myself to survive for a little while. I believe she will be delighted to have been able to help me in this way. Due to present circumstances, she must certainly have suspected that I had neither money nor work at the time she fled Paris. I had nevertheless written to her, but I imagine that this letter never reached her, since I have never had a reply from her. . . . PS. Unfortunately, I made very little money from the sale of these furs, for they were in a pitiful condition.[18]

Irony retained its rights – as well as Fanny's gentle motherly love!

In Russia, Odessa fell that August, Kiev on 19th September, and each of these conquests was accompanied by massacres that bore no comparison to the old Russian pogroms. Victoria and her daughter Elena must have left Moscow before winter set in, leaving behind in their flight letters and family photographs that are lost for ever. This is where the paths of Irène and her beloved aunt divided.

In Occupied France, the litany of anti-Semitic humiliations was never-ending. From 26th April, bank accounts held by Jews were frozen. On 22nd July, a law 'relating to businesses, land and shares belonging to Jews' introduced legalised plundering 'with the aim of eliminating all Jewish influence in the national economy'. This measure would allow three Paris banks, among them the Pays du Nord, to finance the setting-up of an 'Omnium français d'études et de participations' (Ofepar), a company that was intended 'for the eventual takeover of Jewish businesses using the company's funds alone and in association with the state'.[19] From 13th August, Jews were also forbidden to hold a job at a radio station. In Paris that September a sinisterly devised exhibition opened at the Palais Berlitz entitled 'The Jew and France', which would attract almost two hundred thousand visitors. A collaborationist newspaper seriously asked the question: 'Should Jews be exterminated?'[20]

She was furious at being forced to stay at Issy. She longed to return to Paris and reassure herself face to face that Albin Michel intended publishing her new books. Michel Epstein brought up the matter with astonishing frankness in the request he put to the sub-prefect of Autun on 2nd September:

> I have received a letter from Paris informing me that anyone categorised as Jewish may not leave the village where he resides without permission from the authorities.
>
> I find myself in this situation, along with my wife, since, even though we are Catholics, we are of Jewish descent. I am therefore taking the liberty of requesting that you kindly allow my wife, born Irène Némirovsky, as well as myself, to spend six weeks in Paris where we also have a home, 10 Avenue Constant-Coquelin, for the period from 20th September to 5th November . . .

Permission was refused. Irène Némirovsky deliberated. Because she had seen in the newspapers that books had just been published by Daniel Halévy and Jean Fréville, both of whom were Jews ('in the case of the latter, whom I have known since childhood, I am certain of it'),²¹ she could not understand why Robert Esménard was still delaying publication of her *Vie de Tchekhov*. The explanation was as straightforward as it was disappointing: not only was Halévy not Jewish, but Fréville, an ardent communist and a specialist in economic matters, had not published anything since his translation of passages from Marx about the family in 1938.

Esménard replied to every letter, responded to all the author's worries, and agreed to continue paying the monthly advances throughout 1942, but he never dared admit to her that everything stood in the way of publishing her, simply because it would attract the attention of German censorship. 'It is a question of waiting for the appropriate moment,' he wrote to her. 'A suitable occasion will, in all probability, arise shortly and Sabatier will take steps on your behalf with all necessary tact.'²² Irène Némirovsky, whose thoughts 'could only be gloomy', was sustained by these false hopes; 'I now know, thanks to you and to M. Esménard, that I still have friends, and that is very comforting,' she confided to Sabatier on 14th October, taking the opportunity to enclose a copy of a flattering letter from Gibé Films, passed on by Carbuccia, about a film adaptation of *All Our Worldly Goods*. So she had not drawn her inspiration from *Cavalcade* in vain! 'This proves,' she maintained, 'as do other reactions that have reached me concerning this novel, that a well-known name is not essential to the success of a book.' Would not the simplest solution be to publish under a borrowed name from now on? Esménard saw fit to disappoint her with a rigidity that was all the more surprising given that sales of books had never been so flourishing. As in this letter of 27th October:

> . . . I must point out to you that in accordance with very precise instruc-
> tions we received from the Syndicat des éditeurs [Publishers' Association]
> regarding the interpretation of directives included in the German decree
> of 26 April, article 5, we find ourselves in the position of being required
> to send all royalties received from the sale of Jewish authors' works to their
> 'blocked account'. According to this principle, it is stated that 'publishers
> must pay royalties to Jewish authors by sending them to their bank account
> after receiving confirmation from the bank that the account is blocked'.
>
> In addition, I am returning the letter you received from Gibé Films (a
> copy of which I have kept). According to information I received from a

reliable source, a project of this type can only be undertaken if the author of the book to be adapted to the screen is of Aryan origin, both in this zone and the other. I can therefore only be involved in such a project when the author whose work is to be made into a film provides me with the most formal guarantee on this point.

Irène Némirovsky took this brusque approach for what it was: a veiled way of pointing out what steps to take, and it was in the same tone that she suggested to him that from now on her royalties should be paid to her 'friend', Julie Dumot, since she 'is definitely Aryan and can give you any proof of this you may require'.[23] On 17th December, in fact, Julie Dumot, 'writing as Jacques Labarre' – a name spotted in Hugo's *Les Misérables* – signed an author's contract, comparable in every way to the one Irène Némirovsky had, for two novels a year as from 1st January 1942. In spite of this arrangement, *All Our Worldly Goods* would never be published in the firm's yellow covers and would never be brought to the screen.

She had not, however, given up the idea of obtaining permission to go to Paris 'for three weeks or a month'.[24] It was with this hope that on 1st December she collected the manuscripts she had deposited at M. Vernet's practice in April and September, in order to leave them with Sabatier, convinced that they would be better protected in the attic of the publisher's offices in Rue Huyghens, should she and Michel, by any chance, be interned. This collection mainly comprised various versions of *David Golder*, her diary for *Le Pion sur l'échiquier*, those for *The Wine of Solitude* and for 'Le Charlatan', and the first draft of *The Dogs and the Wolves*. To these she would add *Fire in the Blood* and a few unpublished stories, at the beginning of which the name of Cécile was replaced by that of Julie. She now had Albin Michel's assurance that *La Vie de Tchekhov* would be published without delay, thanks to the subterfuge of the pseudonym. But only she could indicate where the necessary photographs could be found, and provide a suitable biography. She did not realise that the one hundred and thirty thousand volumes in the Turgenev Library, where she had so loved to roam around before the war, had been taken to Germany in the summer of 1940 by the Reichsleiter Alfred Rosenberg, the theoretician of the Nazi party, who was very keen on Russian literature . . .

At the same time, she intended to apply for her *Ausweiss* directly from the Kreiskommandantur in Autun, provided that Esménard was prepared to support her request through the necessary authority in Paris. Alas, even Sabatier's endeavours were fruitless; furthermore, Irène Némirovsky feared that they might put her in danger 'by drawing attention to her humble person' . . .[25] There now remained only one way of bringing her closer to her publishers, and this was for one of them to kindly make the long journey to Issy-l'Évêque, where she would welcome him to her new house. This was a large, fourteen-room building, cold but spacious, that overlooked the former livestock market, with a vegetable garden and an orchard from which you could see the Morvan hills. Michel grew lettuces, radishes and beetroot there, and he tended the vines. Cherry trees and pear trees would bloom in the spring. The hens laid six eggs each day. There was even a rabbit hutch. Everyday life was much improved. 'I can't promise you great comfort,' she wrote to Sabatier on 11th December, 'but at least you can be sure that you will eat more or less as you did before the war.' She would, however, have to wait three months before her editor decided to come by train.

A glass of Vichy water

In what was to be her last home, a stone's throw from the police station, Irène Némirovsky's confidence was restored and she clung to every hope. Convinced that her *Vie de Tchekhov* was due to be published, she begged Sabatier to be reassured that there was no possibility this book could offend the censors, 'although I believe it is irreproachable in this respect'.[26] Seated in an armchair beneath the veranda, she scribbled down for *Gringoire* – who would not publish it – the amusing story of the marriage of convenience of Octave, a quiet man who collected porcelain and old glass, to a wealthy American woman, and his subsequent remarriage to the housemaid.[27] This light farce was a veiled reference to the highly colourful divorce, in 1897, of Prince de Caraman-Chimay and the extravagant Clara Ward after seven years of married life. It was probably Julie Dumot who had reminded her of this episode, for she had been employed for a time in the service of the prince's sister-in-law, Princesse Alexandre de Caraman-Chimay (1878–1929), the sister of Anna de Noailles and a correspondent of Marcel Proust's.

For the Christmas holidays, Julie took Denise and Babet with her to Cézac, her village in the Landes, in search of the sun. A Siberian chill had descended on Issy-l'Évêque. Irène had received a few books from Sabatier for Christmas, and Michel was expecting some champagne. Before the spring, he promised himself that he would order some flower and vegetable seeds from Vilmorin on the Quai de la Mégisserie, he was already beginning to earn a small income from the food parcels he sent to their friends in Paris, who were having to endure rationing. A sort of life was beginning again, diminished but almost serene. It was almost six months since the Germans had left Issy. Not everything was rosy, certainly. Michel had begun to drink wine, rather more than he normally did. In the village, some people were surprised that such a large house should be needed for two idle refugees, their children, a maid and a plump cook by the name of Francine.

Not only was her royalty account at Albin Michel in debit to the tune of 120,000 francs, but it was soon apparent that Carbuccia would not run the risk of publishing *Tempête en juin*, for which she was expecting 50,000. 'L'Incendie' would be the last of her stories to appear in *Gringoire*, on 27th February 1942. It is a very strange tale. Mario, a painter with a sarcastic turn of mind, who has retired to an isolated manor house which is none other than the Montjeu farm, pretends to have fled the mediocrity and ugliness of modern times. On his death, in a fire, it was discovered that he had concealed two deformed dwarfs in his house, who follow his hearse dressed in their mourning clothes. His sons. As if it were a puzzle, Irène Némirovsky invites the reader to guess the 'profound significance' of this curious 'spectacle',[28] but what can it be? That an excessive purity may mask depravity? That she felt she was looked upon as a strange animal at Issy? The famous essayist, André Suarès, who read this story by chance, did not provide the key, but he was extremely surprised to come across a story of this quality in the rag that *Gringoire* had become. 'A pearl can be found in a pig-sty. In a revolting news-sheet, I read a story by Pierre Neyret, "L'Incendie". Who is this author? I don't know. I know and read so few. A solid and simple tale, which depicts characters and makes them see. As much sense as there is merit. A story of which Mérimée, with whom it has nothing in common by the way, would have been proud. True in its detail and very good as fiction.'[29] Despite it appearing under a pseudonym, despite it being a potboiler, a story by Irène Némirovsky did not pass unnoticed. She was then at the height of her talent and second to none. For as Mario says: 'I live in obscurity. The eye accustomed to darkness acquires an exquisitely sensitive perception.'[30]

Spurred on by the warm reception given to *All Our Worldly Goods*, Irène Némirovsky immediately plunged into a new family saga that would cover the inter-war years and the victory of Pétainism, up to the autumn of 1941. *The Fires of Autumn* is a twin of *All Our Worldly Goods* only in appearance. Whereas in the first novel she sings of the fearless and irreproachable rural bourgeoisie, in *The Fires of Autumn* she pulls out of the social swamp those who, having dismissed all concern for honour and probity, have plotted the defeat of a France that has decayed because of their selfishness. The lounge lizard triumphing over the Unknown Soldier: what a pretty picture, so much of its time. So very *Gringoire*!

Things are less simple. In 1914, Bernard Jacquelin was a fearless teenager, eager to prove his courage. Four years at the front had transformed him into a jackal. *Travail, famille, patrie*? It was all a confidence trick. While he was bogged down in Lorraine, a Raymond Détang, behind his back, was greasing his palm in the name of '*l'Union sacrée*'. From now on, all that Bernard wants to do is to squander himself, and then to die. 'Just let me get out of there and I will enjoy everything that has been refused me.'[31] Which is what he will do, wallowing in the cosmopolitan post-war Paris. Be it love, business or politics, Bernard respects nothing and shocks his poor father, an armchair patriot who can't understand a thing. And yet it's simple: this life of depravity and corruption, it's merely 'the wartime mentality adapted to peace',[32] the mud of Verdun that settles deeply in people's souls. After the crime, the punishment: because he has deliberately equipped French aircraft with cheap American parts, Bernard is directly responsible for the death of his son, whose aeroplane, a flying coffin, crashes without having engaged in battle at the very beginning of the new war.

This novel conveys a more or less Vichyist moral: the humiliation of 1940 had avenged the defilement of the sacred dead. Corrupted by 'the spirit of pleasure', Bernard is punished by the means with which he had sinned. But the great fire has cleansed his soul. The embers of the lost years will be the manure for moral renewal. Irène Némirovsky comes close to sharing the premonition in Mme Pain's dream: '"You see," she said, "these are the autumn fires; they purify the land; they prepare it for new seeds."'[33] But in rooting her novel in the grandiose illusions of the Belle Époque, disfigured by mustard gas, shrapnel and gangrene, Irène Némirovsky shows that it is the hypocritical cult of war, the sacrifice preached from the pulpit – in a word the ideas of Barrès – that had made the survivors of the 'war to end all wars' the prophets of the future debacle. You do not return from the kingdom of the dead in order to go back there. The Fires of Autumn, moreover, is the development of a story she had sketched out at the end of 1939, 'En raison des circonstances'; even there, René, the soldier on leave, was confusing good sense, anger and nationalist emotions, the poisoned legacy of those who fought in the Great War, misleadingly persuaded 'that it is the shells, the torpedoes and the flames that are the only reality' . . .

So it is not the moral spinelessness of the French people that Irène Némirovsky castigates, so much as the worship of profit, one of the perverse effects of the war: 'I couldn't care a damn, after all, provided I can make lots of money . . .'[34] For in her novel, who is it who calls for 'a firm hand, a leader',[35] who dreams of a dictatorship and a coup d'état, if not the wheeler-dealers and defeatists of Mégève, all of whom are fully convinced of France's military inferiority? Did Pétain talk of 'the spirit of pleasure'? But it was he himself, and all the 1914–18 generals, and their republican war memorials, who had made it so desirable! The Great War was the school of cupidity and disdain for life. Out of victory comes defeat, and it was Verdun that was responsible for Vichy. In a phrase that has a double significance, Irène Némirovsky denies having succumbed to scapegoat politics moreover, and she allows one to see that her gentleness is a trick, possibly intended to mollify Gringoire: 'She accepted the glass of Vichy water that Thérèse offered her with false modesty, and as soon as Thérèse turned away, she got out of bed, opened the window and threw the water into the courtyard.'[36]

A sad kind of happiness

At the end of her novel, Irène Némirovsky describes Bernard moving into a Robinson Crusoe-like retreat, 'two hundred kilometres from Paris', which is none other than her new home at Issy: 'What peace and quiet! There was a small garden, a bench on the lawn, and a little stream that flowed through a field.' Evidently, after a year in which she had been to hell and back, the novelist was persuaded that she would never again return to her former life. This intermediate form of death could be a renaissance. And supposing all this unhappiness, all these betrayals that had helped her to know who her true friends were, had not been in vain? What if the 'purifying pyres of the autumn' had burned the artificial aspects of her success, her Parisian-centred attitude, leaving her only with her most precious gift: her talent? This could well be the one advantage of this war. 'It was a sad kind of happiness, but she was calm and confident.'[37] What is more, she was writing more than ever. Julie had let her use her name, and above all she was going to be published again: in February, Sabatier informed her that she would soon be able to reread the proofs of *Vie de Tchekhov*. The fact that *Deux* had just been authorised to be reprinted was an auspicious sign. And in April, Julie Dumot was still able to buy a copy of *The Dogs and the Wolves* in Paris. It was true that there were no new publications. It was also true that these two books were her bestselling titles by far since *David Golder*.

This mirage would not survive the winter. Harassed by the taxman, Michel, losing all patience, returned a declaration to the inspector of the 7th arrondissement in which every column was marked 'Nil', since the 48,000 francs received from Albin Michel during 1941 constituted an advance, not income. Being stateless, he thought it wise to point out to the inspector that his children were French. It was a ridiculous precaution to take. What would become of his brother Paul, who was staying at Avenue Coquelin, whose rent was no longer regulated, despite a 25 per cent reduction because of lack of heating? Michel could only alert his brother that the bailiff was likely to issue an order for his goods to be seized: but even in such an eventuality, everything would go to the taxman, 'to whom we owe a large sum'. 'I cannot,' he told him, 'undertake to pay the entire arrears on my flat at the end of the war – supposing it amounted to 100,000 francs?'[38] And it was still impossible to go to Paris and deal with these problems face to face!

In February 1942, since neither Sabatier nor Esménard had replied to her invitation, Irène Némirovsky resolved, with extraordinary temerity, to make a last-ditch effort. Forbidden to ride a bicycle, forbidden to enter any public place, forbidden to change her name, an increasing number of round-ups in the Paris area . . . She chose to ignore completely the anti-Jewish persecution and coolly obtain her *Ausweiss* from the Kreiskommandantur in Autun, by writing a letter of disarming frankness:

Dear Sirs,

I am writing to you to ask permission to stay in Paris for one month.

I was born in Russia but I have never been a member of a soviet. Following the Bolshevik revolution, my parents and I took refuge in France, where I still live. Both of my parents are French; I am Catholic but my parents were Jewish. I am a writer by profession and the German authorities in Paris have given permission for my books to be published again.

The reasons that make it essential in my view for me to be in Paris are as follows:

1st My elder daughter, who is twelve years old, suffers from pains in the eyes and her doctor, Dr Morax, should examine her.

2nd My new book is to be published shortly and I simply must have a meeting with my publisher, Monsieur Albin Michel, before publication.

3rd I have a flat in Paris, which I can no longer keep. I must therefore make arrangements with the landlord.

I hope it will be possible for you to give this authorisation and I thank you in advance . . .[39]

This overconfidence may have stemmed from the fact that Lieutenant Kurt Bonnet, the interpreter at the Kommandantur in *Dolce*, was a very real character ('very young, 18 years old, very pale, hands of a drug addict, long, thin, white, big') whose indulgence Michel may have been counting on. Michel had also continued to maintain a correspondence, as cordial as it was prudent, with Spiegel and Hammberger. He did not fear contact with the Germans, and in October 1941, he had gone in person to Autun to hand over Hohmann's watch to the Kommandantur.

So as to leave nothing to chance, Irène Némirovsky also wrote at the same time to Hélène Morand, for fear of disturbing her husband Paul; she probably knew that the novelist's wife was not shocked by collaboration. Might she not be able to intercede with someone she knew at the German embassy, 'so that a one-month pass be granted to me? For your information, let me point out that the aforesaid authorities have given my publisher permission for my books to be sold and reprinted, and for my new books to be published.'[40] In passing, she revealed that she also needed to consult an oculist, because the scarceness of paper meant that she had to write in very tiny letters, and the survival of her household now depended upon her pen. She obtained nothing from Hélène Morand, apart from the address of Monseigneur Ghika, a Romanian like her, who had returned to Bucharest in 1940, and who, on 2nd March, sent her these brief words of sympathy on the back of an 'official postcard': '. . . In my prayers to God I do not forget you or your family. Seek refuge in Him, in all the trials you have endured and that are to come . . . Tell the children that I send them my most paternal blessing, and share this with them, as well as your husband. Yours ever devotedly in X^{to}.' These lines would not reach Issy until September 1942.

It was at the moment that all hope appeared to have vanished that André Sabatier finally announced his arrival, which was expected in late March. It would not therefore be necessary to appeal to that stark-raving mad Grasset, and so much the better: 'You probably know him as I do,' she wrote once more to Hélène Morand on 25th February, 'always ready to accept and even ask for help, but not very willing to give it. That's his nature; there's nothing one can do . . .' Was it in order to make Sabatier feel sorry for her that she wrote to him on 20th February: 'We have been able to get by until now by selling a few things that we had, but this recourse is now exhausted. You can understand how difficult this situation is; it affects my health; sooner or later it will have a bad effect on my work, for it is disheartening to write knowing that so much effort doesn't even ensure our survival, that my children are being brought up like peasants and that the future remains so gloomy. Whereas if I could place some stories occasionally, the situation would be much improved.' This was probably true, but Carbuccia now turned a deaf ear. In mid-March, he offered to intervene on her behalf with Vichy, but this was now no more than a form of words.

By 23rd February, Irène Némirovsky had still not received the proofs of her *Vie de Tchekhov*. Busy with the ending of her new novel, she was enthralled by the accounts – deliberately distorted at the request of the state – of the first hearings of the trial at Riom, which opened on 19th February and was meant to try – or, rather, sentence – those politicians held accountable for the military defeat. Those deemed responsible were Léon Blum, Édouard Daladier and Général Gamelin, but it was the Republic and the Front Populaire, which were suspected of incompetence, that Vichy intended to pillory. We know that the indictment, which was crude and muddled, was made to look ridiculous, and that Hitler himself was angry about this farce of a trial. But Daladier's audacious defence, comparing Pétain to Marshal Bazaine,* and that of Blum, so skilfully argued, demonstrating the industrial effectiveness of the forty-hours-a-week law, were of less interest to Irène Némirovsky than the cross-examination of Guy La Chambre on 4th and 5th March 1942. The former Minister of Aviation explained that when he took up his position, in January 1938, the aeronautics business was 'an appalling sight': 'It was a small-scale industry run by dispirited bosses.' As a result of this, he had to pass orders for material abroad, in particular to the United States, in order to provide France with a fleet of planes worthy of the name. Was he now being accused of having cleverly sold off the defence of the nation cheaply to foreign interests? And yet, La Chambre reminded the court, it was actually Baron Amaury de La Grange, the President of the Aéroclub de France, who had advocated the purchase of thousands of American engines! Senator La Grange, who was called as a witness for the prosecution at the Riom trial, has much in common with Raymond Détang, the lobbyist in *The Fires of Autumn*, who manages to coerce the Assemblée into buying defective American guns. Thus, even in this novel, it is the hangers-on and the opportunists, who were at Vichy that day, who find themselves in the dock . . . As for the failed Riom trial, which was adjourned in April 'because additional information was required', it was the first serious blow to Marshal Pétain's infallibility.[41]

The community spirit

It would therefore be wrong to describe *The Fires of Autumn* as the great novel of ideological resignation that it appears to be. On the contrary, Irène Némirovsky had had quite enough of the National

---

*Who, as C-in-C in 1870, during the Franco-Prussian War, tried to negotiate with the enemy and subsequently surrendered. For this he was court-martialled. [Tr.]

Revolution. Rereading at random her notes from April 1940, she was taken aback to see that at the time she felt a 'sincere and slightly mocking affection' for the French. Taking care to date it, she added this simple equation above what she had written: 'hatred + contempt = March 1942'. It is an about-face somewhat reminiscent of the sudden grudge Heinrich Heine took against Germany, when, having converted to Christianity, he realised that he would not be looked upon any more favourably. It is from this period that we can date the bitter and scathing reflections 'on the state of France', that would contribute in no small way to the posthumous success of *Suite Française*, where they appear – in part – in the appendices: 'My God! What is this country doing to me? Since it rejects me, let us consider it dispassionately, let us watch it lose its honour and its life blood . . . Let us keep a clear head. Harden our hearts. Let us wait.'

Her voice had changed. Hitherto cheerful and bubbly, she had become 'solemn and sad'.[42] She had never been frightened, but she realised that it was other people's 'fear' that made life dangerous for her. That it was the rich who had least to lose from becoming a vassal state, and so they resorted to denunciation. 'Everything that is done in France within a certain social class has only one motive: fear . . . At school, the weakest pupil prefers to be oppressed by one person than to be independent; the tyrant victimises him, but does not allow others to pinch his ball, or to fight him. If he escapes from the tyrant, he is alone, left on his own in the free-for-all.' People who have very little, and who buy and sell on the black market, such as the butcher from Issy, 'who earned five hundred thousand francs in a currency for which he knows what the exchange rate would be abroad (precisely nothing)', they have nothing to fear, whereas a banker would sell his father and his mother to keep his securities, a middle-class man his possessions, a politician his privileges. There is no other way to explain the cringing competition which 'the most hated men in France' displayed, the 'tiger' Philippe Henriot, the propagandist on Radio Paris, and the 'hyena' Pierre Laval, who was returned to power on 16th April: 'you can smell the odour of fresh blood around the former, and the stench of carrion around the latter'. The same men, who continued to advocate national recovery, not only stirred up the cycle of 'terrorism' and repression that put France to fire and sword, but they only pursued their own aims.

The 'community spirit', the ideological foundation of the Vichy regime, was the great lie of that time. In reality, it was a civil war, fought throughout Europe, between the plutocracy and hoi polloi, under the guise of an anti-Soviet campaign. In France, collaborationism was little more than the atonement of the Front Populaire, apart from the fact that it was a stirring of the *ancien régime*. At least, that is how Mme de Montfort views matters, having worked herself into a frenzy over the mistrustful attitude of the yokel Labarie. Very good at insisting that the villagers make up parcels for the prisoners of war, the very Christian vicomtesse would not allow a single rabbit from her estate, which was a private hunting ground, to be poached by peasants. What Irène Némirovsky refers to ironically as 'the community spirit', is simply 'the hoarding of goods for the exclusive use of a few'; for 'these German officers were cultured men, after all! What separates or unites people is not their language, their laws, their customs, their principles, but the way they hold their knife and fork!'[43] Upon values such as these, and a few corpses, Hitler was building the civilised Europe.

In *Captivité*, in which we will find all the main characters from *Tempête en juin* spoiling for a fight, the worthy Jean-Marie Michaud has chosen which side he is on: 'So don't talk to me about the community spirit. I am happy to die, but as a Frenchman and as a rational being, I want to understand why I am dying, and I, Jean-Marie Michaud, am giving up my life for P. Henriot and P. Laval and other overlords, like a chicken with its throat slit ready to be served at the table of these traitors. And, personally, I consider that the chicken is worth more than those who are to eat it.' She was drawn to this rebelliousness, but she felt responsible for Michel and the children. She blamed herself for her wait-and-see attitude: 'For Jean-Marie's political viewpoint to be balanced it would mean that 1) I know what the future holds 2) that I should have a balanced political viewpoint myself, other than one which consists of gnashing one's teeth and champing at the bit or digging holes in the earth to escape.' In fact, her great novel would not reveal any of her own views, nor would it take sides at all. 'Not to demonstrate anything above all. Here less than anywhere else. Neither that some are good and others bad, nor that this person is wrong and someone else is right. Even if it's true, especially if it's true. Depict, describe.' Irène Némirovsky was far more concerned with literature than with saving her own skin, but it was possible that this amounted to the same thing, for: 'What is left: 1) our humble daily life; 2) art; 3) God.'

From 6th to 31st March, Irène Némirovsky was disentangling the guiding lines of the third volume of her 'tragedy on several levels', the general and almost mystical idea of which, already explored by Julien Green in *Varouna* (1940), was that 'the fate of all of us depends on one another'. She moved her characters around, jumbled up their destinies, and tried every combination. The minister, Jules Blanc, who has taken refuge at the Hôtel des Voyageurs, is the victim of a bomb attack. His mistress, 'a sort of Odette Swann, from one drawer down', has a daughter by the name of Brigitte, a well-behaved child who challenges Corte with 'a clear and disdainful gaze'. Corte gives dinner parties in Paris 'where they rail against the workers, the Jews, and the laziness that's taken hold of ordinary people', while all the time providing for themselves on the black market. Borne along by his writer's vanity, 'irritated because his virtues are not recognised', Corte just as naturally appoints himself 'the apostle of the Resistance', but far away from the firing-line: 'it wouldn't be a bad idea to show these sensible people living abroad who earned honour and money by preaching revolt and those who came a cropper.' And, since Father Péricand died on the battlefield, there was nothing to prevent Corte either from being stoned to death by The Penitent Children!

In Paris, due to Arlette's intervention, the directors of the Corbin bank 'do business with the Germans'. At Issy, that 'poor Sp[iegel]' dies. Cécile grows richer on the black market. Madeleine, who sleeps with the enemy, will end up in a brothel. Jean-Marie has a romantic affair with Brigitte and finds himself tied to Hubert through 'a very beautiful, very manly friendship, for which they were prepared to sacrifice their own lives, and which was dedicated to a great cause': the Resistance, to give it its name. But, in 1942, the cause of France has become 'so chaotic' that its supporters have nothing in common between them. Hubert is 'one of the Maréchal's young men, or something like that', Jean-Marie an arms racketeer, and Benoît – who will be shot – a husband who is jealous of the whole world. 'All in all, for my book to hang together, two things are necessary: 1) a short-lived communist revolution in France and 2) a British victory. *Oh, God! Topsy, don't be blasphemous!*'*

Captivité – another word for Occupation or for 'Servage', a title she had considered – is not very different from *Dolce* to begin with. It only

*In English in original text. [Tr.]

really takes off during the spring of 1942. For the novelist was not happy with this 'nebula of chapters' that spun in every direction, from which no 'guiding idea' emerged. '*Tempête* was chaotic; that makes sense, but in *Captivité* something ought to stand out' that is neither 'the effort of liberating France' nor the story of the love affair between Brigitte and Jean-Marie, but which could well be, once again, 'the instinct for survival' that inspires them, just as it inspired so much behaviour that was so contradictory. 'First of all, cowardice. But let us be charitable. Next, a deepening of the soul. The fire becomes more concentrated, burns more strongly, devours the heart: the directors of the bank love money all the more. Jean-Marie and Hubert become more violently patriotic, or party men, if you like . . . Madeleine is more in love than she was with Jean-Marie: she becomes the German's mistress. Benoît does not hesitate to kill him.' The unquenchable fire in the blood!

Upon burning lava

André Sabatier finally announced that he would be arriving on Wednesday 1st April. A car would be waiting for him in the evening at Luzy station to take him to Issy, eleven kilometres due south. It would be a short stay: on Friday, he would return to Paris, via Dijon, where he had a meeting. 'We await you eagerly,' wrote a delighted Irène Némirovsky on 23rd March. 'Mlle Julie Dumot who by a happy coincidence happens to be here, asks that you kindly bring her the 16,000 francs that the firm still owes her. As for me, if you could bring me some weeklies, some magazines and some books, I could not wish for anything more. I have not received the proofs of *Tchekhov*. I hope that nothing has changed on that score?'

On the evening prior to his arrival, she had just decided upon the final format of her new book. 'I've an idea that I think is a good one. I nip Brigitte in the bud. It's all she deserves. I chuck Lucile. That is to say: I *Tempête*, II *Dolce*, then Jean-Marie and Lucie.' This was the birth certificate of *Suite Française*, the still anonymous *roman-fleuve* that would be her *Iliad*, her *Aeneid*, her *War and Peace*. The only difference being that she had no way back. Tolstoy wrote dispassionately, half a century after the event. 'He wasn't bothered. Whereas I, I work upon burning lava. Rightly or wrongly, I believe that this is what should distinguish the art of our times from that of others, it is that we sculpt the actual moment, we work on things that are highly topical. It falls apart, certainly, but it is precisely what is needed in the art of today. If such an impression makes any sense, it is a perpetual evolution, and not something already achieved. *Cf.* cinema.'

Sabatier only stayed in Issy l'Évêque for two nights. On 3rd April, he had already left, taking with him the pile of manuscripts, diaries and drafts that she had asked him to store at his office in Rue Huyghens, where they would lie dormant for sixty-three years. One week later, Denise was in Paris, where her mother had sent her with Julie to visit the oculist, do some shopping, raid the Quai de Passy (where Fanny, alas, had apparently had all the locks changed!) and to pick up from the apartment some chairs, some English books, some sheets, a sewing-machine, a lacquer cigarette case and a few trinkets. It was clearly a mad thing to do, but Denise was only twelve years old and she held French papers: who would think of stopping her? After a thrilling journey, she was greeted by her Uncle Paul, 'a real angel',[44] who took her out to dine on oysters, beef and some fine wines. Restrictions? What restrictions? This brief visit to Paris had a feeling of the holidays about it: Mavlik took her to see *La Symphonie fantastique* by Christian-Jaque, she travelled on the Métro for the first time and experienced two air-raid warnings which somewhat dampened her excitement. 'For me, it was the last word in luxury. My uncle took me to the theatre to see *Cyrano de Bergerac*. It was with hindsight that I said to myself: my God, supposing I had been rounded-up at that very moment . . .'[45]

But Denise only spent two or three days in Paris. On the 12th, she was at Audenge, on the Bassin d'Arcachon, where Julie had taken her to stay in a bungalow until the middle of May, to help her grow a little stronger. There was fresh fish and oysters for every meal, bicycle rides, trips to the cinema and the beach on Sundays: it was almost like the long summer holidays, were it not for school and mass, which Julie would not dream of missing. '[She] is very pious,' 'Nanette' wrote to her mother. 'This afternoon she was plunged into reading a book called *Préparation à la mort* until she almost fell asleep.'[46] Denise had more wholesome reading matter: books in the Bibliothèque de Suzette series and *The Adventures of Mr Pickwick*, which her mother had sent her in the post. In Paris as in Bordeaux, she seemed very surprised to see that young girls of her age were skinny, but it was not long before she understood the reason: if there was no shortage of seafood at Audenge, the bread, on the other hand, was not always fresh, and basic food was scarce. 'Papa and I giggled a little bit on hearing that you were short of butter and pastry,' she wrote to her daughter on 24th April. 'However, Issy-l'Évêque has its good side, I think.' Yet, even at Issy, food supplies were not as easily available as they had been. You could not get anything substantial except in exchange for rationing coupons and 'it is impossible to have an extra gram of meat or anything else'.

Denise was in Paris again in late May, escorted by Julie to whom Esménard confirmed, on the 27th, that 'her' monthly payments would shortly be raised from 3,000 to 5,000 francs, bearing in mind the current difficulties and the continued hope of one of her novels being adapted to the screen. Good news? Quite the opposite: the novelist had hoped that this payment would take effect retrospectively from 1st January. But Albin Michel would not hear of this. 'What petty-mindedness!' she complained to Sabatier on 4th May. '<u>And how wrong he is</u>! So does he want to drive me to the only solution you can guess? (and which is not suicide . . .)' These moans and Sabatier's arguments would prevail over Albin Michel's intransigence, and the publisher went so far as to agree to payments of 6,000 francs for 1943.

Denise only returned to Issy after 29th May, the date of the German decree making it obligatory for Jews in the Occupied Zone to carry a clear, visible sign in the shape of a yellow star sewn on the chest, a measure that had been in force in Germany since September 1941. Only two months after having worn the headdress of flowers for her First Communion, it was one surprise after another: 'Mummy told me that I was Jewish on the day that we were obliged to wear the yellow star. She explained to me that we believed we were Catholics, since we had been baptised, but in fact we were of Jewish origin, and the Germans insisted that we wear this little star . . .'[47] Once again, Irène and Michel could easily have evaded a requirement that only affected them in the village. They subjected themselves to it, however: there was always this attitude 'that consisted of grinding one's teeth and champing at the bit'. As for violating the demarcation line, several Jews attempted to do this: hunted down by the dogs of the Feldgendarmerie, they stagnated in the prison at Chalon-sur-Saône, or at the 'Salengro shelter' at Montceau-les-Mines, guarded by French police officers.[48] Since 6th May, René Bousquet, Vichy's chief of police, had come to an agreement with his German counterpart, Reinhardt Heydrich, about the forthcoming deportation to Germany of five thousand Jews who were held in the prisons of the Occupied Zone. It was the beginning of the Final Solution in France.[49]

The yellow star was Irène Némirovsky's first exercise in sewing, for she had not wanted to allow anyone else to do this job.[50] Only Babet, who was under six, would not wear it. As for Denise, she did not feel in the least humiliated. 'People told me: "It's the law." I wore it until October. At school, no child ever made any comment, but I was very protected by my teachers . . .'[51] Yet who at Issy would have criticised her for not wearing it?

A suite française

'24th of April today, a little peace and quiet for the first time in a very long while. Convinced that the series of *Tempêtes*, if I may say so, should be, is a masterpiece. Work unflinchingly.' The early spring of 1942, with Denise away, was very quiet at Issy-l'Évêque. Irène Némirovsky, left almost to her own devices, made the most of this breathing space to work relentlessly on her great work. She was still unsure whether to call the first part *Tempête* or *Naufrage*, but it was during this month of April that she finally settled on the overall title: 'I must make a suite of *Tempête, Dolce, Captivité*.'

So, a French suite. Why this title, only used previously by . . . Johann Sebastian Bach? Certainly, this was not the first time that she had thought of her work in terms of a musical composition: *The Wine of Solitude* was modelled on Franck's *Symphonie*. As for the 'series of *Tempêtes*', she wanted to give it a sonata form, or else make it look like a symphony in four movements: 'slow, followed by a fugue; allegro in a different but similar tone; adagio, and to end a series of quick dances'. That is to say, four books, of which three were in the pipeline. A cyclical symphony, in which the main difficulty consisted of binding the parts with a common theme or leitmotif.

She jotted down a number of eloquent comparisons: the *Hammerklavier* sonata, *Missa Solemnis*, 'the final scenes in *Parsifal*', the twentieth of the *Diabelli variations*, 'that sphinx with dark eyebrows who contemplates the abyss'. She omitted the instructions for tempo and the subtleties – *presto, prestissimo, adagio, andante, con amore* . . . – preventing us from determining exactly what she had in mind, but it is the contrapuntal art that best defines her concept, a tangle of individual misfortunes and great collective stirrings: 'Bach reduces his material to two contrasting themes, in which a final phase, without any heaviness, creates the synthesis. The melodic line and the subject of the fugue disappear at certain moments like an underground river or only reappear in simple harmonies from time to time – allusions.'

Elsewhere, she compared her characters to the instrumental solo in a symphony, and the crowd scenes to the choruses that give breadth and contrast to the plot. 'On the one hand, the people's destiny, on the other Jean-Marie and Lucile, their love, the German's music, etc.' This is exactly what Lieutenant Bruno von Falk, in *Dolce*, tries to make Lucile listen to when he improvises the sad, universal story of the soldier: 'Drums, trucks, soldiers marching . . . can you hear them? Can you? Their slow, faint, relentless footsteps . . . An entire population on the move . . . The soldiers are lost among them . . . Now there should be a choir, a kind of religious chant, unfinished. Now, listen! It's the battle . . . The soldier is dying, and at that very moment, he hears the choir again, but now it is a divine chorus of soldiers . . .'[52] This is what *Dolce* is all about, and it would be the theme of *Captivité* too: the torture of not being able to hide from what is happening, the illusion of finding a retreat at Issy, sheltered from political emotions and the clamour of the world. Here is the one unanimous meaning of the war: Germans, French, Jews, men have only one mortal enemy, the History that crushes them. 'All in all: the struggle between individual destiny and collective destiny. . . . The German's musical masterpiece.'

This masterpiece without a home, a symphony with piano obbligato, is without doubt *Suite Française*. It is hardly surprising that in 2005 Aulis Sallinen, a composer in a direct line from Sibelius, should have drawn upon it to write a chamber concerto for violin and piano.[53] 'In fact,' Irène Némirovsky seemed to be responding to him, 'it's like the music in which you sometimes hear the orchestra, sometimes the violin on its own. At least that's the way it should be.'

The bitter solitude of rejection

In May 1942, her last hope of seeing Paris again was discouraged by André Sabatier, who reckoned that it was unwise to involve the most powerful means of pressure he had at his disposal: his friend Benoist-Méchin, now Secretary of State in the Foreign Office, who had just applauded 'the powerful roar of the Wehrmacht's armoured divisions, forerunners of the West's great crusade'.[54] 'I understand your point of view,' she replied. 'But, you see, to my mind, both "authorities" are equally hostile to me. That is why I made no distinction between them. I can appreciate that it's pointless to attempt anything ... Truly,' she continued, 'I have no further hopes at the moment. The only possible thing, I believe, would be to publish Julie's book as soon as you are able to do so. That would result in many doors being opened and it would remove a few difficulties.'[55] This book, *The Fires of Autumn*, would remain in the drawer, however. All that Sabatier managed to do was to sell two unpublished stories to the new weekly *Présent*. The second of these, 'Un beau mariage', had been returned to her from *Gringoire*, where Irène Némirovsky had sent it in December; Carbuccia no longer wanted to take any risks, which put a cap on her 'state of bitterness, of weariness, of disgust'.[56] This despondency manifests itself clearly in the first of these stories, 'Les Vierges', which describes the settling-in, 'in a small village in the Centre', of a single mother and her daughter:

> It's life that is frightful. You keep away from life, you are right to do so. Life can only do harm, maim, sully, wound ... Look at me. I am alone like you at the moment, yet it's not because of a solitude I have chosen or sought, but the worst kind of solitude, humiliation, the bitter solitude of rejection, of betrayal.[57]

Présent, a 'political and literary weekly' founded in December, professed sterling support for Marshal Pétain and made no bones about scoffing at the 'talmudic' style of Blum's defence at Riom. On the other hand, it was rarely guilty of anti-Semitism, which no doubt explains the quality of its writers, some of whom were Jews, while others were involved in communist campaigns, and others still had sprung from Action française. In no particular order, they included: Kléber Haedens, André Salmon, Claude Roy, Jacques de Lacretelle, Joë Bousquet,

Edmond Jaloux, Roger Vailland, and even the very young Françoise Giroud. Irène Némirovsky, *alias* Denise Mérande (a double allusion to her daughter and to Esménard of whose name this is almost an anagram) would not see either of these two stories in print, for 'Les Vierges' would not be published until 15th July, two days after her arrest, and 'Un beau mariage' not until 23rd February 1943, more than six months after her death.

One solution was left to her: for Chaumeix, who had got in touch with her again by postcard, also to publish a few stories in the *Revue des Deux Mondes* and, who knows, a novel, in the spring of 1943. But if this could not be done, or was too inconvenient, all that would remain for her would be to 'continue with what she had been busy with for two years already, a novel in several volumes, which she considered to be the main work of her life':[58] her *Suite Française*. It was a false hope, however, and Irène Némirovsky no longer wanted to struggle just for a thousand francs. 'I had many "publishable" things on the go,' she explained to Sabatier, 'but I am well aware that despite all your efforts, I was banging my head against closed doors or if one was half opened to me it was out of a kind of charity, and so I have abandoned all that in order not to think of the future any longer and to work on this work in several volumes that I spoke to you about.'[59]

From May to July, Irène Némirovsky gave *Dolce* the shape we know, and she clarified the contents of *Captivité*. She was now certain that she was writing for the future, 'in the lap of the gods', for she superstitiously expected to see the German troops return to Issy. And so she wore the yellow star. What would happen? She had no further hope except in Sabatier, who had done everything, and in Nostradamus, who had said everything. 'Well, if on 14th July those who promised to arrive do so,' she wrote mysteriously, 'there will be, among other consequences, two or, at least, one part fewer.' It is most unlikely that this enigmatic sentence, written in the margins of the manuscript of *Dolce*, was alluding to any action by the *maquis*. Two parts fewer of her book, in fact, would signify neither reoccupation, nor peace. Furthermore, she no longer believed in a British victory, which is what she would have preferred.

The event that seemed to have brought her anxieties to a head was President Laval's speech broadcast on the radio on the anniversary of the Nazi attack on the USSR: 'We were wrong to go to war in 1939 . . .

I wish for the victory of Germany, because otherwise Bolshevism would become established everywhere.' Ten days later, she noted: 'My preference: the kind of middle-class régime embodied by England. Impossible unfortunately, [but it] at least needs to be revived, for in the end it is essentially immutable; but it will definitely not happen until after I die: left therefore with two types of socialism. Neither the one nor the other appeals to me, but *there are facts!** So one of them rejects me . . . The other . . . But this is out of the question.'

Throughout the month of June, the vice tightened on the Jews. At the Commissariat Générale aux questions juives (the Commissariat for Jewish Affairs), Xavier Vallat made way for Louis Darquier de Pellepoix, whose less legalistic temperament the occupying power preferred. In *Je suis partout*, on 6th June, Lucien Rebatet considered that the new crusaders of the LVF (Légion des volontaires français contre le bolchevisme) were dying as 'victims of the Jews' and of 'Jewish Marxism'. At the same time, the gas chambers and crematoria that were being put into operation at the prison at Auschwitz-Birkenau, in occupied Poland, required the arrest and deportation of tens of thousands of western Jews, including those in the Free Zone. This was done in association with the French police and was agreed without any difficulty by the Secretary of State, René Bousquet. As for the Jews in the Occupied Zone, President Laval left their fate in the hands of the occupying power, only agreeing to offer the help of his police when it was a matter of deporting foreigners. To satisfy the quotas while at the same time salving his conscience, he would merely suggest that children, even naturalised ones, should not be separated from their parents during this distressing odyssey.

I'm frightened, I'm frightened . . .

Irène Némirovsky, of course, knew nothing of these secret discussions that would prepare the way for the arrest of her daughters, her husband, all her in-laws, and herself. There is virtually no mention of Jews in the drafts of *Captivité* – unless it is her regret that she could not call Langelet 'Laangelé' – apart from this strange vision, which expresses

*These words appear in English in the notebook. [Tr.]

both remorse and a premonition: 'For the concentration camp, the blasphemy of baptised Jews: "My God, forgive us our trespasses as we forgive You." – Obviously the martyrs would not have said that.' But the present and the immediate future matter little to her, they are at best the setting for her posthumous work, 'or the victory that I no longer dare think about, or the clash, the battle, the *Pax Germanica*, everything they want, everything that God has wanted, all the individual destinies there will be on one side and the other'. When one walks into the night, one doesn't think of the dawn. But supposing the sun never comes back? It would come back, she believed, but a long time later. 'Never forget that the war will pass and that the entire historic part of it will fade away,' she noted on 2nd June. 'Try to do as many discussions and things as possible . . . that may interest people in 52 or 2052.'

Captivité was getting off the ground. On 17th June, all that she still had left to write were five of the twenty-two chapters of *Dolce*, including the Dantesque party in the grounds of the Château de Montfort, which she would date, in a revealing error, '22 June 1942'. Corte, the opportunist, who had put himself by turns at the service of the National Revolution, who had written for an 'underground newspaper', who had even adopted Aragon's style in order to dash off a *Défaite de la France* and had imagined himself becoming 'the great man of the Party, ha, ha, ha!', suddenly becomes a turncoat, informs on his 'comrades' and joins in the crusade: 'Today the Rhine flows over the Ural mountains . . .' Right to the very end, Corte would be undecided as to whether to take one side or take them all. 'Should a Corte have such cynical ideas? But, of course, at certain moments. When he's been drinking or after making love in the way he prefers, a way that a mere mortal could barely begin to understand . . .'

Meanwhile, at Bussy, Jules Blanc, the former big shot of the Republic, 'shrouded like a corpse', is shaking from every limb. His anxiety and his 'pained astonishment' give Irène Némirovsky away: 'The postman has been. Nothing? Nothing for me? Ah! Yes? A letter, a postcard. No, it wasn't for me, you were mistaken! Not at all, no thank you, it's nothing. Nothing, nothing, nil, *nada*, nothing till tomorrow! And tomorrow? Nothing or worse? God, I'm frightened, I'm frightened, I'm frightened, we have to hold on, we have to hold our heads high.

I'm not just anybody. I have connections.' She who had not shaken with fear since 1917.

And Benoît Labarie, who is now convicted of 'terrorism', who had fled once the Germans had left? Irène Némirovsky sends him to seek shelter in Paris, at the Michauds', but the Gestapo is on his tracks. Through an underground network, he comes across Jean-Marie and Hubert Péricand, who has refused to make use of 'his powerful family who are all collaborators'. They are deported. Jean-Marie escapes and, *happy end*,* flees France with Lucile, arm-in-arm. 'END: listening to Bruno's music.' So *Suite Française* could be 'one of those American films . . . The chase – the lovers – laughter, tears, etc. . . . That's the kind of rhythm I'd like to achieve.' It would initially be 'a fat book of a thousand pages' at least, '*well, well, if I live in it*'.*

For the war was at a turning-point. That same day, in a discussion with someone called Pied-de-Marmite, Irène Némirovsky came away certain that the all-out victories of the Reich and the Japanese aircraft would break British resistance and that France would be forced to 'walk hand in hand with Germany', because there would be no way of coping. She had only one concern from now on: to be still alive in a year's time to describe this 'unforgettable Sunday', when the red death invited itself to the party and the guests told her to get drunk.

In her final notes relating to the composition of *Suite Française*, dating from 1st July, Irène Némirovsky tries to work out Jean-Marie's motives 'vis-à-vis this great game of chess'. Essentially, they go as far as 'the revenge of France' – and this could be the theme of the two last volumes, *Batailles* and *La Paix* – but 'whoever speaks of revenge speaks of hatred and vengeance'. How could the war be won without winning it, with neither victors nor vanquished, without there being 'one that is stronger and one that is weaker' every time'? Two years prior to the events, she anticipated the excesses of the *épuration*, the summary executions, the sadistic violence and the cursory trials that accompanied the liberation of France. In this final part, we would nevertheless take part, she was glad to say, in the 'triumph of individual destiny' over the 'spirit of the hive'. The revenge of the pawn on the chessboard.

*These words appear in English in the notebook. [Tr.]

As if on a raft

Suite Française is an accomplished work that has enthralled its many readers. Irène Némirovsky would have altered it considerably, however, had it been followed by *Captivité* and the two next volumes, *Batailles* and *La Paix* – for, in her mind, the peace could equally well have been imposed by the *Pax Britannica* as the *Sovietica* or the *Germanica*. The *Pax Americana*? The notion had never occurred to her.

Her last short story appears to have been written in late June. The death of old Carillon in 'La Grande Allée' actually has a great deal to do with that of 'poor father Milleret', a peasant from Issy l'Évêque, who died in his little house on 13th June, and whose body, watched over by mourners, she had seen. Old Milleret happened to 'like a drop of wine', and Carillon was the surname of old Grandvin. 'An old rosary was coiled around his hands. His face was peaceful. Beside the body, some women were reciting the rosary, glancing at Marie with a questioning look, while the murmuring continued: "Forgive us our trespasses as we forgive those who have trespassed against us."'

On 1st July, as a subtle form of humiliation, the PTT, the French post office organisation, was informed by the occupying power that Jews – including Jewish doctors – were to be forbidden the use of the telephone. In Paris, Theodor Dannecker and Adolf Eichmann were planning a speedy and massive deportation of French Jews in convoys of a thousand, 'with the aim of totally freeing France of Jews as quickly as possible'. Six convoys of this kind were scheduled to leave on 6th July. In Vichy, rumour had it that these measures would require large-scale round-ups in the Free Zone as well as the Occupied Zone. On the night of 2–3rd July, the German ambassador, Otto Abetz, sent a telegram to Berlin stating that he had 'no objection in principle to 40,000 Jews being evacuated from France to be sent to work in the camp at Auschwitz', on condition that foreigners be targeted in the first place, so as to pander to French anti-Semitism. Laval, who pretended to believe in the creation of a Jewish state in eastern Europe, scribbled down the following at a cabinet meeting: 'It would be no dishonour to me if I were to send the countless number of foreign Jews who are in France to this state one day.' Thus was honour saved . . .

She was, in any case, disillusioned and dispirited. She was almost longing for the bell to chime. '3 July 1942 – Definitely,* and unless things drag on and get worse in the meantime! But please let it be over one way or the other!' On 8th July, the day on which the propaganda film *Le Péril juif* was shown at cinemas in the Occupied Zone, the second Otto list of 'undesirable French literary works' was also published; there was still no mention of Irène Némirovsky's name. However, an appendix made it clear that 'all books by Jewish authors . . . were to be withdrawn from sale'. That same day, a new German decree prohibited Jews from attending cinemas, theatres and all public places. Furthermore, it restricted their access to shops. Apart from internment, their position could not in truth be worse. This was something she clearly expected, for she was rereading Katherine Mansfield's *Journal*: 'Just when one thinks: "Now I've touched the bottom of the sea – now I can't go down any lower", one sinks deeper still. And so on for ever.'[60]

On 11th July, Irène Némirovsky walked up to the Maie woods to enjoy the last remaining pleasures that were not forbidden her. She was feeling cheerful, too cheerful, as if all her anxiety had ebbed back to distant shores. It was a very peaceful, almost miraculous morning:

> The pine trees all around me. I am sitting on my blue cardigan in the middle of an ocean of leaves, wet and rotting from last night's storm, as if on a raft, my legs tucked under me. In my bag I have Volume II of *Anna Karenina*, K. M.'s *Journal* and an orange. My friends the bumblebees, delightful insects, seem pleased with themselves and their buzzing is deep and solemn. I like low, solemn tones in voices and in nature. The shrill 'chirp, chirp' of the small birds in the trees gets on my nerves. In a moment or so I will try to find the hidden Lake.

These were her last words as a writer. 'I've written a great deal lately,' she explained to Sabatier that same day. 'I suppose they will be posthumous books but it still makes the time go by.' Sunday 12th July: nothing. That night, Denise slept badly. The following evening the summer holidays would begin. But she was no longer entitled to travel by train.

---

*This word refers to the previous paragraph in I. N.'s notebook in which she wonders whether she should create one large 1,000-page book, rather than several volumes. [Tr.]

Monday 13th July. The weather was wonderful. At about ten o'clock in the morning came the sound of a car stopping in the Place du Monument aux Morts. There were footsteps and knocking on the door. Two French gendarmes stood in the doorway, bearing a summons. 'I didn't know what was happening, I heard the boots, and I heard my parents go back into their bedroom, all this in a very dense silence,' remembered Denise, who after a few minutes was allowed to kiss her mother. For it was her they had come to look for. She was barely given time to throw a few belongings into a suitcase. In a thin voice, she explained to her daughters that she was setting off on a journey for a few days, perhaps longer. Then she told them to be good. Michel was distraught. 'We adhered to an old Russian custom, which is to remain silent when a member of the family goes away on their own. There was the very lightest of kisses.'[61] No tears. The car door slammed, then silence. Everything happened so quickly that she didn't have the presence of mind to take her pen with her, her reading glasses, or even a book. Katherine Mansfield's *Journal*, for example, which she had been dipping into again. Sensing that her death was near, the author of 'At the Bay' advocated resignation pure and simple in the face of misfortune: 'Everything in life that we really accept undergoes a change. So suffering must become Love. That is the mystery.'[62] How are we to believe it?

12

As on a Shipwrecked Boat
(13th July–9th November 1942)

Live – live – that's all. Then take your leave of life on this earth, as Chekhov did, and Tolstoy.

Katherine Mansfield, Journal, 19th December 1920

Irène Némirovsky was taken to the police station at Toulon-sur-Arroux, about ten kilometres from Issy. From that day on she ceased to be a novelist, a mother, a wife, a Russian, a Frenchwoman: she was just a Jewess.

Michel knew that she was to be taken to the concentration camp at Pithiviers, in the Loiret. He was even informed of the reason: 'general measures against stateless Jews between the ages of 16 and 45'.[1] It was because neither he nor his daughters fitted this category, he believed, that only Irène was taken away. If this reasoning is correct, it does away with the assumption that she was informed against. Yet this is a hypothesis we must consider, however, for why else would the police have suddenly had the notion of arresting a novelist in a small, hidden-away town? Was she denounced? It would not have surprised her, for Bruno von Falk, throwing the packets of anonymous letters that had been received at the Kommandantur into the fire, said: 'People's lives aren't worth much, and defeat arouses the worst in men.'[2]

Before kissing her daughters goodbye, she had time to tell Michel which their most urgent options were. First and foremost, to make use of Paul Morand's, Bernard Grasset's and Albin Michel's German connections. André Sabatier undertook these first steps as soon as he was informed by telephone. In a brief letter, written in pencil at the police station, at five o'clock that afternoon, Irène suggested other paths open to them, all the while trying to conceal her anguish:

> My dearest love
>
> For the moment I am at the police station where I ate some blackcurrants and redcurrants while waiting for them to come and get me. It is

most important to stay calm, I believe it won't be for very long. I thought
we could also ask Caillaux and Father Dimnet for help. What do you think?

I shower my darling daughters with kisses, tell Denise to be good and
sensible . . . You are in my heart, as well as Babet, may the good Lord
protect you. As for me, I feel calm and strong.

If you can send me anything, I think my second pair of glasses is in
the other suitcase (in the wallet). Books please, and also if possible a bit
of salted butter. Goodbye my love!

Senator Joseph Caillaux, the former Prime Minister, and a minister
at various times, was a personal friend of Irène Némirovsky's, and
in late 1941, he had even sent her an inscribed copy of his memoirs.
It does not appear that the support of this pillar of the Third
Republic was sought. As for the worldly Canon Ernest Dimnet,
whose celebrated *Art de penser* was published by Grasset the same
year as *David Golder*, he had been in the United States since 1920;
all hope had virtually vanished when, on 25th September, Michel
received an offer to intercede on Irène's behalf from the ultra-
collaborationist Alphonse de Châteaubriant, the editor of *La Gerbe*.
And even this was not to help free her, but to 'find a good
doctor' . . .[3]

Throughout the summer of 1942, marooned in Issy-l'Évêque, Michel
Epstein moved heaven and earth. He slept terribly, lost his appetite
and his smile, and drowned his sorrows in the Bordeaux wine sent to
him by Julie's parents. Worry and exasperation had made him irascible. When, on the morning of the arrest, poor Francine had thought
it best not to lay a place for 'Madame', he flew into a rage and began
throwing plates around. Denise and Élisabeth, who were consigned
to one room in this house that all of a sudden seemed vast to them,
dreaded his explosions of anger. They were forbidden to laugh, and
forbidden to come out of their room. 'He didn't want to see us.'[4] He
feared being arrested himself and could foresee the day when he would
have to abandon his daughters. 'I fear for the children,' he wrote to
Sabatier on 27th July.

Every day, he tried new approaches, wrote letters, sent telegrams,
circumvented the ban on Jews receiving and making telephone calls,
posted a reply-paid letter to the commandant of the Pithiviers camp.
His efforts met only with failure, impotence or silence. As the options

open to him ran out and the days passed, he grew stubborn and persistent, stooping to the most humiliating, most preposterous petitions, and even considering giving himself up in order to be with her or to swap places with her. André Sabatier had the greatest difficulty – and the greatest sorrow – in reasoning with him, but he did all he could to be of help.

As far as human charity was concerned, Irène Némirovsky knew what she was dealing with. 'In life, as on a shipwrecked boat, you have to cut off the hands of anyone who tries to hang on. Alone, you can stay afloat. If you waste time saving other people, you're finished!'⁵ Paul Epstein, for example, happened to have a meeting on 14th July with Comte René de Chambrun, the son-in-law and close colleague of President Laval. Two days later, Paul was one of thirteen thousand to be rounded up in the Vél d'Hiv.* They would be deported on 22nd July, two days before Samuel Epstein and his wife, whose letter, thrown from a train, remains one of the most uncompromising testimonies of what the squalid prisons at Drancy were really like.⁶ As for Chambrun, he would pay little attention to Sabatier's follow-up calls.

Jacques Benoist-Méchin, Secretary of State to the Vice-President of the Council of Ministers, whom Sabatier literally begged to intervene, would only agree to an unproductive administrative plea. Michel's acquaintance, Hélène Morand, the Princesse Soutzo, who was deeply anti-Semitic, but a fashionable hostess who entertained the flower of Franco-German society at her salon, did her best to discourage any excessive confidence:

> As soon as I received your phone call from Moulins, I spoke to my husband and began to make arrangements to secure the intervention of those most capable of dealing with this matter. We shall do what we can for your poor wife and you must have hope and much patience alas. How was she so mistaken as not to share your nationality? I cannot tell you with what compassion and sympathy I think of her and I shall put all my fervent efforts into pleading her case. I think it is nevertheless my

*Conventional shortening for the Vélodrome d'Hiver, the cycle-racing stadium in Paris, in which Jews were interned in July 1942 before being transferred to the transit camp at Drancy. [Tr.]

duty to tell you that this is extremely difficult precisely because it is a general measure.[7]

Secretly flattered that anyone should imagine she had such influence with Mme Abetz, the wife of the German ambassador, Hélène Morand agreed, however, to coordinate Michel's and Sabatier's efforts. But before involving herself, and, given the current value of friendship, she required solemn proofs of anti-Bolshevism in order to win over the Occupation authorities. As Michel Epstein wore himself out gathering the evidence, he was pleased to be able to remind her that the Némirovskys had been stripped of their rights and expelled from Red Russia, and that his wife's work resounded with her dislike of the Soviet regime. He went further. In a letter 'of great audacity' addressed to Otto Abetz, he paraded the pathetic reference written by Feldwebel Hammberger, assured the ambassador of their mutual 'hatred of the Bolshevik regime' and harked back to the groundless accusations made against Irène Némirovsky, in the hope that this time they might save her:

> In none of her books (which moreover have not been banned by the occupying authorities), will you find a single word against Germany and, even though my wife is of Jewish descent, she does not speak of the Jews with any affection . . . If I may also take the liberty of pointing out to you that my wife has always avoided belonging to any political party, that she has never received special treatment from any government either left-wing or right-wing, and that the newspaper she contributed to as a novelist, *Gringoire*, whose editor is H. de Carbuccia, has certainly never been well-disposed towards either the Jews or the Communists.[8]

Michel did not fail to point out, of course, that Irène was Catholic, that her daughters were French and that her asthma could be fatal; it was information that carried no weight and merely indicated his own feverish state of mind. So much so that André Sabatier reckoned it inopportune to use this desperate letter 'for the purpose its author intended'.[9] A fortnight later, Hélène Morand had still not forwarded it, and she probably never would, for having read *Snow in Autumn*, it did not seem to her to provide sufficient guarantees: 'anti-revolutionary, of course, but not anti-Bolshevik'.[10] It is true that Irène Némirovsky had never been involved with politics, had only written novels, and was not the author of 'Je brûle Moscou'.*

Mavlik, Michel Epstein's sister, urging her brother to have courage and to pray, calmly explained to him that Irène's fame was her main handicap: 'the less well-known the people concerned are . . . the better their chances'.[11] For her part, she obtained from old Count Kokovtzov, a family friend and the former author of a virulently anti-Soviet pamphlet that had an introduction by Poincaré,[12] a testimony of anti-Bolshevism that could be helpful to Samuel, Paul and Irène. It had no effect.

Very gradually, Michel began to lose heart. He had hoped that Professor Louis Bazy, who replaced Pastor Vallery-Radot as President of the Red Cross, might at least be able to reassure Irène about her daughters and to send her a parcel – for he believed she had been moved to a French camp. On 9th August, his anxiety rose a degree: he had just learned 'from a very reliable source' that those interned at Pithiviers, men, women and children, had been sent 'further east – probably Poland or Russia'. He wrote a moving letter to Sabatier:

> Up till now, I thought my wife was in some camp in France, in the custody of French soldiers. To learn she is in an uncivilised country, in conditions that are probably atrocious, without money or food and with people whose language she does not even know, is unbearable. It is now no longer a matter of getting her out of a camp sooner rather than later but of saving her life.
>
> . . . Alas, my dear friend, I am launching one final appeal. I know that it is unforgivable to impose on you and the rest of our remaining friends this way but, I say it again, it is a question of life and death not only for my wife but also our children, not to mention myself. The situation is serious. Alone here, with the little ones, virtually imprisoned since it is forbidden for me to move, I cannot even take solace in being able to act. I can no longer either sleep or eat, please accept that as an excuse for this incoherent letter.

Hélène Morand endeavoured to be reassuring: it was certainly likely that Irène Némirovsky, like thousands of others, had been sent across the Rhine, but to one of those 'Polish towns where they gather up

---

*A short story by Paul Morand. [Tr.]

the stateless people'.[13] The town in question was called Oswiecim, in German, Auschwitz – close by the former Slovak frontier. It was in fact a metropolis, but one inhabited by the living dead. Here Princesse Soutzo's willingness to help came to a halt; all she could suggest, as a last recourse, was to knock on the door of the Union Générale des Israélites en France (the Jewish Union), a 'representative' mouthpiece created by Vichy, one of the purposes of which was to give state anti-Semitism an honourable aspect. In actual fact, the UGIF was a decoy intended to allay the suspicions of Jews or reward them for their support.

On 12th August, Sabatier's letter summarising the situation sounded the death knell: 'All this is very hard, I feel it only too well, dear Monsieur. You must try only to think of the children and remain strong for them, easy advice to give . . . I'm sure you'll say. Alas! I have done everything I can. Your very faithful André.' Michel still continued to make what efforts he could, but he made sure he took no more inopportune steps. He now appeared to be mainly concerned about anticipating the inevitable. The flat on Avenue Coquelin was sold to former servants. On 15th September, having remained silently at home for a month, and now anxious at the approach of winter, he lost patience. He made a fresh approach to Sabatier concerning Hélène Morand, and Sabatier replied: 'It's like banging your head against a wall.'[14] And the walls no longer had ears.

Since 17th July, nineteen thousand Jews had met with Irène Némirovsky's fate, a fifth of them children. It was not mentioned in the press, but the rumours were rife. Monseigneur Saliège, the Archbishop of Toulouse, saved the Church's honour by having the priests of his diocese read out a stirring pastoral letter from their pulpits: 'Jews are men, Jews are women. Foreigners are men, foreigners are women. Not everything is permitted against them, against these men, against these women, against these fathers and mothers. They are part of the human race. They are our brothers, like so many others. A Christian cannot forget this.'

People do not reconcile themselves to the unimaginable. On 5th October 1942, André Sabatier was obliged to dissuade Michel Epstein strongly from attempting to renew his alien's identity card. He believed he would run greater risk by doing something illegal. Michel complied, but immediately began to make the arrangements he considered necessary. On the 8th, he assigned full authority for his daughters to Julie Dumot, in the presence of M. Vernet, the notary in Issy-l'Évêque. Then he sent his one piece of advice to Madeleine Avot: 'Do not forsake the little ones should any misfortune come to them.' Finally, in an extraordinarily calm manner, he asked Sabatier: 'If you think I should provide my children with a change of scene, will you let me know? With best wishes and may God protect us all.' He was arrested the following day.

Having seen his wife and brothers disappear, one after another in the space of two weeks, without any news of them, under house arrest, and half-crazed from worry and insomnia, Michel was expecting to be arrested. Moreover, he had come to desire it. To facilitate it? The astonishing care he took over his final actions as a free man, the serene way he went about them, on the very eve of his arrest, are disturbing. Since his appeals had crumbled in quick succession, all that remained for him was to make the first move. If Irène was not to be given back to him, he would give himself back to her. His daughter Denise could not swear to it, and yet: 'He only became himself again on the day he was arrested. He was ever so happy because he was convinced that he was going to find my mother, or in any case share the same fate.'[15] And his mind was at peace because his daughters would be in the care of 'Auntie Julie', who would now receive the monthly payments from Esménard. There was only one thing Michel was unaware of: Denise and Élisabeth, though French and baptised, and despite the fact that the latter was only five years old, were duly filed among the 'Jews currently domiciled in the arrondissement of Autun and the adjoining district of Charollais'.[16]

On 9th October 1942, the scenario of 13th July was re-enacted: the police knew the way. Father and daughters were taken together to the *préfecture* at Autun. This was where the two scenes took place that would decide the fate both of Irène Némirovsky's daughters and that of *Suite Française*. Firstly, a German officer took from his wallet a photograph of his little daughter, who was as blonde as Denise, and said to the girls: 'I give you forty-eight hours to get away.'[17] Then, Michel's final words of advice before being led off to Le Creusot prison: 'Never part from this suitcase, for it contains your mother's manuscript.'[18] A manuscript that was interrupted, but not unfinished: Michel was not for a moment thinking of posterity, but about the work in progress, which Irène would soon complete. It would be many long years before Denise opened this suitcase, which was embossed with Léon Némirovsky's initials, for it was first and foremost her mother's book.

Michel was detained for at least ten days at Le Creusot, which was bombed on the 17th, then he was transferred to Drancy, the transit camp in the east of Paris. Before sending him to his death, someone took the trouble to rob him of 8,500 francs that he would not need. His daughters did not leave Issy-l'Évêque immediately, and Julie continued to correspond with their father for a while, up until the day at the end of October when, at about two o'clock in the afternoon, two policemen and a militiaman arrived at the village school. Mme Ravaud, the teacher, barely had time to hide Denise upstairs, behind the bed belonging to her mother, a First World War widow whom nobody would dare to disturb. In the evening, after classes were over, Denise was returned to Julie Dumot, who hurriedly tossed a few papers, some photographs and some jewellery into a suitcase, tore up the yellow star and threw it into the fire, before setting off with the little girls without delay for Bordeaux. Bleuette, the doll, and Copain, the puppy, both orphans, did not join them on the journey.

In Paris, on 6th November 1942, André Sabatier sent Julie Dumot 1,150 francs, in payment for the publication of 'Les Vierges', Irène Némirovsky's last short story, in *Présent*. Ten kilometres away, that same day, approximately one thousand men and women, and one hundred and thirteen children under the age of twelve, were crammed into Convoy No. 42, departing Drancy, bound for Auschwitz. Since 17th July there had been thirty-six convoys – thirty-six thousand sentences of death! Hardly any of them would survive, for almost all of them would be gassed upon arrival. This was not how Michel imagined he would find Irène. But he did find her.

From her father, Élisabeth would treasure one particular memento: the comb which he ran through her curly hair, and which gave her a delicious pain . . .

EPILOGUE

A Long Journey
(1943–2004)

Born in the East, Irène went to her death in the East. Uprooted from the land of her birth in order to live, she was uprooted from the land of her choosing in order to die. Between these two pages an existence that was outstanding but all too brief left its mark: a young Russian woman came and left in the visitors' book of our language pages that enriched it. For the twenty years that she had spent among us, we mourn in her a French writer.

Jean-Jacques Bernard, 1946

Julie Dumot was a strong believer. Hidden away in a Catholic boarding school in Bordeaux, Denise and Élisabeth were able to escape arrest for a while, using false names which they had difficulty in remembering. From February 1944, there began a cycle of hiding places, bombardment and fear. Élisabeth had to be gagged so that her laugh should not attract the attention of the German patrols. And her nose had to be concealed because Julie said it was a give-away. Life or death depended on absolute silence. And as a result: 'Because the diet in the cellars was bad for the health, I was ill.'[1] Denise was referring euphemistically to her pleurisy, which would not be cured until August 1945.

On 28th August, Bordeaux was liberated. In September, Denise and Élisabeth, who were destitute, were able to return to school. If André Sabatier did not publish *All Our Worldly Goods* and *La Vie de Tchekhov* immediately, it was chiefly because he believed it 'dangerous to draw attention to her at a time when her situation might be shielding her from reprisals that were still to be feared'.[2] The concentration camp at Auschwitz had still not been 'discovered' by the Soviets at this time and the Shoah had no name. All of Irène and Michel Epstein's friends still continued to hope they would return: Madeleine Cabour, who agreed to take care of their children; Raïssa Adler, who asked for news; the journalist Janine Auscher, who lived through the hell of Drancy;

Canon Dimnet; Mila Gordon: no one wanted to believe they were dead. Julie Dumot, who addressed them by their first names, would even continue sending bottles of Bordeaux to Issy-l'Évêque in April 1945 . . .

At the Gare de l'Est and at the Hôtel Lutetia, Denise and Babet held up their placards until they were ready to collapse. 'She wasn't dead. She was coming home after a long journey. She was pale, weary, weak, her features had barely changed and were still recognisable; they were like the features of loved ones who have passed on, in dreams; she was still dressed in black, she was anxious; in a hurry; someone was waiting for her, calling out for her.'[3] There was only one person who expected nothing: at the age of seventy, Fanny Némirovsky, was still neither the right age, nor did she have the talent, to be a grandmother. When Julie came to appeal for help, she spoke through the closed door of her apartment: 'I have no grandchildren.' She would, however, pay out a voluntary pension, or rather a hand-out: 1,000 francs.

Irène Némirovsky would not come back. In Geneva, in February 1945, Olga Jungelson, the envoy of the Department of Refugees at the Red Cross, could obtain no information relating either to her, or to the other deported writers whom she was responsible for tracking down: Benjamin Crémieux, Robert Desnos, Jean Cavaillès, Maurice Halbwachs . . .[4] And when in June, in a fit of belated remorse, the Banque des Pays du Nord suddenly realised that it ought to make a gesture towards Denise and Babet, it was 'in memory of M. Epstein',[5] who was removed from his duties during the first months of the Occupation. The bank took its place among a 'board of guardians' administered by the Société des Gens de Lettres and Albin Michel, which was to provide for the children's education and support until they came of age. 'I should have helped save her, I should have done more . . .',[6] Robert Esménard would reproach himself for a long time. Initially, it was purely a matter of advances on royalties, but in December 1945, after a meeting of the 'committee of aid to the children of Irène Némirovsky' at the home of the novelist Simone Saint-Clair, a survivor from Ravensbrück, the publisher undertook to relinquish 2,000 francs per month without compensation, so as not to increase the debt built up on the author's account, which at the time amounted to 89,000 francs.

In the same spirit, André Sabatier made it his duty to publish whatever he could. Beginning with *Fire in the Blood*, the short novel – or the 'accomplished long short story'[7] – which in 1945 he intended to place in the monthly review *La Nef*, but which, strangely, he never actually managed to lay his hands on. *La Vie de Tchekhov* would thus be Irène Némirovsky's first posthumous work. It was published in October 1946 with a preface by her friend Jean-Jacques Bernard, who had himself returned from the 'camp of slow death' at Compiègne. This homage appeared initially in *La Nef* in July, followed by a short extract from the book.

Jean-Jacques Bernard was a good prophet: 'Irène Némirovsky,' he wrote, 'does not leave her admirers empty-handed. She worked up to the last moment. Her books do not stop with her. Some precious manuscripts, together with her published work, will reinforce her literary survival.' First, in February 1947, would come *All Our Worldly Goods*, then *The Fires of Autumn*, ten years later. And that was all. Jean-Jacques Bernard, however, believed it to be the case that Irène Némirovsky 'was working on a long cyclical novel . . .' at Issy-l'Évêque, 'of which we unfortunately only have fragments'.[8]

Because of its incomplete condition, *Suite Française* would remain on a shelf for several decades, until Denise Epstein, with the help of a strong magnifying glass, resolved to set about typing it out, spurred on by her mother. It was her mother's voice that she hoped would be listened to, in September 2004, by those it would reach. 'Try to do as many discussions and things as possible that may interest people in 52 or 2052,' Irène Némirovsky had promised herself. Her readers would not have to wait so long.

Fanny Némirovsky died in 1972, aged about ninety-seven. 'She had sold her flat in order to provide herself with a life annuity and lived very comfortably from our grandfather's wealth and from selling her jewellery.'[9]

Victoria, her younger sister, died in Moscow in 1988 at the age of ninety-four. She was the last person who remembered Irotchka's 'previous life'.

Élisabeth Gille, a publisher, translator and writer, died in 1996. She had devoted a moving 'imaginary biography' to her mother, *Le Mirador*, which was awarded the Wizo literary prize in April 1992.

Denise Epstein hoped that *Suite Française*, this novel that had been read by ten people over sixty years, would not be forgotten too quickly. She could not have suspected that by publishing it she would be giving back to her mother the love and gratitude of her readers, which she had been deprived of due to a long period of misfortune. Who can have any doubts today that Irène Némirovsky is very much alive?

Notes

[All references are to first French publication (with chapter number and part number which apply also to English translation where available) unless indicated otherwise]

Prologue

1. J. de Nibelle, 'Israël dans le Loiret!', *L'Écho de Pithiviers. Journal de la Beauce et du Gâtinais*, 24th May 1941.
2. Report on Convoy No. 6 and A. Mercier, *Convoi No. 6. Destination: Auschwitz 17th July 1942*, Le Cherche Midi, 2005, p. 42.
3. Interview with Samuel Chymisz, 5th March 2005.
4. *Ibid.*
5. *Ibid.* One of the fullest accounts of Convoy No. 6 is that by Moshè Garbarz, author of a book of memoirs, *Un survivant. Auschwitz–Birkenau–Buchenwald 1942–1945*, Ramsay, 2006. In the remarkable book *Convoi No. 6 (op. cit.)*, we also find the further testimonies of Samuel Chymisz, Berek Wancier, Joseph Pinta, Bernard Hubel, Albert Abram Wainstein and Moshé Cukierman, some of the ninety-one survivors of this convoy in 1945. The earliest convoys from Pithiviers were less subject to 'selection', so as to replace the number who had recently been gassed and to provide labour for the construction of the camp.
6. J. de Nibelle, 'Israël dans le Loiret!', *op. cit.*
7. *Le Vin de Solitude* [*The Wine of Solitude*], I, III.
8. *La Vie de Tchekhov*, XXII.
9. *Les Chiens et les Loups* [*The Dogs and the Wolves*], XXXIII.

Chapter 1

1. *Les Chiens et les Loups* [*The Dogs and the Wolves*], XX.
2. M. Bulgakov, 'The City of Kiev', *Nakanune*, 6th July 1923.
3. 'Le Sortilège', *Gringoire*, 1 February 1940; in *Dimanche*, Stock, 2000.

4. *Les Chiens et les Loups* [*The Dogs and the Wolves*], IV.

5. *Ibid.*

6. *Le Malentendu* [The Misunderstood], I , *Les Œuvres libres*, No. 56, Fayard, February 1926. We come across this formulation several times in Irène Némirovsky's work, notably in 'Nativité': 'The dawn was breaking, the wind had shifted. As she put her head outside, she felt that *the very fragrance of the air* had changed during the night.' (*Gringoire*, 8th December 1933, in *Destinées*.) But also, in her working notebook for the summer of 1933: 'What I slightly fear, if I describe Finland, is on the one hand, that I have forgotten *the fragrance of the air*, the atmosphere and details of the climate, and on the other hand, that the events, in the main, are trivial.'

7. *Le Vin de Solitude* [*The Wine of Solitude*], I, VII.

8. *Ibid.*, I, I.

9. B. Lecache, *Quand Israël meurt . . . Au pays des pogroms*, Éditions du 'Progrès civique', 1927.

10. *Les Chiens et les Loups* [*The Dogs and the Wolves*], XIX.

11. A. Bely, *Petersburg*, 1912. Translated from Russian by David McDuff, Penguin, London, 1995.

12. P. Nerey [I. Némirovsky], *L'Ennemie*, in *Les Œuvres libres*, No. 85, Fayard, July 1928, IV, iii and I, iii.

13. F. Lefèvre, 'Une révélation. Une heure avec Irène Némirovsky', *Les Nouvelles littéraires*, 11th January 1930.

14. H. de Régnier, *Les Cahiers inédits 1887–1936*, Pygmalion / Gérard Watelet, 2002 (3rd November 1935).

15. 'La Confidence', *Revue des Deux Mondes*, 15th October 1938, in *Destinées*, Sables.

16. *L'Ennemie*, III, III.

17. 'La Confidence', *op. cit.*

18. A. Chekhov, 'She and He'.

19. Card addressed to 'Mme Sprecher, Hôtel de Berne, 90 rue de Châteaudun, Paris'.

20. *L'Affaire Courilof* [*The Courilof Affair*], V.

21. *Le Vin de Solitude* [*The Wine of Solitude*], I, I.

22. *Les Chiens et les Loups* [*The Dogs and the Wolves*], XX.

23. R. Bourget-Pailleron, 'La nouvelle équipe. Mme Irène Némirovsky. M. Joseph Peyré', *Revue des Deux Mondes*, no. 591, 1936.

24. *Le Vin de Solitude* [*The Wine of Solitude*], I, VIII.

25. R. Bourget-Pailleron, 'La nouvelle équipe . . .', *op. cit.*

26. *Le Vin de Solitude* [*The Wine of Solitude*], I, III.

27. None of the replies reprinted in this chapter, or in the others, is imaginary: they come from Irène Némirovsky's recollections that she noted down in her working notebook for *The Wine of Solitude*, preserved at IMEC.

28. *Le Vin de Solitude* [*The Wine of Solitude*], I, VIII.

29. *L'Ennemie*, I, I.

30. Namely, the novel *Les Échelles du Levant* [The Ports of the Levant], serialised in *Gringoire* from May to October 1939, and published by Denoël in 2005 as *Le Maître des âmes* [The Master of Souls], the title we use here.

31. A. Chekhov, *Notebooks* (8th September 1897).

32. An echo of the Nice carnival, which Irène Némirovsky must have been to on several occasions, occurs in *David Golder*: 'They fell silent, as they both remembered the same street in Nice, thronging on Carnival night with people wearing masks who sang as they passed by. They remembered the palm trees, the moon and the shouts of the crowd in Place Masséna . . .' (Chatto & Windus, London.) These masks could still be seen in 1930, in Jean Vigo's short documentary film, *À propos de Nice*.

33. Th. Purdy, 'A French Success' [*The Nation*, 1931]. A little-known critic was even closer to the target: 'The characters are very simple. They lose in subtlety, in humanity what they gain in power, in intensity. They stand out like masks. They all frighten us; none of them arouse our pity.' (M. Hénon, *La Collaboration pédagogique*, 27th April 1930.)

34. *La Vie de Tchekhov* [*The Life of Chekhov*], XXVIII.

35. Prince F. Yusupov, *Memoirs*.

36. A. Rémizov, *La Russie dans la tourmente*, 'L'Âge d'Homme, 2000.

37. Conversation with Tatiana Morozova, Moscow, 28th January 2006.

38. *The Wine of Solitude*, I, I.

39. *L'Ennemie*, IV, I.

40. Conversation with Tatiana Morozova, Moscow, 28th January 2006. In *The Wine of Solitude*, I. Némirovsky alludes to a difference in age between herself and her mother that corresponds almost exactly: 'I am eighteen and she is forty-five . . .' (IV, V). If Anna had really been born on 1st April 1887, Irène would have had to have been conceived when Anna was fifteen; yet she was a woman when Léon married her. When she died on 9th July 1972, Jeanne Némirovsky – the name under which

she had been registered in 1948 by the Office français de protection de refugiés et apatrides, as a 'Latvian refugee' – was therefore aged ninety-six or ninety-seven, and not one hundred and two, as her grand-daughters would choose to maintain, thanks to her egoism and her lies. For, just as Anna/Fanny had refused to take charge of Denise and Élisabeth Epstein, who were now orphans, in 1945, she later disputed any relationship with Irène Némirovsky. 'When we went to ring her doorbell, she replied, without opening, that she had no grandchildren,' related Élisabeth Gille . . . 'Many years later, I telephoned her, saying that I was a journalist, that I wanted to write an article on the writers of the 1930s, that I had just discovered her name in the directory, and wondered whether she belonged to the same family as the novelist. She shouted that she had never heard of Irène Némirovsky.' (*Cf.* Myriam Anissimov, 'Les filles d'Irène Némirovsky', *Les Nouveaux Cahiers*, no. 108, spring 1992.) Anna/Fanny/Jeanne Némirovsky was buried on 13th July 1972 at the Belleville cemetery in Paris, in the Jewish sector, close to Léon and to Iona and Rosa Margoulis. Her tomb bears the Hebrew inscription: 'May the souls of the dead remain always with the living.'

41. Conversation with Tatiana Morozova, Moscow, 28th January 2006.
42. C. Aleichem, *Menahem-Mendl le rêveur*, Albin Michel, 1975.
43. *Le Vin de Solitude* [*The Wine of Solitude*], I, I.
44. Antoine Vincent Arnault (1766–1834), French poet, fabulist and play-wright, emigrated to England in 1792, was arrested on his return and then released. A public official during the Empire, he was once again forced into exile during the Restoration and was barred from the Académie française. He would become its permanent secretary in 1829, following his final return home.
45. These two towns have been renamed Dniepropetrovsk and Zaporozhe.
46. Conversation with Tatiana Morozova, Moscow, 28th January 2006. Victoria Zilpert, *née* Margoulis, died in 1988 at the age of ninety-five.
47. 'Le Sortilège', *op. cit.*, p. 294.
48. *Les Chiens et les Loups* [*The Dogs and the Wolves*], VI.
49. *Le Vin de Solitude* [*The Wine of Solitude*], *op. cit.*, IV, III.
50. *David Golder*, Grasset, 'Les Cahiers rouges'.
51. There is an echo in *David Golder*: 'Children . . . They're all the same . . . and they're the reason we live. It's for them that we keep working. Not like my own father, no . . . At thirteen, get the hell out, fend for yourself . . . That's what they all deserve.' (*Ibid.*)

52. Isroel Rabon described Baluty, the wretched ghetto of Lodz, in *Balut* (Folies d'encres, 2006), without taking anything from the Yiddish picture Irène Némirovsky depicts in 'L'Enfant génial' or *The Dogs and the Wolves*.

53. 'L'Enfant génial', in *Les Œuvres libres,* no. 70, Fayard, April 1927.

54. *Cf.* M. Druon, *L'aurore vient du fond du ciel. Mémoires*, Plon/Éditions de Fallois, 2006. One can also consult *The Thirteenth Tribe* by Arthur Koestler, 1976.

55. *Le Vin de Solitude* [*The Wine of Solitude*], I, I.

56. *Cf.* M. N. Tchirkoff, 'Allumettes', in W. de Kovalevsky (ed.), *La Russie à la fin du 19ᵉ siècle*, Paul Dumont/Guillaumin et Cie, 1900.

57. 'L'Enfant génial', *op. cit.*

58. *Les Chiens et les Loups* [*The Dogs and the Wolves*], VI.

59. I. Zangwill, 'Samooborona', in *Ghetto Comedies*.

60. 'L'Enfant génial'.

61. I. Babel, *Entre chien et loup*, Gallimard, 1970.

62. 'Astonishingly, this street resembled the interior of a farmyard. Apparently the sun never penetrated inside . . . Everyone threw the things they did not want and that were dirty out into the street, giving passers-by the opportunity to express their different feelings about this trash . . . A mass of little Jews, dirty, in tatters, with frizzy hair, were yelling and grovelling in the mud.' (Gogol, *Taras Bulba*).

63. *David Golder, op. cit.*

64. A. Spire, 'Israel Zangwill', *Quelques Juifs et demi-Juifs*, Grasset, 1928. The quotations by Zangwill, taken from *Enfants du ghetto*, are from the same work.

65. The first uprisings of the Zaporozhe Cossacks against the Jewish farmers began in 1638, led by the hetman Pawliuk, but the revolt of Bohdan Khmelnytsky brought about the deaths of 180,000 Jews, not including those from Nemirov, massacred by the *haidamaks*, fanatical partisans who gathered in bloodthirsty hordes. More than six hundred villages were razed to the ground. For the sake of the cause, the Jews were furthermore accused of poisoning the wells, murdering Christian children or causing epidemics. A few Jews from Nemirov sought safety in baptism, others found refuge in the neighbouring town of Toulchin. (*Cf.* S. Asch, *La Sanctification du nom*, L'Âge d'Homme, 1985.) A few years later, General Wisniowiecki, at the head of three thousand men, recaptured Nemirov from the Zaporozhe, thus enabling the 'marranos' of Nemirov to regain their ancient faith. Nemirov became

an important Hassidic centre in the nineteenth century and numbered nearly three thousand Jews in 1896, half as many as in 1648. Note that in 2006, the Yad Vashem Institute registered almost two thousand Nemirovskys who were victims of the Shoah.

66. I. Babel, *Odessa Tales*.

67. For example, Sholem Asch's worthies whom nothing frightens as much as the proximity of the ghetto: 'Who are these creatures so unlike us, down in the Jewish community? How do they live there? What is this language they speak? How unlike us they are! How foreign they are to us! People from another country, from a region so far away, from a place in which one would never set foot! Aren't they Eskimos or some other tribe from an unexplored corner of this vast Russian empire?' (*Pétersbourg*, Mémoire du Livre.) One also finds in the work of Asch, someone who is hardly likely to be anti-Semitic, clichés that would be shocking in other writers. For example: 'A young man was following them who was tall and thin, with very pronounced Jewish looks, emphasised by the bony curve of the nose and the drooping lip.'

68. *Les Chiens et les Loups* [*The Dogs and the Wolves*], VI.

69. *Ibid.*, I.

70. *Ibid.*, VIII.

71. *Lettres de Nicolas II et de sa mère*, trans. Paul Léon, Paris. In his *Mémoires* (Plon, 1921), Count Witte reports that 'the emperor was surrounded by well-known anti-Semites, such as Trepov, Plehve, Ignatyev, and the leaders of the Black Hundreds' (VI), that he 'called the English Jews' (VI) and that he held the Jews solely responsible for the persecutions directed at them, asserting that: 'But it is they themselves, the *zhidy*, who are to blame' (VI).

72. Quoted by A. Spire, *op. cit.*, I. The British parliament had suggested to the Jews that they establish their 'National Home' in Uganda; the World Zionist Congress rejected this offer.

73. Conversation with Tatiana Morozova, Moscow, 28th January 2006.

74. *Les Chiens et les Loups* [*The Dogs and the Wolves*], VII. Sholem Aleichem witnessed the same events: 'Beneath our eyes and beneath the eyes of the whole world, the Cossacks helped to smash windows, doors, locks and to stuff their pockets full. Beneath the eyes of our children, they killed and tortured Jews, women and children.' (Letter to Morris Fischberg, quoted by H. Bulawko, *Monsieur Cholem Aleichem*, Paris, Gil Wern editions, 1995.)

75. Beneath this sentence taken from the 'Diary' of *Le Vin de Solitude*, [*The Wine of Solitude*], I. Némirovsky noted: 'The difference in tone. Health, that goes without saying. But the religious fervour to ask for the daily bread.'

76. *Les Chiens et les Loups* [*The Dogs and the Wolves*], X.

77. It is not known where the Némirovskys lived before 1909; Fundukleyev Street, according to Tatiana Morozova.

78. *Les Chiens et les Loups* [*The Dogs and the Wolves*], VIII.

79. *Ibid.*, IV.

80. *L'Ennemie*, II, I.

81. *Le Vin de Solitude* [*The Wine of Solitude*], I, I.

82. Late 1937 – early 1938, I. Némirovsky also planned to write a life of 'young Napoleon'.

83. This, at least, is what Janine Auscher maintains, 'Nos interviews: Irène Némirovsky', *L'Univers israélite*, 5th July 1935.

84. G. Higgins, 'Les Conrad français', *Les Nouvelles littéraires*, 6th April 1940.

85. *Cf.* Ph. Jullian, *Sarah Bernhardt*, Balland, 1977.

86. *Cf.* J. Huret, *Sarah Bernhardt*, F. Juven, 1899.

87. Vladimir Alexandrovich Sukhomlinov (1848–1926) took command of the Tsar's horseguards in 1876. From 1886 to 1897, he was in charge of the School of Cavalry Officers, which he founded. In 1899, promoted to lieutenant-general, he was appointed chief of general staff for the military district of Kiev, then commander in chief in 1904. In 1905, he was appointed Governor-General of Kiev, Volynia and Podolia, then, in December 1908, Chief of General Staff in the Russian army, and finally Minister for War in April 1909, until he was replaced by General Polivanov on 29th June 1915. Accused of allowing the Russian armies to be unprepared, of prevarication, of sabotaging the supply of arms and of spying for the German armies, to whom he had handed over the Chief of Staff's plans, he was arrested and tried for high treason in May 1916, imprisoned and then released by Prime Minister Stürmer in October 1916, then arrested again, retried and given amnesty in May 1918 in view of his age. He succeeded in crossing into Germany, where he published his memoirs in 1923. 'An insignificant and corrupt man', according to Trotsky, he nevertheless 'favoured the development of communism, or, if one prefers, bolshevism', through his acquiescing to 'German gold', which was indicative of the 'distressing decay of the ruling classes'. (*History of the Russian Revolution.*)

88. 'En marge de l'*Affaire Courilof*,' Radio conversation between F. Lefèvre and Mme I. Némirovsky', *Sud de Montpellier*, 7th June 1933.
89. *Les Chiens et les Loups* [*The Dogs and the Wolves*], X.
90. *Le Vin de Solitude* [*The Wine of Solitude*], I, III.

Chapter 2

1. *Le Vin de Solitude* [*The Wine of Solitude*], I, VIII.
2. *L'Ennemie*, IV, III.
3. *Le Vin de Solitude* [*The Wine of Solitude*], I, III.
4. *Ibid.*, I, VIII.
5. *Ibid.*, I, VII.
6. *Ibid.*, I, VIII.
7. In *David Golder* we come across 'Porjès' (and all the others), one of Gloria's former lovers, 'who juggled enormous fortunes'.
8. *Ibid.*, p. 167.
9. *L'Ennemie*, IV, II.
10. 'Le Sortilège', *op. cit.*
11. F. Lefèvre, 'Une révélation. Une heure avec Irène Némirovsky', *Les Nouvelles littéraires*, 11th January 1930.
12. *La Vie de Tchekhov*, XXX.
13. *Le Vin de Solitude* [*The Wine of Solitude*], I, I.
14. *Ibid.*, I, IV.
15. Janine Auscher, 'Sous la lampe. Irène Némirowsky', *Marianne*, no. 121, 13th February 1935.
16. *L'Ennemie*, II, III.
17. *Ibid.*, II, II.
18. *Le Vin de Solitude* [*The Wine of Solitude*], II, III.
19. *Ibid.*, I, I.
20. *Ibid.*, I, I.
21. *Ibid.*, IV, VIII.
22. *Ibid.*, I, VIII.
23. *Ibid.*, I, II.
24. *Ibid.*, I, VIII.
25. *Ibid.*, I, VIII.
26. F. Dostoyevsky, *Crime and Punishment*.
27. *Le Vin de Solitude* [*The Wine of Solitude*], II, I.

28. M. Gorky, *Vie nouvelle*, no. 106, 2nd June 1918, in *Pensées intempestives*, L'Âge d'Homme, 1975.

29. The name of L. B. Némirovsky does not appear in the lists of the board of directors of the Private Bank of Commerce of St Petersburg published by the *Journal de Saint-Pétersbourg*, a French-language financial paper, in 1913 or in 1914. Omissions excepted, it is likely that Léon Némirovsky did not officially join the board until after war was declared.

30. *Le Vin de Solitude* [*The Wine of Solitude*], II, I, II and III.

31. *L'Ennemie*, II, II.

32. É. Gille, *Le Mirador, Mémoires rêvés*, Stock, 2000, p. 152.

33. Zaharoff is one of the models for the character of James Bohun in *Le Pion sur l'échiquier* (1934).

34. *Le Vin de Solitude* [*The Wine of Solitude*], II, II.

35. *Ibid.*, II, II.

36. 'En marge de *L'Affaire Courilof* . . .' *op. cit.*

37. M. Paléologue, *La Russie des tsars pendant la Grande Guerre*, II. *3 juin 1915–18 août 1916*, Plon, 1922.

38. *Le Vin de Solitude* [*The Wine of Solitude*], II, III.

39. M. Paléologue, *op. cit.*

40. *L'Ennemie*, II, III.

41. *Le Vin de Solitude* [*The Wine of Solitude*], II, I.

42. *Ibid.*, II, III.

43. Word that is hard to read in the preliminary manuscript of 'Mercredi des cendres', from which this extract is taken.

44. *L'Ennemie*, I, V.

45. *Le Vin de solitude* [*The Wine of Solitude*], II, IV.

46. This is how, on 25th March 1934, in the preliminary manuscript of *The Wine of Solitude*, Irène Némirovsky puts the finishing touches to the scene of Mlle Rose's death: 'As a general rule, an idea that strikes me as splendid is useless later on. And yet! Anonymous letter – Scene. Maman is going to dismiss Z. and take on an English woman. Z. kills herself. This explains the revenge well. But make it clear that Z. is no longer in her right mind. So, we must wait for the Revolution . . . Yes, it's a good thing. And what also attracts me is that I can put the nerve centre there. I only have to adjust it slightly, and the light falls differently, in a much more startling way. But precautions are necessary. 1) emphasise the moral support that Z. gives the child 2) show clearly how time weighs heavily on Z. and the beginning of her madness

3) alter the death a bit (also so that it is not too similar to *Les Mouches d'automne*). I don't really know what to do about this: I see the first part, when she goes away, how she disappears into this dark city which slowly disintegrates, a city of dung, of fogs, of shots in the darkness etc. But how to make her die? . . . Or killed by a drunken red soldier? I think that she must disappear and that the child should not know until much later how she has died. Roaming along the bank of these dark canals: she had only just wet her feet and she died from cardiac failure. But the child only knew this much later . . .'

47. *David Golder*.

48. *Les Mouches d'automne* [*Snow in Autumn*], IX.

49. 'Les Rivages heureux', *Gringoire*, 2nd November 1934, in *Dimanche*, Stock, 2000.

50. 'Le Spectateur', *Gringoire*, 7th December 1939, in *Dimanche*, Stock, 2000.

51. *Le Vin de Solitude* [*The Wine of Solitude*], II, V and III, I.

52. *L'Ennemie*, II, V.

53. *Le Vin de Solitude* [*The Wine of Solitude*], II, V.

54. *Ibid.*, II, IV.

55. *Ibid.*, I, V.

56. R. Bourget-Pailleron, 'La nouvelle équipe . . .' *op. cit.*

Chapter 3

1. 'Bulletin' dated 21st February 1917, quoted by Alia Rachmanowa, *Aube de vie, aube de mort. Journal d'une étudiante russe pendant la Révolution*, Plon, 1935.

2. L. Trotsky, *History of the Russian Revolution*, vol. I, *The February Revolution*.

3. It is hard to give an exact date for the episode of the mock execution of the *dvornik* Ivan R. Irène Némirovsky appears to place it during the early days of the February Revolution, although mention of the cheers for the portraits of Kerensky would suggest it was the spring. In any case, in this autobiographical story dated 27th March 1938, in the margin of her work on 'Espoir', Zézelle is still alive, though under the fictional name of 'Mlle Rose'.

4. *Le Vin de Solitude* [*The Wine of Solitude*], II, VI.

5. *La Vie de Tchekhov*, XIV.

6. *The L'Affaire Courilof* [*The Courilof Affair*], XXI.

7. *Ibid.*, XVIII.

8. J. Auscher, 'Sous la lampe. Irène Némirovsky', *op. cit.*

9. In his memoirs, for instance, Prince F. Yusupov is totally convinced that tsarism perished because of 'Jewish commissars, more or less concealed by Russian patronymics' (*op. cit.*).

10. A. Rachmanowa, *op. cit.*

11. M. Gorky, *Vie nouvelle*, no. 52, 18th June 1917, in *Pensées intempestives, op. cit.* Gorky had always declared his aversion to anti-Semitism; for example, in his *Notes and Memories*: 'When one thinks of the Jews one feels ashamed. Although personally I don't believe I have done any harm to people of this race during my life, when I meet a Jew, I immediately think of my national relationship with the fanatical sect of anti-Semites and of my responsibility for the stupidity of my compatriots.' (*War and Revolution.*)

12. *Cf.* I. Deutscher, 'The Russian Revolution and the Jewish Problem', conference on 29th October 1964 given by the Jewish Society of the Students Union at the London School of Economics.

13. *Le Vin de Solitude* [*The Wine of Solitude*], II, V.

14. Z. Hippius, *Journal sous la terreur*, Éditions du Rocher, 2006.

15. Quoted by I. Poliakov, *La Causalité diabolique*, II. *Du joug mongol à la victoire de Lénine 1250–1920*, Calmann-Lévy/Mémorial de la Shoah, 2006.

16. 'La Nuit en wagon', *Gringoire*, 5th October 1939, in *Destinées*, p. 207.

17. F. Lefèvre, 'Une révélation . . .' *op. cit.*

18. O. Wilde, *A Woman of No Importance*, Act III.

19. 'Mme Irène Némirovsky [*had particularly been impressed*] by *The Jungle Book*' ('Le livre de votre enfance', *Toute l'édition*, no. 152, 19th November 1932).

20. F. Lefèvre, 'Une révélation . . .', *op. cit.*

21. Gorky, 'À Moscou', *Vie nouvelle*, no. 175, 8th November 1917, in *Pensées intempestives, op. cit.*

22. F. Lefèvre, 'Une révélation . . .', *op. cit.*

23. O. Wilde, *The Picture of Dorian Gray*.

24. Written in English in her notebook.

25. F. Lefèvre, 'Une révélation . . .' *op. cit.*

26. *Ibid.*

27 J. Reed, *Ten Days that Shook the World*.

28. A. Edallin, *La Révolution russe par un témoin*, Éditions de la *Revue contemporaine*, 1920.

29. Quoted by L. Poliakov, *op. cit.*

30. 'Les Fumées du vin' in *Films parlés*, Gallimard, 1934.

31. *Ibid*. We find another echo of these alcoholic pogroms in *Snow in Autumn*, III: it is on the pretext of discussing the 'sharing out the wine' from his cellar that Youri Nicolaévitch Karine is taken to the village and shot in the back.

32. *Cf. Le Vin de Solitude* [*The Wine of Solitude*], III, II: 'The border was not yet closed, but each train that passed seemed to be the last.'

33. J. Lied, *Prospector in Siberia*, Oxford University Press, New York, 1945. The deal could not be concluded, Lied's colleagues being 'still too far away from a realisation of the revolution to wish to take advantage of the offers' (*ibid*.).

34. *Cf.* E. Jutikkala, K. Pirinen, *Histoire de la Finlande*, Neuchâtel, Éditions de la Baconnière, 1978.

35. *Le Vin de Solitude* [*The Wine of Solitude*], II, II.

36. N. Berberova, *C'est moi qui souligne*, Actes Sud, 'Thesaurus'.

37. The short story 'Aïno', published in January 1940 in *Revue des Deux Mondes*, had been written at the same time as the authentic 'Souvenirs de Finlande', which was probably intended for a radio 'chat' programme.

38. Terjoki (or Terrioki) was a 'small Finnish beach resort, two hours by train from Petersburg' (N. Berberova, *Alexandre Blok et son temps*, Actes Sud, 'Thesaurus', XVII).

39. *Cf.* G. Sanders, *Memoirs of a Professional Cad*.

40. M.-J. Viel [J. Reuillon], 'Comment travaille une romancière', broadcast interview, 1934.

41. These 'genuine memories of Finland', put together during the summer of 1933 in Urrugne, would be used to write the third part of *The Wine of Solitude* and for the background of the story 'Magie' (*L'Intransigeant*, 4th August 1938).

42. 'Aïno' in *Dimanche*.

43. *Le Vin de Solitude* [*The Wine of Solitude*], III, II.

44. 'Magie', *op. cit.*

45. *Ibid*.

46. M.-J. Viel, *op. cit.*

47. J. Bouissounouse, 'Femmes, écrivains, leurs débuts', *Les Nouvelles littéraires*, 2nd November 1935.

48. F. Lefèvre, 'Une révélation . . .', *op. cit.*

49. We should like to thank Anastasia Lester who translated these verses from Russian into French.

50. M. Derroyer, 'Irène Némirovsky et le cinéma', *Pour vous*, June 1931.

51. J. Bouissounouse, 'Femmes écrivains, leurs débuts', *op. cit.*

52. *Le Vin de Solitude* [*The Wine of Solitude*], III, IV.

53. 'Magie', *op. cit.*

54. *Le Vin de Solitude* [*The Wine of Solitude*], III, V.

55. In 2006, this house had become a sweet shop.

56. M. Bulgakov, *The White Guard*, tr. Michael Glenny, Collins/Harvill, London, 1971.

57. Mikhail Gordieyevich Drozdovsky (1882–1919), having formed an army of anti-Bolshevik and anti-German volunteers in 1917, took Rostov-on-Don and died near Stavropol on 1st January 1919.

58. 'Le Mercredi des Cendres', IMEC.

59. M. Derroyer, 'Irène Némirovsky et le cinéma', *op. cit.*

60. 'Aïno', *op. cit.*

61. *Nord-Sud*, bi-monthly Franco-Scandinavian magazine, 15th February 1930.

62. *Le Vin de Solitude* [*The Wine of Solitude*], IV, I.

63. *Nord-Sud*, 15th February 1930.

64. *Ibid.*

65. F. Lefèvre, 'Une révélation . . .', *op. cit.*

66. M. Derroyer, 'Irène Némirowsky et le cinéma', *op. cit.*

67. *Le Vin de Solitude* [*The Wine of Solitude*], IV, I.

Chapter 4

1. F. Lefèvre, 'Une révélation . . .', *op. cit.*

2. R. Bourget-Pailleron, 'La nouvelle équipe . . .' *op. cit.*

3. *L'Ennemie*, I, I.

4. *Ibid.*

5. Interview with Denise Epstein, 10th January 2005.

6. *L'Ennemie*, II, III.

7. *Le Vin de Solitude* [*The Wine of Solitude*], II, III.

8. I. Némirovsky, letter to Madeleine Cabour (IMEC).

9. P. Nerey [I. Némirovsky], 'Destinées', *Gringoire*, 5th December 1940, in *Destinées*. The details given in this story tally with reality: 'Listen: I was thirteen at the time of the Russian revolution, you know. I would remind you that my father was killed . . .'

10. '. . . et je l'aime encore', *Marie-Claire*, 2nd February 1940, in *Destinées*.

The main character in this story is called Olga, just like Olga Valeriovna Boutourline (10th March 1905–14th June 1947), the daughter of Valerian Boutourline (1885–1918) and Maria Oustinov, and wife of Prince Alexander Alexandrovitch Obolensky (30th March 1905–1988).

11. 'Destinées', *op. cit.*

12. This part of the quotation was omitted by Olga Boutourline.

13. D. Dubois-Jallais, *La Tzarine. Hélène Lazareff et l'aventure de 'Elle'*, Robert Laffont, 1984.

14. J. Kessel, *Nuit de princes*, II, I, Éditions de France, 1927.

15. *Ibid.*

16. J. Auscher, 'Sous la lampe', *op. cit.*

17. G. Higgins, 'Les Conrad français', *Les Nouvelles littéraires*, 6th April 1940.

18. We are grateful to Anastasia Lester for providing us with a translation of these verses into French.

19. *L'Ennemie*, III, III.

20. 'L'Enfant génial', *op. cit.*

21. É. Gille, *Le Mirador*, p. 270. This description is based on a badly damaged photograph of Irène Némirovsky wearing a gypsy costume.

22. J. Auscher, 'Sous la lampe', *op. cit.*

23. *L'Ennemie*, III, II.

24. *Ibid.*

25. *Les Feux de l'automne* [*Autumn Fires*], II, I.

26. *Les Mouches d'automne* [*Snow in Autumn*], IV.

27. 'Ida', *Marianne*, no. 82, 16th May 1934; in *Films parlés*, Gallimard, 'La Renaissance de la nouvelle', 1934.

28. *L'Ennemie*, IV, IV.

29. *Le Vin de Solitude* [*The Wine of Solitude*], I, III.

30. Interview with Mme Edwige Becquart, the daughter of René Avot, Versailles, 26th March 2005.

31. *Le Vin de Solitude* [*The Wine of Solitude*], IV, VIII.

32. 'Nativité', *Gringoire*, 8th December 1933, in *Destinées*.

33. According to Oscar Wilde, Ida Rubinstein had danced in *Salome* in St Petersburg before the war; in 1919, she appeared on the Paris stage, for the first time since the war, in *Imroulcaïs*, an Islamic play adapted by her friend the playwright and theatre critic Fernand Nozière (1874–1931), who is mentioned in chapter 6.

34. M. Derroyer, 'Irène Némirovsky et le cinéma', *op. cit.*

35. J. Bouissounouse, 'Femmes écrivains, leurs débuts', *op. cit.*

36. M. Derroyer, 'Irène Némirovsky et le cinéma', *op. cit.*

37. *Fantasio*, no. 353, 15th October 1921.

38. *Fantasio*, no. 346, 1st July 1921.

39. R. Benjamin, 'Les propos de Fantasio', *Fantasio*, no. 331, 15th November 1920.

40. *Journal officiel*, 3rd December 1920; quoted by M. Prazan and T. Mendès France, *La Maladie*, no. 9, récit historique, Berg International Éditeurs, 2001.

41. *Action française*, 9th March 1920; quoted by Michel Leymarie, 'Les frères Tharaud. De l'ambiguïté du "filon juif" dans la littérature des années vingt', *Archives juives*, no. 39/1, 1st semester 2006.

42. *Excelsior*, 17th May 1920.

43. *Le Vin de Solitude* [*The Wine of Solitude*], IV, VI.

44. *Les Mouches d'automne* [*Snow in Autumn*], V.

45. 'Nativité', *Gringoire*, 8th December 1933, in *Destinées*.

46. *L'Ennemie*, II, III.

47. 'L'Ogresse', *Gringoire*, 24th October 1941, in *Dimanche*.

48. Yvonne Comesse, letter to Élisabeth Gille, 15th March 1992.

49. In *La Littérature française entre les deux guerres 1919–1939* (Lymanhouse, 1941), F. Baldensperger mentions David Golder, that 'rough little Jew from Russia becoming a businessman in the United States'.

50. 'But she was more intrigued by what he did not say than by what he related, by his melancholy, carefree, half-hidden soul, both simple and complex at the same time, changeable, multi-faceted, or that at least seemed so to her simply because she was a foreigner.' (*L'Ennemie*, III, III.)

51. Conversation with Tatiana Morozova, Moscow, 28th January 2006.

52. J. Kessel, *Makhno et sa juive*, Paris, Éditions Eos, 1926.

53. *Cf.* Liberty, 'Amour fantôme', *Le Matin*, 1st June 1923, or Nina Mdivani, 'La Princesse Roussadana', *Le Matin*, 30th July 1923.

54. Arthur Toupine, 'La Petite Marraine', *Le Matin*, 29th August 1921. In a press cutting from 1930, Irène Némirovksy went so far as to point out that she sent 'a few stories' to *Le Matin* . . . ('Après "David Golder" . . . Irène Némirovsky', source unknown).

55. *La Vie de Tchekhov.*

56. P. Léautaud, *Journal littéraire.*

57. L. Daudet, *Souvenirs et Polémiques*, Robert Laffont, 'Bouquins', 1992.

58. Marie de Hérédia had married Henri de Régnier in 1896. A poet and novelist under the name of Gérard d'Houville, she was also one of the

most courted women in Paris. Before the First World War, she had been the mistress of writers such as Jean-Louis Vaudoyer, Binet-Valmer, Edmond Jaloux and Henry Bernstein. It seems likely that Irène Némirovsky continued to call on her at Rue Boissière after the death of Henri de Régnier in 1936.

59. Bibliothèque de l'Institut, Henri de Régnier collection.
60. *L'Ennemie*, III, IV.
61. *Ibid.*, IV, V.
62. *Le Vin de Solitude* [*The Wine of Solitude*], IV, V.
63. *L'Ennemie*, IV, II.

Chapter 5

1. On 13th January 1921, *Le Matin* announced the death of Karpoff, alias Lenin, on its front page.
2. E. Epstein, *Les Banques de commerce russes. Leur rôle dans l'évolution économique de la Russie. Leur nationalisation*, Marcel Giard, 1925.
3. *Cf.* F. Albéra, *Albatros, des Russes à Paris (1919–1929)*, Mazzotta/ Cinémathèque française, 1995.
4. Irène Némirovsky told F. Lefèvre in 1930 that she wrote 'L'Enfant génial' 'in 1923, at the age of eighteen', following Grasset's advice to make herself two years younger for the launch of *David Golder*; if the age is incorrect, the date of 1923 is nonetheless plausible.
5. F. Lefèvre, 'Une révélation . . .', *op. cit.*
6. J. and J. Tharaud, *Un royaume de Dieu*, Plon, 1920.
7. O. Wilde, *The Picture of Dorian Gray*.
8. Binet-Valmer, *Quatre jeunes filles et le jeune homme incertain*, II, in *Les Œuvres libres*, no. 70, April 1927. Binet-Valmer, the president of the League of Platoon Commanders and War Veterans, an admirer of Mussolini and D'Annunzio, and biographer of Sarah Bernhardt (Flammarion, 1936), was not averse to anti-Semitic caricature; for example, in *Les Métèques* (Ollendorff, 1907), reprinted by Flammarion in 1922, this portrait of Nicolo, the consul of Chalcedon: 'He, the hideous Greek, more Jewish than a Jew, a huge, garish, offensive nose, a face that avoids meeting your gaze, a mouth made up of tight, protruding lips: two slabs of red flesh stuck between the moustache and the chin; small, slit, fearful eyes, shiny cheek-bones, curly hair cut short; a yellow, bilious, dirty complexion; a frail body, perched crookedly on small legs, on thick thighs.' (XI.)

9. A. Spire, 'Israel Zangwill', *op. cit.*

10. The image of the Russian Jew in French literature on the cusp of the twentieth century is almost always a negative one. 'The stereotype is total. The Jews are miserly and rapacious, as is evident from their tight-fistedness, they are filthy, greasy, servile and treacherous.' (J. Neboit-Mombet, *L'Image de la Russie dans le roman français (1859–1900)*, Presses universitaires Blaise Pascal/Maison de la Recherche, 2005.) The prototype of the 'Ukrainian novel' written in French, before 1900, is *Dymitr le Cosaque* by Étienne Marcel (1883), the pseudonym of Mme Malimuska, *née* Caroline Thuez. Here, the Jews are 'dirty, ragged', have 'claw-like fingers', a hideous 'snigger', a 'nose hooked like the beak of a bird of prey', a 'look that is always shifty'.

11. F. Lefèvre, 'Une révélation . . .', *op. cit.*

12. B. Crémieux, 'Les Livres. Irène Némirovsky: *David Golder*', *Les Annales*, 1st February 1930.

13. The Russian pianist and 'Jewish genius' Rozenoffski has the same experience in Zangwill's 'The Lackeys': it is by improvising on Hebrew themes that he eventually contacts Mrs Wilhammer, even though she had previously refused to receive him in her New York salon. But, having got in touch with her, he immediately forgets his promise to use his genius to help the Jews in the ghetto . . . (in *Ghetto Comedies*, *op. cit.*).

14. *Le Malentendu*, XVIII.

15. *Ibid.*, IV.

16. *Ibid.*, XVII.

17. *Ibid.*, XIX.

18. *Ibid.*, X.

19. *Ibid.*, XVIII.

20. *Ibid.*, XVIII. Note that Paul Bourget was 'Zézelle's' favourite writer.

21. F. Lefèvre, 'Une révélation . . .', *op. cit.*

22. *The Times*, London ('French by adoption', 13th February 1930) would be the first and only newspaper to draw a parallel between Bove and Némirovsky: 'Here is another Russian, after Kessel, Emmanuel Bove and Ignace Legrand, to place among the youngest French writers, and one begins to wonder whether, for good or for evil, the dispersion of Russian intelligence caused by the triumph of the Soviets may not carry consequences scarcely less important to Western literature than the capture of Constantinople by the Turks in 1452.'

23. *Le Malentendu*, I.

24. *Ibid.*, I.

25. *Ibid.*, X.

26. Certificate dated 9th November 1940, signed 'Ph. de Maizière'.

27. Report of the board of directors at the general meeting of shareholders for the year 1924 (30th April 1925). The Banque des Pays du Nord was at this time a limited company with capital of 50 million francs; its net accrued profits for the year 1924 amounted to 6,834 million francs.

28. *Le Malentendu*, XVI.

29. *Ibid.*, XI.

30. *Le Vin de Solitude* [*The Wine of Solitude*], IV, IX.

31. *Le Malentendu*, IV.

32. *L'Ennemie*, IV, IV.

33. *Ibid.* IV, IV.

34. D. Halévy, 'Lœwenstein ou la vie d'un joueur', in *Courrier de Paris*, Éd. Du Cavalier, 1932.

35. *Ibid.*

36. F. Lefèvre, 'Une révélation . . .', *op. cit.*

37. A. Maurois, 'Les œuvres et les hommes. *David Golder*, d'Irène Némirovsky', *Le Spectacle des Lettres*, March 1930.

38. B. Crémieux, 'Les livres. Irène Némirovsky: *David Golder*', *Les Annales*, 1st February 1930.

39. C. Pierrey, *Chantecler*, 8th March 1930. This rumour was taken up again by André Hirschmann in 1931: 'A woman of remarkable intelligence and sensibility, Irène Nimerovsky [*sic*], has been able to capture the life of one of her friends, which she has related in the character of Joyce Golder.' ('*David Golder* or the triumph of cinema over theatre', *Cinégraph*, February 1931.)

40. M.-J. Viel, 'Comment travaille une romancière', *op. cit.*

41. F. Lefèvre, 'Une révélation . . .', *op. cit.*

42. The present-day Rue de Montevideo.

43. C. Pierrey, *op. cit.*

44. F. Lefèvre, 'En marge de *L'Affaire Courilof* . . .', *op. cit.*

45. F. Lefèvre, 'Une révélation . . .', *op. cit.*

46. F. Lefèvre, 'En marge de *L'Affaire Courilof* . . .', *op. cit.*

47. C. Pierrey, *op. cit.*

48. M. Derroyer, *op. cit.*

49. J. d'Assac, 'Maris de femmes célèbres. Monsieur Irène Némirovsky', [March 1935?], source unknown, probably *Je suis partout*.

50. P. Morand, 'Je brûle Moscou', in *Nouvelles complètes*, vol. I, Gallimard, Bibliothèque de la Pléiade, 1992.

51. One of the first words in 'L'Enfant génial' is 'pogrom'. The French had been familiar with the term ever since 25 May 1926, when a young Ukrainian anarchist had assassinated, at a café terrace in Saint-Germain-des-Prés in the heart of Paris, the hetman Petlyura, who had been responsible for the anti-Jewish massacres in 1920. Exactly one month before 'L'Enfant génial' was published, the left-wing militant Bernard Lecache, who had rallied support for the acquittal of Samuel Schwartzbard, published in *Le Quotidien* his instructive investigation 'in the land of the pogroms', completed in Ukraine in August 1926. An apocalyptic picture – 'all paths in the Ukraine lead to pogroms' (B. Lecache, *op. cit.*) – which lacked only one thing: it overlooked the Soviet brutality. At Schwartzbard's trial, in 1927, Joseph Kessel, called as a witness, gave the speech of a French writer who had much in common with Irène Némirovsky: 'Like Schwartzbard, I am Jewish and like him originally from Russia. That is one point of similarity. Another is the fact that, like him, I have had the good fortune to be touched by the incomparable spirit of France, the spirit of liberty, of courage and of justice . . . Even if it was merely to draw the attention of the civilised world to the appalling custom of pogroms . . . Schwartzbard had to do what he did.'

52. *Le Malentendu*, XVI.

53. *Cf.* A. Spire, *op. cit.*, vol. I: 'For the Jew, as does the Frenchman, likes to make fun of people. Polite and full of himself, as is the Frenchman, he likes to scoff at himself out of politeness and pride.' The continuation of the quote seems to minimise the impact of the anti-Semitic cliché, when it is anticipated by the person at whom it is aimed: 'It is as if he were saying to his body: you're not very pretty, you're pockmarked and ungainly; to his arms: you're never still; to his hands: you can't stop touching things; even to his heart: you're not always chivalrous; there's nothing I can do, it's the legacy of centuries of pain, and you need more than one life to change that; but above these slaves of the past sits my liberated spirit, my free spirit which knows them and judges them.' (*Ibid.*) Spire stresses the perverse effects of this way of thinking, which are renunciation and self-denial.

54. For instance, in *Vie parisienne*, on 1st February 1930: 'People have mentioned the late Lœwenstein as a type of Golder. Come now! Lœwenstein was something else.'

55. N. Gourfinkel, 'L'expérience juive d'Irène Némirovsky. Une interview de l'auteur de *David Golder*', *L'Univers israélite*, 28th February 1930.

56. F. Lefèvre, 'Une révélation . . .', *op. cit.*

57. The book, *Oil Imperialism: The International Struggle for Petroleum*, by Louis Fischer – who happened to be a specialist in the Soviet economy – was published in July 1928 by Rieder ('Cahiers internationaux' collection).

58. F. Lefèvre, 'Une révélation . . .', *op. cit.*

59. '*David Golder* . . .', *Revue pétrolifère*, 25th January 1930.

60. *L'Ennemie*, I, V.

61. *Ibid.*, IV, III.

62. *Ibid.*, III, IV.

63. *Ibid.*, IV, III.

64. *Ibid.*, IV, II.

65. *Ibid.*, IV, II.

66. *David Golder.*

67. *Le Vin de Solitude* [*The Wine of Solitude*], IV, V.

68. R. Bourget-Pailleron, 'La nouvelle équipe . . .', *op. cit.*

69. *David Golder.*

70. *Le Bal*, 'Les Cahiers rouges', Grasset, 2002.

71. *Ibid.*, II.

72. *Ibid.*, V.

73. *Le Vin de Solitude* [*The Wine of Solitude*], IV, III.

74. This quotation and the previous ones: *Le Bal*, II and III.

75. *Ibid.*, VI.

76. This connection was highlighted by M. Bernard in the pro-communist newspaper *Monde*, on 16th August 1930: 'This couple strangely resemble those hideous figures that Grosz used in order to stigmatise a class. All freshness is dead in them (though it probably never existed), all human feelings are replaced by petty prejudices and by a desperate impatience to catch up with time lost, in their eyes, in poverty, by hurriedly gathering together the most foolish and most vulgar celebrities.'

77. J. Cocteau, *Le Passé défini II* (11th September 1953), Gallimard, p. 273. In 'Le Bal', the story that appeared on 6th February 1921 in *Le Matin*, Henri Duvernois had already chosen to describe the panic caused by the cancellation of a ball, but wrote that it was due to a death.

78. J. Cocteau, *Lettres à sa mère*, II. 1919–1938, Gallimard, 2007.

79. Insert in *Le Bal*, 1930, quoted in '. . . des livres de femmes', *L'Archer*, 1st October 1930.

80. *David Golder*.

81. *Le Bal*, I.

82. H. Bernstein, *Samson*, IV, V, in *Théâtre*, Éditions du Rocher, 1997. In an earlier version of this play (1907), Samson was 'a Levantine Jew by the name of Melliori' (G. Bernstein Gruber, G. Maurin, *Bernstein le Magnifique*, Lattès, 1988).

83. *David Golder*.

84. 'Le point de vue du mari', *Œil de Paris*, 12th April 1931.

85. Irène Némirovsky had already mentioned *La Semaine de Suzette* in *L'Ennemie*, written in 1928. It is therefore likely that she read this children's publication before she was pregnant.

86. *Le Vin de Solitude* [*The Wine of Solitude*], II, V.

Chapter 6

1. Irène Némirovsky to C. Pierrey, *Chantecler*, 8th March 1930.

2. H. Muller, *Trois pas en arrière*, Paris, La Table Ronde, 1952; 'La Petite Vermillon', 2002.

3. *David Golder*.

4. *Ibid.*

5. F. Lefèvre, 'Une révélation . . .', *op. cit.*

6. S. Duvernon, 'Un entretien avec Bernard Grasset', *L'Opinion*, 18th January 1930.

7. É. Bourdet, *Vient de paraître*, Gallimard, 'Folio Théâtre', 2004, acte II.

8. J. Chardonne, *Matinales*, Albin Michel, 1956.

9. J. Giraudoux, *Bella*, IV.

10. S. Zweig, 'Destruction of a Heart'.

11. F. Mauriac, *Dieu et Mammon*, Éditions du Capitole, February 1929.

12. H. Muller, *op. cit.*

13. F. Lefèvre, 'Une révélation . . .', *op. cit.*

14. Claude Pierrey, *op. cit.*

15. *Les Chiens et les Loups* [*The Dogs and the Wolves*], XXXIII.

16. Letter to Madeleine Cabour, 7th January 1931.

17. 'À la recherche d'Irène Némirovsky, jeune femme russe, écrivain français', *Elle*, 9th December 1985.

18. B., *Vie parisienne*, 1st February 1930.

19. *Ibid.*

20. C. Pierrey, *op. cit.*

21. S. Duvernon, 'Un entretien avec Bernard Grasset', *op. cit.*

22. C. Pierrey, *op. cit.*

23. Hélène Iswolsky, daughter of the former Russian ambassador to France, had begun her literary career in 1925 by writing, jointly with Kessel, *Les Rois aveugles* (Éditions de France), and later a book of memoirs with Anna Kachina, *La Jeunesse rouge d'Inna* (Éditions de France, 1928). A friend of Nikolas Berdyaev and Emmanuel Mounier, she also produced translations of Pushkin, Goncharov (*Oblomov*, 1926), Tolstoy and Dostoyevsky.

24. 'En marge de *L'Affaire Courilof . . .*' *op. cit.* I. Némirovsky would repeat this in 1940, in fewer words: 'Ivan Ilyich is an ordinary man who, one fine day, finds himself face to face with death.' (*La Vie de Tchekhov*, XXI.)

25. R. Kemp, '*David Golder*', *Liberté*, 30th December 1929.

26. H. de Régnier, '*David Golder*, par Irène Némirovski', *Le Figaro*, 28th January 1930.

27. H. Muller, *op. cit.*

28. M. Thiébaut, 'Chronique bibliographique. *David Golder*, par Irène Nemirowsky', *Revue de Paris*, January 1930.

29. A. Thérive, 'Les livres', *Le Temps*, 10th January 1930.

30. Daniel-Rops, *La République*, 22nd January 1930.

31. P. Lœwe, '*David Golder*, par Irène Némirovsky', *L'Ordre*, 29th January 1930.

32. E. Jaloux, '*David Golder*, par Irène Némirovsky', *Le Cahier*, 1st February 1930.

33. A. Maurois, 'Les œuvres et les hommes. *David Golder*, d'Irène Némirovsky', *Le Spectacle des Lettres* [March 1930?].

34. *Action française*, 9th January 1930.

35. 'Le succès foudroyant de *David Golder*', *Le Matin* and *L'Œuvre*, 18th January 1930.

36. 'Une femme de lettres peut-elle réussir sans accepter certains hommages de ses juges?' *Candide*, June 1931.

37. *Ève*, 2nd February 1930.

38. A. Billy, *La Femme de France* [1930].

39. 'David Golder', Fantasio, 15th February 1930.

40. F. Lefèvre, 'Une révélation . . .', op. cit.

41. A. Bellessort, 'Un roman de femme', Journal des débats, 13th February 1930.

42. For instance, F. Prieur in Le Petit Provençal: 'It must be pointed out, firstly, that David Golder, a novel about money and business, is a real gallery of monsters.' ('Chronique des livres', 31st January 1930.) And C. Santelli, in La Dépêche de Strasbourg: 'But does the author himself believe that mankind is really just made up of this? Does she really believe that the David Golders who think only of piling up money on the poverty of others, that the Glorias, an absolute sow decked in pearls, that the Joyces, a cheap tart who offers herself to the wealthiest man interested, in some way represent the men, the women and girls of our time?' [March 1930?]

43. Comœdia, 21st January 1930.

44. A. Redier, 'Un livre à la mode', Revue française, 16th March 1930.

45. A. Ryckmans, 'Les livres dont on parle. David Golder par Irène Némirovsky', La Cité chrétienne, 5th May 1930.

46. G. de Pawlowski, 'David Golder, de I. Némirovsky', Gringoire, 31st January 1930.

47. Le Petit Parisien, 31st December 1929.

48. R. de Saint Jean, 'Chroniques et documents. La vie littéraire. David Golder, par Hélène Némirovsky' [sic], Revue hebdomadaire, 1st February 1930.

49. G. Rency, 'Irène Némirovsky: David Golder', L'Indépendance belge, 3rd January 1930.

50. J. de Pierrefeu, 'Un roman juif', La Dépêche, 30th January 1930.

51. La Volonté, 9th February 1930.

52. Erget, 'David Golder par Irène Némirovsky', Le Libertaire, 8th March 1930.

53. L. de Mondadon, Études, 1930.

54. Erget, 'David Golder . . .', op. cit.

55. N. Gourfinkel, 'L'expérience juive d'Irène Némirovsky . . .', op. cit.

56. F. Lefèvre, 'Une révélation . . .', op. cit.

57. N. Sabord, 'Sur le pavois . . . Sous les pieds du veau d'or. Le David Golder de Mme Irène Nemirovsky', Paris-Midi [1930].

58. N. Gourfinkel, 'L'expérience juive d'Irène Némirovsky . . .', op. cit.

59. Ibid.

60. R. de Saint Jean, 'Chroniques et documents . . .', *op. cit.*
61. P. Audiat, 'Livres à relire. David Golder, Moïse de la finance', *L'Européen*, 8th January 1930.
62. Mentioned by R. Gouze, *Les Bêtes à Goncourt. Un demi-siècle de batailles littéraires*, Hachette Littératures, 1973.
63. 'In literature, disclosure is a common post-war practice. We cannot imagine life except when experiencing jolts like war, interrupted by surprises and attacks. Publishers, confronted with a public inured to fighting, have adopted military methods. They suddenly bring out an author with his fifty thousand brand-new words, as if it were a fresh division. They hurl him at the critics, at the public and, even before they have derived any benefit, they let out cries of triumph and despatch victorious communiqués. And to listen to them, a hundred thousand readers surrender straight away, without anyone lifting a finger. / The reality is not as dazzling as their bulletins, as the least informed of readers have eventually come to realise, and one wonders by what state of grace young authors of shining talent, but whom the public, which has been too often misled, finds suspect, still find an audience among readers who have had their heads stuffed full. / But here at home the stuffed heads still retain enough free spirit to make up their own minds, and the more they are deceived, the more they become curious and perceptive. And this is probably why an apparently legitimate suspicion has in no way deprived Mme Irène Némirovsky's *David Golder* of the success it deserves.' (N. Sabord, 'Sur le pavois . . .', *op. cit.*)
64. Les 93, 'Prix', *D'Artagnan*, 20th February 1930.
65. Letter to Madeleine Cabour, 22nd January 1930.
66. N. Sabord, 'Sur le pavois . . .', *op. cit.*
67. M. Thiébaut, 'Chronique bibliographique . . .', *op. cit.*
68. Thibaud-Gerson, '*David Golder*, par Irène Némirovsky', *Le Courrier littéraire*, 1st March 1930. Franc-Nohain, likewise, was astonished that Golder, even though to his mind he was the incarnation of the Jewish character, did not conform at all to the worship of the home: '. . . that "sense of family", of the "patriarchy" – or of the "tribe" – that is so strong among Jews, no matter what their social position may be, and whether or not they have "smoothed off the rough edges", before or after the "brilliantine", we are surprised not to find more traces of it in David and among David's entourage. David's wife is merely frivolous, grasping and cruel, and his daughter is completely mad. We don't

have any sense of the "Golder tribe".' ('*David Golder*, by Irène Némirovsky', *Écho de Paris*, 16th January 1930.)

69. By Franc-Nohain, for example: 'It is impossible not to be reminded here of the Tharaud brothers, for it is they, it has to be said, who have made these Jews with their long, curling locks fashionable, the same people, incidentally, whom we come across later, with their impeccably glossy hair smoothed down with brilliantine. In *David Golder*, we admire a sort of continuation, a passionate, feverish activity, works that are perfect and precise, but that have the almost dogmatic perfection and precision of the Tharaud brothers. Here we savour, like some exotic pastry or delicacy, everything that is, or that we believe to be, specifically Jewish – the stuffed pike, for instance, in the little restaurant in the Rue des Rosiers . . .' (*Ibid.*)

70. R. Millet, 'Irène Némirovski et le roman français', *Paris-Presse*, 30th January 1930.

71. *Adam*, 15th March 1930.

72. 'Après "David Golder" . . . Irène Némirovsky', press cutting, source unknown.

73. A. Billy, *La Femme de France* [1930].

74. '*David Golder*', *Fantasio*, 15th February 1930. Yet Gloria's real first name is given in the novel: Havké.

75. J. de Pierrefeu, *op. cit.*

76. In this manuscript written in black ink, which bears the title 'Golder. novel', the entire introduction has been considerably amended: ' "No", said Golder. The hands of the man opposite him, pale and agile Jewish hands, gripped the wooden table and twitched feebly with a little grating sound coming from his quick, sharp nails. Golder examined them for a moment without saying anything, in a thoughtful and attentive manner, as if, in the last shudders of a wounded animal, he were measuring how much life remained in it.' What follows is covered in deletions. The 'agile hands' of Jews are a commonplace that we find for instance in the Tharauds: 'The hands, the long, nervous hands fidgeted wildly, in a thousand movements that wonderfully expressed all the shades of thoughts that went through their minds. Each of these long, slender fingers, with black nails at their tips, squirmed about in front of their faces like so many marionnettes, so many little characters endowed with a distinctive life', etc. (*L'Ombre de la Croix*, Émile-Paul, 1917.)

77. J. Blaize, 'Un chef d'œuvre commence l'année', *La Dépêche*, 23rd January 1930.

78. I.-R. See, 'Un chef d'œuvre? . . .', *Réveil juif*, 31st January 1930.

79. J. Auscher, 'Une interview de l'auteur de *David Golder*', *L'Univers israélite*, 5th July 1935.

80. *Ibid.*

81. N. Gourfinkel, 'L'expérience juive d'Irène Némirovsky . . .', *op. cit.*

82. J. Auscher, 'Une interview de l'auteur de *David Golder*', *op. cit.*

83. N. Gourfinkel, 'L'expérience juive d'Irène Némirovsky . . .', *op. cit.*

84. *Le Matin*, 12th October 1908.

85. N. Gourfinkel, 'L'expérience juive d'Irène Némirovsky . . .', *op. cit.*

86. In this play from 1907, Samson refers to Jacques Brochart, an elderly porter from Marseille who has become a tycoon in the Egyptian copper industry, to whom an impoverished aristocrat has been compelled to give the hand of his daughter. When she is unfaithful to him, he decides to ruin his rival by dragging him into a disastrous stock exchange transaction. Like Golder's 'David Town' in the first draft of the novel, Brochart dreams of building a city out of his imagination: 'A real city on the edge of the Sahara . . . Perfectly . . . a city of health, repose, of pleasure too . . . An Egyptian Nice . . . This city would consist of a vast sanatorium, huge hotels, a theatre, a casino, aqueducts . . . And we shall also create, in order to supply our colony, a railway . . . That's a colossal project and a very attractive one.' (*Samson*, I, XIV.)

87. A. Londres, *Le Juif errant est arrivé*, Albin Michel, January 1930.

88. *David Golder.*

89. *Ibid.*

90. H. de Régnier, '*David Golder*, par Irène Némirovski', *op. cit.*

91. N. Gourfinkel, 'De Silbermann à David Golder', *Nouvelle Revue juive*, March 1930.

92. N. Gourfinkel, 'L'expérience juive d'Irène Némirovsky . . .', *op. cit.*

93. '*David Golder*, by Irène Némirowsky, translated by Sylvia Stuart, Horace Liveright', *New York Herald*, 15th December 1930.

94. D. Decourdemanche, '*David Golder*, par Irène Némirovsky', *Nouvelle Revue française*, 1st February 1930; B. Crémieux, 'Les livres. Irène Némirovsky: *David Golder*', *Les Annales*, 1st February 1930.

95. P. Léautaud, *Journal littéraire*, 10th May 1911, Mercure de France, vol. I.

96. Delini, 'Les avant-premières. Avant *David Golder* à la Porte Saint-Martin', *Comœdia*, 23rd December 1930.

97. 'À la Porte Saint-Martin. Avant 'David Golder', *L'Écho de Paris*, 26th December 1930.

98. Delini, *op. cit.*

99. J. Duvivier, radio discussions with René Jeanne and Charles Ford, 1957.

100. J. Duvivier, *L'Intransigeant*, 18th February, 1933.

101. J.-P. C., 'Julien Duvivier va tourner *David Golder* d'après le roman d'Irène Némirovsky. Entretien avec le réalisateur de *Maman Colibri*', *Comœdia*, 23rd May 1930.

102. Reply to an enquiry from R. Groos, 'Do you consider that the cinema has had or could have an influence on the novel? And what is it?', *L'Ordre*, 18th October 1930.

103. In the first version of *Le Bal*, which was published in *Les Œuvres libres* in February 1929, Irène Némirovsky had alluded from memory to two characters from *Les Demi-Vierges* by Marcel Prévost, 'Julien de Roudre and Maud', instead of Julien de Suberceaux and Maud de Rouvre.

104. *Le Bal*, VI.

105. Petrus, *D'Artagnan*, 16th August 1930.

106 E. Langevin, 'Les livres. Du roman cynique. *David Golder*, par Irène Némirovsky. *Le Bal*, par Irène Némirovsky', *Revue française*, 5th October 1930.

107. S. Ratel, ' "Le Bal", par Irène Nemirovsky. Contre la forcerie des talents', *Comœdia*, 1st October 1930.

108. P. Reboux, 'Un livre par semaine. *Le Bal*, par Irène Némirowsky', *Paris-Soir*, 13th August 1930.

109. *Revue des lectures*, 15th September 1930.

110. *Fiches du mois*, 1st November 1930.

111. *Mercure de France*, 15th September 1930.

112. N. Gourfinkel, *Nouvelle Revue juive*, September–October 1930.

113. *Comœdia*, 2nd November 1930.

114. *La Cinématographie française*, 29th November 1930.

115. Letter dated 9th December 1930, published in *La Cinématographie française* on 13th December.

116. 'Curieuse confrontation. *David Golder* au théâtre et au cinéma', *Comœdia*, 18th December 1930.

117. 'À la Porte Saint-Martin. *David Golder*, pièce en trois actes de M. Nozière', *Comœdia*, 18th December 1930.

118. F. Lefèvre, *République*, 12th August 1931.

119. Franc-Nohain, 'David Golder', L'Écho de Paris, 29th December 1930.

120. G. Pitard, 'Au théâtre de la Porte Saint-Martin: "David Golder", de M. Fernand Nozière, d'après le roman de Mme Irène Némirovsky', L'Humanité, 9th January 1931.

121. L'Europe nouvelle, 21st March 1931.

122. 'Ce qu'ils pensent de David Golder', Le Figaro, 6th March 1931.

123. F. Vinneuil [L. Rebatet], 'L'écran de la semaine, David Golder', Action française, 13th March 1931.

124. Letter of 16th March 1931, Jacques-Émile Blanche collection, Bibliothèque de l'Institut.

125. Letter of 6th January 1931, Grasset archives.

126. S. Volonskij, 'A curious conflict about David Golder', Poslednija Novosti, 31st January 1931. Translated from Russian by Irène Dauplé.

127. L. Moussinac, quoted by E. Bonnefille, Julien Duvivier, Le mal aimant du cinéma français. Vol. I: 1896–1940, L'Harmattan, 2002.

128. 'Here we are a long way from those Jewish stories and other vulgar jokes in which the brothers are called Jacob, Isaac, Levy and co. Here we have a tragedy – hearts and souls that suffer, there is no room for the bawdy jokes of a Gaudissart.' (J. Robin, 'David Golder de Julien Duvivier', Cinémonde, 25th December 1930.)

129. NRF, November 1931. 'One needs to have seen Harry Baur with his stomach protruding, his hands hanging from the ends of his arms, his rigid chest, his head turned to one side, and in this head turned to one side an eye that stares out hilariously, to understand the comic heights that can be reached by the clumsy use of conventional, stereotypical attitudes.'

130. F. Vinneuil [L. Rebatet], 'L'écran de la semaine . . .', op. cit. 'Until now M. Julien Duvivier did not enjoy a very great reputation in the cinema world. Some people even labelled him among the recognised salesmen. But this year he has been given the responsibility of illustrating the bestselling novel by Mme Irène Némirovsky, David Golder. No one asked whether M. Duvivier was really qualified to carry out this work. The title of the film appears to have been enough to invest him with great talent straight away . . . Made in the way it has been, David Golder is the kind of film that should best be spoken of in reviews, using words that are dull, solemn and strong, and with a "contained emotion". We confess our incompetence for this type of exercise.'

131. *La Petite Illustration*, 11th April 1931.

132. 'Irène Némirovsky et le cinéma. "Je ne pense qu'en images . . .", nous dit-elle', interview with M. Derroyer, *Pour vous*, June 1931.

133. *Poslednija Novosti*, 1st May 1931, translated from Russian by Irène Dauplé.

134. *L'Intermédiaire des éditeurs, imprimeurs, libraires et intéressés de la presse et du livre*, no. 118, 5th June 1931.

135. 'Film parlé', in *Films parlés*, Gallimard, 1934.

136. *Ibid.*

137. *Ibid.*

138. 'En marge de *L'Affaire Courilof* . . .', *op. cit.* Gallimard had nevertheless published Zoshchenko's *La Vie joyeuse* in 1931.

139. 'Deux romans russes', *La Revue hebdomadaire*, no. 8, 23rd February 1935.

140. R. Brasillach, 'Message de Russie', *Action française*, 26th February 1931.

141. L. Pierre-Quint, letter to Irène Némirovsky, 23rd June 1930, Grasset archives.

142. *Bibliographie de la France*, 1st July 1927. On the history of the 'Femmes' collection, *cf.* François Laurent and Béatrice Mousli, *Les Éditions du Sagittaire 1919–1979*, Éditions de l'Institut Mémoires de l'édition contemporaine, 2003.

143. *Les Mouches d'automne* [*Snow in Autumn*], VI.

144. F. Lefèvre, *République*, 12th August 1931.

145. D. Saurat (and not Marguerite Yourcenar, as É. Gille maintained), *Nouvelle Revue française*, October 1931.

146. *L'Écho de Paris*, 31st December 1931.

147. *Le Temps*, 3rd March 1932.

148. R. Brasillach, 'Irène Némirovski: *les Mouches d'automne*', *Action française*, 7th January 1932. It was Antonine Coullet-Tessier, the author of *Chambre à louer*, who served as a foil to Irène Némirovsky in this article.

149. *Le Bal*, VI.

150. 'Au Gaumont-Palace. Un film de Marcel Vandal et Charles Delac. *Le Bal*. Mise en scène de W. Thiele d'après le roman d'Irène Némirovsky', *L'Ami du film* [September 1931].

151. *Danielle Darrieux, filmographie commentée par elle-même*, Ramsay, 'Cinéma', 1995.

152. *Françoise Giroud vous présente le Tout-Paris*, 'L'Air du temps', Gallimard, 1952. In the German version, the part of Antoinette was played by Dolly Hall.

153. This quotation and the previous ones: 'Irène Némirovsky et le cinéma . . .', *op. cit.*

154. *Bravo*, 'La chance', February 1931. The other replies were from Giraudoux, Colette, Ravel, Maurice Bedel, Moro-Giafferi, Pavlovski, Spinelly, Alfred Savoir, Henri Decoin, André Birabeau, Louis Lumière and Georges Neveux.

Chapter 7

1. R. Brasillach, 'Irène Némirovski: *les Mouches d'automne*', *op. cit.*

2. Les Treize, *L'Intransigeant*, 18th January 1932.

3. E. Jaloux, *Excelsior*, 28th January 1932.

4. M. Prévost, '*Les Mouches d'automne*, par I. Némirovsky', *Gringoire*, 13th May 1932.

5. R. Kemp, 'La vie des livres. Tchekhov et son peintre', *Les Nouvelles littéraires*, 30th January 1947. Kemp is alluding here to a stanza in Paul Valéry's *Le Cimetière marin*, where it is precisely a matter of pride: 'Beau ciel, vrai ciel, regarde-moi qui change! / Après tant d'orgueil, après tant d'étrange / Oisiveté, mais pleine de pouvoir, / Je m'abandonne à ce brilliant espace, / Sur les maisons des morts mon ombre passe / Qui m'apprivoise à son frêle mouvoir.' [Sky of beauty, sky of truth, look how I change! / After so much pride, after so much strange / idleness, though full of power, / I give myself up to this gleaming space, / Over the houses of the dead my shadow passes / Mastering me with its frail motion. [Tr.]

6. Letter to J.-É. Blanche, 25th February 1932, J.-É. Blanche collection, Bibliothèque de l'Institut, Paris.

7. *Le Vin de Solitude* [*The Wine of Solitude*], IV, X.

8. 'La Comédie bourgeoise', in *Films parlés*.

9. *Ibid.*

10. *Le Vin de Solitude* [*The Wine of Solitude*], IV, X.

11. Quoted by M. Fralie, *Le Secret d'Ivar Kreuger*, Nouvelle Librairie Française, 1932.

12. *Ibid.*

13. R. Mennevée, *Monsieur Ivar Kreuger et le Trust suédois des allumettes*, Les Documents politiques, April 1932.

14. *Le Pion sur l'échiquier*, XVIII.

15. M. Anissimov, 'Les filles d'Irène Némirovsky', *Les Nouveaux Cahiers*, no. 108, Spring 1992.

16. *Le Vin de Solitude* [*The Wine of Solitude*], IV, XI.

17. *Ibid.*

18 *L'Affaire Courilof* [*The Courilof Affair*], VII and IX.

19. *Ibid.*, XVII and XXI.

20. Letters from I. Némirovsky to P. Brisson, 13th and 23rd October 1932, IMEC / *Figaro* collection.

21. Insert in *The Courilof Affair*, reprinted notably in the trade magazine *Toute l'édition*, no. 178.

22. *Paris-Midi*, 26th May 1933.

23. 'En marge de *L'Affaire Courilof* . . .', *op. cit.*

24. *Cf.* N. Gourfinkel, 'Irène Némirovsky. *L'Affaire Courilof*', *La Terre retrouvée*, 25th June 1933.

25. Exiled in Germany, Kourlov published a book of memoirs, *La Catastrophe de la Russie impériale* (O. Kirkner, Berlin, 1923).

26. *Le Pion sur l'échiquier*, X.

27. X. de Hautecloque, 'Sir Basil Zaharoff, le magnat de la mort subite', *Le Crapouillot*, 'Les Maîtres du monde', March 1932. The article was annotated by Irène Némirovsky, who drew on it for an early portrait of James Bohun. It is worth noting that in the same issue of *Crapouillot* there is an article by J. Aubry on 'Ivar Kreuger, the king of matches'.

28. *Le Pion sur l'échiquier*, X.

29. *Ibid.*, VI.

30. *Ibid.*, II.

31. Ezekiel, 18: 2, quoted in chapter VI.

32. *Le Pion sur l'échiquier*, V.

33. *Ibid.*, XI.

34. *Ibid.*, XI. Yves Harteloup, in *Le Malentendu* (1926, *op. cit.*, III), already shows some of the symptoms of Christophe Bohun's inability to integrate socially: 'This boy, who for four years had been a sort of hero, was spineless when it came to making a daily effort, compulsory work, coping with the petty tyrannies of life . . . It did not even occur to him that he could do business, fight, try to become wealthy. The son and grandson of rich, idle people, he suffered from being ill at ease and from a carefree attitude, much as people suffer from hunger and cold.'

35. *Le Pion sur l'échiquier*, XVI.

36. M.-J.Viel, 'How a novelist works', interview broadcast in 1934. In this conversation that followed the publication of *Le Pion sur l'échiquier* (May 1934), Irène Némirovsky described her working method in detail: 'I told

you just now, I love telling myself stories; well, it's exactly what I do before writing a novel, I work in a broad sweep, gradually I bring out my characters and I describe their lives, their physical attributes, their education, what their reactions would be confronted with events that are outside the book itself. In this way, I cover pages and pages, I live with them ... I fill exercise books with the features of my most secondary characters. This previous life of a novel is thrilling to me. It's very amusing to make your characters live in childhood; in *Le Pion sur l'échiquier*, for instance, I put Muriel in prison, I made her come out in society. I took enormous pleasure in imagining Geneviève's entire childhood and youth ... for me it's the beginning of the novel, the birth of my characters that form the pleasure of writing, the rest is the real work. . . . I invent all my characters, and those that I don't invent always remain a little hazy. You don't see them as clearly as the others. They are always exaggerated, they are overdone ... Gloria, in *David Golder*, Philippe from *Le Pion sur l'échiquier* and even Muriel for whom I borrowed a few traits. The human being is too complex to enter the framework of a novel, he stands out or he remains less than himself, people whom I could not know well enough to imagine their feelings, their reactions. And so I continue to depict the world I know best and that is made up of unbalanced people, who are outside the milieu or the country in which they would normally have lived, and who do not adapt to a new life without shock or suffering ... Yes, in my latest novel, my heroes are cosmopolitan, except for Geneviève, who is the upper middle-class Frenchwoman on whom the whole Bohun family rely. I have made her a pivot of peaceful resistance, and this is the first time that I have portrayed a Frenchwoman in a novel, my first attempt.'

37. J. Auscher, 'Sous la lampe. Irène Némirovsky', *op. cit.*
38. *La Revue française*, 25th June 1933: 'This kind of fairly repulsive monster required a different pen to that of the author in order to be fearsome and ... lifelike. As such, he's a failure.'
39. *Marianne*, 14th June 1933.
40. M. Prévost, 'Deux nouveaux romans', *Gringoire*, 26th May 1933.
41. Aristide, *Aux écoutes*, 27th May 1933.
42. J. Ernest-Charles, 'Littérature. Une romancière', *L'Opinion*, 3rd June 1933.
43. J. Morienval, *L'Aube*, 14th June 1933.
44. J.-B. Séverac, 'Russie d'hier et Russie d'aujourd'hui. Deux romans:

L'Affaire Courilof, par Irène Némirovsky (Grasset), *Le Camarade Kisliakov*, par P. Romanov (Editions Babu)', *Midi socialiste*, 24th June 1933.

45. *Action française*, 25th May 1933.

46. 'Un déjeuner en septembre', *Revue de Paris*, 1st May 1933, in *Destinées et autres nouvelles*, Sables, 2004.

47. R. Brasillach, 'Causerie littéraire', *Action française*, 30th May 1934.

48. *L'Amour du prochain*, the sixth title in the collection 'Pour mon plaisir', was not a novel but a series of 'reflections on literature'.

49. F. Lefèvre, 'En marge de *L'Affaire Courilof* . . .', *op. cit.*

50. W. d'Ormesson, 'L'antisémitisme en Allemagne', *Revue de Paris*, 1st May 1933: 'There is at least one thing for which we cannot blame the Hitlerites. That is, that in their anti-Semitic activities, they have arrested people without warning. It is even surprising that the persecution of the Jews should not have assumed a more violent aspect when we read the writings in which the nationalist-socialist doctrine parades itself and when we think of the excitement it arouses. It is true that we are merely at the beginning of a campaign that will be carried out methodically. But, on the other side of the Rhine, it is not a question of exterminating Israel by means of pogroms. It is a question of making it perish through asphyxia.'

51. J. Bardanne, *L'Allemagne attaquera le . . . (documents secrets)*, Baudinière, 1932.

52. *Action française*, 18th June 1933.

53. J. and J. Tharaud, *Quand Israël n'est plus roi*, Plon, 1933.

54. J. Van Melle, 'Vacances d'écrivains', *Toute l'édition*, no. 188, 29th July 1933.

55. F. Lefèvre, 'En marge de *L'Affaire Courilof* . . .', *op. cit.*

56. A. Maurois, *Le Cercle de famille*, I, XV.

57. 'Au théâtre Saint-Georges. *L'Homme*, de Denys Amiel', *Aujourd'hui*, no. 275, 21st January 1934.

58. *Poslednija Novosti*, 1st May 1931, translated from Russian by Irène Dauplé.

59. I. Némirovsky acknowledged two other unintentional models for *The Wine of Solitude*: *Le Bois du templier pendu* by H. Béraud (1926) and *La Marche funèbre* by Claude Farrère (1929).

60. It is worth pointing out that Hélène Borissovna Stoudnitzki (*Nuits de prince*) and Hélène Borissovna Karol (*Le Vin de Solitude*) are both daughters of a Boris . . . just like Hélène Borissovna Gordon, Irène's friend and the future wife of Pierre Lazareff.

61. J.-É. Blanche, diary, 19th/20th June 1930, J.-É. Blanche collection, Bibliothèque de l'Institut.

62. I. Némirovsky, letter to B. Grasset, 19th October 1933, Grasset archives.

63. H. Béraud, *Les Derniers Beaux Jours*, Plon, 1953.

64. Interview with J.-L. de Carbuccia, 28th September 2005.

65. *La Vie de Tchekhov*, XVII.

66. M. Anissimov, 'Les filles d'Irène Némirovsky', *op. cit.*

67. J. Auscher, 'Sous la lampe, Irène Némirowsky', *op. cit.*

68. *Ibid.*

69. The working diary of *The Wine of Solitude* is a thick manuscript, kept at IMEC. It is impossible to quote from this extraordinary document in full, but we believe it may be useful to reproduce a significant and representative extract of Irène Némirovsky's method of working: 'I think it will be absolutely impossible to leave Max as he is. *Firstly, he has to be a Safronov. Secondly, he has to be changed physically and morally, made more subtle, more* bogatii mal'tchik i bartchouk [a wealthy adolescent, the son of a rich landowner] . . . *Thirdly*, show the antagonism between him and Hélène more clearly. *Fourthly, no carnal seduction, more of a rape.* Quite the opposite, it would be much more "diabolical" to show Hélène guessing almost instinctively that the time has come when Max *or whoever he is,** is sated with carnal love and will allow himself to be won over by youth, freshness, naivety. *Fifthly* clearly show the night that follows the moment (the storm) when she felt something else apart from pride and satisfied vengeance, how, for the first time, and it is very important, *she has a moral struggle.** Remember Proust's simple, true and noble words, *how we make our own principles and morality, and that they are then mingled with pain, made of flesh and blood, living and panting;* just as Pascal discovers geometry, so Hélène must discover by herself that the *Lord has kept vengeance to himself*, but it is too late . . . *Sixthly*, when she goes to his home, their conversation must contain the following: "Why don't we get married? . . ." or something similar, but to this, she replies: "I don't love you. I have felt affection for you, yes, it's true, but I know very well that it's not love. You see, you're too involved in my past, in my childhood. ~~I should like~~ If I ever marry it will be to someone who is unable to rekindle any of my old memories. I am ashamed and frightened of my childhood, ~~to the point of obsession~~. I want to forget them. I want to change life. I want to go away. Your presence would be unbearable."

*These words are in English in original text.

Seventhly, what becomes of him? ~~That, it's another~~ . . . that . . . Is another matter . . .'

70. P. Morand, *France la doulce*, Gallimard, February 1934.

71. In one of his reading notes from 1934. It is worth pointing out that his friend Tristan Bernard found nothing to criticise in *France la doulce*, and said so quite openly to the author in *Le Figaro* on 14th April 1934: 'Dear Paul Morand, your book is made to serve our cause: it has everything needed to do so. All that it may lack is the possibility of being understood by those who haven't a clue about anything and who will continue to allow themselves to be fleeced, sometimes by con-men, but more often by idiots who delude themselves. However, if this work does not do this magnificent art that is called cinema the favours that we might expect, we still have the compensation of being entertained by a most successful and amusing book, the work of a man who knows how to see the world and who gives us a thrilling picture of it.'

72. P. Morand, *France la doulce*, *op. cit.*

73. R. Giron, 'Conversations: Paul Morand', *Toute l'édition*, no. 217, 10th March 1934.

74. H. Béraud, *Les Derniers Beaux Jours*, Plon, 1953.

75. 'Des écrivains présentent', *Toute l'édition*, no. 233, 30th June 1934.

76. *Toute l'édition*, no. 229, 2nd June 1934.

77. *Le Pion sur l'échiquier*, VI.

78. Discours de F. de La Rocque, 14th June 1936.

79. R. Millman, 'Les Croix-de-Feu et l'antisémitisme', *Vingtième siècle*, vol. 38, no. 38, 1993.

80. I. Némirovsky, 'Théâtre de la Michodière. *Les Temps difficiles*, pièce en trois actes de M. É. Bourdet', *Aujourd'hui*, no. 285, 31st January 1934.

81. *Le Pion sur l'échiquier*, IX.

82. M.-J. Viel, 'Comment travaille une romancière', *op. cit.*

83. This is about the scene in which Yves accompanies Denise to 'Le Perroquet', a fashionable nightclub in the 1920s: 'At the next table sat an American woman; it was impossible to tell her age. She had the sharp shoulder bones of a skeleton and wore pearls that disappeared into the folds of her sagging neck. She simpered while rocking a doll that was dressed up as Pierrot; beneath the powder and make-up, the bags beneath her eyes were horribly swollen and bulging . . . Another woman, who vaguely resembled a toad with her large head and dwarf-

like body, was wrapped up in a heavenly dress. She gazed at a miserable little boy with the terrifying tenderness of an ogress; he was stunned, horrified and resigned as her arms held him tight, like two tentacles . . .', etc. (*Le Malentendu*, XVII.)

84 R. Lalou, '*Le Pion sur l'échiquier* or: Les vertiges de la solitude', *Noir et Blanc*, 7th June 1934. Article illustrated with a caricature of I. Némirovsky by Pol Ferjac.

85. A. Bellessort, *Je suis partout*, 9th June 1934.

86. M. Prévost, 'Romans imaginés et vécus', *Gringoire*, 15th June 1934.

87. R. Brasillach, *Action française*, 30th May 1934. The lunch in question is 'Déjeuner en septembre', which appeared in *Revue de Paris* in May 1934.

88. R. Brasillach, *Action française*, 16th March 1934.

89. *La Vie de Tchekhov*, XI.

90. 'Écho', *Noir et Blanc*, 22nd July 1934.

91. 'Dimanche', *Revue de Paris*, 1st June 1934, in *Dimanche*.

92. 'Les Rivages heureux', *Gringoire*, 2nd November 1934, in *Dimanche*.

93. J. Auscher, 'Sous la lampe. Irène Némirowsky', *op. cit.*

94. *Sequana*, August 1935.

95. R. Fernandez, 'Le livre de la semaine', *Marianne*, 9th October 1935.

96. J.-P. Maxence, 'Les livres de la semaine', *Gringoire*, 25th October 1935.

97. H. de Régnier, 'La vie littéraire', *Le Figaro*, 2nd November 1935.

98. H. Bidou, 'Le mouvement littéraire', *Revue de Paris*, 15th November 1935.

Chapter 8

1. J. d'Assac, 'Maris de femmes. Monsieur Irène Némirovsky', unspecified source, probably *Je suis partout* [February or March 1935].

2. Y. Moustiers, 'Comment elles travaillent', *Toute l'édition*, no. 397, 5th March 1938.

3. J. d'Assac, *op. cit.*

4. 'Une enquête en marge des souliers de Noël. Ce que voudraient lire les enfants des écrivains', *Toute l'édition*, no. 397, 4th December 1937.

5. Denise Epstein to M. Anissimov, 'Les filles d'Irène Némirovski', *op. cit.*

6. *Cf.* R. Groos, 'Estimez-vous que le cinéma ait eu ou puisse avoir une influence sur le roman? Et laquelle?' *op. cit.*

7. R. Fernandez, 'Le livre de la semaine', *Marianne*, 27th February 1935.

8. E. Jaloux, 'L'esprit des livres', *Les Nouvelles littéraires*, 9th March 1935.

9. H. de Régnier, 'La vie littéraire', *Le Figaro*, 9th March 1935.

10. J.-P. Maxence, 'Les livres de la semaine', *Gringoire*, 22th March 1935.

11. J.-P. Maxence, 'Les livres de la semaine', *Gringoire*, 25th October 1935.

12. *Fantasio*, 15th July 1921.

13. A. Chaumeix, speech at the fifteenth dinner of *Revue des Deux Mondes*, Union interalliée, 3rd December 1935, in *Revue des Deux Mondes*, 15th December 1935.

14. 'Jour d'été', *Revue des Deux Mondes*, 1st April 1935, in *Destinées*.

15. *Ibid.*

16. Quoted by G. de Broglie, *Histoire politique de la 'Revue des Deux Mondes' de 1829 à 1979*, Librairie académique Perrin, 1979.

17. 'Silhouettes. René Doumic', *Toute l'édition*, no. 161, 21st January 1933.

18. Quoted by R. Schor, *L'Antisémitisme en France dans l'entre-deux-guerres*, Complexe, 2005.

19. L. Rebatet, 'Les étrangers en France. L'invasion', *Je suis partout*, 16th February, 23rd February and 2nd March 1935.

20. E. Berl, 'Pour ou contre les étrangers', *Marianne*, no. 121, 13th February 1935.

21. I. Némirovsky, 'Théâtre de l'Œuvre. *Les Races*, 8 tableaux de Ferdinand Brückner, adapted by René Cave', *Aujourd'hui*, no. 323, 10th March 1934.

22. J. Auscher, 'Nos interviews: Irène Némirovsky . . .', *op. cit.*

23. A. Chaumeix, 'Revue littéraire. Romans d'automne', *Revue des Deux Mondes*, 1st December 1935.

24. *Jézabel* [*Jezebel*], V.

25. *Ibid.*, prologue.

26. P. Langers, 'Mme Irène Némirovsky, peintre des mœurs', *Toute l'édition*, no. 331, 4th July 1936.

27. J. Auscher, 'Nos interviews: Irène Némirovsky . . .', *op. cit.*

28. *Jézabel* [*Jezebel*], VII.

29. *Ibid.*, XI.

30. D. Desanti, 'Mère et fille: la haine et le rêve', *Magazine littéraire*, no. 386, 1st April 2000.

31. Marie-Thérèse's childbirth recalls the opening scene of *Génitrix*, where Mauriac, in 1923, drowns Mathilde Cazenave in the blood of her miscarriage, in an isolated summerhouse at the family home.

32. *Jézabel* [*Jezebel*], II.

33. *Ibid.*, XIII.

34. J.-C. Daven [C. Descargues], 'Au moment où paraît son dernier

livre: souvenez-vous d'Irène Némirovsky', *La Tribune de Lausanne*, 14th April 1957.

35. *Jézabel* [*Jezebel*], XXII.

36. S. Voronoff, *Vivre. Études des moyens de relever l'énergie vitale et de prolonger la vie*, Grasset, 1920.

37. *Jézabel* [*Jezebel*], VI.

38. P. Langers, 'Mme Irène Némirovsky, peintre de mœurs', *op. cit.*

39. *Jézabel* [*Jezebel*], I.

40. 'Le Commencement et la Fin', *Gringoire*, 20th December 1935, in *Destinées*.

41. 'Hommage à Grasset', *Marianne*, 15th January 1936. The complete list of signatories is given on 11th January in *Toute l'édition*, no. 306.

42. E. Haymann, *Albin Michel, le roman d'un éditeur*, Albin Michel, 1993.

43. 'Liens du sang', in *Dimanche*.

44. *Ibid.*

45. Presentation of *Jézabel*, *Toute l'édition*, no. 328, 13th June 1936.

46. *La Proie*, I, XV.

47. Insert in *La Proie*, May 1938.

48. *La Proie*, I, XII.

49. *Ibid.*, I, III.

50. *Ibid.*, II, XV.

51. R. Lalou, 'Le livre de la semaine. *Jézabel*', *Les Nouvelles littéraires*, 30th May 1936.

52. H. de Régnier, 'La vie littéraire', *Le Figaro*, 23rd May 1936.

53. J.-P. Maxence, 'Les livres de la semaine', *Gringoire*, [June] 1936.

54. I. Némirovsky, 'Le mariage de Pouchkine et sa mort', *Marianne*, 25th March 1936.

55. Letter to Albin Michel, 10th June 1936.

56. 'Les devoirs de vacances de nos écrivains', *Toute l'édition*, no. 237, 12th September 1936.

57. R. Bourget-Pailleron, 'La nouvelle équipe . . .', *op. cit.*

58. *Toute l'édition*, no. 336, 5th September 1936.

59. *La Proie*, II, IV.

60. *Cf.* R. Thalmann, 'Xénophobie et antisémitisme sous le Front populaire', *Matériaux pour l'histoire de notre temps*, vol. 6, no. 6, 1986.

61. Response from R. Doumic to A. Chaumeix, fifteenth dinner of the *Revue des Deux Mondes* at the Union interalliée, 3rd December 1935, in *op. cit.*

62. 'Les devoirs de vacance de nos écrivains', *Toute l'édition*, no. 337, 12th September 1936.

63. 'Fraternité', *Gringoire*, 5th February 1937, in *Dimanche*.

64. *Ibid.*

65. *Ibid.*

66. J. and J. Tharaud, *L'An prochain à Jérusalem*, Plon, 1924; quoted by L. Landau, *De l'aversion à l'estime. Juifs et catholiques en France de 1919 à 1939*, Le Centurion, 1980.

67. 'Fraternité', *Gringoire*, 5th February 1937, in *Dimanche*.

68. J. Delpech, 'Chez Irène Némirovsky ou la Russie boulevard des Invalides', *Les Nouvelles littéraires*, Saturday 4th June 1938. The revival of *David Golder* at the Théâtre russe opened in December 1937.

69. R. Brasillach, *Notre avant-guerre*, Plon, 1941.

70. 'Fraternité', *Gringoire*, 5th February 1937, in *Dimanche*.

71. *Ibid.*

72. G. de Broglie, *Histoire politique de la 'Revue des Deux Mondes' de 1829 à 1979*, *op. cit.*

73. Letters between I. Némirovsky and A. Michel, 7th and 12th October 1936.

74. P. Mourousy, interview with A. Michel, *Comœdia*, 18th September 1936.

75. Interview with Mme É. Zehrfuss, 19th February 2006.

76. J.-R. Leygues, *Chroniques des années incertaines 1935–1945*, France Empire, 1977.

77. J. Van Melle, 'Où avez-vous passé vos vacances? Qu'avez-vous fait de vos vacances?', *Toute l'édition*, no. 386, 18th September 1936.

78. *Deux*, IV.

79. *Ibid.*, V.

80. *Gringoire*, 24th October 1941.

81. *L'Intransigeant*, 4th August 1938.

82. *Gringoire*, 11th April 1940.

83. *Revue des Deux Mondes*, 15th October 1938, in *Destinées*, p. 53.

84. *Action française*, 13th July 1938.

85. 'Espoirs', *Gringoire*, 19th August 1938, in *Destinées*.

86. *Les Nouvelles littéraires*, 21st May 1938.

87. *Excelsior*, 25th May 1938.

88. J. Delpech, 'Chez Irène Némirovsky . . .', *op. cit.*

89. 'Revue littéraire. Romans et critique', *Revue des Deux Mondes* [1938].

90. J.-P. Maxence, 'Les livres de la semaine', *Gringoire*, 10th June 1938.

Chapter 9

1. *Le Maître des âmes*, I.
2. *Ibid.*, X.
3. *Ibid.*, X.
4. É. Zola, 'Pour les Juifs', *Le Figaro;* 16th May 1896.
5. P. Morand, *La Nuit de Putney*, in *Les Œvres libres*, no. XV, September 1922.
6. J. Van Melle, 'Où avez-vous passé vos vacances? À quoi faire?' *Toute l'édition*, 3rd September 1938.
7. *Le Maître des âmes*, I, III, VI, VII, XX. Léon Poliakov has shown that these very widespread stereotypes could be those of authors who were not suspected of anti-Semitism, in particular Lacretelle; we come across almost identical ones in *Les Thibault* by Roger Martin du Gard: 'Skada was a Jew from Asia Minor, of about fifty years old. Very short-sighted. He wore spectacles on his hooked, olive-coloured nose, and their glass was as thick as a telescope's lenses. He was ugly: short, frizzy hair pasted down over an egg-shaped skull; enormous ears; but a warm, thoughtful look in his eyes, and boundlessly affectionate.' (Quoted by L. Poliakov, *Histoire de l'antisémitisme*, vol. 2. *L'Âge de la science*, Hachette, 'Pluriels', 1981.) In this revised and abridged edition of his great work, L. Poliakov has removed the word 'anti-Semitic' used in connection with Irène Némirovsky's name in the first edition (1977).
8. *Le Maître des âmes*, XX.
9. In her working notebook, Irène Némirovsky had underlined in red and in bold: 'Law of 1935: no one may practise medicine in France unless he possesses a diploma from the French state and is a French subject.' A note in the margin makes it clear: 'In a nutshell, he must be French!' Then these two words, in red: 'granted citizenship'.
10. *Le Maître des âmes*, XX.
11. 'La Nuit en wagon', *Gringoire*, 5th October 1939, in *Destinées*.
12. J. Van Melle, 'Où avez-vous passé vos vacances? . . .', *op. cit.*
13. O. Mony, 'Jours heureux à Hendaye', *Le Festin en Aquitaine*, no. 54, summer 2005.
14. Interview with Denise Epstein, Toulouse, 11th January 2005.
15. *Les Chiens et les Loups* [*The Dogs and the Wolves*], XXVIII.
16. *Ibid.*, XXIV. Already Asfar, in *Les Échelles du Levant*, exclaims: 'Useless, simpering Europeans!' (*Le Maître des âmes*, I.)

17. *Les Chiens et les Loups* [*The Dogs and the Wolves*], XXII.

18. L. Rebatet, 'J'ai vu un pogrom', *Je suis partout*, 2nd September 1938.

19. *Les Chiens et les Loups* [*The Dogs and the Wolves*], I.

20. *Ibid.*, VIII.

21. *Ibid.*, VII.

22. *Ibid.*, XXXIII.

23. In his memoirs, Count Witte, the former Russian prime minister, recorded the remarks of a Polish lawyer complaining about the influx of Russian Jews in his country after the Kichinev pogroms in 1905: 'Your Jews have corrupted ours, he told him, just as wild animals infest domestic animals with their uncivilised ways. And, naturally, your Jews cannot help being uncivilised since you refuse them everything that exists in human aspirations and feelings.' (*Mémoires du comte Witte*, Plon, 1921.)

24. *Marianne*, 8th April 1936.

25. M. Martin du Gard, *Les Mémorables*, Gallimard, 1999.

26. *Le Maître des âmes*, X.

27. M.-L. Sondaz, 'Sera-t-elle bonne et heureuse? Ce que disent les astres pour 1939', *Marie-Claire*, no. 96, 30th December 1938.

28. Mgr Piguet, preface to M. Perroy, *Sacerdos Alter Christus: l'abbé Roger Bréchard*, Clermont-Ferrand, 1949.

29. 'Testament' by H. Bergson, 8th February 1937.

30. W. Rabinovich, 'La tragédie du peuple juif', *Esprit*, 1st May 1933, quoted by L. Landau, *De l'aversion à l'estime . . .*, *op. cit.*

31. 'Testament' by H. Bergson, 8th February 1937.

32. J.-J. Bernard, 'Judaïsme et Christianisme', *Le Figaro*, 31st October 1946, quoted by F. Gugelot, 'De Ratisbonne à Lustiger. Les convertis à l'époque contemporaine', *Archives juives. Revue d'histoire des Juifs de France*, no. 35/1, 1st semester 2002.

33. *Les Chiens et les Loups* [*The Dogs and the Wolves*], XXIII.

34. I. Némirovsky, 'Théâtre de l'Œuvre. *Les races*, 8 tableaux de Ferdinand Brückner, adaptation de René Cave', *Aujourd'hui*, no. 323, 10th March 1934.

35. *Les Biens de ce monde*, XXII.

36. H.-R. Petit, *Le Règne des Juifs* (Paris, Centre de documentation et de propagande, September 1937), quoted by R. Schor, *op. cit.*

37. *Le Vin de Solitude* [*The Wine of Solitude*], I, VII.

38. Interview with Denise Epstein, 10th January 2005.

39. M. Perroy, *Sacerdos Alter Christus* . . ., *op. cit.*

40. J. Maritain, 'Les Juifs parmi les nations', lecture given at the Théâtre des Ambassadeurs on 5th February 1938, Éditions du Cerf, 1938.

41. Interview with Denise Epstein, 10th January 2005.

42. J. Maritain, preface to V. Ghika, *Pensées pour la suite des jours*, Beauchesne, 1936.

43. Letter to Mgr Ghika, 7th February 1939. Mgr Ghika had just sent Irène Némirovsky a copy of his *Pensées*.

44. Letter to Mgr Ghika, 27th January 1939.

45. Letter to Mgr Ghika, 25th March 1939.

46. *Les Chiens et les Loups* [*The Dogs and the Wolves*], IX.

47. This final sentence remained virtually unaltered in the final version of the novel.

48. Display advertisement for *Juifs et Catholiques* by H. de Vries de Heekelingen, *Les Nouvelles littéraires*, 4th February 1939. In this book, as in the earlier one by this author (*L'Orgueil juif*, 1938), Vries de Heekelingen, an anti-Semitic ideologue and a fierce defender of the authenticity of *Protocols of the Elders of Zion*, imputes the invention of racism to the Jews, and therefore argues that 'if one criticises German or Italian racism, one should equally criticise Jewish racism'. (*Cf.* P.-A. Taguieff, 'Des thèmes récurrents qui structurent l'imaginaire antijuif moderne', *L'Arche*, no. 560, November–December 2004.)

49. *Le Crapouillot*, February 1939.

50. 'Les Juifs en France', *Je suis partout*, 17th February 1939.

51. Letter to Mgr Ghika, 19th April 1939.

52. Letter to Mgr Ghika, 27th April 1939.

53. These talks, given during the afternoons of 4th and 18th January, 1st and 15th February and 1st and 15th March 1939, were neither recorded nor published in *Cahiers de Radio Paris*.

54. Display advertisement, *Les Nouvelles littéraires*, 25th March 1939.

55. P. Lœwel, *L'Ordre*, 3rd April 1939.

56. *Le Maître des âmes*, I.

57. 'Journal du *Charlatan*', 19th July 1938.

58. Letter to Mgr Ghika, 3rd July 1939.

59. 'Comme de grands enfants', *Marie-Claire*, 27th October 1939, in *Destinées*.

60. Denise Epstein, 'Une photographie', in *Destinées, op. cit.*

61. 'Le Spectateur', *Gringoire*, 7th December 1939, in *Dimanche, op. cit.*

62. 'Comme de grands enfants', *Marie-Claire*, 27th October 1939, in *Destinées, op. cit.*

63. *Les Biens de ce monde* [*All Our Worldly Goods*], XXIV.

Chapter 10

1. *Chaleur du sang* [*Fire in the Blood*].

2. *Ibid.*

3. Letter to A. Sabatier, 13th December 1940.

4. 'Destinées', *Gringoire*, 5th December 1940, in *Destinées*.

5. 'À la recherche d'Irène Némirovsky . . .', *op. cit.*

6. 'Les Revenants', *Gringoire*, 5th September 1941.

7. *Chaleur du sang* [*Fire in the Blood*].

8. 'La Nuit en wagon', *Gringoire*, no. 569, 5th October 1939, in *Destinées*.

9. M. Anissimov, 'Les filles d'Irène Némirovsky', *op. cit.*

10. 'Le Spectateur', *Gringoire*, no. 578, 7th December 1939, in *Dimanche*.

11. 'Comme de grands enfants', *Marie-Claire*, no. 139, 27th October 1939. The manuscript of this story is entitled 'La Querelle'.

12. 'La Nuit en wagon', *op. cit.*

13. All that remains of this unpublished story, entitled 'En raison des circonstances', is a heavily marked draft; some elements of it will be used in *The Fires of Autumn*.

14. The image of the shaker is borrowed from Evelyn Waugh whose description of a rough crossing in *Vile Bodies* had appealed to Irène Némirovsky: 'it's just exactly like being inside a cocktail shaker'.

15. 'Le Spectateur', *op. cit.* Katherine Mansfield, in her *Journal*, which was among I. Némirovsky's favourite reading, mentions, on 18th January 1922, 'a man to remember': 'H. always collects something – always will. China, silver, "any old thing that comes along".'

16. Y. Moustiers, 'Les femmes de lettres et la guerre', *Toute l'édition*, no. 483, December 1939.

17. 'Aïno', *Revue des Deux Mondes*, 1st January 1940, in *Dimanche*.

18. '. . . et je l'aime encore', *Marie-Claire*, no. 153, 2nd February 1940, in *Destinées*.

19. 'Le Sortilège', *Gringoire*, no. 586, 1st February 1940, in *Dimanche*.

20. We owe numerous biographies to Maurois, including one of Turgenev, and to Eugène Semenoff popular biographies of Pushkin

and Turgenev (Mercure de France, 1933). For her own biography of Chekhov, Irène Némirovsky made particular use of the memoirs of his friend Ivan Bunin, 'one of the sharpest and most subtle critics' (*La Vie de Tchekhov*, XVIII).

21. *La Vie de Tchekhov*, XVIII.

22. *Les Chiens et les Loups* [*The Dogs and the Wolves*], XII.

23. *Gringoire*, 4th April 1940. During the phoney war, the caricaturist Roger Roy made fun of Hitler and Stalin in turn, only sparing the rising figure of Marshal Pétain, whom *Gringoire* referred to ardently in these terms: 'Yesterday, a great military leader. Today, a great diplomat. Tomorrow . . .' (26th March 1940.) Three months before he espoused Collaboration, the anti-Semite Philippe Henriot could still be seen condemning, in *Gringoire*, 'the worship of force, cynically practised by Hitler' ('Feu la neutralité', 11th April 1940).

24. G. Higgins, 'Les Conrad français', *Les Nouvelles littéraires*, 6th April 1940.

25. 'L'Autre Jeune Fille', *Marie-Claire*, no. 166, 3rd May 1940. The manuscript of this story was entitled 'Deux jeunes filles'.

26. 'Le Départ pour la fête', *Gringoire*, 11th April 1940, in *Destinées*.

27. Irène Némirovsky would restore the exact quotation from Chekhov in 'Destinées': 'How they suffer, how high a price they pay for us, these people who are above others, who set the tone of European culture.' (*Gringoire*, 5th December 1940, in *Destinées*.)

28. 'Destinées', *op. cit.*

29. In particular: Isabelle Rimbaud, *Dans les remous de la bataille*, Chapelot, 1917; Léon Wastelier du Parc, *Souvenirs d'un réfugié*, Perrin, 1916; Bernard Desuher, *Souvenirs d'un éclaireur*, Perrin, 1915.

30. Advertising insert, *Le Matin*, 24th April 1940; *Les Nouvelles littéraires*, 27th April 1940.

31. *Les Chiens et les Loups* [*The Dogs and the Wolves*], XXIII.

32. *Ibid.*, XVI.

33. *Conferencia. Les Annales*, no. XI, 15th May 1940.

34. *Gringoire*, 25th April 1940.

35. P. Lœwel, 'Les Lettres. De Victor Serge à L. de Hoyer et Mme Némirovsky', *L'Ordre*, 1st June 1940.

36. A. Labarthe, 'La ligne Maginot, bouclier de la France', *L'Intransigeant*, 16th April 1940.

37. Advertisement in *Gringoire*, 30th May 1940.

38. Philippe Pétain, speech made on 25th June 1940.

39. A. Labarthe, *L'Intransigeant*, 22nd May 1940.

40. *La Jeunesse de Tchekhov*, 'Variété historique inédite', *Les Œuvres libres*, no. 226, May 1940; *La Vie de Tchekhov*, XIV.

41. Caroline Wyatt, 'French Novel Survives Auschwitz', BBC News Paris, 27th January 2005.

42. 'Monsieur Rose', *Candide*, 28th August 1940, in *Dimanche*.

43. The line would not be fixed definitively, by means of a topographical survey, until the end of 1941. *Cf.* J. Gillot-Voisin, *La Saône-et-Loire sous Hitler. Périls et Violences*, Mâcon, Fédération des Œuvres laïques, 1996.

44. Marshal Pétain, 'L'Éducation nationale', *Revue des Deux Mondes*, 15th August 1940.

45. F. Brouty, letter to Irène Némirovsky, 27th July 1940.

46. 'La Voleuse', unpublished story.

47. *La Vie de Tchekhov*, XXII.

48. Letter to R. Esménard, 25th September 1940.

49. *La Vie de Tchekhov*, XXVIII.

50. L. Werth, *Déposition. Journal de guerre 1940–1944*, Viviane Hamy, 1992 (8th October).

51. M. Epstein, letter to C.-A. de Boissieu, 16th October 1940.

52. C.-A. de Boissieu, letter to M. Epstein, 14th October 1940.

53. *Cf.* E. Haymann, *op. cit.*

54. J. Fayard, letter to Irène Némirovsky, 14th October 1940.

55. Letter to J. Fayard, 16th October 1940.

56. J. Vignaud, interview with C. Chonez, *Marianne*, 8th April 1936.

57. Letter to J. Vignaud, 3rd December 1940.

58. J. Fayard, response to the questionnaire 'Que pensez-vous de la collaboration franco-allemande?', *Aujourd'hui*, 16th November 1940.

59. Ph. Henriot, *Gringoire*, 31st October 1940.

60. Interview with J.-L. de Carbuccia, 28th September 2005.

61. H. de Carbuccia, 'Mémoire en réponse aux *Raisons d'un silence*', in H. Béraud, *Gringoire. Écrits 1940–1943*, Versailles, Consep, 2005.

62. 'La Confidente', *Gringoire*, 20th March 1941, in *Dimanche*.

63. *Aujourd'hui*, 15th September 1940.

64. 'The Jews did not choose to be who they are, and my contempt is mainly for those who disown their race.' (M. Duran, 'Les abjects', *Aujourd'hui*, 22nd October 1940.)

65. 'Un inédit de M. Louis Destouches dit . . . Louis-Ferdinand Céline', *Aujourd'hui*, no. 177, 7th March 1941.

66. R. Desnos, *Aujourd'hui*, 26th October 1940; quoted by H. Jeanson, *Soixante-dix ans d'adolescence*, Stock, 1971.

67. *Suite française [Suite Française]*, I, 11.

68. *La Vie de Tchekhov*, XXIV.

69. *Suite française*, I, 14.

70. *Ibid.*, I, 27.

71. *Ibid.*, I, 27.

72. H. du Moulin de Labarthète, *Le Temps des illusions. Souvenirs (juillet 1940–avril 1942)*, La Diffusion du livre, 1946.

73. *Suite française*, I, 3.

74. Two years before Hitler, deploring France's bleating pacifism and under-armed state, Lœwel refused to get involved in an argument between fascism and bolshevism and prophesied total war: 'Tomorrow Europe will be put to fire and sword. Millions of men, hundred of cities, an entire civilisation will collapse in an unprecedented catastrophe.' (*Inventaire 1931*, Librairie Valois, 1931.) In 1938, in an article in *Samedi*, he nevertheless considered that the Jews should 'consider with an open mind any criticism directed against them', even if it was the delirious ravings of a Céline in *Bagatelles pour un massacre* (*cf.* D. H. Weinberg, *Les Juifs à Paris de 1933 à 1939*, Calmann-Lévy, 1974).

75. L. Bromfield, *The Rains Came*.

76. *Suite Française*, I, 22.

77. *Ibid.*, I, 22.

78. *Ibid.*, I, 29.

79. *Ibid.*, I, 10.

80. *Ibid.*, I, 6.

81. *Ibid.*, I, 28.

82. Labarie, and not Sabarie: both of these written forms were used in *Suite française*, but Irène Némirovsky formed her 'L's like 'S's. Moreover, rather as she made use of Morcenx and Langon in other books, Labarie is the name of a village in the South-West of France.

83. *Suite française*, I, 30.

84. Letter quoted by M. Perroy, in *Sacerdos Alter Christus*, *op. cit.*

85. H. Pourrat, 'Un mort du 20 juin' (1943), in *ibid.*

86. *Suite française*, I, 25.

87. *Ibid.*, I, 4.

88. M.-J. Viel, 'Comment travaille une romancière', *op. cit.*

89. *Les Biens de ce monde [All Our Worldly Goods]*, XXV.

90. *La Vie de Tchekhov*, XV.

91. *Le Bal*, V.

92. V. Veresaev, *La Vie de Pouchkine*, followed by passages from Pushkin assembled and annotated by J. E. Pouterman, Éditions sociales internationales, 1937.

93. Colette, 'Fin juin 1940', in *Journal à rebours*, Fayard, March 1941.

94. Letter to Madeleine Cabour, 27th March 1941.

95. 'L'Honnête Homme', *Gringoire*, 30th May 1941; in *Dimanche*. J. de Maistre's exact words are slightly different: 'I don't know what the life of a rogue is, I have never been one; but that of an honest man is appalling.'

96. *Suite française*, I, 30.

97. *La Vie de Tchekhov*, XXVI.

98. 'L'Ogresse', *Gringoire*, 24th October 1941, in *Dimanche*.

99. *Les Biens de ce monde* [*All Our Worldly Goods*], I.

100. *Ibid.*, XXX.

101. H. Béraud, 'Et les Juifs?', *Gringoire*, 23rd January 1941, in *Sans haine ni crainte*, Les Éditions de France, 1942.

102. 'Death to the Jew! . . . The Jew is not a man. He's a stinking beast. We get rid of fleas. We fight epidemics. We struggle against bacterial infections. We protect ourselves aginst evil, against death – therefore against the Jews.' (P. Riche, *Le Pilori*, 14th March 1941.)

103. F. Vinneuil [L. Rebatet], *Les Tribus du théâtre et du cinéma*, 'Les Juifs en France', IV, Nouvelles Éditions françaises, 1941.

104. *David Golder*, I.

Chapter 11

1. *Les Feux de l'automne* [*Autumn Fires*], III, III.

2. Michel Epstein refers in a letter to an annual amount of 2,300 francs. The Place du Monument was renamed Place Irène-Némirovsky on 2nd September 2005.

3. É. Gille to M. Anissimov, 'Les filles d'Irène Némirovsky', *op. cit.*

4. *Suite française*, II, 8.

5. Extracts from reports from the sub-prefecture of Autun, Archives départementales de Saône-et-Loire, série W, quoted by R. Voyard, 'Le tragique destin d'une femme de lettres. Irène Némirovsky. Kiev . . . Paris . . . Issy-l'Évêque . . . Auschwitz', Gueugnon, Les Amis du Dardon, 2005.

6. 'Cour de justice. Quand les passions sont déchaînées . . .', *Le Courrier de Saône-et-Loire*, 21–22nd October 1945.

7. *Suite française* [*Suite Française*], II, 20.

8. *Ibid.*, II, 12. It is possible that Irène Némirovsky was remembering Henri Falk, the dialogue writer for *Le Bal*.

9. *Ibid.*, II, 17.

10. *Ibid.*, II, 11.

11. *Ibid.*, II, 3.

12. 'Dimanche', *Revue de Paris*, 1st June 1934, in 'Dimanche', *op. cit.*

13. M. Proust, '*À l'ombre des jeunes filles en fleurs*.

14. *Chaleur du sang* [*Fire in the Blood*].

15. *Suite française*, II, 3.

16. Letter to M. Bergeret, 27th September 1941.

17. 'Les Revenants', *Gringoire*, 5th September 1941. The typescript of this story is signed 'Pierre Imphy'.

18. Letter to W. I. Pahlen Heyberg, 9th August 1941, in reply to his earlier letter of the 6th: 'Madame Jane Nemirovski has asked me to bring back her furs which she had left in the trunks that remained in her flat. Now, these trunks have been emptied and the caretaker of the building told me that you had come and taken away the contents of these trunks. I wrote to your mother to advise her of this. Once again, I have received several cards from her, asking me to get in touch with you, so that you can give me back the things that were taken away. Consquently, I would be grateful if you would arrange a meeting, in order that I may carry out her request.' (IMEC.)

19. Quoted by A. Lacroix-Riz, *Industriels et Banquiers sous l'Occupation. La collaboration économique avec le Reich et Vichy*, Armand Colin/HER, 1999.

20. *L'Appel*, 30th September 1941.

21. Letter to R. Esménard, 4th October 1941. Under his Judaeo-Russian name of Eugène Schkaff, Jean Fréville (1895–1971) originally published a small work entitled *La Question agraire en Russie* (1922), followed by *La Dépréciation monétaire, ses effets en droit privé* (1926). After acquiring French citizenship in 1925, he became a contributor to *Commune*, a reviewer for *L'Humanité* from 1931, a novelist (*Pain de brique*, 1937), and the translator and editor of texts by Marx, Engels, Lenin and Stalin. The unofficial ghostwriter for Maurice Thorez, he would write an ode to his glory set to music by Louis Durey. Just one of his books was

published secretly during the Occupation; it bore the unambiguous title of *Pétain, maréchal de la trahison*.

22. R. Esménard, letter to I. Némirovsky, 10th October 1941.

23. Letter to R. Esménard, 30th October 1941.

24. Letter to A. Sabatier, 20th November 1941.

25. *Ibid*.

26. Letter to A. Sabatier, 21st December 1941.

27. Pierre Lepage [I. Némirovsky], 'Un beau mariage', in *Destinées*.

28. Pierre Neyret [I. Némirovsky], 'L'Incendie', *Gringoire*, 27th February 1942, in *Dimanche*.

29. A. Suarès, *Vita Nova*, Rougerie, 1977.

30. 'L'Incendie', *op. cit.*

31. *Les Feux de l'automne* [*Autumn Fires*], I, VI. Détang is a name from the region of Issy-l'Évêque.

32. *Ibid.*, I, IX.

33. *Ibid.*, II, IX.

34. *Ibid.*, III, VI.

35. *Ibid.*, III, I.

36. *Ibid.*, II, IX.

37. *Ibid.*, III, IX.

38. M. Epstein, letter to Paul Epstein, 23rd January 1942.

39. Letter to the Kreiskommandantur of Autun, 11th February 1942.

40. Letter to Hélène Morand, 12th February 1942, Paul Morand collection, Bibliothèque de l'Institut.

41. The hearings of the Riom trial were adjourned on 11th April 1942, at the behest of Otto Abetz. Those accused were handed over to the occupying power. In his concluding remarks, Léon Blum vigorously reaffirmed the legitimacy of his work, in the 'republican and democratic tradition', and ridiculed the official Vichy doctrine: 'The length of human endeavour does not control the efficiency of an industrial machine, leisure is not laziness; liberty and justice have not made the homeland a defence-less prey; helots do not provide more workers than they do soldiers. Whether it is a matter of using the tool or using the gun, it is liberty and justice that breed the great manly virtues, confidence, enthusiasm and courage.'

42. M. Anissimov, 'Les filles d'Irène Némirovsky', *op. cit.*

43. *Suite Française* [*Suite Française*], II, 16.

44. Denise Epstein, letter to her parents, 28th April 1942.

45. Interview with Denise Epstein, 12th January 2005.

46. Denise Epstein, letter to her parents, 28th April 1942.

47. M. Anissimov, 'Les filles d'Irène Némirovsky', *op. cit.*

48. *Cf.* J. Gillot-Voisin, *La Saône-et-Loire sous Hitler*, *op. cit.*

49. *Cf.* S. Klarsfeld, 'La tragédie juive de 1942 en France: ombres et lumière', *Le Monde*, 26th August 2003.

50. 'Mama never sewed. Except for the yellow star.' (Interview with Denise Epstein, Moscow, January 2006.)

51. Interview with Denise Epstein, 10th January 2005.

52. *Suite française*, II, 12.

53. Aulis Sallinen's *Chamber concerto*, *op.* 87 was first performed on 2nd March 2006 in Espoo (Finland). It consists of three movements: I. *Storm in June.* II. *Dolce.* III. *Delicate epitaph.*

54. J. Benoist-Méchin, *L'Ukraine*, 'Note liminaire', Albin Michel, July 1941.

55. Letter to A. Sabatier, 17th May 1942.

56. *Ibid.*

57. Denise Mérande [I. Némirovsky], 'Les Vierges', *Présent*, 15th July 1942.

58. Letter to A. Sabatier, 4th May 1942.

59. Letter to A. Sabatier, 17th May 1942.

60. Katherine Mansfield, *Journal*, 19th December 1920.

61. Testimony of Denise Epstein, in *Convoi no. 6*, Le Cherche Midi, 2005.

62. Katherine Mansfield, *Journal*, 19th December 1920.

Chapter 12

1. Letter from M. Epstein to A. Sabatier, 14th July 1942.

2. *Suite française*, II, 19.

3. Letter from M. Epstein to A. Sabatier, 29th September 1942.

4. Interview with Denise Epstein, 10th January 2005.

5. *Les Feux de l'automne* [*Autumn Fires*], III, III.

6. This letter from Alexandra Epstein to a woman friend is quoted, without acknowledgement, by S. Klarsfeld in his *Calendrier de la persécution des Juifs en France*, *op. cit.* 'Darling, we are at Drancy. Sam is with Paul. I see them when we are taken to the lavatory. Don't forget us. Natascha is French. We hope that husbands and wives will be sent into exile together. We shall need warm things. Warm gloves, grey pullover,

red triangle, small mirror, toothbrush (hard), shoelaces, knickers, petticoats, bra, books especially, I packed 4 volumes of Tolstoy, woollen socks, winter overcoat, Sam's warm underclothes, his scarf, his blue vest. The lawyer may be able to do something. I have a delightful neighbour. [She] left behind parents aged 86, alone and unable to speak the language. Must comfort them. The address: M. Simon, 123, boulevard Bessières Paris 17ᵉ. The wretchedness and distress all around are indescribable. My neighbours on the other side are nine orphan girls from a boarding school for orphans. The diet is the diet of a military prison. Filthy as a coal cellar. Straw mattress full of lice and insects. Appalling overcrowding. 86 women, 6 taps, we don't have time to wash. There are women who are pregnant, women who are deaf, mute, blind, on stretchers, who have left their very tiny children on their own. Old women of 63. We don't go to the lavatory for 16 hours. We watched the departure of some of the men. They shaved the men in the courtyard. The women recognised their husbands, they shrieked and cried. They carried the men away on stretchers. At night they took the women down to bid farewell to the husbands. Two of them went mad. There are boys kept here who come to help the women. They are Aryans wearing a star and the inscription "friend of the Jews". Tell Natascha, if she doesn't see us again, that she must be brave, that we love her enormously, that we bequeath her our spotless name. May she be scrupulous and honest. Never happy at the expense of others. Search for my parents . . .' Natacha, who had taken refuge in North Africa, would not be deported. She would marry the journalist and writer Jean Duché.

7. Hélène Morand, letter to Michel Epstein, 17th July 1942.
8. Michel Epstein, letter to Otto Abetz, 27th July 1942. The reader is referred to this letter which is printed in full in the appendices of the French edition of *Suite française*.
9. A. Sabatier, letter to Hélène Morand, 29th July 1942.
10. A. Sabatier, letter to Michel Epstein, 12th August 1942.
11. Letter from Mavlik to Michel Epstein, 2nd August 1942.
12. V. N. Kokovtzov, *Le Bolchevisme à l'œuvre. La Ruine morale et économique dans le pays des Soviets*, Paris, Marcel Giard, 1931.
13. A. Sabatier, letter to Michel Epstein, 12th August 1942.
14. Hélène Morand, letter to André Sabatier, 17th September 1942.

15.   Interview with Denise Epstein, 10th January 2005.

16.   The sub-prefect of Autun, prefect of the Occupied Zone of Saône-et-
      Loire, to the head of the Sicherheitspolizei, attached to Chalon-sur-
      Saône, 21st October 1942.

17.   Denise Epstein, to Myriam Anissimov, 'Les filles d'Irène Némirovsky',
      op. cit.

18.   Denise Epstein, Reuters, 9th March 2006.

Epilogue

1.   Conversation with Denise Epstein.

2.   A. Sabatier, letter to Julie Dumot, 9th November 1944.

3.   *Deux*, XXIX.

4.   *Cf.* Olga Wormser-Migot, *Le Retour des déportés*, Complexe, 1985.

5.   Letter from Mme Ginoux to Julie Dumot, 22nd June 1945.

6.   Interview with Francis Esménard, 27th September 2005.

7.   André Sabatier, letter to Julie Dumot, 1st June 1945.

8.   J.-J. Bernard, introduction to 'La Mort de Tchékhov', *La Nef*, no. 20,
     July 1946.

9.   Élisabeth Gille to Myriam Anissimov, 'Les filles d'Irène Némirovsky',
     op. cit.

Bibliography

1. Books by Irène Némirovsky

a) *Novels*

Le Malentendu, in *Les Œuvres libres*, no. 56, Fayard, February 1926; Fayard, coll. 'Collection de bibliothèque', 1930.

L'Ennemie, in *Les Œuvres libres*, no. 85, Fayard, July 1928 (Pierre Nerey).

David Golder, Grasset, coll. 'Pour mon plaisir', 1929; *David Golder*, translated into English by Sandra Smith, Chatto & Windus, 2007.

Les Mouches d'automne, ou la Femme d'autrefois, Kra, coll. 'Femmes', 1931; Grasset, December 1931 ; *Snow in Autumn* (published together with *Le Bal*), translated into English by Sandra Smith, Vintage, 2007.

L'Affaire Courilof, Grasset, coll. 'Pour mon plaisir', 1933; *The Courilof Affair*, translated into English by Sandra Smith, Vintage, 2008.

Le Pion sur l'échiquier, Albin Michel, 1934.

Le Vin de Solitude, Albin Michel, 1935; to be translated as *The Wine of Solitude*, Vintage, in 2011.

Jézabel, Albin Michel, 1936; to be translated as *Jezebel*, Vintage, in 2010.

La Proie, Albin Michel, 1938.

Deux, Albin Michel, 1939.

Les Chiens et les Loups, Albin Michel, 1940; *The Dogs and the Wolves*, translated into English by Sandra Smith, Chatto & Windus, 2009.

Les Biens de ce monde [1940–1941], Albin Michel, 1947; *All Our Worldly Goods*, translated into English by Sandra Smith, Chatto & Windus, 2008.

Les Feux de l'automne [1941–1942], Albin Michel, 1957; to be translated as *Autumn Fires*, Vintage, 2011.

Suite française [1940–1942], Denoël, 2004 ; *Suite Française*, translated into English by Sandra Smith, Chatto & Windus, 2006.

Le Maître des âmes [*Les Échelles du Levant*, in *Gringoire*, 1939], Denoël, 2005.

Chaleur du sang [1941–1942], Denoël, 2007; *Fire in the Blood*, translated into English by Sandra Smith, Chatto & Windus, 2007.

b) *Biographical Works*

'La Jeunesse de Tchekhov', *Les Œuvres libres*, no. 226, Fayard, May 1940.

'La Mort de Tchekhov', *La Nef*, no. 20, July 1946.

'Le Mariage de Tchekhov', *Les Œuvres libres*, nouvelle série, no. 13 (239), 4e trimestre 1946.

La Vie de Tchekhov, Albin Michel, October 1946.

c) *Short Stories*

'Nonoche chez l'extra-lucide', *Fantasio*, no. 348, 1st August 1921 (*Popsy*), unpublished.

'Nonoche au Louvre' [1921], unpublished.

'Nonoche au vert' [1921], unpublished.

'Nonoche au ciné' [1921] (*Topsy*), unpublished.

'La Niania', *Le Matin*, 9th May 1924; Grasset, 2009, edited and introduced by Olivier Philipponnat.

'L'Enfant génial', *Les Œuvres libres*, no. 70, April 1927; *Un enfant prodige*, preface by Élisabeth Gille, Gallimard, 1992.

'Le Bal', *Les Œuvres libres*, no. 92, February 1929 (*Pierre Nerey*); Grasset, 1930; *Le Bal* (published together with *Snow in Autumn*), translated into English by Sandra Smith, Chatto & Windus, 2007.

'Film parlé', *Les Œuvres libres*, no. 121, July 1931; reprinted in *Films parlés*, Gallimard, coll. 'Renaissance de la nouvelle', 1934.

'La Comédie bourgeoise', *Les Œuvres libres*, no. 132, June 1932; reprinted in *Films parlés*, Gallimard, coll. 'Renaissance de la nouvelle', 1934.

'Un déjeuner en septembre' ['Septembre'], *Revue de Paris*, vol. 3, 1st May 1933.

'Nativité', *Gringoire*, 8th December 1933.

'Ida', *Marianne*, no. 82, 16th May 1934; reprinted in *Films parlés*, Gallimard, coll. 'Renaissance de la nouvelle', 1934.

'Dimanche', *Revue de Paris*, vol. 3, 1st June 1934.

'Les Fumées du vin', *Le Figaro*, 12th/19th June 1934; reprinted in *Films parlés*, Gallimard, coll. 'Renaissance de la nouvelle', 1934.

'Écho', *Noir et Blanc*, no. 24, 22nd July 1934, unpublished.

'Les Rivages heureux', *Gringoire*, 2nd November 1934.

'Jour d'été', *Revue des Deux Mondes*, no. 581, 1st April 1935.

'Le Commencement et la Fin', *Gringoire*, 20th December 1935.

'Un amour en danger', *Le Figaro littéraire*, 22nd February 1936, unpublished.

'Liens du sang', *Revue des Deux Mondes*, 15th March and 1st April 1936.

'Fraternité', *Gringoire*, 5th February 1937.

'Épilogue', *Gringoire*, 28th May 1937.

'Magie', *L'Intransigeant*, 4th August 1938, unpublished.

'Nous avons été heureux', *Marie-Claire*, no. 75, 5th August 1938, unpublished.

'Espoirs', *Gringoire*, 19th August 1938.

'La Confidence', *Revue des Deux Mondes*, 15th October 1938.

'La Femme de Don Juan', *Candide*, 2nd November 1938.

'La Nuit en wagon', *Gringoire*, 5th October 1939.

'Comme de grands enfants', *Marie-Claire*, no. 139, 27th October 1939.

'En raison des circonstances', November 1939, unpublished.

'Le Spectateur', *Gringoire*, 7th December 1939.

'Aïno', *Revue des Deux Mondes*, vol. LV, 1st January 1940.

'Le Sortilège', *Gringoire*, 1st February 1940.

'. . . et je l'aime encore', *Marie-Claire*, no. 153, 2nd February 1940.

'Le Départ pour la fête', *Gringoire*, 11th April 1940.

'L'Autre Jeune Fille', *Marie-Claire*, 3rd May 1940, unpublished.

'M. Rose', *Candide*, 28th August 1940.

'La Peur' [autumn 1940] (*C. Michaud*), unpublished.

'Les Cartes' [autumn 1940] (*C. Michaud,* then *J. Dumot*), unpublished.

'Destinées', *Gringoire*, 5th December 1940 (*Pierre Nerey*).

'La Confidente', *Gringoire*, 20th March 1941 (*Pierre Nerey*).

'L'Inconnue' [April 1941 ?] (*C. Michaud,* then *J. Dumot*), unpublished.

'La Voleuse' [April 1941 ?], unpublished.

'L'Honnête Homme', *Gringoire*, 30th May 1941 (*Pierre Nerey*).

'L'Inconnu', *Gringoire*, 8th August 1941 (*'Nouvelle écrite par une jeune femme'*).

'Les Revenants', *Gringoire*, 5th September 1941 (*Pierre Nerey*), unpublished.

'L'Ogresse', *Gringoire*, 24th October 1941 (*Charles Blancat*).

'L'Incendie', *Gringoire*, 27th February 1942 (*Pierre Neyret*).

'La Grande Allée' [June 1942 ?], unpublished.

'Les Vierges', *Présent*, 15th July 1942 (*Denise Mérande*), in *Woman of Letters*, FiveTies/IMEC, 2008, introduced by Olivier Philipponnat.

'Un beau mariage', *Présent*, 23rd February 1943 (*Denise Mérande*).

'L'Ami et la Femme' [n. d.], unpublished.
'Ce soir-là' [n. d.], unpublished.

Thirty-nine of these stories have been collected and published in three anthologies: Dimanche, et autres nouvelles, *with a preface by Laure Adler, Paris, Stock, 2000;* Destinées, et autres nouvelles, *with a foreword by Denise Epstein, Pin-Balma, Sables, 2004;* Les Vierges et autres nouvelles, *with a foreword by Olivier Philipponnat, Denoël, 2009.*

d) Original Filmscripts

Irène Némirovsky donated four filmscripts to the Association des auteurs de films, in Rue Ballu:
'La Symphonie de Paris', 12th September 1931.
'La Comédie bourgeoise', 15th January 1932.
'Noël', 21st May 1932.
'Carnaval de Nice', 21st May 1932.

e) Selected Articles by Irène Némirovsky

['Souvenirs de Stockholm'], Nord-Sud, Revue bi-mensuelle franco-scandinave, 15th
    February 1930.
'J'aime beaucoup le cinéma . . .', Poslednija Novosti, 1st May 1931.
'Théâtre de la Michodière. *Les Temps difficiles,* pièce en trois actes de M. É.
    Bourdet', Aujourd'hui, no. 285, 31st January 1934.
'Théâtre de l'Œuvre. *Les Races,* 8 tableaux de Ferdinand Brückner, adaptation de René Cave', Aujourd'hui, no. 323, 10th March 1934.
'Deux romans américains: *La Mère* de Pearl S. Buck et *Le facteur sonne toujours deux fois* de James M. Cain', La Revue hebdomadaire, no. 4, 26th
    January 1935.
'Deux romans russes: *Complète remise à neuf* de L. Sobolev et *Le Quartier allemand* de Lew Nitobourg', La Revue hebdomadaire, no. 8, 23rd February 1935.
'Deux romans anglais: *Voyage dans les ténèbres* de J. Rhys et *Des étoiles étaient neés* de Barbara Lucas', La Revue hebdomadaire, no. 18, 4th May 1935.
'Le Mariage de Pouchkine et sa mort', Marianne, 25th March 1936.

2. Books Consulted

Not every book and article consulted for the purposes of this biography is listed here, but only those considered to be most useful for anyone wishing to acquire further knowledge of Irène Némirovsky, her work, and the period in which she lived. Also excluded are the numerous press articles devoted to her during the course of the 1930s.

ANISSIMOV Myriam, 'Les filles d'Irène Némirovsky', *Les Nouveaux Cahiers*, no. 108, spring 1992, pp. 70–74.

BELY Andrei, *Petersburg*, 1912. Translated from Russian by David McDuff, Penguin, London, 1995.

BERBEROVA Nina, *C'est moi qui souligne*, etc., Actes Sud, coll. 'Thesaurus', 1998.

BERNSTEIN Henry, *Samson; Israël*, in *Théâtre*, Paris, Éditions du Rocher, 1997.

BONNEFILLE Éric, *Julien Duvivier. Le mal aimant du cinéma français*. Vol. I: *1896–1940*, Paris, L'Harmattan, 2002.

BOTHOREL Jean, *Bernard Grasset. Vie et Passions d'un éditeur*, Paris, Grasset, 1989.

BROMFIELD Louis, *The Rains Came*, London, Cassell & Co., 1938.

CORPET Oliver and WHITE Garrett (eds.), *Woman of Letters. Irène Némirovsky and Suite Française*, with a chronology and introductions by Olivier Philipponnat, FiveTies/IMEC, 2008.

ELLIS LeRoy, *La Colonie russe dans les Alpes-Maritimes des origines à 1939*, Nice, Éditions Serre, 'Actual', 1988.

EPSTEIN Efim M., *Les Banques de commerce russes. Leur rôle dans l'évolution économique de la Russie. Leur nationalisation*, preface by Yves-Guyot, Paris, Marcel Giard éd., 1925.

GALILI-LAFON Jeanne, *Irène Némirovsky, le trouble d'une œuvre*, doctoral thesis, Université Paris 8-Vincennes-Saint-Denis, dir. Claude Mouchard, n.d.

GHIKA Prince Vladimir I., *Pensées pour la suite des jours*, Paris, Beauchesne, 1936.

GILLE Élisabeth, *Le Mirador. Mémoires rêvés*, Paris, Presses de la Renaissance, 1992; preface by René de Cécatty, Paris, Stock, 2000.

GILLOT-VOISIN Jeanne, *La Saône-et-Loire sous Hitler. Périls et Violences*, preface by Lucie Aubrac, Mâcon, Fédération des Œuvres laïques, 1996.

HAYMANN Emmanuel, *Albin Michel, le roman d'un éditeur*, Paris, Albin Michel, 1993.

JAFFRES Bleuenn, 'La relation auteur-éditeur. Irène Némirovsky et les éditions Albin Michel 1933–1942', mémoire de DEA, sous la direction de Jean-Pierre Dufief, université de Bretagne occidentale, 2002–2003.

JANKOWSKI Paul, *Stavisky, a confidence man in the Republic of virtue*, Cornell University Press, 2002.

JEVAKHOFF Alexandre, *Les Russes blancs*, Paris, Tallandier, 2007.

KAPLAN Alice, *The Collaborator. The Trial and Execution of Robert Brasillach*, University of Chicago Press, 2000.

KASPI André, *Les Juifs pendant l'Occupation*, Paris, Seuil, 1991; 1997.

KESSEL Joseph, *Nuits de princes*, Paris, Éditions de France, 1927.

KLARSFELD Serge, *La Shoah en France*, vol. 2, *Le Calendrier de la persécution des Juifs de France 1940–1944. I. 1er juillet 1940–31 août 1942*, Fayard, 2001.

KORLIAKOV Andreï, *L'Émigration russe en photos. France 1917–1947*, Paris, YMCA-Press, 2001.

LACROIX-RIZ Annie, *Industriels et Banquiers sous l'Occupation. La collaboration économique avec le Reich et Vichy*, Paris, Armand Colin/HER, 1999.

LANDAU Lazare, *De l'aversion à l'estime. Juifs et catholiques en France de 1919 à 1939*, preface by Jacques Madaule, Paris, Le Centurion, 1980.

LESSING Theodor, *La Haine de soi. Le refus d'être juif*, translated from the German and introduced by Maurice-Ruben Hayoun, Paris, Berg International éditeurs, 'Faits et Représentations', 1990.

LEVY Jacob, *Juifs d'aujourd'hui*. I. *Les Pollaks*, Paris, J. Ferenczi & Fils éditeurs, 1925.

LIED Jonas, *Prospector in Siberia*, New York, Oxford University Press, 1945.

MANSFIELD Katherine, *Journal*, edited by J. Middleton Murry, London, Constable, 1927.

MARRUS Michaël, PAXTON Robert O., *Vichy et les Juifs*, Paris, Calmann-Lévy, 'Diaspora', 1981; revised and corrected edition, Le Livre de Poche.

MAUROIS André, *Le Cercle de famille*, Paris, Bernard Grasset, 1932; 'Les Cahiers rouges', 1996.

MAXENCE Jean-Pierre, *Histoire de dix ans 1927–1937*, Paris, Gallimard, 1937; Éditions du Rocher, 2005.

MÉMOIRES DU CONVOI NO. 6 et Antoine MERCIER, *Convoi No. 6. Destination: Auschwitz 17 juillet 1942*, with prefaces by Elie Wiesel et Serge Klarsfeld, Paris, Le Cherche Midi, 'Documents', 2005.

MORAND Paul, *Nouvelles complètes*, I, édition présentée, établie et annotée par Michel Collomb, Paris, Gallimard, 'Bibliothèque de la Pléiade', 1992.

MULLER Henry, *Trois pas en arrière*, Paris, La Table Ronde, 1952; 'La Petite Vermillon', 2002.

NEBOIT-MOMBET Janine, *L'Image de la Russie dans le roman français (1859–1900)*, Clermont-Ferrand, Presses universitaires Blaise-Pascal/Maison de la Recherche, 2005.

PALÉOLOGUE Maurice, *La Russie des tsars pendant la Grande Guerre*, 3 vol., Paris, Librairie Plon, 1922.

PERROY Marguerite, *Sacerdos Alter Christus: l'abbé Roger Bréchard*, preface by Mgr Piquet, Clermont-Ferrand, Imprimerie régionale, 1949.

PESCHANSKI Denis, *La France des camps. L'internement 1938–1946*, Paris, Gallimard, 2002.

PLUNKETT Jacques de, *Fantômes et Souvenirs de la Porte-Saint-Martin. Cent soixante ans de théâtre*, Paris, Ariane, 1946.

POLIAKOV Léon, *La Causalité diabolique*, I. *Essai sur l'origine des persécutions*, suivi de II. *Du joug mongol à la victoire de Lénine 1250–1920*, preface by Pierre-André Taguieff, Paris, Calmann-Lévy / Mémorial de la Shoah, 2006.

POLIAKOV Léon, *Histoire de l'antisémitisme*, Paris, Calmann-Lévy, 1951; 1955; 1981.

PRIVAT Maurice, *La Vie et la Mort d'Alfred Lœwenstein*, Paris, La Nouvelle Société d'édition, 1929.

RIASANOVSKY Nicholas V., *Histoire de la Russie*, 5ᵉ édition, Paris, Robert Laffont, « Bouquins », 1994.

SCHORR Ralph, *L'Antisémitisme en France pendant les années 30*, Brussels, Éd. Complexe, 1991; 2005.

SPIRIDOVITCH Alexandre (général), *Histoire du terrorisme russe 1886–1917*, translated from the Russian by Vladimir Lazarevski, Paris, Payot, 1930.

STONEMAN William H., *The Life and Death of Ivar Kreuger*, Bobbs-Merrill Company, Indianapolis, 1932.

THARAUD Jérôme et Jean, *Un Royaume de Dieu*, Paris, Plon, 1920.

THAU Norman David, *Romans de l'impossible identité. Être juif en Europe occidentale (1918–1940)*, Berne, éditions Peter Lang, coll. 'Contacts', 2001.

TOLSTOY Leo, *The Death of Ivan Ilyich and other stories*, translated from the Russian by Constance Garnett, London, Heinemann, 1902.

TROTSKY Leon, *History of the Russian Revolution*, translated from the Russian by M. Eastman, London, Gollancz, 3 vols., 1932–33.

VOYARD René, 'Le tragique destin d'une femme de lettres. Irène Némirovsky. Kiev . . . Paris . . . Issy-l'Évêque . . . Auschwitz', Gueugnon, Les Amis du Dardon, 2005.

WARDI Charlotte, *Le Juif dans le roman français. 1933–1948*, Paris, éditions A.-G. Nizet, 1973.

WERTH Léon, *33 Jours*, Paris, Viviane Hamy, 1992.

WIECZYNSKI Joseph L., *The Modern Encyclopedia of Russian and Soviet History*, USA, Academic International Press.

WIEVIORKA Annette, *Déportation et Génocide. Entre la mémoire et l'oubli*, Paris, Plon, 1992; Paris, Hachette, coll. 'Pluriel', 2003.

ZANGWILL Israel, *Ghetto Comedies*, London, Heinemann, 1907.

ZIPPERSTEIN Steven J., *The Jews of Odessa. A Cultural History, 1794–1881*, Stanford, California, Stanford University Press, 1985.

ZOLA Émile, *La Débâcle*, 1892; Paris, Le Livre de Poche, preface by Roger Ripoll, 2003.

ZWEIG Stefan, *Untergang des Herzens* [Destruction of a Heart]. Translated from the German as *Beware of Pity* by Phyllis and Trevor Blewitt, 1939. Republished by Pushkin Press, London, 2000.

Acknowledgements

If Irène Némirovsky lives in this book, it is due primarily to her elder daughter, Denise Epstein, to whom we owe a boundless debt of gratitude.

Dear Denise, not only did you give a positive welcome to our plans for such a biography from the very start, in the late summer of 2004, but you allowed us to work in complete peace, giving us full access to all the available archives, including your own astonishing memory. We should like you to look upon this book as a substitute for a huge thank you.

We should also like to thank the following: Olivier Corpet, the director of IMEC, and Pascale Butel, who is in charge of the Irène Némirovsky collection there; Samuel Chymisz, one of the three survivors of Convoy No. 6 to Auschwitz, whose welcome, whose story, whose voice, and whose message we shall not forget; Tatiana Morozova, Anastasia Pavlovitc and Daria, without whom we should not have discovered the 'previous life' of Irène Némirovsky; Jean-Luc Pidoux-Payot, our first intercessor; Mme Edwige Becquart, for the affectionate recollection of her father, René Avot, and her family; Francis Esménard, who was kind enough to recall memories of his father, of André Sabatier, and of the Albin Michel publishing house; Irène Dauplé, Irène Némirovsky's granddaughter, for her availability, her Russian and her gifts as a genealogist; Pierre Hayet, the founder and general secretary of the Institut Vladimir Ghika, for his generous help; Mme Anna Kouslik, Boris Némirovsky's great-granddaughter, who helped piece together her family's ancestry; Nickie Athanassi, for her invaluable assistance and precious advice; Jean-Luc de Carbuccia, for his frank and open conversation.

And Malika: this book would not have seen the light of day without your support, your trust, your help and your love. I owe you a great deal. (O.P.)

And my family and friends who have heard me talk about Irène Némirovsky almost daily for over three years. (P.L.)

The publishers thank Editions Albin Michel for kind permission to quote extracts from the following titles by Irène Némirovsky. Translations of extracts are by Sandra Smith:

Le Pion sur l'échiquier © Editions Albin Michel S.A., Paris, 1934.
Le Proie © Editions Albin Michel S.A., Paris, 1938.
Deux © Editions Albin Michel S.A., Paris, 1939.
La Vie de Tchekhov © Editions Albin Michel S.A., Paris, 1946.

Index

IN refers to Irène Némirovsky